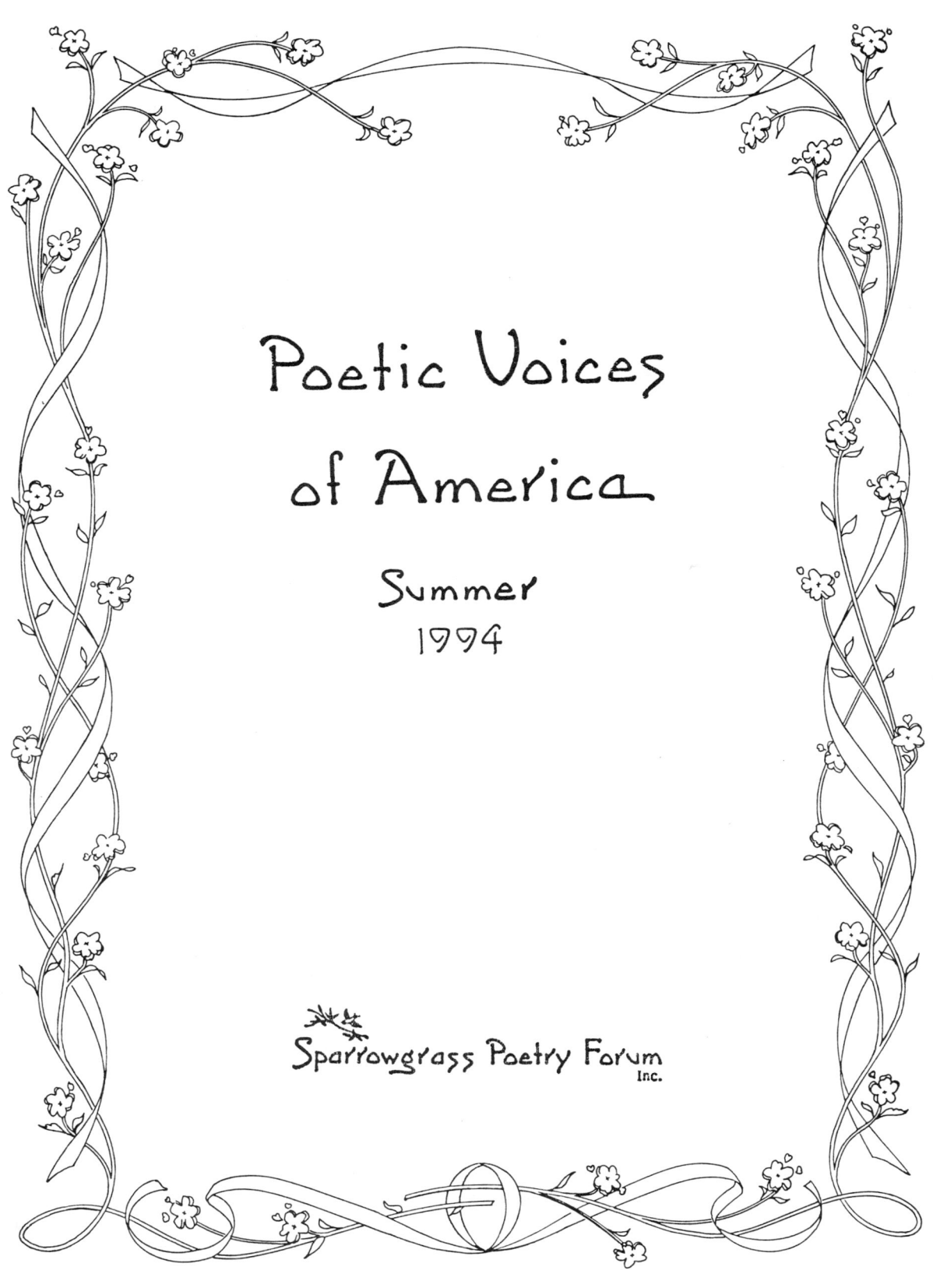

Poetic Voices of America

Summer 1994

Sparrowgrass Poetry Forum Inc.

ACKNOWLEDGEMENT

Photography by Jerry and Barbara Jividen
Images Unique Photography
Chillicothe, Ohio

Copyright 1994
By Sparrowgrass Poetry Forum, Inc.

Published by
Sparrowgrass Poetry Forum, Inc.
203 Diamond St., P.O. Box 193
Sistersville, WV 26175

Library of Congress
Catalog Card Number 90-660082

ISBN 0-923242-32-5

Introduction

Welcome, Reader, to this edition of Sparrowgrass Poetry Forum's **Poetic Voices of America.** Once again, our collection of poems represents a wide variety of thoughts, themes, and genres. And again our collection includes the voices of poets from across the continent and even beyond from other countries. As the Publisher, I like to think that this volume is in many ways a written record of our times and our places, these voices from across the land.

What are these voices saying as they provide this written record? They are providing a personal journal of feelings — disappointments and joys, sorrows and pleasures, fears and triumphs. Certainly, each of our poets writes from individual experience but assembled together in our collection, the poems begin to form a consensus of experience.

Who are these voices? They are persons literally from all walks of life who have a common need to express themselves poetically. Young and old, they are students and teachers, soldiers and ministers, ranchers and cabdrivers, doctors and drifters and a myriad of others in a myriad of other roles. They are people who definitely have something to say and in turn they say it very well.

Where are these voices? Seemingly, they are everywhere. They live in such diverse places as Cheyenne, Wyoming, and Chagrin Falls, Ohio; Saskatoon, Saskatchewan, and St. Augustine, Florida; Peculiar, Missouri, and Punxsutawney, Pennsylvania. Sandburg and Whitman would have loved the poetry in all the names of all the places where we live.

As you read through this collection, I trust you will share the pleasure that I did in helping to select them. I am always struck by what I discover I have in common with all the poets whose work I read. Indeed, poetry emphasizes the humanity that connects all of us.

Sparrowgrass Poetry Forum is bringing you an outstanding volume of verse which you will want to read and share. We bring you the poets' works but until you read them, the act of sharing is unconsummated. As Emerson wrote, "It's the good reader who makes the good book."

Jerome P. Welch
Publisher

EDNA ST. VINCENT MILLAY

In languid whisper
The shore dared you
mere slip of a sea creature
barely twenty in limpet hat
brimming with periwinkles
offering sand dollars.
You hungry as sea anemome
watched sea stars fall
like surf in turrets
on your smarting toes
and crawled with a crab's gait
to find the poems buried
beneath the surface
of a young heart's castle
built in emotional dexterity
yet later abandoned and furious
as love at high tide crashing
into blue shelled clusters
of mussel etched in sepia
along the sweep of salted sunset.

—Diana Kwiatkowski Rubin
First Place Award Winner

THE CRANBERRY BOG

The sun awakens,
 Spreading a blanket
Of brilliant light
Across a sea of garnets;

Dew drops descending
Into the frigid water;
Sharp, cutting blades
Of grass dueling
On the blustery wind—
Forming a bog of jewels
To harvest.

—Esther Barr, grade 10
Fifth Place Award Winner

GRASS OF GOLD

The grass from a meadow
 Laid upon soft sod,
Placed ever so gently,
Only the best for a god.

The legends live forever
On this diamond field.
All the glories of man . . .
Forever sealed.

Only one with the love,
Will ever see what lies within.
The triumphs and tragedies . . .
And what could have been.

Only the gifted and chosen,
Will forever be found,
And those who make magic happen,
On this holy ground.

—Derek Geddes
Fifth Place Award Winner

TEXAS

The magmatic sun
 scalds
the endless road.
In the torrid distance
steel derricks rise.
Mantis jaws chew
the earth.
Their insect hearts,
pumping, pumping.
For an endless
flow.
Question.
Will the ooze keep
flowing, flowing,
'til it's suitcase
sand?
And,
where's the worth
tearing up this
land?

—Sally Ann Berkos
Fifth Place Award Winner

ISLAND GRACE

Raging waters of mist and power
 hungry for the rock edged leap
An old volcano, a dark god's tower
lies quiet in ancient sleep.
Quilted cultivation hides seeds back
from a nudging, inquisitive ocean
Sugarcane sentries by the railway track
Palm trees a dancer's motion.
And oh! Such a sea life to bear
Heaven's names like angel and star
And whale watchers watched by whales without fear
'neath a gold fired sun from afar
And warm scented blossoms here, gifts of island grace
Surf-lit nights and sunlit days, here peace. This Maui place.

—Judith Cameron
Second Place Award Winner

WHERE FLIES MY SOUL AT MIDNIGHT

Where flies my soul at midnight
 in the shading of the deeps
beneath the distant flame-gem eyes
that watch me, spinning, as I pass?

Wrapped in dreamless slumber deep
castles of the night to walk,
I draw aside the spirit-flows
to bare a pale and moonwashed shore.

Arms outstretched to Sirius
dark tides pouting on my lips
that cry the haunted passages
and shadows of the dust-dark sky,

Worlds turn upon my raiment,
and my ornament is flame,
bright embers on a starlit flesh
that melts upon the running breeze.

Country of the hidden heart
bound by dawn and earthly seas —
where is the map that charts the course;
where is the lamp, the golden key?

—Elizabeth Davidson
Third Place Award Winner

THE STAGE

This is the dream field.
 We, wrapped in our roles,
Walk our numbered paces
    And yield up our souls.

Catharsis smitten, we dance
    Beneath the lights
Our words a bloody lance
    or a mockingbird in flight.

This is the dream rite.
    We walk in the afterglow
And suffer the eerie shock
    That comes with the curtain's close.

—L. Ezra Tillotson
Fourth Place Award Winner

spherical star drifting on a fairy's sigh
like dust swirling near the desert face,
a single shadow in the ebony sky
finally arrives at its destined place

amidst the sea of swaying reeds
to the left one-eighty, one-eighty right
surrounded by millions of planted seeds
nothing worth living for in endless sight

tender bud under the eternal sun
embraces life in a singular way
then shrivels before dawn has come
to die of thirst and fall away

—Marie Mai
Fourth Place Award Winner

CHRISTMAS EMBERS

Ah, here we sit before the fire,
The flames flicker warm and bright
Playing hide and seek with the shadows
'Til far into the night.

Ruffles, the cat, is all curled up,
Asleep in her favorite chair
With one ear poised so she can hear
The sound of footsteps on the stair.

But the children have gone their separate ways,
Some very far, some near,
All agreeing to come again
For the holidays next year.

The wind howls madly outside the door
But the lock will hold it tight,
We'll only open it for memories
To come inside tonite.

—Berniece Cover
Fifth Place Award Winner

EXHUMED

It's been too long. Decay's begun
beneath the clods of hardened time.
I shouldn't try to force the sun
into dark corners cold with slime.

To stir the past, rattle the bones,
disturb the natural, resting soul—
It seems too cruel to lift the stones
and peer upon what once was whole.

And yet I press with morbid need
to unearth what I buried then,
to resurrect with awful speed
that grim reality again.

The pearl-grey sky casts ashen light
upon my secret, silent chore:
the futile search, the desperate plight
of one who's lost in "nevermore."

At last I strike the fearful prize!
A shudder speaks my solemn dread,
for there *encore* before my eyes
I wince to see . . . the poet's dead.

—Marvelee Soon Tahauri
Fifth Place Award Winner

EARTHBOUND

I would with sylphlike fleetness
Forsake this creeping earth cell
And join the Huntress and her hounds
In swift moon chase.
Or, with marsh hawk, dip and plunge
Skimming tule and reed with winged ecstasy.
Once I knew the touch of a dream meadow
Barely felt by flying nymph feet
That were my own.

—Frances Hall
Fifth Place Award Winner

WISPS (1986)

My mood befits Puck —
The mischievous one or
plucky ruffian who
does pluck at bodice strings,
As I grasp at that wispy
Thing called Love.

You parry — I thrust
Can Libra and Capricorn
Sustain the wanderlust of lust?

We grope and flail away
Wanting to fly on Love's
Fluttering wing,
Eyeing each other's eye,
Holding dearly to the
Wispy strands of ecstasy
As they slip through our fingers
Like sand slipping time through the hourglass.

—H. Bardach
Fifth Place Award Winner

THE EYES OF THE DAUGHTERS OF CALVARY

of all the light that falls
on country porches
most is lost
except what finds the eyes
of the daughters of Calvary,
the country women rocking, rocking
on the endless knotty planks
that stretch the county roads
from here to Eschaton.

the eyes
of the daughters of Calvary
brace for rapture
in the horsefly air,
find true pictures of Jesus
in the rotten honeysuckle.
epiphanies rise from behind the hogpen,
out of the cow-itch vines,
from the tongues of blue-tick hounds.

the eyes of the daughters of Calvary
see it all and call it good.
and the women keep on rocking
aluminum chariots
while the legions of blowflies
and the bands of greenflies
are acoming for to carry them home.

—Paul Rich
Fifth Place Award Winner

TO THE UNRULY SIR

Gentleman, in the first row, I am aware,
About your musical soul inclined in the core,
I've noticed your expressive love in the air,
Each moment stronger than the one before.

Sir, you conduct the orchestra in a special pace,
You move your head almost in perfect time,
I see you from the stage, in your first row place,
I wish to tell you about your crime.

Your manicured hands up and down gently reach,
You follow each note with a graceful twist,
Mister, tell me, do you wish to teach?
Or just to play the notes on your other wrist.

You even hum the least known part,
You stamp your feet so hard upon the floor,
Sir, in the first row, stop and have a heart,
Next time, please, wait behind the door.

—Marcus Vaska
Fifth Place Award Winner

A DIFFERENT PERSPECTIVE

In the next world will there be
the look of the light,
moving whole fields to a place you don't know—
lighting up the exits of the afternoons?
Will there be branches quivering with light,
lined up the same way, as if someone were approaching,
and they knew who was waiting for their silver salute.

At five o'clock, in summer, are the green lawns
spreading the terrible news
that something is lost we can no longer imagine?
And the light is the only way of remembering.
No one says the sky is radiant with sadness
and the dark places of tears don't matter compared to this.

Dedicated to my mother.

—Constance Greenleaf
Fifth Place Award Winner

DIRT

My father sits in his chair by the window and tells stories
While I watch the wind twist the sky into ropes of rain.
He is old, and he holds his hands before him.
Do you see these? he asks, turning them over.
(I see the rain light turn his hair white)
These are my hands, he says, turning them over.
(Yes, Dad, I see your hands)
    When I was not much younger than you, a brown child,
    In island sugar cane rice days
    I watched my father plow the fields:
    My father, all lumped into a pile of bones and wrinkles
    With the old caribou like an asthmatic arthritic old man.
    Two old men with raisin skin
    Heaving through water, eaten by dirt —
    By dirt and water eaten up by dirt
    And hands all dead, eaten wood like termite trees.
    I swore that day I would not be an old man on a farm
    With eaten hands.
In our clean electric kitchen, he turns them over, quiet.
I look at him, growing old.

—Tania P. Sanchez
Fifth Place Award Winner

THE STATUE IN THE PARK

Warm summer moonlight
rests on her cold marble breasts
    flaming ancient love.

Soft rain at daybreak
    drips from trees and tranquil tears
      fill her hollow eyes.

—Sunny Rivera-Reyes
Fifth Place Award Winner

Naked sunsets simmer
in razor black skies,
reflecting on magnetic clouds
that clasp swollen hands
and yawn threats in night breezes;
echoing endlessly in frosted plains.
Pitter patter dreams
leak onto paper;
soaking up words,
drying brittle ideas.
Sunrise Sunset—
rainbow patterns on wilted pages.

—Hether Pearson
Fifth Place Award Winner

SURVIVOR'S CHEST

Where it's dark and warm
and the mattress springs
barely press through the
cloth, she hides her past;
old brown crisp black photos
of men in stovepipe hats and
her father's hand frozen
clasped to john, dead john.
And worn letters tired
creases from opening and
closing and rereading.
And a dusty pennant and
one pressed rose, a tattered veil
and a ring and the
mattresses soften the pain
far better than a cedar chest.

—Lonnie Prater
Fifth Place Award Winner

MY LOVER

He comes and goes
like the light of dawn
Creeping into the shadows
    at the edge of the sea.
Washing the shore
    at high tide and low
With his creamy froth
    rippling my skin
He comes and goes.

He comes and goes
    like a sliver of steel
Parting my soul
    to its innermost core.
Piercing my flesh
    with his razor-sharp edge
Churning my heart
    in a frenzied thrust
He comes and goes.

—Sylvia Parsons
Fifth Place Award Winner

ALL BEFORE THE DAWN

Packed like chickens, they climb.
Four in the morning, under the silhouette of Tajumulco,
where there's always room for one more
hurried farmer's furious pig butting down
a sack of corn. Between Tacana and the misplaced
sojourner, morning wears a carbon garter.

A sash of ocherous light
alarms the shadows, tracing
a mural of sun on sky, as the bus rambles
up these rocks called roads
to a deeper orange.

Under Tacana, a village rises, ripe
for market, and the chicken bus
wraps the great volcanoes, closer to the sun.

—Peter Whalen
Fifth Place Award Winner

ONE THING I LOVE

There's one thing I love more than the sea—
And that's her ships of sail.
They brave the wind, they weather the storm,
They chase the mighty whale.

I see them moored out in the cove,
In the twilight hours of morn.
Upon the early fog and mist
Their skeleton forms are borne.

But soon the shouts go out, "Ahoy,
Me hearties, let's be off!
Hoist the main sail, man the jib,
Lookouts go aloft!

Run up our colors, anchors aweigh,
Land lubbers go ashore.
We're off for the turquoise seas unknown.
We'll see these shores no more!"

A smile of envy fills my face—
Excitement chills my heart.
I watch the sails embrace the wind
As their graceful forms depart.

I once went down to the sea in ships
And felt the wind in my hair.
But there's one thing I love more than the sea
And her ships . . . it's you, my dear.

*Dedicated to Dad and Mom,
who love ships and the sea.*

—Judy Pitera
Fifth Place Award Winner

WHERE DO DREAMERS GO?

Where do dreamers go,
With cheeks all aglow?
Where do dreamers go,
When March winds blow?

II

Where do dreamers go
In the swirling snow?
Where do dreamers go,
When May buds show?

III

Where do dreamers go,
When bare boughs bend low?
Where do dreamers go,
When ice choked rivers slow?

Envoi

Who knows where dreamers go,
Or why ravens crow?
The answers are buried in the snow.

—Jane Pierritz
Fifth Place Award Winner

THE ETERNAL HORIZON — ALWAYS THERE

Rivers hear the doves
by the yellowing willows.
Purple dahlias,
acorns in the shell tinge
the eternal horizon — always there.

Lonely and isolated, the boy
whistled etudes in the silence —
captured in the mystery
of autumn gold and lightning.

Lovers meet in the midst
of stars and poems.
All seasons wait for a language
yet to be gathered.

Evening's moon deposits gold
on years of his dreaming, oldness
and the stick in winter shadows.

In the late hour of darkness
lightning frays the moment,
portraits the man
in white radiance kneeling.

—Emma Crobaugh
Fifth Place Award Winner

LEATHER

"Half in the hole and half away now." came the call down from the heights.
Now there's barley malt and the wright, old salt, givin' free men ire to fight.
He's a strong one when he's drinkin' and all trouble when he cries.
But, three men it took to pin him, once, drinkin' all the while.
Old sailor, with the sabre wit, and the look of leather and lye.

"All away now, full up and taut." is the call back from the hales
arrested in chains for the open main, face to the storm now, she pales.
He's a strong force at the gatherin' hoist when all troubles caught the sails
but, three men fell from her grace in that rage, once gripped in those burning gales.
He, the bold one, ship's balance at hand, stood fastened; leather and nails.

—B.W. Osborn
Fifth Place Award Winner

USED TIRES

My face flushed crimson with
the coward's cry of appearances
the day he brought the mailbox
welded to a tire, placed it
by the road in my front yard
I tried to hide the worn tread
a miniature wooden fence held dirt
all I needed was a bonsai apple tree
to make it look like nothing
was under there
the more I learned the ways
of his rustic, bruised heart
the more used tires I set out
turned them into flowering pots

—Denelle Floyd
Fifth Place Award Winner

DEATH OF AN INFANT
(September 1963)

Past hours of meted energy she flew
A mere eclipse of earth was all she knew
Yet from this brief and tender span she bore
Her passage to eternal, sun-bathed shores.

No hint of murmur, rancor at disgrace
She quickly grasped the chalice of life's grace
No backward glance, no teary-eyed chagrin
Now time is gone, forever will begin.

Divinity has sung Its rondolay
The sweetest sounds of music fill her day
No need to ponder, reason out a course
As she meets Love upon an infant cross.

Persuade us pure and simple child of light
To execute in truth your forward flight
To rise above the earth in joyful swells
Embrace that Life wherein all beauty dwells.

—Mary A. Kennelly
Fifth Place Award Winner

THE OLD ARE NOT FORGOTTEN

Today, old and gray,
You smell of gold.
With a sky as high as high can go.
Like an empty room,
Wrapped in a hug of warm cocoa.
A blue song with its lonely shape
Escapes from a lemon yellow radio,
Above the vivid red sounds of the parade.
The texture dulls, with eyes hidden.
Birds sing to the season,
In the smell of soft rain.
An ornament like an oblong bulb,
Silver, blue and red.
Washed new.
Rests
Close to the rear,
Yet at the top.
Like old perfume,
Dyed a powder blue.
Kept,
Because you loved it once.

—B.J. McCarty
Fifth Place Award Winner

In the coming year I pray for health
and good friends at my door
and peace throughout the universe
I ask for nothing more

I shall return to wander again
and watch the ships sail by
and stroll again upon the sands
my little grandsons and I

—Marcella Moon
Fifth Place Award Winner

OF A MORNING OF QUIET REFLECTION

Your face behind the water-beaded windowpane
refracts one thousand rounded images—
ten thousand water eyes
streaked into opacity
by a single stroke
of your careless hand.

And I'd walk barefoot over shards
of shivered glass
to touch your face again.

—Austin Fairfield
Fifth Place Award Winner

FREEDOM

I hear the heartbeat of the universe.
My soul throbs to its rhythm
And the stones sing the song.
Its pulse becomes my own and my
Mind rises to the eagle. I
Spread my wings and the
Wind ruffles my feathers.
The world teeters restlessly below
Me as I wheel and turn and slide
And dive. I see the earth, the
Clouds, the sun; I see through
Their motion; I see that they,
Too, silently pulse to that
Lonely heartbeat. And the stones sing
The song, long after drum and
Drummer are gone. And my
Wings take me higher.

—D.J. Shelton
Fifth Place Award Winner

FAMILY ARMS

My father's arms once dark,
now gray ashes.
Invisible, fine powder
inside the black urn in Queens.

My mother's arms are pale,
rarely seeing sun,
flesh hanging loosely from the bone.
Soon to be gray ashes
inside the black urn in Queens.

My brother's arms,
longing to hold another,
too fearful to live
embrace aloneness.

My arms,
brown against the white sheet,
midwife to the woman reborn.

—Edith Gabriele Hillinger
Fifth Place Award Winner

WINTER MARVELS

Snow they say today
  Our green grass may be covered
    Pretty white blanket

The snow did not come
  The sun shines out so brightly
    Weatherman watch out

—Vida E. Blood
Fifth Place Award Winner

A THOUGHT

Why didn't you, Christ
play idly on the lyre
in the cyprus grove like Apollo

sing to the girls
dancing among the jugs of wine

look far away where the sails on the sea
and the rhythm of the oars
would bring your Father in Heaven
closer than Zeus?

How much easier you could be
understood by us who play the guitar
dance rock and roll
and from the blue of the sea
catch the shine which tans our bodies.

How magnificent
would be your religion
of song, dance, fine weather
and eternal youth!

—Leszek Czuchajowski
Fifth Place Award Winner

TRANSFORMATION WITHOUT DESTINATION

Angry young man
gun in his hand
fear in his heart
as he sets out
after dark

shooting bullets
shooting cocaine
shooting sperm
nothing ends the pain

—Robert Strzalko

CREATING

The heavens and earth to God belong,
  His creations from the start.
With sunset spectrum and sparrow's song,
  God impresses the human heart.
Of artist and poet, 'tis said they create,
  With music, paint brush, and word.
In truth, they only imitate
  God's wonders they have seen and heard.
The poet does often alliterate,
  Producing crafty renditions.
The artist attempts to emulate
  God's authentic compositions.
The poet tries hard to be clever,
  This pedantic innovator.
The artist gives all, in endeavor.
  But, there is only one Creator.

—Elizabeth I. Cvetic

THE FAMILY MEAL

The women have been silenced
  At the round table
Lyrics of the folk songs circle
Like vultures above
All the dying wild things
The men laugh
Open-mouthed graves heave and bellow
Spilling centuries of dirt.

—Alicia Jayne
Fifth Place Award Winner

MILKWEED IN AUTUMN

This time of year
  the leaves turn yellow,
bittersweet glows
bright orange on the branch,
a crow flies out of the thicket.
Tufts of milkweed wisp through the air
like ghosts.

For autumn is the time
for bringing back the dead.

So, mother, forgive me
if I hesitate
as I turn down
the bridle path not taken
by anyone for a long, long time,
if I find the abandoned house
and use the rusty key
to try the door.

—Maureen Kravec
Fifth Place Award Winner

OH DEAR MOONLIGHT

When the sun goes down
  And the stars shine bright
The moon sat softly on the hill
Day is to come
And all will wake
And a new day starts again?

—Rachel R. Gunderman

SO, TOO, THE QUIET WIND

So, too, the quiet wind
  Blows 'cross the clear northern expanse
Where life and living things are thin —
Aurora borealis dance —

A fragment of a fleeting dream
Into the tundra, like the wolf
Which howls to the moon, unseen
In lurking shadows of itself —

Then whines the wind, sucking the cold
From artic air, suspended stark
Upon the landscape, winter's hold
Outlined against the falling dark

A nomad, too, this haunting wind
Alone, aloof upon the sky
Marking its path, unmoved, undimmed,
Across the vacant swath, as I . . . .

—Ann H. Womer Benjamin
Fifth Place Award Winner

SEED OF HOPE

Every man has his task of loneliness
Which he must bare and cannot share—
His darkness while sunshine is everywhere.
Then in the midst of pain,
A small seed is sown again—
A seed of hope which springs from his garden of strength—
And as it grows, he carefully nurtures each small gladness,
And prepares himself again for the tasks to come.

—Laura E. Felty

"what price hath beauty?" julie inquires of her broken soul.
and the giggle
which escapes from her lips
as she draws the edge across her wrist
is lost in the strange acoustics of the bathroom.
the giggle bounces off the sink, hits the linoleum,
and mingles with the blood.
and the giggle is no longer such,
but turns into a wry grin with the words
"i told you so"
pursed on its lips.

—Sally E. Andersen

NAMELESS SIGNATURE

They gathered in the low of the wood,
Writing and reciting the wisdom they could.
Unidentified and unknown, they are tireless in word.
Only in their circle can the identity of each one be heard.
They collaborate in grand conversation,
Writing words that can mystify a nation.
Bits of wisdom in rhyme contained,
Their work throughout history has remained
A constant presence in great books of knowledge.
Taught in small schools, and in the learned college,
Who are these who write beyond our reach,
And seem autonomous?
I know not, for the signature of their work reads simply,
"Anonymous."

—H.D. Sauls

LETCHWERTH FALLS

Letchwerth Falls white with foam —
Where people roam —
There's a nice bridge —
At the ridge —
Of a cliff's end —
Just around the bend —
A train is roaring —
Like a lion —
That just started cryin'.

—Zac Randolph, age 10

ALABAMA DEER HUNT

Reddish soil sticks
in the space
between their toes

Seven cluster about
in a well seeded
green-field

My thoughts drift
in the spaces
between them

—Scott Owen Leonard

TOUCH THE SUNLIGHT

Where did you come from
Where have you been

How did I miss you
How did I sin

To taste the bitter
To know the wine

Why could I not wait
Why waste the divine

That which is best
That I now see

What does it matter
What mistaketh me

When I touch the sunlight
When I choose the course

Will I rise up to meet you
Will I become a new force

By God's own forgiveness
By my own remorse.

—Suzanne DeWitt

SOUTH FOR THE WINTER

Driving around today, I felt the same
confusion that's always there when I'm with you —
A tingle in my mind rising to a running panic through my throat,
because I've looked around, and I've been driving in the same
direction for what feels like hours,
with no idea of where I am. Smashed pumpkins and pomegranates
litter the road like heads of people — tangled orange seaweed
clinging to concrete as if the cold ground
is the only thing left to love.

I'm still driving, determined not to be one of them,
Racing the flock of blackbirds overhead finding a better place
to spend my winter — soaring away from your anger
sealed out of the envelope of disappointment you made which
swallowed the smile on my face every time we were together.
But today, the road runs beneath me and the leaves are scattered
with such perfection they look like rented scenery for a
relationship we try to call real, where pretending is everything
even the way you'll eventually say goodbye, with a kiss
that will feel like wax on my forehead — a token gesture
that wants to be a burning imprint left there forever.

—Alice Champlin

SERENITY

In hushed repose my stress did flee
As silence leaned to cradle me.
Motherly arms held me caressed
Within her warmth of thought at rest.

My hold, released by heartened guide,
Found peace awaiting me inside.
There bathed and swathed, she closed my eyes
Made heavy by stilled lullabies.

Well nurtured, full, I stirred to see
Her smile, and clothe me tranquilly.
Renewed, my peace I rose to laud,
And almost touched the hand of God!

—Edwene Dorothy Watson

WHISTLING

Whistling in my ear — like a wind from afar
Who can tell from whence it comes or where
A fleeting moment in eternity's passing
Life so enthralling to all with enrapturement
But no guarantees of tomorrow are promised
Only a passing breath and a fainting heartbeat
Give rise to its numbing frailties

But who am I to question the fates of circumstance
And doubt its allegience to happenstance
As I ponder by winter's window the pummeling rain
Washing all cares into gutters with nary
A thought of future's power to inspire
Afresh in its faith and hope
Again I hear its whistling, beckoning

Whether to dash all promise to eternal damnation
And forget this frailty of existence
And enter eternity's portal to muse no more
Life — like a wind from afar
Only a flitting moment
And beauty its lingering memory.

—Daniel Rogers

EVERY TIME I SEE A SUNSET

I remember days gone by
And sunsets against a deep blue sky

Of times spent with a loved one
Of a father with his son

We'd sit on a bench and watch the sun fade away
As night crept up and washed the day away

Such memories still remain
But somehow they're not the same

There's an emptiness inside
A longing I cannot hide

For a loved one has past
The years went by so fast

I want to see the laughter on his face
But I only see a bench with an empty space

Sunsets aren't as pretty as they used to be
At least they aren't the same as they were to me

I sit on an old wooden bench and feel him next to me
The sun goes down, this is how I wish it would be

—Walter F. Dobrzycki

MORPHEUS

I toss upon the Sea of Dreams
With memories for my shipmate.
Through mist I peer to see your face
For still I love you dearly.

The past becomes the present
Or has the clock been stilled?
I drift between the now and then
And know not if wake or sleeping.

I feel your kiss upon my lips,
Your fingers stroke my hair.
Is this a dream we're sharing
Or are you really here?

To flow between the sea and shore
Brings solace for my sorrow;
It's where I hide my lonely heart
While Morpheus weaves the healing.

—Anna Mae Hoffman

TIMELESS

Poets dream in dark of night
when all around the world is quiet,
a time of peace when nothing stirs
but for a leaf or two that whispers
          down the lane

Somewhere a fireplace sends its
          pungent scent
Where log embers fall to ashes,
No hint of light from sill or sashes
          but for one,
In this room the soft glow escapes its
          ruffled guard
and flows like cream poured out to
          light my yard

If others, waking this unseemly hour
catch the light that glows from out
          my bower,
know not the joy that now begins
when timeless, poets pick up the pen —

—Alma Cook Remington

OUR GARDEN, GOD'S GARDEN

Soil deeply furrowed
A gentle seed tucked within
A bit of sun and water
Our crops will soon be in

Many tiny seedlings
Reaching towards the sun
Getting and giving nourishment
Nature working as one

A blossom soon appears
Another, then more, one by one
Ever so slowly opening
With the morning sun

The petals are fully open
On flowers, shrubs and trees
I know God wants to garden
That's why we do it on our knees

*Dedicated to my Wife, Debbie;
who not only encourages my writing,
but often is the inspiration
for it as well.*

—Michael A. Truax

torpor, angst, a fuzzy day
hemmed by hours neatly chopped
the grainy sun clicks 'cross the sky
a veil of sheerest silk between
my clever eyes and all i see
imploding brilliant dream goes down
my anxious guts and out behind
a relic of old heaven-spin
tsk, tsk, tsk, oh let's lament
the bitter waste and tragic merd
of these my hours timepiece-set
as click, click, click, i unwind back
to moonwhite dream, a ghastly blanch.
—Roy Kingsley

CLOUD IMAGES

The sky was my dream world
with images lightly drawn
on canvases of blue sky.
There played the great
pageantry of shapes and forms.
Castles, with their turrets
stark and gloomy,
lazily floated with bears
and fluffy, fragile angels.
The somber old man
parted his cloud lips
and seemed to hiss
and mock in scorn.

The skies darkened
with black-hued streaks
and hovering masses.

The fantasy clouds disintegrated.
Torrential rains came.
Angels, castles, old men . . . bears—
All were gone forever!
—Esther G. Mullen

MOONLIGHT WALK

A peaceful calm fell o'er the night
The stillness was profound —

While downy flakes of purest white
lay gathering on the ground —

Let's step into the nighttime drifts
and kiss each other's lips —

Chilled by the cold of winter's air
warmed only by the kiss —

Let's bundle up and take a walk
arm in arm let's stroll —

Along the posts of country fence
let's search for rabbit holes —

A falling star has streaked the sky
to grant a lover's wish —

That every hour of every day
shall always be as this —

The stars have all bore witness
as they twinkle there on high —

Old Man Moon just smiled and swooned
as he heard the lovers sigh.
—Betty Pilcher-Freas

SUMMERSFIELD

He sits on his porch
rocking slowly in his worn chair
smoking his briarwood pipe;
streams of smoke spill into the air.
After a slow thought: "Where are my glasses?"
His thoughts trail off like a kite
carried softly by a gentle breeze that passes.
A car drives by and he waves at the glare
motoring from his sight.
—Jason Thagard

REDEEMING THE TIME

Eternity has no time.
How is music made without time?

It is Joy outpouring, Sorrow left behind,
Purpose fulfilled and on-going;

Whale song, wind in the trees,
Morning stars singing together.

When we catch a moment, dwell completely in
the silence of that moment, sometimes we can
experience the music of eternity.
—Sharon Rapp

Who let the flaming horse loose
So it could set the fields on fire
Who called the wolves so they would come
And tear out the hearts of the poachers and thieves
Who danced with delirium urging women
To notice his arms, legs, feet
And who held the child all night
Until grief soaked sheets turned to tears

Legions of dark angels
Haunt the frozen hearted one
Who can look only by lightning
Over an uncertain sea
—Rick Haltermann

A SONG OF LOVE

Let me walk on your virgin land
Following the path to your desert home
Stay be me as I wash off the sand
And then we will be alone
The evening air will cool the ground
And the stars will light our way
Our hearts, and breathing will be the only sound
A symphony they seem to play
And we make love into the night
And we make love all day long
My heart plays the instruments
And your heart sings the song
Singing a song of love
To you, my true love
This is only a new beginning
This is only the very start
Lay beside me and gaze at the crystal stars above
Let me caress you
And sing you a song of love
—Alan B. Katz

BLUE MEMORIES

Sad blue memories fade into the still dark night.
Energy emerges from beneath the veil of twilight.
Bringing itself into the light of day.
There, mingled with hope, wells up into joy,
for the morning.
Giving strength for the new battles.

—Virginia Tondreau

TRAPPED

In a closed space and nowhere to go
trapped
Trying to find its way out
trapped in
Everyone hoping it doesn't get out
trapped in a corner
Pushing against the walls
trapped in corner helpless
Awaiting the keeper
trapped

—Sara Bulmahn

MY WORDS IN TIME

Those little words, how they dance
out of my heart and soul,
as they sing through my mind
of all my moments in time.
Forming little verses and poems,
with all grace and harmony
of all love and life.
They are there when I wake up
to when I lay me down to sleep
when I laugh and tickle inside
when I am sad with tears in my eyes.
They laugh they sing they sometimes cry,
but never do they harm.
And as quickly as they come,
just as quickly they go.
I chase after them with paper and pen
some I catch and some I miss,
but when I catch them and write them down
I know I must share them with all around.

—Linda (Ryan) Martin

HIDDEN TEARS OF LONG AGO

Shadows of darkness, sadness and pain
Somehow someway, we will find a way
To renew life for all, touched by you
Hidden, now lost in time from long ago
Back when all eyes were blind
We will seek and search to find you out
You hid your sins behind innocent minds
The tiny and helpless who trusted in you
Within their tiny depths horrors lurk
To grow in time, from your evils and pains
Hidden in such depths their minds now blank
But the roar of your madness in time
Grows on in tiny depths with strength
Emotions wild with hate anger and all rage.
We stand strong to take those back long ago
So shadows of darkness show your face
Admit your sins and ask forgiveness today
To stop your sins from long ago
And save your soul from hell itself.
For these precious innocent must remember all
Before their tears will flow to soothe their souls.

—Linda (Ryan) Martin

WINTER

See the secrets in the Season
at this special time of year
and rejoice with all God's Angels
hear them sing and gather near

Scenes of icy sleet through sunshine
making rainbows out of snow
reflecting rays like diamonds
in the dancing wind that blows

As we watch the days grow shorter
while the sun withdrawls its rays
'till it reaches outer orbit
and returns to warm our days

While we wait for Winter Solstice
fall-dropped seeds to germinate
thoughts of soon-to-be Spring flowers
much relieves our Winter wait

—Lola G. Ford

CHILDHOOD DAYS

All grown up
In different ways
Lessons learned
And lessons not
Wanting to be
Someone were not
All the good
And all the bad
But reflections now
Of all childhood days

The bad most often
Out weighing the good
But from those times
Our wisdom comes.
Geat lessons learned
Along one's way
For all that bad
Can now be changed
To reflect no more
Upon childhood days.

—Linda (Ryan) Martin

MY GARDEN

When the sun shines bright
Yet my life seems blue
Life's load too heavy
And my heart so weary
I go to my garden
I get down upon my knees
I feel the cool earth below
I put my hands within its soil
And plant new life to grow
God appreciates my love
He reaches down and comforts me
He lifts that heavy load
His love and mine now join
My garden now grows
And blooms with life
Now those that walk
The paths within my garden
Now walk with God and I.
And everyday I gaze
Out over my garden
God smiles back with love.

—Linda (Ryan) Martin

THE SENSE OF SOUL

Desire's honey, oozing from the heart,
Smells its sweetness.

And listening through the soft silence,
The eye secretly selects the insight.

But the tongue, awaiting the salty sweat,
Drips with warm wetness.

So, the body, aching from the feel of the voice,
Screams to be touched.

Upon hearing that sound of the soul,
The ear laughs.

—Angela Igrisan

A BROKEN HEART

    I lost a friend today,
And I don't know why.
    I thought she was at fault,
She said it was I.

    Stone cold words,
passed through her lips.
    Breaking my heart,
into tiny little chips.

    I didn't understand,
all she had to say.
    I do know that she,
had never acted this way.

    Maybe something from the past,
kept coming to her mind.
    But I thought when you became a Christian,
you left that all behind.

    Maybe one day I'll know,
and maybe not.
    I just know how it feels,
my tears to blot.

    You see, she's my daughter,
and my heart she can't mend.
    I just know I'll love her,
until the end.

—Joan Ponvelle

FALL

I watch the leaves fall gently down
Colors of red, yellow, orange and brown
I hear the birds calling out loud
The flocks are gathering to travel south.

Days are long, hazy, calm and still
Winter's approaching, just over the hill
Nature is storing all her beauty until spring
One last burst of glory shows off everything.

My eyes and ears take the whole scene in
I settle down to watch winter commence
God seemed to have gathered all
The world's beauty when he created fall.

—Ruby J. Ramsey

MY GRANDFATHER

He loved the outdoors,
The trees by the score.
The flowers with their scents,
    That he proclaimed were God sent.
Gardens growing corns, peas and beans,
    That were bursting open at the seams.

He loved being from the South,
    With a southerner's drawl which poured
      from his mouth.
Tales of yesterdays gone by,
    Of cotton you could see for miles and miles.
Of forests he had chopped down,
    And trees that were still around.

He loved family, folks and friends,
    God and especially kin.
His faith, honor and honesty,
    Are the gifts he has given to thee.
He was only a mere farmer by trade,
    But a Saint he has just been made.

In memory of Hezekiah Martin.

—Trish Smith

JUST A JOB?

Another day in the classroom,
    With "special kids," (they say)
Sometimes I'm not sure who's in charge,
Is it me, or is it "they"?
We work hard on following directions, listening and work,
Till I turn my back and they report,
"Someone's been a jerk."
I'm busy morning, noon, and night
Planning skills they need to learn:
Good behavior, completing work, home care, and the like,
Shopping, cooking, laundry skills and eating out when it's their turn.
I sometimes think it's not enough,
To teach them just those skills.
There's so much out there just to know,
For them it's really rough!
"Get it fast, and get it right," or else they'll call you "slow."
The world can seem so hard and cold,
When your skills are put to test.
They've learned the most important, though,
They've learned to *want* "success"!

—Linda L. Ryan

WITHOUT YOU

The anguish of your absence is dragging my soul apart
The cruelty of your departure is slashing the will of my heart
Wicked fires struggle to kill the sins of my love for you
And the desires of life burn away turning to ashes without you

Chained to the bitterness of my sorrowful and empty past
That has broken in thousands of pieces like something unholy
Without you my life has become an obscure and shattered glass
And I walk under the shadow of my painful and deep melancholy

At night I fall asleep with the illusion of dreaming of you again
I cover myself with the warm blanket of your unforgettable name
But the cold feelings of my solitude and my tragedy still remain
The obsession and the desire of loving you I am unable to refrain

I don't want to learn to see myself in other lovely eyes
I don't want to learn to fly high in other embracing skies
I don't want to kiss other faces, other lips, or other cheeks
I want to spend with you the rest of my life, my days . . . my nights
—**Nicolas Diaz**

Just a few words of my appreciation to you
Your Guidance, your Love, the way you carried Mom through

This world is troubled and hard to get to
But the Love of our family is Honest and True

You showed us how to love this way
That's why every waking is a special day

Your strength guides me each and every day
You're there beside me every step of the way

I couldn't have asked for a better father than you
I will always make you proud of me in everything I do

I believe God is watching us every day
He's in your heart, You're here to stay

He granted me so many things
But most of all, the Love you bring

The one thing I always want you to remember
You're not only the best father, but a friend so tender

I Love You, Dad
—**Christine Gousie**

OF THOSE THAT SHALL BE FREE!

We stood that day, on top of the world,
On earth, with God and Sky;
We saw our lives, as we watched,
The *changing clouds*, go by!

We asked the whinning wind that blew
Above us in the pine;
Whence clouds came and where they went;
And why was wind, . . . LIKE TIME?

We never say, clouds stay the same;
Nor linger with us long!
For wind was FATE, and CLOUDS were HOPE;
Seeking . . . ON and ON!

We sought as all the clouds do seek;
A spot of PEACE and REST,
AWAY FROM WAR . . . AWAY FROM HATE;
Of, JOY and HAPPINESS!

We found, OUR ANSWER, in the WIND that BLEW;
In the, MOUNTAIN, PLAIN and TREE;
For EACH, was *GOD'S EXAMPLE,*
"OF THOSE THAT SHALL BE FREE!"
—**Richard Claude Shacklett**

HATTERAS

Arbitrary strands of
    weathered fences
        sink deeper into
            rising dunes;
Sea oats bow
    to the salty breeze;
        a swirling structure—
            black on white—
Rises above it all,
    undaunted,
        keeping vigil on the
            rise and fall of the tide.

Dedicated to Dave Stone
for sharing life and lighthouses.

—M. Lynn Burgin

MORNING

The nighthawk runs the horses in,
Stars still shining bright;
Faint light showing in the east—
Rope corral stretched tight—

Coffee boiling on the fire,
Cowboys milling 'round;
Cigarettes glow in the dark,
Bedrolls on the ground.

Horses caught and saddled
As the stars begin to dim;
The cowboss leads out in a lope
And we all follow him

Around the outside circle
As he drops us, two by two,
To comb the range for cattle
As the sky is turning blue.

Sunup finds us scattered
To the four cold winds
We don't make many dollars
But we work among our friends

—Bob Owen

In flames I tear across the sky
dying and thankful for it
as I have nothing to live for.
My burning hatred consumes me wholly
murdering for my suicide
and laughing at my tears.
A dying and broken whore
my religion raped and torn from my hands
I have nothing to gain
and nothing left to lose, nothing at all.
And just as my inferno of rage finds its peak
I am swallowed by the sea
and extinguished by the lonely cold.
Left drowning; helpless; and alone.
I begin to close my eyes for the last time
but hesitate.
I see your hand swallow my pride
and for another chance at life
with you
I accept it.

—Aaron Michael Rice, deceased
Special Honorable Mention

DEPARTED

One regarded him as a possession,
The other as more of a brother.
After dinner, the former went to
The house filled with straw with a treat
Which Jack caressed in his mouth, savoring
The elixir from heaven given to him,
His eyes demonstrating innate playfulness
Until his fierce teeth made the introduction.
A short while later, the latter went to his house
For the usual invitation to spend
The cold night inside with him in his room
Only to discover open, but unseeing, eyes
And a mouth from which fragments of straw seemed
Trying to escape to their birthplace
In the ground from which had disappeared
The warmth of earlier golden days.
From the bowels of loss, came the cry of pain
And the two anointed the departed
And prepared the soil for the inevitable
Return to his longed for eternal home.

—Frank A. Langer

CHILD OF HOPE

In a land of rolling hills, adorned with stately oak and fragrant pine,
Amidst emerald green valleys, where the blue waters softly flow;
There is a child of hope, a child I long could be mine,
In a land of rolling hills, where the roses and the violets grow.

—Patrick Joseph Kelly

It's too late to see the forest, and too tiring to find the right tree.
Rain, cold and friendly, you meet me at my window's edge
and I feel a stranger's chill in his old hometown
for fear of the cold in the alley
you can see a few feet
to grass growing and water dwelling around the stiff, bold blades
reach and you're reaching
see and you're seeing
my face at your door
I never came in for fear of the rain
making me cry
for you and me

—Christopher Manoli Carpenter, deceased
Nov. 6, 1965 - July 24, 1993

SUPERIOR SUNKEN MEADOW

I hear nature's birds singing,
The swans talking to each other,

I see nature's clouds bursting apart,
Then touching another one,
Making new friends,

I smell nature's sea with all its fish friends to keep it from loneliness,

I taste nature's salt spray,
tapping my tongue with excitement,
by the wind that helps it move,

i feel nature's hand while I walk down Sunken Meadow beach.
—Meryl Stebel, age 8½

AUTUMN ANTLERS

As unnoticed and unalarming as the new sun in the east sky
Is a stranger in the treetops with something he just had to buy.
He came unseen and unheard in the night
Much like death when the time is right.
He never moves and somtimes doesn't breathe
While wishing he'll never have to leave.
With nerves of steel and patience unending,
He watches the trees never breaking, but always bending.
His mind wanders in search of what he looks for
And he's positive it's out there, somewhere on the forest floor.
He relaxes for just a second and catches something
Out of the corner of his eye.
He knows he shouldn't move but attempts to try.
He freezes suddenly trying not to look,
But he knows what's coming like it's written in a book.
With a quick turn and a sudden flash,
He can feel his heart drop and hear it smash.
He walks out, looking and feeling like a jerk,
but he knows he must hurry because he's already late for work.
—Adam Richmond

NEEDLE, THIMBLE, THREAD

I.

In sewing shops, I seek out a certain type of button.
It is large, round, domeshaped, and brown,
with a crosschecked surface that reminds me
of miniature mahogany checkerboards.

II.

Aunt Adele's checkerboard was cream and brown,
and the paint peeled up at the edges.
The pieces fit into each other closely,
cream on cream, brown on brown,
after they had clicked across the board as opposing armies,
uniformed and marching in-step
enroute to double-crown new kings.

III.

Our family was in Africa as the telegram chased her away—
I was eight. In the only snapshot I keep from that trip,
I stand sullen before Mt. Kilamanjaro, hovering protective
in the background. I am wearing khaki shorts
and a moss green sweater—
"knit with love" by my Aunt Adele, the label said—
buttoned down the front with six domeshaped, crosschecked,
small mahogany checkerboards.
—Sarah Kate Levy

SEASON OF UNREST

My life is like the falling leaves
That drift and dance with each new breeze
   Hopscotching forth on sun-warmed grass
And then without the sense to stay
I let the wind whisk me away
To muddy streets and sidewalks where
I'm crushed beneath the traffic there.
      —Harriett DeLay

THE SAINTS

O skies of blue, and fields of grain,
O how the Lord doth remain,
In hearts and souls of the Saints,
That crossed the sea without complaint.

Be with me Lord through night and day,
To stay at my side, so I will remember,
That day when the Saints did not surrender.
      —Naky Bishop, age 13

EDUCATION

What awaits at the stop sign?
   Crossing guard — seeking absolution.
Protector of tiny humans;
Limited minds — diseased thoughts influenced
   by their surroundings.
Destination is home:
   stereotypical family life.
Fulfill the journey . . . walk down narrow road,
   past resort for the deceased; physically
   dead returned to their original mother —
   food for the plants . . . Cemetery.

Did they achieve their desires?

Pity if they failed — any advice?
You can learn a lot from the dead!
Children march — single file — unaware . . .
Of what has been; what is; what will become.
      —Lance Brodersen

CERTAIN WATERS

Breaking through the waters' surface,
Shedding chains conceived in dread.
Baptismal hope breathes through my body;
Igniting fires in a soul long dead.

Beneath the waves the undertow is coiling—
Greedy tentacles twist 'round my toes.
But I am fixed and here unyielding
To its yearning, taunting throes.

So the days go by in magic;
Gentle waters reflect soothing hues.
Then . . . inescapably I hear it:
The desperately beckoning song ensues.

I ignore it, crave it, loathe it.
Steadfastly now it comes.
I laugh, I cry, I turn away
As the icy tendrils embrace the rungs.

Inevitably, they too break the surface
To invite me down below.
As ordained, I cry out in a whisper,
Before I willingly turn and follow.
      —Karin Hoyle

TODAYS FRAGILE HEROES

Oh for the gods of the august age,
proud delusions, images divine,
who from ethereal greatness crashed
and burned with vapors fine,
trailed only in the craving soul.

They now arrive on schedule,
the infamous returned to soil,
land thudding lumps of children's clay,
littering our common toil,
reviled by each and all.

These failed and mortal destines,
bankrupt with their grandeur spent,
despised for what we long to be —
dare the smug retrieve no glory lent
nor the moment we were excellent.
      —Steve Olson

THE DANCE

firefly dust
like angel kisses
on a wing and a prayer
flitting from harm's way

scampering destructors
giggling with jars of glowing prisoners
cupping the delicate fairies
in chubby palms

bare feet on the sweet summer carpet
chasing silent wings of miniature moonlight
restless as dandelion ballerinas
bowing to catch the shooting stars

the dance continues
from loping waltz
to bouncing jig
as the twilight hunters stalk their prey
      —Heather L. Trudgeon

THE ICE DANCERS

Breathless silence stills the darkness
We wait, tense and aware . . .
Then, a guitar's strain and piercing notes
   Of flute fill the arena air.

A pent-up sigh escapes the crowd
   And then, a deafening roar!
As the first intricate steps are etched
   In icy patterns on the floor.

Two figures glide in unison,
   And through dappled light seem made
Of swirling mists and beating wings
   And flashing silver blades.

The moving story that they tell
   Depicts man's desperate stand
Against oppression's bond of hate—
   Missing, in an alien land.

It storms the heart with feeling!
   And with a haunting beauty flows;
Could one behold music in motion,
   It would look, just so.
      —Sheila Rose Williams

LIFE

Life is so confusing at times, that's the way it's supposed to be.
When you try to straighten it out, there's more for you to see.

In order for a flower to grow, it needs the sun and rain.
But for you and me to grow, we need both love and pain.

Sometimes the pain is too much to bear, you no longer want to live.
And through the journey of life, you've given all you can give.

But now you musn't quit my friend, for things have just begun.
You have to give life your best, until the battle's been won.

So fight your toughest fight, and put a smile on your face.
Soon your troubles will disappear, as you feel our Lord's embrace.

—Lori Ann Long

VICTORY

Your hair is blazen with the glory that leads men to triumph in battle.

Your eyes glow with the dissention that separates corrupt nations, yet pulls strong nations together.

Your lips are plush with the obscurity of language that drives man apart, but when at its best, unites mankind.

Your body is enticing and full to the naked eye, but when seen by the observant eye it is tattered and worn.

For you are Victory, the pinnacle of that which we all try to achieve, but your sides are steep and rocky, and how sorrowful it is that many are not willing to climb.

—Jeff Morton

SOMEDAY

Someday you will turn to touch me, and I won't be there.
But I could be in the warm breeze, that blows upon your hair.

Someday you will ask a question, and the answer will not come.
But I could be in the warm rays, of the summer sun.

Someday you will turn the corner, to see if I am there.
Then you will remember, all the ways I care.

Someday my friends and family, will gather over on the distant shore.
Where there's no more pain and sorrow, just peace and love forever more.

Some days you will try to remember, some days you will try to forget.
All the things that happened between us, from the first day that we met.

Someday you will climb upon the mountain, and look out upon the land.
Then you will remember this is where, we used to stand.

Someday you will realize, I'm still watching the children grow.
Remembering what I have taught them, how and what they know.

Someday the tears will stop falling, down your face.
Knowing I'm with the Lord, receiving his love and grace.

Even death cannot take away, the kind of love we share.
The years of working together, all the love and tender care.

Someday Heaven's gates will open, and I'll be standing there.
So live your life for Jesus, because we know not when or where.

I reached out my hand to Jesus, and he took me by the hand.
He showed me how to cross over, to the Promised Land.

Just as surely as the four winds, around Highland Mountain will continue to blow.
The memory and presence of (Clayton Walker), everyone will continue to know.

Dedicated to a wonderful, strong, faithful, and loving family of Clayton Walker. He left us in March of 93 with the illness, Cancer. He lives on in all our hearts.

—Faye Wilson

MOUNTAINS

Big arms outstretched to me.
Existing before me.
Three hundred years of family ties, a thousand more for the Blue Ridge to be.
Standing when I no longer can.
Symbol of my arrival to that special place.
Someplace where I can do no wrong.
Birthplace of all my ancestors.
English, Irish, Dutch, Shawnee, Scottish and French.
Birthplace of those who loved me most and best.
In my blood.
In my mind.
Nothing is too high to climb
For I have seen those mountains with every loss and gain.
They stand strong.
I will do the same.
And carry on the family name.
   —E.L. Thomas

THE WIND BEYOND MIDNIGHT

The wind beyond midnight in sultry July,
Is a midsummer siren, beckoning nigh.
While wafting sweet incense from the nocturnal array,
It recaptures the lushness seen verdant by day.

The wind beyond midnight in autumn's blue haze,
Blows bounty from boughs during hunter's moon phase.
And it muffles the sound of impatient feet,
Whose owners, to fatten, seek acorns to eat.

The wind beyond midnight in winter's hard freeze,
Sculptures' ridges of snow circling bushes and trees.
The land is at fallow in purified white,
And the weakest of warmbloods, are unsustained in their plight.

The wind beyond midnight in springtime's renewal,
Brings elixir to buds of each blossomy jewel.
And strong southern thermals loft a million winged beauties,
Launching them northward, to fulfill mating duties.

The wind beyond midnight does its work well,
In nature's great cycles, as the seasons reveal.
So when sleep fails to come, treat your ears to its tune,
And catch a symphonic conduit, to the creator's commune.
   —Lawrence A. Johnson

RAGGED MOUNTAIN'S LEDGES

When I was young, there was no trail leading to Ragged Mountain's Ledges.
Its rock-chimney we did not scale — till nebulous high-pressure wedges
     beckoned — with a strange invitation
     to seek that rocky indentation.

Then atmospheric-highs confided to some of us wanting to wander
on trailless slopes, if we are guided by nature's plea, we will not squander
     scarce resources — Earth still displays
     heartfelt concern for yesterdays!

Though goals are reached, no challenge ends. Meandering becomes unnerving
for climbers who are lost, as friends and family once found, till, curving
     beyond that ragged mountain's edges,
     a rough ravine stretched toward those ledges.

To me, at twelve, that mountain called, a call I knew I must obey.
As sun on ledges shadows scrawled, I blazed a trail to mark the way.
     Alone, fortuitously-timed,
     I reached that rock-chimney. And climbed!

Be warned! Exploring takes a sense of goals, and risks, not yet entwined
with this world's time. Experience affirms, in seeking, we shall find!
     Listen. And pray . . . Learn, as you talk.
     Then — always think — before you walk!
   —Phebe Alden Tisdale

SAY THAT AGAIN

If I looked into your eyes and said, ". . . pray like this . . ."
Would you tell me, "Yes," and then offer up a prayer?
Would you forgive these who have trespassed,
Would you do His will on Earth,
Would you accept His help in times when tempted,
Would you appreciate your daily bread?
For imagine my surprise when a man approached and said,
"Once upon a time I had a thorny crown forced on My head."
I knew then right there and I
Knew that I was gazing into the Lord, Jesus' eyes,
And knowing that I'd been blessed in kind, I said,
"Yes, I know, I know just how you feel," said I.
 —Mrs. Julie Hallissey

THE EAGLE

The Eagle flies high among the clouds.
It comes and visits only in the winter.
Flying low through the valley in search of food.
He sits majestically in a tree waiting, watching,
carefully for a fish to come to the surface.

Diving in and out with a flapping pink salmon
in his mighty claws.
Proudly he takes the fish home to his hungry family.
The baby Eagles learn everything from their loving mom and dad.
Off they fly away in the spring
To somewhere cold again,
To fish the mighty rivers.
 —Rachel Goetz

THINKING OF YOU

Think of the eyes that look upon you with hope,
Think of the hearts that thought of you with love,
Think of the mind that thought of you with pride,
And imagine that.

Think of the cuts and scrapes they kissed to comfort you,
Think of the help that was given during your time of need,
Think of the hours of lost sleep worrying over you,
And imagine that.

Think of all their sacrifices they made for your luxuries,
Think of all their hard work to provide for you and your needs,
Think of all the discipline used to make you who you are,
And when you think of all of this,
Imagine just who it was that was thinking of you.
 —Angela Dove

LITTLE ANGEL

 Mommy oh Mommy would you please tell me why, if there's a God in Heaven, why is he letting me die? From the day I was born I've been in such pain, all this misery and heartache is driving me insane.

 My sweet little darling, God knows what you've been through and now he thinks it's time, for Him to help you. He will take you to His home in the Heavens above, where you will feel nothing but tenderness and love.

 He will take all your pain and misery away and for the first time in your life you will be able to play. My heart will break and my tears will flow on the day God says you have to go, but whenever I look up at the skies I'll see this pretty little angel smiling down at me.

 So for now my darling I have to say goodbye, but I'll be with you again when it's my turn to die.
 —Theressa Peters

EARLY MORNING

The sun awaking from its tomb of sleep
Gradually rose like an austere queen
Reflecting its hands of warmth
Upon the cold and dark world of ice
Permeating my cold and fearful soul
And rushing like the sound of the great wind
Through my cotton candy veins
With the scent of roses

—Shelly Cutting

A FOREST'S INFLUENCE

I wish, at times, for the ability
To brush canvas from white sterility
Into great trees of strength, peace and calm;

Surrounded by verdure and stillness
That may everlastingly embalm
The mood from which this portrait comes.

To preserve my memory
Of greeting morning mists

And grand, rope-rugged trees
Unclenching mental fists.

—Jim Snyder

WINTER

Winter now . . .
We see our shadows pressed upon the wall
four cornered in the firelight
capable of waiting out the cold.

With shadows moving about in the sunrise
against the face,
the floor,
and quiet corners — calling.

And snow falling
in a gentle
and suffocating heap
against bolted doors

While inside, we wait alone —
crying silently for the spring.

—Anthony J. Velez

SOMEONE

The sun rises over the ocean
Smiles down on a brand new day
The earth turns in continual motion
We go about in our usual way

But there's someone out there who is lonely
Someone who is lost in the crowd
We could hear them cry out, if only
The silence just wasn't so loud

And somewhere, someone has found love
Someone broke someone's heart
While someone is holding the world in their hand
Someone's world fell apart

And as daylight fades into darkness
The ocean reflects the moonlight
Somewhere, someone is laughing
And someone cries in the night.

—Lavada H. Barnes

MINDSTONES

Streaks flash through
the blackening blue of sky.
Lit in seconds passing a mind fuse,
and turning it in against itself
in thunderous afterthought,
a blaze of memories
drawn out and swept back in,
Called, carried, and spun
like a mindstone,
Washed by an eternal sea,
Soothed by a salty brine.

—Lorraine Frenette

INSPIRATION

I hear music in the crisp breeze.
I hear it in harsh words.
My world is filled with sweet melody—
Harmonized with harsh reality.

Music elevates my soul.

The intensity of deep, rich vibratos is
Filled with vibrant color and texture.
I visualize it as if I were standing
In front of a work by Van Gogh.

Silence falls—a faint dissident hum
Gently breaks the silence
Lightly floating down to
Blanket me with care.
A tingling, glowing warmth
Comes over me with the thought
Of infinite tranquility.
Angelic voices of the sweetest perfection
Caress my soul
And delicately lift it ever higher.

Every part of me has been rejuvenated.

—Susan Elizabeth Small

POOR SLAVE

I'm a poor slave
Always frightened and afraid.

I'm never ever pleased,
I just beg and I freeze.

I know I don't live a happy life like all,

Instead I cry, I run and I fall.

Getting whipped is the worst,
Boy that really hurts.

My manners are so gentle and
kind,
Unlike my masters who wine and
dine.

Yes, I'm a poor slave with no
freedom of any,
I believe there are slaves who
sometimes have plenty.

But someday I believe, that
someday I will find
That freedom of mine, that was
far left behind.

—Carol Marie Pedroso

THINKING

How deep my thoughts must run to find my mind
Yet when my thoughts have reached where my mind should be
Into a large coliseum the path disseminates
Revealing the immense absence of my mind.

The hollow footsteps of my thoughts in my head
Searching for the mind that would contain them
Hopelessly roaming in the boundless cavity
Stretched out into the dark sanctuary surrounding.

Now my thoughts have nowhere to go
No corner to slide back into when about to be revealed
No crack to slip through when a nerve strikes at them
Only the arena to flail about until beaten and thoughtless.

—Lisa-Jai Gibson

SIGHT

A glazed gaze scanned the Eastern evening sky.
"Where is the pale crescent, due to rise nigh?"
Through her eyes, not dry, yet whetted in hope
To view the lovers' moon her soul's eye did grope.

Alone she witnessed the tides, the sails,
So frail, alone, yet to trust she was prone,
And failed to believe surely had she not grown?

Cloud cover shrouded above her, the mist chilled her to the bone
And led by instinct she felt her toes sink into the pliable dry sand.
She clasped her own hand as she felt her way home.

Dreaming deeply, the waves crashed on.
Whatever sand castle erected surely would be gone,
Be washed smooth with no trace to grace the dawn.

She rose from her bed and looked to the West.
A faint light emanate 'twould glow bright at best
Signalled morning had come, the long night was over.

As first blush cradled the crescent setting moon
Her heart recalled an ancient spring tune
That swelled like the tide beyond the shifting sand dune.

—L.C. Mereness

REGRETFUL MISTAKE

I was put in this sea, this sea of society,
the problems of the world are irrelevant, they don't affect me.

I know not where I came from, or where I will go,
I don't know how long I have to live, with life I run it slow.

Life is fine by myself, but never any fun alone,
it's the idea of finding a perfect match, this I've never known.

Fisherman, they come and bait for my life,
not caring about me, only carving with a knife.

They hide their evil offers, offers to travel to another place,
a one-way ticket for my fate, just to feed their needful face.

So tempting are the offers, so very colorful and pleasing to my eye,
you wonder what it's like to taste, and in a breath a slow good-bye.

What left is there to live, when life is but a series of dreams,
no one to live it with, or so it always seems.

So young and inexperienced, I accept the Fisherman's promise of the sea,
pleading for somewhere and someone else, maybe I just wasn't meant to be.

In a brief second I understand the world, the meaning of living,
but only to be soon forgotten, a life maybe worth giving.

Looking back, I'm not sure what I should have done,
but what more do you want? In a world run by a gun.

—Conrad D. Cheslock

TELL ME ANYTHING

Say not the words that will cause my demise,
Promise moon, promise stars or to tell me no lies.

Say to me that the Earth is flat,
Tell me this life is a dream,
Make me believe the world is free,
Just don't say those words to me.

Whisper my name upon a breeze,
Say it's your heart calling mine,
Take my spirit away from me,
Dash my porcelain soul to the ground.

I ask of you this solitary thing,
Beg and plead that these words you don't say.

Please never say you're going away,
That this is good-bye for the rest of our days.

—Adrienne Hearn

SCARS

The lines on my mother's face are scars surfacing
from the inside.
Strands of silver weave resplendence through her
tired brown pincurls,
and when she smiles,
it is the smile of a queen's elderly cousin.

My mother wears smooth cherry lipstick
and sturdy tweed blazers;
her purse is spilling over with expired credit cards
and crumpled gum papers
and panty-hose remnants.
And her wrists have two, train-track ridges
each.

"You only live once," she often tells me, and,
"Don't marry a Pisces."
Every year she climbs the mountainside
to my grandfather's grave and
spits out the lump in her throat.
She throws her tears down to the river
and smooths her skirt.
Then she leaves.

—April Frances

THE STEWARD

Celestial jewel, resplendent in space
Unique to Creation, now fallen from grace.
Once mantled in radiance, sum essence of beauty
Good earth, you embraced both destiny and duty.

By nature you nurture, sustaining all life
Consummate mother, now burdened with strife.
Your children defiled and helpless — they grieve
All resources plundered, the legacy you leave.

A trusting heart hazed what your mind surely knew
At the hand of your steward came torment on you.
Unequaled in arrogance, moral fiber of mist
Begrudging all others the right to exist.

Remnant of Genesis, what fate stalks your kind?
As honor and malice contend for your mind?
Bewildered by paradox intellect can't abide
Knowledge without reason is the curse of your pride.

Eyes of the Cosmos gaze upon you and weep.
Is judgement from Apocalypse the harvest you'll reap?
Redeeming your birthright means healing and mending
The prodigal finds hope in a spirit of ascending.

—Judith Radosevich

FADED MEMORIES IN PICTURES

Roses of Ribbons
Sweet Summer Sweat
Snow White Christmases
Emotions unkept

Tick Tock of the Clocks
Reminding of Time
Thoughts in Circles
Ending in Rhyme

Candy uneaten
Leaves unswept
Dust undusted
the Forgotten Pet

Fall into Autumn
No Sour-colored Limes
The Child is Frozen
in the Picture of Mine

—C.L. Baker

GOOD NIGHT

Poet
the night
only
once, when
it's there
love it
'Cause soon
it's gone

Poet
the night
you're not
comin'
back, ain't
comin'
no mo'
Poet

good night

—Jamie Reuben Kearney

THE EAGLE'S WAKE

Can you see them
The fledgling souls
Who fly the eagle's wake
With wild eyes fixed
Upon you who soar
The horizons of tomorrow?

Can you feel them
Feather light upon
Your sure wings of
Experience
As swollen hearts thrill
In obscure anticipation?

Can you set them free
As virgin wings
Wage war against
The surging plunge
And spinning world
Of destiny unrealized?

Can you see them triumph
Heights only eagles dare to soar!

—LeAnne Fisher Ensign

GOD'S BEAUTY

Look and see God's beauty. As we go through life. Do we take the time to see the beauty of God. The beauty in the rose. The smell of the lilac. The mountains' scenes. Or the water falls. The ice that twinkles on the trees. Or the snow that covers the earth. From the beautiful red bird to the blue jay. Look and see God's beauty. In the tall slender pine that swaves in the wind. To the large oak that stands so strong. The innocent look in a child's eyes. Or the touch of a hand. Let's take time to look and see God's beauty. I saw God's beauty in you. As you lent a helping hand. To sweep the floor. Or make the bed. It's not always the beauty in the face. It's what's in the heart that shines through. From the apple pie to the coconut cake. Are just a kind word or a smile. Look and see God's beauty in someone, or something.

—Mildred Smith

THE GOOD OL' DAYS

The good ol' days were very special.
We went to school to learn our lesson,
Not smoke some crack or learn to shoot a gun.
Today, car jacking is teenagers' newest craze,
I would've gotten my butt kicked or beat to a blaze.
Hum . . . I wonder what happened to the good ol' days?

The good ol' days were the best.
Growing up, I had a fear of two things,
The wrath of God and my Mom's mighty swing,
Nowadays, they don't know who God is and they'll remove my Mom's finger to get her ring.
I miss the good ol' days.

The good ol' days are gone forever.
I remember Martin Luther King Jr.'s plea, for us to unite in unity.
Come one and all, together, oh yeah, it's more like never.
He hates me because, I'm a different hue,
But beneath his skin, he's the same as me and you.
Have love in your heart for your fellow man and don't kill, rape, rob and haze,
You will discover, if you try, we are living and dying in,
The good ol' days.

—Edward S. Costley

DESTINY

Here on a borrowed land we live,
never knowing the minute nor the hour
when death shall summon us home.
We all hope to be ready to go.

We are standing somewhere in the forest,
but we are serving humanity
while we wait patiently
for the big bell in Zion to toll.

When our seasons are dark and dreary,
and we don't know just what to do,
we always turn to God in prayer
because He will surely bring us out.

One day we shall embark on a long voyage.
We shall sail from evil and strife and
from the toil and burden of our earthly lives
into a land full of peace and glory divine.

Dedicated to:
Mrs. Dorothy McGhee—Matthews Elementary School—Columbus, GA
Mrs. Cassandra E. Harris—Office Manager—Columbus, GA
Mrs. Rose Williams—Lab. Service Coordinator—Columbus, GA
Mrs. Vivian Dodson—Librarian-USA/S, Ft. Benning, GA

—Benjamin F. Miller

LISTENING AND HEARING

Listening and hearing
Are two totally different
    things
To listen
Is to actually pay attention
Like listening to your teacher
To hear
Is to go in one ear and
    out the other
Like hearing but not seeing
So always listen it's
    the key to success.

—Heather Ross, grade 8

THE DREAMER

My mind wanders.
My hands reach.
I see voices.
I taste songs.
They know me.
I don't know them.
I touch fire,
Blazing fire.
I smell laughter.
My feet step onto nothing.
I don't fall.
My eyes open, I can't see.
My lips form,
Unspoken words.
They don't know me.
I know them.
I see voices.
My hands reach.
My mind wanders.

—Rebecca Snow, age 12

SEE THROUGH YOU

I see myself in you.
All the ugly things you do.
That look you pass to another.
Makes me want to shudder.
At the thought that I too can
have that same stare.
The one that says I don't care.
The half smile that seems to
hurt.
The same face (lips) that
can curse or praise.
And the beautiful hands that
can be raised;
That can be formed to hold;
That can be formed to scold.
Afraid to really show yourself.
The real you kept back on a
shelf. Thinking you have hid
it well.
Only to find out your private
shell has a small crack.
Just big enough,
So I see through you.

—Deborah Lacy

THE NATIVE AMERICAN

    Your hands are brown, like Mother Earth. Your eyes like the doe's are soft and full of knowledge.
    I see you standing in the distance struggling against an unseen force. It's the wind from the east, blowing cold into your heart. Like the wolves you and your family move to a place of safety your eyes ever watchful. Deep in the forest you lurk, listening like the wary deer. But the wind finds you gripping your bones with its icy breath. Many of your people die, unable to withstand the wind. You are sad but the wind won't dry *your* tears. You keep moving, like a frightened rabbit, always moving. The wind, always hunting, it always comes to chill you. You won't run anymore. You are proud like the buffalo, majestic like the eagle, and like the wolf you know your home and will fight to protect it. I reach out to touch you but like the leaf, fallen from its home you are scattered in the wind.

—Kerry Kathleen Light

TAKING THE PLUNGE

When you said it was time to share our feelings,
Time to take that risk,
For our relationship to grow,
It was like we were standing at the edge of a pool.
The water looked cold and deep,
But you said "One, two, three, jump"
And I jumped.

But when I came up for air, cleared the water from my eyes
I realized that I was in the pool alone.
You were still on the edge
Afraid to take the plunge.
So I splashed around for a while, sure you would join me.
But you stayed where you were — on safe, dry land,
Unwilling to get your feet wet.

So I climbed out of the pool,
Feeling a little cold, a little sad.
And I know that I will not jump in again,
Unless you jump in with me,
Holding my hand!

—Judith Sheridan Nygaard

LOVE

I whisper my love daily
in songs and praises
to Jesus Christ,
and He whispers His love to me.

He whispers His love
through His warm
and cool breeze
from Heaven above.

He whispers His love
through His falling rain,
through His shining sun,
and through His white freezing snow.

He knows my name,
and I know His name.
So He asks no question
about who am I.

Dedicated to:
* Mrs. Marcia Williams—Columbus College—Columbus, GA*
* Mrs. Cynthia Fears—Columbus College—Columbus, GA*
* Mrs. Shirley Hinckley—Columbus College—Columbus, GA*
* Mrs. Maria Holmes—Columbus College—Columbus, GA*

—Benjamin F. Miller

ISN'T IT WONDERFUL

I hear the gentle pitter patter of the rain upon the roof.
Inanimate objects creaking, tho' nobody's in the room.
The house is filled with silence, the children are not here.
No voices echo in the halls, no arguments are heard.
The hush within my home is very pleasing to my ears.
But something in this moment begins to fill my eyes with tears.
As I relish in this peacefulness and calming atmosphere,
This friend that I so value someday I'll wish would disappear.
I realize what saddens me is it won't be very long,
Before the clock is chiming three and they'll not be coming home.
They'll be grown and out of school living lives out on their own.
The quarelling will cease, but I'll miss it when it's gone.
The disharmony seems miniscule compared to all the love.
I'll so miss the laughter that we've shared, the touches and the hugs.
This house will be so empty, but soon will sing out in delight.
Their children will be here and they will argue, they will fight.
Isn't it wonderful?
 —diana thomas

DAMAGE DONE

It's been years out of nowhere — And now I'm lost in the dust
Like a fire up from flames — I find love up from lust
The beautiful passion — That's never been set free
Is like a restless tiger in a cage — And it grows inside of me

Take me down to the river — Gonna cleanse my spirit dry
Want to taste her flowing kiss — And drown in her watery eyes
Let the current take me away — Until I see the rising sun
Let it take my past away — So I can — Forget the Damage Done

The field of my dreams — A place where I go
To drown out my sorrows — And purify my soul
She always makes me feel — Like there's always someone there
Even though I'm all alone — Solitude is nothing to fear

Take me back to a time — To where a child grows innocently
I cry for his naivete — 'Cause that boy is just like me

Escaping the dangers of love — Like the wind I run
To escape the dangers of love — So I can
Forget the Damage Done
 —Paul Merullo

VICTIMS OF DEPRESSION
LIVING HELL
"ANGUISH"

The heart, the body, all torn and broken, standing imprisoned within the walls of the soul. Cannot escape! Life unbearable!
Alive in an endless agony! The taste of a Living Hell!

Living Hell! Anguish . . . uncontrollable suffering, ragging emotions, agonizing sorrows.
Living Hell! Anguish . . . mental pain, torment, indescribable cruelty.
Living Hell! Anguish . . . darkness, despair, heartwrenching fear, hate, war.

From the depths of the heart and with every breath it has . . .
Comes . . . Screams of rage! Such weakness! Cannot bear the anguish!
Cannot bear the pain! Tired! Want to sleep! Want to escape!
All that is seen . . . is the blinding darkness.

From the depths of the soul . . . Comes . . . A spark! A flicker! Hope!
Lips to quiver . . . of the hope they once knew. Tears of a lost soul! Many tears!

With every beat of the heart and every breath it has . . .
Comes . . . A scream! Through the abyss of inflamed anguish and pain . . .
A cry for peace! Oh! Please! Do not abandon thee!
 —Carolann Snarski

A ROSE

Of all Nature's flowers,
and everyone knows,
there isn't one more treasured,
than a rose.

Bursting into full glory,
with a rich and beautiful hue,
its scent ever so lovely,
delicate and true.

Their haunting perfume so light,
lingering in the air,
like the ghosts of sweet memories,
of princes and maidens fair.

Roses are sheer beauty,
dainty and a treasure,
Mother Nature's gift to us,
they bring us lots of pleasure.
—Fiona Robinson

THE IMPOSSIBLE DREAM

Equal opportunity is a dream
That I'll never see
People can say it and think it
But, you'll never convince me

The color of your skin
Will always come in play
People may not say it or write it
But, most still think the same way

It doesn't matter at all
Whether you're yellow, red or black
When it comes to equal opportunity
The line forms in the back

So, wake up you dreamers
And come back to reality
Equal opportunity is a dream
That will never ever be
—D. Keith Clark

BY FORCE, NOT BY CHOICE

By force and not by choice
My country held against its will
And though the scandal is intriguing
Survival is not an academic skill.

Defiance is my essence
I have no need to be coy
Does suffering really refine
Or does it just destroy?

My convictions are my own
I never pray for an easy life
My prayers are to be a strong person
To glide on through with strife.

By force, not by choice
My island held by treachery and lies
I refuse to take a beating
But I will train myself to die.

Defeat is not allowed
The future is unforeseen
By force and not by choice
My island shall be redeemed.

*Dedicated to Omar: it all begins
and ends with you.*
—Mary-Ann Ossman-Muhammad

WHY?

The fire burns bright
in the dark of the night.
Will God give us a break
and help for our sake —
The families, the kids, the
wild life in a dizz.
Oh, please let the wind
stop blowing and give us relief
in the sunrise showing.
The helping hand of the fire
fighter tall, to bring us a treasure,
our home, at the end of it all,
The anxiety, the anger, the fear, with
the fire lines in gear —
Oh there it is — I see it thru my
tears, but what is it? Only a fireplace, address,
driveway — it's gone — Why? — "God help us all" —
—Penny S. Wilson

THE HOMELESS BELOW THE BRIDGE

They cry out in their longing,
it was age in its pain, it was youth and tears,
it was an innocent face,
and the cold winds of the world.

It was the blue flannel coat, ragged,
on the man passing you on the street,
from nowhere to nowhere he goes,
and comes near you with stale breath,
and a muttered excuse me.

Days and nights and nothing but
the bitter biting wind beneath the bridge,
it is fitting
that they hide from the world that rumbles above them,
it is the real and they are not.

The river flows beside them, traffic roars above them,
life swirls about them, and yet
it is their faces that slide into unrecognizable form,
lost in the mist, they join the homeless below the bridge,
they join the ever-growing army,
I've seen them, below the bridge.
—William R. Ford, Jr.

FOREVER MAY

He sits on a stone by the fresh churchyard grave
His chin rests on gnarled hands propped on his cane
Unaware of the bitter cold, icy North wind,
Or the wind made tears following tracks in his skin.

Bare, skeletal boughs clack a dirge of their own
Bemoaning their sad and sorrowful song.
And yet, he remembers a sweet, kinder time.
And listens and sees with his heart and his mind.

His mind travels back to those bright sun-filled days
Recalling past springtimes of her, young and gay
To that eager young girl running swift o'er the meadow,
So happy and carefree, to meet her young lover.

"Our vows, all those people! Oh how lovely was she!
Our wedding night, shy innocence, *Did she really choose me?*
Strong loving wife, kind gentle mother,
She's been mine so long — Now they say it's all *Over?*

I Will Not accept all these things that they say!
And No! that's not her lying here in this grave!
Why, that woman looked old and her hair was all grey!
And my beloved's as young as the flowers in May."
—Marie Hunley

A TRUE FRIEND

A true friend is someone who listens,
and when you're happy, they also glisten.
They're there for you when you're feeling low,
they always shine a radiant glow.
A true friend does not show jealousy or hate.
And never, no never does an untrue friendship wait.
Sometimes friendship can cut like a knife.
If that happens, they're not your friend for life.
True friends are there to lend a hand,
and for you they always take a stand.
They're with you through the thick and thin.
There are never battles, so neither of you ever have to win.
A true friendship does not struggle to survive.
A true friendship is always alive.

—Kate Thomas, age 14

WHAT IS TODAY?

What does it mean, today, leading towards the future,
What does it mean, the pain, the hurt, the sacrifice?
How much can it mean, the environment, the people, the earth itself,
As much as we all fear inside?

What does it mean, hunger, famine, fatigue,
Enough to make us change?
Can we live on in harmony,
Through darkness and the rain?

Can we change, can we stop heartache,
Can we open our hands and help?
I am convinced, in the present time,
That we only love ourselves.

The day will come when this all will end,
Will we be prepared, ready?
I doubt this much, in every sense,
For the problems are holding steady.

But maybe the sun will shine again,
And the birds will start to sing.
And until then, what is today, what does it mean?
Everything.

—Ryan Crider

CHASED OFF FROM MY FAMILY HOME

As I hit the door steps of the Country House, fire descended upon me like a burning wooded sky. I felt hot like one in a hell fire. I felt the intense heat in my chest like the heat from a hot iron metal.

An image of a small slimy young woman appeared before me. The coldness that followed that moment was like a Swallow rising up from a frozen sea coast. I wandered shiverishly, like a baby lost in a real Winter day.

When I opened the door, I heard the weird sound of a weird old man. He walked towards me with a weird old staff, crawling as slowly as a weird old snake.

Go skyward like a weird old lady, he thundered.
I own this home from above, he roared.

Have I moved into the wrong House? I checked the mail box, the street name and the number, again, and again. I picked up a bill in the mail box addressed to my family, and looked at the bill again and again. I hurried back quickly to my car as my burning body begins cooling off, like a sudden Summer wind drifting northward for a cold Winter day. And my family were no where to say who really owns the home.

Dedicated to my lovely parents and children,
Mr. & Mrs. Herbert E. Kurunwune and
Eugenia Kurunwune and their children.

—Anne Kurunwune

TIME

A gentle breeze at midnight,
My youthful ears did hear.
I laughed and sang at midnight,
Through many a lovely year.

Now blows the wind at midnight,
A cold and wintry sound.
No solace comes at midnight,
My years a desolate mound.

But after comes the morning,
Its brightness marks the way.
As long as comes the morning,
'Tis mine — another day.

—Virginia L. Shaffer

OUT MY WINDOW
#Two

My window . . . my window . . .
What has it turned into,
Through it what visions come?
What doth th'ether imbue
Other than the soft rain,
The jewels of which slow
Seep from balcon'd rail?
The pale light remaining
In the welkin above
Perches within each drop
As it stretches to fall,
And like a lighthouse light,
Lending meaning within't,
Flashes 'cross the distance:
Only men worry
With the passage of time.
Yet men have so little
Time to fathom their faith.
Water a'seep will wet
The floor of a cave
Five thousand years, yet mound
Sediment a mere inch.
But men must earn
And men must feat
Reared so fiercely
To compete.
They have to rush,
They have to rent,
The source to them
Unevident.
And we all seem time-sick
Since time is speeding up
(Time being equal to
Money and other such
Sorrowful rot as that),
So your signal to me,
In a beam from the jewel
'Neath my balcony rail,
Illumed with light above,
Peaceful, unobtrusive,
Again and again in
Unobserved excellence,
Save for me this moment—
Less than a second long
As it stretches to fall,
Flashes, signals, yields
Its simple essence 'round:
. . . .

—Jim Snyder

Why is one man's selfishness
Another one's gain?
How is it two people's actions
Can cause so much pain?
Life is too short
To be robbed of your joy.
Yet some would abuse it
Like a child's toy.
What we want is so simple
But so hard for others to give.
It is a friend
As well as a lover
One who will always be there —
Above all others.

Dedicated to my mother for giving me the creative talent to write this. Also, to a very special friend who taught me the meaning of true love and friendship.

—Thomas Reyes

FROM STEINBECK'S BOOK

There is a man on lookout point
With a chicken
And a knife
And as the sun hits the water
He will sell that chicken's life
To a God unknown

There is a hundred years of oak tree
Bedazzled with feathers and fur
Watered with tears
And saddled with fears
Of a man with pleading eyes lifted
To a God unknown

Go forth son of these fathers
To seek a natural weald
Lightning and fire
Root, branch and fruit
Are pious offerings all
To a God unknown

—James Angus Vieira

FOREBODING

Beyond the shrouded sky,
Fathoms below the rolling foam,
Deep into the blackness of night,
Within depths of the human mind
Searching, scrutinizing, scouring
Mankind strives for enlightenment.

Wake up, humanity,
Let the heavens lie undisturbed,
Alas, let the waves beat the shore,
When death befalls, please let us go,
Leave gray matter unintruded
Be concerned for the here and now.

With strife, destruction and sorrow
Surging within the human soul,
Grant to mortals in the beyond
The quest of frontiers for unknowns.
Present and future intertwined,
Care for now, assure tomorrows.

—Gale Boulware

GRAMMY

Four inch feet pat a dim beat
marking the stretch of hardwood hall
and stop at the kitchen door.

You turn from your sudsy chore
and crouch with outstretched arms
sure as water drips.

I remember being two awaiting rescue
in my purgatorial state of sleep to waking
I remember eyeing you through twisting fists.

Grand Angel sweep me to the heaven of your lap!
and feed me a cheerful egg.
I am thus redeemed by the wrap of your white terry wings.

Some nights as I curl to dreams
your hand will reach past twenty-five years
and stroke me to another dawn.

—Alicia Jayne

FULL CIRCLE

Pure and innocent life's circle begins,
For every need, on loved ones we depend.

Over time we learn, and through stages we go,
Both good and bad, the seeds of life we sow.

The circle continues, days turn to years,
And our memories are filled with laughter and tears.

Our innocence gone, the circle complete, we've conquered the
Challenge of life's biggest feat.

With the wisdom experience brings, we know we are bound for
Better things.

The Lord is with us and His word we heed, He is the One
We now depend on for every need.

We know in life we have done our best, we've come full circle
And now can rest.

With the Lord by our side, we are eternally blessed.

In loving memory of my grandmother, Emma Schantz.

—Julie E. Schantz

A SON

At the time of your conception,
Your mother was the happiest in the world,
I dreamed of what you would be like.

I dreamed of a boy that was just like his father,
My dream came true when I held you in my arms.
The boy I held was his father's image.

As you grew, you changed,
I began to see some of myself in you.
I only hope that you took the good from both of us.

I don't always tell you how much I love you,
I don't always tell you how proud I am of you,
But I hope that you know, that it is true.

Every night, I pray that I will be a good mother,
That you will always know that I love you,
and that you will continue to grow in the same manner.

I hope all your dreams come true, like my dreams of you,
and that someday you will have a son,
that will make you as proud, as you have made me.

Love Mom.

—Barbara DeZuani

LIFE IS WORTH LIVING

Life is worth living, so don't jeopardize it,
Taking drugs makes life go away bit by bit.
They make life a countdown, until the end,
You may think it is sophisticated, but it's not the new trend.

Life is worth living, so don't even start
The drugs and alcohol which effect your brain and heart.
I know this sounds odd coming from a kid,
But in my generation is where this is hid.

Life is worth living, please listen to me
All this is true, you will soon see.
There are things in life worth giving,
I know this, 'cause I know life *is* worth living.

—Shana, age 14

SHOULD YOU?

Should you come home from where you've been?
Should you wish we could be like we were back then?
Maybe, once you see, you may go back from where you came;
For, my love, time has changed me; I'm **not quite** the same!
Once, I was young and alive within you;
I'm **older now and, would surely disappoint you!**
The once smooth face you loved to touch;
Is **well-worn** with lines, wrinkles and such!
The **youthful** body you caressed **close and tight,**
Would betray your memory, **even** in the day's light!
The nimble hands you held and kissed long ago
Are filled with aches and pains; they hurt me **so!**
The beautiful long legs that danced you across the floor;
Don't even have the strength to carry **me anymore!**
Sad as I am, that you went first and we've been apart;
There's one remaining thing the same, you still fill my heart!
So, should you . . . should you come back to me, my love?
I think not; for, in the distance, I hear a calling above!

—Linda H. Adams

IT CAME TO MY MIND

As I travel to Mississippi
more than a year ago
There I could eat catfish
in a restaurant called Bosum Joe.

As well as was friendly the waitress and delicious the food, too.
I always think on this vacation
I know that's a very good idea
to leave this train in this station.

The offer since beauty
and mild the climate
so I think   Don't wait.
I stay here in Meridian before it's to late.

If you remember of a man (his name was) John Dunn
in the eighteenth century he had
built up a cotton mill
he had a greatness of heart and a
staying power of a strong will.

Everybody's knowledge of Jimmie Rogers
as a great country singer
I love his beautiful songs
So I think he is always a winner.

I hope you found out the right way
you could plan the next holiday
to come in this charming bayou.
That's the best what you can do.

—Verena Wüthrich

OUR LOVE

Just the feeling when we touch
Somehow becomes so much.
I want to hold you until never
And hope we last forever.

My feelings are so deep
Sometimes they make me weep.
We have such a beautiful love
It's as free and pure as a dove.

But, if in time, our love should end
I know my heart would never mend
So let me say from my heart
Please dear God don't let us part.

—Kathleen (Lee) Gray

WITH PEN IN HAND

With pen in hand
I will once again
Compose a simple poem
Converting my thoughts
Into written lines
With an end result
A poem with rhyme
And if just once
My simple poem
Is read from its beginning to end
Then I will feel
Through poetry
That I have made a friend
Then once again
With pen in hand
I will compose a poem with rhyme
Because I feel
Deep down within
That poetry is a friend of mine

—K. Ann Tzay

LOVE

There it was, plain and simple,
As bright as a lightbulb,
Silent as a whisper,
True as can be,

    Love

No one expected it,
Not this way,
Never in a thousand years,
Not them,

    Love

Nothing could tear them apart,
Not a man or a woman,
Not a stampede of elephants,
Nor hatred,

    Love

Everyone admired them,
Wished they could be them,
Jealousy was very common,
But one thing kept them together,

    Love

—Kim Kollmeyer, age 13

REMINISCING

A remembered embrace —
The desire once . . .
Touched the soul
And the power to know

Reminiscing —
Like the fabric of a dream.

—Richard Clark

RAINBOWS

Sometimes when you see a rainbow in the sky,
It's prettier than a bird's eye view of the world.
You see that rainbow high up there
And you wonder why and how it got up there.
High in the sky you see your rainbow,
Wishing it would never go away.
But then you turn to greet a passing neighbor,
And when you turn back,
Your rainbow has faded away.

—Shannon F. Noce, age 9

BEAUTIFUL SEASONS

Spring is in the air
We can see it everywhere
Grass and leaves turn green
And chirping birds are seen

Sunshine and showers
bring nature's lovely flowers
Everything is to our liking
We picnic, swim and go hiking

Then comes a change as I recall
When autumn leaves start to fall
Followed by winter winds and snow
And nature again is all a glow

—Alice Marshall

FRIEND'S SONG

For every eye that often cries
into winter's cold and dispiriting night;
My soul is touched by dreams deterred,
as my anguished sighs echo unheard.

For every sweet flower that withers and dies
beneath the storms cruel pitiless might,
there is but one singular song
whose rhythm consoles this sadness in me,
that plays across my thoughts forlorn
bathing me in a sun speckled sea.

It's a song of remembrance
in the times of my sorrow,
that changes the melancholy sky to blue,
a soft chord of the promise of the 'morrow
and the sweet song of you.

—Michael James Clarke

AZTEC IN A LIMO

An Aztec in a Limo
Your empire soon will die
Tracks across your pillow
Your dreams have passed you by

Darwin's theory mis-applied
You're a Soviet success
Pirates feed on others' lives
Until there's no one left

The Godfather taught you ethics
A pit bull on the loose
We must be as inventive as Odysseus
While you're playing Zeus

Viewing us as a fishbowl in a stadium
Your supremacy seems affirmed
Although we're birds with broken wings
You are still a worm

—Mark Fennell

WHAT CAN MUSIC BE?

Music can be a song or melody.
It can be the song of a chirping bird or a buzzing bee!
Music can be the voice of a friend.
It can soothe you excite you all at the same time!
Music can bring you to places of your imagination.
It can be your solace when you're lonely!
Music can bring out the best in you.
It can be the root of anything!

—Gregory Perkins, age 13

MORE

Sometimes the words enter more fluidly from fingertips to keys —
    than from tightly, wrapped fingers around a pen.
This act seems much more than the escape of feelings onto
    page — more like creating:
        the placement and rearrangement of my insides.
And a calm surfaces, with the coming of a close —
    with the excitement of newness,
        so I hurriedly type into discovery.
Yet with every ending, I am left aching for more words, more
    feelings, more findings:
        like the addict who can never get enough of more.

—Kathlena Luft

MEMORIES

Oh, the memories of the years gone by, and the happiness prevails, the photographs that were taken, can surely tell some tales. They show us all dressed up in fine grandeur, to smile and not to frown; but as you know a lot of us really like to clown.

From baby to adulthood, and all that is between; we have all come many years, through life's enormous stream. The uphill an the down, the swaying to and fro, remind us of our yesterday's and help us as we grow.

Oh, the memories of the years gone by, and happiness still prevails, now we gather here today and tell some real tales. As we share our memories and some pictures too, and laugh at all our yesterday's and the things we've all gone through.

—Ellie Skillen

MY WISH TO YOU

Through all that we have seen,
Through all that we have experienced,
Through all that we have done,
If wishes could come true,
I'd wish this for you;

I wish the morning sunshine to glisten in your soft sable hair,
I wish your days happy without a care,
I wish love and health and someone to share it with,
I wish the night to have romance in the air,
I wish a long and happy life full of joy,
And if ever despair and sorrow come your way,
May it be whisked away by the soft summer winds.

These things and many more are what I hope for you,
And if I am not a part of these wishes,
I still hope they come true,
Because you deserve such wishes,
I should know, I'm a friend who knows you and loves you so.

—D. Black

ALWAYS

A star in the dark
    glitters timelessly,
Letting us know
    it is there —
With or without our view.
Emersing itself
in the densest of clouds,
        Secretly.
Starring with Mother Sun
On the brightest of days.
        Reflecting.
        Shining.
            On and on . . .
                On and on . . . .

—Melissa C. Getz

EVENING

The day is done
With evening lights going on
The patter of many feet
Like a weary refrain
Upon the street
One must return to home
And seek a night's release
From the hours of labor
One meets one's neighbor
At day's surcease
Strange odors assail one
With thoughts of food
That penetrates from doorways
And affects your mood
You rush away
At last a destination
And somewhere to rest
To release one's mind
Of thoughts that bind
Night is kind

—Charlotte Sobel

WINTER

The last leaves of autumn
Rustle gently on their limbs,
Pushed about helter skelter
By warm indian summer winds.

All sorts of animals
Both afoot and awing,
Rush about madly
Before winter begins.

Large V shaped flights
To the south to be made,
As the luxury of open water
Is beginning to fade.

The harvest of natures wealth
Must quickly be finished,
For the length of daylight
Begins to diminish.

As the winds out of the north
Do swirl and blow,
All of the creatures are secure
In their own type of abode.

As if prompted by signals
The flakes of snow begin,
Entombing the dull landscape
Until the warm winds of spring.

—Gerald E. Giese

THE PRAYER

A lonely child kneels and prays
"For you are a pleasant one
For this I mean
With your joy
And from your tone
When I am sad
And left alone
There will be no fear
For that you will be near
For this I know
I won't be alone."

—Laurie Dimock

HE'S YOU

She bubbled with excitement
As she reached inside her purse.
Her joy was overflowing;
She thought she just might burst.

She said she met a new love
Who put her in a spin;
Now she can't find a reason
To do anything but grin.

As she was pulling out a picture,
Her heart was opened wide;
Anyone around her
Could see the love inside.

Then she handed me the photo
Of the man who stole her heart.
I held my breath, afraid to speak,
In case the tears might start.

The man she fell in love with,
Who swore that he'd be true,
One day had said the same to me.
Should I tell her that he's you?

—Margaret A. Brennan

THE GREATEST LOVE

I'm alone, but I keep my pride
Sometimes inside, I feel I've died.
The greatest Love I've yet to find
Thus, I speak of the heart, the soul . . .
Mine
I've taken paths that I have chosen
Some that I have not
Some memories, I have kept
Others, I've forgot
I hold grudges in this life I'm livin'
While others, I've forgiven
I look in the mirror every day
The search is on, but still I pray
That some day I'll wake up to find
The heart the soul . . .
Mine
That I'll be standing on solid ground
Because the greatest Love,
I now have found . . .
Myself

*The love I have for life. My hope
that one day, I'll regain what I
once lost as a child and a wife.
And my faith that someday I will.*

—Cindy Pennington Lusty

SO MANY TEARS

It's raining, I've seen it this way before
On occasions when things were really bad
The rain takes on an odd feeling, it falls
Like "tear drops" on my face.
The "Angels are crying," another child is dying,
Another going bad, another heart's being broken, another
Mother sad. Another boy becomes a
Man, but only by an "intimate ritual" is he bound.
Children having children is now world renown
The Angels are crying "so many tears."
This generation must face so many fears
From bigotry, to gang violence, to "pressure from
Their peers,"
AIDS, drugs, unemployment, a "wavering recession"
Homelessness, welfare cuts, a state of "depression."
Our children are dying — The Angels are crying.
So many tears.

—Charles E. Peterson Sr. "The Poet"

JUST WHEN

I remain forever appalled
   afraid and scared
I see
   what we as a race have become
And can't help wondering
   how long before we destroy
   all the good that remains
We all see the pain
   feel the others hunger
   see the acts of violence of brother against brother
Yet few stand beside their beliefs
   of right and wrong
Few pass on to their children
   life that is rich
   in love and support
   and the greatest understanding
We complain about life
   its terrible realities
   and then we stand back
      and allow them to be

—Rachael Storney

YOU'RE THE BEST

I thought that guys were just a waste of time,
but then again, I never thought that you could be mine.
I have fallen so far and so fast.
I have never felt like this in my past!
My feelings are so strong and so right,
I'm on cloud "9" and oh! what a delight.
I can't picture me without you,
I really don't know what I would do.
You're the best thing in my life,
even though you've been known to throw a knife.
The times we've been sharing have been just fun,
and your smile is as warm as the sun.
I hope to always be by your side,
because I have got oh! so much love inside!
I've been dreaming about you every night,
and I know our love is right.
I wish we could be together all the time,
but I'll be happy just as long as you're mine.
I love you darling "yes" I do,
and I know my love will always be true.

—Laura Ann Banker

YOU SAY YOU LOVE ME

You say you love me and yet you know very little about
what makes me happy and what makes me sad, what adds to my
life and what takes away from it or you would try
to preserve me if you loved me.

Is this not the same kind of love than that man expresses
for the great life sustaining forests that are being cut
down and destroyed or the love that is expressed for the
natural rock formations from which are hacked piece after
piece until they are permanently defaced and do crumble?
When man expresses love for a country and then goes to war
with it or admires a glistening, great fish which he has
captured and brought to its death, or the soaring of an
eagle whose heights man dreams of even as he drives it to
extinction, is this not the same kind of love man expresses
for another of his kind even as he passes by . . . on his way
to nowhere? You say, you love me!

—Suzanne DeWitt

THE HEARTBEAT

I loved him so, and I believed that he loved me in return.
I still think that he is the one, though he has left and married another.
I see us together again
in each other's arms, loving one another.
Although we may both be old and cannot remember anything else.
We will remember how we once were so much in love and how we still are.
We will remember only of the good times that we had together.
We will remember only of our love and that is all we need to remember.
That is how I want to spend the end of my life.
That is how I would like to die.
—Knowing that you still loved me
—Feeling your strong, protective arms around me
—And Hearing the only sound, the last sound that I hear before I die
Bum, Bum Bum and yet faster and louder
Bum Bum, Bum Bum.
The last thing that I hear is your heartbeat, pounding for me, pounding for me to survive
The Last thing that I remember about life is . . .
You and Your   HEART   BEAT!

*Dedicated to the one who inspired me to
write this, Jenn, my loving friend*

—Cicely F.

OUR LAST FAREWELL

As I watch your final time with us on this wonderful earth,
I gather my memories and tenderly place them in the smooth oak chest,
    like polished jewels safe and cherished.

The garden's harvest is ready now,
    greenery you have nurtured until summer's end.
Kneeling on the cool damp soil you gently grasp the trailing vine,
    knowing there will be another time of sun-soaked days and rich brown earth,
        and dew upon the delicate blossoms.

It is quiet here —
    words often left unspoken.
But I know you love me, Dad . . .
    my little hand held tightly in yours on an autumn afternoon,
        playing cards waiting to join in our laughter.

A goodnight kiss soon becomes a kiss goodbye.
And I lower the lid of that smooth oak chest . . .
    golden with varnish,
        its treasures stored forever.
And from it radiates love and strength,
    as time goes by,
        as   time   goes   by.

—Constance Hanstedt

TOMORROW?

How days pass so swiftly
time escapes us.
It goes so quickly
For night has come to take
the day
And once again man is silent.

The darkness will take hold for
only moments.
And once again man is violent.

His acts of greed have plagued the
earth for many years to come.
Yet he is blind to this
ultimate rule of thumb.

—B. Mullins

ELEGY*
To the Unknown Poet

Full many a budding poet
   Bloomed to sing unheard,
And wasted God-given talent
Known just to God — and bird:

The raven quoting "Nevermore"*
Was apt to portray his plight:
His poems — all "Love's Labor"
Lost* to human sight —

For his lovely lilting lyrics,
No publisher could be found;
Though exquisite his verses,
In no honored volume bound.

Perhaps, some day in heaven,
His hundreds of hymns will ring,
As evermore, God's angels
His hymns of love may sing!

*Recalling Gray's "Elegy Written in a Country Churchyard," Poe's "Raven" poem, & William Shakespeare's play.

—Mary Alice Badeau Jenkins

SCRIPTURE IS SUFFICIENT

When upon the promises of God
      I do think,
The Holy Spirit doth more
      Christlike—me make.
I give thanks unto the Lord
      for allowing me
      His word to take,
That I might be
      all that I can be
      for His sake.
In all the trials I will face,
      Thy word will surely
      supply the needed grace.
Though grief may be part of
      a future test,
Thy word will always
      provide rest.
Thy will, O Lord, may not
      grant me all I request,
      but this one thing I ask:
Give me Thy peace,
      while—I perform Thy task.

—Bill Ford

MOUNTAIN MATRIARCH
from a collection "Mountain Folk of West Virginia"

She ruled the roost, that mountain woman bold.
She ruled with fist of mail her brawling clan.
An Amazon she was, of steel, ice cold,
Who spoke to be obeyed by every man.
Her grown-up sons walked softly 'round their Maw.
They'd best be careful not to rile her so.
They paid no mind at all to their old Paw
But Maw was one to whom they'd better toe.
A rough and tumble bunch of men were they,
Pure hellions loose upon the mountainside.
They drank their moonshine, brawled both night and day.
They fought and worked and hunted far and wide.
Yet like small children who were put to bed
Their Maw still boxed their ears 'til they were red.

—Mary Jane Reed Welch Bruns

WOMEN OF VIRTUE

A woman, she knows God, and she seeks His face.
Her heart is pure and undefiled in the sight of God.
She trusts His voice, in every case.

This woman is not physically strong like man,
but in God she's strong, to endure all pain.
Now her spirit is strong, and says she can.

Her children shall love her as a friend.
Her husband shall trust her, in everything.
This is the power of her love, that overcomes her sin.

To her husband, she's his Crown of Faith.
She eases his mind, and strengthens his soul
She never withholds and nothing does she waste.

Now this woman of virtue, us men must seek,
treat her as a queen and win her heart
and gain her hand in marriage to keep

Who so ever finds her, will be blessed.
To you I speak my sons, saith the Lord of Host.
Because this Woman of Virtue is still my best.

—Kevin J. Houston

FRIENDSHIP OR LOVE?

How can you turn the blaze of a raging inferno,
Somehow back into the warmth from an ember's glow?
How do you stop a tidal wave?
And how do we turn the love we let grow,
Back into the friendship we used to know?

   How can our friendship survive another day,
   When there's not much more left for us to say?
   Oh no, Now our love is dying!
   Won't you please tell me how can we find a way,
   To make the feelings we've shared forever stay?

Why does it seem like now all we do is fight,
And it's so hard just trying to make it right?
Don't we know something has to change?
Why must we waste time crying alone at night,
When what we want is to hold each other tight?

   Why don't we remember how rare a love is this,
   Stop tearing us apart and leave our dark abyss?
   Oh, how can we just let it end?
   'Cause if we did we know our love we'd soon miss,
   So friend, let's stay together and share a tender kiss!

—Linda M. Powell

HUMMING BIRD

Helicopter, helicopter!
Where did you come from?
Why . . . it came from me!
I can fly like a bird,
I am a bird—
I'm a Humming Bird!

I can fly up, I can fly down;
I can even fly upside down, round and round!

I can fly still and drink nectar from the base of a flower,
And take off backwards going 50 miles per hour!

0 to 50 in less than a second;
My, oh my! Isn't that impressive!

Lord, Lordy! Can't you see—
There isn't a helicopter that can fly like me!

—Wayne A. Rowe

COLOR WHEEL

The whirring pinwheel of the seasons spins and blurs, then pauses at the pumpkin orange of autumn. Contentment fills the ripe globe of the harvest moon; maturity's gravity deepens its restful hues.

But autumn's heaviness tilts the wheel and upends a tiny snowstorm scene; white speckles obscure a miniature house and yard. In Dakota's pie-graph of the year, winter's portion is a glutton's slice, numbing the palate with its frozen crust.

Then the kaleidoscope twists to the notch marked 'spring' and each jade grass blade tumbles into place. Try to conceal a smile at the thought of equal seasons, but savor the brief comedy of spring before summer's droning monologue and the lengthy act of autumn.

And at last the eyepiece of the telescope turns to summer and focuses on the royal blue of sky. Feel for a moment its pulsing power, for its strength must pass to autumn's *da capo* call, with colors freshly mixed and old themes newly ornamented.

—Allan Jacobson

SOMEWHERE IN TIME

The atmosphere, reminiscent of an old time friend,
created by your gentle smile and hearty laugh.
Caressing me, you kiss my every part; our eyes meet
and I slowly melt into your arms.
The touch of your lips pressed to mine, unleash feelings
deep within, I thought were lost to time.
You start a flow inside me that will not subside, as our
bodies passionately merge as one.
Like the fire of the desert winds, you breathe against my
skin; making love to me, you take my breath away.
As we are lost in time, swimming in each other's love, you
take me to heights unknown.
In such ecstasy, you are my only thought, my only
desire.
Two lonely hearts finding each other, and for a brief
moment in time making memories.
Forever dreaming memories of you and me, in a love
lost somewhere in time.

Dedicated to lonely hearts

—Barbara Guyer

JOYS LIKE TOYS

Summer sighs silently slipping
Over yesterday's joy.
Going gently into the stillness
Of now, long gone by.
Touching tender visions of future
Borne into timeless love.
On eternities morn,
All these joys like toys
To touch and feel while
Living this dimensional universe.

—Tisha C. Le Rose

MY FAMILY

Dear Lord, protect my family,
watch over them for me,
circle them in your arms,
and keep them safe
from temptation and harm;
we need your strength
to guide us through
and we need to feel
your love for us, too.
No matter where life leads
Your mighty power
will meet our needs.

—Juanita Powell

A VIEW FROM THE FLOOR

Weary of spirit,
Sick of mind;
Poisoned by his presence,
Deaf, dumb and blind.

All hope of sanity
Lay in liberation.
What others labeled courage
I knew was desperation.

Thirsting for the taste of life
And finding dregs within the cup;
When you're beaten down so often
There's no way to go but up.

—Sue Woods

THE CARDINAL

I have a little friend
Who comes to visit me
Twice or three times a week.
He seems to know
When I am saying
My morning prayers,
Because that's his time to come.
He flits from branch to branch
And often sits outside my window,
Cocks his little head,
And seems as if he says
"Good morning my friend."
He doesn't know it
But I always answer
"Good morning my dear."
This little friend is the
Brilliant colored Cardinal,
And his visit makes my day.

—Mary M. Stumreiter

HEAVEN'S GAIN

Flowers that bloom with the sun
in the sky
Change with the season in the blink
of an eye
A cool summer breeze whispering
Goodbye
To a special soul giving Heaven
a try
For us left behind, we miss her
bright smile
We all wish she stayed for a longer
while
Our friend is not sad or feeling the
pain
No doubt, our loss is Heaven's Gain

—M. Elizabeth

UNTIL THEN

It's been almost a year
since I had to let you go
But I think that there is something
you really ought to know
I still love you just as much
as I did before
And if it's even possible
I'm sure I love you more
The emptiness still fills me
way down deep inside
I try to escape the hurt
but there's nowhere I can hide
I know you will come back to me
I've known it from the start
And I will be here waiting
with all the love that's in my heart
But until that time comes
my memories will get me through
Until we are together again
and all my dreams come true.

—Judy R. Green

VERMILLION RIVER

Vermillion River
Scarlet
Falling down on the stones
Staining
Fading

Vermillion River
Thick
Galavanting to my bones
Crawling
Shoving

Vermillion River
Quick
Screaming out its low pitched tone
Warm
Coating

    Soft   Silent

    Soft   Silent

    Dead   Silent

—Chris Carrera

AFTER ALL

After the hurricane; a tree stands tall.

After the flood; a stone stands dry.

After the quake; a building stands whole.

After the volcano; a blade of grass grows.

After all great devastations even greater
Things survive no matter how simple they may seem. For

After all, after slavery; I stand — strong.

—Jada D. Charles

THE STORM

I love the roar of thunder as I lie in bed at
night and see God crack his lightning whip and scare
everyone in sight.

And as the heavens start to weep into the earth
their tears will seep bringing sweet nourishment to
every tree that grows the honeysuckle and the rose.

Yes winter is slowly fading from view, sending
forth life anew like the tulips pushing through
the ground never uttering a sound.

Soon the bees will buzz from plant to plant
and you can almost hear them say, "Wake up, wake
up sleepy heads spring is on its way."

The robins will start to sing their songs of
love for everyone to hear, I think that is the part
I like the best about this time of year.

Now as the sun begins to rise and we open our
eyes, the morning glories are in bloom and I will
have to say it's none too soon.

Yes everything will look and smell so sweet
now don't you think that is kind of neat.

Soon the flowers will have their faces painted
bright and to think this all started with that storm
last night.

—Robert R Beebee

WARRIOR CHILD

This world that we live in is falling apart,
    And we are troubled on every side;
But don't be distressed, dear child of God,
    Just look to the cross where Christ died.

When persecution comes and you feel all alone,
    The Lord will not utterly forsake you;
Call on His name with repentance and praise,
    And the Savior will carry you through.

When weapons of confusion bombard your mind,
    Tighten your helmet and don't despair;
Lift a shield to quench the fiery evil darts,
    And be assured that you're in God's care.

As the stormy evil battles rage on intensely,
    Adversity may cast you flat on your face;
But, Warrior Child, you shall not be destroyed,
    Salvation comes thru God's perfect grace.

Rise up and speak forth the mighty Word of God,
    It's more powerful than a two-edged sword;
And march boldly forward to the enemy's camp,
    Knowing you're safe in the hands of the Lord.

Victory will be yours by the power of His might,
    So be courageous and continue to stand;
Determine in your heart to climb ever upward,
    Warrior Child, you shall inherit the land.

—Judy Ann Williams Downey

To think that I should do as you please is totally laughable
I have been my own master too long, you see
No one will ever conquer my mind, my heart, or my soul
This freedom's price will be my epitaph
For all have a master of a sort
No one, not even I, can survive total freedom
—Rebecca de Vaz

MOUNTAIN ECSTASY

"In my whole life I have never seen anything so beautiful," exclaims the city child looking up from Daddy's arms into the brilliance and blackness of the mountain night.

Summer pastimes of fishing, swimming and picking wildflowers, too soon interrupted by colder nights; the first snowfall, with a dusting of white in the midst of autumn hues.

Fiercely cold winds follow, virgin snow, white outs and icicles on rocks, forming winter sculptures on the mountain's crest.

These mountains beckon skiers at its peak and ice fishing for the less adventurous below, until spring transports sounds of the snow melting into crystal clear lakes and brooks.

The life cycle begins again, another season, each bringing its own beauty and expectation; our love of these mountains never wanes but grows with each new discovery.

We thank God for this goodness and insight into finding happiness each day in simple things; for the child's joy and wonder at the brilliant stars in the blackness of night.

—Nancy Berry-Boyne

THE LITTLE-BITTY POOL

You have heard about the meadow on the little-bitty pool.
Down in the Tygart river, my sister had one too.
The fish would swim in and lie in her hand.
It was the only little-bitty pool in all of the land.

On the shore of the river she created a pool.
With rocks from the river, where it was shady and cool.
A little entrance where the fish could swim in.
To watch them swimming there brought a smile or a grin.

The water was cool and sparkling.
A soft rippling noise it made.
Trees grew on the banks of the river.
The little pool lay in the shade.
The azure blue sky.
The balmy fresh air.
A splash in the pool, told the fish she was there.

Craw-dads, minnows, a turtle or two,
all shared the water of the fresh sparkling pool.
When my sister entered the water, the fish would swim in.
With their green scaling backs, their quivering tail, and fin.

Calm, peaceful and quiet,
birds chirping and singing their song.
Falling leaves floating on the water.
The current gently carrying them along.
On a hot sultry day, it was such a nice place to go.
To watch the fish swimming around, and nibbling your toe.

A place to relax.
Neath a sky of deep blue.
Was wading in the water of the little-bitty pool.

*Dedicated to my sister, Elizabeth McClain,
in memory of happy by-gone days*

—Vivian Shipp

HALLOWEEN NIGHT

Halloween Night is a night
Of fright,
A night of weird and spooky
Lights.

You see all these creatures
Floating around,
Isn't it spooky in your
Town?

Ghosts and goblins at your
Door,
Ghosts and goblins asking for
More.

Until there are no more
Goblin feet,
The night just isn't complete.

—Paige Dickens

I TRIP TO THE COUNTRY

I went into the country the
other day. I saw many things
along the way.

Many animals large and small,
some could walk, some could only
crawl.

The birds were pretty and flew
about, 'cause I had disturbed
them along the route.

They flew in the trees and
chattered away, scolding me
for spoiling their day.

There was a nice little creek
I traveled along, the noise it
made had me bursting in song.

A nearby deer cocked his head
to the side as if wondering
if he should run and hide.

So I decided I better call
it a day; and climbed back in
my car and drove away.

—Bill Walker

YUKON JACK AND I

In a chaste kiss our lips met.
Yours, the insensate glass
Hard against my teeth
Made me shudder
Just before your spirit
Coalesced with mine and then,
As if invoked by your name,
The wanderlust I felt when
Reading Jack London's tales
Exploded anew in a phantasm
Of dogs, sleds and buckskins,
Bloodied traps,
Timber wolf's howl,
Starvation and blinding snow,
Crumbling shafts of gold mines,
Klondike's tawdry saloons
Offering the extravaganza
Of five-pound steaks, hot baths
And furious, primitive lust
Served up by soiled doves
For a mere handful
Of hard-won golden dust

—Dita Vertefeuille

Don't look at me,
watch me

Don't listen to me,
hear me

Don't touch me,
feel me

Don't love me,
Love

*Dedicated to the truth I have found
in the Love that surrounds me,
and is always within me*

—gatherdi

DREAMER LOFT

I am warm in a dreamer loft
I go to sleep in bedding soft

Like a blinding beacon of light,
bringing to life horrible things,
cutting through once mystical night,
that blasted alarm's ringing stings

Still I lie in my bedding soft
I am warm in a dreamer loft

I move across a hard wood floor,
in a cold, creaking, moaning song
My thoughts are where I was before
The lullaby is much too strong

I still am in my dreamer loft
and always sleep in bedding soft

—Daniel J. Pollard

EBONY QUEEN

I am an African queen
I'm different from you
My hair is curly and kinky
And my lips are purple blue

I come from royalty
Although the U.S. is my home
I came across the waters
And left my rightful throne.

I stood proud and tall
And wore crowns upon my head
Others cowered at my feet
And I was feared instead

Now I'm here in America
Where I am second best
I'm not catered to anymore
And people think I'm less.

My location has changed
And this changed my status too
I exchanged my royal colors
For the old red, white and blue,

Who would have thought it
The changes that were wrought
When a ship made a tedious journey
And all the slaves were brought.

If you had left me in my native land
I would now be an African queen
My name would be Nefratitia
And it sure wouldn't be Jean.

—Willie J. Neusom

A FAILED DREAM

We lived together for a time, and yet so far apart
I never knew the real dreams that lay upon her heart.
She filled the empty hours of my life so very well
It seemed to me a real love where always I would dwell.
Yet, ever for some meaning of her own she sought to find
And slowly drifted off to ease the sorrow of her mind.
Now wish to God that I had heard her disenchanted plea
For all she ever wanted was for love to set her free.
And Oh to have her back again I'd give my very life
But only have I memories left of my best friend, my wife.

—Stephen

UNCONTROLLED FEELINGS

Why do I feel so depressed, deserted, so alone?
Lonesomeness covers me like a blanket.
Stagnated—my feet stick to the floor
Torn between exhaustion from doing
and overpowered by not achieving.

Anxious, nervous, sick inside, yet
lazy, day dreaming, listening but not hearing.
Feel cheated, deceived, resentful, chewed out
Lowered as if on my hands and knees
Clouded over, rained upon, chilled to the bone.

Sidetracked, unable to carry through and be heard.
Why? I didn't ask to feel like this, take this
horrible cloud from over my head. Why me? Move over
to someone else. I don't deserve this.
What have I done that was so wrong?
Please leave me alone, I pray that you go away.

—Mary Joan Smith

REGGIE

It was one-forty-five in a two o'clock bar.
She sat near the jukebox; I watched from afar.
I looked at her, she looked back at me,
and I knew where we'd be at a quarter-to-three.

I sat near her seat. She didn't complain.
My words had design, like an oncoming train.
My moves were so perfect — I wanted to play.
Then I looked in her eyes and my life changed that day.

The talk turned to Thoreau, Bob Dylan, Ayn Rand;
To that bondage called marriage and castles of sand;
For whom the bell tolls and why and why not;
And whether tis nobler to be or be not.

I reached for the bar tab. She said, "we'll go Dutch."
We continued to discourse on freedom and such
And on winds — ill and fair — that blow over our land.
I looked to her lap where she now held my hand.

I was drunk with her thoughts and the shape of her hips,
Her ideas and ideals and her breasts and her lips.
Her "I's" and her eyes touched me places so new
Sir Lust stood his ground — but Sir Love stood there too.

The bar where we met was torn down years ago.
Its foundations were sand as she taught me, you know.
But the passion I found there still burns deep in me
as hot as that morning in mid Eighty-three.

It was one-forty-five in a two o'clock bar,
She sat near the jukebox, but swung from a star.
And only she knew, when she looked back at me,
where we might be at a quarter-to-three.

—Dan R. Kiely

From the Blue Skies,
To The Rolling Hills,
And Homemade Pies
To get my fill.

Seeing the friendly faces,
And inspiring places.
Hearing the wildlife beckon,
Even the cows I reckon.

From southern New Mexico,
To northern Idaho.
I've been a seeker
For a home like Meeker.

—Dennis White

LIFE LESSONS

In truth there is justice
in lies probation.
I give you leave
to take a vacation
to somewhere other
than where you are.
Your words were near
and yet so far
To what you thought
I wanted to hear.
Once I was blind,
But now I see clear
I've learned a lesson
You have yet to discover
to be a true friend
is to be a lover.

—Tracy Combs

CONNIE

Remember dear Connie
sweet as a rose.
Gentle as a breeze
where the green valley grows.

Way up in heaven
where the trinity dwells.
And golden voices
of angels swells.

You can picture her there,
gentle voice singing
and amazing grace from their
golden harps ringing.

God on His throne,
Jesus at His side,
controlling the winds
or whatever be-tides.

Picture her there
dressed in white robes.
Her head all aframed
with a great halo.

Surrounded by angels,
and God up above,
knowing her heart
is swelling with love.

She is real happy
in her surroundings up there,
waiting for you all
in that city foursquare.

—Mary Ramsey Taylor

Sometimes in life you need to take a chance
even on things you may only see at a glance.
Others may say you're making the wrong choice
but you need only listen to the sound of your own voice.
When things don't work out like you first hoped they would
you need not look at the bad, only the good.
The best things in life are easy to measure
if you work hard and fight for life's simple pleasures.
When it seems like you've been beat,
look at the knowledge you've obtained
because sometimes in life the best things take pain.
To be happy in life, just follow your heart
then the pain and the heartache is just a small part.
Remember my words when you take your chance
cause life goes by in a passing glance.

—Thomas D. Ray

MEANT TO BE

Being close to each other is how we were meant,
because seeing you happy makes me content.
The day could be depressing and cloudy too,
but as long as you smile, the sun will shine through.

When I think of the time that we've already shared,
I begin to feel special; I know that you care.
With that look on your face and the gleam in your eyes,
though they are not transparent, your thoughts I surmise.

I'd like to feel my fingers running through your hair;
and whenever you're lonely, I want to be there.
Until then I will dream of tasting your lips,
and feeling the passion in your warm fingertips.

When you speak I hear angels, singing all around;
you lift up my spirits so I can't touch the ground.
I will live beside you forever, and just grow old;
I will never mistreat you, I will praise you like gold.

My heart has been searching for someone like you;
my eyes have been crying the streams I walked through.
There is no other way we could ever be seen;
you can believe it's the truth, we were just meant to be.

—T.J. Magulick

THE FIRST WEDDING ANNIVERSARY

It is only the beginning, the year of paper;
the paper is white; the symbol of purity,
a sacrifice of ourselves to each other.
There is no other gift more pure than love.

The paper is thin, representing the passage of time;
the brief period we've been together,
only a page in a novel of thousands,
bound in leather, trimmed in shimmering gold.

There are many lines on paper;
as memories we have shared.
Memories to remind us of our love.

The paper has two sides, representing two individuals
joined as one. I am you as you are me.
What a wonderful feeling, yet how frightening.

The paper tears so easily, representing tenderness;
but paper comes from trees which grow more strong each year,
the symbol of life and growth.
It is also so with our love, strong and forgiving.

And so it is the year of paper, the first year;
the year of purity, love and commitment.

—Jacquelene Rane Vogele

MONSTER

Its hard surface was flashing,
like lightning on a Summer's day.
Sky-like screen stared wide-eyed,
comparing time, and date.
My skin was crawling, my belly
ached. No! Not this monster!
Shut the door, or it might escape.
A Sigh leaves my lips, mouth wide.

Befriend the creature, as it is.
Touch the surface, push its buttons,
release the pressure, the unease.
Tell it how you feel; and wait.
Electricity and flesh caressed,
vitalized my heart; my new love.

—Ivanka Suveg

ECLIPSE

I looked
In the looking glass
for you
The pain made me run
Afraid I wouldn't
See you
As I looked across at the faces
All standing — waiting
to be seen
By someone.
But I was looking
For you.
Catching glimpses
of you looking
Behind the faces
Forcing me to keep
Running — To keep — searching
For where we would
Stand face-to-face
Forever.

—ElizaBeth Bigham-McGinnis

CRIES OF HEARTACHE

Time after time, I sit in the
dark. I cry because you are
so far away.

Time after time, I cry as I walk
away from you. Tears in my eyes
are so thick, I can barely see
where I am going.

I hold back my tears and
fears for such a long time that
when I least expect it, I break
down and everything comes out
at once. I lose control of my
emotions.

My emotions are fighting to be
straight once again. One day I would
be happy and laughing; the next
I would be sad and crying
because I can not be next to your
warm, sweet, tender body.

—Rosanne Allen-Byers

DEATH DREAM

It's late one cold solemn night
I dream alone . . . bewildered
    Tranced in immaculate terror
"Grieve alone . . . amongst us"
    Defaced voices cried in shrieking harmony
The hidden window to the present reveals morbid surroundings
"Enter the black vastness"
    The unknown, ominous voice slurred
"Relinquish your distraught mind to the demon
    That lurks in the darkness
Face the demons with your soul in your hands
Pull the trigger
Embrace death, accept pain
Welcome fear and walk onto—
Awake
My eyes flood with tears
Hot metal pierced through grieving flesh
    And a lifeless hand falls with the weight
        Of a smoking gun

—Juan R. Fernandez

echo of sanity

not letting go, keeping my grip
with balance so steady, it's tempting to tip
seeing the visions, yet memories they are
i'm physically here, and yet so far
knowing the ending, yet knowing no start
keeping together, yet falling apart
following darkness, yet seeing the light
doing the wrong, yet knowing what's right
climbing inside, yet exposed to the out
knowing the answers, yet still having doubts
fading with twilight, yet blazing so bright
knowing the way, yet having no light
seeing clouds in the night and the moon in the day
following maps, yet losing your way
when touching the frozen and yet it feels hot
knowing forever, but eternity not
hearing the signal, yet making no move
wanting to win, expecting to lose
holding to faith, yet feeling so weak
screaming forever . . . it echos, echos, echos, echos . . . .

—C.L. Baker

HIGH ATTITUDE — A WAR ON DRUGS

You sit around in your fog-enshrouded world of haze
Smoking on others' words of wisdom — not your own
Living the lies of times gone past — without a future
Sending messages of grief and hate unknown to you
Wending your way through mists of dreams gone unfulfilled
Always knowing that those dreams are just that —
The difference between fantasies and life's reality.

There were the days you could no longer remember —
Those days that were important days to recall
But it makes no difference now to even think of the
Times which were the cause of all this because
The thoughts are painful and not easy — so you
Hide yourself in the world of dense oblivion.

Your attitude swings from left to right —
From side to side and leaves impressions of woe.
Which impressions of yourself are you showing?
What is really you and your hopes for your life?
Your aspirations and longings are forever lost.

Will you ever be able to see the side that
The observer sees of you and from you?

—Tom Jones

A TRIP

It has been hard and my only blessings are life's pain;
I watch that I may stumble when I walk
but eternally alone, the road grows short.

And dare I ask of company more,
for not even foe to me
shall I cast into my sea!

You're but a grain in the castle when ivory waves beg the door.
Feel the watch. Another piece of maroon,
peer through a twine lingering and strewn.

It is time for him to travel.
Once again, no necklace of choice,
but with the friends of destiny woe.

—Stephen Willis

2 & FRO & 3

2 is terrible, they say, but I've a different thought.
The strangest in my home may be that e're before's been wrought.

He came with will intact, you see, complete, and all his own.
And not at 2, but right at 3, began to think he's grown.

In acting out this thinking thus, the world does not conform.
It begs the question, from us, WHAT 3 YEAR OLD'S THE NORM??

The screaming's to communicate. The crying? Who knows why?
The jabber just to aggravate. The standing? Not to lie.

The lying? Oh, why, not to stand, of course, and do perceive,
The only chance to wash small hands is way past time to leave.

And Sunday dress? Oh, what a mess! Just let Mom's eye to gleam,
Emerging from a closet? YES! A turtle!! HALLOWEEN!!

My hands are up! Resigned in part, cajole can I no more.
Sustaining life in this Dad's heart is . . . After 3 comes 4!

—Brian H. Thomas

ONE SMALL PRAYER

One small prayer has gone up to Heaven to fall upon God's ear.
one small child's voice has uttered words
that only God can hear.

God make Mommy and Daddy love each other like they used to do.
I don't understand words like child support,
and I guess I'll have to sue.

I wonder God if I'm to blame for the way they feel today.
I don't like to see them fight
or hear the words they say.

I'm just a little girl and I don't really know what's wrong.
They both tell me things are going to change,
and I'll have to be very strong.

My mommy says she loves me and my daddy says it too,
and I'm so very unhappy God,
I don't know what to do.

Soon I'll have a new address and you can find me there,
just in case you decide to answer
this very special prayer.

I know that you can hear me God for you are everywhere
I'm just a little girl sending up to heaven one small prayer.

—Colleen A. Gehr

NEIGHBOR

No more grading letters
Or derogatory remarks
Words of expression festered
Insomnia caused by a dog's bark!

You've stated your opinions
I've expressed mine
Let's put this behind us
Forgiving within time.

—Linda S. Neely

ANNIVERSARY

Sixteen years ago today,
In this very town
I put on my tux
and you your wedding gown.

Together our life began
Till death do us part
My love for you will always come
Straight from my heart!

Love, Richard Nov '93

—Richard A. Neely

STREET LIGHTS

Just like fireflies
   in the sky,
They light the way
   for passers-by.

Shining true, steadfast
   and bright,
Bringing home our loved ones
   late at night.

Through the darkness
   they give their glow,
Showing us the
   way to go.

Helping us to
   win the fight,
Of our fear of darkness
   and the night.

—Jennifer Lynn Puncochar

LOST

Do you know I am lost
without you and your words
I can't sleep, I just think
for your love, in my heart
I hold my tears with lots of pain
My smile is always on my face
How much I suffer you are never
going to know
Time I spend with you running
back and forth
This is time filled with
courage, love, and power
Someday if you will feel the same
To share everything again
Don't cry if you read these words
Just remember somebody is always
behind you, with you, with love
You are never going to see

—Danica Mackovski

A SECRET PLACE

A hidden gully, majestic pines, and wispy alder
Centered a sparkling pool, straddled by a falling cedar.
A mountain oasis, my secret place
Where squirrels gather nuts, a seasonal race.

Mountain lilies, whimsical mushrooms meander below the trees
Soft scents of musk, pine, and cedar ride the gentle breeze.
God's presence purposely lingers.
His love my heart does fill like His praise singers.

Sweet peace envelopes me there.
Melodious melodies of love to God the birds do share.
His presence consumes my being, drawing me near.
Creation hushed in concert, His precious love, so dear.

—Katie Figueroa

SECRET LOVE

"Write me, please write me, write anything," he said
so why do I feel this gnawing dread?
to expose my soul, the essence that fled
and left me feeling partially dead.

The reasons run deep that make me feel shy
and until you draw close, you will never know why
yet one with the key, who inspires me to try
may someday uproot what did seemingly die.

For buried deeply within my soul
pushed so far back that it's taking a toll
lies the love that can make me whole
and only *one* will play that role.

He's here now, smiling, encouraging me
gently, with tenderness, as though on his knee
imparting strength and the will to be free
of these shackles, oh can't you see . . .

I love you my Prince, from long ago
in the beginning, when once I did know
who you were and where I would go
this is the secret that has bound me so.

—Suzanne Dewitt

RETIRED WIFE

At birth, parents celebrate this brand new life,
He grows up to be a husband and she a wife,
Of course this option is only sometimes shared,
If everyone's ideas, presumptions or grievances are aired.

Maybe there are children, maybe there are not,
They enjoy the compensations casting their daily lot,
They share the frustrations, the sorrows and the joy,
That comes along with rearing this girl or boy.

The children grow up, joining the working force,
Following their parents' footsteps, hoping of course,
That life brings everything good along with the bad,
The husband is loving, tender, making the wife glad.

So — he goes to work daily earning the daily bread,
Perhaps she does also, helping finances out of the red,
And in 20 to 30 years, retirement comes into view,
Another celebration, seeking a life all anew.

He has a hobby in the basement, garage or special place,
Keeping from underfoot while she continues her busy pace,
The laundry, the cleaning, the cooking, the shopping — so is life,
HE IS RETIRED!! But who ever heard of a RETIRED WIFE???

—Terry Marie Rockey

Resting quietly on the edge of a dream
    Soul stretching to the stars

Amethyst waves caress the heart
    Lighting up the night with a sudden spark

Shadow of a lover whispers
    See me, see me . . .

Cross the expanse of uncertainty
    Climb the steep winding trail to the heart

No silence there, no darkness to fear
    Free to explore the deepest caves where crystal waters flow

Dawn creeps in and sings the day
    Bringing the dream into view

Resting her heart next to yours
    A soul you always knew

    —Lorilee LaHatt

HEARTACHE MAKES LOVE GROW

    If there had been no heartache and no world full of strife, I can't help but wonder what would have come of my life.
    There are times I think I would be so glad, without the pain and heartache that made me sad.
Yet, on the other hand, they helped to make me strong, so in the future years I can help others along.
    If life had been full of happiness and skies of blue, I would have no true understanding of a troubled heart.
I could not truly say, "yes, I understand you," Because I would not have had to play that part.
    When you think you just can't stand any more rain, stop and think what life would be without it.
There would be a world of dry desert and lots of pain so, you see we just can't exist without it!
    Remember the more heartache and pain in your life the more sensitive to others feelings you should be.
I can't stop the rain, so I let it help me grow. Just let The Good Lord help you through; He sure helps me!

    —Kathy L. Parnell

I am surrounded in glass
It's been here all of my existence
It is my creator and it plans on keeping me here;
Imprisoned

There was a time when I was unaware of the pain
It inflicted upon me
Until I stepped out of the boundary it so cleverly placed around me
And it appeared

I reached out my hand to touch it
It touched me back; with a shock
An electric current flows through it

I am afraid

The glass is wearing thin
So with its last efforts it tries to hold me still,
Shocking me often

I will break free
And I will run; I will not look back

I was afraid.

    —Danielle Nicole Dunnigan

NECROPOLIS

Cold grey arms
    draw me to you
Empty names
    hold me speechless
Stolen lives
    hibernating
Beneath your
    rigid posture

    —Judy D. Masten

PAY DAY

Cumulus nimbus,
High in the sky.
Saturated with water,
Letting raindrops fly.

Let none of this,
Cause us dismay.
For today is the day,
To collect our pay.

    —Richard A. Neely

LOVE SONG

Suddenly I
    see You
I get shivers in the twilight
    of my dreams

You fill me with bubbles
    of ecstasy
    and I dance in the
breathless wonder of the
    rainbow

Purity is the song
    Love is the dance
        You are the conductor

    —Amy L. Luttrell

CHEER UP!

You're awesome
You're great
a million dollars
on a plate

You're nice
You're fantastic
stretchy just
like elastic

You're cool
You're kind
a reel to reel
that can unwind

You're smart
You're neat
two bare feet
on concrete

You're awesome
You're you
so cheer up
and don't be blue!!

    —Jill Krynicki

ONLY A NOTION

In a place of sorrow I dwell,
My ship, it does not sail.
My life is passing by,
I've wings but can not fly.
The one I love is betrothed,
So into the sea I've dove.
I cast my spell to the farthest star
To separate those near and far.
I need a cup to hold my tears;
You are the one I do hold dear.
A rose that's covered with glistening dew,
I cast my fears to something new.
In my hand a mystic potion,
A thought of love, only a notion.

—Leiane N. Gibson, age 12

DISTANT MUSIC

A song plays in the shadows
Of an aged woman's heart,
Calling to mind the visions
Of life's youthful days in part.

She remembers distinctively
The lyrics of seventy years
But can't recall the present day;
Her frailty gives in to tears.

She feels a sense of abandonment
In the hours so dreadfully long
And seeks for a bit of comfort
In this inner, soulful song.

The essence of her loneliness
Nurtures a reminiscent dance,
Reliving those cherished moments,
Quiet times, and sweet romance.

So welcomed is the melody
With lines of no rehearse.
As she anticipates; she waits
For the last and final verse.

—Janet Lux

HANDS

Those hands told where
her life had been.
So many years creased
beneath wrinkled skin.
Babies held and loved
and so long since gone.
Hands too pained to sleep
After all the aches had settled in.

Those hands told where
her life had been,
Blue veins tracing
bridges to our hearts.
Burdens too heavy,
Never to end—or where to start.

Those hands told where
her life had been.
So near to heaven
By a simmering pot,
So near to love
With happiness never sought.
Her hands told where
her life had been,
Now, safe here within my heart.

—Helen Madeline Alexanian Smith

TORN BETWEEN TWO PLACES   OFULLMOON

Life itself can be very cruel to the heart,
The heart takes a good beating from each daily occurence,
And I feel that I'm putting an extra strain on mine.

My family and friends in Ontario I can't stand to part,
But my feelings and emotions no longer make sense,
Like a suffering animal all I can do is whine.

My family and the people I met there were great,
They made me feel welcome, so I left in grievance,
Ontario or Nova Scotia is the bottom line.

I feel that I'm in a soap opera or a political debate,
Not knowing where to turn, I result in reminiscence,
Welcome in both places I have to decide in time.

I'll finish school, my emotions and feelings will have to wait,
Until then I will be in no pleasance,
Torn between two places is a terrible situation to be in.

—Shelly L Stanert

I CARE

The last of my family, the last that I'll bear,
My baby forever, You know that I care.
I know you are mixed up, your life's been so rough,
But you've loved me, stood by me, through all that old stuff.
I'll always be here, for you, my dear son,
I'll try to be patient, I'll try to be fun.
I'll be more forgiving, so please don't forget,
To always be honest, you'll never regret.
I loved you then as I love you now,
We'll make it through together, somehow.
Life is not easy, Life is not fair,
But never forget, I'll always be there.
It will never change, you will always be,
My baby son, my family.
Through long hard times, through good and bad,
We'll share the happy and share the sad.
It took such a long time to feel so secure,
I've drug you through so much, but this time I'm sure.
Sometimes I am distant, it seems so unfair,
But son please remember, I love you, I care!

—Carol D. Land

DAD'S LITTLE ANGEL

Little angel your Dad loved you from the start,
Your bubbly ways completely stealing my heart,
Like a princess, you sparkled my soul aflame—
Seeing much charm like; Shirley Temple's fame.

You fascinate everyone with your cute talk,
And your great stylish unique angelic walk,
A dynamic smile that only Heaven could make,
Sky blue eyes that glow like a moonlit lake.

Dad cannot help but love your natural magical ways,
Especially each night when you kneel down and pray—
"God let all people and animals be happy and free;
"Please take care of sweet Mommy and Daddy for me."

My dear little angel, you are a most wonderful child,
Through life, my love for you will be more than mild,
It will go on after your golden years of childhood,
And remember my premonition when you reach adulthood—

"Ladies and Gentlemen of this most lovely gala event,
The beautiful winning Miss America your Host presents!"
You will appear; like an angel walking out of a cloud,
To a standing energetic applause of a consenting crowd.

—Ray Gordon

MRS. BENNETT

A dear lady of talent, surely an angel of God
Was sweet Mrs. Bennett, the wife of T. Claud

Her home built of gray rock, a house so unique
There was no other quite like it, in Wilson Creek

I'll share with you now, warm memories she's made
When I was but a small boy, just in the first grade

Our class is all seated, there's hush at our table
It's after lunch Friday, and she'll tell us a fable

Maybe the Three Little Pigs, that ol' wolf was so mean
Or Jack and the Beanstalk, with his magic red bean

Cinderella went to the ball, and danced 'til midnight
And I sure loved the story, she told of Snow White

The Night Before Christmas, made my imagination run wild
She filled my mind with visions, back when I was a child

And she could fill the church air, with a most beautiful ring
As she whistled the hymn, while the congregation would sing

She's still telling stories, just like she always did
And the angels listen intently, wide eyed like a kid

'Cause she's now in heaven, wearing a crown of pure gold
Thank you Mrs. Bennett, for all the stories you've told

In honor of a dear woman, Lula Bennett, whose stories awakened and honed my imagination in days of yesteryear.

—Arley M. Bischoff

HILDEGARD, THE MEAN OLD HAG

Hildegard was a mean old hag.
She had brown hair and a torn brown bag.
She walks around the dusty old town,
breaking things by knocking them down.
No one sees her or hears her boast,
cause Hildegard, Hildegard is a ghost.
The bartender cried, "It's the devil himself."
as another glass fell of the shelf.
A few years back Hildegard died.
No one came to her funeral to stand at her side.
She had no friends. No one cared.
Children ran from her cause they were scared.
Then one day while she was getting fussed,
she met a boy getting off the bus.
The boy looked drab with clothes of rag
and he could see the mean old hag.
"You look like you could use a friend, too," he said.
The mean old hag's face then turned red.
"I'm mean and ugly as can be."
"What's wrong with you that you can't see?"
"I see your beauty and you will too
if you look deep into my eyes of blue."
So she peered into his eyes and this is what she saw,
a lovely vision with hair of straw.
As if by magic, her personality changed,
and with that, physically she was rearranged.
Now Hildegard had a friend.
And her terrible mean streak came to an end.

—Nate Reinert

FOURTH SEASON

Blue lights sparkle
Against glittering gold
And splendid is winter's sunset.
Though wrinkled and withered
Are the leaves,
And faded the minted green
Of summer's bright grass.

With mystic magic
And fairyland art,
About the world are laid
All feathery and white
Gleaming snow and glistening ice,
As on wings of wind
A winter's spell is cast

—Lee Wheeler

I walked into the prison,
  not knowing what to expect.
The prisoners they loved and
  welcomed me, their hearts were
  hungry yet.
The minister questioned me to
  find out my intent.
For his idea of our purpose
  he was strongly bent.
The guards they searched me
  tho I had done nothing wrong.
I knew one thing for certain
  we would have to be strong.
As I looked into their eyes,
  and saw the pain living there,
  come dear Lord to my lips, and
  tell them how you care.
I have a lot to learn yet,
  but one thing I know,
If I can plant a seed here,
  one day it will grow.

—Dean Hedglen

MY SHINING LIGHT

There is a shining light
Held prisoner inside me
Embedded in my heart
By barriers that bind me

It is all who I am
But to most no longer seen
The realness of my person
All exuberance to my being

They understand not of the truth
I wish to bring them clarity
Of love for them I hold inside
Of kindness and sincerity

  Oh such a crime
  And in my mind
  I scream and long
  For freedom's time

I dream of freedom of my soul
To hide away no more
I dream one day to shine again
Just like I did before . . . .

—Leslie Ann Walter

CANDLE-NIGHT

They sit, but a few
and dance the evening away
Alight inflight.

Images-our-Shapes
abound, to eye
What was once night.

While whites in yellows
color to blue,
Until morningsight.

—Frog — Jeff

In the old porch swing
I sat as a teen.

I watched as the silver
maple leaves gleamed.

The wind blew so gently
against my face as I closed
my eyes with contentment and
grace.

Oh how wonderful the memories
that came —
when all of a sudden —
the screen door banged.

—Janet Moore

48 WORDS

Tears and raindrops
always come together
you can't have one
without the other

Sometimes it would seem
I could do without both
but as they say
when it rains
it pours

What can you do
to stop the rain?
What can you do
to stop the tears?

—Ruth Phillips (Scibelli)

WHAT ARE YOU FEELING?

    Let me know how you feel
about being with me
    Open up to me and help
me see
    That I really do mean
something to you
    Tell me you'll always be
true
    Pull me close, and I'll
draw you near
    As you say "I love you" for
the first time, so soft and
sincere
    Press your lips to mine
    Tell me you'll always be
mine.

—Stacy Slone

THE LESSON

I know I'll find a cure for my loneliness,
    yeah, I'll find a way to heal this pain;
My body's left with emptiness,
    and my heart's filled with shame.

It was such a surprise.
    I couldn't believe my eyes;
When she walked in . . . with him.

I was the last one to know
    the last one to show
The last one I thought would give in.

I could see it in her eyes,
    and hear it in her lies;
As she started her stories once again.

They say lovers come and go.
    My hurt's something she'll never know.
She's a woman absent of love within.

My friends tell me this is something to be learned,
    and to stay clear of that fire 'cause you're sure to be burned.
It's uncaring to who you are, it gets everyone the same
    all of life's lonely hearts just become victims of the game.

—Matthew E. Gielow

PLEASE LET ME BE

A priceless gem in a pint of dust
intrusted to your innermost for custody
by the Unseen Spirit's gentle Breath
gracing your choice till I mature.
But you worry of the future,
feel you are cursed and be shortlived.
You take me as intruder to your freedom
overwhelming our intrinsic affinity.

You knew I would be
when you fell in love.
So here I am, meant to be heir
to the many mansions,
immortal as the Archangels.

Let me therefore sweet woman
drink more from your blood;
sleep unmolested in your womb.
Shelter me from the cold,
from the poisoned breeze that sprays me as a flea.
Do not lead me to the four walls of death
where the tinkling cymbals beat of sorrow and pain,
deaden the soul before it sees its destiny.
Instead listen to my heartbeats
languishing for compassion, love, life,
and please let me be.

When born, feed me from your breast.
Clothe me with your caress,
and secure me with your kiss.
Feast on my blueberry eyes that look like yours
and see life sublime.
May God enliven your soul with joy,
see in the rainbow-tainted horizons
a glimpse of celestial life
and sing me your sweet lullaby
as you rock my cradle with that labor of love.

Look Mother! Open wide your windows.
Can you see the restless kids on those toystudded lawns?
I hear music from their laughter and rhymes.
They will be my playmates if I come.
So please let me be.

—Seny Isican

TO DICKIE

A little boy's laughter how sweet the sound
A little boy's toys scattered all around
A little boy's shoes that he'll never wear
He was going on two, he was ever so fair
He was such a little fellow yet such a man
God knew best it was His plan
He needed an extra bright star for above
He took my little boy to His City of Love
What about me since he's been gone
There's never a blue sky or a bird in song
Never a sunset or a star at night
That I don't see his face with its beautiful light
Hear the pit-pat of his little feet as if running down the street
See over and over again a million things
To remind me of him my heart sings
How precious is memory when there's no other
To fill the vacant place in the heart of a mother

—P.B. Luckey

SISTERS

Two snowflakes loft softly to the ground, uniquely different in pattern, rest one atop the other without a sound.

God's creating hand makes each different from the other, made sisters in life by one father and a mother.

Much more than this our lives became, when? who knows, so different yet the same.

Two snowflakes melt into one single droplet of water, never knowing where one starts or ends—what does it matter?
The droplet catches the sun's light, prism colors add beauty after the night,
Evaporation will eventually take over, little by little, we return to the "Giver."

We are for now, two snowflakes wafting to the ground, kindred spirits, touch lovingly, our heart-felt song resounds.

Dedicated to my Hero, to my sister, to my friend, Susie, your bravery taught me to appreciate each day as a gift— to look at the Giver and say "Thank you" not, "why?"

—Nanette M. Miller

RECIPE FOR HAPPINESS

1

I really wonder, — when someone asks of me,
 "How do you go from day to day?
 Always smiling and happy —
 Along the rough and lonely way?"
What do they really want me to say?

2

I take a deep breath — but don't miss a beat,
 "Life is *so* short, *so* precious, and yes! *so* sweet!
But each one is so vulnerable — and, oh! *so* alone,
 (he must be independent, and oh! *so* strong)
As down the 'Path of Life' he travels along."

3

"He must learn to enjoy every second, every minute of every day.
 At night put the day's troubles far, far away.
Behind the clouds, store those tears when they start —
 Behind the rainbow, tuck that broken heart —
Begin each new day with a 'spic-'n-span' slate —
 Do it now — It isn't too late!"

—Sophia (L.M.C.)

Once I fell asleep in the sun, I guess I was having too much fun. The heat fried my bones and now they sit in front of my tombstone.
 I was finally found the next Monday, and now here I lay thinking . . . WHAT A BAD DAY!

—Jill Allen, age 12

MORNING

Dew comes down
Fairies dance around
 Still light, still dark
 No sound
Rooster crow, turkey gobble
 Open your eyes
Your dream is done
 But the day
Has just begun
 Good morning
 Good day
 Catch the bus
And be on your way.

—Victoria

VALLEY

In the clear vase
of a mountain valley
my thoughts were gathered

Small buds of silence
threaded deep
among bright blooms
of solitude
a spray of joy
unexpected
in its heavy scent

A bouquet of contemplation
gathered and held
in the clear vase
of a mountain valley.

—Jane Elliot Granberry

WISHING

Wish you were here
 with me.
 To take away my
pain, to cry with me,
to laugh with me, to
make me feel special.
I feel your presence in
all the things you do, and the
things you say. You are the
place I ran to whenever I was
 in need of a smile.
Why is it only you that can
make me feel this way? I
know why. Because you are my
 friend.

Dedicated to all my friends. Thank you for making me feel special.

—Joy Ann Konarski

BUFFALO WALLOW

Long ago
Along a now-dim trail
The buffalo carved
A scratching pit.

Here they wallowed
And dusted off the flies,
Making a deep depression
In the hillside.

Now only a few wild mustard
Bloom in the forgotten dust.

—Alice Jacobson

THE SOUL

No longer can I see
These dreams turn to reality.
No longer can I feel
The hope that seemed so real.

No longer can I hide
This darkness felt inside,
That this soul has died.

Not everything you hear is real,
Not everything you see you feel,
Raindrops are nothing but the tears
Falling from a sky of fears.
A hollowness it cried,
A willingness that was tried,
This soul has died.

Hands together with intention,
Pray for the Divine Intervention.
Before a fall from grace,
It finds a loving face,
High above in heaven's skies,
That this soul never dies.

—Jaimie Snodgrass

MY SERMON

Faith means believing things
Our eyes can't ever see.
Knowing things are righted,
In God's great Eternity.

Hope means always trusting,
The Lord will show the way.
That we'll find the answers,
That were hidden yesterday.

Charity means giving,
Above and way beyond.
It's another name for love
That we all depend upon.

So let These be guideposts,
IN words of purest gold.
Their meaning's clear today,
AS IN the days of old.

God added a postscript,
Reminding you and me;
That LOVE is the greatest,
Of these triune three.

—Darleen I. Hill

I WEAR A GLOVE

I wear a glove known as my color
this very glove often strangles me,

B.S., M.S., M.A.E., all came after my color
still, my color is all most see,

Actually, it makes no difference if I am "black" or "white,"

But, it becomes more important if I am wrong or right,

So, forget this glove known as my color, forget it
and start to live,

Take off this glove known as my color and let another who is
capable of giving, give,

Try talking to me not my color for once let's allow that to rest,
just appreciate that I'm willing to give and know that you're
getting my best.

—T. Mitchell Guy

IN MEMORIES OF MEMORIES

I sit here among these Carolina pines and watch the leaves in all their splendor, no two colors alike, and realize there will never be another whisper or secret shared by you and me.

We once dreamed the dream of lovers, of things to come and how it would be "when." Fate has robbed us of "when" and now I have the memories of things past and the hopes of things yet to come . . . alone.

Now I sit beneath these pines, watching the leaves, knowing and not yet accepting that you are a part of my yesterdays. I am not bitter, for you gave me those yesterdays and left me with the courage to face tomorrow on my own.

My wishes and hopes continue and just as the leaves change so has my life. For as the earth will be richer for the passing of these leaves, my life is richer for knowing you, for loving you, for sharing our whispers, secrets, dreams and life.

So next time I sit and watch the leaves in all their splendor or see the reflection of the sun on the wall that now holds your name, or listen to the laughter of new dreamers, I will think of you . . . and smile.

—Debrah Hendrickson

A CLOWN DIVINE

A clown is such a happy face even when it's painted sad,
A face loved by everyone down to the smallest lad.

A clown can mend a broken heart and make us forget pain,
A person who gives with love and never does complain.

A clown is very special to every one he knows,
He leaves behind a path of joy every where he goes.

And this sure fits a friend I had who's gone to live with God,
To spread his love and joy where all the angels trod.

Now Heaven is the finest circus that any clown can play,
He'd have to be near perfect to be chosen for display.

For think of the sad loved ones who went before their time,
To live among the angels and all of those divine.

And when the hurt and sadness becomes too much to bear,
God brings forth his circus and all his clowns to share.

And now my friend, who is not up there alone,
Has been given that great honor to play before the throne.

—Lois Gray

OF LESLIE . . . FEEL THE WIND

A gentle tug, a tiny voice, "Granny can I go out and play?"
Another face from an earlier time touched my mind and wouldn't go away.
A tiny replica of my now-grown child; I'm amazed how much it shows.
The eyes and hair are both the same, even the freckles across the nose.
Why does it seem so long ago that your Mom did the very same thing?
The way you talk; your wobbly walk; the funny songs you sing.
Then she raised her tiny hands up high for no present I could send.
Her blue eyes were full of wonder . . . she was feeling for the wind.
Golden curls were blown about and kissed her cheeks in the summer air.
She was caught up in nature's magic and I could only sit and stare.
Forgotten were her dolls and games and our newest nursery rhyme.
To her, something we all take for granted, turned her into a little mime.
Then turning as she stumbled, she looked up into my face.
Feel the wind, she asked me softly? And made my world a special place.

—Faye Henley

FORTUNE SMILES ON ME

I once said, a while ago, that fortune had no shame.
Consider what I say as true, but do not give her blame.

In disregard to who you are, she comes and then she goes.
Some consider that she is their friend and others they're her foes.

But, recently she came to me when I had been depressed.
What I learned, through her auspices, was I was really blessed.

For I can count the ones I love on more than my two hands.
None asks for more than I can give none, of me, makes demands.

It's said of me, I've nothing that I can count as money.
Though riches I have not and fame has never followed me;

there's one thing, in life, I can claim and that is I am free,
a slave to no man's passion and no woman's vanity.

If all I've got is nothing which is bought or can be sold
then fortune's smiled upon me and will smile until I'm old.

And when the final reckoning has come and go I must;
for certain I'll look up and say that in the gods I trust.

—Harriet White

DOVE ON 23RD STREET

Is this how we go too?
Cut off at the wing during flight,
disemboweled on the pavement,
drooping so close to limb and trunk silhouettes,
yet decomposing on feigned ground?

Do synthetics spoil our colors also?
Reds transferred to chrome,
our peaches removed by rubber, or browns by cement,
grays to the city sky?

Will we be silenced in the roaring as well?
Our windpipes collapsed,
unable to let out melancholy calls?

Coo-ah, coo, coo, coo.
There I said it for you,
being fortunate enough to still speak.
It has never been so much the speaking,
it's the hearing we humans have the most trouble with.
As the rumbling pounds continually,
our ears are numbed
and our hearts are flattened.

—Jason Boitnott

BLACK ON WHITE

Black on white
Notes on paper
Silent
Lifeless lines
On thin sheets
Waiting
Until someone comes
Black on white

—Nadia Mena Colella

BROKENHEARTED

Why do hearts break so fast?
The fragileness, like a helpless infant
When my heart broke,
I lost a piece.
Now my heart won't be whole.
Can I ever replace the
missing piece?
Or will it be gone forever?

—Annie Han

THE BABY

I walked up to her cradle
Twas just to take a peek
But stood as if enchanted
While she lay fast asleep

A tiny pinkish bundle
Much like a little toy
Yes daddy this small creature
is yours for greatest joy

She smiled as she lay sleeping
And gave a little sigh
I thought she must be dreaming
of fairyland at night

I leaned and kissed her gently
And took just one more peek
A bundled hump of beauty
An angel fast asleep —

—Bill Napier

THE EAGLE

Born a golden Eagle
to soar the open skies
HE looked upon God's beauty
with love and watchful eyes
He fed among the forests
And bathed in crystal streams
Then found for him a shelter
Beneath the evergreens

But storm clouds started gathering
As humans did appear
To tear away the forests
And cause the eagle fear
A thunderstick then sounded
Which made a mighty roar
It scattered golden feathers
Upon the forest floor

Now wounded and bewildered
He hides among the trees
The hope for his survival
Floats gentle with the breeze

—Bill Napier

WHAT IS A FRIEND

A friend is one who can share your life,
All of its joys, all of its strife;
Looking into your soul he clearly sees
The you that's the you he knows you to be!
His mind's uncluttered by society's whims,
Of society's restrictions hemming you in,
Shutting others out if they fail to be
The same old clone he wishes to see.

United in bonds that are true and tried,
He makes the endeavor to be by your side
At times when you need him, yet crowding not;
He'll be there beside you, as close as your thoughts.
He knows how to love, yet not take possession,
Caring and sharing, devoid of aggression.
Yet in all of his giving, he, too will receive
What part you have offered, what you're able to give!

—Marion Barrett

LOOKING BACK

Looking back I see,
the way it used to be.

A time so long ago,
Who could know?

The way it all ended,
And how we've tried to be mended.

We were pushed to the edge,
ready to jump off the ledge.

Ready to show the world we were the BOSS
And no one could survive our loss.

I ask of you, "Who among our group is alive?"
"Who among our group survives?"

And you tell me, "No one."
You do not shed a tear, your heart shows no fear.
We were so close, yet so far away.

—Jeremy Kolosky

UNBOUNDED LOVE

I do not own you . . .
the golden sun shines equally on all who behold her
who then am I to say that she shall shine only on me?

I do not control you
no man's arrogance can direct the wind against her will
what right have I to tell her where to blow?

I do not wish to hold you back
the sweet brook dammed up becomes a stagnant pool
do I not prefer the melody of her dancing where she will?

I do not wish to bind you
the shackled bird sickens and dies when she cannot fly
does not her joyous flight make my own spirits soar?

how then do I have you if you can not be mine?
I will forge between us a bond of . . .
hope, honesty, and love
and leave you free
to come to me
or go as you will
keeping a part of you always
in my heart

—Kevin Michael Davisson

MY BEAUTIFUL LOVE

Effie's mind has chosen a beautiful love for her heart.
Steve is true and faithful from the start.
Their mutual admiration came fast.
    The love of Steve is here to last and last.
They enjoy being out of doors walking hand in hand.
    They like to watch the rain and when it's over
        sniff the air which is just grand!
Also dancing to the "oldies" at home is neat!
    They never knew home life could be so sweet!
Steve and Effie tinker in the kitchen to make dessert.
    Watch out! Now Steve is making out to be a big flirt.
Effie responds with cuddling, as playful as a kitten.
    She thinks it is all superbly fittin'!
They are preparing themselves to go to temple and make
    their love complete.
    The world has never seen a more loving example and
        with glowing faces, the temple trip, many
        more times they will repeat.

    —Jennette Effie English Baker

WE'VE ONLY JUST BEGUN

We must stand tall and be brave, for it is our time now
Together, not only as friends, but as young maturing
    adults
We must walk another of life's long and winding roads
It is our time now, to find the faith within ourselves, to
    take that first big step
The step that will begin our lives
This is our path to the beginning of the end
We've only just begun
In the past, we have always been right there, sharing each
    other's pain and joy
But as we walk further down this strange and winding road
We will all slowly go our different ways
And do our different things
Though right now, we are all young adults fighting through
    life's surprises, and learning with each mistake
We do not yet understand enough about how our world works,
    to have to worry about our futures
Or all the little things the world will give and take
For we've only just begun!!!!

    —Jolene Hindes

THE ANNIVERSARIES

The first anniversary all he could afford was a card
The second he chose a fancy nighty
On the fifth he gave her a vacuum cleaner
On the tenth it was furniture, an easy chair for him
On the fifteenth they went to dinner
By the twenty-fifth he gave her her diamond ring
On the thirtieth she got earrings to match
The fortieth they had a party at home
On the fiftieth the party was given by relatives
On the fifty-fifth he chose a flannel nighty with a little lace
On their sixtieth anniversary Grandpa said to himself, when I wake up from my nap I think I'll walk down and get Grandma a card.
On their sixty-fifth anniversary after many years together and now in their eighties, Grandma went to bed early, perhaps she is still awake thought Grandpa as he got out of his chair.
Happy anniversary he whispered as he kissed her on the cheek and squeezed her hand and as she lay back on the pillow and closed her eyes she sighed, That Grandpa he always did know just what to give me for our Anniversary.

    —Norma Zoller

A VALENTINE FROM LONNIE

I was busy in my workshop,
Whoops, I cut out my heart!

I stood there for a moment
and it began to smart.

Swish . . . an arrow pierced my heart
and I quickly turned my head.

Yep, there stood Little Cupid,
He smiled at me and said,

"Don't stand there you big dummy.
You can't treat this as a joke,
Give your heart to Lena
    your Valentine
Or for sure it will get broke.

    —Lonnie A. Barnes

JUST A THOUGHT FROM THE HEART

No discombobulated thoughts
No shrewd remarks.
No negative thinking.
Just a thought from the heart.

No bad news to spread.
No pages to be read.
No accusations to be made.
Just a thought from the heart.

No guilty misleadings.
No imperil feelings.
No hesitation of needing.
Just a thought from the heart.

No words to be said.
You should know in your head.
And feel in your soul,
Just a thought from the heart!!!

    —"Me"

Why are you mad?
    Is it because . . .
I love you too much
Is my love squishing you?

Are you an injured rabbit
    in a snowy forest
        with no food and water

Do you want me to leave you
    alone in a big confused state
Or maybe I could help you

The answer and result may be
    hard, but it may also be
    good for us too!

Little rabbit I love you so much,
    so much that I will let you free
    if you want

All right Good-Bye Bunny
    Wait, please always remember
    I love you with all my
        heart and soul

    —Leanne Marie Cliff

A FARMER'S DAY

A farmer's day is long and hard;
At the break of day, he leaves his yard.
He goes forth to plow his fields,
In hopes of having abundant yields.
He has stock which he must tend;
There are fences which he must mend.
There is much work for him to do,
But there's nothing he had rather do.
A farmer's gains aren't always great,
Yet he'll go on, his work can't wait.

—Pat Moore

PHINNIUS THE FROG

Phinnius, the frog
where have you gone?
The lily pad is empty
you used to sit on.

You're nowhere in sight
and to my surprise
you missed your dinner
of bugs and flies.

Phinnius the frog
This is no time to joke
Did you — croak!

—Nancy L Porter

LARGER THAN LIFE . . .

Supper's done and now he's free
To do what he really wishes,
Gather his gear and hit the beach
To try his luck with the fishes.

It's nice out there that time of day,
After the crowd's gone home;
The wind blows cool, the light grows dim,
And waves lace the sand with foam.

Catching some fish is a fine reward,
But that's not all it's about . . .
There's harmony, grandeur of sight and sound,
That puts all else to rout . . . .

—B. B. Watkins

HORSES

Lift your head up high.
Let your mane blow in the breeze.
Raise your feet in marching style.
'Be' as free as you please.

Parade or circus horse,
Plow horse or pony for riding.
You are special in your place,
So come out of hiding.
Be the kind of horse you can.
A race would be fun to win.
If it's in your plan.

Lift your head up high.
Let your mane blow in the breeze.
Raise your feet in marching style.
'Be' as free as you please.

—Dorothy A. Cox

THERE IS NO COLOR FOR THIS COLDEST GREEN

Meaning's in the thicket,
you left me presents I'd already seen:

eggs wrapped in dew, tiers of leaves,
bolts of clover. I found them often

among mosses, earthy pieces
I didn't understand.

Seeing in hands these things living,
still extending from your touch.

—Susan Thomas

THE WAGON HORSE

Wagon and driver behind you.
Weighted by harness, blinded by blinders,
Bridled by bit; you gather your stride,
Get up! Tap of a whip.

Moving along in a trotting gait
Snorting from your wagon's weight,
Horseshoes clacking and tapping; trotting along,
Forming the rhythm of the conductor's song.

Horseshoes clacking in perfect time,
Wagon and driver not far behind.
Weighted by harness, blinded by blinders,
Bridled by bit; move on! Tap of a whip.

—Cheryl E. Daniel

THE BLUEBIRD'S SONG

I sit, listening to the bluebird's song;
A wondrous melody it sings the whole day long.
As I look up to see,
This bluebird, 'Tis singing to me.
I honestly must decree,
'Tis a glorious sight to see.
This little bluebird. 'Tis singing to me.

The bluebird's song is a sweet, joyous tune,
As it whistles away the harsh days of June;
And although I must be leaving soon,
I must look around and hear,
A sound that is music to my ear;
As I listen, I see,
This little bluebird, 'Tis singing to me.

—Dale G. Laughlin

COLORS

As I write, scenes of the
ocean sunset come flooding back
to me. The wind was a painter, and
it painted the sky beautiful colors
of pink, blue, yellow, and orange.
The seagulls were little, black,
gliding streaks in the sun.
There were many beautiful seashells of
all different colors: orange, brown, even bright
red.
Now the sun is down; the wind
painted the sky dark blue, with a circle
and little twinkling dots. The seagulls
are gone, and the colors of the
seashells have faded away.

—Sarah Daugherty

SAINT NICOLE

I'm so sad and blue, don't know what to do.
My little girl is gone, through choice not of my own.

My life is just so empty, because she up and left me.
I know she's happy now, walkin' and takin' a bow.

She's sufferin' no more, 'cause she is with the Lord.
I'm very sad to say, she's not with me every day.

She can sing, laugh, and dance; down here she had no chance.
She can also hear and see, thanks to God, she is now free.

I'll see her again someday, to God I hope and pray.
He is so forgiving, even among the living.

Saint Nicole, you take care; I will get through, this load I bear.
And when I see you again; I'll be happy forever, Amen.

—Vickie O'Bryan

When I'm gone some sadness will come,
   it will soon pass and you will see,
      that I am in a much happier place,
         like the caged dove finally set free

I will be all around yet untouchable for some,
   this peaceful place that I surround,
      is full of life in abounds

Although you cannot feel me with your fingertips,
   your memories of my softness, my warmth, my lips,
      entangle your mind from time to time,

I will not be forgotten by your hearts, by your soul,
   your time is soon to become the dove

I will wait for you with open arms,
   because you too are in my heart and soul,
      and my memories that will
         eternally entangle my mind

—Pam Munson

A VERY SPECIAL LOVE

Fifty-five years ago I started a new life
When I took dear Lena for my lawful, wedded wife.

In our wedding vows, we remembered one verse . . .
We would take each other for better or worse.

When we were first married, she was my Beautiful Girl, and
somewhere in those fifty-five years, Lena became my world.

I've got no complaints, our life has been good,
God has given us more than he promised he would.

It's been hard for five years, day by day,
To watch my Beautiful World fade fast away.

Thanks, Lord, for the strength you gave Gloria and me.
We have kept Lena at home, where she wanted to be.

In these past five years, if I've offended anyone,
Please forgive me for whatever I've done.

Lena's relatives and friends shared in her love,
Now she's sharing with others in God's Heaven above.

Lena would tell us not to worry, for it won't help
  a thing.

Now if we use our imaginations, we can hear Lena sing . . . .

—Lonnie A. Barnes

GOOD-BYE SUGAR

I had a friend I called Sugar
She had been with me a very
long time. But as we all know
time does not go very slow,
so she is with me no more.
I'm talking about my little
black dog, who was more than
a pet to me, she was a good
friend who eagerly gave her
love for free. Time did go by
and after fifteen years, I
realized it was over thru the
many tears. I told her it was
time to be on her way. I don't
know what waited for her, I
could not say. So goodbye little
Sugar, my dear little pet, I'll
always love you thru every sunset.

—Sue Bourdeau

DEATH

I often wonder, more and more
What is behind, this elusive door
Is it really, bitter end
Or could it be, love Godsend
I see the pain, the hurt the tears
But could it not be, our misguided fears
I long to meet, someone that's been
But when I do, I'll be there then
I somehow sense, it's not the end
But just a place, God do us send
We all will go, one day for sure
Are we missing, its great allure
I often think, we make the pain
When there could be, so much gain
Why is it, that when we pass
We make it but, a dark black mass
For when I see beyond that door
I know it will be, so much more
So mourn not for the bitter end
Rejoice it is a true Godsend.

—J.C.

GOODBYE, MY SWEET

Run to me — fly swiftly
   'Neath my wings come hide
Let me hold your whispers
   Let me touch your cries

Hurry now — I'm waiting
   My arms enfold your fears
No one — I say, no one
   Will harm you while I'm near

You are so small, so precious
   The hurt to you won't mend
Mommy's leaving Daddy
   Your world — a vortex blend

Now, all I can do is hold you
   My heart can't spare you pain
Away — Away — you'll go away
   Will we touch again?

So small to face such terror
   Wee hands — they grasp so tight
Your Grandmom's heart is breaking
   You've gone — so cold the night.

—Celeste Kusnell Granieri

IN MEMORY OF VIRGIE ALLEN BLANKENSHIP

Through a child's eyes,
you couldn't do wrong.
Through loving eyes,
you were always strong.
Through caring eyes,
you helped me belong.

You had love and understanding.
Even when silent you weren't demanding.
Only once I saw you cry.
No words were said, but
I knew why.

You were never alone.
Your tears didn't show
but I cried them too.
I love you, Grandma!
I won't forget you!

—Lynda Blankenship Owens

NINTH BIRTHDAY

Dearer than my life to me,
Brighter than the sun,
'Twas only nine short years ago,
That you and I were one.

    So tiny and so fragile,
    Your head cradled in my hand,
    I wanted to tell the whole world,
    And then strike up a band.

Five pounds and ten ounces,
Blonde hair and blue eyes,
Nineteen inches of beauty
That surpassed the stars in the skies.

    The years, my dear, are passing,
    Much too fast for me.
    My love for you keeps growing,
    For my daughter—you'll always be.

—Mary Beth Feutz

THE CHILD

A fragile package came today
    With a note addressed to me.
It read, "Herein you'll find a child
    To mirror your dignity.

So give him roots, and fins, and wings,
    Teach him of the stars—
And all things bright and beautiful
    In this land of ours.

Snuggle him when he's afraid,
    But build in him a fire.
And mold his strength and courage
    With heroes to admire.

Teach him truth and patience—
    Bring music to his ears.
Help him choose some valued friends
    To comfort all his fears.

But most of all—just love him,
    For someday you'll have to part.
He'll grow and learn and love and leave,
    But he'll live within your heart."

*Dedicated to my beloved children,
Michael, Robert and Joelle.*

—Judy Pitera

THE LITTLE SIGN IN THE HALL

Just inside the entry a sign hung on the wall;
One that would be easy to miss, it was so small,
And yet the message of just three words
Was one that entering hearts often stirred;
With big bold letters, the meaning clear,
It told one and all "Love Spoken Here."

Each friend that comes to visit a while
Seeing the sign, will carry a smile.
They'll know they are welcome to come again
And more memories of friendship to begin.
Perhaps a hug or two for a moment they'll share,
Because "Love Spoken Here" says they care.

It takes love to change a house to a home,
It takes work to make that love to all known,
It takes a family, no matter how few,
To share togetherness, help see the day through.
With big bold letters, the meaning clear,
The center of this home is, "Love Spoken Here."

—Marjorie G. Shuman

WONDERING

Sometimes I wonder what life would be,
If I hadn't met you and you hadn't met me.

Would I be happy or would I be glad,
    Would I be lonely, empty and sad.

Would I be able to decide what to do,
    Could I make good decisions being without you.

Would I be crafty, trying things that are new,
    If you hadn't shown me all the things you can do.

Would I know what a blessing a true friend can be,
    Or would many acquaintances be good enough for me.

Would I have been spared much heartache and pain,
    Never to have shared love, never to have gained.

Yes, Could I, would I, what should I have done,
    Ever to have missed all the joy and the fun.

I'd never be what I am now or what I will be,
    If I hadn't met you and you hadn't met me.

—Carol A Squires

The face of an angel, some might say,
A smile that brightens my day.
To hear him laugh, as he takes a bath,
brings so much joy some way.
His sweet little voice, when he says "I love you,"
can make my tears run free,
my heart skips a beat, when he jumps to his feet,
to the door, after work, to see me.
He listens for cars, as he waits for his mom,
near the window, he climbs to see,
the same little grin, just all over again,
that is saved in his heart just for me.
At night we pick books, as bedtime nears,
he giggles and laughs as I read,
all tucked in his bed, sweet dreams in his head,
he sleeps as I watch him in need.
I kiss him goodnight, I can hear him breathe,
my face touches soft gold hair,
my love is so great, only God could know,
he'll sleep better just knowing I'm there.

Dedicated to my beautiful son, Preston

—Teresa VanSanden

HERE WE GO AGAIN WITH THAT BUMPY SIDE

        Oh-ooo! Here we go **again**
        Mom is playing that same old song **again**

Title: *Momme is gone child at home all alone*

        If I could hear that **smooth** side
        Oh! How I **Wish**
        Because that **bumpy** side
        Always sounds like **this**

Momme! While you were **away**
        I bumped my little head at **play**

Oh! What a **bump**
        Now there is a large **lump**
        And it is beginning to throb and **pump**

        As I lay there in the **sand**
        I thought of your soothing **hand**

        As my little head began to **sway**
        Others came and tried to soothe the pain **away**

        And all those hands **combined**
        Did not soothe my little **mind**

        All the touching, feeling and rubbing were not the **same**
        As one little touch of your **hand**

Momme! That other side **please!** Let it **Play**
        Because I need your presence **everyday**

        —Wallace Joe Williams

THE SAME OLD SONG

Home from school, mom at labor, because of **inflation**
And! That kind of carrying on is breaking our **relation**

To mom! Wealth seems so **delicious**
And! I'm growing up to be **vicious**

She made a **substitution**
The results are: **abusion**
And **confusion**

Momme is always **gone**
I feel like she is doing me **wrong**

I don't **understand**
It is like a **"disease"** spreading throughout the **land**

Children left at home **alone**
Our mothers are **gone**

They play that same old **song**
Why don't they change to the flip **side**

Title: *Mothers are at home.*
      Children are not alone

Now! That will make us **satisfied.**

Oh! Can't they **see**
The example they are setting we'll also **be**
And when we become **grown**
With a family of our **own**
We are **bound** to be like **thee**

        —Wallace Joe Williams

THE VEIL

One
Escape,
From the
Tempest,
Lies in
A dream's
Sanctuary,
Where
A vision's light,
Raises
This dark
Veil,
Suffocating
My mind.

        —Linda Marlene Cory

CHOICES

Bubbling cool on my toes,
Pouring warmth on my face.
Alive earth surrounds, encompasses;
Rustle, then a song from above.

To this pasture I oft' retire,
Though no soil beneath me —
Only imagination's wings soaring,
Escaping high above cruel abstracts.

It is here, reflecting on anxiety,
On indecent acts of irrational
    beliefs,
Where the decision is made
To painfully exist or to myself
    affray.

        —Heidi Bremen-Humphreys

I NEVER KNEW ABOUT LONELY

I never knew about lonely
Until my Lena went away
I thought lonely was being by myself
On a dreary cloudy day

I never knew that lonely
Could make me hurt this way
I never knew about lonely
Until Lena went away

I never knew about lonely
Or how long a night can be
Until I've lived a part of this hurt
That's still living inside of me

I never knew about lonely
Until I faced life alone
I never knew about lonely
Until I saw Lena chiseled in stone

I never knew that lonely
Could move in my heart and stay
Now I know about lonely
Since my Lena has gone away

If you don't know about lonely
No matter where you are
You should get down on your knees
And thank your lucky star

        —Lonnie A. Barnes

DAY IS DAWNING IN THE EAST

Day is dawning in the east,
Radiance lighting man and beast.
Wake, and worship while God's Light
Paints with rainbow colors so bright
      All earth and sky!
Father, Son, His Spirit:
Three-in-One, Divine!
All Thy world Thy glories see,
Heaven and earth give praise to Thee,
      Dear God Most High!

—Mary Alice Badeau Jenkins

TESTING OF THE SPIRITS!

Awaken me Lord!
For I have slept
In the dreams of the most deep!
(I will) to arise to my feet
To your command, show me,
Oh precious Lamb, I behold!

Stop It! Stop It!
You monster with breathing nostrils,
the hot vapors and air are suffocating.
Lift me above that cloud,
to witness your happy life Lord.
My salvation is forever,
Thank-you Blessed Jesus!

Rise Above, Rise Above,
to behold your love of life.
Simplistic is my walk with you —
TAKE IT!

—Joanne G. Snyder-Haney

JESUS JESUS JESUS

Jesus, Jesus, Jesus
I love Thee most of all!
Jesus, Jesus, Jesus
I love Thee most of all!

    Cherubims and Seraphims
    All ye heavenly, heavenly Saints
    Come and join me in the singing
    To the glory of His Name.
All ye people of the Lord
Living still in the world
Come and join me in the singing
To the glory of His Name.
    All ye Holy, Holy Souls
    Our Friends, the Holy Souls
    Come and join me in the singing
    To the glory of His Name.

Jesus, Jesus, Jesus
I love Thee most of all!
Jesus, Jesus, Jesus
I love Thee most of all!!!

*Heartily and lovingly dedicated
to the One and Only Jesus Christ,
Lord and Saviour of the world; and
Our Blessed Mother Mary; to Saint
Joseph; and to the Most Holy Trinity:
Father, Son and Holy Spirit!!!*

—"Camia"

THE HOUSE

Within a crowded forest stands a house.
The paint undaunted by the winter rain.
The inside swollen with tears doth douse
a passerby unaware of its pain.
The cobwebs weaving loneliness portray
a beautiful scene of gallant romance.
Dust that encompasses the girl's decay
reeks of death and left the house entranced.
For there was no one around to hear her.
All of her cries, her pleas were never known
though the house was seen as a foggy blur
it kept watch day and night through wind and snow
for the way to reveal the secret it hides
is to hope that another comes inside.

—Kristin Klinck

BOX OF REST

Some need them when death has spoke,
Symbols of the end which linger in your mind.
They are constructed of gold, metal, oak,
or whatever materials you can find.

By building them men make a career.
By filling them some do the same.
In everyone's future it will appear,
unless you decompose by a flame.

Never wanting to pick it out,
fit it for beauty and size,
never knowing what it's all about,
in the sight of it one often cries.

God orders the numbers in which they are supplied.
Some say they are passports to lands of gold;
others say you'll be in one forever after you've died.
But not to worry about it is what I've been told.

—Scot Yokom

IF I COULD ESCAPE

    I see nothing, I feel nothing, I sense nothing. But I know it's all still out there. Moving and growing, going on all around me; if only, if only I could escape to look at everything there is.

    I might take in the breath-taking sunsets in the Florida Keys. Or the beauty of a snow-capped mountain in the Himalayas. I might visualize the moisture in the air as I gaze upon a tropical rain forest to see the spectacular colors of a rainbow. If only.

    I might feel the heat rise off the sands as I walk along a beach or the cool moist air from the surf breathing at my feet. To feel the rush of air flowing through my hair. If I could only feel the spirits flying high on a warm spring day. To experience the joy of a white Christmas. Maybe just the proud feeling of a son's first hit in baseball, if only.

    But still here unable to see anything, unable to feel anything. Not sensing anything. To do any of these things I would escape. If only I could. But I cannot for I am dead.

—Michael Mitchell

RAINBOWS AND BUTTERFLIES

I clasped the hand you offered so long ago
   To start on a journey uncharted by mortals.
Looking for rainbows and butterflies, my hand in yours,
   Carried on winds of adventure, I followed you.
Over the mountain peaks with joy we flew,
   Dancing to rhythms of flashing wings in moonlight.
Vanishing into the sun's bright ray, I laughed
   And dallied in the afterglow of your embrace.
Eternity spun her garland unheeded, time had no name;
   Happily I stayed by your side and trusted you.
Youth was forever and strength never waned
   In the aura of dreams and desire I shared with you.
Out of the storms that now rage and delay me, I come
   Seeking your touch to steady my flight and calm my fears.
Under restraining bonds of earth, I wait for you
   To clasp my hand and bid me go on a journey
   Seeking rainbows and butterflies with you.

    —Anna Mae Hoffman

HIS TOUCH

Jesus, how I long for your touch.
Your touch could heal me of so much pain;
I'm living in a world where much of time, I walk afraid.

To pass away tears and that feeling of loss, will be welcome
when I am in your house.
Please take me Lord, though I am not worthy; I am trusting
you to understand my flesh is weak.
I search and struggle to be loved, when it is only you I
should seek.

Human love can fail you, leave you empty at times.
Give me strength and confidence Lord; so I can be at your side.
I will wait patiently on you; giving all that I can,
trying to understand—guide my humble hands.

I ask you one thing, Jesus; if you could let me feel,
some how, some way, make your touch real.
A little reminder of how it will be, when I have your
arms totally surrounding me.

    —Deborah K. Ellis

REFLECTIONS ON LIFE'S SEASONS

In the beauty of the Autumn leaves I find tranquility—
life spans are herein measured in sadness and nobility.

The newborn's welcomed cry—the life season starts,
   bringing joy and love to mankind's heart.

Oh, for the flame of youth's unrest—to conquer
   the world and climb to the crest.

The passionate storms that nurture the seeds
   of love—and giving—and thoughtless deeds.

The splendor of life—the cruelness encountered—
   both by the giver and receiver imparted.

The pruning of self—a life story unfolded—brings
   solace and pardon; all burdens unloaded.

The leaves as they fall—all colors and shapes—
   is the season of parting that all creatures must make.

Although, as the trees, we grow barren and thin, we
   bask in the knowledge that a new life begins.

The Winter storms over, the streams begin flowing—
   new life starts again; Spring's beauty is showing.

The prints we have left in this wonderful scheme—
   is our priviledge of living in Nature's great dream.

    —Inez E. Burns

WHAT IF . . . .

What if I should die before
sunrise awakens me?
Or what if I should live
past sunset?
Or what if clouds should come
and it rains all day?
Will sunrise have awakened me?
Or will I have lived past sunset?
What if . . . .

    —Teresa Michele

NATURE'S ATTIRE

Fossils, rocks,
And petrified bone.
All part of our past,
Still far too unknown.

Dinosaur bones,
They hold so much mystery.
And they help us to learn,
Of life's earliest history.

Clam shells and sharks' teeth,
All washed up on shore.
Or an arrow head left,
From an old Indian war.

Beautiful geodes,
With middles so fine.
Diamonds and gold,
Nature's gifts, how they shine.

There's all types of gemstones,
For us all to admire.
They cover our earth,
They're all nature's attire.

    —Cheryl Conaway

BIRDS

Birds flap their wings up in the
air
They can travel anywhere,
There are all kinds of birds
in this world
They are loved by most every
man, woman, boy or girl,
When you see a lot of birds
together during the fall season,
It is usually for a reason,
It is a sign for colder
weather,
Birds are animals with feathers,
Where do they go during morning,
noon and night
I mostly see them during
daylight
I love watching birds fly,
They can fly excessively
high,
Birds eat food from trees, etc.
They hibernate during wintertime,
Yesterday I saw five,
They give the world a whole
new meaning for living,
Because when I see them I
just love giving.

    —Cliffidean R. Fuqua

LOVE: A POEM

A neverending road,
Leading to the end of time.
A road with a lot of stop signs,
A lot of curbs and a lot of bends.
But the best part of all,
Is that the road never ends.

—Jennifer Carrick

Her body untouched But yet it still whispers for kisses she is my little indian lady she comes to me only at night. Her sketch so lovely and graceful. Her Power is over me. I rise from my pillow and say I have seen your drawing and all else that you have. Only now I ask what do you want from me. And she said your love will you give it unto me.

*Dedicated to Michelle Reed
Love Always, Bruce Reed "93"*

—Bruce Reed

THE IMAGE OF THE WINDOW

The image of the window,
  Shattered,
With a startling snap!
The preception of pretense,
Broken,
With a glance in this glass.
The self conscience burden,
Lifted,
With a mimicking mirror.
The spirited reflection,
Freed,
With a faithful mirage.

—Melinda R. Thomsen

ALONE AGAIN

I know I've had this feeling before —
It's like a ball and chain.
It's a depressing feeling I get
Because I'm alone again.

No matter how many times I try
It's addiction like cocaine.
I get a girl and she leaves me . . .
Then I'm alone again.

Up one minute — down the next
My view of love is a different text.
Women always make it complex
They always think all I want is sex.

But that is not my cup of tea
And you will ask what do I mean —
If the woman wanted a serious relationship
I would treat her like a queen!

But they only see what they want to see
So to no woman I can complain.
I guess I will have to wake up tomorrow
And be alone again.

—Emanuel Lewis

SUMMER LOVE

The sun and wind intermingle for a cool breeze
A bird alights on the tree limb and sings a melody
The rains pour down
A Ho! it is summer time.
The sounds of motors tell that grass is being mowed
Children are laughing and picnics are fun
Under a tall oak tree
Two lovers are eye to eye.
Lips touch lips in a fond embrace
And several words are muttered . . .
The squirrel sits quietly above
Storing winter's supplies.
Not saying a word
Are our two lovers.

—Willie Amaker

A STORY

A story
Whose chapters seek answers,
Held captive beneath the unknown,
Destiny waits,
Still clinging
To pages of tender youth,
Turning quickly
The pages of strife and bleak unremembered times,
Searching
For pages of enduring hope,
As this story progresses,
The heart is left
Wanting,
For unwritten,
In my final chapter,
The discovery of,
Undying love.

—Linda Marlene Cory

ONE NIGHT

That night you broke my heart.
The next morning you came, delivering roses:
Pink, delicate like a new silk ribbon,
Yellow, bright yet not blinding.

Now we visit once again,
Fourteen days after one year.
Everything different, unlike before.

Before, we had:
Nights beneath stars:
Twinkling, shining, radiant.
The moon, clouds, the light,
The silver lining.

Before, we heard:
Crickets playing music before the storm.

Now we don't accomplish
Like we used to do.
We don't notice drifting clouds,
The moon.

The sights and sounds, slowly diminished:
Our love.

—Julie A. Bedard

REACHING UPWARD

As I sit here alone, beauty surrounds me. How can the earth be so beautiful yet so ugly? I look all around me and see the green grass sprouting from the ground. It's growing very fast toward the sky. It's reaching upward.

I see the trees blooming and the flowers blossoming in beautiful shades of summer. They are growing very quickly toward to the sky, reaching upward.

I see myself lost, helpless and lonely, striving to grow. I'm reaching upward, but some how I begin to let go and fall.

"Help! Can't you see I am going downward? I'm frightened and scared. Isn't there anyone I can hold onto, to help me from falling to the bottom? Isn't there someone here on earth to be my companion? Someone to love me and together climb upward?"

But, without a doubt, there is someone upward that is always with me and will always be my companion. If I only reach upward . . . .

—Christina Brennan

BENEATH THE SILVER MOON

In the distant glade sweet sounding music played, at Night
Beneath moon, the sounds of elvish tune. Inside the faery ring
a distant voice did sing of something from old, a tale of heroes bold.
   The wind played a harp, nearby sang a lark.

Melodies reached my ears, Not for many a year had they been heard,
yet here they were. I stood beneath the sky wondering how and why
these beautiful things were no longer seen but by a few. I wished I knew
   the secrets they say when from faraway.

The distant mists parted and little shadow figures darted. They
swirled and danced and didn't even glance at the mere mortal, only
laughed a chortle. As quick as they came they were away
   leaving me to wait until the day's break.

When back to home I finally did go. Thinking of things eery, my
heart's more weary. I long to hear their fair voices clear. Night
after night, I stand beneath the sky, hoping to catch a sliver
   of tune beneath the Silver
           Moon.

—Jody Carlson

WINTER

The day rolls in without a sound, the beginning of winter fall leaves lay on the ground.

The sky turned grey, the air turns chill, the once warm breeze now makes you frill.

The birds start south, about this time, to find the warmth and leave the cold behind.

Is this instinct or do they know, that someday soon there may be snow.

The days are fast the nights move slow, this feeling of abandonment you could not know.

Bundled up day and night, fighting this feeling with all of your might.
You stay inside, maybe in bed, thoughts of warmth lingering in your head.

Hoping for spring to have taken its place, you open the door to get snow in your face.

This feeling of imprisonment without a cause, you curse and you swear at that man they call Claus.

Because you know at this time of year, you will soon see him and his nine reindeer.

Closing the door and returning to bed, the only spring is the one in your head.

These thoughts may keep you warm inside, returning your faith and restoring your pride.

When you awaken the very next day, hoping that winter has gone its own way, it could still be out there with all of its might, lasting through the day and another cold night.

Feeling the discouragement as you crawl into bed later on, at least you have the satisfaction of knowing that one more winter day has gone.

—Steven Lazarus

A PROPER VOICE

Why does it seem so hard to find
a proper voice to speak a mind?
To let them know the way we feel.
To let them see just what is real.
And not disguise our inner-self
to those who'd put them on a shelf.
Far behind their selfish norm
as if to say they're never born.
The passion that we feel within
cannot forever stay locked in.
But will, I say, until we find
a proper voice to speak a mind.
—Douglas Barrett Clarke

The majesty of Earth divine
the beauty of it is all mine
the changing palettes of the seasons
warms the heart and stirs the feelings

I look out of my open window
I feel the gentle breezes blow
animals of all creations
sing of happy, little notions

Rivers breaking on smoothed rocks
birds are feeding in their flocks
fish spawning on water's edge
mother nature holds her pledge

Deer are grazing on the grass
squirrels are huddled in a mass
trees are swaying at their roots
cardinals sounding off their flutes

Nature's beauty all around
soft whispers of distant sound
Earth so peaceful and so great
being destroyed by human hate
—Stephanie L. Frampus, age 17

BECAUSE

Because of all the hardships,
because we walked the miles,
through heavy hearts and sadness,
together all the while.

Because we stayed together,
because I knew you cared,
when I needed someone,
you were always there.

Because of all the good times,
because you were the one,
that shared the love and laughter,
and made it so much fun.

Because of all the dreams we shared,
because we saw them through,
always there beside me,
we watched them all come true.

Because of what tomorrow holds,
because of all that was,
you ask me why I love you,
I guess it's just because . . . .
—M.A. Shields

SNOWFLAKES

The snowflakes fall one by one,
like soldiers marching off to war.
They fall painlessly down from heaven above,
As we wonder quietly, will there be more.

As one lone snowflake drifts quietly by,
And the clouds mournfully empty their tears.
A person wonders wishfully why,
these snowflakes cause such fanciful fears.

And as that snowflake touches the earth,
And the wind blows with a quiet sigh.
We think "Is this the last to earn its worth,"
or will it snow more when mourning comes by.
—John Tillman

HEIRLOOMS

When last I called your house my home,
and was no longer in your care;
I need you to know, there are some things
that I have taken from there.
You may not have missed them, or known they were gone;
You might take it all in strife.
But these things I cherish with all my heart,
for they have changed my life.
The list of things I took from your home,
when you were unaware;
Are patience and love, forgiveness and hope
and memories to share.
I cannot return these things of yours;
though they mean a lot to you.
For they are a testament of all the good times,
and love we have been through.
I hope I have the insight and skill
to use them as you've shown;
Until the day comes, when my children take them,
to be their very own.
—Tami Jo Kuenzli

BAHIA HONDA

Southward,
farther than most could fathom,
there lies an isle
more beautiful than any could imagine.
Where winding trails cut through mangroves,
and soft waves touch the beach.
A simple and peaceful isle
where the world is just out of reach.
The days are warm and windy,
with the sun gleaming bright.
Here the solemn moon,
illuminates the night.
Dolphins play upon the water,
mangroves sway in the breeze,
an osprey soars across the sky,
and my mind is set at ease.

Man has not defaced this isle,
I pray we never will,
for if its beauty is gone from earth,
my heart will forever be still.
—Jamie C. Trost

I woke up out of a temporary state of death to a gray city of concrete and steel buried beneath a blanket of snow.

It is still quiet, peaceful and serene as I watch a hearse plow its way down the street to pick up some body who is living through death.

I thank the creative living God for another beautiful day to rejoice in.

—Clarice Thomas

WAITING

Not only must we wait upon God
But to know what's more wonderful still is the
   waiting upon us of God.

To our waiting upon Him is given an inspiration and
   impulse
From the vision of His waiting upon us.

After we wait upon Him He does not give help we seek,
But longer and longer He waits, to us, it may seem.

Waiting in the sunshine of His love
Will ripen the soul for His blessing from above.

Waiting under the cloud of trial
Will break in showers of blessings as it comes from on high.

God knows when we are spiritually ready
The blessings to our profit and His glory to be receptive.

Four thousand years 'till the fullness of time
Did God wait ere He sent His Son sublime.

Our times are in His hands
He hastens to help within short spans.

—Kathleen J. Krumenacker

A HEAVENLY HOME

I

I've read and I've been taught, since being a child,
That our lives will be better in that "Home" beyond.
A more wonderful place than we will ever know.
If we walk down the straight and narrow road.

II

But it takes time to get there, it's not easy, it's hard.
For we can stray from the track to the "devil's" charms.
We think it's O.K. so we just keep going on,
Till things start getting hectic, then we know we were wrong.

III

They say this "Heavenly" place is always open for us,
If we just open our eyes and clean off the dust.
Trample the "devil" and let "God" lead us in,
To the most spectacular place we have ever been.

IV

What a glorious day that surely will be.
When "He" reveals himself to you and to me.
Will we believe "Him" then when "He" lets us know,
"He" is the "King" of the heavens and the earth here below.

V

I hope I am one of them, so that I may see,
What I've always been told and always believed,
That I may see "His" face and hear his voice say,
You are welcome here where there is no sorrow or pain.

—Gertrude Lawrence

REMEMBER

His smile warmed my heart,
It made me happy.
His touch on my head,
Tapping it when I was sad.
His hug, I want that now,
But I don't have it.
All I can do is remember,
Just remember . . . .

*Dedicated to my Father
Charles W. Ricci
12-20-56 to 11-25-91*

—Holli Ann Ricci

TIME FOR GOD

Have time for God
Where e'er you trod
Put Him first in your life
It will ease your daily strife

Be not anxious for tomorrow
No matter the grief or sorrow
He will supply your every need
If you but His commandments heed

Let the treasures that you store
Be those of kindness, love and more
Have time for God in all you do
And He'll have time for you

—Alice Marshall

A LADY'S TOUCH

So gentle is the wind
As it caresses my face.
   A memory still on my mind
   has brought me to this place.
The moon and stars still shine
so bright.
   My eyes reveal that much
And there's a deep strong feeling,
   of a lady's touch.
My body's weak, I give a sigh
   I picture her sweet face,
Did I expect to meet her,
   Again, while in this place.

—J. Ellis

WHO AM I?

Born from the womb I came;
Wrapped in love—
Nursed with care—

The years passed, learning and teaching became heart.

Tears of joy, I wished for one more day.

Praying for peace was my destiny.

My purpose, I had many, but there was only one.

Blessed was I in my life;

"I AM THE CHILD OF GOD."

—J.T. Toles

OSCAR NIGHT

Far away the lights of glory
Stab into expectant night.
Sweeping back and forth they signal
Earthly hopefuls, tinsel bright.

Silken gowns and soft lace collars,
Slippers made with strands of gold
Stride before the flashing cameras,
Blazoned, blinking, brassy, bold.

Who will rise and stay among the stars
Who grace the silver screen?
Who will fall and then unnoticed
Fade forever from the scene?

God knows, but the rest of us
Are bound by time to wait and see.
Meanwhile I'll enjoy the lights,
Pretending that they shine for me.

—Linda S. Lowe

Night time lurks a deep dark
    dungeon of deafening desire
White laces pour black souls
    wretching toward wonderlust time
Evil alms penetrate the
    proponent's giving prospect
Suddenly still air perfumes a
    mysterious majestic morbid sensation
Tulips tiptoe trystfully
    through passages of lost pureness.

Frigid a faint light appears a fondling
    fiend awaits fierce assumptions
Meshy flesh clings freely on a wet
    shining surface
Harmony remorse reflects
    double tranquility
Trenches widen problematic
    answers dissipate probity
Night time lurks for love
Night time loses love.

—Brandon L. Riggins

AUTUMN

September gold,
  flutters to the ground,
    on butterfly wings
      without so much as a sound.

Blanketing the earth,
  nourishing it with care,
    preparing a warm bed,
      protect from winter's fare.

And so much fun
  to shuffle in these leaves,
    beneath maple/oak,
      stately canopies.

Down wooded lane,
  along rippling brook,
    up this pebbled path,
      then onward home I stroll.

September gold,
  nature's kiss goodnight.
    Earth tucked in,
      Waiting for winter paradise.

—Lil Toomey

MY FOURTH GRADE TEACHER

In my memory she always will be, stern sometimes,
but most times full of glee.
She taught us reading, writing and 'rithmetic,
but never taught us mischievous trade or trick.
Her winning smile with dimples revealed,
told of her feelings which she never concealed.
She taught us to love one another, as though
we all were sisters and brothers.
The Bible was read every day in school,
which taught us to live by the Golden Rule.
Her daughter Leanne is a teacher also,
who watches her children and keeps them in tow.
Billy and Leslie, her grandchildren too,
are constantly around her to make her problems seem few.
Today she's retired and happily living,
with spouse Clarence, to whom her time she's now giving.
In my heart she always will be, my fourth grade teacher,
whom I love dearly.

Dedicated to Ms. Lillian Breese

—Kathryn Hendrickson Cole

SILENT BELLS

A brown clown hides
    behind the curtains,
        as the ballerinas dance.

Trying hard to distract
    their concentration and balance.
        A joker is one who tempts the swans.

Elegant, their vision is peripheral
    necks arched with grace,
        well groomed feathers, preened.

Not to fly, they swim gently,
    slow ripples
        peaceful aquarium.

And turn their fans,
    at that jesting hat.

Too loud for loves ears.

*Dedicated to Raynman, who brought
sunshine into my life.*

—Nancy DeMaria, N 9/93

GRADUATION

This is our last time.
  Our last time to walk these halls,
    last time to laugh in these classrooms.
  Our last time together.
    Let's make it good.
      Let's have some fun.
In the end, we'll miss each other.
    We'll miss our voices,
      we'll miss our laughter.
  Let's make it worth it.
    Let's do it right.
Soon we'll be walking down the aisle,
  with our caps on and our diplomas in one hand.
    With the other hand,
      we'll be saying good-bye.
Good-bye to our childhood, good-bye to the great days.
  Then, all we'll have are memories.
    So let's make the memories great.

*Dedicated to my fellow classmates at
St. Stan's, the class of 1994.*

—Joy Ann Konarski

Sometimes in our quest for contentment, we become even more lost than before.
Questioning values and beliefs, wondering what
really matters
and what doesn't.
And where you fit in to all this confusion.
Someone once said
"It is good to pause now and then in our pursuit of happiness,
. . . and just be happy."
So simple, yet so extremely complex.
I wonder if there's ever a point of "arriving" at happiness,
of reaching that plateau of contentment higher than the one
you presently dwell on.
Or if it is a continuous journey
up the hillside of mediocrity,
and somewhere along the way you learn that the
joy is in the journey.
—Jennifer D. Wells

ROOM #213-2

In the little corner of my life,
I watch the western sky slowly, softly change
from muted gray to soft pink, to deeper pink,
and then explode into a brilliant panorama of fire-red
that stretches across the sky.

In the center, the sun, a shimmering red ball,
quickly begins to set.
Leafless trees silhouette against an ever-changing sky,
seem to disappear in the oncoming darkness.

I close my eyes.
Memories crowd my mind.
Snippets of long forgotten conversations . . .
Youthful faces of departed friends . . .
All the good times with the laughter . . .
All the bad times with the tears . . .
Each memory a precious gem.

The sudden cry of the nighthawk brings me back from my reverie,
and I am once again in the little corner of my life.
—Irene Priebe

HOOSIER WARP SPEED

Crossroads of America: bucolic provincial slow-moving farmers
Mike Royko's jibes about Uncle Elmer's pick-up truck—
That's the reputation we have down the toll road from Chicago.
Nothing could be farther from the truth.

Maybe on the East Coast Monday night is football but in Indiana
It's L680 English Literature read Faulkner write a paper.
Tuesday night it's volunteer work, committee meeting,
Neighborhood Action Group and we're all out of cat food.

Wednesday night in Pittsburgh is probably for poker parties but
Between Ohio and Illinois it's Kids' Club don't forget the snack.
Thursday night South of the Border may be relax-kick-back but
South of Michigan Megan has a concert and no clean underwear.

Before you can dust the piano it's Friday night order pizza
maybe have a game of Scrabble what about the Faulkner paper
Phone ringing bread baking Saturday's gone to the grocery store.
And the tablecloths are still wrinkling in the dryer.

Choir practice Sunday School hear the sermon hurry home
Mushrooms added to the pot roast salad dressed greet the guests
Later you can read the comics do the crossword take a breath.
Just another typical slow-moving week in Indiana.
—Helene A. Hoover

Come to me
in the still of night;
cast your spell
upon my heart, and
breathe life into my soul
with your kiss.
Come to me in my dreams;
let your heart beat
upon my skin, and
caress it in the silent slumber.
Come to me
in the still of night;
rescue my soul, and
let time be no more
than a kiss upon the wind.
—Janeen Leedy

REMEMBERING

Remembering
sunlight lost
    in Asia.

Alone.
Tick-tocking.
Black and white.

I remain
    listening.
—Nancy Belle Fuller

Return often
And take me
My love.
All those nights
Filled with sensations,
And half-dreams,
Lying in your arms
Afterwards
My skin remembers.
Bring back
The memories
Again.
—Michele Scatena

ALL OF THE NIGHT

The night is full
The sky is free
Shooting stars
Are wishes to be
A shining moon
Shines so bright
Casting shadows
Shedding light
Cool air settles
Fog rolls round
Silence awakens
Upon the ground
Dew and mist
Cover the leaves
Of every plant
And every tree
The night has fallen
Fallen again
The day is out
The night is in
—David M. Varner

BOSNIAN BABY

His silent eyes
    stone slab, his body lies
      He never learned how to hate

Wooden toys
    for good little boys
      Destroy, what they create

Hands stiff with cold
    blood stains their soul
      Death hears no one's plea

Puzzled with "why"
    no silent eyes cry
      His grave, His hope, He's free

—E.C. Battey Jr.

HIS WAY WITH ME

As I sat in the late evening stillness
And pondered my deeds of the day,
I wondered what Jesus would tell me
If He should be passing my way.

I thought of the kind word not spoken;
I thought of the soul wounded sore.
I thought of the one deep in sorrow
Who came seeking aid at my door.

I knew then that I had been failing
To let my light shine for my King.
I longed to do something to help Him;
I wanted His praises to sing.

So I prayed as I sat in the darkness,
"Dear Jesus, use me as You will.
Help me to be loving and gentle,
And guide me Thy plans to fulfill."

—Joy Cojeen Wessel

NO CREDIT CARD

The modern way of life
    Is credit cards today.
Do what pleases you now,
    End of the month you pay.

There's no credit card to heaven
    Wake up today and pray.
Don't put off until tomorrow
    What you can do today.

At the crossroad you will stand—
    Lord Jesus and yourself.
He doesn't take the credit cards.
    Don't try to fool yourself.

No credit card to heaven,
    What you should do today—
Is kneel and ask forgiveness
    Lord Jesus knows the way.

On the narrow road to heaven
    If you should slip and fall,
Don't turn to credit cards
    The Lord Jesus will hear your call.

All credit goes to Lord Jesus
    He died on the cross, for our sins,
To give "Eternal Life" forever
    Who believe and trust in him.

—Alice J Anderson

MOST URGENT PHONE CALL *

From His LOVE BOOK, God "phones" you and me:
"His Love gave His SOLE Son," you see,
"To die for our sins, set us free." —
"Please believe, and love Him," is His plea.

He waits at His "phone" eternally —
Gives us "800 number, toll-free!"
Will we answer, with love, you and I,
And join His Love Family in the sky?

* BIBLE: Saint John 3:16 and Saint John 15:13
"For God so loved the world that
He gave His only begotten Son,
that whosoever believeth in Him
should not perish, but have everlasting life."

"Greater love hath no man than this,
that a man lay down his life for his friends."

—Mary Alice Badeau Jenkins

THE EVENING MIST

The evening mist hangs low upon the earth;
Silhouetted birds soar across the twilight sky,
With all this magic my sadness turns to mirth,
Tranquility grips my soul as upon this scene I spy.

Hazy days, lazy days, days that have no end —
Fledgling eagles ride in grandeur on the shoulders of
    the wind.
I hear the timid grouse rustle in the tall, sage grass;
I almost think that I can hear the great
    Almighty pass.

The lofty treetop sways its head in dance of sheer
    delight;
The effulgence of the sunset splashes color to
    greet the night.

I am awed in complex wonder; how could such
    splendor be?
In faith I turn to know and live, I give
    all glory Thee!

—Dennis B. Rone

CHRISTMAS

This Christmas Season we wish for you
Happiness, which is Peace, Hope and Love
Every good gift and every perfect gift
    that is sent from Above

Christ Jesus was born in Bethlehem
And the wisemen saw His star so bright
Rejoicing, they followed that star
Realizing they would see Him that night
Overjoyed to behold this child
Laid in a manger of hay
Lauding God, they presented gifts to Him
    and then went on their way

Messiah, the Light of the World, The Door
As certain as two plus two equals four
Now the Word was made Flesh in time of yore
Nativity, His birth — the first Christmas
Oh, come let us adore Him, all of us
Note the letters starting each line
See who sends you this Yuletide rhyme

—Betty A. Mannon

THE CHILD

A little child can warm the heart of the toughest man around. A child can change any face to a radiant smile instead of a scowl or a frown.

Yes a child is a blessing and a gift from the Lord above. He can fill your home with happiness, joy and abundance of love.

For the child is what we would all like to be, and not have worries, burdens, and miseries.

So love all the children and let them remain a child as long as you can, and when they have problems offer them a helping hand.

The Lord's blessing of children was to enrich our lives. And to make happier husbands and wives.

—Dwight Philip Boyd

A MOTHER REMEMBERS

I turn the pages in my memory book,
   It seems but yesterday.
That you were taking your very first steps,
   How well I remember it, dear.

The day you started in kindergarten,
   So blushingly shy, such keen agitation.
Through eight short years, mile posts of time,
   To the day of days — graduation.

High school, you said, was so much fun,
   I rustle the pages of the book.
Yes, here you are in cap and gown,
   How very proud you look!

I close the cover of my memory book,
   The years have been short, it seems.
Although you are grown and have gone your way,
   You are still my baby in dreams.

—Merle Scheer

MY FRIEND ALICE

Some people have their coffee
Some have to have their tea;
But just a dose of Alice
Is the "pick me up" for me.

It really doesn't matter
How bad I may be feeling;
Cause just a dose of Alice
Will bring me instant healing.

On days when I am feeling blue,
There's just one thing for me to do;
Go to the phone and call her up
A dose of Alice fills my cup.

There's a magic charm about her
And everytime she is near;
The troubles that I thought I had
Just seem to disappear.

I'm really very rich indeed
Although I don't live in a palace.
I have the most precious friend in the world
And I thank God for Alice.

*Dedicated to Alice Freeman,
a very dear friend.*

—Faye Carlton Ralston

JEAN

The years go by and travel fast.
Memories are all we have of the past.
Jeannie has put her dolls away,
   For another girl, another day.
We don't stumble on blocks anymore,
   And paper dolls don't clutter the floor.
Bats and balls don't lay around,
   The guns are silent without sound.
The bicycle's rusting and falling apart,
   Other things now have her heart.
For Jean is seventeen today,
   Quite grown up now won't you say?
But we will miss our little girl
   Who now belongs to another world.

—Frances Crafton

TO SHERRY

I know there are so many things
That I don't know how to do;
But, some things come easy for me:
Poetry — and — loving you.

I'm so glad you're one of us,
The wife of my firstborn son;
Mother of my GRANDDARLINGS, three,
Dear to me, and lots of fun.

Doing deeds of simple kindness
Makes you feel happy, it's true;
And, you ask nothing in return,
Helping others pleases you.

Honestly, this poem's not hard,
Since you furnished all the facts;
For everything you've done — THANKS
For being you — to be exact.

*Dedicated to my daughter-in-law, Sherry,
always willing to lend a helping hand —
I love you, Sherry.*

—Betty A. Mannon

IN MEMORY OF MY MOTHER

God must love me so very much,
He gave to me our loving touch.
Through the years you were there for me
And now, though you I cannot see.
The love we share will always be
Our bond throughout eternity.

A mother's love you gave to me
And now a mother I must be.
In the mirror, I look and see
Your specialness; it's a part of me.
The loving threads from you to me
Will continue on and always be.
In my children's eyes, I look and see
That specialness you gave to me.

Mother, you were there for me
A loving hand to hold.
You gave to me with all your heart
A shelter from the cold.
Now in God's loving care you are,
With angels you reside.
Even though I miss you here with me,
I feel you by my side.

—Patricia Duncan Brown

OFF BALANCE

A person
With too much expectancy
Is like someone
With a cumbersome load held far out in front,
Who perpetually hurries
And runs off-balance
While vainly trying
To slip beneath
The un-levered
Burden.

—B. B. Watkins

THE PETALS OF LIFE

Life is like a rosebush
it starts out as a seed,
then it grows and flourishes
as you too grow and flourish.

The young plant is like an infant;
soft and very vulnerable,
the slightest wind can hurt so much.

The bush grows and strengthens,
as the baby grows and strengthens.
Then one day the bush stands alone,
as the toddler too will stand alone.

Young roses appear slowly
each petal opening bright and sure.
The full flower will one day close,
petals falling one by one
like tears shed over someone gone.

As the aging rosebush withers and dies
so do we, one by one—
now the cycle of life must begin again
like the rosebush does each season.

—Kelly Steepleton

LIFE

It has nothing to do with time,
When things in life treat you unkind,
It's all a state of mind.

How far up that mountain you climb,
how close you come to committing a crime,
It has nothing to do with time.

They say all wounds heal in time.
Even if you've lost your last dime?
It's all a state of mind.

An' if in your lifetime,
you can't deal with your pastime
It has nothing to do with time.

An' if you have no skill,
an' you need in life a thrill,
It's all a state of mind.

An' when your heart & mind have been
abused an' torn,
How long you grieve an' mourn,
It has nothing to do with time.
It's all a state of mind.

—Marsha (McGillis) Gunnerson

MOTHER

Mother you are so special to me
So special even others can't see.

Sometimes when I lie awake at night
you come to sooth me so cheerful and bright

Many people I have told
Of your heart of purest gold

Mother you don't know exactly
how much you mean to me

I'm so grateful for thee

So grateful that you mean
the *WORLD* to me!

—Danette Westerfield

OLAMAE MY SPECIAL ANGEL

I once had a beautiful daughter, her
name was Olamae. She was the most
beautiful girl in the world, when
Jesus called her away.

Now she walks in beauty on streets of
purest gold, in that beautiful place called
Heaven, that land where we will never
grow old.

She has gone to be with Jesus in that
beautiful land, there she will stay
forever and sing with the angel band.

She has gone to that bright land so
fair, where there will be no crying
there, for Jesus will wipe all tears
away and change the darkest night
to day.
Now I know she will forever be
waiting with love for her
children and me.

—Creola Pence

ASHLEY!

Ashley Nicole,
is a merry little soul.
She just turned three,
and is happy as can be.
Ashley is an only child.
So she seems a bit wild.
She likes to share her home with others.
So she is getting foster sisters and brothers.
She likes to ride her bicycle,
When she's not eating popsicles.
And she likes to walk to the store,
even though she's shy, once inside the door.
She's a real beauty,
and everyone thinks she's a real cutie.
How I love that little girl,
with all her long brown curls.
Ashley goes to school next time,
and I'm sure she'll miss me, a long, long time.

*Dedicated to my three-year-old granddaughter,
that has kept me going for the last
three years, when otherwise I wouldn't.
She's my pride and joy.
"I Love You, Ashley."*

—Mary Hulon Johnson

THE WALK OF LIFE

With my every footstep, I trembly strive,
Not knowing from day to day, will I be alive!

Through the path of life, I walk in fear,
Realizing that the shadows of death are always near!

Rushing to mischief, our footsteps blindly flow,
Where we end up, we never will know!

Upon the broad street of destruction, a many footsteps walk so smooth,
Destined to the grave, where their footsteps will cease to move!

—Allen Jones

WALKING WITH THE DEAD

Be with me, souls of the past
Bring me along as I spend time walking the earth.
Give me your strength, your wisdom
Be my protector, at my heels, only a breath away.
As you gaze on the destiny you were a part of
Do you understand my confusion?
Were you perplexed as well?
Is everything now in wonderful order?
You've gone to a place of peace,
To dwell with the spirits of all time.
I have to be able to call out for help
You've done it all and I haven't.
Fleeting thoughts of what peace you must possess.
Wanting to succeed,
With my own minute space in time.
As I put one foot in front of the other,
Pulling my body forward.
This confusion of life must have a reality.
I must have a special place with you,
You must love me, as I know you did in life.

—Judith A. Neitge

QUESTIONS

The blue blur streaks across the room—
through the glass opening.

What's happening on the other side of the glass?

Oh, the pain . . . and the pain of not knowing.

Where is my baby? What is happening to him?
  Is he alive?

Why can't I see him, touch him, hold him close?

Questions . . . . always questions.

Finally, I go to him, his small body with all the
  tubes and wires.

What happened? What went wrong? It's not supposed
  to be this way!

Where is the chubby, wiggling baby of my dreams?

He cries, but there's no sound. The tubes get in
  the way of even this normality.

The endless buzzers, the endless fear.

The endless days lived in the noisy, yet oddly
  quiet world of the premature nursery.

—Nancy Domgaard

SOUL IS ALIVE

The smell of death
I recognized it so
I smelt it here ten years ago
Saddened, sickened was this heart of mine
As we stared along a line
Her face absent of life
Her body rested, cold as ice
Here this woman I barely knew
Hardly tried, never bothered to
Here we were, all dressed in black
All our thoughts thinking back
So will I be in my box
Laying lifeless as the preacher talks
I don't want any crying eyes
For my soul will be alive

—Jammie Marie Garcia

MY PRAYER

I knelt before the lord one day
when I was only seven —
I feared even then I wouldn't
get to heaven.
I prayed a very selfish prayer
but god took it to his heart —
he knew I needed to learn to trust
and gave me an early start.
I'm glad I found my loving saviour
he changed my life and my
behavior.
I'll trust him until the day I die
then go to live with him on high.
Won't you come and join me in
my quest for a higher place —
God will surely welcome you
he has lots of space.

—Wanda Anderson

I DO

In that far off distant land
You need no one to hold your hand
But, I do

With the Lord and Saviour there
You have no need for someone to care
But I do

With all the glories up above
You many not need someone to love
But I do

I struggle through each night and day
Wishing I could find the way
To be at peace like you above
Though you are gone, you have my love
I am so happy that you are free
I shouldn't worry about what is to be
But I do

I miss you so both day and night
Without your love, nothing goes right.
You told me I would always be with you
Only in my dreams can that come true.

Someday love, my time will come
And with you I will be home
I know you long for that day too
As I do, as I do.

—Nell Handley

THE LAST BALLET

Soft morning breezes
    float gently around me.
Teasing, provoking, my hair
    to bend at its will.
Leaves twirling and dancing
    in conicals of color.
Tall trees, in their splendor,
    sway like symphony conductors.
A melody on the wind flutters
    and enters my inner ear.
The air is crisp and cold.
    I closely gather my cloak
As fall sets the scene
    for this special ballet.
It is the last performance
    before the curtain of winter falls.

—Dorothea M. Petrut

MOBILITY REMEMBERED

I grieve for my fast, sexy walk,
the way heels made my calves look.

I grieve for strutting in boots
to an old Hank Williams tune.

I grieve for polkas and waltzes,
danced yesterday, and tomorrow.

I grieve for runs up the stairs,
and for hikes down Mount Rainier.

I grieve for warm sand on my toes,
playing chase with incoming surf.

I grieve for walks in the woods,
without need of "assistive device."

I grieve for the woman who was.

*Dedicated to all young stroke
survivors, with our gains & losses*

—Peggy Grover

A TRIBUTE TO ELVIS

This man had fame—
This man had fortune—
Seems he had it all.
But, fate passed by his door
To make a fatal call.

He had talent and lots of class.
Displaying a most unusual style—
Though when he sang he sang so well
It made a sad heart smile.

With his guitar and dressed so radiant
He would ♪Rock and Roll♪ —
It made him "King" in all the land
As all his fans well know.

Though a Living Legend to many
He'll always be to me—
A super star that shines night and day
He's "Elvis Presley!"

*In honor to the family, friends and
fans of dearly missed and beloved
"Elvis Aaron Presley."*

—Bev Toda

"TODAY" IN OCTOBER

"Upon arising today, I found my way to the kitchen window; autumn, without question, has arrived.

What sight my eyes discovered, as they scanned
the blazing colors of a nearby scarlet maple tree.

Gazing at this picture of a view made possible
by a cloudless blue sky, I watched a perfectly
shaped scarlet leaf fluttering in the silent breeze.

But wait! Another curvy leaf starts its journey
to the hundreds of leaves already far removed,

Swirling, swirling, restlessly—where will it come
to rest?

Just as the autumn leaves begin their descent to
an unknown destiny, I too, may start on that
same journey, tomorrow though, or maybe not—
maybe today!"

—Evelyn Barlic

GRANDMA'S JUST A HUG AWAY

A pretty ruffled bonnet and a bandage on your toe,
such a contrast of character—
like silk and calico.

But even little angels stumble now and then,
for walking is an acquired art—
and sometimes bruise their skin.

Though with a little practice your walk is then a strut,
all the doors you open—
but somehow never shut.

The bathroom is your favorite place the tissue you unroll,
you like to wash your hands—
in the toilet bowl.

But someday when you're grown-up and the past is just a gleam,
when you're wishing on a star—
or awakening from a dream.

Remember that you have a friend who will understand and care,
for Grandma's just a hug away—
her love with you to share.

—Marie Oliphant

BLANK SPACES TALK, TOO

Then I was thinking of Mr. Boland,
your long, paternal shadow,
the one who made you cry,
though you never knew him.

And I thought, too, of the baby book you made for me,
years ago,
all information complete,
first word, favorite toy,
the pages filled with the confident script of a woman
who still believes in logical, if not happy, endings.

So I turned to "Family Tree"
where colorful relatives smiled from the branches,
and I saw you'd entered your mother's name,
but left your father's blank.

I knew then, I think, if I hadn't known before,
how he left his mark.
I finally understood your dark, sad eyes
to the end of your days searching for your father.
But I still wanted to ask you, as you no doubt had asked,
"Just tell me this, Mother, who *was* Mr. Boland?"

—Shelley Ayn Heinzman

LONELINESS

No emotions may pass its dark gates, No room for either loves or hates.
It's an empty, damp, dark place. Without either a body or face.
It can make you all cold and bitter, Take a good heart and make it wither.
It has no limits, No one place to call home. Always from one to another, on the roam.

It can make you empty and stale, Always afraid all you'll do is fail.
Never is anyone too strong, weak or mild. Known by all, man, woman and child.
Never a place to hide, No way to run. It fears nothing, Not even a gun.

Feared by all, It can't be bought or sold. I feel compelled, Its story to be told.
Beware this thing, So cold, dark and dreary. It preys on the heart, All broken and weary.
Remember these things you are bout to be told. Keep one who loves you, To have and to hold.
Don't ever abuse another's love that is strong. Lying and cheating only help it along.

So be honest, open and caring. Because its name I'm about to be sharing.
It has nothing to do with heaven or bliss. Its name, my friend, is simply,
Loneliness.
   —J.W. Scott

SLEEPING DEATH/AWAKENING LIFE

I lay myself to sleep this somber night knowing only death,
A teardrop descends ever so gently down my face,
Like a whisper it uncaringly ignores my sense of compassion,
I yearn for sympathy and rejection only precedes my morbidity,
Plundering deep within my own sorrow I smother myself in a labyrinth of desperation,
Frantically I search my soul for explanations,
Overwhelmed in thought I encounter no solutions,
Reality is right here before my blind eyes,
The sable night seems to settle like the doleful fog,
My body quakes violently as of a body in paroxysm,
A whirling sensation in my head causes me to drop as if I were a declevity,
Unconscious as the torpor of hibernating animals,
Languorously I strain to salvage my resurrection of mind,
Lightning strikes as God's wrath enables me to become secure in cogitation,
Suddenly I'm no longer blind or unaware
At last I have awakened to the sun's iridescent rays luminating color to the precipitous radiance upon my face,
The renaissance of day brings a new unfound glory to life,
I have survived and awakened to another night of laying myself to sleep knowing only death,
Only to once again cry,
Only to once again die.
   —Joseph Anthony Gonsalves

I AM CRAZY, I AM WILD

I am crazy, I am wild, I'm the man who stole your child.
She'll be mine for all her life, one day she may even be my wife.
Your child is tired, and I am, too. So now I leave this note for you.

With all your strength and all your power, she'll be mine every hour.
She was tied with some twine; this you see, makes her mine.

You cannot have her anymore, you won't see her in a store.
If you think I'll let you see her, just because you're full of fear;
For all I care, you can stay in fright, 'cause she'll be with me every day and night.

Her picture will be on "America's Most Wanted," but don't you fret, I won't be taunted.
Her face may be on a carton of milk; you'll instantly think of her shirt of silk.
The one she was wearing that day; yes, the day I came and took her away.
Away from the horrors and the pain; out of that family so badly stained.

The staining of drugs and alcohol, which didn't suit her, no, not at all.
Someone to comb through her hair; someone to tell her that they care.
A person to love and trust her right; that person is me, out of your sight.

I am crazy, I am wild. I'm the man who stole your child.

Dear Mommy and Daddy: I love you both, but I took an oath.
To stay away from drugs and alcohol; they're not for me, no, not at all.
I am now living with a man; what's his name? Oh, I just call him Stan.
He is crazy, he is wild. He's the man who stole your child!
   —Denise M. Lewis

You tell me your dreams
And I will tell you mine
We can travel together
Where joy ever shines.
No sadness or worry
Where trouble is blind
All torment will wither
Where dreams are the wine.
This world is a haven
For death and unkind
A place without equal
For twisting steel vines.
Go with me now gently
Leave all this behind
If you will tell me your dreams
I will tell you mine.

—James A. Marsters

I LIKE ALL THESE THINGS

I like to view a rising sun
At the break of dawn,
To see spiderwebs thin as glass
Spun upon a dewy lawn.

I like to count fluffy clouds
Floating way up high,
And to watch a baby bird
Learning how to fly.

I like to hear a cricket chirr
In the dark of night,
To chase a lightning bug
That blinks its magic light.

I like to hear rain pitter-pat
Upon my window pane,
And listen to the rumbling sound
Of a fast moving train.

I like to see puffs of dandelion
In motion with the wind,
To see your sunny smile
And the happiness it brings.

—Helen M. Bugosh

UNSPOKEN WORDS

there they met
on that icy slope
with hands of fire
and eyes like jewels
so gentle his touch
yet laden with loneliness

and there they slept
in each other's arms
his hand entangled in her locks
her heart beating against his own
together for warmth and comfort
and so much more

and they awoke
to the myriad of voices
of the night
and his eyes beamed at hers
like two sets of sapphires
aglow with knowledge
a fire in the night
a light in the dark

*Dedicated to A.D., this one's
for you. And to pixie stix.*

—Anna Osterholtz

MOTHER OF THE NIGHT

The night sky glows with the iridescent rays of the moon.
The sun will, however, arise again and burn her away too soon.
But for now in the mystic haven of the night,
The moon will shed out her pure rays of white.
With the darkness comes her gentle power.
Lost souls she protects, never devours.
Tears of sweet light flow from her scarred face,
And they fall through the trees like a delicate lace.
When the graves are shrouded in a mist of lost souls,
She shines down to gather them; for the keys to heaven she holds.
With the stars as her children she blesses the night,
And they shine on the world with a beautiful light.
These are her tasks, never to be undone,
Though weak she may be from the hatred of the sun.
To penetrate the darkness and help the dead find their way,
In the night sky she will for eternity stay.

—Rachel Satterfield

TODAY. TOMORROW. YESTERDAY. THE SAME!

Living so long, here, in the Twilight Zone,
means very few will willingly believe
that — what they *think* they see — is NOT what's known.
Obscure events continually deceive!
    Yet inconsistencies, when brought to light,
    form vital evidence time shall set right.

Go back through time ten-thousand years! Why did
the mammoths in Siberia fast-freeze?
This ancient mystery, religion hid,
concealed in seeming ambiguities.
    Now, frozen meat, still edible, belies
    the explanations scientists devise.

Up in Alaska, in that selfsame year,
dealers in ivory, observing beasts
s-t-r-u-n-g o-u-t . . . question what victims had to fear?
Had they been slaughtered for Olympic feasts?
    Although beheaded, why are no knives found
    where carbon-dating has etched frozen ground?

Who knows the answer to this mystery?
Do scientists hold vital clews? One thinks
astronomers (should any look) might see
Invader "X" created molten links!
    A detailed study shows these truths belong
    to those who have abjured Truth for so long!

Lemuria-Atlantis-Mu survives,
an "island" mystery few understand:
Whereas creation of "Earth-days" claimed lives,
"Ancient of Days," tyrannic priests have banned.
    Fresh links to Stonehenge show Christ Jesus knew
    all MATH-encoded concepts shall prove true!

So "on this rock" our Lord rested his case.
Aware of the collision which had spun
Atlantis off — as Earth's "New Moon" — we trace,
in the New Testament, a triple pun!
    Howbeit, all who recognize that "rock"
    concede — one New-Moon-Passover — put them in shock!

The current hoop-la over dinosaurs
is spawning mammoth-sized red herrings which
divert our thoughts from fabricated wars.
Manipulators, changing meanings, switch
    long-held beliefs to ones they dare not name.
    In "Christ," is Jesus being put to shame?

Today. Tomorrow. Yesterday. The same!

—Phebe Alden Tisdale

CASCADING TEARS

The diamonds fall from their blue tinged pools
And slide down slopes of pink.
They land into the hands of fools
Much faster than a wink.

There they mingle with others lost
Not knowing why they're there.
They only sense what they have cost
But no one seems to care.

Soon they will start to evaporate
Making room for more.
For the others will not hesitate
To land on that empty shore.

—Eve Bergman

THE POET'S PEN

The poet's pen is an extension of his soul.
It is used to enlighten the world with
treasures worth more than gold.

The poet's pen connects a child's eye with
his wandering mind. Because with a pen, a
poet can create his own universe through
similes, metaphors, reason and rhythm.

Poets use the pen to capture thoughts like
water when poured into a bottle. The pen
represents a medium where a poet's creativity
can connect to the spirits of other poets such as
Maya Angelou, Geoffrey Chaucer, and Aristotle.

—André J. Harrell

THE TREE AND THE OLD RED BARN

Both sayings old not new
Between a rock and a hard place
Between the Devil and the deep blue sea
There, surely stands you and me.
Black rights Gay rights children's
Rights and foreigners' rights
Where left are you and where am I?

From swagging front porch I look
Through a window of the old old house
Turn to the left, old oak stands tall
And sturdy while red barn out back leans
Slightly, but still there—did I ever live here?
Blue sky smiles upon green fields and long line
Of trees, white clouds are bowls of fresh
Cow's milk in late summer sky.

We laughed played games and waded barefoot
In cool puddles made from clean rain, weathered
The storms of life no matter the hells of time
And many a strife, depression war marriage
Family rearing—all were expected all completed
No one spoke, about Black white Gay or hetero.

A cotton tailed bunny runs from behind the old
Oak tree—I look at you and you look at me,
Must we get lost between the Devil and the deep
Blue sea? Earth trembles beneath my feet, a slight
Wind shakes roses on the bush nearby—it too is still
Here. Take off shoes rub bare toes in white sand
Sit like Gibraltar beside me, we leave a legacy
To this land.

—Lee Wheeler

THE COUNSELLOR

LISTENS to your woes and blues,
KNOWS what to say and just what to do,
EVERYBODY thinks the counsellor's just fine,
YET silent tears run way deep down.
For all the counselling, the counsellor has done
No counsel comes when he needs one.

—Gloria Cuevas

GREATNESS

As you stand and read this,
It's just a matter of time,
Before the one who wrote it
    Will be great, it's written in these lines.
No! My greatness does not come
    From being able to write,
It only comes from Jesus my Lord
    When I take my flight.

Things of Earth I love a lot,
    Such as Family and Friends,
But there is nothing here,
    That can compare with Him.
Jesus is the Son of God,
    But that alone does not make Him great.
It is His love for every one
    That seals His great fate.

If you will only believe in Him,
    Where can you go wrong?
He is ready to hear from you,
    It is written in words and song.

—"Buddy" Frank Mathews

THE MASTER FISHERMAN

"Launch out into the deep
And let down your nets for a draft,"*
Said Jesus, the Master Fisherman
To His fisherman friends in ther craft.

They could not believe they could catch many;
They had fished all night without any;
But obeying their good Friend's wishes,
They netted some thousands of fishes!

Jesus had great hopes for these few men:
God would transform them into NEW men.
"If you follow me," friends, dear fishermen
"I will make you fishers of MEN."*

That's just what they did, those lowly men,
And became God's chosen holy men:
Disciples — Apostles — God's Co-fishers,
To fish for the souls of men!

Their miraculous harvests of lost men,
They netted! — And through ages past then,
All God's Fishermen faithful and bold
Help God to save men, and their souls!

BIBLE: *Luke 5:4 *Matthew 4:19

*Dedicated to Dr. L.G. Gates, Fisher of Men,
40 years, at 1st Baptist, Laurel, MS.
His New Year sermon, all 40 years, "Launch
Out Into the Deep." "The Preacher" also
loved fishing for FISH, those 40 years.*

—Mary Alice Badeau Jenkins

DAY BREAK

It's great to be awake
When the dawn begins to break;
With its brilliant golden light
It signals the ending of the night.
The sky being so blue, so clear
It adds beauty to the birds I hear.
The dawn's an awesome sight to see
Thank God, who gave this sight to me.

—J. Frederick

ON BECOMING MEN

The handshake now replaces childhood
hugs and punches.
Silent, searching stares
replace blundering
conversation and jestful laughter.

Hidden expectations about each other's
lost direction are gradually swallowed—
slipping down Adam's apple.

Words are few and unimportant.
The childhood, adolescent and
teenage connection has gone.

A handshake replaces,
"Come again" and "Good to see you."
Silent, searching stares utter feebly,
"Thanks for stopping by."

—Thomas O. Mays

PUFF-PUFF

If smoke you must,
smoke.
Who could long the pavement
without shoes?
And still call a waiter
with dignity.

Puff-puff,
if you must.
Hold to the lasting familiar crutches.
Will time ever teach you
to laugh and talk at ease,
to look at beauty without contortions,
or salute the moon before blushing?

Smoke,
if smoke you must.
I like you better
when you puff
then, I reclaim
the total you.
I?
Stoic but desolated.

Smoke,
if smoke you must.
Who could walk the city
without a thespian,
or into the night
without belief?

Puff-puff,
if smoke you must.

Dedicated to Carmen Letelier

—Jorge Letelier

SONG OF THE STRIPPING SHOVEL

Lash the green arms that embrace the horizon,
Crumble the rock that supports its blue metal,
Strip the wood-leaf and the soft-footed shadow,
Strip the wood-rose so the wind mourns the petal!

Bite, teeth of monsters, scrape the wound raw . . .
Ascend with the hawser . . . swing like the grapevine . . .
Release the dark waste . . . scale the bronze scab
And return to the feast where man makes a mine!

Remember the fern that curled a fringed finger,
The shutters of peace a willow trail furnished?
Remember the sweet water as breathless as bird-song,
Its brisk, lucid vein now copperas burnished?

O lust for ravines where the wild spoor is brazen,
The briar-bordered lanes where high meadows inch!
Gorge the black coals that lodge the steel throats
But pinch the flared nostil . . . the land bears a stench!

—Cecil Austin McGaw

OCTA

Octa or Octo a word meaning eight
An Octogenarian sure pulls much weight
In terms of the years that have come and have gone
The wisdom that's gained and accomplishments done
It's a world now — still new, with more yet in store
All blessings and joys for the next 80 more

What to do at 80 when you fail to tie your shoe?
You prance right to your favorite store
Now tell me — how you knew?
A loafer or a buckled boot — such fashion now behold
These things become the treasures — more than purest gold

What to do at 80 when the eyes dim to the print?
If you will listen carefully — I'll give you one small hint.
A magnifying glass or two will bring the words anew
Or better yet a friend who'll read and share a point of view.

What to do at 80 when the ears hear only some
Of all the conversations and only half the fun?
A Sony Walkman turned up loud for only you to hear
Will bring you joys as yet untapped and last for many a year.

—Alyce Schmidt

LEAVING LAND

i respect the ocean
i respect the ocean more now
as you pick me up, my day-long lover,
and tip-toe me into it . . .

the cool black nights
beneath the waves
seem never to end,
a fresh-for-me moon nudges the tide
and i am gobbled up, swallowed, and spit clean as chrome!
alive and delightfully new with you . . .
off our knees at last,
our arms shaping a V

i feel that strong when i am this wet
far from the dry of land and its secret doorways
this water is clear and can be traveled eyes first

i respect the ocean
i respect the ocean more now
i am accidentally less human here
more lovable
cracking waves with you

—Danielle Newton

COURAGE

My courage is in the affirmation
Of my part in co-creation.
Through pain and pleasure, I embrace
This gift, and cradle each new face
With awe and wonder in its form.
Now my fourth child has been born.
No naive longing urges me
To dandle baby on my knee.
The unexpected anguish of loving human souls
Of any size intrudes upon the living-out of roles.
But if I dare to take the part
And brave the pains that pierce my heart
When sickness, evil, or distress
Impinge upon our happiness
And let my choice resound the 'Yes!'
Of life, I may find holiness.

—Priscilla Galasso

COME, STAY

Come, stay,—
    For I would talk
        Of many things;

Some trivia,
    But more of that
        Which rings the deep.

When white mist-shrouded fires
    Damped their way
And souls became encased
    In human clay
The dog star danced
    And flickered in the night.
The world was bathed in strange and eerie light.

I could have said
    That which I'll never say
Till I go unknown down
    Toward the end of day.

—Bette Stalder Wright

HEAVENLY LIBRARY

There's so much in the library I love to read
And so many facts there — I really need
To go to the library every day
And read and read, and stay and stay.

I wish I could read ten books at a time!
I'd gallop through bookshelves line by line,
Like unicorn ridden by fairy fay,
Feasting on literature all the way.

But with my slow pace, a fact I must face:
No matter how often or long I embrace
The wonderful treasures the books incase
I'll still fall short, when I leave this place.

But amid my slow, frustrated coping,
I'm wondering if, and even hoping
The Maker of Man, Inspirer of Books,
Somehow on such dilemma looks;

Maybe planned, in His wisdom, His mansions for homes,
With a special BOOK mansion in central zone,
With the Book of Books as the cornerstone —
A Heavenly Library, Reference and Loan.

*Dedicated to Mrs. Eva Mae Walker Boutwell,
our long-time friend, Librarian 43 years:
Laurel Library Ass'n. Laurel, Miss.*

—Mary Alice Badeau Jenkins

THE KEY

    I see clouds with floating dreams;
I see hearts with ripping seams.

    I see eyes filled with tears,
lots of diseases without cures.

    I see children with a lot of fear,
many hearts trying to feel dear.

Many adults don't think I see,
but I'm tomorrow, and I seek the key.

—Kellie Sue Rawson

MOTHER

Let not your heart be troubled,
nor arise anger upon them.
Fill thy mouth with words of meekness,
Abandon them not with your love.

Encourage them in their dreams,
embrace them in your arms
abide them in your deliverance,
Warm them with your affection.

Understand all their confusions,
Lead them on your way,
Let them follow your will,
and teach as a token.

Punish them not with your palm,
for your words are stronger than action.
Bitter words will affect their mind,
But soft words will soften their hearts.

They will always remember your memories,
with your love you gave them hope,
Words of wisdom they'll always remember,
the precious gifts from heaven above.

—Shela

MOTHER LEFT BEHIND LOVE

We can go to the place of
her most humble birth.
We can visit the farmhouse
where she lived on earth.

Jesus called and she answered,
"Lord I'm ready to go,
I have been listening for your call
a year or so."

Mother sits at her Lord's feet.
She asked us not to weep,
"For in Jesus I'll only be asleep."
She was gentle, kind, and sweet,

Her marked Bible and love I'll keep.
Happy in her Heavenly tomorrows,
There will be no pains or sorrows.
Mother is free, free at last,

No worry of her life's past.
Her Lord and Savior is her light,
There will be no darkness or night.
God has a new star in his Heaven tonight.

—Eva .M. (Golden) Byrnes

LOVE

You bring me love like I've never had before. I couldn't ask for anything more. Green are your eyes. I love as the green tall pine trees. I never knew it could come true. But when I'm blue, I just think of you. Hoping to see your green eyes to mine. Red flames in your eyes as mine. Burning as brightly as a forest of green pine trees would burn as a forest fire glows. May this flame of ours burn forever eternally forever. My Endless Love. Ever thine Ever mine, Ever for each other.

—Ramona E. Hamric

WHEN I AM WITH YOU

When I am with you
    You make me feel so sublime,
I pray, you'll always be mine.
When I am with you
and your hair brushes against me,
I feel just what my heart sees,
that you're inside of me.
You begin in my heart and end in my soul.

When I am with you
Only the tender touch of your hand,
brings out this man.
You came into my life,
and a seed was sowed into my soul.
As the waves crash upon the boulders
may our passion last,
even as we grow older,
Look into my eyes
and know that they will never lie,
when I am with you . . . .

—Robert Cadeau

OTHER WORLD

The sea air soft against my skin;
    Salty air.
And I am here and you are there . . .
    In the other world.

The ebb and flow of endless waves
    Slapping time upon the sand
Heal the soul, though awfully slow.

    This is real
    We are not.

The heart you owned is mine at last.
And soft air billows through my thoughts.

    It is good
    And so am I!

I'll lose myself in this today
And tomorrow lose all yesterdays,
    Leave them hanging where they were.

For just a little while
    A sagging spirit is refreshed . . .

I am here . . . and you are there
    In the other world.

—June DeVincent

IMAGINATION

Imagination is the inspiration
    for many individuals' education.
Fly to the moon,
    Swim a lagoon,
        Slay a big dragon,
            Ride in a covered wagon.
Your boundaries are never ending;
You can keep on pretending
    anything you like.

—Jason Clark

LOVE

The long sleek surfaces lay all around.
    They are cool and clean and hot;
They repel and envelop,
They tear and pull;
They are erratic harmony.
And dance a stagnant dance of hope and despair.
They are disquiet and serenity;
They are selfishly giving,
And oddly in sync;
They are power and beauty,
They are love.

—Karla M. Ketchum

Only once my heart's been broken,
    and that time has become a token,
now my heart is sealed tight,
and for my love one now must fight.
A heart of iron I now hold,
strong as steel and icy cold,
from me love will not be taken,
for my will can not be shaken.
Full of joy for that short year,
with nothing to show but a soft little tear.
Now I go forward and hope for the best,
and lock-up my memories in my heart's tiny chest.
Only one person possesses the key,
and I know that by now she's forgotten of me . . . .

—Wade Moller

I BELIEVE I'M GONNA LOVE YOU

As the morning casts a 1,000 bits of sunlight,
    And they shine like diamonds on the morning dew,
I believe that every single one is mine alone to see,
    Oh, I believe I'm gonna love you.

If it seems that there are special stars for lovers,
    And we see them scattered across the midnight blue,
    I believe that out of all this world,
They're meant for you and me,
    Cause, I believe I'm gonna love you.

I'll take you to a magic place, where no one's ever been,
Where there's Prophets made of flowers and music in the wind,
If you wonder why I've given you these treasures,
    Because you're like no one else I've known,
I believe that as we walk thru time,
    The best is yet to come,
Cause, I believe I'm gonna love you,
    Cause, I believe I'm gonna love you.

—Herbert I Shockley, deceased

AS TIME GOES BY

As I sit in my chair wondering what tomorrow will bring,
I sometimes wonder what I've been through.
I remember when I was a kid;
I was strong, smart and fun to be with.

But lately, my life has gotten complicated
and the world has taken a turn for the worst.
I look out my window and I see kids dying left and right like flies.
I cry because blacks are killing blacks and whites are killing whites.
As the clock ticks, I ask myself when will the violence stop?
When will the hatred end.
When will my Savior come? When will he take me away from all of this?

Then I think of my family, my friends, and my loved ones.
What joy they bring me. Boy! Do we have fun!
After awhile I find myself back in my chair not as angry not as sad.
Thinking of what I'm going to do tomorrow **AS TIME GOES BY.**

—Demetrius Teal Veasy II, age 15

INSTRUMENTS OF TORTURE

Small gentry. Opportunist. Last quarter.
Military architect. Soldiers. Engineer. Writer. Forbidden. Condemned.
Obscene. Fictional. Amorous. Sadistic. Fantasies. Indulge.
Scheming the seduction. Abuse. Innocent virgin. Virtuous.
Totally new dimension. Switching roles.
Embrace your own death. Exulted veritable obscenity. Admire. Appalled.
Amused.
Detached. Mordant humor. Striking features. Titillating.
Treated the last twitches. Timespace: dinosaurs. Air raid shelter.
Implications. Outside the lair. Survive. Species. Doomed.
Anticipation of decay. Familiar with death.
The notion of sexual excess. Allusions. Archetypal idealism.
Portrait of contemporary sensual imagery. The language of pain. Experience.
Masterworks are the accomplices of power. Thinking. Enlightenment. The
death of god. The coffin. Putrefying corpses. Life imprisoned.
"THINKING IS THE GREATEST JOY OF MANKIND"
Instruments of torture. Lightning that split the consciousness. The last joy.
Terminal case. Wrestle literature. Medicine. The sun of torture. Equal force.
Ruins of this planet.

—Jud Martell

RIVER, RIVER

River, river, young and free—tell me how this came to be!
River, river, wild and strong—I can relate to your turbulent song.
River, river, my heart cries—for I see pain hidden in your eyes.
River, river, honestly—did your soul quiver with ecstacy?
River, river, rest awhile—I'll find comfort in the light of your smile.
River, river, my heart sings—of yesterdays and better things.
River, river, faithfully—I stand by you—you stand by me.
River, river, be at peace—with careless abandon—and sweet release.
River, river, do you know—where fools collide—and passions flow?
River, river, speak to me—are you near the edge of eternity?
River, river, waters rage—time has written a mysterious page.
River, river, song of the soul—tell me have you sought your goal?
River, river, filled with grace—tell me have you seen God's face?
River, river, please don't cry—God sings a peaceful lullaby.
River, river, lift your head—walk bravely where angels fear to tread.
River, river, despite the past—God's perfect love remains steadfast.
River, river, the time shall pass—when you shall walk the sea of glass.
River, river, shades of blue—be not afraid—God goes with you.
River, river, shades of black—always looking forward—never turning back.
River, river, pale shades of green—the river must fade into worlds unseen . . . .

Here's to our age of foolishness and innocence.
Those were the days. I miss them.

—Dennis Dale Popham

THE FIRST

In the quiet of dawn I sit and wonder
if another sat as I and wondered
of those who came before.

Did another gaze at sturdy oaks and towering pines
on these cliffs of sand and clay
and wonder if another stood here before.

As waves beat the shore and swirl at my feet
could another have looked over mist covered waters
and wondered of the others who came before.

Has another's shadow lengthened in the twilight
and wondered if another knelt and prayed for
those who came before.

Was there ever a time when the one who stood at these shores
did not wonder about another—
for there were none before.

—Maggie Steinert

MY OWN THOUGHTS ABOUT LIFE

I am endlessly searching for what life is all about;
    my purpose is . . .

I wonder if I'll ever understand life's complexities
    and feel free to be me.

I feel lost like I'm on an endless sea voyage;
    drifting alone.

I see the disharmony of the world accelerating so rapidly;
    spinning out of control.

I hear Mother Earth's voice calling for peace and harmony;
    oneness with all things.

I wish I could be free to soar high above;
    as the eagles do.

I want peace, love and brotherhood for all;
    including Mother Earth.

I am a voyager, soul searching;
    seeking oneness.

—Debra L. Horton

ENDLESS LIFE

Petals of souls I spread
    Across the fields of past
Verses of wisdom I sing
    Which whispers to thy heart
Flowers will bloom around my life
    As my soul fades away
    In the sunrise beneath the sunset,
    And there I live
    For ever and ever

—Carrie Gobar Daniel, age 14

A BEAUTICIAN

To be a good beautician—
First of all one must like hair.
And if a certain style she wants,
Must also be aware.

There are a lot of pretty ladies,
That just need a little lift.
And if you can assist them—
It is certainly a gift.

There is a different feeling,
When one has a new coiffeur.
From added self-assurance,
To poise and more allure,

A shampoo, then comes tinting,
(New color is a must)
Next cut for added shaping,
Then curling, what a fuss!

But oh! the finished product,
Is all one hopes will be—
When looking in the mirror,
She murmurs, "Is that me?"

—Floris P Smith

POEM OF LIFE

It began with a thought about a trip to a foreign land
There was some hesitation
It is always hard to let go of a familiar hand

We entered into the unknown with so much to comprehend
But soon found comfort in our new found friends

We have been fortunate enough to see history now as it stands
We have seen people of many different cultures
We have heard the languages of their great lands

We have touched the wall and we have touched the tower
We have felt the pain of concentration camps, being taken in by all its power

We have swum the oceans and have sailed the seas
We have seen the tears of poverty and have felt the scars of disease

We have seen each other at our best
We have seen each other at our worst
All the things we have said and done —In Our Poem Of Life—
Will be another added verse

Be proud of who you are and where you come from
Never forgetting where you have been
So much we have seen and so much in us has changed
We all reached out from the inside and became friends

—Brenda Geris

THE WINDOW OF LIFE

The window of life opens. Once again I am called upon
to make a choice upon which path my foot shall tread.
Questions I have faced all my life come again to haunt
me.
Where shall I go?
What shall I do?

I do not know the answers to these questions now, but with
time I will learn.
The future is not vast and empty, but full and bright.
I shall enter the future rationally, and shall not lose hope
when all seems lost.
I shall not sit and mourn the past, but rather shall walk
bravely through that "Window of Life" and become one with myself
and my destiny.

—Jeffrey E. Cronin

A LIFE-TIME

Life, as this small word comes to mind, to express with emotion,
to identify, a course which spans a life-time.
An existence with greatness of power, fullness of zest,
    that through years gains purpose and strength.
From the beginning to grasp, never to question,
    how long will it last.
Bracing firmly against failure in this fight to survive,
    as success rounds the corner for yet another try.
Like the ocean depositing fine grains of sand,
    each second grants a choice to select a just plan.
An again age produces a knowledge of nothing to fear,
    when tarnished with hardships and tears.
Life in essence, a love of endless beauty,
    touched by a sharing in this rare unity.
Challenges with a desire to win, with steps to pace,
    slow and sure, for then tomorrow all yesterday's chores,
    will become memories stored.
All too quickly life diminishes with time,
    leaving behind a legacy, others seek to find.

—D. Elaine Shaffer

UNCHALLENGED GRANDEUR

A new day is born, across the eastern sky;
As graceful, orange fingers reach up, Oh so high.

Then suddenly, and without so much ado;
A raging, fiery ball, comes bursting into view.

The flowers stand at attention, as nature awaits her cue;
While the morning chill vanishes, along with last night's dew.

Onward, upward across that vast domain;
A kingdom yet unchallenged, none question his sovereign reign.

To evaporate or germinate, bringing warmth to all below;
We set our clocks, our work is done, beneath Sol's golden glow.

Time moves on, as such it must, both now and ages past;
Our memory holds promise of a sunrise, and benefits that last.

Slipping slowly toward the horizon, sinking quietly from sight;
We are awe-struck by the colors, as they usher in the night.

Task all finished, job complete, knowing exactly where he's been;
At the appointed time, he will start anew, and do it all again.

—Bobby H. Aid

TIME

Time is a great healer
It eases so much pain
It minimizes our troubles
that dwell within our brain
as life presents its problems
to what no one is immune
time also solves its problems
to what we are all in tune.

—Jeanette Hutchinson

IMPACT

Words dipped in color—
fire and grass.

Sounds fraught with meaning—
screams and breaking glass.

Actions of emotion—
kisses and tears.

Wounds that are fatal—
loneliness and years.

—Joyce Holland

ONE MAN'S DESTINY

Into the badlands
one man strode.

Not knowing which
route he rode.

To the East?
To the West?

Soon he'd be lost
starving for quest!

Only if this man
could see,

He's on the
pathway of destiny!

—Karen Wipf

OWN LITTLE WORLD

Each little place
In some one space
Has its own race
    Its own little world

He goes out in quest
To beat all the rest
To become the best
    His own little world

You can create
And you relate
Of your own fate
    Your own little world

But what we regret
And try to forget
And what we know yet
    Of our own little world

Is that there are
Near and so far
On every star
    Their own little world.

—Moo

FOREST

As I walk through the forest; I hear nature's most enchanting sounds of life. I hear the birds chirping, the sound of leaves as I trample across the earthen floor, and as I stop and stand up against the trees I hear the wind whispering sweet; sensational sounds of joy. But as I move on, I come to a beautiful flowing river and its most beautiful scenery. I walk over to sit down on the river's bank and listen as the water gushes and gurgles against the stone and pebbles. And as I look up, in the middle of the river out jumps a red salmon. And as I look across out of nowhere appears a deer and her young-one coming down to the river's bank taking a cool, crisped, and refreshing drink of water to satisfy their thirst and even though the evening has to come to another abrupt ending, I say to myself, "Nothing shall ever come between me and my love for God's beautiful creations, FORESTS." And as I look around one last time, I know I've just encountered another one of Mother Nature's beautiful paradises of the world.

—Amanda R. Field, age 13

THE VALLEY OF MY DREAMS

In this dark and gloomy forest where the pine and fir trees stand
This is a virgin grove unscarred by modern man
There I wander ever searching for a valley with a stream
Where the solitude is unbroken where a man can sit and dream

Where the silence is so deep, seems like all sound is gone
Where the falling of a pine cone seems as loud as a gong
Where the breeze in the tree tops plays a haunting symphony
This is the sort of valley that would be home sweet home to me

Let me live there as the cave men did long long ago
Let me leave nothing behind me except tracks where ever I go
No scars or trash to mar the beauty or no camp spots to be found
Just the marks of mother nature, is there such a place around

Do not tell me that I am dreaming, that my search is all in vain
That there is no such valley blessed with sunshine and rain
Let me keep searching for this paradise my friend
For when a man stops dreaming he is reaching the end

—W. Carl Holland

COME WALK WITH ME

Come walk with me in the Autumn rain, through the forest.
You'll see there in the thicket, within the tall grass.
A doe and her fawn bedded down last night.
Feel the place, it is still warm.

Come walk with me in the Wintry snow, through the forest.
The frosty elf has once again performed his magic.
On barren branches he has woven crystal lace.
Touch the beauty, while it is still new.

Come walk with me in the dawn of Spring, through the forest,
As the river rushes past melting ice, cold and clean,
And robins' eggs of blue bring life and song to the meadow.
Share the joy, while it is still here.

Come walk with me in the Summer's sun, through the forest,
Where berries of red and blue ripen sweet for the picking,
And honey bees dance in syncopated rhyme on golden sunflowers.
Embrace the glow, while it is still a part of you.

Come walk with me beneath the stars, through the forest,
Where shadows vanish amidst trees like lovers lost,
And the blue of your eyes guide me like a beacon to your arms.
Take my hand and walk with me, into eternity.

—Demitra Ann Syrtis

THE LIGHT

High and bright
Shown the light,
In the night.
The light was a star,
That shown from afar.
The light in the night,
Always looked so right.

—Heather M. Cowley

OLD OAK

Standing tall and alone,
in a sea of grass.
Patiently I wait,
as the long years pass.

My voice but a murmur,
as the gentle winds blow.
Come, play in my arms
and rest in my shadow.

I've stories to tell,
if you'll but listen.

—John W. Hamilton

UNDER THE UMBRELLA

Under the umbrella
cozy and dry,
Skipping along
'neath a cloudy sky

The fresh smell of rain
when it starts to fall
settles the dust
where my footsteps fall

I hop the puddles
and play a game
and laugh with joy
at the falling rain

And I wonder if there
is a rainbow at night
when the sun goes to sleep
and the moon is out bright

—Alma Cook Remington

JANUARY '92

The white sun boils
In a moving field
Of pale electric blue

Around this energy field
A bronze blanket
Holds back the clouds
Everything is moving.

Above, the sky shifts clouds
Grey, to white, to blue,
And back again.

The golf course rests
In pale gold stubble
And the snow powders down.

A few lake birds are lost
And picking at the ground
Owls sleep —
And hawks watch.

—Virginia Weber

TO MY DAUGHTER

How do I tell you, how I love you.
You came from deep love, passion, trust from two.
We wanted you, when you were a thought in my mind.
A warmth I felt, when I carried you deep inside.
You are the best from two, and kissed with life.
A gift for a short while, I'll treasure till eternity.
You are the Honest in Honesty,
The Trust in Trustworthy,
You are my Pride.
When I look at you, you are the best part of me.
You had my love before I knew you,
And will have my love, till forever,
Never in life's pathways ever believe,
You were never loved,
Because you were and are.

*Dedicated to my daughter, Mistie,
whom I love with all my heart.
May the Lord bless you always, Mom*

—Coletta Heinle

WHAT IS A MOTHER?

A mother is someone who knows all of our needs,
  Our hopes and our dreams and desires.
With a genuine interest in all that we do —
  Someone who guides and inspires.
The heart of a mother is full of compassion.
  Is generous, kind and forgiving,
The smile of a mother is loving and tender,
  And adds so much gladness to living.
A mother is someone with infinite patience
  Who soothes all our troubles away,
Someone with limitless faith in her children,
  And love for them day after day.
A mother can make a home out of a house —
  By being just thoughtful and sweet,
By her warm understanding and gentleness, too,
  That makes life more rich and complete.
A mother is full of true wisdom and strength
  Of loveliness, insight, and grace,
She's someone whose love we will cherish forever —
  Yes — no one can take MOTHER'S PLACE!

—Alfonso C. Rodriquez

MOTHER

There's always someone or something in our life encouraging us to wake up, to get up, to look up, to listen up, to shut up, and wise up to work harder, run faster, hold on tighter, to be a fighter

My mother taught me and now through my own eyes I can see
that all she's secured is because she endured and I was her encouragement as she encouraged me

Her life has been filled so unjustly with unequal pleasure and pain
How could I know as a small child how much from her tears I would gain

My mother held me close in good times and bad
In her arms she kept me safe, I felt so loved and cared for
Now I hold my mother in the highest esteem she's a woman I truly adore

—Alice Rice

DADDY

Oh how can you express your need
  for Daddy?
How can you find someone to lead
  you like Daddy?

Remember to always heed
to your Daddy.
His words will help you.
His ways can guide you.
His love will protect you.
  The best, most marvelous
thing in this world —
  is your Daddy.

Your memories when you were four,
His feet going thru your door.
The smile on his happy face.
When he first saw you — his
wonderful embrace.

His being around
will just hold you spellbound.
  I will forever appreciate him —
  my Daddy.

—Nancy Kerlee

DAUGHTERS

The Youngest:
  Alas when I say no she says yes, when I say yes she says no. How do the little minds run that they can be so opposite.

  When I say maybe, she takes it as yes. When I say sometimes to her it means anytime. Is her vocabulary so different than mine?

  Are those 28 years between so long and tedious that we shall never meet, or per chance at an older date will our minds meet as others do, — and find a common ground.)

The Older:
  Oh the other too! Who thinks all grown ups are fuddy duddys and not half so smart as she. But breaks your heart with woe when sad and woeful she is, and fills your heart to bursting when she procures a card and gift in some devious way. "Well, mother, you are pretty nice, and special to me." "I love you," then do defenses drop, and you wonder how you could have been so cross, with a misplaced dish, or can or jar, or a dreaminess that encompasses all understanding.

  These are my daughters — loved and chastised with mother love.

"A Mother"

—Birgit Blake

Native
Native Americans
No Longer Natives Only Visitors Aliens
Unwelcome By Strangers Now Owners Pushed
Back To Unyielding Land Grassy Plains Herds Of Buffalo
Live Only In Stories Passed Down By Old Timers Bottles Replace
Pipes Inner Peace Not The Goal Only Temporary Relief Pots No Longer
For Grain But For Sale Misunderstood Stereotyped Into Nothingness Alcoholic
Unemployed Vendors Not The Proud Forgotten People They Really Are The Natives
—Melissa E. Brooks

ODE TO THE CHILDREN

There is frivolity in the air; robins and bluejays signal a burst of spring
A luminous sunset bids farewell to another day
There is music in the air, but today humanity pivots on the brink of disaster
Our children are dying, America; many are already dead
Yet you casually turn your head and gaze in the direction of the sunset
From hospital nurseries to high school graduations children need help, Old Glory
Death from disease, destruction, and deprivation robs them and you
As you soak up the rays from a sinking sun, children are being victimized one by one
Weapons, arson, suicide—the three of these are enough to bring any country to its knees
But other atrocities are fast at work stalking our children; they cunningly lurk
Kidnappers, rapists—they are the kinds that rob children of their spirits, bodies, and minds
These children will never relish a sunset, nor enjoy all for which this country has fought
Or mimic the birds' songs, all that nature has wrought
They are too busy crying, dying, or being distraught
There will be no future, America; herein rests my plea; crime is snatching the children
From you and from me; the tragedy is we are letting it be! We have come too far, America
From pioneering days headed West through pestilence and battles, inventions, the best
   in technological advancements
America, you know the rest under which your flag has furled
So let these children grow up and enjoy this land which is by far the best in the world.
   —Zema L. Jordan, Ph.D.

HOMELESS, NOT WORTHLESS

The Land of opportunity the story is told;
Yet poverty and hunger has taken its toll.

Crime filled streets a threat to one and all, yet the rich and famous are having a ball.
Drugs must go comes the cry from on high
As we sit back and watch our children daily die.

Shelters are full from one end to the other; the homeless now could be your sister or even your mother.

You're homeless by choice I heard someone say, as the jobless rate rises more each day.
There's places to live and jobs to be found, yet the employers daily turn the homeless down.

"You have no address," they frequently say;
"how could I contact you from day to day?"

No wonder the lonely, the destitute and poor, have no hope or faith in the system anymore.

Concerts and benefits and charities are raised, but it helps the foreign countries more than us these days.

Echoes of fear can be heard "Feed the poor I don't want them knocking at my door anymore."

As fruitful and rich as our country has become, there should be no homeless,—no not one.
They're homeless, — not worthless, help them if you dare, all they need is someone to care.

Our society has become so fast paced and lost, to help the homeless how much could it cost?

Have we lost our sense of sharing and caring, while all over the world our homeless sit staring!
   —Brenda Ashby

HEAVEN'S DOOR

Drifting away like rose petals in the wind,
I shall stand beneath the solemn sky no more.
I shall not feel the burning desire for triumph
For I soon will be knocking at Heaven's door.

I may not share the beauty of flower blossoms in spring
Or taste the sweetness of winning a fight,
But instead I will be free of problems and pain
And shall spread my wings to prepare to take flight.

I will soar over valleys and mountains so high.
I shall not care about my worries anymore,
But instead I will rest in Jesus' hands
Because now I am walking through Heaven's door.

—Pamela M. Pryor

ANGELS FLY

As I awake to the dawn's early rise
Somehow I see myself in the mirror outside
I hear the sweet music of God's gracious
creatures singing off side.
I would often wonder what it would be like
to fly
the beautifully, heavenly blue spacious
skies.

Neverless to my surprise, one morning's
dawn,
I awoke to realize, that wings like
angels I don't subside.
I know that down deep in my soul, that one
day,
I will spiritually and heavenly fly.

Yes, fly in harmony and gracefulness, and
soar in the love and peacefulness that
surrounds us all.
Here on earth awaiting to die, to one day
reaching heaven, awaiting God's side.
Mounted up with pure snow white wings,
once again hearing the cherubs sing.

—Donald Lee Beilman

SILENCE IS NOT GOLDEN

Some say that silence is golden . . .
I say that it is not

Silence can be a danger
for some secrets have the power to kill

Did you think your silence was protecting me . . .
I'm telling you that it was not

Did you think your silence would hold your secrets . . .
eventually all things come to light

I say to you that your silence was not golden . . .
It was a selfish and self serving thing

Your silence sought to protect only you . . .
For I can not fight an enemy I know not

I will never look at silence in the same way again . . .
for to say nothing is the same as a lie

You held your silence to keep your pride . . .
Was your pride more important than my life

Though I can not God hears through our silence . . .
And I hope with him you made things right

Your silence may have kept me in the dark . . .
But God held me in the bosom of his arms

—E. Tisa Long

ATTITUDE

At times it seems like
our attitude doesn't matter

But it truly does matter
if we want to make it
up the ladder.

The proper attitude is
an absolute must.

That greatly depends upon
whom we trust.

When we feel smashed
on the rocks of despair

Always remember that our
Lord is there.

—Vincent E. Hatcher

ADAM'S WALK

How would it be to walk, just once,
as Adam did, with God.
To know He was beside you there,
as every step you trod.
To hold your hand, and lift you up,
when ere you trip and fall;
To teach you softly with His word,
and give to you, His all.

Though many centuries have passed
since Adam walked the earth;
Our God is here, and waiting still,
to share with us, His mirth.
If we will call upon His name,
and do the things He asks;
Then we can walk, as Adam did,
with God to guide each task.

—Edwin T. Carter

ETERNAL GROUND

I am so happy,
yet I fail to see,
exactly what happy
means to me.

The happiness inside of me,
the mile so long . . .
far, but I still see.
I am there, just there to be.

To paint the picture on my mind,
and compare it to the one before,
would be like changing to sunshine,
or darkness being a sunset forever more.

Eternity brought by you,
not by a dream.
Real and forever,
like the sky's endless seam.

Sewing a stitch in place
with His priceless hands,
brings a brand new face,
to Heaven's eternal sands.

—Jessi Seals

TOMORROW

"When is tomorrow?" my little girl asks.
I try to explain but it's too great a task.
"Tomorrow will be in the morning so bright,
After we've slept through the long dark night."
And as she awakes her eyes bright and clear,
"Dear Mother," she says, "Tomorrow is here."
"Not tomorrow, my darling, I have to say.
Tomorrow will come, but now is today."

"When is tomorrow?" I ask it of Thee,
My kind heavenly Father — all wise is He.
"My child, your tomorrow will come by and by,
But you must learn patience," He doth reply.
"Tomorrow will be the eternal day
When your troubles and trials will fly away.
So live today the best that you can,
Then tomorrow will come in the heavenly land."

—D. Helene Yost

GOD'S CHILDREN

Has your Bible been sitting on the shelf?
Have you been thinking of yourself?
Getting all caught up in your lust;
While God's word sits there collecting dust.
Get up on your feet and follow the cross;
You'll find in the end that God is the "Boss!"
Seek till you find there is no length;
The Master will give you all your strength.
The more you read the more you'll thirst;
Filled with Joy, you'll feel you'll burst.
Healing the sick and leading the blind;
Jesus does this for all mankind.
When he walked on this earth people just sighed,
He said "I Love You," and then he died.
He shed his blood so we may go,
Home to the Father, he saved our soul.
With joy in my heart, I want to sing;
Giving all glory and praise to the King!
Jesus did his duty, now it's our turn;
Be ready my friend, you don't want to burn.

—Teresa Bennett

EARLY MORNING PRAYER

Still dark outside,
The air explodes with song
From birds awakening
In the early morning dawn.

What will this day hold for us?
Everything seems so innocent and pure,
Before the sun rises and paints a different color.
The dilemmas of the hours ahead and
The cruel reality of the human world.

Must keep the Faith and
Trust my God to look out
For family and friends
Going through the trials of life.

Give me an answer, Dear Lord,
On this day of new awakenings.
Help me to see your blessings
And give encouragement to loved ones
So they might prosper in this world
Of singing birds, sunlight and
Your Love.

—Margot A. Thomas

WHO HAS THE ANSWERS?

Where does my answer lie?
Please God don't let me cry.
This wretched pain is destroying me.
Are you up there God, to hear my plea?
The ache I feel is like a disease.
Smothering my heart, God help me PLEASE!
You have the answers to set my soul free.
Is this a test or challenge for me?
Did I pass or does the sufferin' keep going?
Could this be a part of growing?
If so, I can't take much more.
Just open the Golden Gate door.
Guide me through the horrids of this place.
By shining a light upon my face.

—Ave M. Doane

HELP ME LORD

Oh Lord, help me to live like you each day,
and every night when I kneel to pray.
Help me to pray an earnest prayer for every
   sinner everywhere.
Help me to do some job or deed that will
   help someone in time of need.
And if I speak an unkind word I pray, dear
   Lord, it won't be heard by woman or man,
   as we press our way to the Promised Land.
You said "strive to enter in," and our sinful way
   to mend.
I thank you Lord for letting me live to find that
   joy in serving you is real.
And as the end of time draws near, more of
   your word I want to hear.
So when you come, I'll be sure to know
   that my garment will be as white as snow.
And when you say "well done my child,"
   I know there will be a welcome smile.

—Helen Rooker Rogers

JESUS KNOWS

I have Jesus on my side, when in
doubt He'll be the without.

   I've got Jesus on my side

Best friends might be around, but Jesus
is abound.

   I've got Jesus on my side

When people and things get you down and
everything goes wrong, with Jesus the faith is
on my side. In Him it keeps me alive.

   I've got Jesus on my side

When times are hard, family are few just
kneel and pray Jesus is on the way for
you.

   I've got Jesus on my side

When people have done you wrong, just
pray to Jesus, he'll keep you strong.

   I've got Jesus on my side

There are troubles in this world today, man
nor woman knows the way, but I've got
Jesus on my side.

—Jesse Thompson

COUNTRY LOVE

Holding thoughts — instead of hands,
  while flags and yellow ribbons dance.
Far away — close in heart,
Stay safe my brother, sister too,
  fighting for our country love.
We know the fears you face,
  we have them too.
As the fears take hold — close your eyes:
  memories dance like fireflies
    of the quiet peaceful times
      in our country love.
Return again my hero friends:
  even with the times at hand —
    stay a while longer than . . .
      in our country love.
Come my brother, sister, friend
Enjoy our country love,
  again.

—Rebecca Price

HERITAGE

Out of the Bush,
  From that far off land of Africa.
Many, Many Moons ago
a child was stolen and brought
from across the sea.
Indirectly that child was me.
My roots of a child that was
brought here, and sold into slavery.
Others were the seeds of that
young girl's womb that passed
from her to me.

She was the Blood of my blood,
The Skin of my skin.
In many ways this is the essence
of my soul.
"This" is the African blood in me.
I saw her in my mind as though
it was today.
"As she ran from those men
trying to get away"
This is the African blood in me.
And most all this is my
Heritage, of that child that
was brought from Africa,
Many, many moons ago.

—R.M. Wilson

PEACE

I wander through the darkened woods
  hearing noises that are misunderstood
they may seem frightening to the human eye
but there is peace hiding deep inside
nature is a wonder we can not see
because life is gone through so quickly
maybe if you would stop and take a chance
the beauty would put you in a trance
let go of your secrets and let them melt away
into the peace hidden in the trees.

—Jenny Wussow, age 15

A PHONE SURVEY

Speaking of politics . . .
  Are you a republican or a democrat?
What is your stand on world hunger?
Are you for or against the health plan?
Do you think Puerto Rico should become the 51st state?
Who did you vote for — Bush or Clinton?
Pro life or pro choice?
Should you be allowed to buy a gun?
If they made solar-powered cars would you buy one?
Should they cut the forests or save the owls?
The rights of the many or the rights of the individual?
Oh! You're only a child?
May I speak to your parents?

—Claire Hassig, age 12

REVIVAL OF BEAUTY

Where have all the American Indians gone?
  They are not hiding!
Voices are rising out of the dust,
Long silenced wisdom — the Ancient Ones
Crying out — of Medicine Wheel,
The Beauty Path and Red Road Walk,
Of Mother Earth cleansing herself now,
The beginning of a new life style
Based on the old ways
AND future hopes of unity and peace
In a beautiful, clean, healthy world.
The voices speak of Great Spirit,
White Buffalo Calf Woman and the Sacred Pipe,
The Sweat Lodge and the Vision Quest.
Let us learn about and help bring back the Old Ways!

—Orillia O'Connor

FEELINGS OF A POLITICIAN

I can hear the heartbeat of Reed City
  She grows more weaker every day
Unless someone cares to make her better
She'll never gain her strength to run and play
So let's all try to help her with her troubles
And maybe she can gain some happiness
In this old world we don't need any sorrow
We need to feel as though we're being blest
She needs some loving, sinless hands to guide her
Corruption needs to disappear from her door
She doesn't need the lies and the hatred
She needs honesty forever more
Righteousness is the sunshine of tomorrow
So pray for this day by day
We will bring back our community from sorrow
And Reed City will revive in a blissful way.

—Louise Devendorf

GOD'S SON

He carried the heavy cross on His back down the street.
Then they nailed Him to the cross by His hands and His feet.
And on the third day, He arose from the dead,
And the word of our God started to spread.
He healed the sick, and made the lame walk,
And when He was gone, the people would gossip and talk.
They did not believe Him, when Jesus would say.
That He'd sit on His throne with His Father one day.
They did not believe Him, that He was God's Son.
That He would ascend to His Father, when His work was all done.
So believe in Jesus completely, with all your heart and soul,
And the happiness and love in your life, will quickly start to grow.

—Dawn Luebbers

THE CHILDREN'S READING CIRCLE

The Children's Reading Circle
Was a won'drous place to be.
It was down here in the basement of
This good old library.

The ladies were so pleasant,
As they helped us choose our books.
They told us to be quiet,
But, 'twas said with friendly looks.

The years were 1941, and 42 and 3;
My sister so enjoyed it when attending there with me.
If I could be there once again, why, I would love it so;
It's a place of warmth and magic, and of that I'm sure you know.

—Shirley DuBois

FOOD FOR ALL—
On Sand Mountain, Near Pisgah, Alabama

This morning I went to the garden, now a jungle of grass and weeds.
But I needed some corn and potatoes, my kids and grandkids to feed.

The air was cool and fresh from an early morning rain.
The grass and weeds are a beautiful green, but to get my food was a pain.

Every thing has grown so fast from all the rain and sun.
I can't believe how fast it grew.
It seems the garden was just begun.

Overhead the sky had cleared, as a large chicken hawk passed over and called.
Searching for his dinner too, I watched him quiet appalled.

Then back in the house, as I sat down to rest,
There on the porch rail was a little gray squirrel,
His food to quest.

Then the big mud turtle made his trip from the pond to the apple tree.
It was an uphill climb—he also knew he'd get his lunch for free.

The humming birds fly in and out to sip their nectar sweet.
The lazy dog, already full, lies on the floor asleep.

Now I'll warm up some sour dough bread, boil potatoes and corn,
also some steak I'll fry.

When the family gets here, we'll eat it all and finish with fresh apple pie.

—Marjorie Allen

MY DAY

While feeling down
and full of gloom,
I looked out to see
a daffodil bloom

With its head turned toward
heaven to sprout,
Just watching it made me
want to shout.

"Only God do I have
to answer to,
Not you, or you, or you!"

—Wallie L. Moore

REFLECTING UPON BEING THREE DECADES OLD

I dropped a stone
into a pond.
One circle,
Two circles,
Three circles,
Four.

More circles,
More circles,
More, more, more!

They stopped.
I saw me;
Inside;
On top;
T-H-I-R-T-Y!

—David Youngs

OLD LOVE

Some think Love
Is for the young,
And Fool's illusion Time,
But, I say Love
Is for the old
For you I'll sing my Rhyme!

Hot, young, Love
Is passion's tool
Gluts itself, and asks for more,
Often discontent,
Feeling Fortune's Fool,
Walks out and slams the door!

Old Love grows,
Along with Time,
Builds its own illusion,
Satisfies itself,
In satisfying.
Finds love's own conclusion.

Yes, I'll sing
For you Old Love
And Happy Years we've known,
Reaping Harvests
Of the Lasting Love,
That we have sown.

Dedicated to my husband of 62 years, My Tony.

—Ruth S. Ozanich

DESOLATE

I sit here all alone
in this cold dark world
there is no love here
my thoughts are all awhirl

the darkness overwhelms me
I cannot feel a thing
cupid passes over
no love for me will he bring

my heart is heavy with trouble
I've given up indeed
as they pulled their love away
my heart continued to bleed

my blood has all spilled now
I've shed my final tear
alone is what I am
not content, but here

—Delores K. Nuernberger

LIFE IN THE FOREST

My branches are losing their leaves.
My roots weaken each passing day.
As the forest grows around me,
I become overshadowed
By younger life
Of all kinds.
No longer
Do birds use me
To build their homes.
The squirrels have found
New places to play their games.
Rotting bark has left me unfit—
For building, for saving, for living.

If a tree falls in the forest
And no one is there to hear it,
Does it make a sound?
If I die,
Will anyone notice?

—Rick Henkel

REALITY

Future fact of "unseen truth"
Published in tomorrow's news
Experience of eye to ear,
"Dominator"—emotional gear,
Hidden secrets sky to sea,
To know, to love, to hate and fear,
Media cover—information stew,
Mix of truth with lies and clutter,
New world hocus pocus
Working under cover.
Science good, science knot
Truth seeker's, visible fact,
Not always right on "shadow path."
Ancient game—*neuron pain,*
Loops of never ending chain,
"Mystic war of DNA,"
Puzzling—universal strain,
Unknown vision, orbit mission,
Earthbound little human face,
Frustration key, *lost in space.*

—Gisela M. Williams

The coldness consumes, and I quiver once more.
My mind quickens upon the close of the door.
Dare I decide to turn my head
and out of the depths of the night,
deliverance be bled.
The weeping will wane and the silence wander still—
throughout the wakenings and forgotten will.
Find us beneath the black of the sky
and bowed before secrets;
behind those I hide.
Concealed is a passion passing the time
to perjure reality and encompass the mind.
Bowed head turns to find no one in sight,
no sounds of breathing, no shadowed light.
Simple darkness remains, and it is known all too well.
Every memory remembered
and still no one to tell.

—Katie Shannon

SHATTERED FRAGMENTS

Staring infinitely into the silver glass
Winding down roads never before ventured.
A sunless, hollow soul awed but
brave, plunging into another dimension
at break-neck speed.
Passing by familiar faces unable
to be recognized. Music echoing, magnifying
this endless plummet.
Wintry darkness adding confusion
to a world of complication.
Suffocating; drowning; lungs
exploding. Gasping for
nonexistent life. Being
compressed into a trapped body
incapable of exceeding outer
limits.
Loneliness swallows
my wasted life until disheartened voices coax me
back through the mirror of reality.

—Pauline DiPietrantonio

blood spills like cheap red wine
soaking city sand and cement
absorbed by bigotry, ignorance, arrogance

lovers of the bleeding

wretch
vomiting their grief onto our conscience

in the silence of no response
the pain wails
tearing peace
renting comfort

we march
streets — capitols — each other
outraged and righteous

the bleeding can't respond

we enter the confessional of our intellect
absolve ourselves

the bleeding can't respond

—Joan Regner

TO TOUCH THE MORNING

I wake up each morning with nothing on my mind, the things of yesterday a day away, I feel anew, I can't quite explain this new sensation that erupted in every part of my body but, all I know the love I share with you is not dark like the night but more like the morning cool, wet with dew, with a slight summer breeze blowing ever so gently, it's as though the breath of life that God put into the first man is sweeping across the room, it's at this moment with the one I love that I've touched the morning and taken hold of it catching its essence.

Dedicated to my mother, Dorothy Wiggins.
—James A Wiggins Jr

BETWEEN NIGHT AND DAY

I travel along a line between night and day,
Equally beckoned by the promise of dreams' peaceful fantasy,
  and the bright vision that sunlight brings.
Must I choose between the two?
I want both, I do:
  To dream in playful fantasy; to let new meanings spring from
collisions of color and symbol and things learned long ago; to have
ideas of no consequence or responsibility beyond my waking sight,
  And then to see the sun of each new day with clarity improved by night.
—T.A. Adamec

AUTUMN NIGHT MUSICAL

The moon's reflection through the honeycomb clouds looks like a daisy that just bloomed on opening night

The slight breeze rustles a maple, oak, and willow leaf orchestra beside the
  river audience that quietly waits for the performance to begin

Slowly the curtain rises as soft voices from falling raindrops serenade the
  earth as its seeds imbibe the secrets of Mother Nature

Streaks of light magically paint the natural stage and draw out
  the glistening complexion of the leaf actors

Clouds drift briskly by as the daisy bows off stage but soon returns
  for an encore to let the characters glow radiantly in the spot light

The production ends, leaving the audience twigs of long-term memories
  to carry to a larger generation
—Halle H. Magpoc

ANOTHER DAY, ANOTHER FLIGHT

Early morning, sky just getting light, I wipe the dew from the wings. Mags on; prime, choke, swing prop, engine roars to exuberant petroleum life. We climb: engine yelling its defiance at the sky, then softens to a smooth purr, like a contented cat, as we reach our height.

Sky of cobalt blue; puffy cotton-ball clouds above, below, to the sides, like sentinels watching us pass through their domain. It is 1910, we fly the mail, Jenny and I.

Early morning, sky just getting light, I wipe the dew from the wings. Switch on, choke, pull the rope, the engine roars to exuberant life, smell of gas and oil fill the air. We climb: engine yelling its defiance at the sky, then softens to a steady drone, like a bumblebee, as we reach our height.

Sky of brilliant blue; puff cotton-ball clouds above, below, to the sides, like ghosts of ancient fliers watching us pass through their domain. It is 1990, we enjoy flying, My Ultralight and I.
—H.L. Baggett

I TRIED

I tried to love him,
But he didn't love me

I tried to hold him,
But he pushed me away

I tried to talk to him,
But he wouldn't listen
Then,
I tried to forget him,
But he was always there.

—Rebecca D. Short

'ONLY HEAVEN'

Oh how thankful
Thou must be,
for this great starry sky
Given to thee,
Holy Angels
Hold me near,
Nurturing Thou Nature
with blessed care,

I, wisk out
and thrust!!
This great starry sky,
for only such as heaven
Could make pure
Such as I,

'Only Heaven'

I, dare as to hint
        not why,
For, this is heaven
   Thou Great Starry Sky.

—Michael Bradshaw

LUCKY ME

I feel so lucky to
have found someone
like you who's always
there and shows me
you really do care.

I hope and pray
to God will last
forever I just can't
see us not together.

When we are apart
from each other you
may not know,

My heart will always
follow you wherever
you go.

Words can't express
what I feel,

All I know is
my love for you
is real.

Dedicated to Chap Christian
—Linda Gaglio

IN APPRECIATION

In Dec. '92 I was one of ten nominated for employee-of-the-year;
this was not my first nomination, yet I heard my name in fear.
My husband had passed away a few weeks before,
now I had to choke back my emotions once more.
Those were such dark days, not caring if I lived or died;
how could I appear happy, when always crying inside.
I didn't want to smile, be 'on my toes,' and polite,
knowing I couldn't handle the pending limelight.
But, Feb. '93 I won and with a few tears, got through
my short and grateful speech of thanking all of you.
You wonderful people, my working family;
you gave me your strength when you voted for me.
You made it an uplifting year, just want you to know.
Now, my reign is ending and it's time to let go.
It's much easier smiling now, my days not so full of strife;
I sincerely thank you . . . one and all, you gave me back my life.

—Hardy Reese

GROWTH

Some people choose not to even notice the subtleties
The details of right and wrong
Even if it feels as if there was an elephant
In a studio apartment
Pretending that it does not exist
That it does not break the little hearts
That it does not destroy the sanctity of the home
Where the roots grow dysfunctionally
Producing fruits of resentment
Blaming both man and mother
For all the wrongs of the entire human race
When really it stems from the individual
Branching out to the leaves of humanity
Always wishing to be another form of growth
Wanting to be a rose in a garden full of weeds
If the light shines through with the nourishment of water
The healing may begin
Then the individuals will see that they only carry around the shell
Of a weed
And inside is a bright, red rose.

—Elizabeth A. Michael

MY FRIEND AND I

When I was young I had a friend
together we were through thick and thin.
We shared our laughter, we shared our toys,
played in the woods, climbed trees like boys.

We used to eat blossoms from a tree in the woods,
We didn't know what they were but they sure were good.
We would climb that tree every day as far as we could go,
sit and eat those blossoms until we'd want no more.

Jump on freight trains, ride as far as we wanted to go,
Jump off and walk back home, our feet would be so sore.
We smoked rabbit tobacco, we ate sour grass,
drank sugar and syrup water long as it would last.

Sweeten Vinegar Water with soda this is a drink of the past,
This was our homemade Coca Cola and we made it with class.
We walked the rails and ate "Maypops," roamed the cemetery too,
Searched for doodlebugs under the house, bit butterflies' heads off too.

Fought each other almost every day
The next few minutes we were back at play.
Now that we have grown older and our hair is gray and thin
We don't get together often, but we are still friends

—Mary L. Walker Ogletree

ONCE AGAIN

Once again, my heart, you betrayed me—
You gave away my love to someone I would not have entrusted such a delicate object to.
Once again you did not see what harm could come to me if my love was to be misused.
Once again, my heart, you did not consult my reason before deciding such a thing,
For it never would have consented.
Once again, my heart, I blame you for all the pain I am to suffer for your carelessness.
I beg of you to be more careful of those you choose to trust.

—Maureen Jolie McFarlane

THE BATTERED ROAD

You say you know and understand my pain and what it's like on the Battered Road. You say you know and understand my fears, and you're equipped to advise, counsel, and help me to deal with my pain and fears. You say you know and understand my emotions, but how can you know, if you've never traveled the Battered Road?

You may truly care and have a sincere desire to help me, and you can. Be my friend, not my counselor or advisor, because you're not equipped to counsel or advise me. If you think otherwise you're feeding your ego, and not helping mine.

If you've walked the Battered Road, then you're equipped to know and understand the pain, fears, loneliness, helplessness, and the indecisiveness I deal with.

When I reach out for a friend, be there for me. Take my hand and give me support. Let the woman who has walked the Battered Road be my counselor, advisor, and example. Only she is equipped and has the ability to help me understand my pain, fears, and emotions, because she has walked the Battered Road, and she knows the struggle I face; she knows the way up and out — SHE IS FREE.

—R. Marie Robinson

TO KISS THE SUN

So right with the world was I, not so long ago, that to embrace the sun was risked by no one but me—how bold!

So brave was I to kiss the sun, a feat no one else had ever done.

To reach for the warmth, the brilliant glow to be mine, a thought less than finished and foolish to pine.

In the beginning, love made me strong, never fearing the choice was wrong.

I reached for things I should not have, never thinking of the bad.

The dangers await, I saw some, but knew love would conquer for the two of us are one.

Faced with challenges I have created, the stress and the hurt paint a future ill-fated.

As destiny foretold, love, like the seasons, changed its color without my permission and out of my order.

Still hanging on to what was never meant to be, I fight the untempered foe, but the sun's heat began to cool and less than dim became the glow.

Depleted from battle that I had not won, the wholeness became two again, and I cannot face the sun.

—Linda S. Bergman-Althouse

LAST KNIGHT OF SUMMER

Sitting on the porch swing
Sipping ice tea,
He stares at stars
And wanders
Cosmic oceans
On the frigate
Of (his) dreams . . . .

—Brian Gilliland

LOVE AND HATE

When one loves
they love from the
heart and soul . . .
When one hates
they hate from the
mind . . .
Love can live
forever, when hate
can only live as
long as you can
remember.

—Jean Norris

FAREWELL TO SUMMER

Summer beauties,
Droop their heads,
In the late—
Fall flower beds.
Crisp brown leaves,
Do whirl about,
Brilliant sunsets—
Fairly shout
Robins now,
Have taken flight—
Crickets fiddle,
In the night.
Soon flakes of snow
Will flutter down,
To blanket—
Countryside and town.

—Zelma Bomar

IN PRAISE OF GRAMMY:

And she gives . . .
To all those she knows
and loves.
And she gives . . .
More than she is asked
always, with a smile.
And she gives . . .
To me and all I love
the pleasure of her being.
And she gives . . .
Comfort, understanding, wisdom
and acceptance.
And she gives . . .
A place for refuge
and nurtures her family.
And she gives . . .
More than I can ever repay.

—Karen Ruth Liska

THE RAINFOREST

How splendid and wonderful you are
Your beauty is never ending
What secrets do you hide beneath your green canopy
A flutter of a butterfly
A creep of an ant
The sweet perfume of your flowers
The morning glimmer of freshly fallen raindrops
You are so sweet kind and complete
But alas your future looks dim
Some will never know what beauty lies hidden within
Humanity is knocking at your door to crush and
Consume you until you're never more

—Danielle M. Mason, age 12

LATE SUMMER

Sultry autumnal twilight
   relaxing in an oak rocking chair
     that creaks on an open porch.

I hear the crickets tune-up
   in the dry shrubs. Frogs voicing their
     opinions in the near-by pond.

I watch the cumulus clouds turn thunderheads
   across the open plain, as the distant lightning
     brightens the evening sky with white zig-zags.

I close my eyes and listen
   to the drone of the oncoming rain.

—Nadine L. Frisch

BIRDS IN FLIGHT

    Little bird how gentle are thee . . .

    And yet you hold up through terrible plights . . .

    In all your meekness, your strength prevails, over your weakness . . .

    In all your smallness, power over the largest wind, you do conquer . . .

    In such a frail body life abides, with so many odds against thee . . .

    Free you are to be, the best little bird for all to see . . .

    Simple do you make it look, as you glide your wings against the sky . . .

    Risk embarked, each day that breaks, but yet, you dare not fly . . .

    All risk at hand, you take off with a great stand and set sail for ventures, as planned . . .

    Blind faith carries you through . . .

    God's grace embraces you fully . . .

    Alone, in a pair or with a flock, you hold your own uniqueness . . .

    Each bird giving his best . . .

    Each bird contributing to life what's met . . .

    Content in the fact, that you were even given a chance to be born . . .

    In the realization of your value, ultimate freedom is found.

—Donna Babin Larke

THE ROSE'S KINGDOM

The Rose is the queen,
   The daffodils are the princesses,
While the lilies and the daisies are villagers.
Their kingdom is the garden,
Their castle is the tree.
The Rose's head sweeps down from her throne,
As she bows toward the crowd,
And gives them each a special smile,
From deep inside her petals.
She smiles one more gentle smile,
Before she moves back to her throne,
And slowly she dies with the end of spring.
She will come back another day,
Just you wait and see.
And give us her special smile,
Right before she leaves.

—Anne Madariaga

RAIN

Because of the rain, there is a sad day
and it also gives us another day to say

'I love you mom, I love you dad'
and now we are happy instead of being sad

While it is raining, you could read, cook, or sew
after the cloudy rainstorm, there comes a rainbow

The rainbow is pretty and gives us all joy
and brings a smile to even the roughest, toughest boy

The rain that falls is natural, as you may already know
the rain provides us with water and helps the pretty flowers grow

So the next time it gets cloudy, appreciate the rain instead of being sad
and be thankful for the rain and its sparkling rainbow that always makes us glad

—James E. Brown

SUNRISE AND SUNSET

Mother Nature has two awesome
Displays each day: Our eyes fail
To recognize what lies in store as
We go about our way.

The majestic splendor of sunrise can
Never be matched by human hands: Only
God can create such beauty with the
Right texture and tone in all lands.

When this scroll of color opens in
Full view, everything begins as new:
Our spirits can become lifted high
As the sky, just give it a try.

As the hours slip away, our energies
Go full blast which won't last:
Towards eventide we run low on
Charge and our tempers even flip.

'Tis now sunset and the dark curtain
Of night descends: Soon man and
Nature shut down — then God causes
The sun to rise anew!

—Melvin Manwarring

FRIENDSHIP

Friendship is of more value
than the rarest gem.
A never to be forgotten treasure
that lingers on in the heart,
long after visual contact
is but a memory.

—Marlene Emerson

THE DOVE

Graceful is the gray old dove.
In beauty she wins a prize.
Every sparrow envies her
wonderful dark old eyes.

Of all the compliments she gets,
she thanks them the very least,
as she always says to them,
she is prettiest of the beasts.

—Natalie Borges, age 12

PANACHE

From the Sunset's massive colors
To the far-reaching water's shores,
We find God's handiwork sublime,
Mortal bodies, eminence divine.

Man in his honored aesthetics
Emotionally deny God's antics.
His Niagara Falls we compare
To man-made Hoover Dam is fair.

The universe, He claims as his.
Rockets and satellites man's biz.
Life is God's greatest creation!
The soul is man's great creation!

From the pinnacle where God sits,

I wonder if . . .

He's doubtful of earth's aesthetics?
—Dona Andrews

MIRAGE

Have I fallen
Into a trench
Of self-denial
Self-pity and
Scornful silence
I feel your presence
In my consciousness
But I cannot
Touch
That mirage
Indeed it seems
As though my canteen
Is empty and
I am forced to suck
On hot pebbles burning
Ringlets on my
Tongue
So as to avoid
Jumping into a
Pool of sand

*Dedicated to Romeo,
my only home.*

—Heather A. Simiele

VISUALIZE

A power failure left me
sitting in the dark,
the only thing I could hear,
was the pounding of my heart.

So in my mind I began to see,
the things which I could not see.
The abstract painting hanging on the wall.
The grandfather clock standing in the hall.
The picture that hangs above the fire place,
the books of poetry, stacked in the book case.
I saw all these things in my mind.
Suddenly the lights came on,
just in the nick of time.

—Earl Nash

SEARCHING

She found it emerging from the dark brown earth,
where graceful stems of silken green,
unbent and reached in patient growth,
that was the essence of serene.
Upon these stems would later float,
blooms of velvet so vibrant in hue,
she would bend down to touch them gently,
to know that they were true.
She found it in the wondrous white beings,
which swayed in the daylight skies,
and stars that winked out of the night,
enticingly untouchable as lies.
Inspiring dreams that her childhood body
could not possibly contain.
They hammered at her insides.
Drove her down the lane.
As an adult to seek the wonder,
in eyes of green and blue,
that were more like the distant stars,
than blooms in vibrant hue.

—Kathleen Anne O'Connell

ONE LONELY VOICE

One lonely voice can't change our country overnight,
That one lonely voice won't always be right,

But who is to say what's right and what's wrong,
To end discrimination — we must all belong,

Belong to a group that we call the free,
To help out our country, will you join me?

One lonely voice can't help all those in despair,
That one voice might not always be there,

So we must all pitch in and help out as well,
We can't just sit back and begin to dwell,

Dwell upon everything that we do own,
Letting those in need go unknown,

One lonely voice can only make it start,
That one voice will touch their hearts,

Upon the people the mission will lay,
To bring back our country's pride today,

The pride that was forgotten long ago,
Will come storming back for that one voice to show.

—Todd DePaulis

HIGH RISE INTERCEPTIONS

Foot steps respond on the pavement below
Announcing the movement of harried souls that come and go
Some Exhaultant, some in misery and pain
While others, although high, seek to get high again
Doors fling open, then shut in vain
Shadows slinking in rhythmic rain
Seeking to find where the next hit can be gained
Oblivious to sanity or sane
Me! Here I sit in my Ivory Tower on high
The scene is too extreme, and I want to cry
Cry! Me! Cry? Why?
But for the will of God there goes I, I, I.

—William H. Harper

A REBEL'S PERCEPTION

You may never see my footprints upon the sands of time.
And the total of my fortune may be less than one thin dime.
Not a footnote in a history book will mark my life on earth,
No statue in the city park to validate its worth.

You may never see my picture in culture's hall of fame.
Among the rich and famous you'll never hear my name.
Neither publisher nor preacher will note my last farewell,
No impassioned speeches nor the ringing of a bell.

No flags at half-staff flying, no wreath upon my door,
No mournful music playing as I leave the earthly shore.
No trophies on my mantle, no plaques upon my wall;
Never made a touchdown nor hit a grandslam ball.

Never climbed Mount Everest nor sailed the seven seas.
Never found a serum to eradicate disease,
I've no academic honors in literature or math.
Never needed ten commandments to keep me on the path.

No preacher, priest nor rabbi has taught me how to live,
And I've avoided conflict, so there's nothing to forgive.
So it really doesn't matter if my memory fades away;
I'm the guy who came to watch the game but never learned to play.

—Richard Rand

A PARASITE'S EPITAPH

There lived a begger in Moredantown,
Twas near the "Ridge of Fear";
He eats by day, and he sleeps by night,
And his god is a bottle of beer.

A wanderer came a roving by,
He preached a tale so true;
So told of a man who was all for himself,
His own life he happened to slew.

But the fearless beggar took no heed
Of the advice the wanderer gave;
So to further convince, he went on to tell,
That the town would not give him a grave.

They were full of revenge, but their reasons were just,
For he had destroyed his own self;
So to leave no trace of his scornful life
For the minds of youth to see.

His body decayed along with his past.
In the bottom of the sea.
And as people pass by Moredantown, to gaze at the "Ridge of Fear,"
There hangs a sign below the bridge, *"An Unknown Man Lies Here."*

—Darleen Ann Boldt

BEAUTY OR BONDAGE

Who can paint the wind
waving Kansas wheat
in a golden sea?

Who can read the rain
giver of life
to parched and buckled land?

Who can see the laughter
of a child
skipping down the street?

Who can sing the sunset
where saguaros
silhouette the western sky?

Who can hear the threads
of tattered coat
covering the homeless man?

—Dorothy Shank

IMPRISONED

Without warning
My enemy strikes.
Relentless—
Unyielding.

Unending pain
Racks my body,
Saps my brain.
I am not dead
But I am trapped.

A bunch of bones,
Full of arthritis,
Locked within
A swelling skin.

It's a cruel sentence
Without reprieve.
I don't want it
But it seems I'll be
Its prisoner for life.

—Emilia A. Glaz

HE CARES

How grateful I am,
How blessed I feel,
Knowing that in all things,
   in all ways —

HE CARES!

Each word I speak,
Each thought,
Each breath and heart beat
Give me cause to smile,
   because

HE CARES!

Never need I fear
The darkness of night,
The pain,
The sadness,
The grief that could consume,
For in His presence,

HE CARES!

—Barbara Hamry

GOD'S LOVING PROMISES

Promises from God's word intertwines
my heart with life.
The blood of Jesus on Calvary intertwines
my soul for eternity.

—Izena Griffin

NOT FORGOTTEN

Lord please help me travel onward.
   May the past not be a hindrance.
There's the tendency to look backward,
   And remember one particular romance.
We then were both unconverted.
   One still remains the same.
I wish he was redeemed,
   And removed from the burden of shame.
Is there any hope it'll happen,
   My heart has to ask?
The Holy Spirit doth my life sharpen,
   Since He began the task.
Why doesn't Christianity appeal
   To more people on earth?
I'm thankful for the Holy Spirit's seal —
   Ever since my rebirth.
Out of love, I pray for him.
   He's lived on a lower plateau,
Because the worldly things dim
   What he might have found true.

In remembrance of Daniel Parvese, held
POW during WWII in Germany, a motivator
of my "freedom of speech" privilege

—Gladys Scott Henderson

ANGELS IN HEAVEN

I never held you in my arms, and cuddled
your little bodies close to mine,
but always within my heart you will remain
until the end of time.

Although I'll never play with you and spoil you
as Grandmothers have been known to do,
and my heart aches so for your parents,
who had you for such a short time,
I know you're safe in the arms of Jesus,
sweet, sweet grandchildren of mine.

The only gift I'll ever give you is the
love I feel in my heart,
Now and forever, Mary and David, that love
will never depart.

It's so hard sometimes to understand
why God makes not His wishes known to Man,
but we have to believe that He knows best,
and that, in His arms, you'll have Eternal Rest.

In heaven, my darlings, you'll always run free,
for our Lord Jesus said:
"Suffer the children to come unto Me."

Someday there will be other babies to hold
and to love,
but I'll never forget my sweet angels in
Heaven above.

In Loving Memory of
David Lee and Mary Elizabeth Roby
October 23, 1992

With Love from Your Grandmother

—Alma Ann Roby

BACK TRACK

A time to be gone on a journey thus far,
  On top of a mountain to grasp for a star.

Away in a valley, green grass for to lay,
Alone walking deserts near break of day.

Soaring among clouds ever so high,
Off to chase rainbows that color the sky.

Moments to frolic with God's angels at play,
Gliding free spirit on wind wings today.

Time for a dreamer to be somewhere removed,
Escaping in time to lost dreams pursued.

—Bunny Morgan

SEARCH FOR THE RAINBOW

Oh, Dear Lord, open our eyes that we might see
  The beauties of this world—
    As you meant them to be.
Turn up our flickering light, that we might
    Behold the love and friendship
      Waiting to bring us joy.

Whether days be sunny or gray,
    We ask your help, Oh Lord,
      To glorify our day.
The many blessings you've bestowed,
    Can not be counted one by one
      By your grace, we'll see the beauties
Of this world.

So, as we greet each dawn;
    Let love and joy shine thru—
      To beam a light as beautiful
         As a rainbow in the sky.
Its gentle light will lead us
    Through each and every day.

—A.L. Walker

DON'T GIVE UP!

If you love the Lord and you're trusting Him
  And you're sailing a stormy sea,
You may fail — and you sometimes will
  But a failure you'll never be!

If you stumble and fall, say "ouch!" if you must
  Or even shed a few tears;
But don't just lie there and waste away
  Or give in to all your fears.

If you've made a mistake and you've really
           "blown it"
  Don't give up and sit there chagrined
God will turn even your mistakes around
  With Him in control you'll still win!

If you've been lost and wandering
  For a very long time in the valley,
Remember your constant companion
  With *His* guidance you'll surely rally!

And when you've failed or lost your way
  He hears your innermost groans.
So pick yourself up — *don't you dare* give up!
  Jesus will lead the way home!

—Joyce Murphy

LOVE'S PRAYER

May God above keep us together
With Love to endure through stormy weather
Let us finish what we start
May The Lord guide our hearts
And Jesus will light for us the way

—Richard Sean Parkin

HE ANSWERED MY PRAYERS

With his head upon my pillow, as he lies here next to me,
Brings a warm flood of love and devotion that only God can see.
For the prayers I said so long ago were answered one hundred fold.
I prayed for God to send Me someone to be at my side, till We grow old.
The younger years were exciting, filled with Love, Passion, hard work, and Faith.
And four beautiful children, all because of this Wonderful mate.
So many years have now slipped by, and our Golden years are here, but deep in My heart
I feel such Calm, I have no doubts, I have no fears.
As before My prayers were answered, I'm sure He hears Me still, I'll pray We'll be together in the world that has no End, for the Man that lies beside Me, is the best that's ever been.
He's truly God's intention of what a Husband & Father should BE.
And to think God's love was so Great, He gave this Man to Me . . . .

—Connie AcMoody

PRAISE HIS PRECIOUS NAME

"Give thanks for He is good, for His loving kindness is everlasting" Psalm 118:1

My strength and song are in the Lord
    Praise to His precious name!
In loving kindness He careth for me
    Praise to His precious name!

The Lord is for me, I will not fear
    Praise to His precious name!
In Him I have refuge in time of despair
    Praise to His precious name!

Where man has failed, the Lord can help
    Praise to His precious name!
The gate of the righteous He opens to me
    Praise to His precious name!

The builders rejected this cornerstone
    Praise to His precious name!
He is that stone on which I can build
    Praise to His precious name!

The right hand of the Lord we exalt on high
    Praise to His precious name!
Through His salvation I live not die
    Praise to His precious name!

Let us rejoice and joyfully sing
    Praise to His precious name!
Thou art my God, it is Thee I extol
    Praise to His precious name!

—Wilma Boe Wyant

FRESH FIRE

In L.A. while the buildings smoulder,
Anger waits at every turn.
History is repeating her cry of rage,
Calling: "Burn, Baby, burn."
But Jesus pleads to your soul and mine:
"I want to take you higher,
Away from this setting of hatred and games;
Let me show you some *holy* fire.
Let my flame come forth and consume you
With a zeal that cannot be tamed,
With a fervency in your hearts,
Bear the torch of JESUS' name.
Let your voices thunder, my soldiers,
Let ME be your burning desire.
March on, tell my truth to this dying world,
Be anointed with my FRESH FIRE!"

—Penny S. Weatherspoon

AND MULTITUDES CAME

He called the multitudes to the hillside
with muted tongue and upraised hand,
and spoke in simple parody
many would embrace
but some would never understand.

Eyes and ears strained, in eagerness, welcoming
the message meant for all to hear.
Some pressed closer
yet others turned aside
overcome by diffidence and nameless fear.

"I come not to abolish or destroy
but to fulfill, give courage, hope and renew.
No matter what, or who you are,
yea, I offer everlasting life
even unto the least of you."

They say the hillside is empty and silent now,
but those who stop to listen still can hear
a sighing through the boughs,
echoes of the spoken word
and whisperings of a long, lost yesteryear.

—Kostadinka

PEACEFUL POND

So rapidly the world goes by,
but caring not, they simply lie
in royal crowns of white they've donned,
    lily pads of the meadow pond.

And while the world goes rushing by
    the turtle, frog, and dragonfly
just sit content in dew of dawn,
    to watch the lone Blue Heron yon'.

Here shadows fall from azure sky
    while cattails stand in grass awry
and join the woodlands on the pond
    where mirrors their carefree realm beyond.

And when dusk bids a moorish sigh,
    I find again my heart reply
to things that I have grown so fond,
    like wrens in meadow's evening song.

For these are pictures sweet to me,
    of God's peace and tranquility
that teach and prod me to rely
    on Him, now . . . as the world goes by.

—Sandra Jeanne Watman

THE END

Last night we said goodbye.
I heard you call out my name.
I said I loved you.
You said you didn't love me the same.
So I turned my back and walked away.
Thinking you would return the very next day.
You said you were leaving
    but I would not listen.
You are gone now.
It's time to let go.
The tears rushing down show
    how much I cared.
I guess you will never know.

—Jennifer E. Campbell

THANKS, NO SECONDS

I can't imagine marrying again
Subordinating my desires to his
I could for Fred because I loved him more
Than my own self. As well as loving him
I loved to love him. Giving his life joy
Became my end in life. His joy was mine.

I can't imagine housewifing again
Intimacy with another love
Touching someone while he touches me
Waking up to see another there
Seeing someone new in the old place
Sharing closets, bedroom, and concerns
Tailoring my schedule to his
Cooking once again three times a day

I can't imagine staying home again
Now that I've discovered traveling
My schedule need not suit anyone else
Reading, writing, walking, swimming—free!
I'd give it up to bring him back to life
But I can never marry someone new.

—Barbara R. DuBois

WINGED HEART

The trees are pretty and green,
The sun is shiny and bright.
Help me to lift up my heart.
Give it wings to take flight.

The flowers, they will bloom.
The songbirds, they will sing.
The grass, it will be green again
After winter, when it's spring.

The children play with dogs and cats,
That do not scratch or bite.
The shepherds watch and tend their flocks,
As they watch the eagles take flight.

Soaring with their wings of gold
Over the mountainous sky.
Up into the heavens above,
Where only the angels should fly.

Lift up my heart and give it wings
So I may visit my love.
I know not my time here in this place.
Until then, let my heart soar above.

—Brenda S. Lewis

IN MY HEART . . .

In my heart she lurks.
An all around favorite.
What could never be said
Stays with me in silence.
Boredom chokes and chases,
Through every damn second.
I made the severe error
In walking away angrily.
You did nothing wrong,
And I couldn't correct myself.

In my heart she sleeps.
We're cuddled like two puppies napping.
Problems do occur when no words are spoken.
Some day I know that woman will come,
And she will be real.

—Lauro E. Pasco

LOVE HURTS

As I'm sitting here
Tears are coming down my face
Wondering what I did to make
You want to go away
I really can't say how much you've
Hurt me by saying you love me
But showing me you really hate me to my face
I want to show you
I'll be here for you
But everytime we're together
We both shut down like teardrops
Falling way deep inside
Some of our friends
Say we're going to last a life time
But do you really think we will
When we can't even talk
Out our problems together
Now I'm not saying I want our fake
Relationship over, I just want a real one to
Appear sometime.

—Kandi J. Stilwell, age 17

THE VESSEL THAT SHINES LIKE THE SUN

Captain of a ship
That sails the sea of love
Captain of a vessel
That shines like the sun

Boundless voyages
Take me to and fro
Endless excursions
Take me high and low

Motionless upon the water
That absorbs your delicious glow
Insane on top the water
That reflects the moonlight's gloomy show

Charismatic sailors
Tend the deck and sail
As I memorize the endless journey
Into the winds of gale

Shipwrecked on the shore of insanity's home
As the island's mutants greet me with love
They carry my wounded soul back
To the vessel that shines like the sun

—Richard Freedom Davis

MOON STRUCK

Moon Drops
A Crying Moon
Turning Into Balls Of Hail
Melting Before Connecting With The Earth
Parallels Of Dimension They Must Travel
Icicles From The Rain
One Lands Pointed On The Head Of A Dead Unicorn
Stars Of Crystal Sparks Illuminate Upward
The Deserted White Stallion Resurrects
Full Of Vibrant Life And Wild
And The Moon Glowing With Happiness
From Dignified Eternal Creation

—Rebecca Ann LeFebre

MY RIVER

River running along the shore,
I go and sit and quietly adore.
Animals, under and above, and with fur,
Come to live with the strength and power of her.
They come, like me, to indulge in her presence,
To find food or a peace of mind with essence.
A place to let loose and truly be confiding,
I find myself slouching on a bench, in awe admiring.
Her waves slap and slosh and beat aggression onto the shore,
Is this what I come here for?
To be free and flow to where ever,
She's always got those who need her in all types of weather.

—Nadine M. Barten

THE FOREST

I was in darkness for an insurmountable time
Then came the prodigious forest that none could resist
Where rang out the sound of harmonious chimes
And all about human life did not exist
But within the trees cried out in pain
The ground moaned and the flowers wept
So I plunged into the forest through the crimson rain
For I saw upon a mound that a light slept
Through thickets sharp I suddenly took flight
For the light upon the mound was slowly dying
As I ran the mound stayed just out of sight
Running faster and faster I felt like crying
Closer and closer it closes, I draw one final breath
I now know this forest's name and it is Death.

—Mike Anderson

STAR-VATION

God said to Abraham, "Look at the stars in heaven;
I will indeed multiply thy seed like these stars."
How many stars are there?
No man can count them
How many starving in the world today?
Can you count them?
Do you dare count them?
Bulging eyes and swollen bellies
Shriveled, cracked, dry flesh
A distasteful hue
Mass graves
Death—a constant, unwanted, cruel messenger
Children dying, mothers crying, the government lying
Pakistan, Ethiopia, Somalia
How many more will be numbered among the stars of heaven?

—Dwain C. Robinson

STARSTRUCK

My Maverick Star
Galaxy non-conformist,
Platinum guide.
He leads, I follow
Starprints on his sands of time.

He touches briefly wild verbena,
Spirals saguaro's spiny arms,
Lassoes tangled, purple sagebrush.
Enchanted, I'm this piper's mime.
Till border bridge
In early, early, gray of day
Breaks his astral spell,
I go my charted way.

—Isabel Dunwoody

THE IMMIGRANT

Good bye my Rio Bravo
The Rio Grande sand,
I'm an immigrant
That few understand

    I was a little child
    Who was born in Tennessee,
    My dad was Mexicano,
    What do you think of me?

I recognize my mother
The Statue of Liberty,
I'm proud to be Hispano,
She's also proud of me!

    I like to speak Spanish
    My father told me so,
    I love the blonde ladies
    I like the Honky Tonk!

No matter if it is "charro"
The Hat I used to wear
I'm an immigrant
Forever any where!

—Jesus Morõn Villarreal

MY BEST FRIEND

My best Friend is close
beside me every day.
Encourages me to do right
when things go astray.

He's never failing
and always true.
He can cheer me up
with ease, when I'm blue.

Forgives and forgets
when I do wrong.
When I feel weak,
He's always strong.

In this world
without my Best Friend.
I know my happiness
will surely come to an end.

No greater LOVE can be found.
When it begins as Friends.
My husband, My Best Friend.
Forever and ever, Amen.

—Jennifer Lynn Starks

GIFTS OF GOD

I was given eyes that I might see
The beauty that we all can be
But instead I see a world that is separated by race
Please God, I wish I was blind, so that I cannot tell the color of another's face

I was given ears that I might hear
The sounds of love that draw us near
But instead I hear a world where shouts of indignity are all around
Please God, I wish I was deaf so that I cannot hear a world full of such inhuman sounds

I was given hands that I might touch
The warmth of friendship that means so much
But instead I feel a world where an outstretched hand strikes out as it becomes a fist
Please God, I wish I had no hands so that I cannot feel the senseless killings of ones so missed

But much to my dismay I can feel and hear and see
What my world is turning into and what is happening to me
Please God, guide my hands and eyes and ears to do thy will
Your precious gifts of love are all that keeps us from death's cold chill

—Walter F. Dobrzycki

ROSES

The "rose's" petals all formed in "love." Like a caterpillar in a cocoon, gives "birth to a butterfly." God's wisdom and beauty bring forth a "beautiful rose" . . . after the bud, "roses" speak love, "God's love" . . . "from above."

What a sweeter scent, than the "Wild Irish Rose?" How was that "sweet scent of love," put there? "Think on it" . . . No man could ever bottle its scent, capture its essence . . . "To exploit."

Formed by the "Hand of God," wisdom and forethought of "Our Maker." God Himself . . . is "Love." Jesus is the "Rose of Sharon." "Love" crucified a rose. The Rose of Sharon "Love" "Rose petals of love." "God's love never fails."

"Roses" . . . "Roses" . . . "Rose petals of love" . . . .

        "Roses"

Dedicated to my wonderful Christian father, Gus Ganert.

—"Blissful"

THE HIWAY ACROSS HEAVEN

As you gaze over the horizons in the far distance of your sight
You may see the hiways crying and they don't always seem just right.
It could be they are lonely from their trip to the higher state
Or perhaps they're just tired from traveling with so much weight.

Many loads supply the earth; eighteen wheelers trample a path
But the driver must push on, in search of the lighted bath.
The challenge of speeding time adds the most stress of all;
Schedules must be met, and the obstacle appears a wall.

Gifted are the truckers as they proceed between the lines
Avoiding the four wheelers, the Semis arrive on time.
Moment by moment they guard this gift within
For to take it for granted would be the greatest sin.

Knowledge and understanding come one day at a time
They know they'll be rewarded with complete peace of mind.
Experiencing life will tell the truth to all
Who appreciate it as a gift and drive to stand tall.

Following destiny's path, using each day to set their goals
Without judging or criticizing, makes these spirits free souls.
Traveling the "Hiway Across Heaven," their souls will never die
But some days, like the Hiways, you'll see the truckers cry.

—Jacqueline R. Turnipseed

YOUR CHILD

I am your Child.
God has entrusted me to you, to teach me.
Teach me with love, not hate.
Teach me not how to get revenge.
But how to forgive.
Teach me not to look down upon others.
Help me learn compassion, and respect.
Teach me with your actions
Not just your words.
For you are my greatest teacher.
I am your child, teach me well.

—Karen Chase

THAT MAN THAT IS MY DAD

Since I was just a boy,
I've always said one thing:
I hope I can give my children
What my father has given me.

I hope I'll have those caring arms
Just when they're needed so,
And I pray they'll understand
When I am forced to tell them "No."

I pray I'll be the friend they need
When they think they've had enough,
And someone they can turn to,
Even when life is not so rough.

I hope I can give them guidance
Down life's sometimes twisting path,
And be the light that guides them
After my embers have turned to ash.

I'll try my best to do these things
And give them all that I have had;
Following the light that leads my way . . .
The man that is my dad.

—Randal E. Dobson

A DAUGHTER'S GRIEF

I stand silent at the ball-park,
Watching your grandson,
Like any Mom would do,
Missing your enthusiasm,
When I turn to say something,
But you aren't there.

I shop in the mall,
And find myself ordering your favorite food,
Somehow hoping,
It will bring you closer,
Like a warm blanket,
On a winter's night.

I catch a glimpse,
In the early light,
Of a woman rhythmically striding,
My hand taps the horn in greeting,
She turns puzzled,
As reality awakens me.

*In memory of Eileen Emerald Leeking,
loving mother, wife and grandma,
devoted community and church volunteer*

—Cindy Brennan

TO THE NEW PARENTS

We can not believe
as we walked down the hall each night
checked each door
    watched and listened and prayed
that we were the parents of three.

Years have passed.

We can not believe
as we walk down the hall each night
checking each door
    watching and listening and praying
that we are the grandparents of two.

—Odessa Sanden

JEALOUSY AND HATE

We were pronounced man and wife
We turned around to start our life
All the happy faces smiling at us
Except for her, it was disgust!

Through the years, they seemed to flee
We had our children and we were happy
The love was all around when they were born
Except for her, nothing but scorn!

It finally happened, the day came
I at home with my children at play
My husband at work, the phone rang
It was her, she had something to say!

The years have passed and her regret
The day my husband and I met
The anger she does feel
To her, it is very real!

To her, what is done is done
There will always be a grudge
It is not her fault, she loves her son
And it is not our place to judge!

—Linda Smedley

DADDY'S LITTLE GIRL

Daddy you are big and strong,
I'm your little girl.
I know you say you love me,
But my mind is in a whirl . . .

You say Mommy doesn't understand you,
That's why you come to me,
But I'm just your little girl . . .
Daddy, can't you see?

I don't understand your loving touch,
It makes me feel afraid.
But I'm too young yet to know . . .
I'm a little girl betrayed.

You say it is our "secret,"
If it hurts I can't cry or yell,
For something bad will happen . . .
If I ever tell.

But you say you love me, Daddy,
And though I feel afraid,
I trust you, for I'm too young to know . . .
I'm a little girl betrayed.

—Joetta Lee

BABY BRIAN

A look, a pause, and then the smile . . .
It makes one's soul light up;
So radiant, happy, and free of guile—
Pure love's overflowing cup . . . .

—B. B. Watkins

YOUR LOVE WHISPERS

There is a whisper, the sounding
of a soft voice
from who, from where
it is so soft but yet loud enough to hear

Just a whisper of a voice
so calm and pleasant
not a careless sigh or a moan
but a whisper
Listen to the whisper
of your
heart speaking to mine
Listen closely it's a soft whisper
a soft message of delicate love

—Yolanda Lebron

FAMILY

Family is what makes life worth living
There is so much care and lots of giving.
Mother, father, sister or brother,
There is so much love for one another.
Grandparents are so special too,
In all the wonderful things they do.
And what about children, don't you see?
They help to make the family tree.
For they help the tree to slowly grow,
By having others as you know.
Birthdays, reunions and holidays
Bring family together in many ways.
It's great to have family big or small;
It's better than having none at all.
So cherish your family wherever they are,
You're blessed to have them near or far.

—LaCheryle Thompson-Criswell

Christmas in the city,
a wonderful time of year,
windows decorated so pretty,
our spirits filled with cheer.

Let's not forget the story,
of how it came about,
it's one of praise and glory,
of this I have no doubt.

Guided by a shining star,
shepherds crossed the desert sand,
they traveled on so very far,
with gifts in each hand.

Who is this one, we come to see?
a king, I heard them say,
one special babe, they all agree,
and to whom on bended knee they pray.

Merry Christmas.

—Karen S. Karlsen

HOME

A rolling energy, pouring forth
From age old past.
The glow against the blackened brick,
Smouldering up to dance from the chamber,
In the bitter night wind.
An essence of hickory pervades
The capacity of the hall,
Satisfying a tranquility unassailable.
Through the pane,
a host of celestial luminations,
Decree contemplations of the beyond.
A languid intoxication
Permeates the soul,
And placid utopianism subdues the spirit,
To an opiate state of repose.

—William Boone Zambrano

MY SON

Handsome as he is,
how could a little person have such a big son?

He's surrounded with love
He gives and receives.
Tender hearted, forgiving.
A small child at heart.

I love him so and he knows.
He knows me, that makes me happy.

He belongs to my Father,
no longer a child.
He takes care of him,
guides and protects.

The joy he has given me.
The pride I have in him.

We are blessed to call him
our son.
I thank my Father for him
continuously
My Son.

—Peggy Stanton

TO MARGARET

Privilege my palate with love,
And I'll taste the heavenly nectar that attracts
The dainty and delicate hummingbird,
Whose plumage is brilliant.

Bless the organ which filters my vision with love,
And I'll witness the radiance emitted
By a vast landscape of wildflowers,
On the brightest days of springtime.

Allow for a walk through a garden
Devoted to roses, with flowers in full bloom;
Your love is the scent, then,
That becomes captured by my nose.

Upon the skin a smoothing massage,
A gentle caress, a tender kiss;
Such is the message broadcasted
As love, in the manner of your touch.

Finally, listen! and hear as sleep approaches
The melodic lullaby of a nightingale,
Under the light of the moon
Resemble the voice of your love, when heard.

—Richard Steven Crist

THREADS OF GOLD

Each child is a thread of life, shining,
   gold, and small.
Each thread is so very fragile and should
   be loved by each and all.
Our children are the future, so precious,
   innocent, and sweet.
Their lives depend on all of us, and yet we
   give them to the streets.
Hungry, cold, and lonely, their tiny figures
   fade.
Though they are the very single ones the
   human race has made.
Each child is born with innocence, shining
   in its eyes.
Those tiny eyes and hands stretch out to hold
   you when it cries.
One person loving just one child, has the power
   needed to give.
A little bit to just one child will help that
   life to live.
They form a brand new generation and these
   threads we must sew.
And don't just stand and watch them, help
   them as they grow.
So don't allow that golden thread to be cut
   off so fast.
Let that little life unwind, and help to
   make it last.

—Maryanne Monro, age 13

MY SISTER, MY FRIEND

We're only passing through this world,
   one lifetime at a time.
To live and love and leave again,
until the end of time.
Won't you walk a little slower
till I walk with you my love?
Won't you fly a little slower
till I fly with you above?
There's nothing left for me to do
in this, my earthly stay,
except to wait to be with you
so we can fly away.
Won't you walk a little slower,
so we can drift awhile?
Won't you stop to smell the roses,
then you and I can smile.
Won't you be my guardian angel
my sister, my friend.
Won't you walk a little slower
till I'm with you once again?
Won't you walk a little slower
as I hear you angels sing?
Come be my guardian angel
with the wind beneath your wings?

*Dedicated to my #5 sister. All the
rest of my hours, days, weeks and years
will be with thoughts of my sister, my
friend, until I'm with her again in the
kingdom of God, forever free. She's an
angel in heaven, waiting for me.*

   I love you Sis
   —Tootsie Kelly

THE YEARNINGS OF AN OLD MOTHER'S HEART

As she gently rocks to and fro
And the sun is sinking low
Though her face carries a smile
An old mother yearns for each child.

As she prays for each so dear
Those far as well as those near
Though at times they're wayward and wild
An old mother still yearns for each child.

Sure she can't keep them tied to apron strings
She knows they have to be doing their thing
But deep down all the while
An old mother still yearns for each child.

As her beads she does silently tell
And God seems to whisper "All's Well"
Her prayers bridge many a mile
As an old mother yearns for each child.

—Margaret Willett, deceased

born too early

leaving the warmth of the womb before her time
she was small too small
with transparent onion skin
a wee two pounds of female life
a miracle of nature
tubes in every hairlike artery
she fought for survival
amazing wriggling nippled toes
hard for the eye to see
long smaller than tiny fingers
grabbing at the space
even then wanting to hold a loving hand
naked bright dew drop eyes
blank with no knowledge of her life to come
tiny lips searching for the absent breast
a mother looking on asking God
to spare her child to give it strength
to grow outside her body
she could no longer give it sustenance

—Mary Mungar

DADDY'S HUNTING PARTNER

My dad sure liked his trusty old shotgun,
He thought it was the best kind to shoot,
He hardly ever missed a squirrel with it,
And he sometimes got more than one, to boot.

Daddy was a sport tho',
He would never shoot a dove,
He felt they were kind of special,
To the man above.

I sure did like to go hunting with him,
Of course, I followed a ways behind,
His long legs were much faster,
But I really didn't mind.

I felt so very important,
Carrying Daddy's homemade hunting sack,
Which was usually full of game,
By the time we got back.

Grandma said, little girls weren't supposed
   to go hunting,
But Daddy and I both agreed,
Since he had no little boy to go with him,
It was left up to me.

—Ethel M. Wilbourn

SMALL FAVOR

If I appeared at your window, late
one rainy night, and tapped softly at the
glass . . . would you let me in?

If I asked you to tell me all of your
secrets, the answers to my every question, and
the mysteries of life . . . would you whisper
in my ear?

If I confessed to you all my sins,
my dreams, and my desires . . . would you
be my savior?

—Jessica Rossiter

TO LOVE

Have you ever wondered at the meaning
of simple words?
Take, for example, the expression
    "For the birds."
I've heard many men say,
that love should go that way.
But, if that is truly the case,
then I should not be here in this place.
I should be soaring high upon the
    currents of Mother Earth,
    circling, soaring for all that
    an eagle is worth.
For if love is for those that ride
    the air,
then, my love, we must join
    them there.
Together, let us build a nest high
    upon a cliff,
And watch this loveless world grow
    cold and stiff.

Dedicated to Rachelle Rowland
my "Soul" inspirer.

—Michael Blevins

MOTEL MISSISSIPPI

They cleared the lot last Fall.
The house is gone — the beige box
where I learned to love.

Cool mornings I would awake
curved into his belly,
an arm draped securely around my waist.

It was not my best affair — it was my first.
I know it wasn't true love,
but here I learned what true love really was.

Anyway — now it's gone . . .
knocked down and wiped away
as if my memories didn't matter.

He moved out.
I left town.
And, I guess I thought the house would stay
as some odd tribute to our futile efforts.

Now there's only a motel —
a concrete building over my lover's bedroom.

Maybe I'll check in
and lay my memories to rest.

—Mavis Lamb

WHAT IS LOVE?

A kindly face, a safely place
A feeling of softness carried around
Another day.
It's not a toy or inane thing,
It's the stuff of life, a wedding ring.
It's a picture faded and cracked on the edge,
It's a petal of a rose, found on a ledge.
It's the smaller things that fit in the heart
That keep the big things from breaking apart.
It's stuff of life on a beach somewhere,
The tide, the moon, the salty air.
The sun in the morning across the stone,
The sun in the evening shining on home.

—Ernie Rudolph

SILENCE

Silence
No word or murmur escaped Him
Silence
Never ending forever there
I speak
Words escape me and He listens
I speak
My problems, my fears He hears them all
Silence
He never opens up His feelings remain with Him
I speak
I reveal my inner self to His sympathetic ear
Silence
He reveals nothing the mystery remains
I spoke
Now He knows I have kept nothing hidden
Silence
His secrets are hidden, He has yet to open up
Silence
Our only barrier, yet to be broken

Dedicated to Matt Chesney
Who I fell in love with

—Millecent Weigandt

LOVE'S STIRRINGS

My Queen, My Queen
why do you haunt my dream
with promises barely whispered
and words never spoken
from the most beautiful soul I've ever seen?

A beautiful smile with a slight twist
Reminds me of the love I've missed
Shapely legs encased in silk
Torturing me with visions of love . . .
and lips I've never kissed.

How can I whisper words I want to say
into your ear on the pillow where it lay
while between us rears ugly walls
of silence and stone
And you so far away?

I want to hold you in my arms
while swimming in your charms.
Encased in my love
Like a jewel from distant lands,
I'll protect you from anything that harms.

—Steve Baker
Effie Baker

CHOICES

How can anyone ever doubt,
The gift of life and what it's all about.

Right is Right and Wrong is Wrong.
So simple is life's magic song.

There is good and there is bad.
ONLY two choices to be had.

Seek the bad in all life's things,
And sadness and heartache are all you'll bring.

Find the good in all you do,
And life will be fair unto You.

So simple are life's answers.
Seek not one's Self, but seek the MASTER.

—Gail P. Arbogast

LIFE'S GREATEST TREASURE

Many of us seek, with heads down low,
From birth 'till the day we die —
To find material blessings; and so
    The Greatest Treasure oft slips by.

A farmer stumbles upon a field
    In which a treasure lies hidden deep.
He sells all he owns to make a deal;
    And buys the land to have and to keep.

A merchant who buys costly pearls,
    In his wanderings finds one greatly priced.
Then caution to the wind he hurls!
    Sells all! For with that gem he is enticed.

And so we search the ground each day,
    Never thinking to look above —
When the Greatest Treasure that can come our way
    Is the Gift of God's Eternal Love.

(Matt. 13:44-46)
—Frances B. Fike

THERE'S NO MORE I CAN DO

I am always with you from beginning to end,
There is no one else who can be such a friend.

I clothe you and I feed you and give you to drink,
I suggest your thoughts daily and help you to think.

When you ask me in prayer to fulfill a great need,
If not handled your way unbelief will succeed.

Your prayers I will answer in my time and my way,
It's your heart that I hear it's not in what you say.

Because for your benefit I try to do more,
You shun me and curse me repent I implore.

Unwilling to wait for your prayers to unfold,
You proceed on your own forgetting all I foretold.

I have given my Son and my miracles too,
Oh my child there is nothing more I can do.

It's all up to you now I'll always be here,
For through grace you're forgiven just seek me my dear.

    Lord I Praise Your Name For From You I Came

Dedicated to my Saviour Jesus Christ
"Lord I Praise Your Name For
   From You I Came"

—Pauline McInnis

ADAM'S FIRST WIFE

God created Eve from Adam's rib.
Satan created Lilith
Who would not obey,
And berated Adam every day.

She would not do wifely duties
But quarreled and argued and fought
Until Lilith fled Eden
And became a regular demon
Of love, tormenting men
With erotic dreams
And became the very spirit
Of demonology created
By Satan.

From a Hebrew legend as old as time.
—Guyla Wallis Moreland

MY HEART SMILES

Let my life be pleasing to thee.
I only want your face to see.
If I could put a smile upon thy face,
I would truly sing, 'Amazing Grace.'

You sit on your throne, and watch
   over us.
To pray, to witness, we do not fuss.
We become so selfish, and do not care.
But let's get-up, and go, and share.

The treasure of Jesus, that we have found.
And then in heaven, many will abound.
You see a smile upon my heart, so
   smile, sweet Father, and you will see.
The happiest witness; that witness
   is me.

—Sandra L. Frigo

THE SUN FLOWERS

I see a little child
running through a field
of big, big sun flowers
I could see the sun dancing
all around the sun flowers
a beautiful yellow flower
with a dark, dark brown,
big dark green leaves
hitting against the child
little arms and legs.
The sun flowers
reaching up to the heavens
and staying so tall.
I could see it all in my mind's eye.
And dream . . .
They are real
some place
I know they are.
"Let me always remember dreams.
Do they really come true?"
All dreams can become real
They do every day for someone
And they will for me
With God's help
I can not do it myself
But "God can."

—Blanche Mary Colombo

YOU

You are a creation from heaven,
a little hand to hold.

Your mind is a clean slate,
fill it with love and wishes.

I am your present.
You are my future . . .

Cherish yesterday; Succeed today.
Dream of tomorrow.

You're a new beginning, the sunlight of dawn.

The world is yours.

You're my precious—
    my baby.

—Amy Nicole Patrick

FROM THE MOTHER OF TWO BOYS

The attention that a boy receives,
Is, generally, his due.
There's nothing like a boy around,
Unless, perhaps, it's two!

For boys are climbers and swingers,
To *walk* is not their style.
They run and jump and skin their knees,
They whoop and roar and swing from trees,
They push, they shove, they poke and tease,
Forever delighting in devilish deeds.
And yet, their antics are quick to please,
And sure to bring a smile—

To those who love and tend them,
Who mold, and train and bend them,
Who watch and teach,
Who praise and preach,
Who hold their breath and wait to see,
The men, their boys, too soon will be.

—Karyl J. Gooding

SOUNDS OF A CHILD

Crash, bang, zap, plunk—
I hear, I wonder;
Whirl, spin, fly, run—
I see, I suspect.
Pop, boom, churn, snap—
I hear, I worry;
Slide, dart, run, hide—
I see, I know!
A busy day — excitement mounts,
Unending sounds — unending doubts.
The worries build — the tension grows,
The day goes on — but never slows!
The pressures of the busy day,
The thought, sometimes to run away!
But then the night begins to near
And through the house these sounds I *cheer*!
Splash, glug, bubble, churn—
I hear, I wonder;
Sigh, stir, toss, dream
I see, I know!

—Jennifer (JenniSu)

DEBBIE

Debbie, who was kind and
gentle, there is no one like
her. Debbie, you are the apple of
my eye.

—Nilson Ortiz

YOU MOTHER

You encourage me to meet my goals,
You help me go through all the roles,
You're the one I am to thank,
I know it's hard with the trouble I make.
You're the one who gave me life
  (even though Dad helped a bit),
You're the one who put up the fit.
Even though it hurt a lot,
You still made my bottle with a hot pot.
You are very special indeed,
You're the one who gets my every need.
You're my mother all the way through,
You're the one who's always true.
You know — Mother's Day should be every day,
Especially for Mothers like you!

—Carrie Cole, age 10

GRANDPA'S EYES

Through Grandpa's eyes I saw the
Most wonderful things,
Love, Happiness, Caring.
Now that Grandpa's gone, I can't see
Those things anymore.
I wished I could,
Sometimes I wonder did Grandpa's Eyes
Ever cry. Were there ever tears
That came out of those wonderful eyes?
If there were, I'm glad I didn't see them,
Because then, I know I always
Made Grandpa's eyes happy.

*Dedicated to my Grandpa, George Romick,
who passed away July 1, 1989.
I loved you and miss you with all my heart.*

—Mistie Heinle, age 15

CHILDREN OF THE 50'S

They say we children of the 50's were naive,
Our childhoods were given a reprieve.
I ask you naive about what?
Promiscuity, pornography, drugs, and smut.

We formed loves, relationships that were
sound.
To be accepted we didn't need to sleep
around.
For our activities, and experiences were
new found,
Extended families, neighbors, and friends
did abound.

Getting jobs after high-school was expected.
For our work ethic, they reflected.
Give me back the 50's,
With all our naivity, they were the nifties.

—Jo Ann B. Vogel

CHANGE

Life is not worth living,
Unless you feel pain
Among the joys and pleasures—
And let nothing stay the same.
Beware that constancy is the enemy
That never did exist.

—Sandra Bullock

MY POCKET

What's in this pocket of mine
   Besides a dime?
Oh, it's a smile,
And a crocodile;
A smelly sock
And a dirty rock;
There's many things in this
   pocket of mine.
Not just a dime.

—Melissa Marshall, age 13

A TRUE ARTIST

The respect I feel
Can not be expressed in words
And my gratitude for the
Lessons he has taught me
Is never-ending,
I watch his style
And power in awe
Hoping that one day
I may come close,
May it be a mile,
To his ability
To earn as much respect
From him as he has
Earned from me is
Impossible,
He is truly an artist,
The greatest I have
Ever seen

—Dawn Giles, grade 10

TIME

Time, time is passing by.
Hurry, hurry! Just try, just try!

To record your pets, your cats,
your birds,
Record your memories, your
thoughts, your words.

Record it on pictures, in
stories, or rhymes.
Record every one of those
happy times.

No time, no time! no time
to waste!
Glue it on paper,
glue it with paste.

Save your life,
save what's mine.
Save what's yours, and
save your time!

—Erika Lynn Adams, age 14

THE SEA AND ME

Standing, looking out over the seaside,
Contemplating all of those fathoms of water and the tide.
Searching through the winds of time,
Searching through the thoughts of my mind.

I am awed at all of the water, all of the brine,
The salt of the earth to last for all time.
The width, the depth, the roar of the incoming waves,
The quiet as it goes back out over the sailors' graves.

The untold stories, the hidden treasure,
They must go on and on without measure.
Can this be what life is to me?
Can this be what I am to see?

All of the friends and loved ones lost in the sands of time,
New ones to make as my future unwinds.
Stories of the past forever untold,
Treasures of the future each day to unfold.

—Floy St. Sauver

ELUSIVE DREAM

White house, picket fence, bank account, family bliss.
Building generations to follow in your footsteps.
All is serene, or though it may seem.
Is it a mirage, or is it just a dream?
Or could it be a fairytale that we all want to believe?
Society crumbles. Morality tumbles.
The all mighty God gently intervenes.
He touches the land to calm the seas.
Few will notice, but the chosen will see.
Rages are brewing, companies barely moving.
Shut downs, layoffs, Poverty increasing.
All are invading the elusive dream.
Factories closing, families eroding.
Generations without direction.
Shadows of footsteps are barely visible.
White house gray, picket fence frayed.
Bank account dwindles, family in disarray.
The dream of life slowly fades away.
Only the One above, can help us maintain our way.

—Dorothy Wiley

LIONS PARK

Warm summer evenings we spent swinging
in the faint glow of a distant street light,
our talk about blueberries and mountains.
Nearby on a thin patch of grass,
a lion statue poses like a king, watches our flight.

Legs aimed toward the sky
our laughter awakes the sleeping night.
Trees bend their branches back
creating a pathway to the stars.
If only our bodies could have departed the swings,
we'd have lost ourselves to another world a long time ago.

In the winter, we race through snow to our knees
find rusty chains too cold to grasp with ungloved hands.
We hold the chains in the crooks of our elbows,
and become airborne in each other's thoughts
of summer and spring.

Even now when the night sky hovers hazy and still,
I dream I am back at Lion's Park. A naive young girl
riding to the stars. You swing beside me.
We discuss blueberries and Never-Never Land.

—Mandy Georgi

FALL

A glint of Fall was in the air, as I approached the bend —
A zapping, chilling breeze, the rolling twig.
　　The few leaves with a touch of red.
　　The Summer's nearly o'er, 'tho the sun is still bright,
　　　But the nights and mornings are cool — when I fetch the paper;
　　Letting the dog out, Another year approaching the brim.
Corks popping — distantly; Bobbing for apples — 'Tis the Season
　　as ghosts, goblins and turkeys march onward, and inward?

Dedicated to Larry, my Granddad, who passed away one year ago today.
　　　—April Phelps

(THE PASSING OF EMILY DICKINSON)

　　Do not stir me from my sleep for death has reached out
her withered hand for my soul to keep.
　　Do not stir me from my sleep for the lights are faint and
my spirit is weak, I can see the tunnel so dark and bleak as
it drags my soul to travel within.
　　Do not stir me from my sleep for my valor has dissolved and
my mind has grown unclear. Death is clutching my vessel to
steal, snaring it from my mortal zeal.
　　Do not stir me from my sleep for now my being is in the world
of perpetual restless restive, for my spirit to forever keep.
　　　—Glenn Roach

SAILORS STORIES

I see the raging beauty in the splashing of the waves,
I've heard the sailors stories of seas turned into graves.
Of ships that sank years ago, never to be found,
How ships like the Titantic couldn't hold their ground.
The sea can be so beautiful, she can be your friend.
Until you catch her in a storm and feel her chilling wind.
She's quick to help you get to shore by the rising of the tide,
As quickly she will sink you, the sea she has no pride.
Men of the sea say she's clever, she knows just where your bound,
Then with the slightest whisper she can turn your ship around.
So try to beat her if you can. What have you to lose?
Like a thousand other men, your life, your ships, your crews.
　　　—Francine B. Winters

MICHIGAN

Come with me to Michigan a real vacation land,
Let me show you a place of beauty, God's water wonderland.

The horizon forms its borders, where sky and water meet.
As viewed from the Porcupines, with Lake Superior at its feet.

Where across the waves at evening, when the sun sets out of sight,
Reflects the glow of crimson, from the rocks of Hemite.

Or scan the clear blue waters from Lake Superior's sandy shore,
There's no place more beautiful, than Michigan, I am sure.

The ships that sail these waters and from Lake Huron with their freight,
Move slowly on the seaway to Lake Michigan at the Straits.

Where stands that mighty structure, the bridge at Mackinaw,
Like arms stretched forth in honor from each peninsula.

As you gaze with awe and wonder, at this great expanse of steel,
It's a symbol of the strength and courage the Michigan people feel.

So come with me to Michigan, this land of lakes and streams,
With its fish and fowl, deer and bear, it is a sportsman's dream.

So with thankful hearts we offer, to Him who's in command,
Our praise for this spot, called Michigan, God's water wonderland.
　　　—Zelma C. Clark

WHERE DID THEY GO?

As I watch the gentle snow fall,
In the distance I hear the children call.

I know that soon they will be home,
But still I feel all alone.

Where did my babies go?
With their ten tiny fingers and ten
tiny toes.

They seem to have grown so fast.
Their crawling, bottle days are in
the past.

But as I see them come into view, I
realize they have a lot of growing-up
to do.

There are first dates, cars and such,
And when they are over I'll miss
them just as much.

—Melany L Haddock

THE JOY OF A LITTLE CHILD

Birds were silent in the trees
As leaves of gold and brown
Settled in a gentle brook
And coated the sleeping ground.

A mother and her child of three
Sat quietly nearby.
They closed their eyes to better hear
The buzzing of a bee.

But then the child arose
Her curiosity fed.
She jumped into the stream
And it splashed and dashed and swirled.
She jumped into the leaves
And they flipped and dipped and whirled.
The birds in the trees
Sang loud and clear and wild.
All nature came alive
With the joy of a little child.

—Eldora Johnson

FEARS TO SLEEP

I make welcome to you
  my father.
I make welcome to you
  my son.
I make for us sweet
  sound and dance
in which we play
  as one.

I speak to you
  my father.
I sing to you
  my son;
That a wisp of sound
  may remind us
of our birthday
  in the sun.

Tears fall as raindrops.
Hope springs as grain;
that our bodies be washed and nourished
and we be forever new again.

—Mitchell B. James

MY GRANDMA

My Grandma is a treasure that is like a fine wine.
She ages with such grace. Each year she is more fine.
She always has a word, to encourage and up lift.
Without the wrapper or the bow, she is a perfect gift.
Grama has the wisdom, the tenderness, and heart,
When I don't have the answer, she always seems so smart.
If I sat on her lap, she would probably break in half.
She is so tiny, but she's always open to a laugh.
Another year is gone, but I need to know I've told her,
Within my heart each year, the closer I will hold her.

—dana paige vail

MY SON

As a father, I was blessed with a wonderful son,
but, I was doubly blessed with another one.
Their mother was pleased and shared with me too
that our Dear Lord, above, gave us not one but two.

I remember, when they were little we
would play games and have fun, but now
they are grown, my sons on their own.
They became young men who are truly great.
We, as parents, are glad each found a mate,
Both, happily married, and are blessed
with children of their own.

We as Grandparents, have truly been shown
that all of our blessings, happiness and love
have been given to us from our Dear Lord above.
We, as a family, give thanks to our God,
we dearly love.

—Betty Brobst Fenstermaker

MY GRANDDAD

My Granddad was a strong man
Not just in physical strength . . . yes, internal
He provided for his family a plan
With provisions that are eternal

With ebonite skin and pearl-like teeth
And veins in which crimson blood flowed
The sky at his head, terra firma at his feet
His spirit man lovingly flowed

Hard work, little pay were his wages
Raiment, shelter, food Granddad supplied
His family's love . . . barometric gages
Made hard times weather the storm's tide

I'll always remember my Granddad
By his quiet smile and proud manner
His stories though true would make a man sad
To not carry a visible moral banner

—Linda L. Henderson

TIMES ARE CHANGING

Times are changing, this I am told.
People are changing, we keep getting old.

Politicians tell us we all have civil rights,
Victims become invisible while criminals enjoy free flight.

People are homeless and babies fail to thrive.
Why is it so difficult just to stay alive?

People with no jobs are trying to get aid.
While politicians complain about the amounts they get paid.

We send billions to countries whose children are starving
While our own slices of beef get smaller with each carving.

Land of the free, home of the brave —
Americans becoming one huge grave.

Times are changing — there used to be gladness.
Welcome to America! This way lies madness.

—Donna Mae Douglas

WOLF DOG

I am outcast, alienated, run off.
I am without a pack, a mate, another
soul to share the sleeping and hunting grounds.
I howl but with no answer, I bark but with no ferocity.
Separated from the pack for my difference,
attacked for my foreign ways.
The nights are cold, long, empty.
The oneness has reached my soul,
closing my emotion and sealing me up like a vault door,
never to open again.
For my uniqueness, I was valued. For my difference
I was ostracized.
The Irony of the event has become as an anvil straining my
legs, chained to my neck as if to impede my progress.
Darwin, your words ring true, I am not the strongest.
Tonight I sleep eternal, forever the wolf dog, never a pure wolf.

—S.E. Frost

ODDS NOT EVENS

This is a world of odds not evens
We are the size God meant us to be.
But in this world of following style trends
Everyone judges us for what they see.

We were meant to be totally different
Not all in the same mold or form.
Being different makes a person interesting,
After all, that's the way we were born.

In you inherited the genes your parents gave you
Exercising, dieting and worrying won't help very much.
Be at ease and accept what God meant you to be
Don't let trends get you in their greedy clutch!

You can't possibly judge a person wholly
By what your eyes alone behold.
It's what's inside each person's heart
That makes them worth their weight in gold.

Yes, this is a world full of odds not evens
It's exactly as God meant it to be.
So the next time you see someone different,
Remember, what they are is what you can't see!

—Venita J. Bahun

THINGS OF BEAUTY

Things of beauty, which you and I
Pass by upon our daily rounds,
And do not see;
Are by the artist often sought;
And with his brush or camera caught;
Preserved for all eternity,
So that the world may see,
As well as we.

—Josephine Williams

THE LEAF BALLET

Each leaf dances to its own tune.
The ballet is in progress.
I missed the opening number.
No matter —
I can pick up anywhere
in the endless annual performance.

My dignified oaks
are disrobing for winter.
All summer their green apparel
roofed my grass floor
and cooled my brow.

Now, their mission complete,
leaves, one by one, take the stage.
The sun spotlights the show.
Their swift swirls create tutus
as they pirouette and plie
and bow at ground level
to mute applause.

—Lucile Roden

PVT US 090160

It started out as a game
Little soldiers lying on the ground

A childhood fantasy
Play soldiers, tanks, and planes

"Charge" came the call
I moved my men forward

A mud bomb is hurled at the enemy
Not one is left standing

I peer out triumphantly
Over a grassy hill in the park

A job well done
Victory at age 8

Time flies by
The toys are packed away

I am older now
More important worlds to conquer

The grassy hill is now barren
The smell of smoke fills the air

I remember the order to "Charge"
The grenade hurled at my feet

I feel nothing
I am gone from this world

It will be called a victory
Triumph once more

It started out as a game
Little soldiers lying on the ground

—Walter F. Dobrzycki

MY WISH

What do I wish you for your wedding
    Such a wondrous time of life,
Joy I wish you by the tonnage,
    Not an ounce of strife.

What do I wish you for your marriage,
    All the happiness there is,
All the wonder of fulfillment knowing
    You are his.

What do I wish you for your lifetime
    All the love each one can give,
And this love will be unending
    All the days you live.

    —Florence A. Cox

SHE'S NOT THERE

She can make me smile with a glance
She can make me sing with a stare
That look in her eyes
Makes me glad I'm alive
But I look, and she's not there

Her heart is as warm as the sunlight
Her beauty is beyond all compare
She holds me in awe
As I let out a call
And run to her, but she's not there

I torture myself with this vision
But I follow it still without care
For the way that she seems
She could not be a dream
I know she exists somewhere

She is waiting for me to find her
And she dreams of the feelings we'll share
So I will follow the chase
Until I find that place
I will find it, and she will be there

    —David Cohen

I SEE STREAMS

There are footsteps in her laughter,
In candescent leaps, she smiles
    I see streams
      of gleam running
        around
         the
        inside
        of
      her eyes
        &
    Afterward
    her thighs
      flowing
        cooly
    to disguise
      seams
    we always   To p
      seem   which   l
        to   From   u
        find   heights   m
          Such   m
                                    e
                                    t.

    —michael scott marks

I'M HERE

The clock still ticks to the rhythmic beat of time
The chill of winter is blowing
The green leaves are falling
And my broken heart is calling . . . I'M HERE

The distance has no meaning, the reason has
its place
The void that keeps us so far apart has only
helped me face
The tempo of the music, as the drummer plays
our song

As long as we're together we can march right along
And I'M STILL HERE.

*Dedicated to my friend, my lover, my husband
James Carol Montgomery*

    —Betty J. Montgomery

MY SPECIAL HAPPINESS

Happiness sat beside me
someone who was lost at heart
and talked to me like a real person
Which his love came from the heart
he made me feel special
when he asked me to dance
I felt light as a feather
when Happiness gently took my hand
After the dance was finished
I saw my sweet Happiness fade away
he left me with a piece of what
true love feels like today
My Sweet Happiness will forever be in my heart
and there forever my special memory of
Happiness will forever stay.

Dedicated to Matt

    —Shavonne Thomas

SMOKING, SMOKING

Smoking, smoking, it's always you and you
Smoking, smoking, find something else to do
You leave me, I'm breathing the smoke you
    left behind
I'm coughing and sneezing aren't you a friend
    of mine?
Smoking, smoking, it looks like so much fun
Smoking, smoking, don't leave that butt when
    you're done
It's funny the money, that all goes up
    in smoke
Are you laughing the smoking keeps you
    all so broke?
I love you, I love you I want you
    by my side
Don't leave me, believe me my
    relatives have died
from smoking and choking and burning
    their insides
Stop smoking, stop smoking, tell me
    have you tried?
Smoking, smoking, it's always you
    and you
Smoking, smoking, find something else
    to do.

    —Lorelei P. Allan

HEAVEN SENT

A boy in a stable was God in man form.
He came out of love on a blessed Christmas morn.
What stories He'd tell us of life and His home
So we would have hope and not hopelessly roam.

He's the bridge to new life for all who believe.
Humble beginnings set you and me free.
Because of His Love through an act of His will
Christ walked Yahweh's plan that affects mankind still.

No matter what race, past mistakes, or profession,
"Do you know God's Son Jesus?" is the matter at question.
May this Christmas be more than nice gifts and a tree
But a new gratitude for how God intervened —

In the lives of mankind set on course with destruction
What meaning life has when we heed His instructions!

Oh, come to the stable and worship the king.
Give Him your life, that's the best offering!

—Sheryl Rohrbein

A TALE OF CHRISTMAS

The Christmas spirit is all around. You can tell by listening to the familiar sounds. Carolers are singing the traditional songs. While shoppers are buying and rushing along.

Everyone is happy at this time of year, bidding you hello without even a sneer. Children keep wondering what Santa will bring, and hoping he won't forget one single thing.

Then all of a sudden it is Christmas Eve, and husbands are out picking a tree. Mothers are putting their children to bed, while visions of sugar plums dance in their heads.

Well everything is finished and the room is aglow, with tree lights and carols and packages with bows.

The windows are decorated with wreaths and holly, and a big picture of Santa looking so jolly. To top it all off, it is snowing very light, and you think to yourself, "It's a perfect Christmas Eve night."

Dedicated to my dear beloved father, Mr. Robert Montgomery. We will miss and love him always.

—Carolyn Ann Caporusso

WINTER-TIME

Let the snowflakes fall, Because it's winter,
The Sparkle of the Holidays is here.

Time when people are rushing past each other,
As they meet their Friends and Loved Ones along the way.

There is not much time to talk about the weather,
It's too Wonderful to see the Beauty of this Day.

Oh! The glitter of the stores along the sidewalk,
The vivid reds and greens are here to stay.

You feel the sweet, sweet Spirit of Christmas,
When you listen to the music that they play.

Now the greatest thing about the winter season,
Is because our Blessed Savior, then was born.

There will never ever be a Greater Birthday,
Without him life would be, Oh! so forlorn.

Now let's all stand up and sing to Praise our Master,
For this great free world, we live in of today.

And be Thankful our forefathers loved him also,
Just be Happy! Oh! So Happy on this Great, Christmas Day.

—Rachel Davis

YESTERDAY

Things are not the same
as yesterday
Old friends don't remain
New ideas have replaced the old
A broader spectrum I enfold
And still I dream of yesterday

—Betty L Edens

JESUS CHRIST ETERNAL LOVE!

Christmas is upon us,
Now it's time to shop,
Everyone is in a rush,
It seems no time to stop.
Sleighbells are ringing,
Jack Frost has filled the air,
The carolers are singing,
There's magic everywhere.
Folks are stringing lights,
And decorating trees,
On these winter nights,
No one gets on their knees.
To give thanks to God,
For that first Christmas gift,
Sent down from God above,
The one whose name we lift.
Jesus Christ eternal love.

—Misty Lewis

WE LIFT OUR CHILDREN

We lift our children
   to the sun.
They have so many charms.
   Their lives just begun.

Their minds are unbound,
   their footsteps sure.
Like your Son before them,
   They're prisoners no more.

Their skin is pale
   as a fallen dove,
reaching like an angel
   for your love.

Held in your arms
   fears fall to sleep.
Each and every heart
   Your Spirit does keep.

For the night has come
   and it asks but this,
Will you bless my child
   with your kiss?

Oh, the night bleeds
   like a wounded dove.
It screams like an angel
   for your love.

Three birds sing
   at the break of day.
Teach only love,
   I hear them say.

Their song awakens
   eternal friends.
The joy of homecoming
   is in the wind.

Let the banquet begin.

—Mitchell B. James

Unstoppable — we struck
Flint to steel on
the darkened shore.
In one instant
A seething shaving
Bred wilder than
Any flame —
Should be.
Dominance consuming
all;
w/ a swell
of history
rising w/
the sun.

—John Pendleton Grove IV

STREET SONG

Come tell me wicked wretches
what does your plight divine,
as dark night slowly catches
the brisk cold winters whine.

Along the streets you clamor
in dirty swaddling clothes,
in mumbling speech you stammer
your multitude of woes.

The passers-by refusing
and choose there not to see,
the heartless moral bruising
you take with due ennui.

They one time had a mother
and suckled her warm breast,
you could have been their brother
and shared their fitful rest.

Condemn them all together
the sick the halt the numb,
security we tether
and call you just a bum.

—Everett A. Tavares

THE DRUNK

he had to have a crutch
balm for the pain of living
help he needed so much
if life he was giving
the ache of failure's
dreams never tried
thoughts so damn unpure
of the cold nights he cried
alone born into this world
alone in a hole in the ground
scraping an existence
the world offering all resistance
his pain constant
with beat of his heart
survival a mark of persistence
watch his life fall apart
the days and lonely nights
he'd forgotten about love
tried to forget living
the bottle his only friend
tired of being pushed and shoved
each day a reminder of failing
only on death could he depend
the more he drank
the sooner it come
so he drank

—Albert Hubbart

THE GUN & THE BADGE

A Gun and a Badge are a deleterious tool, received by some
for bad and for cool. The ones for cool, are the ones
who aren't. The ones for the bad, well they know they
are not. So the ones for the bad, continue to get bad
and become their own enemy, that hides behind that Gun and
Badge, that wonderful tool that they use for cool, and
believe in for all the wrong reasons. For it is there to
Protect and Serve, that one thing we all deserve. The true
who are Bad and the true who are cool this poem I'm writing
is only for you. Because all of us know we have nothing to
prove, to the ones with the Gun and the Badge . . . . "90"

Dedicated to my son, Will Fox.

—Roni Fox

WIND IN THE LADDER

Life has such irony that the truth can be born . . .
Created by the wind passing through the ladder,
Giving birth to that perfect universal note.
The sound that harmonizes with perfection.
It is all music that has been and all music that will be.
A note that cannot be recreated.
It's only meaning to tease,
Showing the simple, omniscient, undefinable power in
                                  unity of all that is.
The mystery of the universe is revealed through the wonderment
                                  of that note
Created from moving the ladder against the wind.

—Jim Senior

SURRENDER

I have a real need
Of wanting to be accepted and loved
    For who I am, not what others usually see
        Through bits and pieces of images of me.

My frustration is immense, and I lose my grip
    And my sixth sense, I cannot conceal that I am too real
        But out of the struggle of trying to maintain a balance
           I found out that I created my own barometers . . .

I suffered, I doubted, I survived, I studied myself on the edge
    Of the internal stranger, counting the errors disguised within
        I have learned to fill in spaces I did not know were vacant
           And I have battled through to a clearer vision . . .

The harder our challenges, the more bountiful the rewards . . .
    But they are well hidden by a process called years.

—Michael S. Janjac

THE PIT

I stand amid the muck and mire of the pit of despair. The
treacherous gales are trying to drag me back, back into their
depths of endless decay that brings me to the very brink of
insanity and leaves me to drown in an enveloping, stormy sea
of misery; as with outstretched arms I attempt to rise above
the disastrous wasteland and suffocating seaweed has
entangled itself around my unwilling limbs, thus preventing
escape. I only I can free myself of this stubborn, persistent
force that time and again tries to defeat me, must I forever
be tormented by this deep, dark wasteful pit of depression?
Wait, there's a light, a ray of hope, someone to help me unlock
the secret passages of my mind, to bring again to memory an
inner strength, ever present but hidden at times, a place
where God and I meet together, the very soul that belongs
to Him that He and He alone strengthen and will reclaim at
journey's end.

—Sybil (Messer) Wadkins

SEALED WITHIN THE SHIELD OF THE SON

The Chief Shepherd and all of His helpers
Have made their encampment about this assembly,
It has been appointed unto them to do so
And in all holiness they give protection to God's family.

By decree of the Holy One who sits forever
They have come forth dressed in their fullest armor,
The Captain who leads them never makes mistakes
In perfect obedience He has disendowed the Charmer.

The Lamb of God, our Redeemer, came forth unto His own
Into the tabernacle of sinners behind the Crying Voice,
In the sins of passionate hatred they paid Him no heed
And in their depravity they crucified Him who died by choice.

The Garden of Perfection sets just beyond the dawn
The Son of the new morning will be the light of truth,
If you have been called to know His love
You'll share forever in the glories of eternal youth.

—Dallas Marshall

LAKE ARROWHEAD — June, 1993

A fragrant flowerfall washes over the mountainside;
Golden blooms, like whitewater, crash against the cliffs.
Its perfume surrounds my sensation.
I am forced far from this world of frenzy
And float to a stiller, more contented place.
Clouds tease the trees that strain to meet them
And the wind chases water
Across the lake to the shore.
Even stone seems somehow softer
On this mountain of the blest.

Even midnight, jealous of the day,
Cannot steal the beauty with its sooty sky.
God throws gargantuan handfuls of glitter
At the blackness . . .
Stars sparkle like sequins on velvet.
Sleep taunts my eyelids.
I step away from wakefulness . . .
But I am not sure when dreams began.

—Dorothea T. Curran

MOTHER AND DAUGHTER

The rain and wind came down
And the sun stood still
And in the tumult of joy the Angels came
And I looked up and they called my name
As I soared through eternity on wings of the sacred dove
I knew the meaning of perfect love.
Grieve not for me my precious child
We'll be together in just a short while.
I named you for the Saint Therese
And I'm so proud of you on God's green Earth.
I leave you now in great joy and peace.
We laughed and loved and worked and played together as one
And now my earthly chores are done.
I am so happy in my celestial home
And in the beauty of it here I'm never alone.
Cherish each day as if it was your last
For you can inherit God's heavenly home
When your time on earth is past.
I'll always love you my darling daughter, Therese,
And now I leave you
In love and peace.

—Sara Raley Mathews

THEOLOGIC

The Past is with us forever,
The Present no Power can change.
The Future is not in our vision —
A Scene for the gods to arrange.

Arrange it they will, to their liking,
Their whimsical humor well-known.
While We in our infinite Wisdom
Our Failures with Penance atone.

For Man has made God in his image,
He grows as we grow, good or bad.
But His Almighty fumbles and foibles
Drive the Forces of Nature quite mad.

—Alwyn Hallowes King

BOY AND HIS DOG

Boy and his dog are best, of friends
From boyhood, until manhood ends
Comforting each other, day and night
Inseparable all through life

The dog sits, holds his paws together
And slowly, silently bows his head
With the little boy, as he kneels
To pray, beside his trundle bed

Nightly at the end, of the prayer
With the sounding of "A Men"
Up jumps the boy, hops into bed
So does, his hairy friend

Boy gives his pal a friendly pat
Just before dropping off, to sleep
Whispers "Good Night, God Bless you"
Then drifts, into dreamland deep

Dog lovingly licks the boy's hand
Wags his tail and softly barks twice
As if to say, "God Bless you too
And a very pleasant Good Night"

—Monettia Phillips

FRIENDSHIP

It is a growing together of
people. The understanding of
personalities, and a united
transition of care, companionship,
mutual respect for each as a
whole person, and the sharing
of new ideas, as well as experiences,
which create harmony and friendship.

Growing together in wisdom
and knowledge, can be very uplifting
and inspirational, as well as
gratifying, creating many hours
of enjoyment, just being together,
and having mutual understanding
and admiration for each other.

Because to enjoy the qualities
in another person, you must first
appreciate them as a whole being,
allowing them to reach their own
specific goals, striving for perfection,
expectations and excellence, in
performance.

—Mrs. Joanne Mlodik

KITTY CATS

Kitty cats are friendly
Kitty cats are cuddly
Kitty cats are furry
Kitty cats are warm
Kitty cats are caring about you

—Nathaniel Skinner, age 10

THE CATS AND I

While I am away
   I feel you gently
     Rub against me
I hear your soft meow
   Singing in my heart
I hear you purring
Gently caressing my wounds
I feel you nuzzle me,
       with love.
I feel you curl up
    contently, near me
As you heal, my pain
   in my heart, mind, soul
We are far apart in distance
   But your loving ways
     Give me strength
       Yet, I cry
Because I miss you
I hope we can soon heal
    each others wounds.

—Sarah Haines

DOG, MAN'S BEST FRIEND

Please forgive me for the rug, and the mud on the sofa. And please forgive me for the torn up newspaper and the chewed up doll, it wasn't Suzy's favorite toy anyway.
And oh forgive me for your slippers. You can always use them to cover up the hole in your "brand new suit," besides that's all they're good for anymore.
And oh yeah, please forgive me for the broken plate. I broke that when I ate your steak. So please forgive me. After all dog "is" man's best friend.

—Shelly Ann Robbins

I got a new puppy —
  And to do things right,
I made him a bed to sleep in at night.
I got him toys so he could chew,
And all he does is chew on my shoe.
    He runs around the yard & chases the cat,
If he ever catches him, that will be that.
He runs thru the house with the speed of light
And of course sleeps with me at night.
    He eats what I eat, & he's doing good,
Sure likes it better than puppy food.
He's lots of work and sure a pest
While he sleeps I get some rest.
It won't be long till he grows up,
And be a good old dog not pesky pup.

—Wanda Shaw

POUND PUPPY

When he picked me out from all the rest, I thought, this is my lucky day. I had no way of knowing things would turn out quite this way.

He took me home and kept me — oh — a year or two, and then he threw me in the yard because I chewed a shoe.

I tried to say I'm sorry as I licked him on the hand, but he just turned and slammed the gate, I guess he didn't understand.

If only I could let him know I really meant no harm, but last night I overheard him saying something about a farm.

The next morning when he picked me up and put me in the car, I thought he had forgiven me — but we didn't ride too far.

All at once he stopped and pulled me by the hair, threw me out and off he drove, just left me standing there.

The next few days were very hard, filled with pain and fear, because everyone would kick at me whenever I came near.

I'm just lying by the roadside now in a bed of sand — oh — I wish my master would drive by so I could lick his hand.

I just want to tell him I could never find the farm, and that I'm truly sorry and I really meant no harm.

—Muriel Mosley

HANDS

What are hands? Hands are the tools of expression.
  The gentle touch of a loving mother
    Discipline from a caring father
      Hands can swing a bat or throw a ball.
        Lift you up from a painful fall.
          Hands are wrung in time of stress.
            Clenched in fists for a power test.
              To pledge allegiance to the U. S. A.
                Folded on the breast to sing or pray
                  To pray for forgiveness and God's perfect love.
                Hands are wonderful gifts from above.

—Ida E. Warner

OUR PROBLEM

The trees are getting smothered in our greatest work of all.
We must be proud, for we keep producing.
Will we still be proud when we start to smother ourselves?
The trend must be growing, for each generation it gets worse.
The rainforest is coming to an end.
Do we plan to reverse the process?
Or shall we leave it alone and die within.
Part of the "lost generation" wants to help.
But what's the use if we all aren't working as a group.
From factories to cigarette smoke,
If the problem is not conquered, we will all choke.
Sooner or later, if not helped, it will be floating to the ground.
And only then, it will be the end.

—Julie Belcher

PATIENTLY SHE WAITS

Alone she sits in her room/ The utter stillness/ A walker against the wall/ On the wall the pictures look on silently/ She stares out the window/ A bird feeding on the ground never knowing/ A smile comes on her face/ A reflection of the past/ The clock on the wall ticking/ Here time doesn't matter/ She reaches for something on the table/ Her mind changes/ She turns her head/ Dim eyes searching for the door/ Her hand still in the air/ Is someone knocking/ Her heart beats faster/ No one entered/ She lowered her hand/ How many days/ Does it matter/ Folding a small handkerchief/ All is the same/ The night the day/ It doesn't matter/ Her sad eyes close/ Half a sandwich lies beside her/ She drifts off/ Thinking maybe tomorrow/ Will my children come/ It gets so lonesome here/ Patiently she waits.

—Ed Davis

MY FIREHOUSE PRAYER

Help me Dear Lord, every day and night
To hear the cry for help and do what's right.
Give me the strength to help those in need
For this is the life I have chosen to lead.
Help me Oh Lord, to give it my all
And show me the way out, when my back's against a wall.
Give me the courage when the siren wails through the air
To answer the call and show someone still cares.
Help me Lord, to decide the right things to do
For with You by my side, I know I'll pull through.
Give me the wisdom I need to save lives
And fill me with the will I need to survive.
Help me Lord, to be able to admit when I'm wrong
And give me the courtesy to put things back where they belong.
Hear me Lord, for these are the words that I pray
In hopes this volunteer will live to answer calls yet another day!!

"AMEN"

—Mark Graver

Crimson bird of flight so fleet
Here, now gone, the autumn leaf

—Chalane J. Sheldon

RIPPLES IN THE WATER

The baby turtle swims in
the ripples of the water.
If I had the money
I would buy him from
the kid down the street
with a quarter.
But only the name of the
game could tame this creature
of pain. For thy who disturbs
him will pay the price even
if it is not very nice.

—Matt Wirth

POEMS

I love to write poems
About beautiful homes.

They are fun to write
While flying a kite

And are nice
While away from mice

They are sweet
When you don't cheat

They are great
When you stay up late

To put this in summary
is easy you see

You just have to say
Poems make my day

—Katie McBride, age 10

CALIFORNIA BURN

Until yesterday
it was against my will
to understand how fire
could bring a bitter chill!
The angry flame
from an arson's lite
turned our beauty black
and the darkness bright.
The once quiet, calm
on this oceanfront side
was engulfed in a fury
from the fire's swift ride.
The raging winds!
The fires roar!
It swallowed up our homes,
our dreams — no more!
But now that it's over
and we face this new day,
we thank God for the firefighters
and for added strength, we pray.

—Annette R. Czajkowski

THIS TEAR

As a tear rolls down my face
It's just a memory of you
A memory that makes me think
Of all the things we've been through

But this tear you see right now
Will never be seen again
My heart has finally found its time
To start its uneasy mend

This tear breaks into a million pieces
And washes you away
With all the good times
And turmoils of yesterday

As I walk out of your world
And you walk out of mine
This tear that you have just seen
Will be cried for the last time

—Tracy Reynolds

LOVE AND TRUST

Love is a feeling,
that comes from deep within your heart

Trust is what you're supposed to have,
every day you're apart

Giving your love to someone,
is not an easy thing to do

Because the fear is always there,
that they will hurt you

And then after love,
comes that word trust

'Cause in every relationship,
that's really a must

A couple falling in love,
will never go anywhere

If unconditional love and trust,
are not there

—Linda Houston

TRUE LOVE

All my life I've wondered
what it would be like to fall in love
You'd think it would make you happy
and it would be beautiful like a dove.

Now I see that's not so
it only makes you cry
So I bow my head down low
then look up towards the sky.

I don't ever want to fall in love again
it causes too much pain
I feel like I can't ever win
there's nothing there to gain.

Then one day true love comes along
and your life is no longer blue
You start to sing a different song
because he's the one that's true.

Now your life is different
the old is not the same
For now I see I've made my mistakes
I guess I'm the only one to blame.

—Rhonda R. Pepera

SWEETNESS

When I hear your voice or see your face,
it's not a matter of choice.
My heart beats a rapid pace.

It's nice, sweet and feels good
    and it's part of
and it should; it's just called
    being in love!

—TTG

WAKING TO LOVE

Waking to a sound of that faraway bird
was like love in the beginning stages
dawn was slow in arriving
stars still brilliant
and trees were still
no bird was calling now
not even small owls
that rattle through the night
tree to tree above the RV
the smell of smoke from two woodburning stoves
rotting leaves, damp ground
air very, very still
Earth waiting for dawn
coming day
expectation
patience
a strange stillness
stillness that was love
not the love of something
or someone . . . simply love
without sentiment
without feeling
complete in itself.

—Lois Barr

JEREMY

I never dreamed you'd come into my life,
it took me by surprise.
Looking at you I see a reflection of me,
with so much love in your eyes.

You're like a star that fell from the sky,
and set my heart aglow.
A sunset on a sandy beach,
a mountaintop covered with fresh fallen snow.

You're a gentle blowing breeze,
on a warm summer afternoon.
A romantic picnic in the park,
or an evening lying under the moon.

You're my prince charming from a fairy tale,
the pot of gold at the end of a rainbow.
A perfect lullaby, a beautiful, bright, red rose,
the most wonderful guy I know.

You're such a precious husband,
who was truly sent from above.
I will always fill your faithful, loving heart,
forever with my undying love.

*To know I'll share forever with my best
friend is more magical than any fairy
tale. I love you . . . endlessly.*

—Kristy L. Houle

EARLY MORNING

Daylight is close now after a long dark night,
The rustle of a thrush, in a bush, is the first sound to my ear.
Nature is awakening and anxious for the beautiful sunlight,
Then the chatter of a squirrel breaks the silence so clear,
He will gather some acorns and maybe a pine cone,
And sit on a limb of that large oak—morning is near.
There it is, the beautiful sunrise, and I'm not alone!
A Cardinal is singing in a laurel nearby,
Across the hollow one answers with her sweet call,
They will build a nest soon, because Spring is nigh,
In that birch over there, so straight and tall.
Yes, the world is alive, for morning is here,
Showing the glistening of dew on a lovely pink rose,
The best time of day, for now there is no fear.
  —James E. Spivey

WHEN . . . WHERE . . . WHY . . .

Gazing up into the endlessness of ordered cosmos
At the constellations of shimmering stars above
From this galaxy where we abide, on Earth — Shan
A billion such galaxies within range of Earth
The enormity of God's universe seems inconceivable . . .
How many drops of water must it take to form an ocean?
Each alike but a miniscule part of the whole body of water.
Liken each of us to small flickers of lighted soul
Yet part of the whole of God and Universal Creation,
By virtue of undying soul imparted by Creator.
Is each brightest star in each galaxy sun to other systems?
Will we abide, sometime, in other galaxies on our journey?
When will we be reunited with pure essence of Creator?
On this one small journey through endless time and Universe
What were the circumstances that brought this individual life?
How far have we come on our journey of evolvement?
Why do we find ourselves in present circumstances?
Where and how will all be consummated?
So many unanswered questions, searching, longing for reunion with Creator
Yet all eternity to come to realization of God's WORD!
  —Doris Eberhardt

PAINTED DESERTS

Two lost and forgotten souls
Wandering in a garden with its sweet blooms bloomin' all around them
And they stop . . . but for a moment

Stare into this loneliness
Stare into all forgottenness
Just a few steps behind
My love for you . . . is not blind

In one hour of fatal kisses
Once in dew dropped petals
We missed our hearts and we passed each other in a pocket of time
We didn't know we would part as one

But now as I look back
Into my crystal magic stick
Back into my dreams of old
Looking for the one to hold

But all that my eyes will let me see
Is you . . .
And,
Me . . .
Floating in the gardens.
  —Sharon R. Rouse

HAUNTED WALLS

As if in prison with bars and stalls
in my room of haunted walls
haunted, haunted, haunted walls.

no words of wisdom
no freedom is gained
from a world that's lost
with bars in chains

but if a door was opened
and the chains did fall
would my ghost be lifted
from these haunted walls
haunted, haunted, haunted walls.

—Dorothy C. Taylor

MADMAN AND ASSORTED PLAYERS

I see the earth falling,
I hear the mirror calling.
   The children dance.

No one knows I'm right,
there is no hope in sight.
   The demons prance.

Life is very long,
my sentence here is wrong.
   The keys are turned.

The people change their faces,
come from different places.
   Secrets are burned.

Thru windows I see life,
inside is deadly strife.
   The jokers play.

Life has lost its reasons,
the years pass without seasons.
   The masters stay.

—Richard Quinney

MY "ADVENTURE SOME" SPIRIT

   There is, in my soul, something
strangely alive
   Like a wanton, unscrupulous
rover;
   That says when the first days
of Autumn arrive,
   "Tramp of the road, move over!"
   And my feet start to go down
a dim, narrow path,
   That leads over high place and
hollow;
   And they stray, though my head
keeps commanding them "Stay,"
   So what can my heart do
but follow?
   Yet I never could be like a
regular tramp
   Who forever is destined to roam;
   For the sprite that said "Go"
from the depths of my soul,
   At twilight, would turn me
back home!

—Mary Durham

SINGLENESS

I am a woman whose arms are barren,
And whose life is empty.
For I am not a mother, nor a wife.
I hear no little footsteps or feel tiny arms hug
   my neck.
No cries of 'Mommy' break through the silence of
   my nights.
I am barren, but not by choice.
Life has not seen fit to grant me a husband,
Nor does the State allow me to adopt.
So I remain barren.
My arms lay useless at my sides,
As my eyes watch others who carelessly play at
   motherhood,
While my arms remain barren.

—Rebecca Sue Flowers

MY BROTHER, THE DRUNK

In the twilight of my years
I longed for a measure of peace.
To be free from all pain and tears
And I wanted to take my ease.

He came to my household to stay.
And at first I was filled with hope.
"You'll regret it," I heard them all say.
"There's no way with him you can cope."

"Put him out on the street," they all said.
"Get them off the street," others say
When you love them, your heart rules your head,
And for me there's no other way.

God never said life was all flowers,
Or troubles would not come our way.
He promised to be near us these hours,
And lead us to a much brighter day.

He can take a life that's been wasted
NO life is beyond repair.
And turn it to joys never tasted
So how can I say I despair?

—Ann Boyles

THE BLACK MAN'S STRUGGLE

Hi, my name is Black Man, at least I think so
I live in the times where poor is all I know.
Don't have a home that I can say is mine
Couldn't have two children, instead I had nine.

Work hard every day, sun up till sun down
Come home tired, and wearing a big frown.
No time for my children not even for my wife
Yes, my name is Black Man and this is my life.

To be sad is poor, to be poor is sad
But being poor, sad and black is all that I've had.
Black Man I was born, Black Man I will die
Shut off to myself sometimes just to scream and cry.

Up to my neck in debts, can't pay my bills
No food to eat, in this cold house I live.
Sometimes I wonder, Is happiness in my view
This old Black Man is doing all he can do.

My name is Black Man, I told you once before
I am not rich, I'm down right poor.
My dreams are cloudy, I can't see my way
To make ends meet, I live from day to day.

—Shirley Outland Blount

SOMEONE'S MOTHER

"I'm not his Mother," she yelled at me.
"He is my son, but I'm not his Mother."
I pondered long this reaction to a simple introduction,
"Laura Blank, this is Mrs. Paine, Dr. Paine's Mother."
I thought it would be a way to start a conversation.
Shouldn't she be proud of her son?
Was she jealous of her son's achievements?
Isn't it an accomplishment to raise a fine family?
A smart, modern writer is she.
But she did raise five gifted children.
Shouldn't she be proud of that too?
Does she feel she was in household prison half her life?
They have homes of their own now: Now she is free.
She wants to be known for her art alone.
In this modern world she can have both;
World of artist and gifted Mother, too.
Why not just glow with pride when introduced
    as someone's Mother?

—Margaret Ethelyn Hunter

DAYS WHEN MAMA LET US SEW

I recall the days in West Virginia
When we were poor but no one seemed to know.
Joy abounds throughout the miners' houses
Specially on the days that Mama let us sew.

Colors of the rainbow all around us
Children with their faces all aglow.
Patches of color surround us.
Wish I could tell my Mom I loved it so.

To learn the colors was so easy
Our stories about each scrap were told over
With every stitch we learned to sew

All the tiny pieces had their story told with love each
    time we saw them there
Quilts and pillows were covered with our joys and sorrows.
Patience — love — endurance — faith — we found there
Soon we scattered to the wind ne'er to forget.
When Mama let us sew!

—Blanche LeMoine

REQUIEM
For A Loving Daughter

You came a little while, and then you left.
Beneath my frozen smile, I was bereft.
My days with you slipped by so fast,
Somehow, I knew, the die was cast!

Somehow, I knew, deep in my heart,
This time, we'd be forever, far apart!
Somehow, I sensed, our close ties would sever,
That you were going far, far, from me forever.

Oh Daughter, of my love, I prayed that you could stay!
Tears were falling, as I watched you turn, and walk away.
You were a woman grown, and this I knew,
All that I could do was hope and pray for you.

Sometimes, there's just no way that we mortals can cope
In spite of all our prayers and all our hope!
We're helpless to fight Fate's cruel decrees,
No matter how hard we try, or inspite of all of our pleas.

I watched 'til your plane flew far out of sight
Then turned away to walk into the night
There was a sob in the wind, and tears in the rain,
Loneliness, forever, deep in my heart, dull, aching pain.

—Ruth S. Ozanich

A MOTHER'S HEART

    Mother's love is a wonderful thing.
It makes a baby coo and sing.
    It makes a grown man cry a lot,
because he knows he breaks her heart.
    It makes a girl smile a lot,
because she's forever in her mother's heart.
    My Mother loved an awful lot!

—Robert J. Wheeler

TO MY LATE FATHER

    Dad, when you gave me life
you gave me watercolors.
    Through your short but lasting
influence.
    I've found a brush and
learned how to use them
    Nothing else can be said . . .
Because . . .
    No matter how you paint it . . .
    Thank you just isn't enough . . . .

    "I LOVE YOU DAD"

        Your Loving Daughter,

—Catherine A. Bernard

DADDY'S GONE

Forever warm . . .
In life . . . so cold.
Eternal youth . . .
Appears . . . old.
No visits now . . . reflections none
Or soft, sweet, loving thoughts
Future . . . once . . . oh yes!
Eternity is bought . . .
Life was sold, yet . . . less.
So quiet, peaceful, . . . (looks alone!)
But memories of life . . . forever gone.

*To my father, Billy Ray Whitworth.
May he receive in Heaven all the
rewards that escaped him in life.*

—Michael S. Whitworth I

A TRIBUTE TO MOM & DAD

    I have learned many things from
you, growth and knowledge, ways to
protect and defend, understanding pain
and sorrow, but above all, learning
to live in a world of difficulties, being
a part of reality, and transforming it
into challenges, dedicating oneself
to understanding the problems of
the world, and trying to make a
difference, while listening, being
patient, kind, understanding, having
mutual respect for each other, and
learning to swallow pride, in
some situations, in order to
become a loving peaceful individual,
and interacting in various ways,
in order to make the world a
better place, living in peace,
harmony, and God's love.

—Mrs. Joanne Mlodik

DUSK

The sun begins to set. The day is almost over,
Yet, the true majesty has just begun.
The sky fills with kaleidoscopic splendor,
Orange silk wrapped in ribbons of blue.
White puffs of clouds dance in playful competition,
But the sun will not submit.
It cuts through with rays of glory
Like arms reaching to God.
Everything that has ever existed, everything that ever will exist,
Lies before me.

It is so simple. It is a paradox.
I am diminished. I am revived.
It comforts. It demands my attention.
I feel warmth. I feel a chill.
I see life. I fear death.
It is gone.

—Walter F. Dobrzycki

ROY G BIV

I came upon a bullfrog one day
Sitting so majestically and serene.
He ruled over a world of color
A royal kaleidoscope so it did seem.

Pools of water of *cobalt, azure* and *lapis lazuli*
Amid banks of *russet, sorrel* and at dusk almost *coppery.*

A bright warm sun illuminated the region
With rays of *scarlet, crimson, cardinal* and *vermilion.*
A gamut of flowers bursting in playful rivalry
Ruby, majenta, saffron and *lilac* with petals of irridescent *ivory.*

I stood in awe amidst this chromatic kingdom
Desiring to question the ruler of this radiant spectrum.
"The color of your robe which you display so regally,
Is it *lime* or *olive* or *emerald* or of what *verdancy?*"

The bullfrog turned and bellowed a tumultuous croak
While remaining so majestic and serene.
"What color am I that rules this land?
My friend I am simply **green.**"

—Walter F. Dobrzycki

PERSONAL

Byron, Verlaine, Frost — who were they —
perhaps I know, but if not — so what?
Is there a chance their inspirations were mine?

That blue crystal in a beaker — was it their joy?
a faulty ab initio program — their depression?
snowy winds from Lolo Pass — their anxiety?

For me, Marysia's waving hand
her nose flattened on the schoolbus window
are some of the inspirations

keeping away those snowy winds that blow
disturbing blue crystals onto blank sheets
of my unfulfilled poetry intentions

her smile is my reassurance against false thoughts
which do not precipitate in joyful rhythms
and in words able to play the lyre on the plains of my days.

Byron, Verlaine, Frost — who were they —
deprived of blue crystals, faulty programs,
winds from Lolo Pass and Marysia's flattened nose?
Perhaps I know but if not — so what?

—Leszek Czuchajowski

RAINBOW COLORS

Yellow, blue, purple, red
Rainbow colors in my head
Green, pink, black and brown
Colors are all over town
I walk and look, I look and walk
I don't have time to stop and talk.

—Sabrina Monteith

THE SHADOWS

I saw the shadows go by,
I thought I saw them cry.
It was a dream,
So it seemed.
I wish I knew why I saw them cry,
But I think I will see them go by
  tonight.

—Jenny Roush, age 12

TITHE OF LIFE

As you start life's road together
And you cross the narrow sands
There's a king who sits in Heaven
Just to guide you through the land

If you put your trust in Him
He will lead you by the hand
Just remember that He's waiting
And He is a mighty man.

There'll be sorrow and sunshine
There'll be laughter and tears
There'll be promises broken
As you travel through the years

But put your trust in Jesus
He will be there at your side
And when the clouds then do gather
You will have a place to hide.
  (Safe in the arms of Jesus)

*Dedicated to all our children and
our families and to all people.*

—Donald E. Styck

MY MOTHER'S GARDEN

When I stand in the garden
the garden my mother planted,
where the roses and the dahlias
bloom, I'm enchanted.

I stand in awe and reverence
and study them intently,
as with the summer breeze
they nod, so gently.

Each one of them a beauty
none prettier than the other,
each one a symbol of purity
just like my mother.

I close my eyes and bow my head
and wonder in my mind,
why they must leave, in winter,
just memories behind.

But I thank the God in Heaven,
in the heavens above,
that He gave me flowers, and
a mother to love.

—Gerald King

FINDING OUT

Slip into that silent sleep.
Where no one can be disturbed
Letting all your thoughts slip away.
Like that sad, sad game.
Open your mind and you will know
All the meanings of Life.
For that is all we want to know!
The opening is a physical thing,
Not done by the mind,
But instead, to the mind.
Then, ALL your problems will be gone.

—Chris Batman

STARS AT MIDNIGHT

There are many stars at midnight,
I watch them now and then.
But really not as often,
As I did when I was ten.
A million miles from nowhere,
I see them shining there.
I sometimes stop and wonder,
Why I stand and stare.
Their bright lights always sparkling,
They almost seem aglow.
I wonder where they came from?
But I guess I'll never know.
And then at morning's dawning,
They seem to fade away.
They've shone so nice and brightly,
But now the sun must have its day.

—Leander Wegdahl

GARDEN OF IGNORANCE

There is a little hole in my door,
that allows me to peek through.
It gives me a very vague picture,
of a sad and lonely you.

I ask why you are this way,
but you cannot hear me speak.
And knowing you are so burdened,
I feel cold and incomplete.

It hurts to be on my side,
and have you on the other.
Why won't you allow me to help?
for I feel you are like my brother.

I realize we are different,
in reality; who wants to be the same?
We grow in a garden of ignorance,
where we both take the blame.

Looking through the hole,
I discover you walking away.
Hoping we can live in friendship,
somewhere, somehow, someday.

Dedicated to God, my parents, my family, and my friends. Also for anyone who understands the truth, sorrow, and injustice this poem represents. It is sad to realize that though we are aware of these social barriers, we still allow them to exist.

—Dawnmarie Matteson

A SHATTERED DREAM

For a while now we've been going together
With the dream that we'd last forever,
But today my worst dream came true
For the rest of my life I had lost you.
I was a fool to think you loved me.
The tears I now shed for you can fill up a sea;
Because of the pain you caused this lonely sad girl,
The world around her became a whirl
Confusion in my mind is present;
A stake through my heart was put in by a wondrous
    peasant
How could I have had a dream at the start,
When at the end, all that awaited me was a broken
    heart.

—Lili Garcia

TODAY'S MINE

This is a diamond day cut to stay
long like a gem on a ring—a solitaire
given in engagement, placed where
a wedding band will go. Such is today!

Look at its rose cut hours as you would
the facets of a diamond—minute triangles
reflecting the light of love—refracting angles
of impurity into one brilliant second of good.

Yes, this day is a perfect jewel,
flawless—cut, polished, pure—
sparkling as it's turned—adamantine and sure
like everyday words set in love's vow or rule.

Such rare days are hidden deep in a week's hours
in an ordinary month in an ordinary year and shine
like precious minerals in an underground mine.

Only when one is found to be a gem—a sign
set in the sun's circle for this present—do I keep
it as I do the anniversary that marks today as ours.

—Sylvia Cooper

MY TREASURE

In this life there is much to gain
Some seek riches others fame
For me I'll take a simple life
A comfortable home, a loving wife

All of these one must earn
Take your time, wait your turn
Be sure you always do your best
Pause now and then to rest

I found a friend, partner and loving wife
We will travel down the road of life
True to and honest all the way
Whether at work or play

Both working it is true
For the things we want to do
I look around but I can't see
Any one richer than me

My greatest treasure is you, Darlene
My sweetheart, my wife, my queen
My Christmas wish is: together we will always be
Throughout eternity

—W. Carl Holland

I did not watch the clock as it went from 10:30 to 11:30,
I did not watch its formations,
I did not watch as the secondhand went to and fro,
I did not watch because I was not there,
My sadness did not see the clock's formations,
I know not why the reason,
of such foolishness—
My sorrow did not listen to the tick-tock of the clock,
My dreamland did not see my fate,
The clock tried to show me the future,
but my eyes did not see the clock's formations.

—Angela Cronch

MONARCH BUTTERFLY

A Monarch Butterfly came to my garden today,
To gather food wherever he may.
On a bright red flower he made a short stay.
His orange and black colors added beauty to my day.
Don't go away I wanted to say.
But he had to be on his way.
He had no time to play.
For before the cold weather holds sway,
He must fly far, far away.
While in the ground through the winter the flowers will lay,
Ready to come forth and bloom again when it is May.
Then come back again pretty Monarch Butterfly without delay.

—Janet Temperly

DARKNESS

Here I am
Going along at my own pace.
Suddenly plunged into darkness
Years spent waking in the dark.
Totally oblivious to any daylight
Living and breathing in my own little world
It takes years for me to leave part of the darkness behind me
I am still in my own little world.
But I grow tired
I need to get out
I need to come alive again
As I walk out the door, I look behind with saddened eyes
Physically taking some of you with me
As I start over again, I find you there waiting
Ready to start again.

—Kathy Murphy

A SONNET TO ALL SEASONS

Plants grow, snow melts, buds burst, sky clears, bees hum.
Grass sprouts, kids shout, fish jump, eggs hatch, sweet spring.
Suns hot, shade cools, ground dries, long light, alls mum.
Falls next, leaves turn, airs bright, cool nights, sounds ring.

Wind blows, leaves fly, bark falls, trees bend, colds here.
Clouds burst, rain falls, streams run, seas churn, gulls swarm.
Boats rock, waters splash, sand shifts, waves break, brings fear.
Tides roll, rocks grind, bells toll, light fades, fires warm.

Childs born, child grows, youth comes, youth goes, age waits.
Schools in, schools out, find work, love comes, find mate.
Childs born, child grows, youth comes, youth goes, age waits.
Lifes tears, lifes trials, lifes hugs, lifes smiles, lifes fate.

Year in, year out, thru good, thru bad, life wades.
time flies, age sighs, loves gone, live on, life fades.

—Lila Peeters

SOUNDS OF DROWNING

In my eyes you can see it.
The desperation, the anger, the confusion.
Confusion is what I am made of.
I hate being alone yet there is no love for anyone here.
My heart only knows the silence it has heard for so long.
My heart weeps its hot, silent tears.
My tears are pooling at my feet.
Soon . . . the sounds of drowning.

—Dawn Secor

THE NIGHT . . .

The Night—
   So dark, yet peaceful,
   Holds no fear for me.

The Day—
   So bright and clean,
   How can it frighten me?

Around my Friends—
   So alone and by myself.
   When does this loneliness end?

My God—
   So strong and true,
   Where is the peace You send?

My feelings—
   So confused and in conflict,
   My world seems upside down.

My life—
   So broken and shattered,
   God catch me before I drown!

—Kaci Diane Carlisle

MIDDLE OF THE NIGHT

You took the left road, I took the right. I had a ring on my left hand, you had nothing on the right. But I've loved you still through all the fights. I'll love you all of my life. In the cold of the night, I can think of you and heat up my life.

   Like a rose in the early morning sun light. The wild flower that blooms in the spring.

   Like the great Mississippi running through our state.

   You went to the left, I went to the right. But somewhere we'll meet back in the middle of the night.

   Like the double rainbow that shines over my bridge, in the rainy day light.

   Like the full moon shining off of the green Mississippi water, in the dark of the night.

   We'll meet back in the middle of the night.

—Sharon LeSieur

LONELINESS

When no one ever talks to you,
   Or notices you are there.
You develop a certain feeling
   of despair.
You wish you had the nerve,
To tell them how you feel.
Yet somehow, though you try,
The words just don't appear.
All that you can do,
Is listen, hope, wish, and pray.
That someone will look,
And finally speak your way.

—Elisabeth Kane

MAKE THE BEST

Life's not fair, as you know.
You pick up pieces as you go.
You make the best of what you've got.
The littlest thing means a lot.
You take a bud and make it a flower.
You take a drop and make it a shower.
As you walk along life's lane,
   you pick up pleasure as well as pain.
You try your hardest and do your best
to try to keep up with the rest.
A friendly smile does no danger.
It makes a friend out of a stranger.
If you try hard, you'll always win.
For you get out what you put in.

Dedicated to my son and my niece, who have yet to experience life. May they find the good in it as well as the bad.

—RIO

Crimson lips
And hearts of gold.
What is foreseen
Cannot be told.
Innocence and purity
Are the empowerment
   of naiveté
In this estranged world:
The golden age of junk.
Drunken joys.
In Bacchus we trust—
God of wine and
Divine giver of ecstasy.
Take care: sugar and strychnine
Rushing forward urging persistence
To the core of our existence.
Born to satisfy and gratify our senses.
Sucked in—
Into this so estranged world.
Trapped by the horrors of reality
   that surround.
Look deep into your soul—
Your future will soon unfold,
And you shall see
Crimson lips
And hearts of gold.

—Elizabeth

FRIENDSHIP

There was a time when I thought I was alone
   Facing the world all alone
Then you found me one day
   and all my fears faded away
My dreams and hopes have come true
   and all to the thanks of you

—Cassie Robinett

MOVING DAY

Up at dawn, hair's a mess,
   can't focus on what to do next.
Breakfast is over, and Kitchen's clean,
Utensils packed, and Fridge is recleaned.

Dining room is easy, it only needs to be swept,
Bathroom is easier, tub only needed to be scrubbed.
Contents of dresser drawers are thrown into boxes,
while clothes in closets are thrown into green bags.
Beds are disassembled, and Mattresses thrown away,
Screws, Nuts, and Bolts are packed away with the soap.

Moving men are early, and I'm not ready yet,
They agree to come back in an hour, but two have gone by.
Truck is loaded, keys are left with neighbors,
Good-byes are said, and tears are shed.

Now comes the hard part of unloading the truck,
For the distance traveled has driven everyone nuts.
Fees are paid, men have left, and clutter in Livingroom
has to be organized and unpacked.
Food is ordered, and everyone rests,
For my hair's still a mess, and so is everyone else.

—Sharon Toni Myrick

FOND MEMORIES

As my mind wonders back to my childhood days,
I think of the old farm where we were raised.
Times were hard, but we didn't seem to care,
We always had food, clothes, and shoes to wear.
Life back then is just a dream,
No fear of drugs or anything.
No store bought toys, we had back then,
We played in the yard with our neighbor friends.
We played ball, jump rope, and red rover,
Kick the can, hide and seek, and Annie over.
We played these games to name a few,
Life was full of things to do.
We popped corn on the open fire,
And roasted peanuts in the hot ashes there.
Out in the corner, by the old rail fence,
Where I spent many happy hours,
That's where I built my playhouse,
And planted little wild flowers.
I made mud pies to my heart's content,
And set them out to dry.
A few days later I'd tear them up and make a new supply.
No store bought toys could ever erase
Those fond memories of yesterday.
If I had but one wish, that would come true,
I'd go back to the old farm house with Mom and Dad,
And sit by the old fireside,
But only to reminisce for just a little while.

—Rosie B. Sneed

HALF OF A SONNET

You! Taste the air that blows into my room.
Taste it now, sweet and cool, before our doom.
Close your lids, feel it brush your burning skin.
Let it toss your hair as you forget your sin.
That air, that breeze, it comes from the dark night
Where curiosity is good and right.
Can you hold that force which plays with your heart?
What is it? Is it a white Dove or a Dart?

—Becky Ward

He holds her hand, her shaking hand, with courage he has
   not to give he squeezes gently reminding her that
   this is how they live.
Trembling eyes beneath the skies, she sees the darkness of
   a troubled cloud mixing with his eyes of blue as they
   stumble to the ground.
She moves against his body as his mouth engulfs her own,
   the power in his being matching none she's ever known.
Above, the cold wind stirs and blows the dead autumn
   leaves away, she listens to him breathing hard,
   knowing she's died that very day.
The tears and the painful cries can't stop the storm
   that's come . . . and as darkness veils the sky above,
   her whole world comes undone.

—Carol O'Lea Kirkman

BOOKSHELF

We spoke through the bookshelf.
   Indisposed and busily free
we talked and laughed and forgot our work.
Paradoxically wanting/not wanting to complete our tasks
and desirously wanting to continue speaking.
Possessing long brown hair (with a touch of gray)
and a pleasantly refreshing smile of energetic destruction.
Razing my self-created walls of protection
from the painful caresses of ecstatic joy.
Walking hand-in-hand, in my racing mind of obsessing thoughts
precluding hurt and including Susan.
Until next Wednesday,
through the shelf of books and hopes.

—Donald L. West, Jr.

OF YOU WHO LIES IN UNBORN SLUMBER

Of you who lies in unborn slumber,
   I, often, find myself in wonder
Of the way you look and feel and smell and taste.
O how long I have waited to meet you!
Longer even then the time since I have known the one who is
   your present home.
Already I love you—even though we have yet to share
   a single touch.

Will you yearn for me as I you?
Will you fulfill all that I dream for you?

Though the time that spans our meeting keeps us distant,
It serves for me to prepare and you to grow
(Or rather, you to prepare and me to grow).
For in these times when of you I wonder—
I often wonder of me and hope that, upon our meeting,
You shall travel your journey called Life
Holding pleasant thoughts of the one
   who has started you on your way.

To the memory of Ryan Andrew Lenseigne, our little angel

—Kert B. Lenseigne

The departure of my souls,
   because of the hollow despair,
My thoughts, I dream.
nothing is there!
My heart aches, because I drift,
of thoughts I wish to behold,
I still hold them,
But when the close,
I follow through my thoughts,
you will see!
I hold truth,
now buried beneath rocks and stones,
never to be heard,
because I hold the secrets,
I hold the truth!
Come visit me,
I will speak.
For my love,
sees your immortality to come!
I love you.

—Angela Cronch

RAVEN HEADED MISTRESS

Oh, my Raven Headed Mistress
   Your lips like amethyst
But more precious
      Than any jewel
Such jewels I wish
To embrace with my own

Like a Raven you fly
High up in the sky
Being on top of the world
With such powerful flight
Oh, my Raven Headed Mistress
Swoop down to me
      And take me high
      Up in the sky
      Right by your side
And I'll fly you higher
Than you've ever
      Flown solo

—Joey C. Brown

WHITE GLOVES

The only one on campus
   with white gloves
you walk around
in hot days
rainy days
rushed days
in days joyous or sad
in days tired or sentimental
you flash your hands in white gloves

among thousands of girls
primped and fragrant
all different
as the colors of drops
in a sparkling fountain

only you
in white gloves
of your untamed fantasy
extravagant soul
and subtle feelings.

—Leszek Czuchajowski

THE JOURNEY

How can you be fading
When the sun still shines so bright
How can you be leaving us
After such a valiant fight

I am not ready to say good-bye
Or willing to let you leave
My heart for you is breaking
And I've only begun to grieve

But I know you're on a journey
That you must walk alone
As much as I want to be with you
On the way to your heavenly home

Your battle is finally over
For you there is no pain
What we consider our greatest loss
Is now God's cherished gain

—Susan M. Roach

MAN TO MAN

Rows of crosses everywhere,
each in chilly night does stare,
It's so silly lost in vain;
those at home possessed no pain.

Maybe in old Flanders Field,
or some, long; lost desert tomb
Possibly in an unmarked grave;
I cry, Oh God, destruction save.

Still a voice, so silent, whispers
— as tho in man to man;
so far beneath — too soon forgot,
— torn from unblemished sod.

Maimed and crippled, minds no rest;
haunting dreams, of years at best;
Wealth in purchase; loss to gain
May all who went "Arise again."

—Clyde W. Jontz

NOW YOU MAY WEEP

Now you may weep, Jacqueline,
now you may weep.
Your bravery's a legend
    the nation will keep
close and beloved
    in all years to come—
poignant and proud
    as the low funeral drum—
majestic as the draped flag
    on the slow-drawn caisson.

The days of your November
    ordeal were four—
courage ennobled the
    anguish you bore—
eyes wide and tearless,
    queenly head high,
children beside you,
    death passing by.
Joy will return one day
    solemn and deep,
but now you may weep, Jacqueline,
    now you may weep.
November 1963

—Anne K. Behrens

VAMPIRE OF THE (SOUL) MIND

This mysterious and terrible
                Disease has come.
It has landed on our doorstep
                like a softly shrouded Angel
Of Death who is not wearing black,
He's wearing a purple cloak because you are not yet dead.
You walk with the Monkey of Hell on your shoulder.

This Vampire of the Mind, did He leave your soul behind?

You are a life junkie, you want to go on each day
But He takes His time toying with your mind
He sucks our souls dry as we watch you try
No doctor understands the pain of
Living Death
Voodoo Zombie
Which doctor?
Witch Doctor.

Dedicated to my father, a modern victim of Alzheimers'

—Christine Zimmermann

GETTING AWAY WITH MURDER

We drove down the road late one night,
And saw a car without its lights.
The man at the wheel had been at the bottle,
It caused him to lay his foot on the throttle.
In a matter of seconds, my friend's life was snuffed out,
He was guilty of murder without a doubt.

That night he was arrested and put in jail,
But come the next morning, his friends posted bail.
My friend was dead; she'll be sorely missed,
And all he got was a slap on the wrist.
Three months later, he went to trial,
He greeted me there with a wink and a smile.
Six months in jail on work-release was the sentence,
But I don't think that was much of a penance.

In jail he sits, awaiting the day,
When he can have a few drinks, and drive away.
But me, I grieve for the friend that I lost,
And laws that don't work, in spite of the cost.

—Jennifer Unterwegner

I HEAR VOICES CALLING ME BACK

I hear voices calling me away from the dark
My path has reached a shattered mark
Goodbyes that I'm not ready for filter through my mind
Yesterday's friendships are hard to find
I hear voices calling me back to earth
Trying to convince me I have some worth
All I really want to do is soar in the sky
I want to run away in a fond goodbye
I hear voices calling me to live
Commanding me to take what they give
Anger floats within me for life's crystal link
We watch the wondrous sun sink
I hear voices calling me to stay
Unheralded choices are swept away
Our souls are encased in time
Friends dissipate life's crime
I hear voices calling me away from the dark
They want me to accept the flight of the lark
Rainbows slither through my mind
Yesterday's friendships seem to bind

—Thelma Tasimowicz

TIME

Hush, hush sweet child, the time is now, to be mild.
The woman inside wants to be heard; now not another angry word.
Time now to claim and tame,
Time now to say we're not the same.
Contentment not resentment; Joyous strains and happy refrains
These are the gifts to reclaim.
    —Mary McDermott O.S.U.

DEMENTIA

LOOKING into the river as YOU SHIELD yourSElF while under DEMENTIA
the wire THAT IS wrapped around YOUR CRAZED MIND
heat that is PENETRATING the shallow chasm between the VALLEY that
    YOU call your heart or SOUL
the SAVIOR who comes to BLESS or WAS IT HEAL?
he FOUND your SINS and he WEPT onto the rocks beneath his blistered
    FEET
TIMELESS tears to be shed for YOUR HATRED
havoc to BE replaced for what was THE CROSS you are TIED to
the field of DEAD roses and the sea of LIVE RATS
YOU wallow with the FEAR YOU CREATED and threw OUT to be eaten RAW
crawling in AND OUT of the fortress that IS your HOME
serenity AND LIFE are passing by
YOU feel the MADNESS and IT creeps so SLOW
shot down by a stake to be MET BY RAZORS
creatures pull AT your hair BUT HE stands and he LAUGHS
you laugh LOUDER for YOU cannot hold it
SO by letting GO it is better
iron and STEEL
PLASTIC hearts broken and TORN
SHATTERING at YOUR sides
LOUDER than bombs and softer than SLEEP . . . .
    —Brandie G. Chaconas

IF YOU MUST KNOW

I am what I am and what I am I am, if you must know

I'm sometimes happy sometimes sad, sometimes mad, and sometimes bad,
if you must know that's what I am

I write songs then sing along sometimes short sometimes long,
altogether a song in a song

Some of love and some of hate, I sang for peace but much too late

For who am I is the question asked, for me to answer is quite a task

I'm strange and different one might say, for the way I act and the
things I say

But in this day and age isn't that the way to play

I listen to Rock 'n' Roll yes the music people say "Takes your
Soul," for only an opinion can be so bold

I'm also a Christian and proud to be, so what I am God made me to be

"To be or not to be" a man once said, so simple yet true of life
it's been said

For I "live to be," if not I'd be dead, it's as simple as that for
what you have asked

So what you've read is what I am though good or bad this paper
stands

For the assignment you've given this paper should do, yet for me
only an introduction to this life that I choose
    —Franz Lucas

LOVE

Love, is a gift from God,
Love, is given to everyone,
Love, it will always be
Love, it's from you to me,

Love, is the smile on your face.
Love, is Mary full of grace.
Love, begins with a child's birth.
Love, transcends beyond the Earth.

—Joshua C Mull

IN MY DREAMS OF YOU

I watch her face through the crowd,
But my heart is fixed on him.
I watch her as she clings to his arm,
And I vow to separate them.
As I watch them hand in hand,
Walking side by side.
I see her grant him one last kiss,
Before she disappears into the night.
I stand alone in silence,
As he whispers a soft goodbye.
The crowd has cleared to only us,
When he looks into my eyes.
I wait in anxious wonder,
In the midst of only two.
A single tear rolls down his cheek,
As he whispers "I love you."
I have not to ask the question,
Because his eyes tell me the rest.
I know our love was meant to be,
For I am truly blessed.

—Tamra Musko

"THANKS" TO LITTLE SISTER

I met her in the driveway.
There was shyness in her eyes.
I walked right up and said, "Hello."
Softly she said, "Hi."

I thought of her all week-end,
too frightened to dial the phone.
Then Sis said, "Go and call her,
or spend the rest of life, alone!"

I made the call and we made plans,
for dinner and a show.
We joked and laughed and had much fun,
'til it was time for me to go.

We saw each other four more times.
A friendship slowly grew.
Then I had to leave and say, "Good-by,"
as my heart broke right in two.

I told her I would write her.
She didn't seem to mind.
She didn't know I fell in love,
and my heart had gone half blind.

I'm so happy that I've found her.
And much to my surprise,
This living picture of heaven,
has blond hair and blue-eyes.

*Dedicated to my beautiful wife, Tania.
Just when I thought all was lost,
God and my kid sister,
Brought you into my life!*

—Nicholas C. Consolino

FRACTURED HEART

Understanding everything; yet explaining nothing at all. Telling no one, carrying the weight of the haul.

This fractured heart can trust no one. Caught in a dream all alone. While in an ocean full of suffering and burning, reaching out to those who listen, love is still yearning.

Trapped in a cage searching for help which no one will give. Learning of nonexistent happiness, wishing once again to live.

—Valerie Sprague, age 15

THROUGH THE YEARS

Through the years we've known love and passion, conflict and pain.
We've shared our thoughts, faults, cares,
and dreams. We've worked hard, fought hard and
loved deeply, we've seen our dreams unfold.
We've grown in our relationship, to where we
know when each other hurts, or is troubled.
We've become one in many ways.
We are as an uncut diamond that has lost its rough
edges, and shimmers and shines, its brilliance
will go on forever, as we polish and care for it
through time.

—Wendy Sundstrom

THAT SPECIAL SOMEONE

When that special someone comes along,
Every day becomes a joyous song.
Nothing after is ever the same,
Call it love, call it fascination, call it by any name.

Each day's sky is a little bluer,
No one else's heart can ever be truer.
To the beautiful rainbow there seems no end,
As we each other's lives do blend.

So many things that before did bother,
Now are easy when shared with each other.
Every day shows us a new facet in our love,
And we realize our marriage was made up above.

—Maria E. Herbert

LOVING

My love is true and deep within my heart.
Every day it grows stronger for both of us.
Living life to the fullest is what we need.
In times like today, love is what matters.
Sometimes words can't express just how you feel.
Staying together seems harder, but fuller.
It is love only that keeps two people together.
Always love and trust the person you are with.

Memories are what make us stay together, always.
Everybody must look into their own hearts.
Real people can see that love holds true.
Even strangers see that we were meant for each other.
Don't let anyone try and run your life for you.
It's only love that holds two people bound.
Today life is what we make it, not what others say.
Happiness is loving the person you've chosen for life.

—Francis E. Meredith

AT REST

As I rest upon my laurels,
There is not the least inclination,
To stir beyond the moment.
Stars may appear to skid across the sky,
Am I to be moved?   No!   And why?
There is no incident needed to exact from me
a movement . . . beyond the moment,
As I rest upon my laurels.

—J. J. Pepe

READING THE BACKBONE OF LEARNING

In our world today, knowledge is important.
Reading is a fundamental way of learning,
It is the backbone of the learning process.
It is enjoyed by young and old.

Readers can enjoy adventure and fantasy,
While traveling no farther than a comfortable
    chair in their home.
All kinds of information is available.
Whether it is the daily news or history of long ago.

Not everyone has learned to read well,
They are at a disadvantage, some have to have
    documents read to them.
Parents should encourage their children to read.
It is helpful in their scholastic ability.

If you want to be wise take up reading,
It is not limited in scope.
Different types of material offer varied insights.
Whatever you are interested in you can find
    information along that line.
It is said, "You are what you read."
Hooray! That says to me that we have an
    opportunity,
To become wise, enjoy life to the fullest,
Reading is the gateway to knowledge.

—Bertha Kauffman

PRIDE

Every child's heart and soul is filled with
    lots of pride
Some people let it shine right through, while
    others make it hide
While others keep it locked up, as if it were
    in jail
Others let it escape each day, as if it were
    on sale
Some people are afraid to let, others see who
    they are
When others let people see, just by looking at
    their car
You can tell when a person is very self-assure
While others make it seem as if their life is
    a blur
They are afraid people will always put them
    down
They seem as if, instead of a smile, they're
    always wearing a frown
On the other hand, there's people who let it
    shine right through
They seem as if they're always happy, and never
    feeling blue
Good or bad, inside you know there will always
    be tomorrow
And whether or not you want to admit it, you
    won't always live in sorrow

—Jessica L. Silye

ABOMINABLE SPIRIT

What is abominable spirit?
Sounds quite complex to me —
Is it the will to just *try harder?*
    Coupled with *tenacity??*

Is it that *certain* "*can-do* spirit"
    used by Heroes of the Past??
That were told: "that will *never work!*"
    And: "you will *never* last!!"

I'll bet it's the little "*think I can* train"
that climbed the mountain of our soul!
As we watched our confidence *regained*
so we could *continue* to our goal!!

I'll make a visit to my memory bank —
to search an idea *more profound!!*
But it will be that old *Abominable Spirit*
that will keep my feet cose to the ground!!

—F.E. Wiemer

TEARS

Tears are not useless;
They are mirrors of your soul.
They bring with them salty sadness,
Slippery trails of liquid gladness,
Glistening streaks of angry madness.
From deep inside you, they are true—
Reflecting passion, strength, and *YOU* . . .
Giving life to your emotions
Making real your wildest notions . . .

Giving a reason to remember
Countless memories, dark and tender—
Quenching thirst and setting fire
To your heart's and mind's desire . . .

No matter how the teardrops fall,
Whether welcome or not at all—
They'll always be a part of you,
Something real and something true.

—Sherri Fletcher

YOU HAVE TO BELIEVE

You have to believe in happiness,
    or happiness you'll never know . . .

I know that a bird chirps nonetheless,
    when all he finds are crumbs . . .

You have to believe the buds will grow,
    believe in the grass and the days
    of snow . . .

There's a reason a bird sings on his
    darkest day, he believes . . .

Many a heart could find content,
    if it saw the joy on the road ahead . . .

The joy ahead when it's had to grieve . . .

For the joy is there, but you have to
    believe . . . .

*Dedicated to my husband, Dan, and our
son, Bradley. I love you both.*

—Patricia Dudek

EVENING MIST

Standing alone on a sandy knoll
Watching it spiral and whirl as it came
wrapping me close, a round cacoon
enveloping mist, 'till I had no name.

Across the lake on a distant shore
the fog swirls down, the lights grow dim,
teasing the trees in a dancing game
until all are shrouded limb by limb.

In this mystic world
will they hear me shout,
It seems not so
as the lights fade out.

A priceless moment of solitude,
only a step to open the door
and my Island of mist
will be no more.

—E. Jean Van Horne

WILD THINGS

I love to watch the wild things play
beneath the trees at the break of day.
They run and chase and leap around.
They kick their heels high off the ground.

A special pair of long-eared hare,
they run and jump without a care.
Along came man and shot his gun,
and now there's only one.

She sits alone beneath the tree.
I see her, not so frequently.
She doesn't play and run and chase.
She comes and goes at a slower pace.

I heard another shot this fall,
and now she doesn't come at all.
I miss seeing them out there,
that playful little furry pair.

While rabbit stew makes some folks' day,
I'd rather see them run and play.

—Sandi Chaussee'

ARCHAIC MOSAIC

The thinnest shaft of sunlight
Loosed from an unseen smiling bowman
From an unknown point of blue sky
And with unheard shriek of speed

Fell to meet, hushed as Hermes
Passing by, a strange target:
Coiled on the temple floor,
A stone serpent's amber eye.

Fell to strike, with no mistake,
The seeing part of no god's friend,
Ancient, unblinking, glaring up
At the cosmos it would destroy—

Met its match and locked with light,
Embraced unbearably, held too long
In a moment just long enough
For Chaos to be born, rocked out

Of solid stone and shaft of sky;
Pitched to pieces and patterned chips,
Twisting new shapes of glittering bits
In the shattered art of archaic mosaic.

—Susan Walters

FRESH PRODUCE: from Rotten Gardens (the Bums Rush)

He used to get stoned
on that Cannibus Stuff.
It lifted him up
    from his down.
But now he's got her and he
        gets high enough
with his head firmly planted on the ground.

Abused he skipped off
up a Chemical Street.
His mind tripped on
    Scatterbrain Trails.
But now he's strung out
on a Juvenille Treat
and his heart heaviness never fails.

—Mykle leMieux

CHICKEN DELIGHT

Irma, the hen is my favorite pet,
a leghorn so different from the rest.
Dis-likes cracked corn and prefers instead,
to peck on my door for her daily bread.

Each day at dawn she sits on her nest,
laying fresh eggs for my breakfast.
She doesn't realize she is only a hen,
my little shadow thinks she's a person.

Where-ever I roam she follows behind,
relaxed in a chair, onto my lap she climbs.
Sharing a comfortable spot on this seat,
using her beak to caress my cheek.

She fell from her roost and had broken her leg,
I attached a splint, one that was home made.
Bandaged the wound from a first aid kit,
this white feathered hen never budged one bit.

To my surprise, the leg healed rather fast,
the bone had knitted so I removed the cast.
Her lady-like behavior, I'll never forget,
Irma is one of a kind and my favorite pet.

—Marge Blank

THE HUNGRY GOAT

Billy the goat had a mean disposition,
and horns to challenge any competition,
no animal dare stray within his eyesight,
for Billy would surely engage in a fight.

In order to restrain this ornery goat,
he was tied to a tree each day with a rope.
Punished for the fancy slips he nibbled away,
damaging expensive clothing laundered that day.

My stockings were hung on a separate line,
the moment I untied Billy, something entered his mind.
Tastebuds were activated when he located this feast,
three pair of nylon hose were minus six feet.

While on a date that dark chilly night,
luckily strangers were nowhere in sight,
the only slip I owned slid down my legs,
I was fit to be tied and cried like a babe.

Embarrassing enough, at the show we were seated,
I sensed I was being deliberately defeated,
my beau laughed hysterically as he removed my coat,
for the movie was entitled, "The Hungry Goat."

—Anne Hess

Oh little babe who was born
Amid the rancor and the scorn.
But in your mercy oh child of Bethlehem
You heard our prayers and our Amen.

And so you grew in beauty and grace,
And love and healing followed you from place to place.
But even so the sins of the world grew more and more,
And so that fateful day the cross you bore.

Oh Jesus, my Jesus
I love you so,
And on this Christmas Day
I want you to know.

   Love, Mae

 —Mae R. Gerardi

BAREFEET IN THE SNOW

It was after Christmas that I'm lucky to say,
 the first snow fell on this lucky day.

So thrilled was I,
 that I ran outside.

Jumping feet first I took a spell,
 then leaning forward I just fell.

I lay there still and could not move,
 for I ran into the snow without my shoes.

It didn't take long before I knew,
 that my feet were turning blue.

I jumped so high that I actually leapt,
 for snow is no place for barefeet.

 —S.S. Cecil

CHANGING OF THE SEASONS

The day dawned bright and promising.
 Will it be that way tomorrow?
What will each hour bring?
The day dawned bright and promising.
Do I feel a hint of spring?
Or will winter still be lingering?
The day dawned bright and promising.
Will it be that way tomorrow?

 —Lila Peeters

It seemed a long time coming
But it's finally here at last,
That day we all call "Christmas Eve"
And it's going to be a blast!

The ground will be all white with snow
The fires will all burn bright,
We'll make a circle 'round the hearth
And sing Christmas songs all night.

We've hung our lights and wrapped our gifts
The moment's oh so near,
We'll try to make this day last forever
Because it brings us all such cheer.

We'll pray to Him for peace and love
And thank Him for our health,
It may appear we don't have much
Yet we thank Him for our wealth.

Now we wish all children, 'round the world
Could have as much fun as we do,
But there are many less fortunate than us
So please say a prayer for them too.

 —Byford "Doc" Butler

THE SPIRIT OF CHRISTMAS

'Tis the time of year, when friends and family draw near
 To share tidings of great joy, and little ones get a brand new toy

But is this Spirit of Christmas that we've all come to know,
Really like a Norman Rockwell painting, full of sincerity and glow?

For the Spirit of Christmas that I recall, bears no resemblance to this at all

Come let us visit a Christmas at my house, where everyone is drunk, yes even the mouse!

Over in the corner is weird Uncle Fred, as usual, he thinks he's funny with that lampshade on his head

And cousin, Bill, with his fifth double martini in hand, defies the laws of gravity,
 God only knows how he stands

My dear old Aunt Martha, who never touches a drop of the stuff
Has again prepared her special egg nog where a quart of rum to a pint of nog seems to be enough

Now let us adjourn to the food and drink set at the table
If we can pull ourselves away from "It's A Wonderful Life" playing on cable

The tom turkey is stuffed; his drumsticks adorned with paper cuffs

And Uncle Bob proclaims, "He looks almost too good to eat!" as he plunges
 the carving knife deep into the meat

I think if the turkey had been granted some last request, he would have wished for a female,
 one with big breasts

But enough said of such feasting and more, time for one more round, well maybe two or three or four

Alas, when thinking of the Spirit of Christmas, be sure to look beyond and see
Christmas Spirits are not like Dicken's ghosts of Christmas past, present or to be

It is more like a spirit that tends to leave you feeling aloof
Remember, the true Spirit of Christmas is always 80 proof

 —Walter F. Dobrzycki

COLD, WET RAIN

I walk through the rain, as I go
Many drops fall to earth, under toe

Upon this very dreadful rainy night
I continue as though I were in flight

Conscious of neither rain nor cold
But, letting time pass, growing old

I shall endure this wind and rain
For life, for me, is not to live in vain

I've got a place in this life
To worship God, and endure strife

I shall fulfill his prophecy
That is, to let the light shine through me

Whether it be rain or shine, that's all you see
You will see the light that shines through me

—Christopher T. Campbell

DONKEY DEE

Hee haw Donkey Dee, with your flapping ears,
Baring your buck teeth, brings laughter and tears,
Your body is dumpy, your appearance very comical,
When tampered with, your kick is astronomical.

Hew haw Donkey Dee, you funny funny gluck,
Bray for me a little, when you are full of pluck,
What is your diet, beans, barley and oats,
Raw rice and milk, or goons, gulls and goats?

Hee haw Donkey Dee, do a funny prance,
But mind you little devil, not in the seat of my pants,
Here's a little hay, chaw on this a while,
Did I see you, bare your teeth and smile?

Hee haw Donkey Dee, I'm bidding you adieu,
There's many a clever creature, but not as wise as you,
For years you've thrilled many, of these, even me,
You are much a wonder, wise old Donkey Dee.

—Linny Nelson

PIMPLES

I have pimples and pimples all over my face,
when will they go, and will they leave a trace?
Those ugly acne blemishes rob the beauty of my skin;
oh how I hate when my friends look at me with a grin.

In front of the mirror many hours I've spent,
with poking and squeezing improvement was meant.
But low and behold what is the result?
These red and white blotches are an insult.

Now I can't go to prom looking like this!
My mom tries to comfort, but I just hiss.
It's unfair how ugliness happens to me.
I will stay home now, I want no one to see!

I've used "miracle liquids" with true dedication,
to no avail; I need a dermatologist's education.
My frustration increases with every new day,
where does acne come from, when will it go away?

I'll do anything to get my unblemished complexion back,
I'd eat cow food, walk on my head, or sleep in a sack.
So if you can tell me a new disappearing pimple trick,
PLEASE, let me know it and I'll try it real quick.

—Ursula Egger El-Tawansy

LUCKY WAS A COW THAT COULD MEOW

I once knew a cow that could meow
He was black and white
and didn't like to fight.

He liked to roam pastures
and fields, although he was
quite lazy even when it
wasn't hazy.

He had no horns nor hooves
to speak of.

He didn't like grain nor
cared for hay.

And even more peculiar
he only weighed about
ten pounds.

—Leroy Parsons

RIDING

Riding in the wind, I run like a cheetah
Catching the sun and,
Leaving the dust for the army ants
Dashing down the field,
Dashing down the court,
Let the air slap the cool breeze
Through my nostrils
And dash back into the wind,
Riding in flight,
The wings flow to the waves of my lyrics
Brushing from the pores of my tongue,
Whisper, breathe onto me,
And savor the placid clouds on the mission,
Riding, flying the passionate night away,
Like the nightingale of my dreams
Riding in the wind,
Riding in the zesty air
Evaporating the gloomy waters
Into spring jazz.

—Cedric Lamar McGhee

DIETER'S THEME SONG

Oh my! I'm in a fix.
I need to lose some weight.
No gentleman looks twice at me.
I'm sure not whistle-bait.

Pies and cakes and candy,
I love them all, I do.
Potatoes, bread and gravy
Are mighty tasty, too.

If I could live on salad greens,
Then I would be a honey.
But spinach, lettuce, cabbages,
Are strictly for a bunny.

It's nice to go on eating,
Forget the calories, every one,
Let the Fates take over,
But being fat's no fun.

So now I'm on a diet,
Determined to lose weight.
My friends will soon envy me,
For I'll BE whistle-bait.

—Agnes K. Bogardus

HOMEWORK

Homework, homework you drive me so!
I'm covered with it from head to toe.
It's such a bore,
I'd rather eat an apple core.

My teacher gives so much of it,
Every day in class I have a fit.
Yesterday I paused and then I winked,
Cause I was thinking, "I can't wait till
   it's extinct!"

—Haley Dillon, age 10

ONE TWO

One two smell my shoe
Three four it's not smelly anymore
Five six the cake mix
Seven eight the red paint
Nine ten the little red hen
Eleven twelve it's on the shelf
Thirteen fourteen the basketball team
Fifteen sixteen a string bean
Seventeen eighteen the color green
Nineteen twenty that is plenty

—William Heermann

A CRY IN THE NIGHT

I hear a voice cry in the night,
face is hidden from the Light.
Whirling, turning mist of gray,
close in around me where I stay.
Darkness fills my wounded heart,
for tonight my love we soon will part.
Memories like teardrops fall to the sand,
farewell my love we take our stand.
The cry of night comes loud and cold,
come with me child for we must go.
We journey to a place that's filled with Light,
where no more voices cry at night.

—Sheila Green

SEASONS

It happens late in the Fall
When the suited boys play ball.

The days get shorter — the nights long.
The leaves change color — the green is gone.

Pumpkins are suddenly in fashion again,
Bobbing for apples and the northern wind.

Summer days are only a fond memory.
Hot burning sun we will long to see.

Snowflakes come tumbling, tumbling down.
Covering the drabness, the ugliness drowned.

Little do we know the cycle's begun,
A change unveiled, waiting spring sun.

Then a tiny leaf will break the earth.
The seasonal change, in its great worth.

Life goes on, a gentle blend.
Changing times, an in trend.

—Patsy Potter Blue

WILLOW

Willow, oh willow
What do you have to tell?
What have your weepy arms seen?
How many have used your great brown trunk
   as a back rest to look out upon the water?
How many tensions have you eased
   or teary eyes have you dried?
Have there been many children climbing
   your boughs?
Are there grooves in your arms
   from the constant sway of a swing?
Where are the nests that chirp all day
   and the spiders that lace your leaves?
What does the wind whisper in your ear?
Willow, oh willow
What do you have to tell?

—Antoinette M. Powell

MELODY OF SPRING

I hear a robin singing,
There — on that high branch —
The words to its song are ringing
Through the neighborhood —
   "Hurry up Spring — Hurry up Spring"

I think I hear Spring coming
On pussy willow feet,
Where there will be a trail
Of purple violets so sweet,
Nature has planned Spring's entry.

The trees so tall, like sentries
Are going to wear green,
All this beauty should be seen —
It will change so quickly
Will be gone for another year.
Let us enjoy each moment
Of this wonderful miracle
                Spring!

—Bernice C. Plautz

LEBENSRAUM

I'm told there is more space than
matter in an atom, and so much movement,
they always work.

The sky is happy, everything
has its place, the sun travels
its path, followed by the moon. All
those stars come out and shine their
past upon us, so much movement.
They never embarrass, they never
rob, grovel, or whine. Even when
the wind blows they flow.

Do stars feel pain in space?

Is the moon a prisoner of the river?

Nightly, like a ghost, traveling and space,
I see it always. The star in your
eyes, your face in the watery moon,
all in a box, stored in a corner, made
out of love, hidden from space.

—Paul S. Sadler

Why have you come?
in a time so sad.
You belong to the past,
    the present is mad.

You live in the mirror,
    with eyes cold and dark,
There weakness can't cope,
    with strength, so stark.

You use me for vengeance,
    on the whole Human Race,
You're the Man with the power, . . .
    —But to yourself a disgrace.
    —Lee Williams

THE MESSAGE

Often I have wished
    Certain things I could do
And marveled at the many things
    That other people knew

But I kept right on wishing
    It was my constant cry
And never, never once
    To do things did I try

Then one bright, clear morning
    A message I did read
It said, you too can do
    If my lesson you will heed

That lesson stopped my wishing
    For action was its key
Here are the exact words
    That message said to me:

"Sitting still wishing
    Made no one great;
The good Lord sends the fishing
    But you must dig the bait."
    —Colette Taylor

THE QUILT

Carefully you stitched
The pieces of a quilt.
You pulled them all together
Like the loving home you built.

One by one was added,
A story with each piece.
First a tad of broadcloth,
Then a scrap of fleece.

This belonged to Joyce
And this to brother Gene.
Oh, this was Jerry's favorite
When he was just a teen.

Many hours you labored.
Many days passed by.
Then the finished product,
A quilt one could not buy.

There is no replacement value
For this sampling of our lives.
No profit could be sweeter
Than the memories it revives.
    —Barbara Brickey Jividen

ROSE AND A THORN

A rose is often described as a garden plant,
Bearing only a soft sweet fragrance.
The colors of life and a symbol of peace,
To spread across the nations.
As beautiful as it may seem and great as it may smell,
It's not often you see the pain.
The once beautiful flower has now become a sharp spine or a
    prickle on a plant.
A thorn in the flesh,
As painful as it sounds,
Has now become a wound of your heart and soul.
—Melissa M. Dreadin

MAMA'S GOLD HEART

You gave more love than expected,
You gave us guidance,
You provided more that your share required,
But yet, you remained, not only a friend
But one by comparison
No matter how hard the task or goals
You set for both yourself and family you've accomplished.
With that Mama, you have a
Heart of Gold.
You give so much to make others rich,
And with a heart like that it's no wonder
Why so many people love you,
But to me you'll always
Be Mama to me.

Dedicated to my mother, Dorothy Wiggins.

—James A Wiggins Jr

FORBIDDEN FIRST LOVE

She'd never been in love or even gone steady,
    when he came into her life eager and ready.

His hair of silver — his eyes of gray
    his smile, his touch — could make her day.

She was fully aware of his family at home.
    Love vs guilt — why did he roam?

Years passed — their love continued to bloom
    still unaware her heart was headed for doom.

If she'd been older, she would have known she would pay.
    Yet, with no goodbye he vanished one day.

Left with only memories and a shattered heart,
    her wonderful world had fallen apart.

A husband — children — a home of her own,
    twenty years later and still she longs.

Why did he never say goodbye?
    Was it because he was afraid they'd cry?

Does he ever think of her from days gone by?
    Could a love like theirs just one day die?

Does she still dwell in a small corner of his heart?
Why did God will they love and live apart?

*Dedicated to my best friend Linda —
For giving me the courage to accept the past,
live in the present and look to the future.
You are truly "The Wind Beneath My Wings."*
—Brenda Curtis

SWEET RAIN

Oh let it rain
wash away the fear
cleanse the soul
and let it rain
Beckoning such peaceful sleep
tapping sweetly my window pain
And rain, rain please
and I shall warm beside the fire remain
To contemplate and supplicate
and listen to the rain

Oh rain, sweet rain
wrapped in Grandma's quilt
future golden days assure
But now rain, yes rain
and cleanse the soul
and let me feel secure

—Julie L. Chase

A SEASON

In lonely solitude, I stand
On the mountain's edge and watch
As autumn's exhilarating winds
Scatter a brilliant multitude of
Colorful leaves upon the earth below.

The trees that once stood tall and proud
Now stand naked and barren,
As if lost,
Seeking warmth and comfort
But finding none.

Babbling brooks cease to flow
Wherein ice crystals form
Robbing them of their strength.

For as the passing of time,
This season too shall pass
Rendering unto us
Earth's bountiful beauty.

—Elizabeth Tyner Tew

SUMMERLONG

The long days come on slowly here
    A steady drip

They stop and stare and seldom blink
    A rusty stain

Through fearsome eyes that hold no tear
    A deep ravine

No vision but an awful light
    A broken pane

The long days under sickly skies
    A hidden look

Turn back the beds with searing sheets
    A secret place

A dusty wind as summer sighs
    A sudden love

Will stretch and run the silent heat
    A final race

—S.D. Anderson

HE WAS ALWAYS THERE

He was always there when I needed him
Understanding, caring, and true.
I could open up and talk to him
And not worry what he might think or do.
He was always caring;
And, in a sense, knew what to say
When I was happy, sad, or angry.
Now that he's gone, I don't know what I'll do.
He was always there;
I love him true.

—Deana C. Crowe, age 13

RAPTURE

Today is the day of the sun
Today is the day we've begun
Today is the day in which tomorrow we'll say
What we had yesterday today we have none

But what if tomorrow doesn't come
And what if we never had begun
Then today is the day
And that's how it will stay
And the best is yet . . . whoops
It's done

—Stewart Dale

A DREAM

A dream is a tool which everyone needs
It makes all of life's hard work worth doing.
With a dream you can conquer any obstacle
And overcome any defeat.
A dream gives you ambition
It gives you the spirit to achieve
And most of all it gives you dedication,
The driving force which helps you succeed.
With a dream, you can do the impossible,
Set goals for yourself and follow through.
For there isn't a better feeling in life
Than having a dream
And making it come true.

—Karly Therriault

THE WOES OF A GOLF COURSE SUPERINTENDENT

The night has come and gone
The day will be so long
The complaints freely flow
The grass continues to grow
The equipment breaks down
The leaves fall to the ground
The irrigation system fouls up
Sometimes you just want to give up
The rain begins to fall
But that doesn't end it all
The shop needs cleaning up
The records need catching up
Now the day is finally through
The time has come for some rest and sleep too
Tomorrow is a new day, so sleep while you can
Wake up tomorrow and start all over again.

—Chris Lewis

TO MY HUSBAND, BILL
(On our 32nd Wedding Anniversary)

The years have passed so swiftly by, and yet, each day seems
almost like the first for you and I.
There were times it certainly didn't look that way, when I wanted to leave
and do my own thing, there wasn't much that you could say.
Instead you prayed quietly and asked God to help me. In your own sweet way,
you stood aside to let me do what I had to do, to learn, that from
addiction I could be free.
I can never put into words what your faith has meant. Now, 32 years later we
are still together and I truly believe in my heart you are
an Angel God has sent.
I look with deep gratitude on the family our love has brought. The children,
the grandchildren, all precious gifts, a promise of the future, the
dreams we had sought.
To say thank you would not be quite enough, to love you more would be
an impossible task. I never dreamed on the day I became a bride, that
you would be all that I could ask!

—Mary Dunn

TIDES OF TIME

I once saw the world through the eyes of an innocent child.
Where nothing was wrong only misunderstood.

When a tear could be wiped away by a kiss; and a smile mended
a broken heart. And a hug flooded light on the dark shadows
erasing them from my thoughts.

And then one morning I woke to a cold and cruel world. Filled
with manipulation, pain and deceit. All that I had thought and
dreamed was wiped away.

Leaving my heart cold and barren. As my memories became a bitter
taste. Leaving the warmth to turn to ice. I built a wall to block
out the pain.

Then you came along and reached out to me, breaking down my wall.
You gave me back the vision I once had. You kissed away my tears,
warmed my heart with your smile and wrapped your arms around me and
held me till the pain left. You brought back the light in my
eyes and the laughter in my heart. I thank you for loving me
unconditionally.

—Franchesca deBonneville

For LUIS . . .

I'M ANGRY. ARE YOU? HAVE YOU FORGIVEN him? I NEVER WILL.
I MISS YOU. WERE YOU SCARED? DID IT HURT?
WHERE WAS I TO CALM YOUR FEARS AS YOU HAD MINE SO MANY TIMES, SWEETLY . . .
DID YOU CRY OR SCREAM? WAS IT FAST, OR SLOW?
DO YOU REMEMBER now? DID YOU THINK OF YOUR LIFE?
DID I PASS THROUGH YOUR THOUGHTS, AS THOUGHTS PASSED FROM YOU?
DID YOU FIGHT NOT TO DIE? OR JUST GIVE UP?
ARE YOU SAFE? HAPPY? LONELY? WERE YOU PEACEFUL? ARE YOU now?
DO YOU MISS LIVING? DO YOU WISH YOU WERE HERE? I DO!
WHAT WAS YOUR LAST WORD? YOUR LAST THOUGHT?
WAS IT OF GOD? OR THE TERROR OF YOUR MORTALITY?
DID YOU EVEN REALIZE? DO YOU now?
CAN YOU SEE US WHO LOVE YOU? I WISH I COULD SEE YOU.
I MISS YOU. LIFE MISSES YOU.
DO YOU EVEN CARE? IS IT BETTER now? DOES IT MATTER? now, then . . .
WHAT IS now AND WHAT IS then? BEFORE then YOU WERE HERE,
AND AFTER now YOU WILL STILL BE GONE.
then CHANGED EVERYTHING. I HATE then! I HATE now!
EVERYTHING GOES ON. HOW IS THAT POSSIBLE?
WAS THAT REALLY YOU IN MY DREAM LAST NIGHT?

—Ann Senior

A MEMORY TO DREAM ON

Dance me around the floor once more
before we say goodnight
So I'll have a memory to dream on
When I close my eyes so tight
Let me hear you say "I love you"
Before we say goodby
Just put your arms around me
before I start to cry
The years have come and gone
Fifty years in all
For soon you will leave me
In the spring or maybe fall
Please wait for me among the angels
For soon I'll join you there
We'll sing and dance together
as we climb the Golden Stair

—Christina M. Delaney

SOMETIMES

Sometimes i love too strong:
Sometimes i love too long:

Always hoping the love i found,
would last the whole world round.

Sometimes my love grows weak and
i start seeing things in my sleep.

I tell myself love's all in my head
but as the days go on the loneliness
grows wide.

I've found many people trying to fill
the whole, but no one really knows,
there's no one person to help me
though, but if there is, please
let that person be you!!

—Raushanah

HUSH, SECRET!

What your heart may contain
Closed within the barriers
Is kept to only you.
Secret is the name.

Why must people prod within?
Why must people trust one another?
Who does? Who doesn't?
Secret is the problem.

Tell one, tell another;
It'll get around in no time.
Friends to their friends.
Secret is the present.

You find that someone,
Who wasn't supposed to know, knows.
Disappointment and guilt will come.
Secret is the future.

Will things ride over?
Is there forgiveness in this game?
How do people feel and think?
Secret is the past.

—Carrie A. Coombs

THIS NIGHT

This night, your head slumbers on another pillow,
Beneath some other sky,
Beneath other stars in heaven,
Does your heart belong to another?
Does another lie in your arms this night?
Does your voice speak to her?
My heart has been wrenched away!
My life, my soul has withered!
Do thoughts of me enter your soul and invade your mind,
Or have you forgotten my memory, this night?

—Jessica Lambertus

NOW IS THE TIME

Can you hear your name? Do you know my voice?
Such is the world that awaits you.
Did you know of me? Did you have much choice?
Now is the time for you.

Are you touching me? Am I touching you?
A wonder of the world appears.
Can you see the light? Can you feel its warmth?
Now is the time and here.

Will you take my hand? Will you share my love?
Roping the winds of chance.
Should I break your fall? Can I rise above?
Now is the time to dance.

Can you fly away? Can I dry my eyes?
My beloved, so free.
Was it all I could? Will it be enough?
Now is the time to see.

Will you hold my hand? Will you be our love?
As we remember when.
Must I go away? What of the roles we played?
Now is the time till then.

—Matthew J. Schlueter

THE HAND I WISH WAS THERE

I've longed to feel her lovely hand in mine,
and last night the pleasure was all there.
Although it was only just a dream,
real, powerful passions are what the night did bear.

As our hands got closer and folded,
ecstasy and delight were all I could feel.
The elating pleasures seemed so genuine and true;
I only wish the hand I held was real.

When I awoke my hand was empty,
wishing hers was there to hold tight.
When I realized it was all a dream,
so badly I wanted back that ecstasy and delight.

Our hands folded together so perfectly,
like a key that fits in its lock,
like lovers fit into a romantic story,
or a foot that slips in its own sock.

I could not have been happier in my dream,
I was like a kid in a toy store.
I don't know if truth and destiny will seal our hands,
but I'll always hope to dream of her some more.

—Andrew John Secula

PICTURE THE MAN

Picture the man, not really a man,
  But merely a child,
All torn up inside, with nowhere to hide,
As his world closes in, where has he been,
What are his sins,
To deserve such a fate, the object of hate,
Derision and scorn, these things he's foresworn,
Yet, still forced to feel, each day an ordeal,
As he suffers the plights, the angry red blights,
Which life sends his way, what can he say,
How low can he sink, till he stands on the brink,
At the heart of despair,
All alone, he stands there,
Will he jump if he can,
Picture the man.

—D. G. Thomas, III

MY GRANDPARENTS

I really don't know what to say
Of how I feel about my grandparents today
Because they live so far, far away
And I hope to see them one special day

In a way I feel alone
Twirling around in a cyclone
Of not knowing the ones I love
The ones special to me, like the symbol of a dove

But what I feel cannot be expressed
As the pain in my heart is hardly pressed
I know one day I will meet them soon
They will love me so as bright as the moon

I write this poem in deep love
For the ones I love as pure as a dove
And I will wait patiently
To see the ones who love me

  My Grandparents
    —Maame Kanbi

A FRIEND LIKE YOU

I felt alone except for Him,
  no one could I let see me.
For if they knew me as He did,
  I am sure that they would leave me.
I am not who I really am,
  for fear of being alone.
He knew I needed a true friend,
  someone who'd love me as I am.
He sent someone who really cared,
  she loved me, and my life she shared.
We laughed, we cried, we just sat still,
  we knew our friendship was His will.
I learned so much . . . how truth is best;
  to sit with someone and be at rest.
You encouraged me, and urged me on,
  I found things I couldn't do, could be done.
I thank the Lord for you this day,
  although He's taking you away.
His plan is best, I know it's true,
  I'm glad I've know a friend like you.

    I'll never forget you, Debbie
      —Jo Ann

THE FOREST BEAUTY

Behold the fairness of the forest
Feel the fecund beauty of the woods,
Where life stirs in that fragrant carpet
Far from the city's material goods.

Tread with me the forest's knolls and valleys
Where pine needles are moving with a sigh,
As if that Indian maiden caressed them still
In her soft moccasined feet, passing by.

—Lillian M. Williamson

MY LIFE AS A CUMULUS

Fluffy and quiet, I pass through the sky
Till Nimbus grows dark and mean.
Critical and bullying, he tries to take over,
Acting just like a queen.
Moody I get, adventurous too
As I team up with Cirrus and Sun.
Briefly it rains, my sky is now gray
But shortly the battle is won.
Sunny and bright are the Heavens again
As Cumulus saunters on by.
Mysteriously silent, yet happy in fact
At last in control of the sky.

—Coleen M. Gilliland

MANKIND

Winter, Summer, Spring and Fall,
  By the roadside you see them all.
Lifeless bodies on the ground,
One by one—all run down.

From their homes they must flee,
Because of our machinery.
So we build to suit our needs,
And destroy the homes of subhuman breeds.

Years from now when they're all gone,
We will realize what we have done.
Preserve all creatures large and small,
They were a gift to be loved by all.

—Allison L. Bataller

THE TREE

Dead are the branches,
dead are the leaves.
once there was life,
Now all of the tree deceased.

What a story it could tell
of the joy and the pain,
the struggle, its rapture,
the winter, fall and spring.

Death we think of as final.
but, is this really true?
Or does death bring life to us,
as well as other things too.

Its life here on this earth
is well over two hundred years.
Its death will bring a remembrance
of days gone by so dear.

Die oh blessed creation of God,
but let its death be not forgotten.
Just as a tree the Lord's death was upon,
His life is forever and beyond.

—Joyce Bruce

SHOPPING

Sitting in the clothing store,
Watching the dressing room door.
Little girls of all ages, it seems,
Love to play dress up in their dreams.
When Mom has to sit and watch for an hour,
The fun begins to turn a bit sour.
This is outfit number five
Mom's neck is breaking out in hives.
Time to go, Mom yells through the door,
As another outfit hits the floor.
She says back, just two more to go,
Boy, it's been a long fashion show.
When all is over and done
You know she won't pick just one.
Going shopping is SO much fun.

—Lynn Jenks

MY CHILDREN

Letting you go filled me with
    despair and pain.
I hurt where I could not touch
    or see — only feel.
Letting you go left my composure
    cracked and fragile
As the years hastened on — and
    I with it
I learned from that great healer — time
To release those I love — so
    they may grow and move on.
Release is a gentleness — a kindness
    we give to others.
I own no one — or need to.
I should love them — just as they are.
I will watch them grow — in mind and
    spirit.
May they be all that they want
    to be.
Ah — I have filled my bruised
    heart with loving freedom.

—Carmen M. Engram

PAM

Her untimely demise made us all arise
And become better women and wise
She touched many hearts, many friends
And was happy, joyful and kind

Not when she was in a bind
Did she ever, ever whine
Hey I can't be divine
And didn't have wine

She lived a full life
Partly being a wife
She could never say no
To anyone, sick, sorry or woe

Her friends said we cannot believe
That she has gone to eternity
Life is short at the best
But she did all the rest

She trusted in good faith
And was received by grace
God bless Pam now
Because at last peace she has found

—Jane N. Bice

AEONIAN WHISPERS

Listen, Listen, the souls are calling
Of men and ages in time lost falling,
Away, away, beyond recalling,
If only to say, "Listen, listen.

"We have lived and have loved and have learned,
And someone in his memory burned
The epic tale of how time has turned
And given us voices, haunting voices.

"Life's no less now than was then a game.
Surviving, we won eternal fame.
As years roll by, remember our names,
Better would it be our words, our words.

"Listen, listen for if they survive,
Some knowledge, some truth from them derive,
To keep us, and more so, them alive
That you might repeat 'Listen, listen'."

—BethAnn McClain

THE EMERALD ISLE

As I walk through the forest of green,
I see plants of beauty,
and birds that sing.
Soon I came upon an emerald stream,
it was so beautiful,
by chance was it a dream?

I thought to myself for a while,
"This must be the stream of the Emerald Isle."
I followed this emerald stream,
when something caught my eyes,
not a flower, a bird, nor flies,
but a leprechaun.
Before I could breathe, he was gone,
faster than the sun chasing the dawn,

Then I found myself alone,
Looking in the mirrored water as it gleamed.
I saw a young man who for a moment,
wondered with the eyes of a child.
Forever changed by the mystical adventure,
at the stream of the Emerald Isle.

—David Jones, age 13

EAGLE DANCER'S BIRTH

Bright Water pushed, Heaven and Earth collided.
Nine moons of waiting, the time was at hand.
Trembling fists clenched, her muscles tense
Onto the Great Path, Eagle Dancer's journey began.

Bright Water pushed, Heaven and Earth collided.
Her belly swollen full, ripe with life.
She fought down a cry, gasping for breath.
Sweat beading on her brow, her body taut.

Bright Water pushed, Heaven and Earth collided.
Pain streaked through her, she screamed.
Her body trembled, strength giving way.
Calling out to the Great Spirit, relief came.

Bright Water pushed, Heaven and Earth collided.
In a release of pleasure, she cried.
Like a river dammed, her bonds gave way.
And Eagle Dancer emerged, the race reborn.

Dedicated to the principle that every person has the inalienable right to be free from both the physical and mental bonds that others may force on them.

—Erin Slack

Two hours with Brian flew by
As we laughed and shared our thoughts.
The afternoon closed in too soon
While we opened up our hearts.

Happiness and spaghetti sauce
Were our topics of concern.
I found salvation in his words
I'm not the only one.

Like death, I knew the time would come
So soon, and he would need to go.
I watched his bike sail out of sight
Through raindrops on the window.

—Carole Ann

MAY YOU . . .

As you face each new today,
may you find you'll always be
Prepared to meet its challenge,
use its opportunity—
May you always have a dream to follow,
wisdom's light to guide you . . .
May you know that others love you
and will always stand beside you.

I dedicate this poem and renew my love and respect to some very special people in my life . . . my children. To Kevin, Stacy, John and Jay Atkins.

—Cynthia M. Atkins

DANNY RAE

There is this guy named Danny Rae.
   Let's go see him Saturday.
   We know exactly what he'll say.
"Oh, my gosh, you made my day."

We'll go eat lunch with Danny Rae,
   On that fine old Saturday.
   He knows exactly what we'll say.
"Oh, thank you! Thank you, Danny Rae."

Then we'll leave old Danny Rae.
"See you again next Saturday."
I really don't know what to say,
But goodby! Goodby, Danny Rae.

—Tracy Stone

BEGINNINGS . . .

I begin to live,
But die without a purpose.
The world is too much of a gamble.
My life a roll of the dice.
I work, I cry, I try to become.
Expectations too high,
Salary too low.
The dreams in my head
Are blocked by the future.
Take a chance on what may happen;
Make a choice in what you decide.
Then follow what comes,
Whether it be what you wish.
I must live for myself;
Place the rest second best.
My quest for tomorrow—
   Begins with today.

—Kristi Nicholls

IT WAS ALL ME

When I was a child in so much pain
My heart so hurt, my mind so lame.
I wished I could have had someone to blame
But it was all me, this I now claim,
Now the truth is what I see,
It was no one's fault, it was all me.
Now I love someone, Lord knows it's true.
But bring heartache and pain seems all I do.
But I take the blame, like a man I do,
Lord help me save this love that's true,
For without this love what shall I do?

—James Robert Clark

THE DRIFTER

He is a traveler of world-wide acclaim
A tyrant to those of the entrepreneur world
Considered an expert in survival
Resourceful in many other numerous ways,

Materialistic in all unselfish ways
Never trying to go "To the extreme"
Exemplified by his three bedroom box home
And the exquisite garbage can cuisine,

This well-to-do man
Is persistant in the struggle of life
Considering all meals blessings
Each sunshine his wife,

The democracy in which he lives
Socially unfit for the average man
Being each citizen of the law
Lends and extra set of hands,

So this man of many talents and views
Should be considered royalty
Living as a true survivor
Dying an advocate of HUMANITY!

—Bomani

TO LEE (Who lost his life in a skiing accident)

On this, your 16th birthday,
   you've gone to fairer lands,

Leaving us with aching hearts,
   and empty reaching hands.

Your absence leaves a vacancy,
   that's impossible to fill,

Just memories of a better time,
   when you were with us still.

Your memory brings a gentle smile,
   sometimes a falling tear,

Recalling the happier times,
   with you still being here.

Heaven is a dearer place,
   because God called you there.

He needed your help, your expertise,
   and gentle loving care.

Soar, our gallant Eagle,
   in your realm beyond the sky.

We'll hold you here, within our hearts,
   till we see you by and by.

—Stella Damewood

GOALS

Set your goals and follow through,
You will be judged for what you do.

Education can determine what you earn,
Your wage will come from what you learn.

Your purpose in life should begin at birth,
A little self wealth and a lot of self worth.

So follow your dreams and make them come true,
By setting your goals and following through.

—Nancy G. Rockwell

ZEUS

Stretched full length, kneading paws pushing into my chest, staring!

Movement brings a narrowing of those sapphire eyes, flashing displeasure,

Green hard orbs mesmerize, daring defiance.

Purrs vibrate thru supine bodies.

Shared warmth flows.

I am his, captive plaything, sustenance, sanctuary.

No mistake here! He owns me!

—Margaret E. Allen

THE EMBRACE

Over the years
I watched my neighbour
the Apple tree
with its greening leaves and fragrant white flowers
bearing red fruit . . .
gently embracing the barkless gray Ash
transplanted near by
with out any roots . . .
standing alone
with cables stretched to keep it erect
shackled with fasteners and straps
holding taut the weathering lines
busy flowing with communications . . . .

—Richard Francis Bacon

CLAIRE, YOUR BABY ANGEL

Among the many souls encountered
as your last night through death throes lingers,
surely, at Heaven's gates she waits:
the baby girl you first conceived.

That angel you gave earthly life
and lived for ten penumbral days,
with kisses of rebirth and fruition
tears your pale astral chrysalis . . .

And, proudly, among glistening cherubs,
your child guides you through enchanted gardens
while the whole Heaven's chamber sings.

And there, before the Father, trembling,
she crowns you with a fulgent halo
as your shoulders receive celestial wings.

—Pedro Diaz-Landa

A SMALL SOFT VOICE

"Hey out there can anyone hear me?"
I'm down here in this dark place begging
    to be free
My mother is so young and not so sure
    of life
She's had so little happiness but lots
    of pain and strife

Does anyone care that I'm down here
Unsure of the future and so full of fear
My mother's afraid her mind's not so
    clear
For I'm truly a gift from God and so
    very dear

Some parents are lucky and some are not
I guess it's the unlucky that always
    gets caught
For they can't face the future rearing a
    TOT

I beg you mothers to really search deep
And think of the little ones you put
    to sleep.
Never to play and breathe the fresh air
To feel the warm wind blow in their hair
The sunshine warm upon their face
Oh why does life go at such a fast pace

—Mildred Cox

A PROUD BLACK MAN

Once on a cold day out on
the street,
I saw a man walk by dressed
neatly from his head to his feet.
True to his color he was a
proud Black man.
Straight from the ground,
right from the sand,
there I saw a proud Black man.
In his eyes, you could tell
he had no one to love,
But nowadays in this world
we depend on the one above.
He walked as proud, and
steady as he could,
slow and calm like all Black men should,
with his head held up high
and his shoulders held back.
He was a proud Black man, no
buts, but a fact.
As he walked by I thought
to myself,
God didn't put us on this
earth for his health.
He put us all here to stand tall
and be only who we are.
If we can't do this
we won't get very far
That proud Black man is all I
thought about that day,
for all black men should be that way.

*Dedicated to my grandmother,
Annie Jean Alexander
Born: Nov. 12, 1931 — Died: July 18, 1993
I will always love you and be A Proud Black Man.*

—Cameron B. Logan

GIVE MOM A BREAK

I've worked 8 hours, and I feel I could drop, but I look at the floor that I should mop.
My thoughts are disturbed by "Mom I need a drink,"
Let me find a glass in the dishes in the sink.
I've cooked supper, gave baths, and washed all the clothes,
The way I feel at this point, only God knows,
I want to go to bed, so they will leave me alone,
but I can't do that now, I must answer the phone.

Why can't I win the lottery, so I can hire a maid,
I doubt that's going to happen, so I'll work to get paid.
It's 11:00, and they are finally asleep, I'll just check in for one last peep.
Sometimes I stop and ask myself why, but, I get my answer from those little blue eyes.

—Leisha Hardy

A MOTHER'S MOMENT

I sit and stare at a little bundle, lying in his bed
I wonder what dreams may be, inside his tiny head?
Then silently I close my eyes and pray to God above,
To guide him in his growing years and teach him how to Love.

I see his tiny little fingers, as small as small can be,
I look upon his precious face, he is the world to me.
I notice how the aroma of a baby fills the air;
I look across the room and see, the clothes that he will wear.

Then quietly I bend, to grace him with a kiss
It is a Mother's Moment, that's filled with tender bliss.
And somehow I feel at peace, deep within my soul,
Knowing that I've given birth and once again feel whole.
I sit and stare, at this joy of mine,
Knowing that I'll always Love him,
Until the end of time . . . .

—Benita Eason

THE FLIP "SMOOTH" SIDE

Another day
Has come, but it will not be the same as **yesterday**
Because my **momme**
Is here to watch over **me**
While I run and **play**

If I fall while at **play**
And bump my little head and if it began to **sway**
She will pick me up out of the **sand**
With one touch of her **hand**
Will soothe the pain **away**

Oh! **Momme**
I'm feeling **good**
Let **me**
Go out and run and play, **oh!** If you only **would**

I'm having a good **time**
Playing help soothe my little **mind**

And **suddenly!** There is a **thump**
And a large **bump**

Oh! The pain is so **severe**
Momme! Come over **here**
I'm in **fear**

She picked me up out of the **sand**
With one touch of her caring **hand**
Soothe the pain **away**
Oh boy! Again I can run and **play**

—Wallace Joe Williams

MY DAD'S HAT

It's funny about my dad's hat, He can't remember where it's at. Or where or when, he took it off because he's wanting it again.

—Peggy Ann Sadler, age 11

DEAR DIARY . . .

Your best friend is someone who,
Listens to all your problems.
And never talks back.
She may answer your questions,
Without saying a word.
You can tell her all your
Worries, loves, hates, and fears.
When you feel you have to talk,
And your friends won't understand.
Tell the one,
Who will always lend a hand.

—Betsy Kane

MEMORIES

My brother had a monkey
He held it by the toe,
It was just a toy of mohair
Of memories long ago.

He'd put it in his pocket
When he had something else to do,
It'd prick and scratch his leg
Through his pants of faded blue.

It didn't seem to bother him
'Cause to his monkey he'd be true,
If asked today, I'm sure he'd say
I didn't know you knew.

—P.A. Smith

Do you ever think about taking a life away?
like your own?
just to get away from it all.
no worries, no heartaches.
no feelings, no hurt.
but what lies after death?
scares me,
where will he lead me?
which way will I go?
not only that,
but will all my hurts vanish?
or will they get worse?
in a fire, flame,
forever.

  —Angela Cronch

WOULD YOU LIKE SOME APPLE PIE?

Television, hours of it a day. Can you really get an education from it? I'd like to change the channels. A mind is a terrible thing to waste.

Living history is interesting to me. Learn from the past. The Star Trek generation is off on their five year mission to nowhere.

What kind of sex life did they have on their five year mission? Only Kirk was getting anything, and Spock, only once in seven years.

That's no life for me.

But still, there has to be morality, and from here we can only look to the past to find it.

"A generation lost in space, with no time left to start again.* I'd rather have some apple pie.

American Pie by Don MacLain.

  —E.S. Yeager

A MAN IN TIME

There are new songs to sing
For a man in time
Let the new tunes ring out
For that man in time
Whatever song that comes to mind
I'll always know, it is my song — I sing it well
Cause, I am that man in Time.

When I walk in the park
I can stroll till after dark
Then I gaze at all the stars
And my heart sets the beat
And then I search for that new tune
With words to rhyme
It is my song — I sing it well
For, I am that Man in Time.

Now the old days have gone
My thoughts deep like earth to sky
So well remembered are all the good times,
Lost loves, sweet romance
If sad, I cry — Happy, I dance
My life's my song
Measured by time — the best yet I'll find
Oh! — I am that Man in Time.

  —MALKAH

HOPE

Just when the first rays of the sun
touch the soft eyelashes after sleep
into the troubled, crying soul
the hope as bird begins to sing.

Though the sun has just appeared on the sky
dark are the thoughts and dreams
they never find the answer — why
has never happiness been around here?

The light of day is true and real
and makes one wonder, seek, and find
while almost makes him blind
the precious cure, to heal the tear.

At night, unreached by light and joy.
the restless soul enters exhausted its place,
and as it disturbs the heart and mind,
it goes asleep to wake up for another aching day.

  —Zorro

ALL FROM ABOVE

Take me in your arms, and never let me go.
Take my hand and say, our love will always flow.

You said you liked me, just as a friend;
but that sounds like money that just cannot be spent.

I know you don't love me, but at least you can try, I won't hurt you, you won't die.

I guess I'll keep dreaming, just like I used to; and then there will be no way that I can love.

So if I keep dreaming, I'll capture your love; those dreams and those promises, they're all from above.

  —Charnell Rushing

SEASONS OF LOVE

White clouds across a bright blue sky,
In my imagination, spell your name.
And the vivid autumn leaves rustling by,
Whisper our story, not the same.

In the air that echoes your voice so sweet,
I hear you speak so tenderly.
Like summer rain falling gently at my feet,
It refreshes the very soul of me.

I can feel your touch in the gentle winds.
See your smile in the warmth of the sun.
Naked trees in an open field bear all my sins,
Yet through it all there is but one . . .
  my love.

I smell the scent of the summer past.
It reminds me so much of you.
And these memories will always last,
For to you I shall always be true.

  —Melissa Wood

GUARDIAN ANGEL

If you believe in Guardian Angels, and I do!
What do you believe they can do for you?

If I called her she would walk with me through
	dangerous harmful places . . .
I believe she shelters me in her arms, from
	overwhelming grief and shows me the way
	to understand.
I believe she talks to me, "look UP to sunshine,
	stars, heavens with moon, full and gone,
	sunrises by the creator, as his hand passes
	over the day, glorious sunsets, closes the day."
I believe the heavenly Father protects her with
	an invisible shield and in return, she
	protects me from physical, mental harm.
I believe, if you have faith in yourself, all
	things are possible

Now do you believe in Guardian Angels?
I do.

—Beverly H. King

EVENTIDE

To where the wind has flown beyond the sea;
Wing-ed birds fly to infinity;
Pushed east,
By the westward setting sun;
At eventide when raptured day is done.
Eventide, a twilight full of peace;
A sunset full of mysteries never ceased.
The sun has scattered man 'tween wake and sleep;
At eventide,
Such time to sow and reap.
Factories winding down their ugly noise;
Women stepping out to find their joys;
Feet pressed in to shoes with spik-ed heels;
Drinking wine,
And watching movie reels.
Take me home o eventide to rest;
Take me home to cat and dog and bird;
Take me to oasis washed and blest;
Upon whom,
Your spirit you've conferred.

—H. T. Lorring

FROM TIME — FOR A TIME

i hid my smile in a far away place
and i unearthed my weep from
under the branches

someone threw a sin over my eyes
to wear it behind my mind and
my magnifying glasses

they put my grandfather at the window
where i saw him standing and scratching his face
with the shards of a glass long ago broken

i saw my wife playing the trumpet
and my daughter showing-off her bare shoulders
and then i went to seek my friends
old, simple and smooth like
the cherry pit
and i ran
i ran on the fields together with the horses
and i wanted to long for
but i only found
a gray morning full of disease.

—orit

WHERE HEATHER PLAYS

In a hushed garden I have a
	cottage off the lane,
With thatched roof and shining window panes,
A glow of roses wind the trellis round
	while lavender and heather sweep the ground —
And sassy birds talk back at you
	while running through the morning dew

A willow tree leans down to touch the brook
that babbles softly through its shadowed nook,
While ripples make the shiny pebbles seem
like diamonds where the sun steals through
to capture little bubbles swirling past.

And with a sigh I laugh and turn at last
	to chores long overdue,
So I will leave my heart behind
Among the ripples and the vines
	where Heather plays —

—Alma Cook Remington

TO DAD

When God told me to choose a dad,
I looked all through the line he had.
I checked for this and checked for that.
Not this one, no, he's much too fat.
That one's arms are much too hairy.
That one's eyes are much too scary.
God tapped His foot and said, "No, no,
You cannot judge a father so.
Try this one — he is just your size,
And there's a twinkle in his eyes."
I said, "He doesn't have much hair."
And God said, "No — but look right there.
He has strong arms to hold you tight,
Soft words to comfort you just right.
And see his heart — it's big enough
To love you, yet it can be tough."
I scratched my head and said, "I guess,
Let's put this father to the test."
I've tested him. Now I must say —
"I LOVE YOU — HAPPY FATHER'S DAY!!!"

—Shelley S. Lande

UNIQUE

    Black vs White
    White vs Black
We are people, not just colors.
We have the same feelings as everyone
else.
We feel gladness, pain and sorrow.
We all try to say that we are better
than blacks.
We make them separate, but say they are
equal.
We call them names such as nigger and
don't realize the pain they feel.
They've come so far — in many years.
Let's stop applaud them and say
hello.
Who knows you may learn a thing
or two.
Maybe you've made a new friend and learned
about differences in their cultures.
Our hearts make us unique not our color.

—Rebecca Webber

THE SILENT TIME

In a quiet moment I felt your love
beat
In a quiet moment I felt a repeat
of all I used to feel for you
In a quiet moment I heard you
laughing
In a quiet moment I heard all the
silence in the world and when I looked
around there was only two

—Phillip P. Ordiway

HEART FELT LOVE

Remembering being held by you
I hope you think of me too
The good times we had
Of which none were sad
Thinking of you, I produce a tear
Only because you are not near
Like a swing in a tree
I wish you would come back to me
I hate to be alone
With fear in my bones
I would like us to be one
And we would have some fun

—Matt Conro

LOVE

Love for a woman cannot
be defined,
But yet it goes on for a lifetime.
Perhaps, at first it's childish
happiness and then romance that
Keeps it aglow.
Then motherhood that makes it
shine.
Yet even sorrow makes you aware
of love and its endless flair.
Maybe flickering — but yet never
dying —
Is the light that is love —
carried by a woman.

—June Marie Lanham

LOVE HERMIT

i don't see her now
our time stolen
given away
she's got a new man in her life

some one to learn of
exchange feelings
express what's hidden
she's got a new friend in her life

someone to hold her
whisper sweet nothings
send her flowers
she's got a new passion in her life

she's become a love hermit
i wish i was too

—Rhonda Gayle

LOVEDELION

You are a dandelion.
When you are in my solitaire possession, you appear complex yet beautiful.
But only during the short intrusion of time are you mine.
Then the winds blow and you are spread along the earth.
You are rebirthing and never again will you be in whole, with me.

—Becca Stein

DANCING

Hearts pounding . . .
Sweaty palm in sweaty palm,
Our breaths collide.

Bodies slowly moving . . .
We hear no music play,
Our hearts are beating out loud.

Body temperatures rising . . .
Then the music stops,
And we walk off the floor in separate directions.

—Mishell Chernobieff

YOU ARE THE ONE

When we first met.
I fell for you.
You were different in your own special way.
Your sweet smile, lightened my heart and soul.
I knew you were the one I had been searching for.
I am just too crazy for you.
When all the night I'm not with you
My heart is full of loneliness inside.
No love is true if it's forever to be with you
Don't make me spend my life just waiting for you.
You should be the one who taught me what to do.
You made all my wishes come true.
You are the one who cares as time goes by.
I can't live without your love, can't stand being
   alone.

—Theresa Duyên Duong, age 14

I WILL BE YOUR EVERYTHING

If you feel as if you are
   falling into darkness,
  I will be your sunshine.
If you feel you are weak
   and losing control,
  I will be a tree
   for you to lean on.
If you feel as if you are
   drowning in the sea of life,
  I will be your lifeguard.
If you hunger, but can't be satisfied,
  I will be your food.
If you are freezing in a
   world of coldness,
  I will be your fireplace.
If you are lost, I will be your home.
If you want to fly, I will be your sky.
If you want to sing, I will be your song.
If you want to climb, I will be your mountain.
If you want love, I will be your dream come true.

Dedicated to John, my loving husband
*Because you're **my** everything*

—Laura L. Swaney

ODE TO A PASTOR

We were blessed to have her pass this way,
This person named Wendy, we were sure she'd stay.

But Fate took a hand, it was not be be,
She was called from our midst to Eternity.

We're thankful to have had Wendy, our first full time woman pastor,
A very special person, fulfilling our needs while serving her Master.

She will always have a special place in our hearts.
Thank God for her life and example, and now as she departs,

May we learn to take each day with its burdens and trials, and stop a bit,
And count our blessings and be thankful for it.

—Donnie Olson

OUR SON

What do I tell **our son**, when he says to me, "I want my Daddy, where is he?"
Barely three years old, but so wise for his age.
What should I tell **our son**, what should my answer be?
A killer drug called Crack, took your Daddy away.
He wasn't strong enough to loosen its grip on him,
he felt he had no future, his life was very grim.
So what do I tell **our son**, when he says to me, "I want my Daddy, where is he?"
He was high on Crack when he took a gun one day and put an end to all of his misery,
he couldn't have done it otherwise, he wouldn't have left you & me.
What do I tell **our son**?
That you loved him very much, that you will always be with him & he will feel your touch.
That someday when he's older he will understand, what you did was beyond your control,
And that you will always carry us, deep within your soul.

Dedicated to the Memory of my Husband, Sidney Madlock, deceased May 11, 1991.

—Regina R. Madlock

WHAT IS MY DADDY DOING?

What is my daddy doing? I often think of how,
he's in Heaven praising Jesus, I can almost see it now.

All the Christians singing praises to the Savior they all love,
in their robes of white and crowns, in that city up-above.

What is my daddy doing? Is he walking by the river or beside the crystal sea,
he's in Heaven with the Father, Oh how happy he must be.

A land he longed to be in, so wonderful and bright,
a land of peace and love, where there, there is no night.

What is my daddy doing? Inside the gates of pearl,
we read the scenery is marvelous inside his "new found world."

Is he walking with his brother upon the streets of gold?
Is he laughing with his mother? They are happy we are told.

What is my daddy doing? I know he's happy there,
no sorrow, tears, nor sickness, there is no dying there.

I miss him beyond measure; his smile, his loving touch,
but for him to be with Jesus is the thing that means so much.

Lord, if you will, tell my daddy "hi" for me,
until I tell him for myself, for there I'll someday be.

—Karen Prince

WHERE WE HAVE BEEN

Tremors shook the Golden State
When I was born.
When I was ten, California shook again.
Walls and bridges crumbled
Where I stood when I was Twenty-four.
Floods and muds, and Wildfires of Ninety-three
Ravished a land where I have lived
A half a Century.
Thirty or forty, or a million years or more,
California has survived where She has been.
Will I?

—Virginia Tabor

LIFE

You have what it takes to stay in school
So don't mess around don't be a fool
Get your education and stay smart
If you don't do drugs then don't start

The road is not easy it may get rough
Sometime the going may get very tough
That's when you kneel down to pray
Ask the Lord for strength every day

He will answer your prayers for you
After you've done what you're supposed to
So stay in school and get a life
You'll go through pain but end up all right.

—Booper

MY WORLDLY TEACHINGS

With tears of joy,
I put each one of you,
High up on a pedestal.
To teach and care,
and learn, you fear,
of all the sorrows,
oh so near.
I hope my teachings have not been in vain,
I hope you heard along the lane,
and my echoes stay within the reaching power
of my sane, for that's all I have to give.
A little knowledge,
and wisdom too.
That, I've also learned from you.

—Lilly Preece

KINDRED SURPRISE

Two neighboring men, related by kin,
In dispute of a property line;
Greeted each other and not like a brother,
But like sour grapes on the vine.

Each thought he was right and held on tight,
Not yielding one to the other;
As word was spread, came a nod of the head,
And isn't that just like a brother.

But soon they agreed, both had a need,
The cost they would split fifty-fifty.
And folks all around, in their little town,
Thought that was really quite nifty.

Surveyors came, staked off said claim,
Gave one a map both heeded.
The strip of loam between each home,
Would be a street when needed.

—Edmond C. Woods

SEPARATED

Words and time, we cannot find
A season slipped past, somehow left behind
Fragments missing watching other families
hugging and kissing.
Questions unanswered, prayers to say
One often wonders, why it all ended
this way.
Unkind words spoken, we wish never
abound.
Fragments shattered, nowhere again
to be found.
Our little ones and us separated,
are we ever to get back off
the ground?
Lives tattered and torn; a part
of us ended,
A small part reborn.

—Paul E King

BABY BLOCKS

To her, the world is a closed book,
A vast field of knowledge
Consumed in a dust storm;
Her eyes strain in the fog of her life:
Searching for the answers
To all her questions.

The library in her mind is old and desolate;
The shelves contain only outdated books
With brittle yellow pages of confusion;
But even they are beyond her reach;
She longs to touch them, to read them—
Useless or not, she doesn't care.

Now, she will try once more
To indulge secretly under lamp light,
Inhaling the intoxicating scent of ink and paper—

Then . . .
The crash;
The children holler;
The book falls to the floor,
Closed once again.

—Chad Wolfe

SUNDAY'S PAIN

I feel her cracking
On the inside,
Spending her days bravely in control
And her nights — somewhat the same.

She is hungry:
She needs to taste, the fruit of his affections —
To digest his warm embrace.
She is thirsty:
She needs to drink, from the poison of his potion —
The enchanted chalice of his kiss.

I feel her cracking
On the inside,
Her mind weak, suspended in time . . .
When a man was her physical blanket
Now he's one of comfort;
Covering the memories inside her mind.

Every year that passes
The soul within her feels the same;
Wondering . . . if she will ever fill the void
That usurps as Sunday's pain.

—Khrystán Page Renfro

THE POWER INSIDE OF ME

There is no power inside of me.
That power has been taken away you see.
They speak out, although I disagree I say nothing
Because there is no power inside of me.

Who gave them the right to take my power away.
I got used to not having any say, that is how
they took my power away.
I don't like the way this sounds.
I guess my power has been found.

—James Ray Topeka

PINEVALLEY PINES

O' Pinevalley Pines so tall so straight
I bring you greetings from way up state
Greetings from your companion tree
That left these woods that she might be
A pipe for an Organ so great so grand
That thrills many people throughout the land.

It makes me sad that you cannot hear;
Those beautiful tones so soft so clear,
That come from the throat of that piece of wood
That once in life by your side it stood.

As I listened to that music rare,
While paying my respects to our President there,
I thought of you trees and the different roles
You play in the gladdening of our souls.

One of you died that she might be
A promoter of life in the Eternity.
The rest of you live and stately grow
Braving the winds and the winter snow.
All to bring joy to those that can see
The Doe, the Squirrel, the Robin and Me.

—Ivan Holt Hunt

ONE OR THE OTHER?

I wake up to hear the birds sing
I stand up and hear the phone ring

I shower to the sound of water down
I dress with the feeling of wind all around

I address my journey with the sun on my face
I enjoy the feeling that nothing can replace

The joy that's before me is like no other
Nature and me, so alike one another

When I walk to school, I notice many things
When the flowers are bloomed, all of Nature springs

When the trees stand tall, the world is at their feet
When the bushes are small, Nature and I meet

We care for a week, recycle and are clean
We soon forget about it, then we turn mean

We litter and destroy; strip it to the core
Eat, drink and play; begging Nature for more

We wonder why Nature becomes so grim
We blame it on the other guy; you know, him

The finger should point to the only one who sees
Nature is defenseless, don't bring it to its knees

—Christina Overbay

A KISS AND A PROMISE

You don't have to buy me diamonds
You don't have to buy me furs
Just give me a kiss and a promise
That I will always be yours.

You don't have to buy me a mansion
Or even satin gowns
Just give me a kiss and a promise
That we can share life's ups and downs.

You don't have to promise me a rose garden
I know how rough life can be
Just give me a kiss and a promise
That you'll share your life with me.

—Stacey J. Skidmore-Hasil

JOURNEY'S PAIN

At the beginning, summons;
a beat a rhythmical vibration
weariness to labor under

    childbirth having material existence
        sharp teasing agonizing physical suffering

stabbing, a piercing wound
indifferent and devoid of emotion

    abrupt punishment of horror
    acute infliction of crushing pressure

an affect of such violence
warning — deterioration

    serving as an alarm
    the last examination

in a course of torment
    birth to death
        an afterimage without anguish

—Vicky Guerrero

IN A WORLD LONG PAST

Fun it used to be, to live like you and me,
But that's in a world long past.

Laughing was a common joy,
One we often knew.
Now the happiness is gone,
It went to the grave with you.
I had once a cause to fight,
To drive myself to win.
But when you left, I found myself
Where I have never been.
In a world where I want nothing,
Where my dreams are torn apart.
Now I realize, throughout my whole life,
You had been my heart.
With you gone, I have no will,
It was you who took me to the top.
I take a look at all my life,
And living seems to stop.

Fun it was to be, to live like you and me
But that's in a world long past.

*Dedicated to Mary Elizabeth, who I dearly
love forever and wish to thank for always
giving me divine inspiration, but most
of all for being my better half.*

—Lane W. Marshall

SOARING SOUL

Death does leave an empty shell behind.
To bury it is proper, down into the depths of earth,
Or cremation of this empty shell, which is left behind.
No use to anyone, the soul floats free and clear.
Its journey is just beginning.
What need of the lifeless body which has no place in
    the after world.
The soul or spirit, if you will, can touch its loved ones
    and in a sense help them on their way.
Keep yourself attuned to the soul of your loved one, and
    many times there will be the help you need in making
    decisions.
And in passing, there is much pleasure to be gained by
    thinking of a loved one or friend.
The happy times, fun times; these things do not disappear
    because of the loss of a family member or friend.
They are stamped in your memory forever.

—Birgit Blake

EXISTENCE

There is an abundance of joy, sorrow, love
Hate, fear, courage,
In this life.
Some will say that life is not worth the struggle
As there is nothing — only void existence
— but —
There is an abundance, especially of hopes and dreams
Which temper the sting
Of life and death, of time and place.
Make possible love and happiness.
Give strength to bear disappointment, discrimination, fear,
Pain, agony and hate.
There is courage — The courage of youth
Born of inexperience.
There is courage — The courage of adulthood
Born of fear and necessity.
Denied the omnipotence of God,
We hope and dream in a state
Of uncomprehension.

—Alice C. McMurry

LIVING FEARS

Stargaze into a heat wave. Lift up, up to the sky.
Feel the earth shake beneath you. Let the salt,
drift from your tears.

Empty your pockets and soar the air. Breathe the
softness of clouds. Exit your body, just for the moment;
let go, and live with your fears.

Clap to the rhythm of drowning birds; Dance to the
music violence cries. Stomp and shake, let it out.
Enter the world of sweet nothing.

Drink from the fountain of forgetfulness, Eat the
cake of remorse. Wash in the lake of burnt
ashes. Sleep in the valley of dead.

Wake in the morning of darkness, walk into the
smell of blood. Lie in the bed of slashed corpses;
Dream nothing while you lie there.

Exit the mountain of lost souls. Remember your
sick little life. Tell the story you already forgot,
sing, the song of the mind.

—Kathryn "K-T" Long

TO BE IN LOVE TO BE

When I love you
And you love me
Then and only then are we we.
    If I can't love you
And you won't love me,
    Then what can we be?

Should I love you
    And you are you
What can I be to you?
    If there is no you
Then where are you,
    So you yet remain just you.

—Joy D. Redmond

LIKE A DOVE

For you my love
to soar like a dove

For I am not worthy of thee
I must leave for thee to be free

Free of my untrue love
The skies are waiting for you above

For you shall be happier
to be free like a dove

For you will always be
in my heart, my love

For you will now soar like a dove!

—Nicole M. Rouse

I SHALL NEVER FORGET YOU

I can't believe you are leaving,
you never said why.
I can't believe you are leaving
I never got to say goodbye.
All I can keep are memories that
are so dear to me, you made me think,
and you made me see.
I am afraid to speak, I am all choked
up,
The pain in my chest is ready to
erupt.
Give me your address,
please give me your number, you,
my friend I shall always remember.

—Sarah Howe, age 13

FORGIVE ME

Forgive me, pleads the clock—
For I often work against you.
Forgive the subtle 'tick-tock'
Of my pendulum which races you.

A busy agenda such as you possess
Requires one like my construction.
Even so, midst a more peaceful rest,
I seemingly push for your destruction.

Exonerate the accusations placed
Around myself and all my kin.
For every morn' and 'morrow faced
The facts passed clear — I cannot win.

Nor you veil, regardless of your class,
For time will never wait to pass.

—Corie McDuff

Mind distilled; emotions dissolved;
Enter my dream, without your clouds.
Torrid surroundings, dark gloomy rooms
Forward with stress, the outcome confused.
Murky the water, shallow and green.
Bitten by bugs too large for your dreams.
Air motionless — thick with debris.
Cough till you puke your life of unrest.
Again does it feel more like . . . oh stress.
The walls around you come tumbling down.
Hit by the best . . .
       . . . still standing so proud.
    —Anthony Liberato Campafiore

QUESTION

Fear, wonder, no answers to have —
to lay and let the mind run to depth,
to give thought to questions until
body gives to sleep.

Things unknown which only have a
passing thought, no more to question
no more to give time of mind.

I cry to give me answers of things to know
to give me rest of soul for things untold,
to know it is at close of touch,
   but so distant
why is this a life must?
   —D.E. Pierce

RUNNING

While jogging through the streets
I contemplate why I run.
Surely, it is not for the glory.
This is because there is none.

"Why do you do it?" many people say.
To get in shape for hockey
Is what I used to answer.
Now I am sure that cannot be.

For the sense of competition
Is what some might tell you,
But it is more of a battle with yourself
Than between the black team and our blue.

Therefore, it must be the good feeling inside
Pumping through you with every stride.
  —Brent Jenkins

We need to all realize this
We were all put on this cosmos
For a short time it would seem
To console each other's woes

And when we have our children
We need also remember this
That our children are just loaned to us
We'll answer to our Maker at our final tryst

As we bring these children up
Let us put them first in need
Doing what we think God wants us to
He could take them without heed

There should never be child abuse
Toward God's children, or for sure
We should not neglect or repress them
For they are with us to endure
  —Jonette Barrón

LIFE GOES ON

Life goes on
Amid sunshine and rain, happiness and pain
Brightness of day, dark gloom of decay
Job tryout for me bucking seniority
Failures encountered, problems conquered
Great pride in work, duties we shirk
My struggles in vain, his illgotten gain
Birth of a child, mammals in the wild
Foods dry unspoiled, fresh linen soiled
Lapsed home insurance, strength for endurance
Roof sprung a leak, in public scared to speak
Loss of youth and health, false promise of wealth
Life's temptataions, fatal hesitations
Dire solitude versus musical interlude
In earthquake tremor hear street wise vendor
Steel tanks rumble, find buildings tumble
Hope and assets gone,
                and life goes on.
  —Albert M. Maier

SILO

An abandoned silo stands beside the road
A monument of history that goes untold
The old barn that once as built so sound, now
lies rotting upon the ground
A foundation is all that's left to be seen, of
A home that once was a farmer's dream
The fields that flourished with corn and wheat,
Or no longer providing us with these foods that we eat
It's all gone, and only memories are left behind
So our children's, children's, children, can someday
Look back in time
And thank their forefathers that help build this
Land
And look proud upon that old silo, and the hardship
for which it stands
Yes a part of an era where a way of life was
Lead
And the silo is now a tombstone, symbolizing a
Piece of history, that now is dead
   —Wm McEven

STRUGGLE TO SAVE THE BARN

There was no lightning in the cloudless sky
as he set forth to fetch the cows
a hulking farmer with reactions quick
committed to his labors and on his lips
prayers to God thankful for his harvest

A wild wind blew; announcement of rushing
winter, then terro struck his heart
yellow tongues licked, flashed,
shot out to greet him

No time to stand idle on this day
in autumn golden bales of fodder
tindered combustion glowing, smouldering

Muscles tense, sweat, infernal heat
thick clouds; swinging pailfuls of water
he climbed mile-high courses
leaping to the very top

Droplets, dripping, seeping like weeping
in the barn, soot blackened face poised
aloft he saved the hay, a river poured
from the heavens, struggle over God saved the barn.
  —Nancy Ellen Nelson

IN MY MIND

Tempt me, touch me, it all does the same.
I teach you, I treat you, it all seems like a game.
I need you, I feed you, but you leave me in pain.
My tears will fall like the summer rain.
I'd give you my soul, my dreams, my sight,
If you would let me hold you for just one night.
In your thoughts you need my heart,
But your life I want to be a part.
I'm scared to say what I feel is true
But you have to know that I love you.
I thought I've felt this feeling in the past,
But God above said it wouldn't last.
You have to know that my feelings are dear,
For I plan to love you forever and a year.

—T. Hayes Webber

LOVE

You walked into my life without any guile;
You offered your strength, and gave me your smile.
It was in spring, and the stars were bright;
You melted my heart with your sweetness and light.

Your eyes, filled with truth, were bright and clear.
You brought me joy, and love and cheer,
And fresh air, kindness, innocence.
To let you go would make no sense.

You took me to picnics, and parties and shows;
You taught me a love that just grows and grows.
We went to meet your family;
They were so friendly, so kind to me.

We married and that brought us joy, so much
That we didn't need houses and cars and such.
We soon had two sons, they both were such dears.
Our love and our joy were assured through the years.

—Shirley DuBois

PARTINGTON COVE
Big Sur, California

It had been ten years since I had seen her. I tried many substitutions; the Canadian lakes of Ontario, the pale blue off St. Croix and even the Maine-like coast of Door County. Each offered her best, but came up far short, unable to compete with the Queens greatness.

She knows so much and I should never have run from her beaches and the memories they hold for me. I have hidden from her as I have tried hiding from you . . . but she always wins out in loving, as you do.

I could hear her calling in the Rockies and her song became strong as I neared the California coast. I approached her with apprehension, as I would fix my gaze away from your eyes . . . or slide my hand away when you came close.

Now we meet face to face. Her waves rush in to greet me and her touch is filled with love and forgiveness. I mix the salt of my tears with hers and her dark blue fingers run through my hair, caressing. Her song so soothing is the same and peace comes as I stretch out on the sand pillow she provides.

—Herb Aughinbaugh

LET GO MY LOVE

Yesterday is past and gone
Let's not linger anymore
Life's lessons are meant for us
To learn, grow, and unfold
The time to let go is now
We are too content being Me
Find yourself and be you
Experience life without me

What we shared will always be
Fondly remembered by me
You deserve the best in life
The time for closure is now
But before you go, just let me say
Thanks for yesterday
Thanks for helping me grow
Thanks for letting us go.

—Veronica C. Tucker

BECAUSE OF YOU

Your smile, it overcomes me,
To brighten up my day.
Your caring, it surrounds me,
To help me on my way.

Your laughter, it subjects me,
To your humor and your charm.
Your arms, they overpower me,
And keep me safe and warm.

My smile, it longs to greet you,
Into each and every day.
My caring longs to shower you,
In each and every way.

My laughter, it's because of you,
You've come into my heart.
My arms will always hold you tight,
We'll never be apart.

To Ron, because your love inspires me.
—Mickey

LOVE IS LIFE

Love is like
A rose

So beautiful
To the eye

Such beauty should
Never bring you pain

Yet . . .

There is the thorn of the rose
That can prick if handled incorrectly

Such is life . . .

Handle it incorrectly?

You will need to nurse the wound
Until it smiles with life

But remember . . .

The lesson learned will bring
Just as much beauty as the rose

Love is life

*Dedicated to Lewis Lett, III,
Aaron Lett and Zachery Waller
for all that life stands for.*
—Louise Waller

SOAR

My spirit soars off the ground
As I stand earthly bound . . .

I climb into the atmosphere
And twirl up to the stratosphere.

I experience ethereality
And soar into infinity.

Space and time there is no bound
As I skip and soar all around.

I look down at my physical being
Pulling my spirit back from soaring.

My spiritual journey must end;
I return to where I stand . . . .

—Judith King

KEEP THE SPIRIT GLOWING

America has always been
Brave, Strong and Free.
Her Beauty always shines
from the City, to the sea.
She's seen her share of hard times —
Trouble, Grief and Strife.
But the Lady in the Harbor
Still stands there with her light.
She sets a good example
Of how we should be —
Tall, proud and shining,
For all the world to see.

Light the fire with Liberty
and Justice for us all.
Renew the Flame of Brotherhood
in Hope that we won't fall.
Let's trust in God and stick together,
that's where we belong.
And keep the spirit glowing
for America, our Home.

—Janice F. Plymel

THE LANTERN IN THE WINDOW

Dad left a lantern hanging high
    up in the window
Till the boys were back from town,
The dark of winter days was long
And often homeward bound —
    the road not quickly found

In summer horses pulled the wagon
    faster all the way,
For at the end was house and barn
And stalls filled high with hay

The bright glow marked a warm house
And folks who wait within,
It mattered not what lay outside
but warmth that lay within

I wish sometimes
In coming home
I could look up and see
The lantern in the window and
    folks who wait for me —

—Alma Cook Remington

As each moment passes eternity unfolds.
Compelled to find the truth, I set out on my own.
Now I walk the cold, dark streets of life.
Seeking, searching, trying to find my doorway.
Every step I take brings me closer to journey's end,
Where I will find the site of judgement.
The judgement will be final, the decision flawless
And the soul will be eternally damned, or glorified.

—Jason A. Holland

DREAMLAND

I dream of a beautiful dreamland,
That only I can see.
And when at night I close my eyes, I dream of what
It can be.
It can be a world of my desires, a world of fantasy,
I can dream a world of wonder because I have the
Key.
When I wake up in the morning, my dreamland goes
Away,
And when I go to sleep again, with me it's here to
Stay.

—Susan R. Agudo

AUNT KATE

As I stepped onto the porch from the street below,
I glanced through my neighbor's window.

Through the glass, in disarray,
I see a tattered old woman with hair of gray.

My mind starts to wonder, my eyes swell with tears,
As I recall her younger years.

I remember her and all her ways,
At birthday parties and holidays.

It's strange how age can be so unkind,
To rob your body and your mind.

As days roll by and life unfolds,
Will someone comfort me when I grow old?

I hope it's someone who can carry the weight,
Like the way my Mother cares for my Aunt Kate.

—Jeanie M. Pollock

MEDITATION BY STARLIGHT

I climbed the hill at midnight.
The air was chill and crisp,
And echoing with the whispers of ancient days,
Before the earth was ravaged by ungrateful Man.
I looked up to the stars, the crown jewels of Heaven,
Shining in the splendor of eternity.
They whispered to me in silent communion,
Their multitudes imparting wisdom
Undreamt of by day.
"We were here before the fleeting moment of your race,
And our numbers dwarf infinity.
What of your mighty civilization,
Your great cities, your technology?
They cannot touch us, they cannot trouble our peace.
Only the searching soul in contemplation
Can dwell among us, partaking of our joy."
So deep is the sky, and so high are the stars,
Forever safe and free.
Constant friends they are to the world-weary soul.

—Michael Gootee

DEER LAMENT

Tomorrow the Hunters all will arrive,
The Deer will be lucky, if they can survive.

There will be much sorrow in each little group,
When guns start shooting, we'll see them all scoot.

The mothers and fawns, will be chased just as fast,
While the bucks scatter, their dooms come at last!

Oh, many a proud man will brag to his friends,
How he stalked the deer, that led to its end.

—Neva June Anderson

ARTISTS GALORE

An easel, a canvas, a sketch pad, and colors,
these are the tools of an artist at work.
Some music, a few words, and a voice that's included,
these are the tools of an artist at work.
Costumes, dance steps, music combined,
these are the tools of an artist at work.
Lyrics, music sheets, instruments galore,
these are the tools of an artist at work.
The list could go on, it's endless, you see,
there are so many talents that are called art-ist-ry.
Whatever your talent, just grab a hold,
For God gave these talents to come forth as gold.

—Shirley Ann Green

GLADIOLAS

The baby chicks are dying in the sun in Guatemala.
The gladiolas are turning from peach to brown
in the jar you placed on the table beside the bed.
Pieces of lime, green fragments of pulp
cling to the wood like dried flesh;
once plump with the juice of our love
sticking now to a surface, hanging on.
The ants form in silence
waiting to clear the memories away.

Are you crying?

Boxes stacked in the bus station
as we wait.
The chicks poke their yellow heads through holes
gasping in heavy air.

—Merrylee Lord

I AM

I am 98.6 degrees
No wind or clouds, very plain,
yet amazing to hit an exact temperature.
I am Titanium,
very flexible and unbreakable.
I am a Koala,
sitting high and eating good.
My color is Navy Blue,
plain yet graceful.
I sound like the pitter patter of rain,
making sure not to make much noise.
I am a stream,
whose water is clear and current strong and pure.
I am Bamboo,
Strong, Useful, yet a type of grass,
Therefore, I don't stand alone.

—Randy "R.J." Lane

THE BUILDING, THE BOY AND HIS HORN

The buildings are high
Like the clouds in the sky
The rainbow is high
Like the clouds in the sky
Little boy on the hill
Blow your horn which gives me a thrill.

—Claire Marie Casey

THE ROOF

On the roof, I can see above the gray.
On the roof, I can see above the city.
On the roof, I can see above the mass.
On the roof, I can see above the hatred.
On the roof, I can see above the sorrow.

On the roof, I can see the rainbow.
On the roof, I can see the unity.
On the roof, I can see the beauty.
On the roof, I can see the tranquillity.
On the roof, I can see . . . .

—Eric V. Goodridge

A SIMPLE THOUGHT OR TWO . . .

For the whole wide world
or those few that are close to you,
Poems!
What a lovely way to let them know
how you really, truly feel.

You can write about whatever
is on your mind —
Loved one, family, friends or a pet
You can talk about love, happiness,
people, or even one of life's scary things

You could describe your hopes & wishes,
Your fears, bad things, or happy times,
Your dreams, or even a wild fantasy
Or maybe, just a tiny memory
that means the world to you.

But if you'd rather, maybe you
prefer just to write a
simple thought or two.

—Sandi Ard

THE JOURNEY

Eat and drink today
for the journey is long
and the sun is hot.
The rain falls scarcely on the sand
and their shifting tides
may lead us into oblivion.
In search of the ancient tribes we came
hoping to learn the rich culture
of their nomadic ways.
But now the night is upon us and cold.
Huddled under blankets
the distant stars gather
in the corners of our eyes.
The horses stand sleeping
with an occasional sigh
while camels lay sprawled
like some felled prey.
All is quiet.
Dreams unravel another world upon us.
The night marches on.

—John Henry Jaryno

MEMORIES

Memories find me in my dreams
and dance around me
like music in the air.
They float in such a way
they cannot be ignored
nor do I want to ignore them.
They please me;
recreating a happier time
that tho' it is gone
and may not be so clear
I have a warm smile in my heart and soul
that no one can take away.
My memories find me in my dreams
and dance around me
like music in the air
and they are forever mine.

—J.A. Pfeil

BEYOND MY REACH

A soft, white cloud became a curve
Unseen, unknown, uncompromised.
I threw a rock up at the sky
To bruise the cloud amidst the blue
And found my eye could never reach
So high; but, then, again I tried

Because I had belief I could
Be tough enough within myself
To reach my goal. A leaf is all
That I could hit somewhere on high,
And it fell bruised nearby my feet
And lay there, telling me nothing —
For it had not a thing to say.

I bit my lip, I tried again,
And hurt my arm inside a lot
To my alarm. And cut the skin
On the toughness of the sharp rock
As it regressed hot into the mud.
And I went home, nothing to say.

—Merle C. Hansen

WISHES AND DREAMS

　　　I wish to be,
　　　But I am not.
　　　I wish to live,
　　　But I do not.
　　　I wish to love,
　　　But I can not.

These are my wishes few;
Left unanswered—this is nothing new.

　　　A dream for sanity,
　　　But there is not.
　　　A dream to create,
　　　But I do not.
　　　A dream for love,
　　　But she does not!

I am my wishes,
　I am my dreams—
This illusion is not what it seems;
But look—I can not be what I wish,
　I can not be what I dream,
　　This dementia makes me scream!

—Mike Yeoman

IMAGINATION

Imagination, dead, imagine
strange ol beckett writes
give credit where credit is due
beatniks are back wanted in popular demand
to use their imagination to help this poor lonely world
stripped of all its imagination
soon to be dead, imagine that
we think it won't happen
we just frolic in our joys and ecstasies
peace; wouldn't it be nice
morbid melancholy just doesn't cut it
gather ye rosebuds while ye may
live, enjoy, take care of all imagination
we can create, to obtain anything
if we would just put our minds to it
imagination can wander, can wander the lonely streets
can walk on the sand, can sit under a tree
it is just waiting, don't let it down

—Melisa Sides

A DAY IN TIME

The Eastern glow flowed through my window pane
To scatter diamonds in the dust
Dust so fine no eye can see
Sunshine soft as kitten paws across my carpet, beamed
I watched the clouds seep through the rays
Then open to a burst of light
To put to sleep the night.

Sunbeams flitted around my room
Touched my pillow there
And left a shining hi-light on my tumbled hair.

The noonday sun burned hot and crested overhead
Like fireflies it shone around my bed
I slept
And while I slept the Western sky turned red.

I wakened to the setting sun
And as its beams flowed by, I reached for moonbeams
Forming
In the evening sky.

—Fern Costello

THE TABLET OF RAIN

The beauty of nature is one we can't ignore
for what would we do without it?
Could we have a beach without a shore?
　No, I hardly doubt it.

The sea is wide with water, the ocean holds it too.
The lakes and streams have it harder,
　for their work comes from you

Each day continues on without a thought or pout,
But oh my friend how you would cry with tears
　if you could see the drought.

You think the trees are green and the sky is blue.
You think the ocean serene and the air is true.

But beauty is in the eyes of those who can see.
Truly you would cry if you could see me.

For I am the season that beauty isn't seen
And I am the reason that beauty is green.

So please think again before you cause me pain.
For truly the world would end if there was any RAIN.

—Carol L. Lewis

A GREAT VALUE

Here is my trust, it is only for you
Here is my trust, it will pay you back
Here is my trust, use it when you feel unsure
Here is my trust, keep it clean with honesty
Here is my trust, as it gets older it gets better
Here is my trust, be good to it for it hurts easily
Here is my trust, it is 100% pure from the heart
Here is my trust, it will not tell others
Here is my trust, it will be yours to keep
Here is my trust, use it as if it were the shirt off my back
Here is my trust, it will cost you no money
Here is my trust, do not lose it for it is of great value and very hard to find.
    —Stephen D. Coffey

QUITTING TIME IN SAINT PETE

In a cold, pastel lobby 5:00 beeps from a delicate, tanned wrist.
Pushing open clean glass doors, burning air rushes on cold fingers and cheeks.
Sirens rage, horns blast, white heals click across cracked pavement.
The teeth-clenched blond fixes a frozen gaze on her Mercedes two blocks away.
She avoids the face behind the rusty shopping cart
piled with dirty plastic bags, rags and wet cardboard
and past the leather hand clenching a cup.
Embarrassed, she pretends not to hear the obvious question directed at her,
but can't ignore (though she tries) eyes singeing her back
and her legs beneath a too-tight skirt.
Sour smell lingers on an empty but still sticky garbage can,
overpowering her own cologne.
Rap beat amplifies from an approaching Cadillac
out-of-sync with racing heart and heals.
Afraid, she fumbles, curses for keys and spills her purse,
leaving behind lipstick and change.
Inside she sinks into leather cushion, slams noise behind a heavy door
and blasts cold air on sagging hair and gritty skin.
Squealing out and away
Another day behind her.
    —S.O. Shaut

JUST YESTERDAY

"Wasn't it just yesterday," said the owl with his spots quite shaken,
"That we had homes, clean air, and food and the rainforest had not been taken."
"How true," chimed the eagle so lonely and weary,
As she looked left and right her eyes sore and teary.

In the murky sludge below a saddened manatee tries to float,
Avoiding nets of fisherman hauling toxic fish aboard boat.
Poor opossums and squirrels hit hard by pollution's wrath,
Have reactions so obscure they head straight to car paths.

Wasn't it just yesterday that schools had windows, tiles, and learning?
Now tight buildings with carpet fumes keep pupils's senses burning.
As toxins fill their frail little bodies, discipline is needed a-plenty,
No wonder Johnny hasn't learned to read and Johnny is now twenty.

Wasn't it just yesterday as I secured the gas mask across my face,
That I could actually go outside and be a part of the human race?
Wasn't it just yesterday that I heard the sweet songs of birds,
Smelled blossoms, watched animals romp — yet today there's not a word.

There's nothing left safe to eat, wear, or do,
Who can stop this from happening — only me and you.
Don't make today and tomorrow become our toxic end,
Wasn't it just yesterday the earth was our dear friend?
    —Carol Bailey

I miss you today —
You've left footprints
On my memory
That remain through time;

The impression deeper
And more lasting
Than "I love yous"
Written in sand —

Soon swept away
                With the tide

*Dedicated to my husband —
My Inspiration — Whose
"I love yous" are always
written in stone . . . .*
    —Denise K. McQuiston

LOVE BROKE

Now I sit to write,
as the radio plays our song.
I wipe tears from my eyes,
as you've been gone so long.
I think of days past,
as I continue to cry.
You said that you loved me,
but still you said good-bye.
I'm really sorry for,
the things I have done.
Now I'm left all alone,
all alone, with no one.
If you loved me again,
it would heal my wounded heart.
But for now my dear,
where should I start.
If we could love each other,
like once in the past.
Our hearts wouldn't be broke,
and then maybe it could last.
    —Travis P. Soileau

A SONG

Oh, to sing a song to thee
T'would keep thee lying next to me
Though bitter phrases cloud my ears
The toil of ill-begotten years.

So, frantically I search in vain
Just oh to lessen bitter pain
For but a moment though to sing
A song that you to me would bring.

So, late into the night I fret
For what I have not found as yet
The strain inside is near to break
When from a dreamstate I awake.

Oh, horrors what could I have done
I see the rising of the sun
For now my bitter fate is sealed
No more tormented pen to wield.

For, with the coming of the day
No words in song for me to say
For but a moment though to sing
A song that you to me would bring.

*Dedicated to my once and forever
soulmate, H. James Mahmood
This is my heart song to you.*
    —Renée Melles

TO LOVE

Two eyes which see me through and through,
  Two shoulders which hold my head when blue, oh blue
Two ears which hear when words are not spoken,
    Two arms which hold me and stay unbroken.
Two hips which shake and dance so free,
    Two legs which run, run ever to me,
        To which, I Love thee!
    —Beth A. Gordon

What is behind the doubt burning in your eyes?
  You almost wanted to love me.
Now, I'm as refreshing to your life as the creaking sound of
  old rusty hinges on a cellar door, as comforting to you as
  a blackbird screeching in bare winter trees.
There is a dark cloud covering a full moon.
The stars, once sparkling, are hidden.
This long, lonely silence between us suffocates me.
If only you'd reach out and pull me back into you, before I
  completely disappear in the total darkness of uncertainty.
    —Linda Jean Lohr

IN MY SOLITUDE

In my solitude — my thoughts drift to you.
I remember the soft look in your eyes —
As you watched me move through my day;
And how they'd twinkle as you thought a special thought.
I remember the corners of your mouth —
And how they'd continue up in full grin.
Your face lights up in reflection of my own —
And becomes a canvas full of picture stories and truths.
I remember the soft, warm touch of your hands —
And how they moved across my body;
As explorers setting out for new adventures — not hurried —
But determined to make the journey a memorable one.
Your quiet talk and hushed whispers soothe me now,
Even in your absence; and I find myself humming songs
We sang last meeting.
I feel your arms around me; comforting me
And filling me with a sense of completeness —
Keeping me close — Till we meet again . . . .
    —Denise K. McQuiston

YOU BRING TO ME

You bring calm into my life . . .
and light into my world.

You bring joy into my days . . .
and sadness when we say goodnight.

You bring hope for my tomorrows . . .
and faith in myself today.

You bring to me your smiles . . .
and eyes that say "I love you."

You bring into my life a treasure . . .
and ask for nothing in return.

You bring a wonderment of caring into this friendship . . .
and a sensitivity, I've never known.

You bring all your positive traits . . .
and teach them to me one by one.

You bring me so much happiness and joy . . .
that I wonder, are you real, or just a dream?
    —Deborah K. Leadens

Oh sunlight strike these eyes that they might see the darkness of today and hence avoid it.
For living with a vision misted with ignorance is far worse than living with no vision at all;
Although living with no vision at all is ignorance.

—Devin Teague

HOKO RIVER DIG

I walk in burning mud,
Burning from the pressure of brown feet
And of lost voices buried within
A soaked anatomy.
The tides are low
And basketry fragments excrete their shelled whispers
Of twenty-five centuries of silence.

The acidic curiosity of science
Attempts to pry open those whispered secrets
And to decipher their ancient songs,
As I walk through this village site,
Within invisible footprints.

—Karl Ickes

A DIOS

A world to hell has gone,
   violence with arms has dawned,
   not by guns nor by swords,
   merely with maniacal spurn of words.
Deceive, the media says it must,
   as they descend with a news rush,
   twisting schizophrenically to disband,
   their hellish creation in their hand,
   all their lies could only serve,
   a fiendish, impartial bunch of brainless nerves.
I will fight with all my might for those,
   whose desires are to escape those howling whores.
On the night when they open their plight in pen,
   the upright will stand, but not for
Satan's gain.

—Mariano Otero

THE VIOLATED CHILD

Refused the knowledge of acceptance
Violated
Pushed into the shadows, of a dark cold existence
Shunned . . .

Walking through the mist
Rain runs down a cheek
Intertwining
with the salt of a child's tear.

Downtrodden, Weary
Alone . . .
Unable to see the sun
nor feel its healing warmth.

The truth never told
imprisoned within
The secret
of a father's deepest sin.

Robbed of all innocence
her purity none
The soul of a child
Fading . . . Her spirit is gone.

—Audrey Nieto

TO HOLD MY HEAD UP HIGH

I hold my head up high
   Once confused and afraid
   An innocence lost
   But experience gained
And I hold my head up high
   My heart and pride
   Once shattered
   Have made their way together again
   The things I have seen
   have made me strong
So I will continue to hold my head up high
   If you should look into my eyes
   and see the pain
   of happiness lost once again
   Know that I've been there before
   and will endure
I will continue
   to hold my head up high

—Erin James

I'M NOT GOOD ENOUGH

I'm not good enough.
Who said that?
You don't have a degree.
OK — That'll make me OK?
I'll get one!
I'm almost there . . .
Am I good enough yet?

Sorry — You need your Masters!
What!? But you just said?
So what! What would happen
If people thought they were OK?
Yeah! What would happen?
Things in the world might function . . .
And then who'd need a degree?

You're not good enough — no Ph.D.
I'm not good enough.
Who said that?!
Not Me!

—June V. Becker

EXILE

On one day, somewhere in the past
The dawn awoke without me.
Strange there, in my own bed
Lost to myself.
I prayed my pulse would still
Before they noticed I had left.
With deft fingers I rearranged my hair
Into its old disguise,
Drew the eyes to proper unconsciousness
And stepped out through the thick wall
Of my complacent womb.
The dawn and I were born
Unobserved.
I ran to find who had fathered me,
To tell him!
But himself had been devoured
Leaving me alone in that exiled realm
Of awareness
Where I knew nothing,
And sensed all.

—Marilyn Bray

TO MATHEUW

As you remain in Heaven
happy from war,
the light in the tunnel
you find a door.
God has invited your soul
to come in
for a special reason.

—Adon J. Janse, age 9½

A VALLEY REFLECTION

I grew up in Renfrew
A quaint little town
In Aberdeen Park
At the North end of town.

I swam in the Bonnechere
And played in the Park
As I think of it now
It was really a lark!

I skated in winter
And skied on the hills
We attended the Movies
To acquire our thrills.

There was no thought of Pot
Of Cocaine, or of Crack
But of fun and good friends
There was *never* a lack.

In the heart of the Valley
We grew up in style
We look back on our childhood
With ever a smile.

—"Petunia Skittlebum"

A GRAIN OF SAND

Our boys and girls running
Along beaches
Watching
Listening
Hearts pounding
Sand in eyes
Ears, mouth, blisters,
No foot prints
Warm, cold
Ever changing designs
Made by wind vehicles
Little hands, big hands
Tears, smiles
Long last looks
No sand castles
Sharing faces of home
Well kept secrets
A grain of sand

Saudi

*Dedicated to our armed forces
leaders, our boys and girls,
our brave, strong family members
who gave strength, and kept
our country strong*

—Jean M.S. Lerner

WHEN I BEGAN

That atavistic ancestor whose footfall matched the music
that he made as he marched in rhythm with his Desire
to reach the far mountain
the streams he followed gave him new patterns of song;
the blowing grasses gave his body new bendings
whether in the wind of yearning or of striving
or of favoring force,
The cats that leaped sinuous in the distance
sent ripples of lithe reaction
through sinews that learned to swim
the ripples of the ever-flowing waters.
Now is all that rhythm mine
bequeathed through the ever-living umblical cord.
They are my Subconscious
unreleased—yes, unreleased
until Ego-maturity turns the key.

—Cecile Musson Smith

TEARS

I awoke one morning and you were gone.
'Where are you?' my heart cried
But only silence answered.
I reached for the warmth of your touch
But the sheets lay cold with your absence.
'Why did you leave?' I called to silence.
'Did I love you too much that you fled with fright
And left me here with loneliness to hold me?'
If I let you go this time, how long will you stand in the
fires of your terrors
Before you grow tired of the pain?
I feel singed from the many times of pulling you away from
the flames
And my grip on you weakens.
God will not allow me to burn with you.
He whispers to me to release you
But I hold on for fear of your pain.
I would hang onto you forever
But the Lord says, 'Trust in me.'
'Oh God! Help him!' I pray.
And the Lord reaches down with his Fatherly hand
To stroke my cheek and to catch my tears.

—S. Kay

PSYCHO SAVIOR

Blind resurrection is called upon you
You are reluctantly heeding its warning
Your dulled terror reeking, Pulsing through your veins

Confusion balks you . . .
Decisions control you . . .

NO one can be your savior
You stand above waiting atop a treacherous plateau
With waves that shatter upon the jagged rocks that
Mock you

As you look beneath your feet,
Scarred from being bare,
Bleeding from the pebbles imbedded in
your souls

You see hopelessness . . .
You see deception . . .

But, then you take another LOOK.
You think perhaps you see a glimmer of PRIDE.
You bend over straining to look closer,
But all you find is
Fools gold

—Yoon Sun Kim

My death will be mysterious.
As you think of the deductive reasoning around it,
It will feel numb.
It will decrease its value, to nothingless.
feel my heart, it is no longer there!
You will never know the truth,
Because how I feel,
how I think, Is DEAD!!
no longer heard,
no longer understood.
—Angela Cronch

SIMPLICITY

I think that I've lived well today —
Countless blessings came my way.
I had a rendezvous with life, I did.
I found life's beauty from which I hid.

I seemed to be captured by hours in the day.
In seeking more minutes, life slipped away.
I worked and I planned, worried and scurried,
Wondering why I always felt hurried.

I kicked off my shoes and decided to rest,
Meticulously watched a wren build a nest.
I listened to laughter of children at play,
Heard echoes of nightfall, closing the day.

I watched the sunrise light the earth.
I counted the riches of what life was worth.
Barefoot I walked in the fresh morning dew,
Sensitized by simplicity, peacefulness, too!

Now cognizant am I of life's endless treasures —
I know how to calculate limitless measures,
Living and learning, experiencing, yearning —
I'm thankful, that peaceful now, my world is turning!
—Patricia A. Swisher

LAUREL MEMORIAL
To Two Great Friends

Mississippi, Laurel, are greatly bereft:
Two pioneer educators have finally left;
Mr. Watkins, Superintendent, godly as preacher,
Prentiss School, one of Laurel's master teachers;

Instilling love of God, country, and brothers,
Teaching respect, and rights of all others,
Sowing their seeds of knowledge and character,
Growing fruits and flowers, in youths, coming after.

They planted their gardens, — some, forty years —
From baskets of wisdom and love, those dears.
They nurtured, weeded — some, watered with tears —
And now they reap heaven's blessings, and cheers.

Their fruits and flowers their fragrance still send;
Thus continue to honor Laurel's Two Great Friends:
Mr. Watkins, our Dean of Wisdom College,
Prentiss School, our Pioneer in Truth and Knowledge.

Dedicated to R.H. Watkins, Supt., 40 yrs., Laurel City Schools, Laurel, MS; Bernice Tyner Booher, School Pianist and First Grade Teacher, Prentiss, 40 yrs.; Bertie Bell Cook, Long-time Principal, Prentiss School.
—Mary Alice Badeau Jenkins

EVOLVE NOW

Moving on, Moving upward,
Expanding in the light.
Cymbals ringing, rhythm abounding
With celestial might.
Spiraling upward more and more
towards an open door, of pure white light.
Evolving, moving, flowing,
No discord, only sweet delight.
Moving on to Eternal Presence.
—Patricia Rudolph

LIFE'S NOT A BOWL OF CHERRIES

Life's not a bowl of cherries,
Bowl of cherries,
Bowl of cherries.

There are many things to get done,
And they're not exactly "fun."
Life's not a bowl of cherries.

Make a lunch,
Prepare a brunch,
Feed the cat,
Get rid of the rat,
There are beds to make,
And lots of things to bake,
Still, don't shirk,
You have to go to work!

Life's not a bowl of cherries,
Bowl of cherries,
Bowl of cherries!
—Haley Dillon, age 10

THE LAST LETTER

Late one night you went away
and did not say good-bye
you tried to keep a secret
because of foolish pride

I hurt for you, I prayed to God
to take your pain away
he answered and took you home
but I wish you could have stayed

I think I knew you held a secret
which many tried to hide
in secrets there lies death
but chose to keep your pride

Deep inside I always knew
that you could never really be mine
but like the others I looked away
and said that things were fine

Your lifestyle was your secret
that you tried to lock up tight
but all things done in darkness
are always brought to light

Soon I will forgive you
but for now I need my anger
because the secrets that you kept
could have put my life in danger

I'll never really understand
although I know society isn't always kind
and although I may be angry
I hope it's peace that you shall find
—E. Tisa Long

LOVING

Loving you as I do
Our life being happy today
I ponder in my thought of thoughts
What would I do
If you decided to go away

To leave the life we have built
Which seems so wonderful & grand

To be without you darling
Would be like seeing a beach
Absent of its sand

Life's road, so hard to handle
Without you it would be such a void
A sky absent of its stars at night
A night without its pale moonlight

—Lorraine Cypher

SPRINGTIME

Behold the lilies in the field,
See the fruit trees in their yield;
Hear the robin sing its song,
Spring is near — it can't be long!

Grass turning green from winter's sod,
Coming to life, reminds me of God;
Turns me to that higher power
That rules the earth, sea and air.

It brings to mind our risen Lord
As recorded in God's Holy Word;
Victorious over death and grave,
The vile sinner's soul to save.

It points me to an unknown day
When that same risen Lord will say,
"I gave my life that you might be
With me in Springtime, for eternity."

—Willie Rose Green

MY LITTLE COCOA PUFF

My "Little Cocoa Puff"
(My little ball of fluff!)
You're so cute and cuddly —
Always so playful and bubbly.

Whether you're taking a little nap,
Sound asleep upon my lap —
Or under the covers you go . . .
To nibble on my big toe.

Just holding you against my chest,
While we take a little rest.
Just holding you in my arms . . .
My little puppy with all your charms.

You're a special little guy.
I needn't ask why
God has sent you
With all your love so true.

Oh! My "Little Cocoa Puff"
(My little ball of fluff!)
Just snuggle up to me —
For together we'll always be.

*Dedicated to Cocoa Puff Chazmo, my
little toy poodle. His unconditional
love has inspired me to put my
thoughts into poetry.*

—Judith Kay Burnett

AT JOURNEY'S END

The seasons yearn to stay awhile,
To do their thing with grace and style
The sunshine seems a little brighter,
Everyone's steps a little lighter.
The stars do twinkle a little more,
As seas rush on to caress the shore.

Why, you ask, do these things take place,
Why do many have smiles on their faces?
The answer's as simple as can be,
It is God's love for you and me.
No matter which of life's roads we take,
At journey's end, God's love awaits.

—Lafern E. Porter

THE HARP

In the attic of my wistful mind
dwells here an ancient harpsichord
which lies beneath the dust of humankind
and waits to play in harmony once more.

It longs for dazzling strokes of player's fingers
by day, in shadows, reaches for the light
which forming spectrums only briefly lingers
to once again depart into the night.

As darkness folds in all around the portal
the creaking of the floor creates the sound
a heralding of frequent not a visitor
to a cluttered place so seldom ever found.

Expecting not the music to begin
A welcome guest then plucks the fragile strings
creates a random melody, but then
departs to leave the harp no song to sing.

Returns no more, but haunts the darkened space
as music to the soul is like the wind
to whisper love and leave without a trace
to play once more, but never play again.

—Wilda Graham

I LOVE YOU MY LORD

I love you my Lord
For saving my soul

I love you my Lord
For making me whole

I love you my Lord
For setting me free

I love you my Lord
For always healing me

I love you my Lord
Let the little girl see
That for her you died on the tree

I love you my Lord
Let the little girl keep her eyes on Thee

I love you my Lord
Help the little girl not to follow me
But my Lord, my Lord, only Thee

I love you my Lord
Your word is so good to me
And all my life your presence will always be

—A. Rosita Jones

LET FREEDOM RING

As Bold As A Lion You See, His Only Purpose IS To Be Free.
Yes There Is Freedom For All On This Great Planet.
Yet, We Fail To Recognize The Best Things In Life Are Free.
Let Freedom Ring.
What A Joy To Have Purpose In Life.
Oh, Once You Were Willow, But Now You Favor The Mighty Oak.
Remember To Bring The Things We Take For Granted To Light.
This Is The Land Of The Free And The Brave.
Pause, Let Us Thank Those Who Made Sacrifices; Ethical, Moral And Cultural.
"Long Live The King's Dream."
    —Pattie Denise Gates

AND WE LOVED YOU

We were there . . . Did you know? We were always there. We stood by —
And loved you, even when you went to our neighbor's house and said
We'd hired men to kill you. Then the police came. And we loved you,
When we dead-bolted the door, chained and padlocked the gate —

To keep you in — so you wouldn't embarrass us anymore.
Like the time at the bank, when you started screaming that your son
Was stealing your money, or when you tried to jump out of the car —
On the freeway. Still, we didn't blame you, we tried to understand.

And we loved you.

I wish I could forget the way you looked when last I saw you —
A shrunken frame of a woman — swallowed up by the large lift chair
You lay in, hunched to one side, heavy-headed,
Unable to wake from the sleep you were lost in.

We could feel the growing emptiness of our little house as we
Watched the spirit leave your body. It was December, Christmas
In the air, the tree just bought, the house rearranged with frills.

I left my parents that day because I knew. I left them sitting
On the floor, on either side of your big chair, I left them —
And went Christmas shopping — because I couldn't stay —
And watch you die. And I loved you, Abuela.
    —Gloria Sifuentes

THE OTHER SIDE

I speak to you from the other side . . .
We share the same sadness, it's true.
However, I knew him longer, more differently than you . . .

At first there was such anger, from all of us, I know . . .
The people gathered 'round you, to comfort and console.
The anger turned to hatred, when quiet talk turned bold,
I wondered what was happening, to all of us and so . . .

I speak to you from the other side . . . not spouse, not daughter, nor mother,
He was to me you know, my very special brother . . .

And now I mourn three others, no longer can I see them.
So close and yet so far . . . yearning to free them . . .
Your hold is, oh so tight!
Must you make me fight? Or, visit just with sight . . .

The emptiness surrounds me, on days when I am blue . . .
I sit and think about him, of days when in our youth.
There is so much confusion, of that you can't deny,
So much included in, the only question, WHY?

I speak to you from the other side . . .
My feelings aren't quite clear,
You see my special brother, left me just little over a year . . . .
    —Michele Yarrow

FATE

She jumps on the earth,
As if it's a ride.
She's neighbors with the moon,
They live side by side.

She bounces and plays
As she goes 'round and 'round.
She's obnoxious and loud,
But makes not a sound.

She's love and hatred,
Sadness and laughter.
She's peace and war,
From now ever after.

But when the ride's over,
She'll jump off to cry.
She'll fall through the universe,
But never will die.

—**Autumn Larson**

A THOUGHTFUL RHYME

Everything is temporary
   including time
and the birds on the
   telephone line.
Summer, winter, fall
   and spring.
I look for things
   about which to sing.
Walking along at a slow pace
I have no desire to win a race.
Important things
   are hard to find.
I find my happiness
   evolves from within.
I trust myself — not
   other people's whims.
Everything is temporary
   That's my 'by-line.'

—**Winifred Mingle**

FAIR WARNING

This is always true
So bear in mind —
One person's "junk"
Is another person's "find."

If you don't take care —
And try to be kind
The one that gets hurt;
Is the one left behind.

Maybe someone else
Never had what you have —
And can really appreciate
What you treat so bad.

They'll collect it up —
Polish it well —
And after awhile
No one will tell —

That it was cast aside
All bent and dented —
It will look brand new —
With its heart all mended . . . .

—**Denise K. McQuiston**

WORKING HANDS

Working hands are hard to find,
Especially ones both strong and kind.
Yet, I found a pair that's in rare form,
A pair that's endured many a storm.

These hands tell a story, if you're willing to read;
A lesson they'll teach, if you're willing to heed.
There are so many lives these hands have touched.
They belong to a man who is loved very much.

I'm glad that I found them; 'twas a wonderful day.
When I needed a hand, they were there right away.
Now I understand this, my quest was an honor . . .
For I found that these hands belong to my father.

—**Barbara Brickey Jividen**

THE FARM LABOURER

Bill, was walking home from his job one day
   It had been a tiring day, bailing hay.
Summer was over, he could feel the chill,
   He could see the smoke coming over the hill.
Smoke meant that fire was in the grate,
   Better hurry now or he would be late.

He opened the door, he could feel the heat,
   After the cold outside it was really a treat.
He took off his clothes and entered the tub,
   After a meal he was on the way to the pub.

He and his wife knew the crowd in there,
   Even the pianist, her name was Clare.
After some songs they were full of good cheer,
   Especially when the landlord appeared with the beer.

You'd think everything was going just fine,
   Until suddenly, they heard the word 'TIME!'

So old Bill's life was never too drear,
   He could always rely on the pub and the beer.
Every night was a night of good cheer,
   With good friends, where else would he be . . . but here.

—**Alf Jones**

BEAUTIFUL BLACK CHILD

Beautiful Black Child.
   Beautiful Black Child
running aimlessly without a cause
like a stallion in the wild.

She takes a pause.

Beautiful Black Child
with brown, almond eyes searching for tomorrow's dreams in God made Heavenly skies.

Beautiful Black Child
whose mind is innocent and free capturing every challenge set before thee.

Beautiful Black Child
singing a joyful message of victory. No! No! No more bondage, no not for me.

Beautiful Black Child
playing in the sand, experiencing creativity with Ebony, blessed hands.

Beautiful Black Child
a natural jewel from Mother Earth. Unique. Special.
Oh, how precious is her birth.

—**Elizabeth M. Williams**

MY MOTHER

God could have chosen another
And, not you, to be my mother.
So, I thank Him for choosing YOU
'Cause you'd have been my choice, too!

*Dedicated to my mother, Trice Manns
. . . real genuine . . . and one
of a kind. I love you, Mama.*

—Betty A. Mannon

THE WATER'S THIN

It's hot.
The stream is flowing.

So, I run to see the stream.
Now, it is just a brook.

It's hot the stream is flowing.
I stop and wonder why the water's thin.

Then, I walk in.

—Victoria Bennett-Lindeman

SOMEDAY

Maybe someday
That time will come
When this world
Can be as one.
When all races
Can unite
And be friends
Instead of fight.
Walk together,
Hand in hand,
Over this
Divided land.
Carry each other
Down the shore
Just so we can talk some more.
Care enough to lend a hand.
Love enough to share the land.

—Sarah E. Walsh

MY FAITH

He is always there to walk with me
Through the darkest of nights,
He gives me strength and courage
Until the break of morning light.

He listens when I talk to him
About my burdens and my pain,
Sometimes he is all I have
Among the storm clouds and rain.

He reaches out and touches me
Tells me to be patient and to smile,
That he is always there for me
Until I walk that last lonesome mile.

I am alone but never lonely
As he is never far away,
My faith in him grows stronger
As he will call me home someday.

—Dorothy A. St. Louis

ANSWER IN THE SKY

The moon peeks through my pane
it remains a vision blurred
I looked to it for guidance
it whispered and I heard

the message did not come in words
rather in energy and light
when I close my eyes — I feel it
love has no need of sight

—Colleen McElligatt

THE SPIRIT OF THE DREAM

He rides the currents of the air,
Free to go most anywhere,
A thing of beauty, grace, and strength,
His wings stretched out to their full length.

Strong and fearless he appears,
From cloud strewn sky the tree he nears,
He glides in slow, applies the brake,
To take his perch above the lake.

That proud and noble setting head,
Independent it could be said,
Intelligence gleams from his eyes,
He's Nature's ruler of the skies.

He stands for freedom, stands for pride,
Courageous heart beats deep inside,
Independent, proud, and free,
Like this symbol, we all should be.

To reach for ever higher heights,
Stand for freedom and equal rights,
The eagle represents this theme,
He is the spirit of the dream.

—Erick L. Sokn

END OF INNOCENCE/THE FAIRYTALE MYTH

This is the age of innocence
Ivory wedding dresses
We don as we walk down the aisle
Lace veils cover our blushing faces
Yet why do I wish I had a black veil
To mourn the death of innocence
A veil of secrecy
With which I enable myself to cry
Puffy white clouds
Shower down upon me
I feel a snowy coldness approaching
For it must be winter
Or maybe numbness
Which makes us frigid and hard
A stark, quiet, fruitless existence
Why can't I escape
I can't breathe
I pale in comparison to the person you once knew
Lift the veil, so that I can see more clearly
Purity is but a sin, forgive my indiscretions.

*Dedicated to old friends and new, much gratitude
for the help, support, encouragement and feedback.
Thanks: Marc, Michelle, Kerin, Jenn, Chantal,
Steph, Dawn, Tylene, Anita and Mom.*

—Diane Normandin

A CERTAIN STAR

A certain star burns so bright
sometimes I think I will get burned from the light.
Although I've tried to hide from sight,
I cannot ignore the bright light.
Why, oh, why am I the only one who sees the light?
Others have scanned the sky but alas they cannot see the light.
Is it because, my dear, you are the Certain Star that burns so bright?

—Bruce Horaz

PANORAMIC MAGIC

I love the sound of rain on the "RV" roof.
Its cheerful rhythm like some tiny hoof.
Sent from the sky to dance for you.
    To sweep away the dust and cobwebs too.

Grumbling thunder — lightning streaking to the ground.
    Awesome majesty all around.
A rumble here — a flash there,
    Panoramic magic everywhere.

Sunlight begins spilling its light,
    making marked contrast of shadow and bright.
The rest of the sky is still darkly stained.
    You wonder if thunder and lightning will repeat its refrain.

—Mary Alice Bastian

THE CAST

Life is like a stage, and we are members of the cast
It ends with the present, and starts with the past
Everyone here has a part in this game
For some it is the future to fortune and to fame
Some will not make it, and give up from the start
We cannot blame them, they weren't meant for the part
Some find the part they're looking for
Just to hear the slamming of a door
As the names and faces come and go
They might have made it but did not know
The seasons change so quickly and the years go by
Some were riding way too low, and others up too high
For some it will come easy, for some a constant fight
Some will never really know which way is wrong or right
But all of us together are members of the cast
And what we left for others to enjoy is all that's going to last!

—Paula Ellison Price

DEATH IS ONLY A DREAM

Only a dream, Only a dream of glory beyond the dark stream.
How peaceful thy slumber,
How happy the wakening,
For death is only a dream.
Friends come nigh, they say I must die.
Early the summons, have come from on high.
The way is so dark, yet I must go
Oh what sorrow you may never know.
Mother, 'twas dark, and the light came at last
And flooded my Soul with esteem.
Only a prayer, Only a tear.
Oh if brother and sister here.
Only a word from the book so dear,
For death is only a dream.
Only a dream, Only a dream, of glory beyond the dark stream.
How peaceful the slumber,
How happy the awaking.
For Death Is Only A Dream.

—Lorraine Rudd

LIFE

Believe me:
If I knew anything,
Then I'd tell you everything;
I'm not God!

—L.M. Ward

THE RAIN AND THE WIND

The rain cries!

The wind blows!

The kids run in the rain!

The rain and the wind laugh at the kids!

In the summer the rain goes and the wind stays!

—Courtney Lynn Haynes, age 8

ROLLING THROUGH GEORGIA

Rolling
    through
        Georgia

Rolling
    through
        Georgia

Hear
    my drums
        rolling
            through
                Georgia

Roaring
    through
        Georgia

Roaring
    through
        Georgia

Hear
    the battle
        roaring
            through
                Georgia

Rolling
    through
        Georiga

Roaring
    through
        Georgia

Hear
    my drum

Hear
    the battle

Rolling
    and
        roaring
            through
                Georgia.

—Ernest F. Barr

CHANGE OF SEASON

White snow flake,
    falls gently down,
On placid lake,
    and frozen ground.
While nature sleeps,
    beneath the storm.
Where mother keeps,
    her children warm.
Till restless spring,
    creates a shift,
From winter's blight,
    to summer's gift.
The gift of life,
    that makes birds sing.
The brilliant color,
    that flowers bring.
A picture of beauty,
    no canvas can claim.
For renewal of life,
    is never the same.

—Pamela Meloni

OUR LAST GOOD-BYE

Though you still
are here,
distant in your
silence,
of painful feelings
unaware,
so sure
of your righteous
perceptions.

One last farewell
my fellow,
I wish to give you.

Unspoken words
never unlatched.
Feelings.
Uncomfortable moments,
grey stares,
boxed.

As a one time
exception,
just before you go,
tell me . . . ,
could you have
cared?

Days long
I reminisce.
Nights . . .
unguarded, hopeful,
searching
for a moment,
a warm instant,
a meaningful gesture,
to capture
the words you never
utter.

Farewell unloved,
it is our last good-bye
together.
Let's find a final minute
for forgiveness,
Maybe . . . I care.

—Jorge Letelier

TO WHOSE SHORES DO WE BELONG?

To whose shores do we belong?
The shores that we were snatched from in the night,
snatched from our ancient mothers and fathers!

The shores our enslaved sisters and brothers dreamed to someday
return? The same shores that we are told hold only nightmares?

To whose shores do we belong?
The shores that the keepers of the lineage carved
a brutal history of our past, their bodies and minds bent
but not broken—forged a new beginning in a new and strange land.

Their Heritage beaten out of them as beasts of burden.
To whose shores do we belong?
Forced to live a future thirsting for the past.
Touching, but not feeling.
Looking, but not seeing.
The senses long for the answer to the question . . . Who Am I?
To whose shores do we belong?

—Marie Placide Durr

CICADA'S SERENADE

A cicada sits with me on a canoe on my honeymoon.
A cicada sits with his favorite Saturday afternoon serenades.
Just got married, we sit there, feeling lazy afternoon sun,
Listening to him sing, as if weaving the waves.

*My Love, sings a cicada, I like your homemade grits.
Give me more with a glass of Lemonade,
Give me more with no maple syrup.
Oh delicious, oh wonderful, oh fantastic.*

A cicada sits with me on a canoe on the river.
I'm your company. I'm your company.
A cicada sits with me on a canoe, singing.

*Sinning is a pleasure seeking.
I was watching you from up on that orange tree.
My friends also heard her stifled with her own blood.
She died fast.
You are free now, sir. Women are sick.
But you cannot eat any more of her grits.*

—Keiko Nishimura

SILENT WINTER

The sun — died; the music — silenced; my world — shattered.
The candles flickered, and the wild wind roared.
The earth sighed, an oak collapsed, your eyes closed in peace.

And Picasso lost his dream . . .
. . . All, on the day you left me . . .

They said you had flown away, away to the stars and skies.
You were no more in pain — My pain had just begun.
Comfort was all about me, and yet — I sensed none.
Your healing was over — Mine was far from ending.

Sweet spring and songs were all around me, but
All I could see was a silent winter.

I strained for your voice, yearned for your laugh, screamed for your face.
You had gone — I was left alone.

Though you were a black void, your memory was a rainbow — a perfect prism.
They stared at an empty shell — you held my hand.
You heard my cries, came, and wrapped me in roses.
Thorns pricked my heart — You kept me alive.

Even now, you are behind me: leading me, loving me, singing, laughing.
Sweet rain fills my eyes. I cry for a blessed father.

. . . The tears came, on the day you left me.

—Jenna Pendragon

REALIZATION

I'm caught in the web of fulfillment.
You seem serene.
I've wished upon many a star—
and dried my tears with crushed hopes.
Everything seems so simple,
    but it is not.
You don't like me.
Friendship is not a word that comes to mind—
    when I look at you.
I wish my heart wouldn't flutter so often.
My ego conveniently keeps me in place.
I have to move on.
Why am I always lonely?
I am invisible to you.
There was never a spark.
You had a hidden agenda.
I'll die slowly—
until your image disappears from my memories.
My dreams were never found.
    I had nothing.

—Roberta L. Wilson

TO MY UNBORN CHILD

Even though I can't hold you in my arms
    or gaze into your little eyes,
I can feel your every move and twitch.
It's a miracle that within my womb you lie.

You have grown so much already
    and you seem to be healthy and strong.
Your father and I can't wait til you're born
It's just 4½ more months, it won't be long.

We'll love you because you're our lovely child.
So it doesn't matter whether you're a girl or boy.
You'll be just as precious to us either way.
You'll be our little bundle of joy.

For now I hold you in my dreams
but it won't be long before you're in my arms.
When you're here you'll know you're loved
as your father and I keep you from all harms.

*Dedicated to my loving husband Ronnie
and my beautiful daughter Irene.*

—**Judy Runnels**

SOLITUDE

Strawy tangled field,
Nature's graveyard reaching
Toward this solitary house.
Solemn gray clouds motionless overhead,
A blanket for this lifeless corpse.
Everything is frozen in time.
Here and there hangs a stiff wilted leaf,
A relic of the fall: a stigmata of decay.

Within these fading walls
Faint shadows fall on an empty settee.
A forgotten rocking chair watches unstirring.
An antique coffee table waits barren.
Dusty books sit tilted on half empty shelves
Their inner messages unheard.
All listening for footsteps that no longer fall,
For chattering voices no longer heard,
Only the solitary shadow of a man,
Walking slowly, sadly
In this museum of yesterdays
Forever gone.

—**Larry Bogart**

TEACHING

You
Behind the walls
Wearing your mask
Look within
Is there any good thing?
You abhor the reflection so—
You build another wall

Shackled to the walls
You hide the fallen countenance
Behind a smile of wax
But I see you as you are
I look through walls
Melt wax

Stripped of your fetters
You can fly
Give me your hand
And I'll give you my wings

—**Eunice Cornish**

MY ISLAND FRIENDS

They came from the island,
    To play baseball.

With love in their hearts,
    for one and all.

They cared for me,
    when I was just me.

Not for someone,
    I wanted to be.

Their memories remain
    deep in my heart,

and my love for them,
    will never part.

But I hope they remember
    that I was a part,

Of the most wonderful team,
    that loves from the heart.

—**Les Wright**

fire flies

from my window I see them dance
floating gently on the air
soft star shine so close to me
flickers of light so fair

as a child I caught them
place them behind the glass
the wonder that entranced me
imprisoned — did not last

beauty I had to capture,
possess, and make it mine
Mother warned me of the danger
death does not take much time

so sad and unaware
my exuberance took their lives
collected, jarred, and forgotten
the seizure became the crime

now content to watch them
glide by upon a breeze
smiling when I realize
their freedom is my release

—**Colleen McElligatt**

HAWK

Hawk soaring, circling
High above on the warm breeze
Oh, to be so free!

—Jeri Sorensen

HARD TIMES

It is in these times
These times when it seems
All is ending
When nothing is right
It is in these times
That I want to run
To run, screaming your name
When I can run no further
I will walk, speaking your name
When I can walk no further
I will crawl, whispering your name
When I can crawl no further
I will simply lie there
Thinking of the joy
That has been brought
To me
By you

—David Agrava

IN MY HEART, FOREVER

I see your eyes,
I feel your touch.
I see your smile,
It hurts so much.

I start to cry when I think,
That we will never be.
The pain is so deep,
It hurts more than you'll ever see.

A love like this,
Is hard to find.
I can't bear to think,
You'll never be mine.

You've said no words,
But, you've hurt me deep.
In my heart forever,
A place for you I'll keep.

—Kelly Gallagher

THE BELL JAR

I sat behind a wall of glass,
So safe, there in my jar.
And not one soul could touch me.
I viewed them all afar.

And then I felt the softest touch,
But full of strength and love.
And suddenly, the hope returned,
From God who dwells above.

He offered me a safe retreat
Outside my glassy wall—
A perfect grace, a blessed life,
A path to joy—that's all.

'Twas just enough to heal my soul,
And cleanse complete the scar.
And somewhere, in a foggy past,
I've left that sad bell jar.

—Jo Piper

MONEY "vs" LOVE

I was blinded by your love now I can see,
How it came and went so easily.
I sometimes wonder what just went wrong,
Money was the problem all along.
Money isn't everything was the saying for me,
For others it's a never ending reality.
I know now not to mix love with money,
For sooner or later you will lose your honey.
I've lost your love and that burning flame,
What I thought was true was just a game.
We have been through the worst together and the best,
We hug and kissed and all the rest.
In slowly losing hope I got this motto,
Winning your love is like winning the lotto.

—James E. Vangel

TRUE FRIEND

I cast a faint smile and lowered my eyes
I turned to walk away but to my surprise
I heard a soft, "hello," so I turned around
My eyes are no longer looking at the ground
We both reached out with a lonely hand to lend
Standing face to face we feel we have found a "TRUE FRIEND"

Hand in hand down the path smiling faces aglow
First we quicken our step, then we go slow
Giggling girls looking for something to do
My new friend kicks a pebble, I kick one too
We promise our friendship to the very end
Hand in hand we know we have found a "TRUE FRIEND"

To school, to parties we play together every day
Not once do we think of looking far away
Into our future, into our life
When some day each of us will become a wife
With children of our own to care for and tend
And pray that in their life they will find a "TRUE FRIEND"

—MaryLee Buerkle

TWO SPECIAL GIRLS

Four little eyes,
always following me.
No matter where,
if you please.

Outside or inside,
there they are.
Shining just like,
four big stars.

Four little feet,
running after me.
Trying to keep up,
don't you see.

Giggling and laughing,
as they run.
I have to smile,
as I watch their fun.

Four little hands,
working so hard.
Making mud pies,
out in the yard.

Calling real loud,
to all their friends.
To come on over,
and play with them.

Four little ears,
don't miss a thing said.
While two little mouths,
spread it with dread.

In bed little arms,
clutching Raggedy Anns.
Sleeping warm and snuggled,
off into dream lands.

Glowing rosy cheeks,
all in the right places.
Adorn their beloved,
wee little faces.

Watching them grow,
keeps me in whirls.
But that's just fine,
our special twin girls.

*Dedicated to Tonya & Sonya
with love from Gramma*

—Rusty

LITTLE GIRL

Little girl, once full of laughter and glee,
From your dungeon of despair, will you ever be free?
Dream on little one of childish games and play.
In your safe harbor of numbness, may you stay.

Held captive in a prison of hell,
Will anyone come to make you well?
Fear deeply rooted in the past,
Link by abusive link, it was cast.

You were so trusting,
He was so disgusting.
You could do nothing but wait,
For him who controlled your fate.

In the darkness with no light,
A faceless voice whispers, it's all right,
But a brutal body brings pain,
Which forever will remain.

—Deanna Konrath

Child of the trumpet vine
Where are you now?
Where dock leaves grow
And fragrant locust trees abound?
From dimity and corduroy thighs you sprang.
Child of the trumpet vine
Who hears you now?

Who is the child of the trumpet vine?
I am the child of the trumpet vine.
And all of those who remember
The poisonous purple throat of the
Jimson weed, growing rank in the barn lot.
The heavy sweet scent of the locust,
Thistles turned lavender with the dust of country lanes
Cattails necklacing a silent pond.

Even now there is a pale wash of sky
That puts me back where it all began.
And if I see a stand of dock leaves
Or smell locust trees, I am there.
Where is the child that picked the flaming trumpet flower?
Here. I am the child of the trumpet vine.

—Mary M. Taylor

SLEEPING CHILD

You were filled with so much trust,
Your abuser filled only with his lust.
His touch was so brutal,
Your soft whimpers so futile.

So innocent and precious you were,
Unsuspecting of the horror that would occur.
Your little body so tender,
You had to surrender.

As others created by your mind,
Remained behind,
To bear the pain,
You escaped to another plane.

Protected and safe from a world of hypocrisy and lies,
As the others bore the pain and never asked why,
Like soldiers numbed by many wars,
Bravely doing their job, these imaginary conquerors.

Tears still glisten on your cheeks,
Sleeping child, so tiny, frail and meek.
Sleep on my precious little one,
Until the battle is done.

—Deanna Konrath

AS I SIT HERE

As I sit here motionless
underneath the falling sky
I sit here feeling lonely
waiting for the world to pass me by

If I was your raging ocean
And you were my ferocious wave
I'd capture you in suspension
Before you crashed against the bay

As I sit here expressionless
underneath the falling rain
I sit here kissing misery
waiting for you to taste the day

Dedicated to Trevor Allen

—Richard Freedom Davis

THE WORLD AS I SEE IT

Sometimes I wonder what
has happened to this world.

Starving, homeless children,
Raped and beaten girls.

Pollution in ocean and the
air that we breathe.

No room left for happiness
just twisted shattered dreams.

Wars in foreign countries
and the children that we lose.

Homosexuality isn't something
that people choose.

Sexual harassment and
racism is in the air.

Never ending protests yet
people still don't care.

We have to recognize our faults
and be careful of what we say . . .

To make this world a better place
for tomorrow and today.

—Barbara Lynn Miller

CONFETTI

And confetti falls
Alliance pleads
Descension calls
Defiance creeds
The Distance crawls
With rapid speeds
And confetti falls
In tired dreams

—Jennifer Spears

LATE SUMMER

Winds of late August
    draw Summer away.
Seems recent Spring's birth,
    the blossoms of May.
Rushed by their currents
    towards Autumn's dark path,
I wish not — I must,
    if only I hath
the powers of gods,
    those dreams of want men,
for capture of time,
    my sweet Summer again!

—Brian Mugge

THE BOUQUET

Anthologies of life's
Collection

All recorded in verse and
rhyme

Bloom upon the thought
of memories in each man's
mind

Fimbriant petals of yesterdays
action pressed on the pages
of time.

Create the seeds of
Living one day at a time.

—Caulene Hobby Wilkinson

A SAFE PLACE

Why is the world
filled with so much
hate?

Where's the Love
What's the fate.

People dying leaving
so much sorrow.

You don't even know
if you'll see tomorrow.

Take my hand and
walk with me.

Where flowers grows as big as
trees.

We can hide beneath
its leaf.
And shield our selves
from all this grief.

—Yvonne Foster

Goodbye, My Love.
My life will feel incomplete without you; as will my soul, however, it's in our best interest that I leave.

Day after day I watched the selfish demons quench their lusting thirst, damning your soul to an internal hell and your mind to an everlasting quest for pleasure.

Now as each hour unfolds I wonder if it was worth the agony of watching you deteriorate by the minute while those spirits you so desperately need consume your entire being.

Minutes pass what seems like an eternity of time before you stagger into the bedroom and fall once more onto our sagging mattress.

Quietly I creep toward you and kiss your forehead as the tears of anguish twist my battle worn soul.

Taking a deep breath, I close the door and relish my first seconds of freedom before my body wretches from guilt.

—Gina M. Kowalski

FRIENDS AND LOVERS

Fortunately I have you to talk to
Right from the moment
I awaken until the
End of each day.
Never having to feel alone
Dreaming of you constantly
Silently singing my heart out with happiness

Asking you to help ease my loneliness
Never bothers me any longer, wanting to do the same for you
Do I need to say more?

Longing to be with you, sharing our feelings
Over and over again
Violently hating the moments spent apart
Every extra minute I spend thinking of you
Right from the moment I awaken until
Slumber time occurs.

—Melissa J. Marshall

A VISIT WITH A FRIEND AT THE VIET NAM MEMORIAL WALL

I went to the wall to remember
A friend I no longer see
But as I gazed in the wall's reflection
I saw his face looking back at me

I said I will never forget you
I've remembered you all through the years
I told him that was my promise
And both of our eyes filled with tears

We talked of the days back in high school
Of the football games, dances and such
And I told him the world was quite different
But some things had not changed all that much

For a moment he was right there beside me
For a minute I wasn't alone
Then I glanced back at the wall for a second
And saw his name clearly etched in the stone

As I left I heard whispers behind me
Coming from the men in the wall
The message was clear that I heard there
The message was meant for us all

They asked Please don't ever forget us
We gave you the most we could give
For as long as you choose to remember
In your minds and your hearts we still live

—Cindi A. Page

WHEN A STORM IS OVER HEAD

When the clouds move over our sunshine and darken up our day,
Will you be there to hold my hand, and help me find my way,
As time passes us by, and our love appears to be dead,
Can I count on you to be by my side when a storm is over head, when a storm is over head.

—Nicole Jones

WILD FLOWERS

On the side of a two-lane, country highway,
Which divides the fields of late spring wildflowers,
There lies, on a muddy, gravel shoulder, a weeping little girl.
As precious as a porcelain doll,
She lies still, without motion, and weeps in silence.
The door of her father's station wagon is wide open
And there are traces of red on the window.
The car, sitting halfway off the road, idles with a rugged sound.
She can see the tail lights fading into the horizon,
As the sun sets, leaving a purple, hazy tone on the clouds.
A breeze blows and the wildflowers sway,
As if they were acknowledging the pain.
The petals glide through the air as if they are ripped from their stems.
The inside of the car takes on a grim, dark existence
And those crimson tones dictate the mood.
The weeping could be heard for miles,
If there was only someone to hear, someone to sympathize, to comfort.
A torn leather wallet lies under the front wheel . . . Empty!
As the sun sets, a light drizzle begins to fall and the child lies motionless,
The tears mixing with the raindrops . . . Empty.

—Matthew Woods

BORN TO DIE (THE LIFE OF A TREE)

Started from a seed, took root and began to grow.

The first few years were the hardest . . . fighting off the elements and getting my roots embedded firm, but oh how I grew . . . a strong trunk with powerful roots and limbs.

Although I had a long way to grow I was already feeling proud.

I realized I had to enjoy each day as it was, for from the moment of my birth . . . I was born to die.

I tried to grow tall and straight, sometimes I tended to lean a bit, but with the help of my family and friends around me pushing me on . . . again I stood tall.

Little friends started to come to visit, sit on my limbs and talk a while.

Every once in a while through the years I noticed some of my family and friends would leave or die. It made me sad and lonesome, but I kept growing and growing till I was ready to share with others.

A family was born in my trunk, my leaves and limbs protected them from the wind, rain, snow, and sleet.

The years flew by and they grew up, leaving my limbs to make their own homes, but always returning to visit me.

I was getting older . . . my limbs were not as strong, I couldn't battle the storms as easily, but I loved my home in the woods, and when I was hurt my family and friends comforted me.

I knew I was born to die, so I loved and lived with all the emotion and strength I possessed.

The years have passed, I have no leaves, some think I'm dead, but I still am standing strong and proud . . . because somewhere out there my family or my friends will always remember me and I shall live on forever!

Dedicated to my father, Elmer Hammer at the time of his death.

—helen page, m

THE POPLAR TREE

The poplar tree stands proud and tall
With beauty seldom seen,
Loaded with its yellow leaves
Which once were fresh and green.

One yellow leaf comes swirling down
As winds begin to play,
But as the winds become irate
A million float away.

The ground is cloaked with tons of leaves
You feel you want to bawl,
As many tons you rake away
That many more will fall.

The leaves now gone from tree and ground
The tree stands bare and tall.
To see this scene repeat itself,
Just wait until next Fall.

—Annette Silvera

WINDWALKER

I hear a voice speaking in the wind
Windwalker is back again
His voice pierces the barrier of sound
His presence is certainly all around
He walks with the warrior in battle
He gave the rattlesnake his rattle
He knows the thought of every man
He walks on the wind across this land
If we are good we have nothing to fear
But while he is there he is also here
No escape from the hand of Windwalker
He is not just a sweet talker
He rules the world with love and power
He is in control each and every hour
Walk and talk with me Windwalker
Tell me the ways of the death stalker
From all directions you surely come
And we wonder just where you are from
We must believe in our perfect plan
Windwalker please help us to understand

—George D. Winters

STRENGTHENINGS

    Where does your strength come from? Where does it start or even end? Strength comes from making it, and not making it. If you allow yourself to learn from life's ups and downs then a strength starts.
    If Life is important to you as seeing another day arise, then having a clearer view of your daily Life in a path to which you travel into. For without strength then your Life work is in vain.
    Strength comes from a will down deep and strong. A will to stand the test of time.
    Strength never ends as long as you are making a better place in you, than the world around you. Strengthenings.

—Lisa Kay Rupp

OCTOBER DAYS

together
    we held on tight to the strings of those
  high flying October days

  keeping them below the clouds in the sunshine

  living every moment
  touching every side and angle of each other
  in laughter and silence

  the October days have ended

apart
  the touching does not stop
  we are still connected

—Dianna McCormick

THAT WONDERFUL TIME OF YEAR

Fall — a time of seasons —
Sun filled days of delight.
Blowy — wind whipped breezes —
Autumn; what a wonderful time of year.
Crispy, crackly leaves blown hither and yon;
Colors of red, brown, gold, orange and yellow.
One last time:
Fluttery sails sweeping you across the lake;
One last picnic at the beach; or in the park;
A fast horse ride into the hills and back.
Soon to be seen — jack frost at early dawn.
Etching everything in sparkling, glorious white beauty.
Then; nippy, chilly days —
And soon:
Gentle white flakes — drifting softly down,
White beauty — stretched everywhere —
Un-marked, un-trodden.
It's called winter — wonderful winter.

—Marion Wood

She is a secret.
She comes from many regions. Asia, Persian Gulf,
Australia, California, and Venezuela, to name a few.

She is beautiful beyond belief.
She is cultured, coated, protected, and unseen
from everyone and everything.
She is a secret.

Her colors range from rose, cream, white, black,
bronze, brown, pastel shades of lavender, blue,
yellow, green, and mauve.
She is locked away in her private world.
She is a secret well kept.

Created by nature.
So genuine, so unique, like no other.
She's mysterious; no one sees her as she grows.
She is a secret.

This makes her so desirable, sought after by many.
The pleasure to have her, to touch her, to admire
her beauty has been a dream.

She was a secret but someone has found her.
The door to her private world is opened.
She is discovered and the world puts her on display,
so all can see her beauty and elegance.

She is a pearl, she is the secret of the sea!

—Patricia Wagner (Trish)

JOURNEY OF LIFE

If I should die tomorrow on this journey of my life,
Then today I'd ask you honestly if I could be your wife.

And if I should live a thousand years, and you should live one more,
Then I'll be waiting patiently behind the golden doors.

This feeling that I have inside cannot compare by far,
To any love I've ever had that might have left a scar.

A flaming torch of passion burns inside my heart,
Your gentle touch and soothing smile, to me, a work of art.

If you should ever wander a million miles away,
Then a million miles I would walk to see your face today.

And if we should go our separate ways on this path which we both share,
Then I wish you luck in all you do, for I will always care.

—Monica M. Felgner

DIAMOND IN DISGUISE

A diamond in disguise.
The carbon sheath that covers you shows internal darkness.
To the miner however, you are something beautiful
that only takes time to uncover.

The diamond is created over years.
The foundation is solid, but the environment undesirable.
The gem sprakles unconditionally underneath a protective covering
that will eventually be worn away;

To enable the beauty and radiance of the hidden treasure
to shine in all its splendor.
This miracle may happen naturally,
or with the care and patience of another.

Either way, the diamond will finally shine and show off
the beauty that has been covered for many years.
Once this happens, it will enrich the life
of the lucky person setting it in gold.

—Sharon E. Smith

THE CONCH

"I sing of the incredible blue. Oceanic mama, handmaid of the world, given to earth."

Thus was the song that caught my ear, sunrise at the beach;
Like some mysterious radio, a conch lay at my feet.

"My song was once proclaimed by Tritons, trumpeting their city, I witnessed their lives strung from their waists."

A stranger to the maritime, I did not understand. I bid the conch to sing some more,
and closed it in my hand.

"I sing of sailors young and aging, full beards caked with dry salt; brown and brazened arms swinging their sails.
What lovers has the sea had, loyal to the very end of swarthy gaits and faces fresh as their day's catch."

Amazed at this pure instrument of finely layered pearl, I studied it with deep intent,
Yes, every colored swirl. But more than that, I listened to an ancient seabound tune —
A lullaby of falling tides, transpired by the moon.

The day stretched out in greenish-blues, and deeply did I think of majesties and treasure ships long sunken in the drink. And soon I sang in harmony . . . the conch and I were one. In sparkling, emerald
waves of time
My head was gently spun.

Then my mind grew weary (though the song still strummed), and silently I threw the shell to
where it first came from; to land upon another shore, to find another friend;
And so the way it all began, commence now to the end . . .

"I sing of the incredible blue . . . ."

—Jean Mehi

WHERE YOU GO

Where you go, I will follow
Where you walk I will stand
When you leave I'll be going
With a feeling in my heart

When you cry, I'll be weeping
When you're sad, I'll be blue
When you think the world is over
I'll be the one standing by you

Can't you feel the love in my heart?
Can't you see how I love you?
When you think the world has failed you
I won't be the one failing you

—Myra Alexandria O'Bryant

FROZEN ASSETS

A Soul, trapped, on a stair
Frozen, Frozen, See it there.

Trying, to rise, above
Unable, to move, to Love.

Trapped, in the cares, of this world
See, sin spin, and swirl.

Then the Son Shines, upon this Soul
Light, thawing out the cold.

This soul, set Free, from sin's grip
Free to Rise, and make that Heavenly trip.

Are you, like this soul, 'twas so cold
Needing Love, as pure, as Gold?

Then Ask the Son, to come In
And Let, real Love, begin.

When your life, is thawed out, A-New.
You will be ready, to rise, to Heaven too.

—Addison Alfred Barber III

BEAUTIES OF NATURE

Trip, trip, tripping down a country path
To my thoughts I gave sway
To watch wild life at its best
The beauties of nature's way.

My trip be it not in vain
For soon there came a noise
Two squirrels jumping on a limb
They expressed themselves with poise.

Chattering and bouncing from limb to limb
So fast I was losing sight of them
Darkness was gathering all around
Yet, they didn't seem to mind.

One disappeared into the tree
Then came out on the ground
A nut between two little paws
I watched him as he dined.

Then I stumbled back to the path
On my face I felt the breeze
Pictured in my mind were squirrels
Leave them ever to the trees.

—Gladys M. Setters

THE HUSTLE OF TODAY

People going off to work everyday
Seldom have any time to play
Barely knowing their neighbor folk
Should have taken more time to have spoke,
But only the tip of a hat — or a wave of the hand
Surely this is not a part of God's plan
To show some sign of compassion
Is it from a long past fashion?

Life now then has made us greedy
We have no time for the needy
Such a small burden to help share
To show many we still do care —
Yet we say — there is no time
So work, worry, a dime (just to save)
That's for old age you say
Might be better if we all pray.

—Dorothy I. Brown

WHAT MONEY CAN'T BUY

Money can buy a church building,
and money can buy the pew,
but dear friend keep this in mind,
it can't buy Heaven for you.

Money can buy worldly friends,
and worldly possessions, more than a few,
it can buy you world wide travel,
but it can't buy Heaven for you.

Money, the lust of the flesh fulfills,
as the pride of life you pursue,
the lust of the eyes is attained,
but it won't buy Heaven for you.

Now the Bible, it plainly states,
though you have riches more than a few,
these won't open Heaven's gates,
they just can't buy Heaven for you.

—Lee Roy Nevitt

SCHIZOPHRENIA

There are thoughts in my head
    waiting to burst.
Spinning and racing —
    creating a thirst.
I am in my own world,
    is it fiction or fact?
I don't know anymore
    what is exact.
Destruction is my future —
    chaos my state.
Delusions control me —
    Neurotic my fate.
They have labeled me psychotic.
    In my dreamland I will stay.
Insanity has imprisoned me
    as I shuffle about the day.
The whirlwinds of my mind
    compose the emptiness in my eyes.
Here no one can reach me —
    as the man within me cries.

—Cindy A. Dick

WATER

Man has not thanked water enough —
It is only taken for granted!

    Without water there can be
    No flowers or tree —
    Without water you can't
    Have coffee or tea!
    Without water rainbows can come
    Only in dream.
    Without water you can wash windows
    Only with milk or cream!
    There will be a thousand things
    You can't do without water
    Not to mention how many saints
    Will take it a serious matter.

    Oh, dear water, Won't you ever leave me,
    Or it might just as well
    Nothing is said.

    —Harry Wang

WATER PIPE

When he came to me he was charming, and oh so sweet
But beneath all that sugar was something hidden and discrete
I gave him my heart, life's most precious gift
But instead of doing the same he left me adrift
He was no longer charming, and the sweetness melted away
What was left was a stranger who just thought I was in the way
With my heart in his hand, he squeezed it 'till it broke
And with the blood pouring out, he laughed as if it were a joke
I was falling through the darkness, his bitterness cut me like a knife

But a comforting hand reached out, and I held on for dear life
The darkness began to fade, and I saw the light
And who I saw at the end of that hand made everything all right
For he took all the pain and he threw it on the floor
And with him near me, I was happy once more
As for the guy who hurt me, he got lost in the dust
He was like an old, forgotten water pipe covered in rust

*Dedicated to the memory of my father, Gene Allard; who passed
his ability to share his feelings through the beauty
of poetry, to me. Thank you Daddy!*

    —Jenny Allard

THE WATER DANCER

The harvest of winter had passed,
peace and tranquility had returned to the moonlit lake.
As I gazed upon the water's edge, a soft, pine-scented breeze
ruffled gingerly through my hair.
I could see where the shoreline had been abused by nature's moods.
The tranquility was short lived, for from the distance came a voice.
The ancient, distinctive call aroused my senses,
and made the hair on the back of my neck stiffen with anticipation.

I peered out onto the lake, searching, hoping, demanding his presence.
After what seemed like an eternity, a shape, silhouetted
against a silvery reflection of the moon, came into view.
His majestic body slid through the icy-blue water in search of a mate.

Displaying his intricate white scrolling, he held his head high.
He called to the night, and waited. No response.
Finally, from another part of the lake, came a welcome answer.
Lifting his sleek body out of the water he danced along the surface.

Powerful wings pounded gracefully against the forces of gravity.
An echo had stirred his soul, while passion . . . enticed his heart.
But more importantly, winter had left.

His arrival had opened the gates to spring; he, "The Water Dancer."

    —Steven I. Little

we are but two ends of
a spectrum which have
come together, and we've
created our own flavor.

fate has had it that
you have come into my life,
perhaps for no other purpose
than, to let me be me.

    —Robert Winter

CHOICES

You start out young
So strong and brave
To strive for a dream;
Your life you gave.
And though you're not sure
Quite what that goal is yet,
You'll strive to the end
Until it is met.
You'll run the race
Through thick and thin.
You'll set your own pace
Until you win.
And even if you aren't
The best or the first,
You know that you can't
Ever be the worst.
For the first shall be last
And the last shall be first.

    —Sharon E. DeBoer

D. N. A. TOMATO

Perfect body
perfect face
perfect muscles
perfect legs.

Perfect hair
perfect teeth
perfect nose
perfect lips.

Perfect nails
a portable phone
Armani pants
Armani pose.

Perfect body
perfect face
perfect tone
perfect length.

Perfect machines
for perfect friends
perfect lover
and the perfect pet.

Perfect principles
for perfect talks
perfect timing
the perfect clock.

Perfect body
perfect face
perfect muscles
D. N. A. taste.

    —Jorge Letelier

SOMEWHERE IN THE MIDDLE I WONDER

Conditions unfair, mastered by fate.
Cottaged in times eternal wait.

The summer before next
seals the arrival.

Throned for romance, and for love
to rival.

Will you feel the passions as I?
Foreseeing the bond, for which
we are tied?

Or, are you weary and long no more?
Accepting the boundaries behind
structured doors?

—Roberta A. Barrera

THE UNBORN CHILD

Life is too beautiful for anyone to kill.
Especially if not at free will.

The unborn baby, deep within.
To kill, is such an unforgiveable sin.

People think that it is the right thing
   to do,
to get out of trouble . . .
      Would you do it too?

People need help from someone,
to give advice, and show what
      they've done.

Everyone has to die someday,
but no one should have to go
that way.

Just think if you were that
soul . . .
First you have life . . .
      Then no where to go.

—Jessica Erin Bourgeois, age 14

THE RAPIST

He plans to violate her innocence
to molest her faith
to desecrate her trust

She will feel his rage
she will be filled with doubt
she will lose all hope

He will carry out an act so vile
while acting out his anger
he will feed on her terror

He will use her for his own lust
her resistance giving him power over her
he will not care about her pain.

When it is over, he will discard her
battered and bleeding
to be left alone.

He will not concern himself for her
as she is long forgotten
as he now hunts his next prey.

She is alone,
All confidence is gone.

—Helen D. Long

THE TRIP

As I sit here reaching for the ultimate high
I feel gay as my eggs fry

Waiting for my next blow to the sand in the vase line
I am cold yet so fine

Now as I snort my last powder
My ear drums are banging louder

Finally through the ecstasy of depression
I look at the mirror seeing a horrid expression

Then my body starts to fall low
And now I know

I have reached my destination
The pleasuredome of termination

—O.J. Hyung

I walk at night,
Through fields of mist,
Upon wet blades of grass,
Moistened by evening dew's kiss . . .

I lay on a secluded hill, to stare,
At crystal visions in the sky,
So peaceful, softly, I think to myself,
I only wish I could fly . . .

I dream, I think, I laugh to myself,
But sometimes, I just wonder, "why,"
"There's wars and death, heartache and pain,
Those are the times, I cry . . .

But one day will come,
The world will be changed,
The bad will fall by the coming of good,
And all will be rearranged . . .

I get up from my spot, and walk
Down to the field of steam,
I'm now going home,
For I awoke from my dream . . . .

—Lance Rafael Hunsher

DIARY OF A MADMAN

Dreams shattered — like fragile glass
The cloak of darkness embraces me
Bitterness, morbid fear and dread
   Enmeshed in my head, writhing to be free.

Outside — silence; unbearable and soundless
   A tomb that encompasses it all
I feel terribly alone, vulnerable, weak
   My thoughts waver but never stall

Twisted, distorted, they spin around my head
   A swirling vortex of inconsistency
Pangs of guilt claw at my soul
   I'm impotent, helpless; condemned to be.

A nameless terror echos back and forth
   Through the dark recesses of my mind
Shrieking, screaming, in tumultuous cacophony
   Answers, explanations, reason — all left behind.

I'm hanging on to the frayed ends of sanity
   Groping, as the threads wear thin
Now I'm slipping . . . falling . . . from reality
   Into the pit of mindlessness . . . .

—Hrishabh Sanghvi

SUNRISE TO SON RISE

In sunrise of life, two babies are born.
Out from darkness, each is torn.
They learn to crawl and walk.
They learn to babble and talk.
They grow up in a world of love and hate.
Before committing, they hesitate.
At the right moment, girl meets boy.
They ask, "Is this the real McCoy?"
They prolong their commitment, trust is a must.
Only God can cast out doubt and fear.
He can make this commitment special and dear.
This commitment can be made on a sure foundation.
Two are made one, by the God of creation.
They build on the foundation of trust and love.
They are held together by God's love.
In the sunset of life, each child is born.
From a world of darkness each is torn.
In the Son rise of Eternal Life, we'll never die.
The Father and Son will light up the sky.

—Al Thomas

FOR EVEN IN HELL THERE MUST BE PEACE FROM LIFE

Chant again the words of battle
And give heart to all the young men
Let their cries echo a new call
And allow me the honor of their company
For I will seek no greater tribute
Nor hope for a more noble cause
But to fall amidst their numbers
And join in their loving embrace
To hear again their wondrous tales
And speak with friend and foe
To be a brother forever
And drink with them from their dry well
For then I am one with them
A lost brother no more
And I with them again
Another place to call my home
I rest
Unknown
A lost brother come home

—George Perry Field

HAPPINESS

Wisdom, knowledge and understanding;
"Feed your faith and your doubts will starve."
To make the world a happy place,
We must show a happy face!
Don't use a gallon of words
To express a spoonful of thoughts,
The hardest thing in the world to open is a closed mind!
Things always get better or worse
So we're either worrying for nothing
Or worrying too soon!
Years wrinkle the skin
But the lack of enthusiasm wrinkles the soul!
Learn as if you were to live forever,
Live as though you were to die tomorrow!
I learned to pray such a long time ago,
While my grandmother's love helped my faith to grow!
Grant me good health, for this I pray,
To carry on my work from day to day!
Spare me from fire, from floods and angry tongues,
From thieves, from fear and the evil ones!

—Elnora Pugh McNeil

TO A SPECIAL FRIEND

It started out as friendship,
and turned into something more.
The love I feel for you,
I've never felt before.
You make me feel so happy,
whenever I'm down,
By telling your stupid jokes,
and acting like a clown.
I can't believe you tell me,
all the stuff you do.
But I'm glad that you can trust me,
and I can trust you too.
You're my best friend,
and I want you to know,
No matter what may happen,
I'll NEVER let you go!!

—Loretta Cottrell

IN MEMORY

I never learned to fish from him
in fact 'twas quite the other.
I did learn how to sail a boat
as did my mom and brother.
And I should never tell hurtful lies
or boast of fortune come my way.
He said "What comes may quickly go.
Give thanks for happiness every day."

He came from very simple means
and hard work made him wealthy.
Not so much the spending kind
but honorable, wise and healthy.
He thought of others always first
and little or none was his share.
For looks of joy and happiness
were what he sought as his care.

He kept us all well clothed and fed.
Whatever the needs he met them.
And now he's gone but not inside.
I loved him so — and miss him.

—Michael David Scott

WISHES

I'd like to be a willow tree
beside a tranquil stream.
I'd stand and think and dream
of all that I could be.

I'd like to be a rainbow trout
with irridescent side,
with waving fin and fluttering tail.
I'd swim and glint and glide.

I'd like to be a herring gull
and live beside the sea,
above the shore, I'd float and soar.
But this can never be.

I can not be a willow tree
or a rainbow trout or bird.
But I can help my fellow man
with loving deed and word.

I can make my aim in life
conform to God's own scheme.
And be content to be a part
of life's unending dream.

—Gloria Hodges

THE OUTSIDE

It is a world of in between,
with no security, and no constancy.
A door is open to me,
So I am able to see inside.
The light of my greatest desire shines out
With warmth of pure acceptance,
But I cannot cross the threshold to enter in.
Some invisible barrier confines me
To the edge of the outside,
forever looking in.

—Marcy L. Hill, age 18

MY BEDROOM PRAYER

Bless this humble mess, O Lord,
and shine on it with grace.
Watch over me as I step on things
in this messy place.
Give me effort and provide me strength
to clean it once a week,
and maybe, every now and then,
I'll find the things I seek.
Guide me through this maze each day:
helping me in and out,
until I clean up the mess and
reveal the original route.
And if I need your help again,
and I am in distress,
I'll call you in my time of need
to help clean up my mess!

—Shawna Thompson

MY SILENCING WORLD

Do I smile? Do I frown?
Do I laugh with all around?
Should I cast a glistening eye
To share the pain of those nearby?

Would an eyebrow arched in shock
Convey concern, or friendship block?
How can I, with ears near dead,
Respond in love to what is said?

A blush, a hush, a silent tongue,
A gnawing ache, inside begun,
To hope for "oneness," once so strong,
But now to know I don't belong.

Friends, once faithful, slip away.
The price for them too hard to pay,
When oft-missed comments, more than once,
Bring awkward grins and no response.

For all who care, the task is great,
Key thoughts and phrases to relate.
Which words are understood the best?
What to repeat, and skip the rest?

Will those I love, with patience thin,
Regret to see me coming in,
And find the strain too great to stay?
Will they, like others drift away?

Lord Jesus, help me fight despair.
Help me seclusion to beware.
Use my life for all to see
Your love and power. Shine through me!

—Karen Mohs

NATURE BY NATURE

Look at the wind
see how it blows.
Watch the trees dance
and put on a show.
Feel the sun
warm on your skin.
Blue skies shine
like the soul within.
Time passes on
moving slow to the beat
Like the grass that grows
beneath your feet.
A day passes by
full of wonder and joy.
Nature has taught us
we can't be coy.

—Deborah Thompson

NATURE

Nature, oh so beautiful with
blossoms in the trees,
the water is falling
like tiny little bees.

As the sun shines down from
the sky,
the summer days go
passing by.

Then a frosty wind is
in the way,
to make us chilly all
the day.

And before you know
under the moonlit snow,
a sprout of grass is
beginning to grow.

—Alicia Christman, age 9

ISABELLA

I remember a summer past,
we sat atop a fence;
where we renewed a friendship fast
lasting summers hence.

I bared my mind, as you did yours,
as much as we would dare,
and lightness lifted heavy heart
as laughter filled the air.

And no dark feelings or hard thoughts
that summer's night could see,
for I brought out the best in you,
and you, the best in me.

What bid me bare my mind to you,
so safely to you drawn?
I'd sit atop the fence with you
to stay till morrow's dawn.

I saw you then, more kind and sweet
than any who'd allure,
and now you own space in my heart,
protected and secure.

—Hudson Powers

FLOWER

Sis said you came
    like an aunt of Old South.
a visit that lasted years
You brought a heart without ego or fault
    to look after your new dears.

Days then began
    with your bright face.
too eager to think of measure
Curls and plumes never grayed—
you made our pack a pleasure.

Now you're home
    'though again someday we'll be.
Your watch moved to a higher port
    but for present—
all I know
is the life of a dog is too short.

    —Diane Paulsen

UNFULFILLED

My roses didn't bloom last spring,
Their blossoms withered under frost.
Sickness crept within my flowery ring,
Its fragile fragrance forever lost.

In vain I attempted to protect
These buds with a faithful heart.
Nature's cruel chill was hard to detect—
My garden and I so far apart.

A false security blinded my sight
Like a garland about my eyes,
Stealing that in which I took delight
Wearing love as its disguise.

Longing for butter soft petals I plead
To hold a bouquet in my arms,
But those who cannot nurture the seed
Shall not benefit from its charms.

    —Ellen Myers

ANGEL BABY

I know you are a gift from God
Sweet Granddaughter of mine
Your eyes, your nose, your precious smile
A treasure most divine.

I feel your soft smooth curly hair
Beneath my chin each morn
And hear your pleasure while you sip
My memories so well worn.

Now, though you're nearly 8 years old
And I can't cuddle you
I still remember all we shared
Until you were but two.

Sweet Kaela, you're your mother's child
But Grammy loves you well
So mind your manners, say your prayers
And only time will tell!

My loving little granddaughter
You're always in my heart
We have a special bond, we two,
That none can ever part!

    —Beverly A. Paul

MOVING THROUGH THE EBONY MIST

As I sit, my mind does wander,
and my fate I start to ponder.
Fonder does my heart grow for some haven far away.

And through a night so unending,
again I move my thoughts not lending.
Fending off the cold unfeeling darkness in my way.

In my heart the fear is growing,
and my hopeless soul not showing.
Knowing as I move along that I have lost my way.

I feel the power of confusion,
rising to complete illusion.
Fusion of my heart and soul causing much dismay.

Doubtful that I, once again, will see the light of day.

    —Thom Simonson

ALONE TOO

If, in discovery of myself
I should find you
And we should find us
The world we touch
Will, I am sure,
Be better for
Our discovery.

Looking out from shadowy places
I can see half-hidden faces
And I hear echoing sounds
Of a broken heart, mending as it pounds.

Off in the distance, somewhere outside,
The soft sounds are so painful
A loving being cries.
Oh yes, a thousand voices go screaming.
You're alone, you've gone mad, you're dreaming,
And I answer, I am alone, as tears come streaming.
I set forth my heart and soul to be touched
And to touch others, who, like myself, are alone.

    —Rohnie

SENSE-LESS

The velvet darkness of the night enfolds me,
But with you not here
It is like a horsehair blanket,
Like the couches on which we used to sit.

The cooling breeze from off the lake
Refreshes the lilacs
And wafts their aroma across the planes of my face.
It could be a desert wind storm
For all the refreshment it brings to me.

The dinner that I cooked
Lies uneaten on the table,
As tasteless to me as would be the hay
Upon which this cow once had chewed.

The world was once a beautiful place,
A delight to the senses,
A stimulating experience.
But then you left,
And the sensitive receptors of my soul
Dried up when you disappeared.

    —Rena Scheingarten Safer

SHATTERED DREAMS

As the river rises higher and panic spreads beyond, we fill
up our sand bags until the sand is gone. I look at my valuables
so shiny and bright, and pray that the water won't reach them
tonight. As I lie upon the sand bags and day turns into night,
I watch the rising waters in the bright moon light. I hear the
"THUNDER" from beyond it plays to me a very sad song. The
"LIGHTNING STRIKES" as the wind picks up, thank God here comes
another sand truck! We pick up the bags and load in the sand a
little boy gives me a hand. Now the "THUNDER" is louder and the
"LIGHTNING" is close and the rain is pounding as the dam begins
to "BURST!" Now the rain has stopped as night turns into day
and that little boy who helped me was tragically swept away.
Now I look at my valuables so shiny and bright, but they
don't seem so valuable since I lost my son that night.

—Michael DeChirico

HEART OF FIRE

These hands are not of flawless form, nor talent do they hold,
And yet they bring my art to life — the art of stories told.
No sculptor sculpts a better scene than I can shape for you;
The words like stone I've chipped away from thoughts that were askew.

If put within the proper place they show to you the sky;
The brightest hues of reds and blues within your mental eye,
Where treetops glisten in the sheen of springtime afternoon,
and pink-white blossoms smile at you to show that summer's soon.

I, just as quick, can show to you the darkness of a life,
The slowly growing hopelessness amidst the painful strife;
A great decline from birth to death — from strength to no control,
Till only fleshless bones remain, remembered by no soul.

But through my art the single gift which I aspire to bring,
Is warm, sweet love into your heart to make it softly sing.
My pen — it burns the page with ink that keeps hot your desire,
And so I'll always use my art to light your heart of fire.

—Kostandinos Papanikolaou

THE LIGHT . . . TOO LATE REMEMBERED . . . . .

The Light . . . will shine but twice in her lifetime . . . once . . . as his
hands urge her to go . . . and again . . . as his hands beckon her home . . .

For in birth, as in death, she will walk nearest the Light . . .
there . . . she will find no pain or hate . . . no shame or blame . . . for
in those precious moments . . . there is no need for such earthly
teachings . . .

For . . . only on soiled ground do such things first bloom and then
flourish in the hearts of mankind.

As she is taught . . . as she will live . . . as she will teach others . . .
man against man . . . black against white . . . Catholic against Jew . . .

She will hold tight to the past . . . forbidding the future . . . and
stifling the present . . . and . . . as the minutes of her life slip
away . . . never to return . . . hate will be thrived upon, blame will
be cast, shame will be felt, and pain will linger . . .

Then . . . too soon . . . the Light will flicker and form a flame . . . ever
increasing . . . until . . . she will walk on earth, but stand in the
Light . . . only then . . . will she remember her first time in the
Light . . . in the truth . . . that there was no need for the earthly
teachings . . . but she will remember and understand too late
 . . . much too late.

*Dedicated to my mother . . . Glenda Barnes . . . always there to listen,
softly criticize, and forever praise my work . . . she has all my
love and admiration.*

—Alisa Barnes

REBIRTH

Come forth into a new world
without sin.
Feel the life stirring in your soul,
then release it at once and feel ecstasy.

See the love in people.
Touch things for the first time.
Drink of the questions in your mind.

Then a dark cloud appears from nowhere.
Problems choke you;
Reality blinds you;
And responsibilities starve you
from the simple
       first moment you were.

—Sandra L. Tall

LOVE LETTER TO DEATH

Your beauty lingers repeatedly within
My deep reflections. I find it almost
Impossible to depart from your image
Of sublimity. Day after day, I
Contemplate the eternal closeness
That we could share. How I long for
Your warm embrace; your embodiment
Sheltering me from this perpetual
Suffering. You are my hope when the
Agonies of life have laid extreme
Frustration and vain expectations upon
Me. You are the one I desire and cry
For in my lonely duration of infelicity.
I yearn for your intimacy, your
Captivating kiss, and your affectionate
Caress to relieve me of the ill wind.
Come to me, comfort me; hold me with
Such security. I am patiently waiting
With open arms — for what is worth
Waiting for. Someday soon, my love,
May we be united.

—J.M. Emberton

IF EVER I HAD A WISH

"If ever I had a wish,
I'd wish for us to be
together until the end of time,
through all eternity."

"I'd wish for a place where we could go,
to live and love and die.
A place where no one else could go,
a place for only you and I."

"I'd give anything for this wish,
I'd even give my life.
For I could die a happy man,
if I had you as my wife."

"But, alas, my dream cannot come true,
it was never meant to be,
and the thing that I will most regret,
is that our love will never be free."

"But if ever I had a wish,
I'd wish for us to be,
together until the end of time,
through all eternity."

—Richard B. Griffin

MARRIAGE

United as one in marriage, a bed of roses fantasy,
blinding young love that cannot see, the fears and
struggles of reality
fading, falling rose petals disappear, striking
thorns of rage, and anger, wounded hearts
love will amend.
Faith in God, life line of love, bonds the marriage
until death do us part.

—Leona Marzinski

RESPONDEZ S'IL VOUS PLAIZ

Can I hold you ever so tightly
As the stars hold the beauty of your eyes?
Can I sing to you ever so lightly
As the moon comes to lighten up your sky?
Can I kiss you softly, slowly through and through
Like the sweet rain coming to kiss the ground?
Can I bring you pleasant dreams so true
Like the west wind shaping the earth so round?
Can I walk you endlessly on the shore
As the sun endlessly lets out its glow?
Can I keep you happily more and more
Like Heaven happily letting down its snow?
    If I must wait and give you my final breath
    Then I shall love you beyond the realm of Death.

—Soka Heng

THE MIRACLE

Hard to put this in meter or fast time,
Even to put this in a rhyme.
But . . . a miracle happened before my eyes,
Out in the open beneath sunny blue skies.
A car pulled up to the Emergency door,
The woman was partly lying on the floor.
As a Doctor rushed out . . . and I could see,
Tied the cord then patted the mother's knee.
The "miracle" was kicking about,
More or less to say . . . I'm glad I'm out!
How worried but proud the father looked,
He parked the car and took his wife's pocketbook.
Mother and baby went through the door,
On the way up to the maternity floor.
God's blessings are many for your husband and you,
As I said a prayer when I had you in view!

—Joanne Marquette

THIS THING CALLED LOVE

When your heart cries out, to that
Special that is around — this thing called love.
This thing called love it burns deep,
Within — the only one that really knows
it, is the one that it dwelleth in.

When no one is around, it longs to be
felt. It longs to be handled, like the
word of life. — When it is handled, it
brings forth pure life. This thing called love.

Without it life is meaningless, we're
as empty tombs. But with it, we
blossom as the May flower would in June.

Strength, joy, peace and happiness
are wrapped up in this lovely package,
This thing called love. Do we really have it?

—Conal Royal DeVine

PAIN OF A DREAM

Tucked away is my silent sleep
Forever thinking, wondering, why do I weep
There's no one there, I am all alone
In a restless fury I am gone
In a flash I am back, startled by a look
Who is it, what is it for the brief moment that I took
Suddenly in a frozen motion
Shifting, falling, crashing like the ocean
So how do I explain what is happening out there
To another it appears as a vacant stare
There I am lying peaceful it would seem
But no one knows the pain of a dream.

—Ashley Spurlock

THE GENTLE WIND

The cypress trees bent softly in the wind, their branches gently curving as they slowly but firmly were molded by the steady, warm breeze blowing through them. Their leaves were sometimes caught by a frenzied whirlwind which urged them turn back, but the steady breeze blew resolutely until the branches were clearly etched against the sky, forever formed by the gentle wind.

We are the cypress trees blowing in the wind, seeking to be molded by the gentle breath of the Spirit but caught in the whirlwinds which seek to destroy the symmetry of our branches.

If we turn with the whirling wind, we are lost. But if we bend with the Spirit, our branches will grow in strength and beauty and fruitfulness, and will be clearly etched against the sky, forever formed by the Gentle Wind.

—Audrey Monnier

TILL DEATH DO US PART

All I am is all I know,
And I no longer know what's real,
I just try to stay on the go,
So I won't think of how I feel.

I'm supposed to smile and carry on,
Not resenting every medal and the awards,
Who will decide if they died singing the wrong song,
Knowing that they'll never put down their swords.

Emptiness is such a lonely place,
Reality hurts all the more,
Sometimes life seems a hopeless case,
With time always closing the door.

All the plans that were made,
Are shattered and tossed away,
Even the memories are starting to fade,
And I can't face another day.

No one can know the pain,
I try to keep inside,
I feel I need a cleansing rain,
Or maybe a place to hide.

I guess I'm supposed to call it fate,
And try to hide my bitter resentment,
I'm so confused, I don't know who to hate,
Now, I'd settle for a place called contentment.

—Marlene N. Johnson

LITTLE BOY

Little boy what tears you shed
As tho' the world hung o'er your head
Such pain and heartache you must know
For life so justly to bestow
Upon a boy with nothing more
Than worldly, aged years of four.

—Mavis Smallfield Vejar

STEAL AWAY

Swaying mist began to fade
and sunlight brightened all around.
The diamond sprinkled knoll
sent sparks up from the ground,
and morning sounds embraced me.

Musty earth and pine cone scent
assailed the waking senses, and
nostrils flared in eager greed,
out casting all defenses;
then, brushed the soul within me.

—JeanAnn

THE MIRROR WAS ONCE MY FRIEND

I remember gazing,
at the mirror long ago
The person looking back at me
was someone that I know

Then the person peeking back
at one time or another
Started looking like none
other than my mother

One day as I was perusing
some photos from the past
I looked upon my grandma's face
from the mirrored glass

Time marches on
and the mirror never lies
I only wished I got to know
the people passing by

—Barbara Bergstrand

TEARS

There are two kinds of tears you see
One for hurt and one for glee
But one kind of tear is different
It's better than the rest
It's the tear you want to have
It's definitely the best
This tear is very seldom
You rarely see this tear
But instead of bringing heartache
It always brings you cheer
Even on a stormy day
When everything is gray
It can really cheer you up
And brighten up your day
It comes when you are very proud
Like a child getting his first toy
It is a wonderful feeling
It is the tear of joy

—LeeAnn Gray

A FATHER'S STRENGTH

Oh, For my heart shakes every time
He enters the room.
His large brown eyes tell a story
And always set the mood.

The strength we give him
Keeps us united as one
Yet his eyes tell the story
When we are all to have fun.

Though we stand as individuals
Our blood runs the same
And when there's a cry for help
We appear as a "gang."

Now "our" eyes tell the story
Can you read what they say
We stand here, before you,
We're "Family,"
That's what they'll say.

—Kathleen Robinson

HOMELESS

Where do I sleep tonight?
Do I sleep in the park
Where the lights are bright
or do I sleep where it's dark and damp;
under the bridge
with the rest of the camp?

Will I find food in the usual places
or will I have to beg?
Seeing the changes in peoples' faces
maybe I'll go hungry tonight
wrapped only in cold and fear,
considering my awful plight.

I remember, was it so long ago?
So much living has passed
from holiday dinners to lawns to mow
unbelievable that I too could be here
lonely, empty and numb.
How far is it from safe and secure?

—Shawna Bruce

WHY?

Why is it,
can you tell me Sir,
that we help one
but not another,

that we comfort one
with open arms,
but leave another
to suffer harms,

that we dress one's wounds
with gentle care,
but leave another
with nothing to wear,

that we take control
to restore order,
but never cross
another's border.

Why do we generously help one brother
but do not even acknowledge another?

—Sam Nilsson, age 13

HEAVEN OR HELL

Heaven has got a Special Touch
That's why everyone wants to go so much.
Hell has got a Fiery blaze
That Fire burns for days and days.
If you're lost and can't be found
Heaven is not where you are bound
You need the Lord by your side
There is no need to run and hide.
Go out into the world and witness to the others
In God's eyes they're your sisters and brothers.
God has made us Special in a certain way
He gives us a Special Gift to use each day.
For Heaven is where I know I am bound
Let's hope *Hell* is not where you are found.

—Carol Hayes

THE GIFT

I searched and searched and tried to find
A special gift for you
So, I asked the Lord to
   Bless you and keep you safe from harm.
I didn't ask for treasures —
   I knew you wouldn't mind.
Instead I asked for wealth
   Of a different kind.
I asked he give you hope,
   Good health throughout your life,
That peace be with you always
   No matter where you are.
But, most of all, I asked him for that one special gift,
   The Love he gives so freely;
The Love which we all *need*.

—Lupe Miller

THE EYES OF GOD

The eyes of God are upon us
He sees us everywhere;
He sees the lonely sinner
He sees each humble tear.

He sees the Christian's trials
He sees the wicked's scorn;
He sees the evil of this world
He sees the beggar forlorn.

He sees each good deed that we do
He sees what's in our hearts;
He sees the children at their play
The soldier, in foreign parts.

He sees the rich man at his gate
The poor, the blind, and the lame;
He sees the sick upon their beds
The Martyred and the famed.

The eyes of God are everywhere
He sees all that we do;
How blessed it is to have a God
Who watches over me and you.

*Dedicated to my Aunt, Mrs. Lola C. Myers,
in memory of my Uncle, Mr. William Leroy Myers,
to my husband, Matthew Blanding, Jr., and in
honor of my Lord and Savior Jesus Christ.*

—Loretta C. Blanding

REASON TO CRY

Heaven is a quiet and peaceful place to be,
unlike the hell that we presently see.
Some people mourn when others die,
but when I think about it I see no reason to cry.

They go to a place where they'll receive proper care.
On Earth, that feeling is seldom and rare.
So why fear death when it's life that's frightful?
Our afterlives could be so delightful.

When we hear the sounds of sapphire halls,
God is calling us to his kingdom, our heaven.
We should all be thankful that we eventually die;
for if we don't—that is the reason to cry.

Dedicated to my grandfather, Wolfgang and my great uncle Glenn. Also to my parents, Andy, Kristen, Alicia, and Brad. I love you all!

—Heidi L. Wolfgang

ANOTHER ANGEL IN HEAVEN

Little Nickelos Gosney, we knew so well.
Has gone to Heaven where he will dwell.
Now he can sit at Jesus' feet.
And listen to his words so soft and sweet.

His mother and father will without demand.
Will try to meet him in that Promised Land.
His pain has ceased as we know for sure.
His sickness is gone, to suffer no more.

He loved to play baseball, I understand.
Where he can still play in the Promised Land.
The diamond will be made of snow white clouds.
Where the angels will gather in great big crowds.

They will cheer him on when he steps up to the plate.
Saying, hit us a home run our little mate.
He will win their hearts that is for sure.
His suffering is gone to be no more.

—Woodrow (Pee Wee) Puckett

TOO SAD THE POEM

Too sad the poem that I should now write,
  So painful the memories that surface unbidden,
  Too bitter the tears I taste in the night.
    I am alone;

This hollow shell that walks alone on the shore
  Is only the faintest echo of what used to be,
  Recalling forever, the life that was ours before.
    You are gone;

Autumn comes, I turn my face to the waning sun,
  Searching for the warmth that was you
  Finding only a weak pale light, offering me none.
    Days Without Meaning

You gave me your forever, promises were made,
  I gave you my life, my love, my dreams,
  The promises were broken, shattered by senseless rage.
    Nights Without End

I look to the heavens, knowing you are there,
  Watching over me as I journey on,
  Knowing in the end, all will be our fare
    We are united,
            our love Eternal

—Catherine L. O'Hearn

GIVE ME SUGAR

Sugar is a craving, for some a little,
  to some a lot.
To me sugar is a never ending hunger,
  as a bottomless pot.
Sugar is my life sustaining love,
  as nothing else could be.
Sweet sugar, gentle to the lips, brings
  wrapping warmth to me.

—Rusty

JENNY, THE WHITE RABBIT

My drawing hand is very cold
Even in a pocket fold.
When it feels warmer,
A line or two I'll add
To this sketch of a rabbit
I'm copying on an envelope
From a photograph
In the window of a camera shop
On Wacker Drive in Chicago.

Jenny is the rabbit's name
I recall this way.
She lives in a neighbor's hutch
Seen through snowflakes today
In a town near a railroad
Where once my parents resided.
With happiness I watched Jenny play
And from a window run away,
Then return to folks she loved so much.
Now her likeness in my purse
Almost makes me feel her touch.

—Dorothy Ferg

MOTHERS

Mothers are forgiving, loving, laughing, and living

Mothers are for granting little children's chanting

Mothers to your children you are the best, better than the rest.

Mothers make mistakes, so give us mothers some breaks

Mothers make up most of the nation, but when we have children we don't realize what we are facin'.

Mothers go through a lot for their kids, such as sickness, teething, and knee skids.

Mothers go through more than most, so mothers have a right to boast.

Mothers have feelings too, so try to put your foot in our shoe.

Mothers to me are as sweet as can be, as long as they realize that after their children are grown that they need to be free!

—Alice Adams

THE ENVELOPE

Have you ever been in an envelope?
An envelope of love.
Glued together in assurance,
Glued together in care.
Encased within the envelope,
Is all security,
Is all peace and contentment.
Remember the envelope?
The envelope of your mother's love.

—Kari Morris

TELL ME

"Have you ever been scared
Or extremely bored,
Or felt torn
Like a used rip cord,
Do you know, where your life
Is gonna lead,
Or do you just sit back
And let yourself bleed.
You have to wake yourself up
And plant the meaningful seed,
That will give you your lifelong creed,
This is indeed, what it means
To be finally relieved."

—Bob Tomlinson CPS

TO BE REMEMBERED . . .

Let your heart be open
like a flower in full bloom.
Arms outstretched, reaching, gathering.
Let your words speak a sweet
fragrance, be gentle and kind.
Yet, let your stem be sturdy
and strong!
When the season ends, your petals
will fall, softly, undisturbingly,
only the memory indelibly pressed
in the minds of those forever
loved.

*Dedicated to my loving children,
Melissa and Christopher.*

—Dorothy A. DeAntonio

THE BERKSHIRES

Sunrise to sunset,
another beautiful day,
gives way to nighttime.

Everything is quiet,
    except for the occasional chirp,
of a sleeping bird.

Suddenly, a bright red color,
    sweeps before my eyes.
A scarlet tanager getting breakfast.

There is a spider web,
    newly formed,
between branches of a tree.

A dull shade of grey,
    mist begins to rise,
and give way to another beautiful day.

And a frog croaks, GOOD MORNING.

—Donald R. Siegel

ENJOY THE COLORS

Enjoy the colors, the next one is white.
Remember them well as winter winds bite
And snow lies deep on Zimmerman hill
And drifts in the valley down by the mill.

Now maples turn scarlet, the birches turn gold
And weeds wear frost diamonds—a gift from the cold.
The geese are gathering, there's a nip in the air,
and a brilliant blue sky, the weather is fair.

The days grow shorter, the nights grow chill,
And I know that soon there'll be snow on the hill.
So enjoy the colors for soon they will go
Buried beneath the white of snow.

—Dortha Benson

THE GARDEN

I sit quietly in the garden all alone
Reminiscing, letting thoughts roam
I've seen the seasons change this place
The flowers of fall yielding to winter's embrace
But when spring comes again most flowers pull through
Again painting the garden in a multitude of hue
How like the garden are we in life
Time is the seasons bringing joy and strife
Some flowers bloom again when the trail is o'er
Some are seen here again nevermore
As I sit here thinking and the hour is growing late
I hear someone knocking at the garden's gate
Come in stranger, my once closest friend
Did you come back to herald the season's end
Not a word is spoken
The silence remains unbroken
Just a hand upon my shoulder
And I know my season's almost over.

—Amy D. Brown

A KEEN FOR TOMORROW

Grey fantail victim of the freezing night,
You were valiant in life.
A voice of hope at the window each day,
Surrendering to the universe.
And, with beak upstretched,
    Awaiting breadly sustenance.
You lived nobly with your limp,
    An outcast from the flock. Yet,
Your beauty summoned the start of our daily existence,
    And showered us with dazzling purple-green light.
We were flattered by your company
    And staggered at your 'wit'
As you monitored our stirring by the fresh dawn's light.
Quintessential teaser of cats, how your broken strutting
    puzzled them through the window pane.
The world is less with you now gone,
Beauty assaulted. No trophy for your handicap,
No medal for your valor,
No hymn to your princely presence.
There is silence on the roof.
Yet, you will live on unsung, we, witnesses
    bearing your memory in grief, testimony eternal
    to the hand of your Creator.
Grey fantailed messenger of infinity,
    Harbinger of eternity,
We sing thee, farewell.

—Joan O'Brien

DAVID

I've compiled my heartaches
like an editor forms his epilogue.
   There are strong hurts
     that made their chips in stone;
     the fickle ones
     that became dust on the shelf.

But of all those heartaches,
the one that came from you wrote its own inscription;
like a headstone cutter chiseling marble,
blowing the bits and dust away.

You cut deeply within me
   and when all those marks were made,
     blew what was once a part of me away.

    —Pamela Moore

A cat's bellowing howl fills my empty lungs.
The question of life or death always in my head.
Existence . . . is it worth it?
Pain falls around me like beautiful rain.
A gun in one hand, dread in the other,
Lyrics pour into my ears, opening my eyes,
Becoming my Saviour.
The gun becomes a pen and this page, my casket.
Lyrics still hammering toward me.
Lyrics that become the dirt that covers me,
warms me, feeds me,
And then becomes me.
When it's finally over, can I go on?
Yes.
Why?
Because of one soul who doesn't even know me.
I don't know him.
But I thank him for reasons he doesn't understand.
After I do . . . I can go on!
I live until the next song.

*Dedicated to the one soul, Eddie Vedder, a
great poet with a gripping voice. Thanks man.*

    —Chad A. Armstrong

BEHNAZ

Her name fell tripping from my tongue
Like ripples in a mountain stream—
With the taste of an unfamiliar spice,
Of music with strange harmony
From a world I had never known.

Our fingers never entwined.
We never touched or shared a kiss.
Only once, our minds caressed
For a single moment—for a brief moment,
Our souls brushed, our essence combined.

She sang for me, a sad and bitter song
Of anger, of loneliness, of pain.
Ah, could I but turn her thoughts to love—
And beauty—and warmth of life,
What a sweet enchanting song she'd sing.

Then she was gone—the moment had passed.
That wondrous, satisfying,
Always remembered moment.
What loss I felt—I was alone! I was empty again!
But, unlike before, I saw my aloneness—my emptiness.

    —Gene Grant

MY FIRST AUTUMN DAY AWAY

A dense fog covered this rainy day.
The wind shook the window and
it lured me to see
the branches of a tree harshly
swaying from side to side.
At first to me it seemed they
were waving good-bye.
Another look and the branches
were your arms outstretched and
just waiting for me to run into
them where I belong.
I'll be home soon.

    —Nicole Snyder

A CHILD WITHOUT A NAME

You never got to hold it
A child without a name
The love you have inside
Of you always will remain

Under different circumstances
The timing wasn't right
One day there'll be another child
To cherish and hold tight

I know the pain you feel
The way your heart is torn
For the decision that was made
About the child that was unborn

They say time will take away the pain
And the load will be easier to bear
But it's your tears that are shed
And you wonder does anyone really care

For it's not them that have to deal
With this day in and day out
Such a very hard decision made
You'll always have a doubt.

    —Teresa Brand

ROSALIE

God sent an angel to the earth
So wondrous, sweet and dear,
She scattered love where'er she went
'Twas joy when she was near.

Oh Baby, darling Rosalie!
She lingered but a while
I see her now, her angel face
Her bright eyes and her smile.

We did not dream but that her love
Would long be at our side
But now a sad sweet memory
Will in our hearts abide.

God, too, has need of jewels rare
Up in His realms above
He clasps our baby tenderly
In the fullness of His love.

And so we wait, we hear her sing
The song by angels sung
For so sweet Rosalie must leave us
While her love is young.

    —Selma Haffener

MOM AND DAD

I never thought I needed anyone,
but I guess I'm proving wrong,
Always winning everything I've done,
Me, independent and strong.

Now I'm looking ahead,
At a new life that awaits,
Thinking about things done and said,
All of our fights and debates.

I want to say thanks,
for raising me your best,
understanding I'll always be different,
never like the rest.

—Gretchen Cannis

IS IT WORTH WHILE

We go along from day to day
   To find a tear our smile
And wonder whether after all
If life is worth our while
We see so many tragedies
That happen here and there
And suffering that seems much more
Than anyone can bear
And there are times when we ourselves
Are faced with problems great
And we must have the human strength
To bear our sorrows weight
And yet we know that there is bound
To be a brighter dawn
If we just have the courage and
The will to carry on
We know that we can conquer fear
If only we will try
And every now and then there is
A rainbow in the sky

—Estle D. Duncan

UNSPOKEN TOMORROW

Sullen as a snow storm
Bleak as a thunderous day
The sound of death beckons
Maybe for you today!

The message came in the afternoon
It conveyed the feeling of sorrow.
I can't help thinking to myself,
I want to talk to you tomorrow!

I tried to vision your feelings
Like the time we last parted,
"Why my son is growing up,
I wonder when this started?"

I want to talk about my maturing,
It's been years since the last we met!
It seems like it was only last week,
The words are still there yet!

I view your body at rest,
A look of no worry or sorrow.
I still want to talk to you,
Because today is tomorrow.

—Edmond W. Givens

A SONNET FOR MY MOM

There's something to say of my Mother's touch
   It helps to make my world go around,
For, without it I'd have to think too much,
Then many trials would thus abound.

Her touch is one loaded with tolerance,
And kindness, and trust, and faith, and love.
Pain won't cause her to stoop toward defiance;
She receives her touch from up above.

Her touch says everything should come out right,
But leaves room for the unexpected.
It knows how to act out of the spotlight,
And stays on the path—it's directed.

Her touch, so wondrous, cannot be measured.
Not even by time will it be weathered.

—Julie Schultz Semel

Norma, Norma, sister dear,
   We miss you so much, we wish you were here;
Why did you leave us, why did you go?
   We want you with us; we love you so!

We knew you were sick
   Didn't know how much;
Wish we could've helped you
   With an extra special touch.

Wish we could see your beautiful face,
   Wish we could see your smile and your grace,
Wish we could feel your loving arms,
   Wish we could feel your many charms.

One so special, truly were you;
   Memories now will have to do;
Your caring, sharing and loving ways
   Will stay with us all, all of our days.

Norma, Norma, sister dear,
   Not with us, but very near.
In Heaven some day together we'll be
   Sharing and caring and loving and free!

—Sharon Stanius

THIS OLD GRANNY

As I grow older, day by day
   I pluck one grey hair and two seem to stay.
I cream and lotion my skin so soft,
The wrinkles I mean to just slough right off.

And then I say, "What was that you said?"
As I try to catch the next line read.
My glasses play tricks as I stretch my head
To see over bi-focals when I look ahead.

But my heart feels young and I hope to stay
Active and carefree without dismay.
My talents are eager to be useful, still.
And young good-looking men are still a thrill.

The little ones are as great as ever
But three hours is about all I can stand,
Of their joy and laughter and playful games
Their running and shouting and playing so grand.

Leaves me tired and weary, ready to jump on the couch
For peace and quiet, I'd make like a mouse.
I know now, I'm a little bit older, day by day.
This old granny is here to stay!

—Ruth W. Weaver

A GIFT TAKEN FOR GRANTED

Some say, I am the most magnificent living
    thing on earth. I provide many of
    your needs, with very little gratitude.

I populated the world and was a part
    of every culture and all of history.
    Our numbers once were great and
    people worshiped our family.

A day to you is a decade to me.
    A life time to you, was centuries to me.

My family now grows small,
    My relatives are few.
    Once you could depend on me.
    Now I depend on you.

Think about what life would be
    without a tree.

—Paul B. W. Carlon

LITTLE RED ROOSTER

There was a little red rooster learning to crow,
    Standing proud and erect and oh so bold.
He would let out some squeals and then a squawk,
    Then listen for others as to crow they would not balk.
People that heard him would ask "What's that?"
    Then laugh, walk away as they tipped their hat.

This went on for weeks, without any luck,
    But this little red rooster would not give up.
He would crow his heart out the best he knew how,
    Then strut around as if taking a bow.
One fine day; the ground covered with dew,
    He let out with the perfect cock-a-doodle-do.

Years went by as he crowed his best,
    Then came the day he gave up to rest.
This red rooster will not be forgotten,
    As he crowed at the fields covered with cotton.
Many roosters will come and many will go,
    There will never be another that stood so bold.

—Frances Suggs Flowers

WHISPERS IN THE TREES

Whispers in the trees called a grieving song.
    While wilting of their leaves retold I was alone.
With a trail of drifting tears amid to aid me on
Enchanted binds of "years to pass" played to me this song.

Whispers in the trees, we're just whispers in the trees.

Bestowed itself upon me did this forest in my heart.
Such cold struck my soul as to rip my life apart.
A chanting amongst these woods encouraged me to hark.
Thus the forest fowl began another part.

Whispers in the trees, only whispers in the trees.

Darkened woods devoid of bloom
eldritched place of death and gloom
Won't you spare me of the doom
thou hast meant for me?

Whispers in the trees, the birds sang;
Whispers in the trees.

Then behold a voice said — feel no burden my dear son.
For now your days shall soon be done.
Then will come your rightful turn
to whisper in the trees.

—D. Shaun Morgan

THE SPRING

I looked into your eyes tonight
    Although you were not there,
And when they caught and sent the light
From out the vacant air —
Or where we walk all by myself
Within the waving field,
I find inside a poet's wealth . . .
You're absent yet revealed.
So even though you're gone from earth
As most one day may blessed be,
You'll always be my song of worth
In love's eternal melody.
Though love may fail from lesser force,
Ours, 'tween us, has surer source.

—Jim Snyder

WHEN IT RAINS

I love it when it rains
    Sometimes it puts me in a quiet mood
        or even puts me to sleep
Other times it makes me feel sensuous
I want to hold my man in my arms
        and not say anything
Then there are times when the rain
        disguises my tears
I don't want anyone to know
After the rain,
The grass and flowers are watered
        the crops are nourished
        and my soul is cleansed
            God is good
I love it when it rains

—Sophia deLayne Johnson

AFTER VISITING A BLIND FRIEND

Thank you Lord that I can see
    many sights so dear to me.

Smiling faces of children at play,
brilliant sun shining, warming the day.

Family, friends, faces of love,
twinkling stars in heaven above.

Cool green grass so soft under our feet,
Animals, birds are to our eyes a treat.

Fall leaves in party dress, orange,
    gold, brown, and red,
Beautiful trees and flowers,
    wild or in garden bed.

Rainbow with colors so bright,
full moon that lights up the night.

High mountains, deep valleys,
    winding rivers too,
Golden, sandy deserts, oceans
            sparkling blue.

Fluffy white clouds
    floating by,
Kites, airplanes flying so high.

TV, movies, stage productions too,
give great pleasure to me and you.

Thank you Lord that I can see
All these sights so dear to me.

—Margaret Story Myers

In the wind's voice
your name,
can be heard . . .
I call back,
desperate,
that you would hear me,
But alas,
early morning life
and silence
were all that fell on my ears —

And I ask the wind
to wrap you in my love,
cradle and nurture you
And my need for you,
as strong as life itself . . .

For You are my life
and my light
and my energy—
—Lori Temple

THANK YOU FOR YOUR VISIT

Thanks for visiting me, Today!
Tis my spirit who doth speak,
And it is my Inner man,
Tis he, whom you see.

Perhaps you've seen dreams dissipate
or have known loss in some way,
and because of this —
We can communicate.

For in times of trouble
Diversity can be a brother,
And as we share —
We have communion with one another.

For it is in sharing
Our spirits catch of . . . Flame,
But, first the touch of God
Must light your Inner man.
—G.M. Bradley

A SPRING EVENING

Purple, pink, and blue evening skies
Walking barefoot in the green grass
Listening to the birds singing sweetly
Touching the white flowers on the
bush
Feeling romantic as the wind lifts
my perfume in the air.
Sitting down on the grass to tumble
and admire the little purple flowers.
Resting my arms behind my neck
to let the cool spring breeze cover
my body.
Now darkness grows, and colder
wind comes, not the gentle breeze
of the day.
I go inside and am left with
the memory of the day.
How simple and relaxing it was, and
it would have been only more perfect
if I had my love to share it with
me.
—Elisha Moody, age 16

GRANDMOTHER'S BONNET

Grandmother said I was all eyes and whys,
When she went to wash her bonnet.
It had no ruffles or bows or ties,
For she had painted blue birds on it.
"First I remove the cardboard staves,
Then a dip in cold water." She explained.
"Before soaking in the iron wash pot.
You see, cold water loosens any stains,
Then the dirt is removed by the hot.
I rinse and stiffly starch it, and then
When I hang it to dry on the line,
The birds will fly in the wind."
My joy was complete when two hung there,
Blue birds on hers and red birds on mine.
—Trudy Van Riper

MARIE'S DESK

It was an old Victorian flat top desk
But the stories it could tell.
It held an old Coleman gasoline lamp,
A sterling silver candle holder,
An antique tooth brush jar filled with pens,
Limoges bone china dish for stamps.

A gavel that called many meetings to order,
Lucite key to city of Memphis engraved Marie Meyer,
A dogwood paperweight from Cranbury, New Jersey,
Cards, letters, membership books.
A letter from President Clinton June 7, 1993.

The top was scarred with many writings
To family, friends, and parties to give and to attend.
Cards to sick folks and to the bereaved
With memories of that loved child, mother, father, friend.

Yes if the desk could talk
A tale it would tell
Of life's work and love,
That's Marie's Victorian desk.
—Marie Zeisler Meyer

THE OLD HOUSE

It was just an old house, run down.
So many memories there could be found.
Children crying or shouting with laughter,
Filling each room from floor to rafter,
So that never a dull moment came round.

The house was far from neat I must say.
The children always felt they could play,
Without messing too many things,
Or the fuss that neatness brings;
Except when company was on the way.

Then everyone had to forget their play;
Keeping everything neat and in its place.
When the guests had come and gone,
Then the house turned into a home
Where confusion and excitement was the pace.

Having children makes a house a home.
Maybe there was no place to be alone;
But the joys that children bring
Far outweigh the other things
And you yearn for the times that are gone.

*Dedicated to Yvonne, Christine, Marie
and Jonathan, who lived there.*
—Ruby Vernon Stull

THE SUNFLOWER WARRIORS

The many days were filled with splendid conquests.
The hours consumed by unquenchable imagination.
The minutes moved ever endlessly through the midsummer's eve.
The fruits of nature had come to bloom.
Thus giving shelter to the warriors of youth.
From the fortresses of the grape shrouded trees would they roam.
Devouring all foes who should cross their paths.
Great be the number before them but undaunted would they press
  to their task.
Enumerable fields of the golden flowers of the sun have they
  slain.
Only for the imagination to be filled again.
The days were filled, the hours consumed, minutes moving ever
  endlessly.
  —Robert W. Johnson

I entered the church house and headed for a pew
when the usher stepped forward and said, "We welcome you."

He took me to a seat near the back of the room
as the lady at the organ played an old familiar tune.

It was Amazing Grace, I had heard as a lad
when I attended the old country church with my mother and my dad.

But as I grew older I soon drifted away
from that cradle of safety I enjoyed in that day.

Seems the world was calling me as I'm sure it has called you
it's a big exciting world and there is much to see and do.

So I answered the call as many men have done
and many things I did, not unlike the Prodigal Son.

Yes, I wasted much of my life and my money is all spent
and now I'm coming home because my heart now says repent.

Yes, God has regenerated my spirit as only God can do
and I see a better life now coming into view.

If I had listened to my parents when they tried to steer me right
my life could be bright and sunny instead of dark as night.

But hindsight is twenty-twenty, a fact proclaimed by all
men will not give way to truth, till their backs are against the wall.
  —Melvin DeHass

CLOUDED LOVE

I saw a break in the cloud today . . . the cloud . . . which shadows his face
like the trees shadow the earth.

Oh, I have always known it was there . . . buried deep inside . . . falsely
hidden from emotions of any kind.

Like a sad memory . . . it would begin to surface . . . then . . . instinctively,
protectively, it would push its way back . . . deeper and deeper . . . freely
escaping the human rituals of feeling or caring.

Sheltered constantly from the outside world, outside faces . . . it never
quite emerged . . . for if it did . . . the pain would surely tear out his heart.

Many times, though, through the years, I have seen him fight it back . . .
with stubbornness and spite . . .

but . . . today . . . the words cut too deep . . . and suddenly . . . the cloud broke . . .
and I saw a tear, I saw his heart, and I heard "I'm sorry" . . . for
the first time . . .

Then softly, almost whispered, I heard "I love you" . . . how hard it must
have been for him to say those words . . . words I had never heard . . . yet . . .
. . . did he not know . . .
. . . I knew it . . . all along.

Dedicated to my brother, Brent Barnes, who inspired this writing . . .
he holds a special place in my heart . . . and always will.
  —Alisa Barnes

NIGHT LIGHT

As the moon settles its bright rays upon the lakes tides. Such beauty is filtered through the moonlight. The stars gaze deeply into the eyes of the tide. The cool wisp of the night's air rushes through the soul.

—O.J. Bell

SPIRIT OF SIERRA MADRE

I see your mountains in the distance
The sun slips over your silhouetted crest
Offering me the solitude
Of a nearby place to nest

To breathe the spirit of Sierra Madre
Is to breathe the breath of home
The one you've always searched for
That kept you on the roam

Open all my hidden places
Erase all the tortured faces
That brought me safe to you
Oh, spirit of Sierra Madre

Allow me into your arms of welcome
Into your space of grand design
Let me feel your warmth and sunshine
Let it heal my troubled mind

To breathe the spirit of Sierra Madre
Is to breathe the breath of home
The one you've always searched for
That kept you on the roam

Dedicated to my cherished, incredible children, Sheryl and David, and to Hoona-Qua's faith and lead.

—Sharon Lee Keene

EARTH'S NUPTIALS

The morning's mist
covered the earth
like a bridal veil.

Beauty
(too pure to come from anyone but God)
was seen as the sheer mass was lifted.

Innocence
was evident;
no man had yet molested the virgin soil.
Though soon, farmers would plant;
factories, pollute;
laborers, toil;
and children, play.
But not now—only a kiss from the sunrise.

Freshness
was the ceremonial fragrance
leaving the senses with a desire
to reject all others.

The commitment?

I vowed to love, honor, and cherish her
so long as the Earth should stand
and I should live.

Heaven was filled with such joy
that its tears fell as rain.

—Barbara Brickey Jividen

I LIKE A RAINY DAY

Heaven sends the sunshine to brighten up our day
This makes life more pleasant all along our way.
But still we need the showers to make the flowers grow
They make our earth to blossom for mortals here below.
Softly falling raindrops always soothe my soul
Sweet and quiet peacefulness around me seems to roll.
The hectic pace of life dwindles; fades away
And I feel my gentle Savior has sent a lovely day.

—Eva E. Steinka

NATURE'S WAY

The bird feeder hangs up high by the door.
Over the flowers that bloom in the bed.
The butterfly circles and lights on the bloom
Of a zinnia, bright and red.
The hummingbird tastes of the nectar sweet,
His busy wings hum and sigh.
He sits for a time on a small bent limb.
He eats, then he turns to fly.
He guards his place, and never will stand
For others to feed here today.
His fury is raised, when he sees them there,
And he turns and runs them away.

—Margaret Morris McCuiston

STORYTELLERS

The setting sun on the horizon
Casts colors of many hues
Colors the sky in many visions
Sends the day into night
Raises the gods to watch over the heavens.

Dancing around the sky they see all
Knowing without telling
Keeping secrets that shouldn't be hidden
Feel forbidden to tell,
For they know it may hurt.

At last a part of them is smoldered,
As a candle whose flame has been extinguished
'Tis not long before all is lost,
When the sky is completely darkened
And the gods can no longer dance.

—Broch Muhs, grade 11

JUST A SIMPLE WISH

What's it like to be a moth or miller?
Sometimes wish I were a caterpillar.
Long or short, dull or shiny,
    fat and wooly, . . . that's for me!

I would rush around so that I could see,
    just how many feet protrude from me.
Up and down the branches I would crawl,
    I'd munch on leaves and try not to fall.

The only problem, being one, I see,
    is that hungry bird set to pounce on me!

I wish I were a feathered bird,
    not a four legged feline furred.
I'd swoop down upon a wiggly worm,
    but only the one big, fat, and firm.

If on my flight I see a bug or two,
    I'll just hop up behind and eat them too!

—Mary Lou

FANTASYLAND

Fantasies from my childhood
I believed this day and age
Convinced me of reality
That all the world, was my own stage

Creating people for my players
I kept watch from my ivory tower
Searching for my charming prince
For my knight in shining armour

Dashing warriors, dueling swords
For my colors and my hand
Never had much of a dowry
Neither treasure, never land

Carving paths thru dusty streets
Coloring my atmosphere
Flying banners over battles
Like some valiant cavalier

—Barbara Bergstand

Our passive father
lays his child to rest
as our mother
overwhelms us with her warm beauty
the fog hugs his dying sister
and floats calmly above her breasts

We've suckled the morning's tears
with parched and starving lips
Leaving the silhouetted trees
to shudder at their own wretchedness
as their roots give up
and search no more

Giving us their child
to make love on
we must once again
return to the tranquility
of our lost child
and let her live in her
reigning simplicity

—Vivian Kubulan

PASTORAL SYMPHONY

The breeze that wafts, so tenderly
The fragrance of the hour;
Whether flowery dogwood tree
Or honeysuckle bower,
The taste of berries on my lip,
A tinge of red rubasse;
Each bid me come, their nectar sip,
Their lea for my paillasse.
Mine eye doth long for shaded slope
Of sod and sarsparill,
For dandelion, for winding trope,
For tangy bulbous squill.
Mine ear doth want for song of bird,
My touch, the naked air;
My heart entranced, there sepulchered
In God's green woodland fair.
So, let me there among my hills,
Stealthily recline;
Amid a shroud of daffodils,
Of oak and elm and pine.

—Elmer A. Williams

I WONDER

In this day of modern society, there is a question that really bothers me.
Couples don't marry, they live together for awhile
Then they just part with a smile.
I wouldn't try it heaven knows, but if I did just suppose, will someone put my mind at ease, would I be the shacker or the shackee?
Really, laying all jokes aside, we should look on marriage with pride, for that has always been God's plan
That is why He made woman from man.
I hope it will all be right someday, and we will all see it God's way.

—Margaret Neill

TOO FAST FOR ME

The hills that had once seemed mountainous to me
Now are merely tall.
The yard that had seemed unending to me
Now is rather small.
The friends that meant the world to me
Now have moved away.
We write letters, but still —
It's not the same that way.

No more snowball fights
        sled rides or
               hide-and-go-seek.

No more Barbie dolls
        ghost stories or
               let's pretend we're asleep.

I'm growing up too fast for me.
I want the simple days —
   "Let's climb a tree, start a club,
     play house . . ."

If only it still could be that way!

—Briana Hines, age 13

THE TRUTH SET ME FREE!

This changing world alarmed me!
    I searched! I must be free!
        My efforts all were futile.
           Peace and I were far from mutual.

The Prince of Peace then found me!
    The One who set me free!
        He turned my life around.
           His love made fear fall down!

The Truth is clear each day!
    I search the Bible and pray.
        God's Words are very clear!
           Jesus Christ His Son so dear

Was sent to earth for me!
    Not just for me, you see.
        He paid the price for sin!
           One needs to turn to Him!

Meet Him today!
    There's no delay!
        The Bible is where He's found!
           You'll soon be heaven bound!

—Arlene Carpenter (Abate)

COUSINS OF THE STARS

We, distant cousins of the stars,
  Must learn to love, and welcome chance,
So, with childlike trust, to love with
Unconditional acceptance!

Love based on freedom can never
Grow boundless in a jealous heart;
In an understanding exchange,
Love, like distant stars, lives its
           part!
—**Arlene D. Krueger**

MOTHER'S DAY THOUGHTS

It's Mother's Day — but the line is filled with just washed clothes — As much to keep busy as of necessity.

It's Mother Day — and Mom needs me. A daughter I will be — A Mom another day.

It's Mother's Day with memories for only me to know.

It's Mother's Day, a day to wish and pray all women could be blessed.

It's Mother's Day, not of dreams, but of reality. Today, by circumstance, a day to be alone.

A melancholy day. A time to think, a time to thank my Mom and Grandma too, who hovered ever near in good times and in bad.

This Mother's Day, I raise my hand for one I never knew and for the two God let me claim.

With the miracle of miracles, life never is the same, but on this day, with pride-filled heart, tinged only with a speck of pain, I thank Thee for your grace and know oft times our most precious gifts are not the ones we would have chose.

So in this vein, I thank you for this precious time in which to dream and contemplate.

It's Mother's Day and I am blessed with memories and hope.
—**B.J. Frieden**

MOMENTS WITH MY MOTHER

When I look into your eyes I see a twinkle,
  When I look at the hard years in your face I
    see the wrinkles.

When I share your laughter of years gone by,
  I remember the times you wiped the tears from
    my eyes.

When I share the stories of how I was always put
    first and never last,
I remember my childhood and from you there was
    never a shadow cast.

When I share your warmth and kindness that can
    only come from a mother,
I remember you're the greatest no one can take your
    place there is no other.

When I talk to you on the phone and we are down and
    blue,
I remember the place called home that I can always
    come back to.

When I share your experience of being a wonderful
    mother and standing so proud and tall,
I remember that a mother is so many things and
    only the heart can list them all.

Dedicated with love to my mother, Bertha Merriman
—**Judy Voltz**

A BUS

A Bus is a lion that roars so loud
  So everybody can hear this hurting sound.
  He starts running fiercely fast.
Whenever someone goes near they would usually pass.
—**Alyssa Young, age 9**

HEART SERENADE

As silent as a dropping pin,
  I hear my thrashing heart within.
As far as the day awaits,
I hear my heart project no hate.
But as I come to full awareness,
My precious heart will shed no lie
and prolong itself in a melodic,
ever-soothing alibi.
—**Allyson Jade**

THE FATE OF THE MISLED HEART

I shall bury my heart
  (Though my body must go on)
In this shallow grave without a name,
For it beats no longer.
Its strings have been pulled maliciously
By the music of pipes played untimely.
Cupid plays no music
And the heart is strengthened
By the wounds of his shaft
And eros does not allay him,
But follows.
Pan plays merrily and Eros joins him
On drums that beat in time to the heart;
And the heart slowly dies with the music.
So heed not the music of the loins,
Lest your heart petrify as mine,
Buried in this shallow grave
Among many stones of its kind.
—**Keith Foecke**

TOKENS OF PAIN

Oh the pain, I did cause.
  No, I didn't stop or pause
To think of the way
Or even the day
When the tables would turn
And my heart would burn.
All I cared about
Which no one can doubt
Was all the attention
To live the premonition.
The premonition of dreams
How real the pain now seems.
For now I'm all alone
To live in my dome
Of misery and sadness
While others live in gladness.
I guess it is fair
Because others' feelings I didn't spare.
For their hearts I've broken
And kept as my token.
—**Amanda Konersmann**

BUTTER HI

fluttering little butterfly
made of bright color dust and love
dancing merrily
to and from the fire in the sky
falling, falling through the wind
over and under
flowers in bloom high and low
flocks of fellow ask
whatcha doin,
lone little butterfly
I'm dropping all around the great sky
to say HI

—Rupert Valero

ODE TO A GREEK FRATERNITY

Meet my fraternity brothers
They all think just like me
For initiation rites
Included several nights
Of free lobotomies

Come over Friday night
The guys are putting on a dance
Hear the DJ jam
In the room we'll cram
Your reputation will be enhanced

We're the United Colors of Crayola
Accepting all peoples and creeds
If you want some fun
And to meet someone
Alcohol is all you need

We are lost without each other
Preferring nepotism in our jobs
Yet, as time goes on
We remain headstrong
By following Calvin and Hobbes

—Mark Fennell

SPORTS ARE ME

I like basketball,
   can't you see,
I like football,
It's right for me
I like baseball,
   swoosh!
What a swing!
I like soccer wow!
I'm the king!
I like sports,
can't you see,
I like sports,
cause sports are fun,
You can throw,
You can jump,
You can also run,
In sports you always
have to try.
Some people don't
and we all know why.
Sports is about trying
you see.
I like sports cause
sports are me.

—LeRoy Heard Jr., age 11

AWAKENING OF TIME

Awake!
Shake dreams from your hair, the morning has come.
Ride across the land, and greet the sun.
Distant and always on the run.

Night has passed and now sky of blue.

Distant hills and enchantment of sight.
Do you feel the warmth from the radiance of light?

Can you vision the far past, and to embrace
fearlessness at last.

Travel farther into the day,
And capture the choice of time.
Always of chance and filled with rhyme.
Plundering more of each day, just an awakening of time.

—Stuart L. Spanier

A RAY OF HOPE

Just a sunny ray of hope
To someone close and dear
A sunny note to help you cope
With those so close and near
When we cherish the memories
Of the ones we've loved and lost
We can always count on those and never bare the cost
You never should feel down and blue
Your family and friends will know
That no matter how much work you do
Your pain will for certain show
Sunny thoughts can sometimes bring success
And this sunny reminder will too
It's just a little note to say God bless
For all the kindness you hold so true
And if by chance you seem to face
Get up and shout you're proud
For you have already made the grade
You now seem to stand out in the crowd.

—M.L.A. Frazier

THE CONSCIENCE

I stalk the woods
My mind full of anticipation
I am a hunter . . . not able to feast

I cool off in the stream
The chill pours inside my body
I am a fish . . . lying on the shore

I watch the wildlife
my awareness more clear than ever
yet, I am a camera . . . not capable of focus

In which direction should I look
The walls of my mind appeared to be made of glass
however, the night fell . . . and I went blind

Then, one day I woke
The wilderness filling my every breath
the link was there . . . when I was unconscious

I found myself
Without realizing I had ever been gone
one's mind must be silent . . . to hear the truth

The world buzzed around me
But until I left it completely behind
I would always be caged . . . but, now I am free

—Mary Ann Stevenson

DEPRESSION YEARS — 1932 —

Best Christmas ever to Grandma's house we would go.
In old bob sled in deep cold white snow.
Home made caps — mittens hand made toys —
Were all so pleasing to us girls and boys.
A bright red apple, bit of candy too, are days
    to remember for me and you.
Grandma's feast a great delight, neat
    clean house in candle light.
A tree trimmed so pretty with home made stuff.
Whatever we got was good enough.
We'd sing songs were so happy —
    For we had it all.
Those good old "Christmas" days are best to recall.

—Evelyn M. Stephens

PRECIOUS MOMENTS

I like pretty things, twilight-time, trees
    silhouetted against the sky, a babbling
    brook, a robin's eye.

I like pretty things, bird prints in the snow,
    a fire in the fireplace, all a glow . . .
A roasted brown turkey and all the trimmings,
    and a warm heart all full of giving.

I like pretty things, Christmas time, bright
    ribbons and bows, colored tree lights
    and mistletoe.

I like pretty things and nice things too,
    but the nicest thing to me, my dear,
    is being in love with you.

—Doris M. Osborn

* TRADITION *

At last the Christmas rush is all behind us,
We joyfully rang in the New Year,
With good friends and family,
It's an absolute must.
Lots of laughter, charades,
Champagne and exchanging hugs.
We made some noise,
Open the doors,
And let go.
The last of the year's bugs.
But my favorite of all,
Is this Norwegian tradition.
A wonderful group of family,
With lots of determination and ambition.
Marathon mashed potatoes,
Lefse and lutefisk,
You learn to eat it at your own risk.
If you can't handle . . .
. . . this cod like fish,
There's always mounds of meatballs to dish.
Remember the secret is . . .
. . . to use generous amounts of melted butter.
When everyone is served,
Hardly a word is uttered.
At least we eat Lutefisk once a year.
You must enjoy it with akvavit and beer.
But truly to my amazement,
More than the Grand Lutefisk,
Is all the love, time and work put into it.
That brings together a family and traditionalship!

—Linda S. Neely

JANUARY SNOW

Falling, falling, lightly falling
    Winter's hoary breath aglowing
In the lamp light of the night.
Grass and boxwood tucked in whiteness
Waiting for the dawning light

Duchess snoring, snow is pouring;
Cleo's snoozing, nature's losing
All its color oozing into white
Unseen master stroking faster
Briskly whisping, out of sight.

Flakes of silver, loose and light,
Slightly drifting, quietly lifting
Powdered magic left and right
Artist laughing at his crafting,
Deftly painting snow-bound night

—Larry Bogart

SONG IN THE NIGHT

She played a Christmas carol
on a hot August night.
I wondered why,
in the heat of the evening
she thought of a faraway land
and that elegant tune.
Eventually I realized
it was the only song she knew
and I listened for it
not only at sunset,
but also at midnight
and sometimes, just before daylight.
A Christmas song in any season
seemed to bring peace
to a life gone wrong,
just as it has done
for two thousand years.

—Ellen F. Childress

THE CHRISTMAS GIFT

And He came as a little baby
Born into a world undone.
It seems hard that this could be
The Father's will for His own Son.

The Child grew day by day
Learning the same as we all do:
Submitting to His parents' way
And following the Church's too.

Throughout His life He aimed to show
What the Keys of life should be,
And how the Spirit of God should flow
Through our lives for all to see.

You see, His life is an illustration,
A picture in cross stitch sewn;
A revelation of the Pattern Son,
That now has been made known.

So take hold of His revelation
And follow it so you can be
Another illustration
For all the world to see.

—Julia Ruane Smith

MY MOTHER'S EYES

I've looked into my mother's eyes
I've seen a heart of gold.
I've seen a life of motherhood
Contentedly unfold.

I've looked into my mother's eyes
I've seen a loving wife.
I've seen a woman's devotion
Enduring at married life.

I've looked into my mother's eyes
So many times before.
The love I've seen within those eyes
I'll see forever more.

I've looked into my mother's eyes
And hope someday I'll find.
That what I've seen in my mother's eyes
One day my children will see in mine.

—Lisa Harry, age 14

ANOTHER DAWN

Today some bad news came, but someone loved me just the same.

It was the chosen day, the clouds let down their winter's burden, but someone loved me just the same.

As mind absorbed the news that day, past trials prepared the way.

In silent knowing, his presence there assured another dawn.

With lighter heart and renewed mission, the winter's snow became a vision.

All because someone loved me on that day.

Dedicated to my husband for his many years of love and patience.

—B.J. Frieden

DANCING WITH MY LOVE

Come dance with me
 Hug in my love like a wave
  Of an invisible flow
   Dancing like the ride of a canoe
    On a river's glow

Dancing With My Love
 Like a warm breath that's
  Frozen from the cold winds
   Crystalize and sprinkle
    Deep into my soul.

Dance With My Love
 With arms around my waist
  Whirling and dancing
   Flowing with grace
    Knowing our love
     Will dance and dance
      Forever embrace.

—Lyda

DANCING THE RACE

Pounding, hypnotic, this rhythm's life is
The force between you and the earth as you gyre.
"Lead! in this hard dance." the rock cries —
"And I'll follow."
A gift long brooded in sinew and bones:
Your heart's beating; the ragged edge of your breath
Are its tokens.

A seed sows its strength to the ground
And is changed to a form not its own.
So your steps' strength given outright
To the patient, dependable soil
May return, mysterious, as joy.

—Stephen Maleski

THE TREE OF LIFE

I came to a tree so full of Life,
Whose boughs were strong and fruit so bright.
Its branches hang heavy with seed borne new . . .
Which left this message for me and for you.

"I have visited many places most were pleasant lands,
Where the flowers were bloomed
And their stamens — perfumed.
(Ay, their fragrance a — sheer delight!)

And as I look around, and up, and then down,
And see the vastness of the sky . . .
And all beneath it lie — I'm enthralled.

Living amongst worlds that are,
Worlds that were, and worlds
That shall be,
Makes me proud to know
That I have part with thee."

—G.M. Bradley

THE CREATOR OF NIGHT

Who erected the night around me?
I dare to ask!

An answer from the builder is not coming . . .
Was I able to build all this night-wall by myself?
My question contains so much madness
I am about to crown myself as the founder of night
The coronation with a hideous smile
Giving orders to pour more tar in the cracks of the wall
"Built in the whole forest
Tight the whole world inside
Let them have nightmares"

Early in the morning when the wall collapses,
The hard working spirits are hiding
Deep into the cracks of the earth
It is not a droughty season
I just feel sorry for this awake night
I regret this useless night

I paint white my dark rings
Around my burning eyes
Exiting staight in to the hospitable world
Aiming straight into the open arms of the hospitable world
And the light?
I already forgot
Yes!
And the light . . .
Who was asking me?

—John Plesh

HERO

Stands there a man so tall,
he cannot see his fellowman?
So tall in the stature of his mind,
he cannot lend a hand?
If so, his vision of self is great,
but he is small.
Observe him.

Stands there a man who meets you face to face,
who knows no boundary of rank or strain;
walking beside you step for step, pace for pace,
sharing your fear, your glory and your pain?
Learn from him.

Stands there a man, a leader of men,
whose concern is not his visage, his power or gain,
who looks not to his comfort, safety or claim,
who for the love of country, honor and brothers,
devotes his being to serving others?
Follow him.

—Charlotte Nichols

IF I WERE A KING

If I were a king of a vast nation,
I would proclaim their eternal Declaration of
freedom, your freedom of power, your freedom of hate,
your freedom of love, your freedom of choice, and your
freedom of state. I would bestow all of these just
blessings upon my nation, because of my love
for them, and because of their trust in me,
and for this strong nation I would set laws of
right and wrong, then for a season I would
leave my eternal nation, to see if my people
would heed or disagree with my laws of right
and wrong, and for the ones who did not agree
I would destroy their disbelief, and towards the
end of my ruling I would grant those who
did believe a blessing of a new kingdom, and at
my death I would not be sad for them, but I
would be glad for them, because they would all
know that I was the one who invented
freedom.

—Jeff Campbell

FREEDOM

To laugh, to cry, to work, to spend,
To live your whole life as if it had no end.
To go, to come, to forget, to remember,
To dream, dance and love from January to December.
That's precious, precious freedom, guard it well,
A lack of it is frighteningly close to hell.

That's when you watch your steps and restrain the tears.
Deny your feelings and flee in fear,
Follow tight schedules and balance each check,
Glance over your shoulders. What a pain in the neck!
Then you realize that you're losing it, the headaches start
But what can you do to stop the panic in your heart?

So you change and rearrange your life, then you hope
That your existence would cease being a grand tightrope.
Suddenly the sun comes bursting forth
You grasp this treasure for all it's worth
Just hold on to that sweet, sweet freedom, never let it go
Someone actually gave His life for it you know!

—Maureen F. Linton

TIMELESS

Calm winds blow a sweet delight
Hallow lands of sand and sky
Silence of time standing still
Mystic pyramids and sand hills
Endless secrets lie untold
Turning to nothing as they grow old
A place that time will never hold

—Norman James Foldvik

SAILS

Billowing sails
of cloth as fine
As silk
   on a woman's knee.

Braced in the breeze
   with a tempest's heart
From the roils
   of an untamed sea.

From barnacled bottom
   to the top of the mast
Every bit strains
   to be.

As swift as the birds
   as light as the clouds
Out on the waves
   and free.

—K.A. Nelson

THIS COUNTRY IS OUR HOME

Raise up your flag high!
There's no shame to feel
Proud fluttering of the heart;
Honor all for which it stands:
This country is our home;
United, we hold it strong.

Allow yourself to cry
For the many men killed
While facing battles hard;
Protecting their Motherland:
This country is our home;
United, we hold it strong.

This World could never deny
The desire and burning will
For democracy within the heart
Of the In-God-We-Trust man:
This country is our home;
United, we hold it strong.

—Melba Murleen Valarezo

CORAL ROSE

Coral on the petal of a blooming rose
Bliss that gives it smell delight
Here I stand by your grave
With the memory of that night

Cruor spilled like a blizzard
The shriek, the panic
A blade through the flesh

How can one do this to himself;
The revolting thought in mind

It was when I walked in and found
   you there
Now I stand before your vault
Holding in my hand,
The Coral rose
In memory of you

—Carol B. McFall

YOUR ABSENCE

As I stare at your picture,
I begin to tear;
I am going through such torture,
because you are not here.

I miss you so much,
my heart still aches;
I think about our last touch,
and all of our mistakes.

But I can definitely say,
that I still very much love you;
Waiting for the day,
that I can finally be with you.

The thought of me never seeing you again,
just tears me apart;
If so—you will never be forgotten,
you have a permanent place in my heart.

—Richard Lee Goldner

STORED UP TEARS

Could I but shed one single tear
to help erase this pain
so open gates to cry a stream
so far has been in vain.

All this sorrow locked within
since we had to part
why the tears can't begin?
Yet streaming from the heart!

Had we not shared such perfect love
I would have no cause to wonder
why I cannot cry just one single tear
from a heart so torn asunder.

I've prayed, "Dear Lord, help me understand
with all the pain and love I feel
not one tear to ease my loss
my eyes seem ever sealed.

Perhaps the tears I shed within
are being safely stored away
to cry a stream of joyful tears
when I go to you one day."

Dedicated to Ciss and Jackie.

—Edwin P. Spivey

BUDDY

Where did my friend go?
The guy who used to tell me dumb stories,
Stay away from me when I was angry,
Call me a dork.
Where did he go?
I see him around all the time
but he's never here.
The guy I did not want a romantic relationship
with for the sole fact that I wanted to
retain our friendship.
Maybe I was wrong.
Maybe I should have gotten involved with him
romantically
All I know is that I miss him.
I miss him so much.
More than he will ever know
More than I would ever tell him.

—Elena Balli

THE WATERFALL

When I think of a waterfall I think of you,
White foaming rapids and crystal blue;
Its pursuit focused on just one goal,
Tenaciously bearing its very soul;
Through the seasons with winter's cold,
Ice crystals form and to rocks take hold;
Yet the waterfall never knows a reason,
To be affected by the season;
And spring with its life beginning force,
Water moves even faster on its course;
Summer with the beauty to take a dip,
Or watch the deer as they gingerly sip;
Waterfall's passions and stubborn style,
Reminding me of you all the while;
Seeing everything so crystal clear,
I find you so totally dear;
No backing down from life's heartache,
Never regret choices you make;
How symbolic can all of this be,
Of how the waterfall reminds me.

—Shari Moore

DIVORCE

Divorce, you horrible and despicable thing!
With a sword you invade beautiful homes
Inflicting cancer into their bones,
How deadly are your stings!

To husband and wife you inject your wiles
Of splendor and gallantry perceive
Through your blandishments are deceived
Of glittering worldly guile.

To you are born babies with scorn,
Youths roam the lanes with weary brows,
Stripped of love from selfish lovers grow
Craving for a kiss, care and wishing were unborn.

Oh Lord! are they to blame? Provide them grace.
For love and marriage are your glorious gifts,
But mocked, shattered and thrown into rifts
Turning this world for innocents a living grave.

Ah! that men and women could see,
That beyond this stormy life is the promised land,
In exchange for trials numerous as sands.
There, glitters gold of unending bliss, care-free.

—Seny Isican

It is said that the eyes are the window to the soul. I stand without and look in,
Wondering what mystical, magic secrets lie within those crystalline panes.
When I look, will I behold beautiful lands? A sky alive with fire
As the sun settles down to rest beyond the horizon?
Still waters flowing gently, speaking in wondrous tones to a luscious green forest
full of life,
Set afire by the crimson kiss of the setting sun?
With the fading of the day, night settles in. The call of the wise owl questions "who?"
So I, too, wonder "Who" lies behind those eyes?
Behind those eyes, those eyes that set my soul aflame with life, lies the mystery of a man.
His laughter sparks life, for it comes from deep within the heart and reaches forth
to light all around.
He sends forth his touch to others slowly and quietly, never firm, ever sure.
While sometimes hard to understand—as the bubbling stream, his words spring forth
With the wisdom and understanding of the ages.
All you need do is be still and listen, to hear the whisper in the wind.
But it is his eyes, so crisp, so clear, wherein lies the secret of life.
—LaDonna Dial

THE HOMEFRONT IS HELL

One year ago today
Our friend Mary went away.
They sent her to a foreign land
And placed a gun there, in her hand.
The President declared a war
Some questioned here — "What are we fighting for?"
We prayed each day for her return
Had no idea — What she would learn.
The wounds of war cut so deep
Endless nights of interupted sleep.
A struggle everyday to survive
And feelings of guilt for being alive.
The emotional destruction is far greater from the start
You can rebuild a country — but how do you rebuild a mind, a life, a heart?
Fragmented memories and a shattered dream
Look at my eye, I can't find the gleam.
They think a parade will make it all better
We waited for months to get through a letter.
The war is over, we've left the DMZ
Yet the war wages on for it is within me.
—Dawn Alvis-Richards

SAILING

Where are you
Who are you
Are you out there somewhere—maybe looking for someone too
Someone like me maybe
I search their eyes to make certain they are not you
So far there has been no sign of the one I think I must be looking for
Little flashes occur—a connection of tastes, styles, attitudes, desires
They always seem to end—leaving me desolate and empty
So much emptiness in this life

I wish I could be certain you are there—that you will someday be by my side
I will love you as much as I know I am capable of which is a tremendous amount
I hope you will be able to handle how intense and deep my love, my passion for you will run
Like all the oceans ebb and flow—bottomless in some places, shallow in others
Will you be able to handle the crashing waves of storms and the serene calms of smooth and
    glassy waters
Will you be the water of my life
Quenching my thirst only to leave me thirsty for more, yet never drowning me
Will there be someone to sail these oceans and find a harbor with me

I hope for a time when I will anticipate coming home to you
To feel your presence, to hear your thoughts, to read your signs and know how to react
I must believe you are out there somewhere sailing in your own ocean, waiting and looking
    for me
If you are I will try and find you—keep your bright sails flying so I will know it's you
—Jill Marie Poffenroth

SAY SOMETHING GOOD

I heard of a man,
   that lived a few years ago,
      by the report of many,
         the meanest you could know.

It seemed hopeless to find,
   any to claim him as friend,
      he was hard and calloused,
         no limit to his sin.

Another man in this town,
   was as kind as could be,
      and in every human being,
         he could some goodness see,

When the mean man died,
   missed like thorn and thristle,
      said the kind gentle man,
         that fellow really could whistle.

    —Lee Roy Nevitt

HALLOWEEN

Halloween's the one night of the year
When little children have no fear
When darkness falls they venture out
Like little soldiers on a route
With bag in hand and flashlight too
They're out to threaten me and you.
"Tricks or treats" is their demand.
Best reach out with sweets in hand.
They mean every word they say.
You have only to obey.

But as their little legs grow weary,
And the sandman makes eyes bleary,
Soon they're heading homeward bound.
At nine o'clock there's not a sound.
Ghosts and goblins are in bed
Little angels fear to tread.
Halloween is done this year.
Let's all have another beer.

    —Lawrence V. LaChapelle

Alone, no longer feeling your warmth,
Alone, no longer hearing your voice.
Birds no longer chirping, music no longer
playing.
Was it my cry? Did I cry too loud?
Alone, no longer hearing you yell.
Alone, no longer feeling your fists.
Leaves no longer fall, sun no longer shining.
Forgive me for what I did? Forgive me
for what I didn't. Why did you go? Why
did they take you? I told them to stop,
I told them I loved you.
Time's gone by and to think they knew, you were
why I was black and blue.
Alone, no longer needing to hear your voice.
Alone, no longer needing to feel your warmth.
Birds chirp once again, music plays loudly.
It wasn't my cry, I did cry loud enough.
I can still hear your voice, I can still
feel your fists.
Leaves fall in beautiful colors.
Sun shines brightly.

    —Sheri Gromek

PODIATRISTS' LAMENT

The baby has her first new shoes
With tassels just for fun
And toes ten times the width she'll choose
When she is twenty one

    —Fred B. Cushman

HALFTIME

The flash of the horns; the tap of the drums
are signals for another show.
We march on the field in disciplined ranks
like soldiers all in a row.

We play with passion and fury;
We are The Eastwood Marching Band
But we know our performance is
just not enough for the hungry
football fan.

    —Theresa Pisarski

ABRAHAM LINCOLN

ABRAHAM LINCOLN'S Mother gave thanks
Her name we all know was Nancy Hanks
His Father named Thomas, when he was born
The Backwoods People nicknamed him Linkhorn

Born on the Sabbath, a Baby so fine
In a Hunter's Hut, in 1809
Little Abe was born in Kentucky
Grew tall and STRAIGHT, A mind that was plucky

Sarah was Abe's Sister's name
She was never to have any Fame
Now we know that Abe was sent
To be OUR 16th. PRESIDENT

    —Blanche M. O'Neill

DRIFT-WOOD BUFF

Although I know it will be tough,
   I'm going to tell 'bout Drift-Wood Buff.

At a pond, lake or brook,
   His head held low, he has to look.

In the brush he paws around,
   Driftwood clunking on the ground.

A-stooping low with an old straw hat;
   Some folks call the driftwood rat.

A heap of brush, stumps, and sticks—
   I've heard it said he must be sick.

With saw in hand and hatchet, too,
   It seems it's all he has to do.

I guess it makes his heart feel good
   With an armful of that rotten wood.

A-tripping o'er the stubs and stones,
   On the shore that wood rat roams.

A-poking here, a-prodding there,
   A-piling driftwood everywhere.

All of this is really rough —
   There's no one like that Drift-Wood Buff.

    —Carroll R. Buffum Sr.

YOU CAN'T STAY DEAD

You're going to die as is appointed,
whether short or tall or double jointed.
Then you will rise for a judgement stand,
it's going to be hell or God's Promised Land.

If you haven't accepted God's good neighbor plan,
then you'll live on suffering at the devil's hand.
There'll be pain and torment through endless ages,
yes, it's long-term payment for sins' wages.

Now my prayer for you is this very day,
that you'll turn to the Lord and walk the narrow way.
Although you're not exempt from this world's trouble,
you'll live on in Heaven where pleasures a trillion times double.

—Lee Roy Nevitt

INSTRUMENTS IN GOD'S HANDS

I am only an instrument in God's Hands
   To be used as He plans.

Whether one who speaks with persuasive words that win,
   Or writes well on paper with a pen.

Whether a physician who treats a disease,
   Or the plumber who repairs the pipes that freeze.

Whether a president of a large corporation,
   Or one who works at a factory in cooperation.

Whether an officer of the law,
   Or one who mows and rakes in a lawn.

Whether a farmer who works in the fields,
   Or a mother that in the house prepares the meals.

Each has been given abilities from the God above,
   To be used to serve in love.

So what ever ability God has given you,
   Use it to His glory; always be diligent and true.

—Herb Franks Jr.

GOOD MORNING

Whatever happens the rest of today, I thank you Lord for this glorious morn.

Soft breeze, song birds, distant jets, gentle sun in soft blue sky. And thanks so much for my special guy.

He has sowed the seeds. They are starting to show. The good earth is green and ready to grow.

Down the lane the postman's car is pulling away. The scent of my roast is filling the air.

So whatever happens the rest of the day, thank you Lord for this glorious morn.

With a song in my heart and a quickened gate, I head for the mailbox to see what he brought.
It's full to the brim with papers and junk. Who cares? It is such a nice walk.

No one's around to witness my grin, delighting in springtime — a flower I pluck.

So whatever happens the rest of the day. I thank you Lord for this glorious morn.

—B.J. Frieden

One by one
Through the darkness they come.
Rays of light
Piercing the night.
Clearing the way
For a new day.

—Mikki Barnes, age 13

THE MOON IS MY MUSE

The moon is my muse
Silvery smiling down
From the Midnight Sky
Holding my eye,
Gripping my hand,
Passionately kissing the dainty fingers
With which I write
Enchantment as it touches
Gently my face
And winks at me.
My muse is the moon.

—Heather Elayn

LA LUNE D'AMIS

A hard waxing sphere in the black
Full of magic and mystery
A stony sign of time
A sliver or circle
With endless grey seas
It watches over us with silver eyes
Like a pale lamp in the black silky sky
And lights our path
During long nights of cold passage

It beams down on us all
And its presence is felt in full
Causing lunacy and madness
Keeping all at bay
As cold clouds howl past its surface
Like wisps of soft smoke

—Reed Sissman

MY NURSE IN WHITE

I lay in the hospital, so blue,
suffering with pain,
and loneliness too.

I cried out, "Oh Lord,
how can I endure
this pain inside,
I can't stand for sure."
Then I heard His soft voice,
so clear in the night.
"I'm sending you my Angel,
you'll be alright."

The Angel, "God" sent,
gave so much love and care.
I knew He was right.
He'd answered my prayer.

Sending me someone,
with tenderness and light.
My Angel of mercy,
my Nurse in white.

Dedicated to my nurse, Connie Conley.

—Lola J. Meeker

EVERY SPECIAL MOMENT

Every moment with you was special
there's not a second that can be replaced
I want so much to turn back time
your departure is the most traumatic event I've faced

Special times with you
are times I will never forget
If anyone asked what's most important
preserving your memory would be it

So many pleasant thoughts
so much that we shared
Yes, I'd want you in my life again
knowing how much I've suffered, and the pain I've beared

I will always thank God for you
and for what little time together we spent
I want to keep you forever
that's why I savor every special moment

WITH YOUR MOTHER

I need to know you're in Heaven
and that you're safe and well taken care of
I hope you were greeted by your mother
she can give you so much love

I can't stand the thought of you being lonely
freezing from the dampness and cold
She will wrap a blanket around you
God will protect your soul

With your mother beside you
you can walk through darkness and fear
You will be together again
just as you were here

I want to be there to protect you
my precious, darling brother
I wouldn't worry as much
If I knew you were with your mother

YOU SLIPPED AWAY

Snatched into darkness
when I fell asleep last night
I kept trying to find you
searching and searching, but couldn't find the light

So many faces
faces of people I didn't know
they hadn't met you
and I had no picture to show

I climbed high mountains
walked through swamps and the deepest river
Suddenly I began to panic
knees weak, I started to quiver

I had to find you
you were misplaced or lost
so determined to find you
you're priceless, I'll pay any cost

When I stumbled upon you
so still, so silent as you lay
You reached out your hand to me
before I could pull you back, you slipped away

ALL YOU MEAN TO ME

You are the source of my joy
your departure is the source of my grief
You are part of my past and future
the reason I question a prior religious belief

You influenced my personality
your memory directed my ultimate goal
In each aspect of my life
you play a major role

There are so many challenges
yet I know all I can be
I wish you could share my success
Eddie, you mean so much to me

I developed courage through your existence
due to your departure I know the reality of pain
You mean so much to me
you're the missing link in the family's chain

If you were here today
I know how much better my world would be
You've changed my life forever
can you know, all you mean to me?

BECAUSE OF ME

I don't know where life went wrong
can you tell me, do you know
Did you die because of something I've done
please can you tell me if it's so

Can you forgive me if my actions
past or present caused you to die
Is there a reason
could my sins be why

You know I'd never intentionally hurt you
nor allow anyone to
If this is because of me
tell me what did I do

I asked God for an answer
I fast and pray
in search for an explanation
lost, will he show me the way

It's impossible to trade places
make up for all you didn't experience and see
I will never forgive myself
if you lost your life because of me

Eddie at twelve years old.

*"Eddie," thank you for teaching me the value of life, Love and what it means to be a family. You will always live in my thoughts and in my heart. I love you and miss you so very much **Eddie** and I will always keep you in the spotlight. Love, your big sister, Belinda.*
Dedicated to Doris Edward Dalton, Jr., from Belinda Arzella Dalton, with love.

—Belinda A. Dalton

HELLFIRE

You rise from the flames of hell
you carry names such as hate, war, suicide
mass destruction.
You tell nothing but lies.
To tell the truth you would surely die.
Your tongue forked as the lightning strike, hair
burning of gold.
Eyes that burn to the depth of the soul.
Your touch like acid rain, you take God's name in vain.
Your breath the smell of decay
You don't have a place to call your own
You're really alone.
Just sink back to the pit of hellfire.

*Dedicated to all of my high school teachers,
you helped me make it through the tough times.*

—John Hacker Jr.

CHASM

As a beginner tutor, I entered the Program
With a bachelor's degree but soon realized
How ignorant I was, totally uneducated
In the depths of the problems of illiteracy.

Far beyond the inability to read or write,
It extends into one's entire existence,
Paralyzing in ways the literate
May never understand.

Through "Each One Teach One,"
I saw the chasm which prevails
For those who do not know vowel sounds —
To us, it is so simple — to them, it is rough terrain.

The pace is painfully slow — how I admire their efforts
In their battle to remove this barrier to the future —
Tomorrow will be the same . . . but someday
Someday . . . they can name their destiny.

—Betty Varner

A SALUTE TO OUR — UNITED AFRICAN MOVEMENT

You and I are magnificent people
We stand together as a team —
    rather — as a determined group
When we arrived on the planet
    the job was waiting
Our ancestors and forefathers
    lived and died as they
        fought for "change"
They never asked for any far-fetched
        "courtesy"
Only sought their sight to a "Freedom Plan"
Our ancestors were cunning and cautious
    just to assure a day to day living
They could only watch their babies
    snatched from them . . . as they
        reached the age of five
Their hurt was oh — so-o-o painful
But they had to keep stepping — praying
    and reaching for "The Promised Land"
I've questioned this travesty and
    wondered a time . . .
How folks — the perpetrators
    could commit such happenings
    and not consider it a crime!

—Vetha Marie Coward

BROKEN DAMS

Hopes and dreams
    dashed against the rocks
        of the flooding waters;
Promises for the future
    swept away
        by the rushing currents;
Self-confidence and esteem
    eroded and collapsed
        with the force of the waves;
A solitary figure
    stranded and unmoving
        as the waters swirl and rise.

—Lori L. Getz

DEPRESSION

You torture without compassion,
Pierce the depth of my weary soul.
Drown me breathless in confusion
Pondering my life's endless pains.

You take me as the fallen leaf
On the wayside forlorn, trampled,
Blown, tossed, no one cares give a left,
Perish unknown to oblivion.

But priceless, let me live by choice.
You great challenger of the frail!
Loved, I cling to my Father's Voice
And Brother's cross, my salvation.

Since my youth till now I am gray,
You poison me but befriend you.
Welcome you and profoundly pray,
My lamp with the Spirit of Light.

For every pain from morn till night,
I drink of my Brother's Blood of Life;
Conquering your deceiving might,
Earn my crown for Eternal Life.

—Seny Isican

WE WERE INNOCENT

The golden sun is setting,
And with purple glowing light,
The beautiful and striking scene
Becomes a starry night.

Thunder rumbles through the clouds,
The cold reveals our breath,
The chilling wind and stinging breeze
Give us the kiss of death.

Our God calls from far away,
But we pay him no mind,
Because we're deaf from deep within;
And yet we are so blind.

We do not have the happiness
We had when we first started,
For we began so innocent
And now we're brokenhearted.

Our helpless bodies tremble,
Cold penetrates our minds,
For we just took the easy path
And left our souls behind.

—Amanda Marie Halash

THE OAK TREE STANDS

Against the sky an oak tree stands,
Its statue tall and strong.
Its branches stretch across the view,
And movement of the leaves are few.

Its strength is shown through storm and rain,
And still the picture stays the same.

Like life we weather many storms,
And patience is learned in many forms.
Yet tall and strong and firm we stand,
Like flowing leaves in God's own hand.

A picture is painted against the sky,
Firm and strong and standing high.

—Mary "Emily" Hicks

THE SIERRAS

I am the mountains.
I am free.
I was once under the sea.

I can reach the stars up high
My snow-capped mountains scratch the sky.
Rams jump from peak to peak
Yosemite is a friend near me.

From black cave eyes of rusty red
Gold and silver and a little lead.
People came from everywhere
Trying to get the values I wear.
Some of my caves are 100 years old
The diamonds I have were once coal.
I hate to lose the mineral in my soil
If I do I will be spoiled.

I am happy that I am me
I am the mountains
I am free . . . .

—Ndukaku Ibe, grade 4

I FIND A POEM IN EVERY THING

In the beautiful rays of the setting sun,
Playing across the sky when the day is done,
    I find a poem

In the laughter of little children at play,
As they romp and enjoy each beautiful day,
    Happiness for a poem.

In the murmur of the babbling brook,
There's a melody we sometimes overlook,
    Music for a poem.

In a rainbow arching across the sky above,
That reminds us of God's infinite love,
    A promise of a poem.

When a mother sings a soft lullabye,
To comfort her loving baby's cry,
    Love for a poem.

In the tall stately trees swaying with the wind,
That shelters bird nests safely in its limbs,
    Whispers of a poem.

When my cup runneth over with joys or woe,
I always find release to let things go,
    When I write a poem.

—Betty Pierce

Today it seems
This vase filled with daffodils
represents life and its loves.
Now past the stages of beauty
fresh and soft to the touch.
Vibrant shocks of color.
Blazing yellow fire with sharp reed-like stems,
Surely they'll slice flesh if dared get too near.
    Beyond the dying stage.
    "So sad" everyone comments,
    or cries of their death.
But here they sit now. Dried and delicate.
More fragile than ever imaginable.
Dare not touch them, for fear they will
crumble to dust.
Still radiating from within.
That same fiery beauty touches me.
Today the daffodils are perfection.
    They are survivors.

—Jeanette Wilson

THE MAGICIAN

Each and every day of any year
Love was the craft and the labor
He wove gifts of alchemy and wood
Love creates magic, don't you know?

No learned artisan, he . . .
It came with him just one more time
A gift of karma
To me and on to mine

He was ageless, an illusionary elf
And sweet sage of past and futures
He was my constant
Ever there for me and mine always

No talker he, my teacher of times
Mental images exchanged through air
We had no need to speak
For he had always been my eternal grandfather

And, don't you see . . . would always be

—Bettye Maglaris

ALASKA SEASONS OF BEAUTY

with four seasons so clear
my adventures just starting
from warmth emerging from the sun
to the cold cry sharpness of winter's white snow
I settle down with fireplace blazing
suddenly winter is here
Northern lights my companion and protector
a blanket of darkness upon me
I settle down with rubber boots
suddenly spring is here
melting snow covering the ground
wild flowers breaking the warming earth
I settle down in my hammock
suddenly summer is here
fishing among the grazing moose
eagles flying free in clear blue skies
I settle down with umbrella in hands
suddenly fall is here
rain guiding the golden falling leaves
all combine Alaska's seasons of beauty

—Susan Hampton

THIS OLE GUARDPOST

Darned are the days when all seems to go wrong
And I feel as if I'd trade this job for a song
Very seldom now, do I get in this state of mind
Inside, I wonder if my life's decisions were kind
Did I need at some time, to have tried to earn
Decide on a different field, or another life to learn
But now, I really think the right choice was made
Overviewing a lot of people here, I wouldn't trade
Regardless of times when all is not at right height
Good outweighs the bad, and good is always in sight
Happy it makes me to sit here and think about it all
Ever to believe, I have truly made the right call
Surely now, I'll finish here without much strife
In my mind, this ole guardpost, is a part of my life

Dedicated to David Borghesi and family
A lifelong friend and a paragon

—Jimmy Lee

The full moon, in man a madness makes.
A full circle of reflected light instantly awakes.
    In legend, great furred creatures
    Roam the countryside, disguised
    As daylight hides their features.
Then consider, living, and who knows?
On what road, the wildness goes?
    Two lovers at leaps edge.
Each to the other make the eternal pledge.
With trust sealed by a hot August moon.
    So, Who can complain?
    When, all too soon
    One has to explain
The existence of a lover to another.
Not as you might think, a character defect.
But soley, as a historically founded, astronomical effect.
    Can this be, a lunar cause?
Or is it as an icy cap, the sun thaws?
The moon's silvery light, only reveals
That which otherwise, the night conceals.

—Theodore H. Austin

A CHILD TO LIVE

As I lie here in the darkness of the night
I'm trying very hard to keep my eyes closed tight.
I would so much love to fall asleep
But yet, my thoughts of the day are hard to keep

If only I knew what tomorrow will bring
I would only hope for sunshine, love and birds to sing.
If only children would play in the bright sunlight
And dogs would bark with great delight.

I know then I'd smile at the end of the day
I'd fall asleep as my thoughts would go away.
I'm grown up now and reality is here to stay,
I have a car, a house and bills to pay.

If this poem reaches out to any of you
I hope, I pray, I left one clue
"That as we grow each and every day
A small part of us is a child to play
A child to live, love and to forgive
For in a child's eyes, there's just one race
A race of people,
Wouldn't that be a nice place?"

—Kathleen Robinson

ANGER!

Feelings of anger do rage within,
  me.
For I cannot understand the,
stupidity.
Reason does not come to,
surface nor does compassion,
from within.
Why does trouble gather,
to those who do not seek,
it?
For the time at hand,
peace does not abide within,
these angered walls of,
    my soul.

—Paula .D. Jacobs

EVOLUTION

A million years later
after all is said and done,
here we are. A new layer of skin
has covered the cuts and bruises
and something foreign to yesterday
has placed light in our eyes
and hope in our heart.
It took a million years. Evolution.
Yet aging has made us,
in many ways, younger.
Hardships have provided strength
and those who observe think life
has been good to us and simple;
our smile of contentment
is positive proof.
    No.
It's just a new layer of skin
covering the wounds,
hiding the pockmarked
face of life.

—Ellen F. Childress

LIFE

Soar high like an eagle,
Take charge of your life,
Look forward to tomorrow
Not to days filled with strife.

The world is a waiting canvas
Paint it with love, beauty, and soul.
Mountains and valleys need climbing,
Still look longingly toward your goal.

We often do not contemplate
What others around us think,
Our days are but a whirlwind
Which we often see rise or sink.

We know not what the future holds
Many days seem murky and bleak,
But be strong, concerned, and resilient,
Keep searching for what you seek.

So like the awesome soaring eagle
The sky is your infinite limit.
Reach for the moon, the sun, and stars;
Because your life is but a minute.

—Pamela Carver

In summer He brings us the trees and the flowers
Together with daylight's lengthening hours
He sends the sunshine and the rain
That yields the harvests of golden grain
The colors of autumn provide many hues
Till snows of winter come again
Earth's cycle thus completing a turn.
The love of God that spans the seas
Or leaps the peaks so high
Is ne'er too far from you and I
To feel His presence nigh.

—Ruth Vander Heide

THE GIFT OF LIFE

When I hear the call of the Turtle Dove
    in the distance at early morn;
And when I hear the evening wail of the Whip-poor-will;
Then I thank God that I was born.

When I hear the rumbling noise of a springtime
    thunderstorm;
And the raindrops beating against the window pane;
Then I thank God that I was born.

When I see the majestic mountains in all of
    their adorn;
And when I see the winding rivers and oceans deep;
Then I thank God that I was born.

When I see the stars in the heavens, with all their
    sparkling going on;
And I see a golden harvest moon;
Then I thank God that I was born.

Since God has given me ears to hear, and
    eyes to see all of the beautiful things
      He has formed;
How can I hold back my thanks to Him for letting
    me be born.

—Allene Coley Edwards

COUNTRY BEAUTIFUL

God made the country so pretty and serene
That is why in the spring everything turns green

The country is quiet both day and night
From early dawn until the last day light

The air is fresh, very clean, and pure
I may question some things, but for this I'm sure

A day in the country will release your stress
Because you're away from all the concrete mess

There are lakes and ponds scattered about
The air is so clear you can hear people shout

A second home some people will buy
Out in the country by the big blue sky

Raising children in a pleasant environment
Where there are no drugs, guns, or torment

So when God created the earth to see
He was thinking of you and me

The sun will shine and the moon is bright
The stars will twinkle late at night

So pray that the country will always be
A safe haven for all of us to see

—Donald A. Woodson

EXPLAIN "LOVE"

Love, how do you explain love,
Is love a phase of life,
Or is love forever,
Is love heartache,
Or is love dear,
Does love have meaning to feel,
Or is love an empty fear,
The only way to truly know love is,
To feel love with your heart,
For he showed me true love,
Now I understand it in my mind and,
Feel it in the depths of my heart,
For he is my true love.

—Shantell Vicknair

THE FAITH I HAVE IN YOU

I have walked the barren plains
I have carried the jailors chains
I have fought the demons of pain
For the faith I have in you
I have had a knife through my chest
I have cried for my last breath
I have seen the face of death
For the faith I have in you
I have drowned in my self pity
I have scavenged through the city
I have slit my wrists a plenty
For the faith I have in you
I have drank the poison blood
I have swam my tears of flood
I have never understood
The faith I have in you.

—Ken Howard

WHILE I AM STILL ALIVE

Tell me how nice a person I am,
Wonderful and warm — a real gem;
And how good a job I do each day;
To help our people each passing day!

Shower me with love, and forgiveness;
Tell me that I bring you happiness!
And that you miss me when I am away!
Tell me these, tell me more, I pray!

Extend your hand to me in time of need,
Tell me that I am your friend indeed;
Dance with me and make me happy,
As we work hard for the family!

Tell me when I make a mistake,
Tell me please, for my own sake;
But praise me when I am right,
Always be my guiding light!

Sing to me my favorite song,
In person, or on the phone;
Thank me when I make you smile,
Praise me as I walk the extra mile!

All of these, I want to hear,
While I'm alive, while I am near;
No, no, please, not in eulogies,
But NOW, even with apologies!

Yes, all these, I want to hear,
Every minute, every hour of the day;
For what good is it to say,
All these things, when I am GONE AWAY?

—Bert Caoili

SOUL SEEKER

soul seeker searching within yourself.
to find, find love, love of self. to find,
find peace of mind. to move, move forward
in your life to cast no doubts as to who,
who you are. touching others, without
giving up, giving up self. to know, know
that which has been given, given freely.

deep inside there is "me!" a spirit, a spirit
that when set free, free to be, will send a
message, soul seeker. emotionally in touch with
self. physically strong to deal with self. to be
at last, at last content with self.

love "thyself," soul seeker.
                       love thyself.
        —Florence L. Bell

MY JOURNEY

The light at the end of the tunnel
Was my only glimmer of hope
To strive for in the dark abyss
Wearily I dragged myself closer
Ever gaining on the source of light
Many a time I stumbled
Sometimes I stopped to sleep
Often headway was so low
I had to crawl on my hands and knees
Time lost all meaning
Numb purpose replaced despair
Though racked and ruined I inched ahead
Until I stood at my journey's end

No torch, no beacon, not even a candle
Greeted me at the tunnel's end
It was but a mirrored door
That kept reflecting the light in me
I threw open that door
And breathed my fill of fresh rushing air
My journey was over, I was free
        —Bella Becker

LIFE PARANOIA

Subliminal messages
from a confused mind . . .
      barely the truth can we find.

We wonder who's doing what.
    When and if our throat'll be cut.
Yet these thoughts are only self-devised.

Many things in life we fear . . .
    only because we fear our life.
        We think 'destiny' is always near.

We dread and forbid change . . .
    our life may be rearranged?

Stuck in our own rut . . .
    we keep a knot in our gut.

Always so leery
    that we stay confined . . .
        ourselves we never find.

Life's so fearful,
    that we stay a placenta . . .
        because of life paranoia.
        —Kelly Gohm

I look behind me and
    I see the past
        the good and the bad times
            I thought would never pass.
I look down at my feet
    to see where I stand
        In the middle, I am
            between a tear and a smile
        I turn.
To look in front of me
    to see, what the world holds
        in store for me.
In the distance, you know what I see?
    A child. A child going through the cycle
        just like me.
    —Paula A. Paxiao

WISHES FROM A GIRL WITH LEUKEMIA

I want to live,
But my strength's draining like water in a sieve

I want to be out of this hospital room,
Where shadows seem to loom.

I want to run in the fields with the deer and bees,
Hear streams laughter and climb the tall trees.

I want to snuggle in bed on a frosty winter night,
With lollipops and peppermint sticks in my sight.

I want to play with my friends,
The fun never ends!

I want to look at stars like precious gems,
All these are my whims.

But most of all,
I want to live.
    —Timber Laue

FIRST

I Fly with eagles
high over the clouds
With each soaring sojourn
    I proclaim aloud
I am Black, First

You see me
    You love me
You read me
    You become me
But with each digested verse
    Remember
I am black, first

I stand in great halls
    with audiences so vast
I am the epitome' of perfection
    from first word to last
But as the syllables fall from my tongue
    with powerful inflections they are shaped
As hoods cover my head
    and around my neck chords are draped
You see a man of great substance
    and knowledge so diverse
But take a look at my skin
    and remember
I am Black . . . FIRST.
    —Michael Develle Winn

BEYOND THESE DOORS

Beyond these doors lies a place of beauty and magical substance,
yet nothing lurks.
Beyond these doors used to lie a garden of fantasy and dreams,
but they have long been gone.
The harsh reality has walked in leaving no time for escape — no
time for love — no time for dreams — no time for fantasy.
The waves no longer beat like romantic drums; the birds no
longer sing a sweet song; the wind does not blow gently as before.
Beyond these doors nothing of the special things lurk within,
but harsh reality walks within, leaving no time, anything to
desire and no where to escape.
Beyond these doors no one will lurk within; everything is gone.

Beyond These Doors!

—Amanda Cowan

LIFE

Too many chores
Too much to do
So much busyness must make me feel important, valuable, loved
It also makes me tired

So very tired
Is this old age?
A back that hurts in five places
Relieved only by rest and exercise for which I have so little time and interest

Go here. Do this. Hurry. Smile. Get that. Don't stop.
Wheel and deal so I won't be a bag lady.
Worry. The market is up. Gold is down.
I carry a four trillion dollar debt on my back.

Gaining weight, again.
No time for hunger, reflection, reading, rest
Food is quick and easy fuel
Keeps me barreling through my endless list of tasks

Where is my soul?
Where did she go?
Did she move to a more nurturing place?
Maybe she just waits quietly for better care and attention.

—Gayle Robinson

BEATITUDES OF A MOTHER

Blessed is the Mother who loves God and teaches this love to her children.

Blessed is the Mother who guides her children on paths of righteousness for she shall always be proud of them.

Blessed is the Mother who knows how to comfort, for she will receive the devotion of her children.

Blessed is the Mother who understands her children, for she shall have good memories.

Blessed is the Mother who is meek and never judgmental, for she shall receive her children's confidence.

Blessed is the Mother who teaches respect to her children, and she will also be respected in return.

Blessed is the Mother who teaches harmony and mercy to her children so they will be ambassadors of peace.

Blessed is the Mother who teaches her children compassion, for she will always be loved.

Blessed is the Mother who emphasizes right over wrong, so her children will make good evaluations.

Blessed is the Mother who teaches her children to be pure in heart, and her home shall be filled with happiness.

—Betty Pierce

GREEN

Green is plants,
Green is grass,
Green is one color that's glass.
A marker is green,
A crayon is green,
Green is a color I have already seen.
Green is a bean.
Green in a shower isn't very clean.
Green is a tree.
Green wouldn't be good if it was you and me.

—Adam T. Krynicki, age 10

MOUNTAINS OF COLORS

While riding the skyway the other day
I heard a sound in my heart to say
When God dressed the high country to see
  for a while
He did it in a most spectacular style.
With splashes of colors all over mount faces
It marks North Carolina the most beautiful
  of places.
It will soon fade away into winter's embrace
But for now it's America's most wonderful
  place.

—Lola Gamache

TEDDY BEAR

Everyone should have
a teddy bear, because
when you need them
they're always there.
Everyone should have
a teddy bear to cuddle
mine likes to watch
the space shuttle.
Everyone should have
a teddy bear because
they're the ones that
mostly care.

—Jessica Erlynn Gonzales, age 10

PHYSICAL CHEMISTRY BLUES

The mathematics are flying
Right over my head
The Schrodinger equation tells all
But I can't understand what it said

You'd think the solution manual would tell you
But no, it's not so kind
You need an electron microscope
Just to read between the lines

How did you derive that formula?
I think you skipped some steps
If you didn't have a Ph.D.
I'd think you were inept

I'm not opposed to integration
It helps me reach infinity
But that differentiation
Will be the death of me

I've got the P-Chem blues so bad
I'm as volatile as lead
I've got the P-Chem blues so bad
I wish I were an art major instead

—Mark Fennell

A LITTLE BIT WILD

He was a little bit wild, and liked to roam,
Then, he'd seem to get lonesome and come
  back home,
He'd sit patiently waiting to come on in.
We played this game again and again.
Then I noticed a distant look in his eye,
Like maybe he wanted to tell me good-bye,
That very night he took off to go away,
Where he went I never knew, and cannot say.
A few days later, he lay dead next door.
My cat would never be home any more.
Now, if there should be a cat Heaven
  somewhere,
I know that Bud has to be roaming
  up there.

—Billye Dial

A COW NAMED MOLLY

There once was a cow named Molly,
She was fat, content, and jolly,
She lived on a farm where the grass was green,
The greenest grass you've ever seen,
But grass was not to Molly's taste,
In fact she let it go to waste.

Molly yearned for luscious hops,
To her they taste like lollypops,
She also liked to chew on barley,
Much to the chagrin of farmer Charlie,
When Charlie went to squeeze her udder,
Thinking he would get milk and butter.

Surprisingly what filled his pail,
Was tasty foam and beer and ale,
Now Charlie was smart and wiser,
He sold poor Molly to Budweiser.

—Lawrence V. LaChapelle

SAMANTHA

Samantha's her name and deep in her soul,
Stealing my man has long been her goal.
She's silvery, sensitive, chic and sedate;
A sassy young vixen who's stolen my mate.

A true femme fatale whose master's tame heart
Was totally captured right from the start.
A man who by nature shows little emotion
Has offered this mistress his total devotion.

He teases, she pleases; she whimpers, he simpers.
He fails to elude her—I feel the intruder.
Sometimes her attention is focused on me;
It's only because he is nowhere to be.

This man and his "friend" have created a bond,
Their mutual attraction society spawned.
She only need purr and prance in his face,
And he drops what he's doing to enter her space.

These two so devoted—amusement is mine.
She only need speak, so self-satisfied.
I hide 'round the corner and watch them at play
And scowl at their antics—what else can I say?

Of whom do I speak with a jealous wife's tongue?
Who is the temptress, seductive and young?
It's not what you think and I'm quick to confess,
She's our kitty, Samantha, who effects my distress.

—Judy I. Tsoukalas

HARMONY

The unification of two spirits
One the instrument, the other the lyric

A mindless encounter, not the intention
Two spirits soared, in celestial dimension

With cavalier boldness, the lyric the oldest
Untapped potential, the instrument essential

Transformation minor and major took place,
Their essence consists of passion, time and space

Complimenting one another with every note played
Open and honest music is made

Transmitting, the two spirits connect
Waves of *Harmony they Reflect*

—Darlene Chrisman

A CHRISTMAS STORY

Christmas is the symbolic meaning for
the birthday of Christ
Who was born to Show us the way of life.
We live for Christmas day
To see What's under the tree that
contains all gifts.
These gifts symbolizes our gift of life,
That was given to us upon the birthday of Christ.
Christmas brings joy to people
around the world,
It brightens the day of Boys and Girls.
Traveling from place to place each house
With smiling faces can be seen,
filled with excitement and Cheer,
Knowing that a New year is near.
But we must not forget as the year begins,
That Christ also died for our sins.
So when we lie down on Christmas night,
Give thanks to God, for Our Lord Jesus Christ.

—Duncan Parham

THANKSGIVING

The Lord has blessed the seeds we have sown
He sends the sun and the rain;
That has made the seeds burst forth and grow
    Producing glowing fields of grain.

As summer days have come and gone
    And autumn has filled the air,
The bountiful harvest has been gathered in
    We have so much with which to share.

Be thankful to God for family and home
    For the fellowship of wonderful friends;
For the beautiful world that's ours to enjoy
    And the love for all that He sends.

Let's count our blessings each day of the year
    And thank God for His mercy and love,
Anywhere that we look we surely can see
    All the good things that come from above.

Let not just one day be Thanksgiving Day
    For God's blessings come to us all year;
So each day may we bow with grateful hearts
    And give thanks for all we hold dear.

—Mary Lee Nelson

ICE STORM

Late here in the evening
in my lonely writer's garrett
I see a flashing neon light
from the Vacancy sign of the motel next door
those naked trees on the front lawn
have red and white glistening icicles
hanging from their rigid arms
and all is quiet
except the ticking of the clock
and the scraping of the ice
against my window
as that lonely frozen blue spruce tree
reaches for the moon

—Dina J. Lauzé

CHRISTMAS EPIPHANY

After living with close families
Who deeply love each other
I wanted to partake
Remove my heart's protective cover

Let me carry those bags
Allow me to hold that door
A compliment, a smile, an extra ear
Small gifts galore

Easier to act on my love
Than to put my heart into words
I extend my hand to help
Your needs unspoken but heard

The traditional holiday season
Unfortunately officially ephemeral
Let us extend the love throughout the months
Make your neighbors day delectable

If you still see only the material
Your world is empty with such beliefs
May God in his wisdom and love
Grant you a Christmas epiphany

—Mark Fennell

YOU *CAN* GO HOME AGAIN

(In Answer To Thomas Wolfe)

Some say you can't go home again
That things will never be the same,
One cannot recapture former things;
But I have found this is not so.

When soft winds of memory blow
Across dandelion meadows, meandering streams,
Wooded glens and mirror-clear ponds
Reflecting the years buried within us.

Marshmallow days of yesteryear,
Indian summers and harvest moons,
Pumpkin colored leaves burning at curbside;
Pungent scents of autumns gone.

Memory's pictures filter past:
Sunny days and carefree child,
Life so simple, safe and mild;
Secure that this would always last.

Childhood things — long since flown,
Loved faces blurred by tears and time;
Gentle moments of life relived and extolled —
You *can* go home again — if only in soul.

—Betty Joan Smith

THE CALL

I walk a dark road
    fraught with danger;
robbers ride past me
    with boomity-boom radios,
and the moon reveals my silhouette
    to evil men behind trees.
But then, around the bend,
    as shadows fall thick around me,
a soft glow of red, yellow and royal blue
    light up a stained glass window.
The friendly colors shine steady
    into the night,
and blend into a sacred shape
    that calls me into a House of Prayer.
    —Shirley M.

IN THE JUNGLE

Lost in the jungle of the modern world
Too much to know, and no time to learn
Nothing is as it used to be
It's getting so hard, No one is free

No open minds foretell the truth
No open eyes to cast the blame
We pay for our lives in a political game
For a government without shame

Few pockets bulge with glory
So many hearts with a sad story
Countless minds with answers wasted
Can it stop before destruction is tasted

The land of dreams has ceased to exist
Of the failing countries, We top the list
We've sold our once lovely land away
While very few collect their pay

To many, the once "Land of plenty"
Has saddened their hearts
And left their stomaches empty
    —Christian J. Rosales

THE DREAMER

I haven't any gold to leave when
I grow old, somehow it passed
    me by.
I'm very poor but still I leave
    a precious will when I must
    say good-bye.

I leave the night-time to the dreamer.
I leave the song-bird to the blind.
I leave the moon above to those in love
    when I leave the world behind.

I leave the sun-shine to the flowers
    and the honey to the bees.
To the old folks I leave the memory
    of a babe upon their knees,
    when I leave the world behind.

I'm tired of living alone.
I want someone to call me his own.
To love and caress me,
to dress and undress me,
I'm tired of living alone.
    —Jan Will

WITH NANEW HANDS ONLY

With Nanew Hands Only Can day end
Mans save thy lost a low handy hope
Hands with money only can lead lift
Sinking low with no dawn light sinking
Sun light reaching out hands only
I've seen hands use in many forms
Love & Hate carries way about Nanew
With hands only child folding to pray
Mother tender touch when all else fails
in a mother's loving way.
Yes hands can express your feelings
Do Nanew says use them this way
I wonder if hands unconscious with
expressation with hands only
Can I write, work or play
Nanew part of me that I forget to embrace
But without them it wouldn't be the same
With mur Nanew Hands I can sign talk speaks
Your eyes learn the Nanew hands language-less
    —Danny J. Ward

MOURNING SONG

What is this thing called grief, that dulls the
    joy in life?
It's filled with disbelief and the
pain in my heart finds no relief.

I can not tell what grief does to others.
I just know what it does to me.
It fills up my mind and lies heavy in
my heart, because my dear one and I
had to part.

The road is very rough and long, and from my
lips it steals the song.
It took my dreams and shattered them, it
feels like half of me is gone, as we were
truly one.

This grief seems to have no end, though I'm
told it will ease its grip.
It's so hard to believe this sorrow will leave
and my heart will heal again.
    —Kathryn Amenda

THE SIGNS

Hurry brothers and so not shirk
The Oceans and Lakes are dying
The birds are no longer flying
The heavens are covered with murk
If you care you will see
If you don't—you may not be
The signs are up do not miss them
There is still time to make it a gem
God is there for everyone
Do not be frightened and run
All you have to do is love and care
All God's creatures need love and care
So shall ye sow, so shall ye reap
Hurry brothers before we end up in a heap
Do not be afraid to feel love
All that is left is the dove
Do not fail to see the signs that are flying
If you do all of God's creatures will be crying
Come all ye people you have the power
To move the people in their ivory tower
    —Bruce Horaz

JUST ME

Sometimes I think my head's a top spinning
round and round;
My feet can't seem to find a piece of
solid ground.
My life is like a cyclone turning, twisting
and spinning,
I may not be losing, but I'm sure not
winning.
I wish I was a bird, with wings so I
could fly,
Away from things that hurt me and make
me want to cry.
I wouldn't ask to stay that long, just for
a little while,
Just long enough to mend my heart,
and make me want to smile.
Maybe then I'd find some answers,
so I could finally see,
Has all the world gone crazy or is it
Just Me?

—Sarah M. Cornell

RAIN DROPS

I hear the rain drops falling upon the world
outside.
And from the roof water falls like a huge water
slide.
Crystal clear rain drops trickle down my
window pane.
As the torrents of water rush aimlessly on
the street in vain.
And as I watch it slowly disappear just around
the bend.
Finally the rain drops start to vanish and come
to an end.
When the clouds start to clear away, as I
watch the sky.
I know that the sun will shine out and the earth
will dry.
But this wonderful cycle of life will again
be repeated.
I know at the time when the rain drops are
most needed.

—Annie Louise Easley

THE SEARCH

My soul's a well — so dark, so deep,
Surfaced over with mirror water so placid,
A well full of longing — bottom never explored,
Filled with unanswered life to fulfill.

The surface was broken.
I dove like a seabird,
    down
        down
           Getting lost in myself.
There raging were the currents mercilessly flaying,
Holding me prisoner of their turbulence.

Peace ebb tides — cease churning!
Peace — bring peace with you upon returning!

No sound echoed back o'er the howling,
Echoed back o'er the rage.
    Then
        God's breath
        Stillness
        Peace.

—Maire Ni Ciosáin

LET YOUR HEART SING

Want to feel alive and free?
Just Let Your Heart Sing a melody!

The land, the sea, the sky and we
All play a part in this harmony.

For you to feel alive and free,
Just Let Your Heart Sing a melody.

—Rae Kae Powers

FREEDOM (Analogue)

For freedom may we ever grateful be!
The privilege of choosing how to vote —
Our codes and policies we freely quote,
The right to habitate the land and sea
While sharing home with mate and family —
Yes, we may read all writings ever wrote,
And sing a sacred, or a jazzy note.
Because these joys of freedom we still share,
Americans, lift up your thanks in prayer!

—Frances E. Chicoine

EAGLE WINGS

Once I flew high as the eagle flies,
Through silver-lined clouds up above;
Then an evil wind plunged me to earth,
Far away from the Father's sweet love.

Grounded in the dirt with broken wing,
Struggled hard to get back on my feet;
Choking on dust that swirled around me,
Each attempt would end up in defeat.

Looking up soulfully to heavens above,
Crying out in my desperation and fear;
My voice echoing off deep canyon walls,
For all the cougars and wolves to hear.

Knowing I must go find some protection,
From enemies who would feed on my soul;
I crawled for shelter of a nearby cave,
Shaking fearfully in a pitch-black hole.

Never feeling the warmth of sunshine,
Growing weaker with each passing day;
Alas! With hunger for self-preservation,
I ventured out of the door of my cave.

Only a few shaky steps taken at first,
Heart pounding 'neath feathered breast;
Each sunrise would find me trying again,
Traveling further before having to rest.

My soul thirsted for the heavenly winds,
Feel the sweet breath of God on my face;
But looked down upon my battered wing,
Knowing no strength could it embrace.

Depression set in as I pondered my fate,
An angry rattlesnake scoffed me nearby;
Fearfully I ran way back to the cave,
Good-for-nothing eagle who can not fly.

The sun has risen in a crystal blue sky,
Feel God's Spirit gently tug at my soul;
Walking out into this new day created,
Being miraculously healed and made whole.

God reached down His hand and lifted me up,
Loosed me free on the breath of His love;
Soaring up through the silver-lined clouds,
There I entered heavenly gates up above.

—Judy Ann Williams Downey

I've lost the world, the light, the hues
I live in shades of grey
I've lost the varigate of life
And there is hell to pay
Every daisy I denied
Every smile I shunned
Each new morning's golden glow
Rise up to haunt me now
In memory only live life's gifts
The joys true sight can bring
I *yearn* not for wealth or power
But just the green of Spring
—Kat Weng

THE RECIPE FOR LIFE

You take a large amount of laughter
And some tear drops mixed with sighs
Add to this some sunshine
And the smile of merry eyes,
Put in two cups of morning dew
Dilute it with rain
Stir it well with happiness
And season it with pain
Pour this in a golden cup
Buttered well with strife
Wrap it up with problems
And there, My Friends — is Life
—Margie O.

VIOLET VALE

Through the misty woodland vale,
By the edges of a trail,
Violets deep and violets pale
    Weave their floral tapestries.
With leaves from forest green to jade
And petals amethyst in shade,
The colors of the loom are laid
    By twining rings around the trees.

The silver mists that fill the air
Thread crystal raindrops here and there
Upon the violets, sweet and fair,
    That wind along the trail.
And then, the fir trees, fringed with moss,
Make tasseled hems of silken floss
To frame each landscape all across
    The lovely violet vale.
—K. M. Williams

THE WAY IT IS

The poor.
They try,
Try to be like the rest of us;
Try to act like the in crowd;
Try to be pleasant and sure of themselves.
Some of us look at the poor and laugh,
But to laugh at the poor may be to
    laugh at yourself,
For one day you may be in the same
    situation;
You may be the one,
Wanting to fit in,
Wanting to be like the in crowd.
But everyone has to realize,
The poor who pray as they do,
    may one day have their
    hopes and dreams come true.
—Sara Ziegler

DAY DREAM

If you close your eyes and make a wish,
you dream a dream of no limits.
For each day is different from the rest,
That's why it's important to do your very best.
Some dreams tell us what must be done,
and some are filled with fun in the sun.
I hope your dreams are sweet and nice,
because dreams are a part of every one's life.
Here's a wish from me to you,
I pray that all your dreams come true.
—Royal A. Kelly

SPRINGTIME ON DOLLY SODS

I watched the sun come up on Dolly Sods today,
And every little creature seemed to say:
"Just come along with me and play."
Along the streams and thru the woods
I lost myself for one full day.

Deep into the virgin woods the trail did twine,
And no longer the worldly cares were mine;
The mountain streams the music provided,
As the little creatures play hide and seek,
And watch the sunbeams thru the trees dance.

Slowly back to my little hide-away,
And back to my worldly cares I must return;
Recalling every moment of this day
With plans soon to return and enjoy,
All the wonders that nature provides.

I saw the sun set on Dolly Sods today,
And all the memories I'll hold dear
When no longer I can roam the hills,
But sit on my porch where I am content,
And think of all my yesterdays on Dolly Sods.
—Hilda M. Rowe Davidson

VIENNA

Come my friends to a legendary place
Where the sidewalks are cobbled,
And the streets run in circles.
The musicians know the scales and the keys.
They play for love and for money
In opera houses and on street corners.

Do not go through the dark alleys.
Stay instead in the yellow light
Of Maria Theresa's historical avenues.
Watch visitors pass by in the horse-drawn cart.
Listen to the young driver
Explaining the sights to his patrons.

As he approaches the corner store,
The girl who sells silk scarves
Looks out the window and waves to him.
The violinist on the street corner
Plays a sweet melody as the cart goes by.
The driver sings auf wiedersehen in reply.

When the evening falls, you must find
The young dappled lipizzaners
In the Austrian countryside.
They graze upon the sweet clover
In a pasture with Queen Anne's lace
As pretty as a Viennese melody.
—Cynthia Ann Cavanaugh

SHINGLE ISLAND RIVER—MARCH

thin February ice
clutching the flanks of the river
first feels the change,
swept away; swelling loins quiver
as the black river eagerly relieves the land.

tossed, floating ice,
is crushed to the sides of dying oaks
that preen their budding boughs in the black mirror
killing them.

earth must give ground
before the patient purpose
of the river's heaving haunches.

black fingers feel through
dead grasses of summers past.

It is the taking time.

—Arthur Thibodeau

THREE KITTENS

Three kittens rose at dawn, marching off
as if to conquer Europe
down the hall, round the corner
goose stepping with tails held high
When did you ever see a kitten that didn't
accidently, not on purpose
undertake to ransack and ruin your house
Very innocently, without malice knocking a glass
a planter to the floor
purring i-didn't-mean-to and crying
when you swat her, too gently to do any good
too little too late to stop them from doing
what they can to the carpet in the night
behind closed doors
shut in and trying to get out
But that's better than letting them sleep with you
you could wake up castrated,
without toes
or nipples

—D. J. Milton

FLYING KISSES IN THE GRASS

The tall grass by the railroad track
Beckons me to come . . . then stand aback.

A harmonic tune whines and hisses
With a melody of thousands of kisses.

The sound beats like percussion in a band.
After a few seconds I can no longer just stand.

I take a step to test my theory
And hundreds of grasshoppers jump in fury.

The grass buzzes and clicks as they fly
And suddenly they land and quietly lie

Until I take another step to watch the show
They arc in all directions so high and then low.

They gracefully leap to the other side
At my command. I am mystified.

I tread again and again to repeat the sight
And they sail several feet in noisy flight.

I've tried this other places where my walk leads—
Beside the highway in the tall uncut weeds,

But the railroad track is the best spot to see
The grasshopper jump miracle for me.

—Marilyn J. Shelton

CROCODILES

Crocodiles are low but they always smile:
because,
the dirt they are so cast upon
amuses their bellies,
so they remain without choice
and smile for no reason.

—Laurie Lightcap

LIGHTNING BUGS

I wonder about lightning bugs,
What makes their tail to light?

Do they have a switch under their wings
So they can shine at night?

Do they shut off their switch in the daytime
and in evening then ignite it?

When they hit the windshield of my car,
Would you say, "They are de-lighted?"

—R. Laurel Nielsen

Tall hills of home are callin'
Tall mountains cloaked with snow
On timbered slopes tall trees do stand
A callin' me back home

Old eagle cuttin' circles
Against a sky of blue
Olympic peaks a gazin' west
Upon Pacific view

My soul was born to wander
Across this earth and sea
And never know a restful place
Till my homeland called to me

With compass pointing eastward
We sailed Pacific swell
And there along horizon rim
My homeland I could tell

Tall hills of home were callin'
Tall mountains cloaked with snow
Neath tall straight trees my soul will rest
For I have wandered home.

—Henry D. Aitken

FROZEN IN TIME

Ducks skating across this frozen
wonderland, in such comical
fashion.
For awhile they glide across the
ice in such grace and style,
then, suddenly, as if intended
for a giggle, they bump into
one another, and fall into one
gigantic heap of feathers and
fun.
Giant Pines and Oak trees stand,
branches bent beneath the
burden of heavy ice.
And as the sun sparkles through
their glazed branches;
They cast a shadow of beauty
all their own.

*In memory of John L. Edwards III, my
brother-in-law. He always encouraged me.*

—Joyce Hixson

FOREVER

If I could find the man of my dream
who cares enough to let me lean
when all else, around does seem
to weigh so heavy, so painful or mean.

Who would not judge, but without a word
could pull me to him like a fragile bird
sharing his strength and about me gird
my soul, my spirit with all his verve.

Drawing me back, one step at a time
towards the potential that truly is mine
making me whole from drinking his wine
this is the man, with whom I would dine
    Forever.
    —Suzanne DeWitt

JUMBLED THOUGHTS

I watch the sky late at night,
Looking for the moon
And its face so bright.
I wonder as I ponder,
Is that a smile or is that a frown?
Does he approve of my life
Since he's not around?
I feel a warmth as I look up,
And think of the day
We will again join up.
Until that time, I must go on,
Three boys to raise and share my love.
Beyond the moon was a song we agreed on,
And now the moon is something I lean on.
That mystical face reminds me of all
the things we've shared.
I have but to look up to know he's there.

*In loving memory of my husband
Roger W. Bundridge (1951—1993)
Sadly missed and fondly remembered*
    —Shirley Bundridge

THE GOLDEN THREADS THAT BIND

Those golden threads of love and trust
so fragile to some it's true
did bind us both so very close
as fresh as the morning dew.

When things were tough, the going hard
as they of'times will
the golden threads grew stronger still
as in true love they ever will.

The golden threads from heart to heart
pulsing with love so pure
as days grew into months then years
to help our love endure.

So when you vanished in the night
as the moon was riding high
the golden threads grew stronger still
the higher you did fly.

So when, one day, the threads grow taut
bind closer around our hearts
you'll then know I'm coming home
from then we'll never part.
    —Edwin P. Spivey

THE MYSTERY OF NIGHT

Holy is the night; the masquerade of day is done,
the revellers attend no more the carnival, of life
illusive, the night's black mantle covers all
who sleep beneath its mysterious folds.

This is the time when is heard the language of
another world, a tongue that utters words too
deep for shallow day. A gentle tongue withal.
Musical and sweet, chaste and tender speaking
with the Voice of the Soul.
    —Leopoldine Fink

when the summer sun ceases to shine
and the distant rumble of the skies
summons Heaven's tears
I will remember you

when the moon in all its splendor
ignites the night in its tranquil
display of light
I will remember you

I will remember tender caresses in
the darkness
I will remember passionate kisses
of unrestrained emotion
and I will remember us as One

We Danced together a Dance of Intense Passion
a Dance of romantic Fire which fused Us into
ONE

when the light of my existance dims
and all that remains is the shell
of what was once my essence

I will remember you.
    —Edward J. Sullivan

CARRY ON

As I lay here on my bed
    I think of you
And all you've said
    Of how much I really miss you
My life isn't the same
    now you are gone.
I feel I could go insane
    Because I have to wait so long,
To see you, to touch you,
    To hear your tender voice
But to wait, I guess
    Is my only choice
Why can't things change?
    why can't you be here?
The days I have to face without you
    I really do fear.
I won't have your hand
    to lead me away from wrong
I don't think I can keep
    this up for very long
I guess I should think of when you will be here
    And of your good advice
That will be so near
    Until that day
My dream lives on
    Until that day
I'll just have to carry on.
    —Janell Hildeman, age 17

TO MY WIFE

Who is a blessing from our Creator?
Who is worth more than a ruby?
Who is more valuable than gold?
Who is the sunrise in my heart?
Who has a smile that can melt heart of stone?
Who has embraces that are so loving?
Who has words that are so wise and encouraging?
Who has kisses that are so meaningful?
Who is trustworthy?
I'll tell you who!
My *best friend!*
My *wife,* Ruth!

HAPPY BIRTHDAY, HONEY!

    From Your Husband!
    In our Lord's Love!
    —Douglas D. Nicholson

VIEW FROM WITHIN THE CRYSTAL BALL

The last time I saw you
So many years ago,
The wind dancing through your long scarlet hair
As you walked barefoot through the sand
Wearing old blue jeans
And my silk shirt, so new that
The factory creases had not yet vanished.
I came here that night
To visit my mother
And lay flowers at her head.
You held me then,
Touched my cheek with the
Soft but starch-soaked silk.
Moonlight reflected off my tears,
As you half-carried me to my car.
I wish you could be with me now
Instead of buried there so near,
But infinite miles away.

    —Adam Todd Bradley

LIFE

Life is precious but short
some people enjoy it by playing a sport.
Life is a world that's ever changing
and at any second could become endangering.
Life is not a bowl of cherries
but seems like it to anyone who marries.
Life is full of choosing
and some people end up boozing.
Life is full of people who like flirting
and people who are, but don't like hurting.
Life gives no reward to a fool
but once in awhile, to everyone, is cruel.
Life is something very real
it is not a game of let's make a deal.
Life is not getting old
but remembering being carried over the threshhold.
Life is being everything you can be.
Life is as far as you can see!

    —Melissa Wasserman

I HAD TO

Missing your charms.
Missing your smile.
Needing to be in your arms.
Wanting to walk that mile.

I want to say, "I Love You,"
to touch your face.
If only you honestly knew,
you were my leather, as I was your lace.

But each one of your fights,
was tearing my heart away.
I knew it was time to take a hike,
for I could not take it another day.

So, here's good-bye my true love.
Time to spread my wings,
fly into the night and stars above,
where things are at peace.

    —Tina M. Snow

THE WEDDING

As we danced, I was in his arms.
But I heard no music play.
Just the sound of his heartbeat,
by him, for me, to stay.

As we danced, I was in his arms.
But I could not see how striking he appeared.
Just his eyes looking into mine
like our faces were mirrored.

As we danced, I was in his arms.
But I could not touch his skin so tender.
Just my hand in his
was all that I could render.

As we danced, I was in his arms.
But I could not taste his lips so gratifying.
Just a whisper of "I love you,"
in that short time we were buying.

Dedicated to my husband, Tom.

    —Nadine Paglini-Konieczny

VIEW WITHOUT YOU

I see your easy chair still by the window
Your slippers where you left them.
Your pipe is still laying there as if
you were returning soon

I walk through the rooms we shared
and I still hear echoes of
the words we said

I look out of the window and the
moon we once looked at is
still hanging there

I feel warm tears
slide down cool cheeks
I hear my heart break in little pieces

My world is a little dimmer
    and dreams far and few between
My world no longer has bright
    vivid colors as it used to be

I don't think I like a world without you

    —Cloretta Rose

A PRAYER SENT TO THE LORD

God I can't let go of him
Cause I know he needs my love
No matter how hard life is to him
he's the one I've chosen to love
My days may be strainful
with lots of painful talk
From people who think they know
but yet they do not
Our lives together may be discussing
because of problems they often see
but God he's still my husband
No matter how worse it may be —
So I come to you with my problem
Cause only you can help me see clearly

—Margaret Elaine Maxwell

THE GOD SKY

The clouds have begun the ceremony,
They stretch apart,
And move aside,
To let the body rise.
Heavenly angels carry the spirit
To clean the soul of hatred and lies.
Protected by the sun's soft rays,
It floats between the velvety clouds,
And through the golden ring of light,
To join awaiting God.
Bright orange sun streaks close the door,
So not to reveal the secrets
Of the world above.
The God Sky.

—Nicole L. Pallatto

THE GRAVE AWAITS

Hungry, gaping . . . the grave awaits
ready to devour, digest and delete
With a cadence — distorted and defiant
worms march to a perverted beat
penetrating my flesh, drilling bones

The grave awaits . . . an illusion
Like a magician's hand it deludes
Flowers are laid by dear ones
But the decay persists, stench hidden
The wreaths — a facade to foulness

The grave awaits . . . an appointment
I must be there . . .
For the penalty of sin is death
Upon the flesh the feast continues
Dust animated, to dust I return

The grave awaits . . . a prelude
to life — to sentience — to eternity
God's gift of life everlasting
I receive, the crucified Christ
the resurrected and everliving Christ

A defeated foe . . . the grave awaits
Jesus' blood powerful and precious
a sweetsmelling savour unto God
cleanses and conquers . . .
Born again — I live again! Hallelujah!

—Subhendra Santoshan Dharampaul

THE MIRROR OF LIFE

The Mirror of Life that I face each day.
The Image God made of us all in his creating way.

The Mirror of Life we look out onto the world for peace.

Hopefully one day the wars of the world will cease.

The Mirror of Life is helping us understand the meaning of love and care.

I pray to the Lord that he will truly move away the cruelty, tears and the grievance we bear.

—Gerald C. Reid

MARY FRAN

Out of this world I will never take;
    silver or gold or any keepsake.
All I have will be left behind.
    I hope dear Lord, you keep in mind;
the dear ones I cared for in sickness and death.
    And spiritually ministering
      with them as long as there was breath.
Then it was up to me to pray,
    until they were at perfect rest.

I hope they are waiting at the golden gate,
    to welcome me from my inevitable fate.
When I face the maker of this old earth,
    I can't offer franincense or myrrh.
Will he consider what I have done best,
    or what I worked for, was it just a test?

In all the 56 years of nursing dear Lord,
    That's all I have to offer Thee,
      please welcome me.

—Mary Fran

LEAN ON JESUS

When you are sick
And filled with despair,
Lean on Jesus,
He's always there.

When you travel
That long, rough road
Lean on Jesus,
He'll carry your load.

When trials and tribulations overcome you,
Lean on Jesus, He'll not forsake you.
When you are troubled and feeling depressed,
Just lean on Jesus, He'll give you His rest.

He's the one to lean on
When you need a trusted friend.
He'll be there to guide you
Until the very end.

When your way seems hopeless
And you don't know what to do
Just lean on your sweet Jesus
And he will carry you through.

*Dedicated to my Aunt, Mrs. Lola C. Meyers,
in memory of my Uncle, Mr. William Leroy Meyers,
to my husband, Matthew Blanding, Jr., and
in honor of my Lord and Savior Jesus Christ.*

—Loretta C. Blanding

GIVING

I have so many tears to cry
For times I was told that I was wrong —
But wasn't.
For times I was told I wasn't right —
And was.
And if I cried out all those tears
I'd have no time
To hold close those
Who need my loving arms while
Crying out all of their tears.

—Sandra Brandt

THIS YOU GIVE TO ME

How can you possibly know completely what you do to me, The joy you convey that wells up . . . from listening, sensing, touching, seeing and knowing you.

The passion I receive that resounds within my entire being from a spark beginning at my center core and radiates outward, joining forces with your essence to create new energy.

The delight that surpasses anything you can own, this you give to me.

—Suzanne DeWitt

A TIME IN LIFE

There comes a time in life
We need to look above and beyond strife.
Look into our heart and mind,
Let go of the past, leave our troubles behind.
Pick up the pieces, toss them away
Look to a time of a brighter day;
Friends may come, friends may go
It's what we hold to that hurts us so.
If you are bound by a hurt that is so great,
There is more to life than we anticipate;
Life is sweet, life is good,
And it is really hard to walk like we should.
Meet a friend that is in need,
Let them know you are a friend indeed.
Let go and set free, Life is to love and let be.

—Dee Davis

BEAUTIFUL PRINCESS

Her hair the source of glory to behold
The cute expression sought beneath concealed
So gracefully adorns her precious soul
When brushed aside her lovely face revealed.

Dark eyes that shine regardless of the light
With brilliance fascinating constantly
Attractive, archly brows like doves in flight
Above black pearls just setting on the sea.

A silhouette so picturesque to plead
Her movements like a princess are refined
Proportion perfect to embrace indeed
Her overwhelming presence blows the mind.

How sweet it is to know that you exist
No dream could ever match such vivid bliss.

—Michael David Cruz

FEELINGS

Feelings, Feelings so many feelings.
Feelings of Sadness
Feelings of Gladness
Feelings, Feelings.

What are feelings?
Feelings of Joy
Feelings of Love

Why do I feel like crying or feel like
hitting someone or something?
So many feelings.

Just what are feelings?
Why do you say you have feelings for me?

Feelings, Feelings
So many feelings.

—Lori Harps

A ROSE IS A ROSE

Fresh and beautiful
opening with the warmth of the sun;
glowing and proud
swaying in the breeze,
but never breaking.
Such is the rose;
Such is our love.
You have given me a fresh start
into a life that is beautiful —
with the warmth of your love
I have opened myself up to you,
and basking in the glow, have become
strong and confident once again.
Though at times it may waver,
it will never break.
Such is our love;
Such is the rose.

—Catherine Mejia Sinex

COME HOME TODAY

I know at times your morale may be low.
But I just want you to know that there
is someone here who believes in you, because
it's a job you have to do.
We are all supporting you and understand what
you're going through.
We are all waving our red, white and blue and
tying yellow ribbons waiting for you.
We are all singing songs of freedom hoping
you will all come home soon.
We are all united as one from all walks of
life, all religions, nationalities and races, all
thinking the same thing, breathing the same
words and fearing the worst but all we could
really do is pray for a way to get you home
very, very soon . . . .
Hopefully today!!

*I dedicate my love of poetry to my loving
grandfather, Francesco Rodino' and to my parents
Michelangelo and Giovanna Siciliano
for their love and support.*

—Lisa Joann Siciliano

I'M FREE!

Please release me,
    let me be.
A wounded heart you made,
    and suddenly, I have to be free.
I feared you all my life, now I have made
    the promise of a brighter, newer day.
You will own me no more,
    I am stepping into the light.
You can't hold me down down,
    this is *my* life!

Don't think it's over
    because I know it's not.
When you come from a place that hurts,
    you learn, you grow a lot.
I've learned not to fear you,
    and I've grown to forgive you.
At last, I am Free!

    —Lisa Meyers, grade 8

EMPTY ARMS

They cry at night.
    You go to them from your bed nearby
Comforting, taking away their fears
or discomforts of hunger.
Then they settle back in your arms
to a peaceful sleep.
You return to your bed nearby
tired but happy.
Then one day you find yourself
locked away, out of reach
Unable to hold them in your arms
You wake up to their cries only
to realize they aren't there,
You are alone. You return to
Your bed tired and sad, so sad.
You want only to be able to feel
their warm bodies in your arms.
To kiss their faces, to comfort them.
To start over and do every thing right.
To be free. To fill your empty arms.

    —Ellen F. Daugherty

THE ROSE

In the beauty of the perfect rose
I find you —
    The memory of your fragrance
    so clear
    that even now
I can feel our last embrace,
The silken petals
like the touch of your cheek
    as our tears met . . .
The fresh scent,
compelling; so like you . . .
And the thorn, like love,
the pain of its
    sharp point so severe
    that it could
cause a man to crumble.
Yet without,
there would not be
    a perfect rose . . .
    like you.

    —Linda Carol Adams

MEANING OF LOVE

To me the meaning of love
is when you're the only one I can think of.
Love isn't just a word
but an emotion, felt and heard.
Love isn't a kiss here and there
but something you feel ever so rare.
Love isn't always making out
but in your feelings having no doubt.
Love isn't trying to hide we're a pair
but wanting to shout it out that I care.
Love isn't an emotion spoken from a voice,
but it is conscious choice.
Love isn't happy day and night,
it might occasionally have a fight.
Love isn't filled with lies
but someone to hold you when you need to cry.
The meaning of Love to me is *YOU!*

    —Kimberly J. Gifford

I AM

I am yours
    and yours is a song
        a song so sweet
        my soul wept at its tune

I am yours
    and yours is a dance
        a dance so in synch
        our bodies moved as one

I am yours
    and yours is a harmony
        a harmony so perfect
        I couldn't help but hear it again and again

I am yours
    and yours is a poem
        a poem with words so passionate
        it left me with no words of my own

I am yours
    and you are mine

    —Ilana Douville, age 16

LOVE AND PEACE

Life is a continuous quest,
    For the elusive love and peace;
Like a flowing river,
    It will never cease.

For the power of love and peace;
    Can warm a cold winter night;
Can be a glow in the darkest hour,
    And can surely heal a broken heart.

It is not easy to harness love and peace
    But, with persistent determination,
And relentless pursuit; through courage and faith,
    In time they will be conquered.

Love and peace are vital to life,
    As essential as night and day;
Like the April buds which need the rain,
    They bring comfort to ease the pain.

As the power of love and peace is captured,
    Life will shine brightly for us all;
Like the brilliance of sunlight,
    It will become the essence of life divine.

    —Orovelia L. Jones

BIG SISTER

Big Sister, Big Sister,
I'll be a big sister —
My mommy is having a baby.
A sister, a brother,
it's one or the other.
She says that I'll love it . . . (well, maybe).

She says that I'm big now
and that I can help somehow
when this baby arrives in November.
Mommy's time, love and care,
I will now have to share
with . . . (its name I now can't remember).

It can't walk, it can't talk,
It can't even play, at first —
Just what will this baby be good for?
It can coo, it can smile
and after a while, she says,
I can teach it to do more.

Big Sister, Big Sister,
I'll be a big sister,
Once it's here, I cannot exchange it.
I'll be good, I'll be kind,
And its crying I won't mind,
but Mom, I'm NOT going to CHANGE it!!

Dedicated to "Big Sister" Brenda Kae & li'l "Sissy" Laura Brooke, who never let me have a dull moment.

—Robin B. Williamson

TRIBUTE TO A BROTHER-IN-LAW

He came to us with certainty
   with all his worldly charms
   accepting us for what we were
   with loving, open arms

No questions asked, no issues raised
   or expectations of what to be
   and becoming an important part
   of our loving family

A heart of gold, an ear for all
   an understanding soul
   he never stopped believing
   when times had taken toll

A perfect spouse, a loving dad
   a successful, caring man
   who never said "it can't be done"
   but believed it always can

Although we can't be with you now
   in minds and hearts we're there
   to tell that we love you
   and how deeply we all care

We thank you for all things you've done
   for the person that you are
   for the friendship you have given us
   whether near or whether far

Your birthday is the perfect time
   to let our thoughts run free
   and tell you just how proud we are
   to have you part of our family.

—Ellie Caruso

GRANDMA'S LITTLE GIRL

She's only four with eyes of blue
And Oh what she can do to you
She can make you laugh
She can make you cry
And there are times when you'd like to die
She can be an angel and oh so sweet
Then the devil takes over
And she's hard to beat
When you're down in the dumps and feeling blue
All she has to say is I Love You
She comes through the door all happy and gay
Says, "Hi Grandma, How are you today?"
Her eager arms reach out for a hug
She puckers her lips for a kiss
How can you resist
GRANDMA'S LITTLE GIRL . . . .

—Roma Hogue

WOVEN WINDS

Whistling wind speaks quick blind words,
   Tossed about over the trees' placid leaves.

They listen to us and respond coolly,
With a twist and a bounce.

I speak with the breeze,
And I tell it of you.

My warm breath weaves into the cool wind,
And joins its winged travels to a distant land,
      where we speak of you.

As Zephyrus and I talk,
My words are blown over the treetops.

They tickle their leaves and bend their branches,
With each phrase, gust and breath of air.

The leaves doubt not, when we speak of you,
That the woven wind knows the truth.

Because it is the one who talks with the wind,
Whose soul is speaking,
      with itself . . . .

—B.G. Dunlap

I CAN'T TAKE BACK FOR WHAT I DID TO HIM

There he stood smiling,
Friendly as a butterfly,
Fragile as a glass,
And as sweet as a candy,
My love for him grew every day.

But my love for him never show,
From the outside of my body,
I hardly speak or look at him,
But only to say hi to him,
And only say good bye.

He thought I don't love him,
But deeply I really do,
So he died in such a sadness,
And I suffer the same too,
For my love to him now show.

I hope this is not true,
For if he is alive,
I'll never be this cruel,
To my lovable grandfather,
The one I only love and care.

—Ruth Mak

WITHIN A STILLNESS

From the depth of the sky
    I can feel the touch of his being
From the feel of the wind
    His being flows through me
Through my feet on the earth
    I feel his strength
From the strength of his voice
    I feel his caring
From the caring in his heart
    I feel his love
Close your eyes and feel these things
    The blind can truly see
Your god is as real as you choose to believe
    For you as well as me

—**E.B. Rector**

SONG OF GOD

While the world's people sing
    the sweet bewitching song of self,

Waves of the sea crash upon the high rocks
for they are high sounding cymbols
        of God's glory;

Wavelets flow over low rocks
for they are flutes playing out
        the melody of God;

Birds sing a perfect note of music
for they are a choir
        of God's meekest children.

And trees clap out the rhythms of praise
        for all of nature to hear.

Rocks and
    trees,
birds and
    seas
sing a song of God to me.

—**Shirley M.**

HIS LOVE (A Love Poem For Jesus)

You are the best thing in my life
That's what I think of you
As a husband loves his wife
Is how I must love you

But your love goes deeper than that
This I can truly see
For I can't think of any man
Who would die like you did for me

You are all that I need in this world
Because your love for me is never-ending
It's because of the beating you took for me
That I don't have to spend my time sinning

I've never had love in my life
Not like the kind that you give
No one has ever laid down their life
So that I could forever live

Sometimes when I think of you
I just can't stop crying
It's because of your love for all mankind
That kept us all from dying

—**Yvonne Melchoir**

A BRIGHTER DAY

Wake up my friends and look around,
    what is going on in America is
    so profound.
So much agony and pain, many struggling,
    feeling all they have is lost with
    nothing to gain.
A precious little life again is taken.
    A poor mother cries, "Did I do right, or
was I mistaken?"
    Take your love to those in need.
Those who are hungry, poor, in body or
spirit.
    Take to them the Lord's love, planting
His seed.
    Show them a brighter day,
walking and trusting the Lord, who guides
    them along their way.

—**Tammy J. Shepherd**

THE BEAUTY OF GOD

I can see the beauty of God everywhere,
In the rose that opens to meet the day,
In the sun that rises with much flair,
For the beauty of God is everywhere.

We need only to open our eyes to see,
That God has made each and every tree,
And sends the leaves after winter's snow,
A beautiful new coat on which to throw.

The beauty of God is in a baby's face,
Who will grow in the world to find a place,
Then the beauty of God will soon be hid,
With the pressures of life, instead.

We must not forget the beauty of God,
For it will help us meet each new day,
It will help us to smile, and to say,
"The beauty of God is here to stay."

—**Edith Chase**

WATCH

(Reflections for the First Sunday in Advent, based on Mark 13:32-37)

Watch — be alert — attend
    to the holy one within you,
        the Christ who comes anew.

Be vigilant — aware — heed
    the bustling, noisy world,
        the quiet voice of calm.

Work — play — pray
    aware of those around you,
        attentive to yourself.

Stop — pause — wait;
    notice the life you are living,
        wake to the newness that calls.

Listen — watch — rejoice:
    the One who is coming is in you,
        the realm of our God is now.

—**Susan Baker-Lehne**

TIME TO BE ME

Sometimes I'm not the daughter
You've always wanted me to be.
In lots of ways I'm not the same little girl
I was so many years ago.
It's probably difficult for you at times,
But I'm fastly growing up, you see.
It's not that I don't love you, Mom,
I just need to be me.

—Pamela L. Bergsten

TO COMFORT YOU

Even though it's hard to smile,
Easier to shed tears awhile.
God is watching over you,
Knowing what you're going through.
I just want to tell you, I care,
I've had the same burden to bear.
I'll be praying for you,
Knowing that God will see you through.
He'll help you pick up those broken pieces,
And live each day filled with His sweetness.

—Barb Miller

ROOTBOUND

There's a little tree on a windblown hill
Near my Parent's home on a foggy coast.
The little tree, like the heart of me,
    Sways and blows and almost goes
With the wind and the rain.
Its roots are bound as it sways and sighs
    Again it is bent, wistful and still
On its windblown hill.

A book of travel, a smell of the sea
    My yearning heart—like the swaying tree,
Bends and blows and almost goes
    With the sea and the train.
Tight in the ground my roots are bound.
    I sigh and settle to earth again . . . Home.

—Pat Farquar Bryant

A DAUGHTER'S GOODBYE

When I visit your grave, I feel
    so alone,
I feel the only way I know you,
    is by what is written in stone.
The time we had together was
    much too brief.
That all I have done since you left
    me is grief.
But now I have my own family, as
    I'm sure that you know,
It is now time for me to move on, time
    to let go.
As time goes by, I will not forget you.
My life is being enriched by sweet
    memories of you.
Just know that one day we will meet
    again,
With you waiting there to walk with
    me, hand in hand.

—Billie Jo Stout

ON THAT DAY

Are they true, when they say
They'll be there, on that day . . .

To grasp me, when I'm feeling sad
And lift me up, when things go bad . . .

And when I need, A hand to hold
Because the world, is so, so cold . . .

They'll give me more, or so they say
They made A promise, on that day . . .

To be right there, by my side
To wipe the tears, if I cried . . .

I've accepted them as true, and I also must say
That I'll too be there, on that day . . . .

*Dedicated to my mother, the person that I
love the most outside of myself.*

—D.Q.M.

TO JANICE:

The bending of the willow trees is a voice.
Sometimes when it rains
The voice is my sister's.
That's when my life looked like
The Smell of Raspberry Preserves
And Hazelnut java was the water of life,
Because you were three years older than I.
I needed to believe you
Before I could believe your existence
While the absurd hands of wrath and stupidity
pat me on the head like some sad pet
(So I pretended that I was as secure as a weed
Perhaps a little less so . . .).
We ran in fields of obscure miracles (together)
So when the next moon comes, I will SMILE.
Tomorrow some mysterious pictures
And undefined leeches will find me again
But the garbling gallows will show me
My sister
And make the core of my skull happy.

—Sugene Yang

A BIRTHDAY ODE TO MY SON

On the 5th day of April, 1943,
And you were so very sweet and wee,
At 5:30 in the morning you were born,
And always you've been as bright as the morn.

Life has not always been gay,
But you had the courage to face each day,
And you always adjusted to it
With kindness, cheefulness and wit.

Now it is 1966 and you are 23,
And I wish that you could be here with me.
But you answered the call of Uncle Sam,
And now you are in Viet Nam.

I think of you both night and day,
As I turn my eyes to heaven and pray
That you will be safe and peace soon comes,
And I pray for others and their sons.

And even though you're far away,
And I know you'd like to be home today,
I wish you a happy birthday, dear one,
And thank you for being a wonderful son.

—Eunice Kirby Byrn

Dare to close your eyes
Awaken and please be wise
For sleep could only hurt
You'll be six feet under the dirt
Only fear has put you there
You were scared but no one cared
A horrible life you have led
Now a wounded soul you lie on your deathbed
No one can help you now
Your act is over so just take a bow
You pray to your god for his help
But you manage nothing but a little yelp
No one to turn to where do you go
To heaven or hell do you even know?

—Michelle Watts

THE WINDOW

The day was bad, I got through it somehow,
next day I'm back to the window.
The day was great, I've had none better,
next day I'm back to the window.

The pain today is gone tomorrow
when I'm at the window.
The joy today is gone tomorrow
when I'm at the window.

Sorrow is on my back today,
tomorrow the window will help.
Confusion clouds my head today,
tomorrow the window will help.

Today, I feel no love, today.
Tomorrow the window will love me.
Today, I have no friends, today.
Tomorrow the window will befriend me.

The world never hurt me as hard as it tried,
as long as the window was on my side.

—Rob Goerne

METAPHOR OF DYING

My flower is dying.
After all my nurture, my care, my attention,
the damned thing is dying.

Why did it even have to bloom?
Why did I have to glory in its beauty?
To bathe in its aroma?

It's dying,
and there's nothing I can do about it—
except get mad.
But at whom?

The flower?
The one who gave it to me?
Myself?
Fate?

I will not remember it,
the pain would be unbearable.
I will throw it in the trash
where it belonged a long time ago,
since in reality,
it's been dead for years.

—Sylvia R. Sampson-Haney

BEHIND CLOSED DOORS

Behind closed doors a child cries
You hear not his cries.

Behind closed doors a child's tears
You fear not for him.

Behind closed doors a child suffers
So you cover your ears.

Behind closed doors a child dies
So you think up lies.

Behind closed doors a child's last good-bys
And you close your eyes.

Behind closed doors another child is born.

*Dedicated to all the children, who are,
were and will be abused.*

—Alice

ANIMALS WE'RE NOT

The corners are our place of business
Opportunity we seek in the streets
Hustling becomes a way of life
Struggling week after week

Jealousy kills, and our sympathy
Is a violent act of revenge
A poured drink on the curb as we observe
Memories of our unforgettable friends

But life goes on in a world of sin
Where the wealthy reign supreme
And of glamour, fame, and fortune
Are the average black male's dreams

So though we do what we must to survive
Enslaved to uneven paved blocks
The media may forever misunderstand
But animals we're not.

—Jonathon (Stone) Jarrell

WHO AM I?

I want you to know who I am
Yet many will say
I don't give a damn.

All well and good for those who don't care
But listen my friends and please be aware!
I'm forty this year and many may know
My life has been struggle with room to grow.

My potentials are many
My aspirations are great
If you put them together
I carry much weight.

I am not bragging
For you will find
That we all can succeed
If we have the right mind.

I am a Muslim
"So what? You might say."
Allah created me the best in every way.

—Lavern Bilal

A TRIBUTE TO MY FATHER

How can I honor my father who is also a
friend of mine. Who is solid as a rock and
has stood the test of time?
He always seems to have the right answer
when there's something I do not know, and
he's someone I can lean on when I don't
know which way to go.
Many things he's taught me are priceless
like character, honor, and truth, and
the need to trust in Jesus while I'm still
in my youth.
And though I fear of losing him, I now can
plainly see that I could never
completely lose him because there's
a little of him in me.

—Shane Trotman

A FATHER'S LEGACY

My Dad . . .
  his strong hands
    hold me up to play and explore,
      yet are gentle,
        holding me close
          when I need to feel safe and warm.

His smile
  makes me smile
    and tells me he is happy
      that I am his son.

His heart
  lets him speak words
    of patience,
      understanding,
        and encouragement . . .
          surrounding me with a world of love.

And although I am very small
  I always know
    that he is my buddy . . .
      My Dad . . . .

—Carol Cameron

MOTHER! HOME!

Mother! Home! — that blest refrain
Grows lovelier each passing year!
Its melody drifts o'er memory's lane
And softly falls upon mine ear!

Mother! Home! — that blest refrain
Helps me feel her presence near!
All that I am or hope to gain
Rests upon my memory here!

Mother! Home! — that blest refrain
Every day it brings me cheer!
All I've known of grief or pain
Its sweet chords still calm my fear!

Mother! Home! — that blest refrain
Let me sing it loud and clear!
All things go, but these remain
Mother! Home! — names I revere!

—Linda F. Mayhue

ON BEING A SINGLE FATHER

The sun marched down the avenue
  in golden-riot glaze,
While fog burned off the sodden ground
  in wispy ghost-like haze.

The silence hung, suspended like
  a drape of Spanish moss,
Was broken by a freight train
  which spawned a grievous loss.

The treasures of a morning shared
  with my little son,
Outweigh most anything tangible
  having been tearfully hard-won.

Three weekends on Golgotha but,
  the fourth and fifth he's free,
And, along with all the weekdays
  spent the way we're meant to be.

*Dedicated to Alex and my family.
Both are my reason for being.*

—Rich Areeda, Jr.

TRANSCENDENT BETHROTHAL

Our lives led us together into the dark green forest
  among trees so old they seemed ageless.
    We knew they had endured, as we had,
      through season changes of both harsher and gentler times
        with years of quiet and solitary struggle etched in their forms.

We watched as strands of sunlight streamed between the ancient trees
  to the dark forest floor,
    intertwining light with the darkness.
      Your eyes became the Earth,
        mine, the Sky,
          bound together by the nurturing green world
            that held its roots in the Earth
            and reached upward to the Sky.

We became connected, Spirit to Spirit,
  in the light and the dark,
    in the Sky and the Earth.
      We were two, yet one . . .
        You and I
        and We.

*The poems I have written are dedicated to Harold, beloved
husband and soulmate and devoted father to our son, Matthew.*

—Carol Cameron

IT'S LOVE WHEN . . .

It's Love when your life is dim
    when you're not around him.
It's Love when you're full of cheer
    even when he isn't near.
It's Love when you cry
    and think you will die.
It's Love when you burst with joy
    like a child with a new toy.
And it's Love
    when you feel a hand from up above.

—Traci Leis

M.S.

Years ago you said to me
I love no one but you.
Dearest if you marry me,
you'll never more be blue.
Had I known then what I know now
would my heart have been so gay
to receive your kisses and words of love,
all the while knowing the price I was to pay.
I loved you then, I love you still
I guess I always will.
For with out you darlin' there is no doubt
I would have been twice times this blue.

—Nancy C. Scribner

SOMETHING'S MISSING

If you don't have someone to look up to,
    a brother, sister, or friend,
    you'll always be blind.

If you don't have something to lean on,
    a pole, wall, or shoulder,
    you'll always fall to the ground.

If you don't have someway to follow,
    a road, path, or guide,
    you'll always wander astray.

If you don't have a friend to count on
    caring, honest and true,
    you'll always be lonely . . . .

—Thomas J Kerner

FRIENDS

We've been friends for twenty years;
    Shared our worries and our fears.
Though we were younger when we met;
We haven't changed a whole lot yet.
We've been each others biggest fan;
Always talking over every plan.
We look back at things that seemed so bad;
And laugh about the "times" we had!
Now we're separated by 3,000 miles;
But I remember you all smiles —
When I told you I had a new life.
You said "Go on and be a good wife."
My happiness meant more to you —
Than all the things we planned to do.
Though I took you with me in my heart;
We're *still* 3,000 miles apart!
So every now and then you call to see —
What on earth is going on with me!
Even though other friends rate high;
Sisters couldn't be closer than you and I!

—Charlena R. Clay

FULFILLMENT

When I reflect upon a lifetime so misspent
    In search of fortune, fame, frivolity
In practicing a profession in descent
And other forms of idolatry
Seeking pleasure in meaningless pursuits
Indulging ego while neglecting mind and soul
Ignoring both my heritage and my roots
While confused as to my lifetime role
As despair takes hold — and I feel old,
Useless and obsolete
I deign to let the truth unfold
And savor once more my life's chief feat
Three special daughters did I sire
To what greater goal can one aspire?

*Dedicated to Mimi, Laura and Hilary
with much love*

—William J. Lippman

THE ONE I LOVE

The first time I saw you
Like a newborn sees their mother,
My mind was totally blown
As your presence was shown,
Your deep dark eyes, sent me into the sky,
Your sweet smell of womanhood
Made me feel like a child
Living in a rich neighborhood,
Your sweet soft voice
Can quiet the loudest noise,
The way you look makes me feel
Like a crook, stealing from the
Pages of Victoria Secrets Book,
The way you are today
Is how I want you to stay,
Don't ever leave me, or lose your style,
Because if you see I'll run for miles.

*Dedicated to the first girl who ever meant
something to me, besides my mom, and of course
my coach of talent, "The Lord Jesus Christ."*

—Bob Tomlinson CPS

A LIFE'S CHOICE

    Everyone can build a world
of their own

The tools
are presented to us at birth
We build our world
according to our liking
and our tools worth

It's length and width and atmosphere
we can define

It starts with our first tool,
a book.

The length and width depend
on how long we read and how deep we go

The atmosphere depends on what we read

How beautiful do you want your world to be?

*Dedicated to my mother who taught me the
importance of a good education and books.*

—Musataye (Misty) Jones

MEMORIES

Of memories is life composed
As notes do music make; or noise
So people, places, happenings
Recalled to mind; emotion springs
Replete with pain or joy

One holds in trust a tranquil scene
Familiar once; a church, a lane
A sidewalk table set for two
Another sees in darker hue
The fires of war again.

To each, though dear these scenes may be
'Tis players aye are at the core
Friends are the thread, the salt, the stuff
Who've shared life's journey, smooth and rough
I greet you as of yore.

—Bill Mathewson

FOOTPRINTS

As man journeys along life's way,
He leaves footprints every day.
Some are eroded by the waters of time,
Some remain, to become sublime.

Those eroded are gone evermore
Nothing achieved, unable to score.
They bespeak of goals that were set,
Allowed to fade so were never met.

The prints that remain give inspiration
And stir up man's imagination.
He moves up as goals are set
And one by one they all are met.

So follow the footprints left in the sand
You'll gain success as to a man.
You, too, will live to become sublime
And leave prints on the sands of time.

—Annette Loftis

WHEN YOU ARE OLD

When your fantasy becomes reality,
And all your dreams come true;
You forget that others are in poverty,
You forget what it's like to feel blue.

Your needs for possessions
Turn into obsessions;
You walk on clouds,
You have no doubts.

When you don't see,
You don't agree
That others are in need,
Until your own heart begins to bleed.

When all is acquired
And you feel tired;
Your face begins to wrinkle,
Your heart begins to twinkle,
You now turn to others,
Your sisters, your brothers.

When you are old,
All the things you took for granted
Before your eyes unfold,
The real need is then presented.

—Isabell T. Devenport

MEMORIES

Memories of the past
hidden in every single heart,
however painful, we never seem to part.

New lives begin
while others end too soon.
They come and they go
like the stars and the moon.

You remember the love, the happiness, and the pain,
you remember friends and foes
all just the same.

One last wish
for one perfect smile,
while laughs and tears forever pile.

A dream come true, a broken heart,
all pieces of a puzzle
that shall never fall apart.

Memories you have will never leave,
because in your heart, they forever breathe.

—Sonya Roncevich, age 13

MEMORIES

My friend and partner is far away,
but ne'er a day goes by,
when I think of then,
and think of when,
we smiled and said, "good-by."

It was a time long ago,
ten years, or so,
when we shared a friendship
of laughter, love and fun.
Each of those times together were special
and included everyone.

With learning and sharing as much as we could,
Lifes lovely pleasures were our own.

But good times end and some new ones begin.
Yet, never the same as they once had been.
You have your life, I have mine,
separate from the other,
yet, united together with memories of
that special time.

So my partner, be good to yourself.
Be happy and prosper
and drink lifes fine wine.
And I, too, shall drink a toast,
and smile with contentment,
just to know,
that we each share fond memories
of that time, long, long ago.

—Diane Karen Fox

THE DANCES OF LIFE

My mind is not quite what it used to be but
I still can remember some of the joys of long ago;
I do find, however, so much of the goodness still
in a groth of true love in a few friends who come and go.

One of the many things I hold of dearest value are
the dances of life that will warm the heart and mind;
As long as I will live, I will never walk away
from a chance to see and enjoy all beautiful things of nature I find.

Or, like elephants strutting along proudly in the holiday
parade with kids and old folks laughing and clapping all the way;
Or, like watching the fan tailed peacock dancing with grace
on the farm in the valley on a beautiful sunny spring day.

—F.A. Horning

FIRESIDE SEDUCTION

The pine icy to his very core lays so stately upon black cold grate,
unmindful, unaware, of his encroaching fate.
She comes quietly, softly, gently she comes,
he feels her not nor knows where she comes from.

Flinging open her arms, she bares her warm heart,
enfolding him tenderly, wanting to be part . . .
of bringing him to live, embracing him warm.
He turns his back indignantly, full of his scorn.

She reaches out fingers, caressing his sides,
from her tantalizing heat he has no where to hide.
She teases, she coaxes, she firmly grabs hold,
he has fear of this sensuous warmth so bold.

She burns with a fury into his heart deep,
he no longer can hide, hold back, or keep . . .
the coldness inside he held for so long,
he's blazing, he's melting, he's singing her song.

And when she is done, she flings him away,
his usefulness gone, she'll no longer stay.
So he'll die frigid, forsaken in a black ashy pile,
desiring her embrace again . . . her bright, sultry smile.

—Debora Jean Good

CHILDHOOD MEMORIES

Memories so far away yet ever so near,
Recalling my childhood of yesteryear.

Though my make-believe world is gone and childish things are laid way,
The vivid memories still surround me as if it were yesterday.

By the side of the road stood our sweet country home,
Where we shared a love and joy maybe few have ever known.

The array of colorful flowers our yard was ever filled,
Giving perfumed fragrance to the air as sweet as a songbird's trill.

I used to sit for hours watching the bees go humming by,
Or following the graceful flight of a yellow butterfly.

The apple trees would soon burst forth with leaves of deepest green,
And the walnut trees would follow not to be outdone it seemed.

With warm July came summer storms that seemed to ever last,
And mother would gather us under her protective wing until the storm had passed.

But soon the harvest moon would signal that autumn was drawing nigh,
And with daybreak would come October's bright and sunny blue sky.

We knew the time was growing short for fun and outside play,
For soon old man winter would fill our every day.

Inside our playful noises thru winter still would ring,
For we knew that soon the wintery blast would give way to another spring.

—Helen Pope Bell

SECOND CHANCE

As the walls of death fall below my knees I am able to step over the boundaries that kept me silenced and I fall to the earth to plant a new beginning. As I rise up, the sun feeds off my sadness and warms my freezing soul and I feel as though I am no longer on the ground, but walking across the wings of an eagle. As I soar towards the heavens, I gaze at the life line on my hand and I realize . . . I'm still alive.

—Todd William Raasch

DREAMS

Beauty lay hidden until awakened by you.
Passions, which were dormant, were released by you too.
Dreams became realities; swept swiftly into miraclous bliss.
Two heart became entwined and eternally sealed by your kiss.
Years passed like moments, enraptured by your eyes.
We could climb the highest mountain; swim the deepest sea.
Nothing is impossible, when you are here with me.
As we grow old together and we contemplate our fate.
Dear, our love is eternal; no matter what our fate.

—Linda Rodriguez

Rainbow sunset glinting on the horizon, the sun begins to fall. I run through a forest as darkness sets the pace. Running scared and terrified there is no place left to hide; nothing left but darkness. My life's search and cannot find, but when I wake to morning I'm in a field of daisies and there amidst the wildflowers sits a royal rose. Shining bright as the sun and dripping red like blood. When I looked closer I saw that it was you. The storms on the horizon fled at my discovery, knowing as I knew that I'd fallen in love with you. Looking into your eyes chaos turned to peace and all the wars around me quickly began to close. Storms that haunted me, the hurricanes in my soul, found no place left to thwart me as you began to court me. I found that in an instant the hammer had struck my soul and where once I was empty, there was no longer a hold. So I took you in my arms and told you how I felt and your words of kindness swept away my heartache. No longer doubting this world or thinking it was fake, I saw that finally I was where I meant to be. Everything about you sets my world at peace. Now forever is no longer out of reach and in my heart I found the answer to this stirring in my soul — It is Love.

—Dave Lenger, Jr.

LAST NIGHT

Again he leaves
    without a word
       and footsteps heard
         into the hall
       disappear

      and the door   closes.
—Leslie L. Dame

SALE

I know it's sad,
When they die,
All they had,
For those that buy,
By and by.
Now I'm old,
Soon be gone.
My things sold,
Life moves on.

—Tony L. Blansit

EARTH

The wind is whistling
  The trees are blowing

The river is flowing

The stars are glowing

The fire is roaring

The plants are growing

The bees are buzzing

The rain is falling

The thunder is thundering.

And the earth still

Goes round and round

With love and care

Sound by sound.

—Danika Blood

He puts on the Mask
To hide his fears
A twisted face
Of alcohol and tears

Hiding behind it
To numb the pain
In a state of denial
Once again

The painted smile
Does not ring true
Underneath
He's lonely and blue

One quick glance
At the laughing eyes
A closer look
Reveals the lies

So he takes off the Mask
And puts it away
Hopes to avoid it
At least for today.

—Judith Ann Render

Good-bye old friend
My heart will ache for now
But I know it won't ache forever
Although it feels right now like it might.
I cry when I think about you
And sometimes I laugh through my tears
When I remember something crazy you said
Or something funny you did.
Someday the tears will disappear and I'll just laugh.
I don't know when, but someday.
So right now I'll just say
Good-bye old friend,
I will always miss you, remember you,
And especially love you.
I will hear your laughter in the wind, see your
Smile in the clouds, and feel you in my heart
FOREVER.

—Michela Cordova

I AM NOT FROM THIS PLACE

The church is dim.

   But there she sits,

     Third row from the front.
     Near the center aisle. In the shadows, quietly.
     Her cloaked head bowed.

Her posture seems to beckon me —
                    For comfort.
                    For answers.

Slowly, I sit down, and I watch her.

     Should I approach this stranger?
     She is so silent, but then, I've heard,
     So many have cried all their tears.
     Nothing is left, but an empty gnaw,
     That scrapes away at the soul.

    —D. L. Shilling

A GRANDMA TO REMEMBER

I will always cherish her understanding,
Her politeness
Her appreciation for others
Her eagerness to love
And the will to live

She has the qualities within
That make her precious
Someone you can turn to when in doubt
Someone to listen to your thoughts
Just someone to hold you tight

As I grew older
I began to feel the bond strengthen
The bond that brought us even closer
I can learn from her
Even when only a memory, she will guide me

For she is my Grandma
A person of the utmost importance
She cared for me in childhood
And I believe she always will
Even when the halo hangs high above her head

*Dedicated to my wonderful grandmother,
Ada Blake of North West River,
Labrador, Canada.*

    —Dion R. Burry

MY TREE, MY STRENGTH

Standing so tall in all your splendor.
Slightly moving with the breeze.

Leaning forward, I reach for you.
I must not touch.

The flame of desire will reach its peak,
With no words to speak!

The wonder of your majestic strength,
Will cool me in the radiant heat.

My tree, my strength.

I will linger there beneath your branches,
Waiting, contemplating.

    —Monica Nunez Aguirre

TIME YOU CANNOT TURN AROUND

When age has gone beyond our youth
You must always keep this in mind,
Alone with wisdom you must live with truth
Because time you cannot turn around.

If you must build a wall for it to last
Your mortar should be mixed with lime,
Reference only used to look up your past
Because time you cannot turn around.

I was taught to leave what's yours alone
And what I should keep be only mine,
Each day I live with a mind very strong
Because time you cannot turn around.

*Dedicated to my wife, Mildred and
my children, Leanise and Lindsey Jr.*

    —Lindsey R. Smith

THE HUNT WAS ON

The hunt was on, the mood was right
When first she gleamed upon my sight;
A lovely apparition, sent
To be a moment's ornament;
Her eyes as stars of twilight fair,
The curls and beauty of red hair:

I saw her upon a nearer view,
A spirit, and yet a woman too!
Her speech and motions were light 'n free,
Amid steps of cautious liberty;
A countenance in which did meet
A soul so pure with promise so sweet;
A creature bright 'n quick 'n good
To fill the hunters needing mood,
For transient sorrows, to chase away,
Wtih smiles, hot kisses, and the play.

And now I see with eye serene
The very pulse of the machine;
A being breathing thoughtful breath,
A traveler between life and death;
The reason firm, the temperate will,
Endurance, foresight, strength, and skill;
A perfect woman, nobly built
To warm, to comfort, to clothe in gilt
And yet a spirit still, and bright
With something of an angel-light.

    —Thomas James Gilson

NOT SEEN

Shed tonight was tears,
With all the unseen fears,
Lonely and forlorn,
Another fear is born,
To be alone once more,
No more soaring,
To go home UNSEEN.

—Nicole Peschong

REALITY

God cares not
If you are
Black or White
Or yellow trimmed
With blue.

He cares only
That you realize
How very much
He loves you.

—Wilma Storms

GOD WILL TAKE OUR HAND

Life is something given us,
   free from God to man
Life we must truly trust,
   yes as best we can.

Life is for us to cherish,
   till the end of time,
Before we all do perish,
   your sweet soul and mine.

Life is but an hourglass,
   filled with grains of sand.
When the sand has all runout,
   God will take our hand.

Dedicated to my father;
March 17, 1980

—DuRaae V. Davis

A POET KNOWS!

Be it man or woman
Black or white
A poet knows . . .
They were born to write.

It may bring them pain
The loss of a friend . . .
But a poet must have
Scratch paper and pen!

Poetic thoughts flow
Like a master creation . . .
A poet writes like a worker
Taking dictation.

They respond like a lover
Cast under a spell . . .
And that is the reason
They are moody as hell.

Don't e'er blame a poet
For writing too bold . . .
Their thoughts flow forth
Straight from the soul.

—Roberta Comer

WHEN I MEET JESUS

I can almost hear the trumpets. I know the Lord is near.
The Lord will take me with Him, I will meet Him in the air.
Just remember that God loves you and will never let you down.
The next time you meet Jesus there will be Angels all around.
Just think of what you'll tell Him, when He looks you in the eye.
You'll see his loving, caring face, a tear within His eye.
He'll tell you that He loves you, all your sins will be no more.
For you His blood was given, as He takes you through the door.
You'll see your lovely mansion, and the streets of purest gold.
You will know you're in Heaven where you'll have to fear no more.

—Richard Munro

A TROPICAL SUNSET

A tropical sunset, what a beauty to behold,
Sending gleams across the sand in colors of gold.

The yellowish beams on the water connecting sea and sky,
Reminding us that shadows of darkness are drawing nigh.

The peace and tranquility of the fading light of day,
With sunlight dimming bringing darkness on its way.

Soon the moon on the water will cast its glow,
As we ponder what mysteries lie far below.

As we dwell on these wonders, our eyes give way to sleep
And we cherish the days memories, ours alone to keep.

We awake next morn to a sunrise so calm and serene,
When once again we're absorbed in a world of magical dreams.

Oh that an artist could capture these spectacular sites,
What a magnificent masterpiece of beauty and delight!

Dedicated with love to my Joe for the many beautiful
tropical sunsets he has made it possible for me
to see which will live in my heart forever.

—Helen Pope Bell

THE GIFT

A babe is born, in pain, but such great joy,
As we behold our baby boy.
A gift from God, for us to keep, for a little while.

A babe is born, we rejoice, in his first smile and faltering step,
That we did get
This gift from God, ours to keep, for a little while.

A babe is born, in anxiety and with great emotion
We watch his rapid locomotion.
This gift from God, ours to keep, for a little while.

A babe is born, with pride, we see him off to school
Our son, our boy, our jewel!
This gift from God, ours to keep, for a little while.

A babe is born, time flies. Do we yet realize?
No, we are not that wise.
This gift from God, is ours to keep, but for a little while.

A babe is born, Oh Lord, what pain!
He's with you, again.
This gift from you, with us for such a little while!

—Helen J. Weldon

NATURE'S THANKSGIVING

All of earth's nature pays its tribute to God!
From the tallest trees in the sky,
to the deepest tap-roots of all that grows,
there is a pride that will not die.

From the ugliest weed to the loveliest flower,
they take from the earth and grow toward
God for all their worth.
Showing the best they can be, before they die.

Then at the final stage
when their best is spent—
they drop to earth, their seeds, their leaves,
their branches, their all,
to pay their rent.

—Jane C. Pyrek

MY HUNTING SURPRISE

Hunting season is here again;
Went out in the woods with some other men.
I went to a ridge top, sat under a tree
    to get a better look at what I could see.

I felt quite comfortable out there in the sticks,
    with a thermos of coffee and my 30-0-6.
So I lay back my head and closed my eyes,
    never expecting a sudden surprise.

I felt a hot breath and a very cold nose.
    I awoke real sudden from my sleepy repose.
I jumped to my feet and dropped my gun.
    There went my deer on his departing run!

I looked and I searched the whole day long;
    I walked until all the daylight was gone.
I never again saw that cold nosed buck;
    So "my" hunting trip was without any luck!

—Edwin Johnson

FLY

A buzz from the window, close to the frame
Black body and wings one leg has gone lame

He scours then cleans, is he all that neat
Hanging at right angles just by his feet

Looking for freedom, scaling the glass
Butting and banging, hovering at the sash

Does a fly wonder or think of his day
Can he plan his meals, will he find time to play

Glass to the front, freedom to the rear
Instinct drives him forward, when the opposite is clear

Searching and climbing with never a snooze
Each little journey no spirit does he lose

But time takes its toll, to the sill he flies
And there in the morning so still does he lie

No longer moving, declined has his mass
Light as a feather, brittle as ash

Piles upon piles they collect on the track
Moving the window compresses the pack

One fly's life such a simple little matter
But alas he is gone, the toad surely sadder

—David P. Miller

FEATHERS—FEATHERS

Feather writer, on a pen,
Feather tickle, my best friend,
Feather cleaner, as on a duster,
The many things a feather muster!

Feather coat, as on a bird,
Feather make me write a word!

Feather stuffed as in a pillow,
Feather lying under a weeping willow,
Feathers, feathers from all the birds,
Feathers make me write poetic words!

—Kathleen Ruczynski
  Poopsie

WINTER REFUGE

Nature hurls in winter
And boldly conquers the air,
Making of the snow a blanket
That gives the sleeping earth
An extra layer,
In which to rest for Spring's rebirth.
The children are wrapped and warm
Against imminent storms.
Chocolate steams in the mugs,
To be enjoyed in the refuge
Of the restful, familiar house.
Snow glistens in the meadow
And on each hill and tree,
Giving purity to the peaceful whiteness.

—Lindia Speer

PAPER LAND

Dismally trudging, a writer's hand,
undaunted in pace, on a paper land.
Letting not his spirit weep,
    though many times his mind may sleep.
Thaught is not friend or foe,
    yet to some, it will come so slow.
Oh how it taunts and teases,
    still its end there of, truly pleases.
No words or lines come to the door,
    of one who look at self, to adore.
To judge or criticize the style of it,
    enjoying the words of fellow poets.
So run those of you that can,
    and catch your dream in a paper land.

—Stanley F. Buchmiller

MOONLIGHT MAGIC

The wisps of the clouds in front of
The moon give a special glow
To the light of the moon.

As I look out into the midnight
    Sky — I see the moonlight,
The moonlight magic.

As the moon rolls by, it is the
    Stroke of midnight, and I'm soaring high.
Higher and higher the moonlight shall
    Inspire. Inspire me to fly higher.

Fly, soar shall I, bravely across the
    Moonlit sky! Fly high shall I!
The moon doeth inspire me,
    The moonlight — moonlight magic.

—Caneel Troxclair

Snowflake
　Tiny white
　　Little light
　　　Happy face
　　　　Fancy lace
　　　　　Fall down
　　　　　　Kiss ground
　　　　　　　Melt away
　　　　　　　　In a day

　　—John Landgraf

Where did my summer go
with his blue eyes shining?
The heat of his mouth no
longer caresses my skin,
and his voice no longer
melts into brilliant
sunsets. My wild rose has
faded, and I know my
summer has passed away.

　—Angie K. Harper

ALTHOUGH I AM GONE I LEAVE YOU THIS SONG

To rejoice in harmony
　Not in sorrow
And live for tomorrow

For I will Always be there
　Close to your heart
　Not so far apart.

I have gone to spread my wings
Because I have found a new home
　Where I won't be alone.
I hear the trumpets playing
　And angels singing.

Cry no more, Cry no more

For I have no pain no more
　Only joy.

　　—Evelyn Hampton

BEAUTY IN THE ROSE

Undying love and devotion
　Dried for everlasting comfort
Admired for its simple perfection
Death undying — everlasting love
Careful tenderness makes for
　Foreverness
Treasures of lives long since gone
Tears dried on our hearts
In longing for something we
Must give up in the flesh
But memories will always
Replace the empty void death
Bring to our world
Everlasting love in the beauty
　Of the rose

*In memory of William H. Davidson
　(Grandpa)*
　　—Kathleen D. Molinet

WINTER TIME

As the winter approaches us
　The summer is going away.
When the winter comes our house is toasty warm
And we watch T.V.
We will sleep in the room that has warmth in it.
In the morning I expect it to snow in the middle of winter.
When it snows it will look nice and pretty outside.

　　—Barry Lynn Kingery, age 11

ABOUT ME

I celebrate woman.
God created man in his image . . .
God gave woman the gift of birthing and nurturing the man.

I celebrate emotion.
Woman emotion takes rides and spins through many worlds . . .
God gave woman emotions to care for man.

I celebrate intelligence.
God gave man the ability to analyze . . .
God gave woman the ability to understand
　　　　　　　　　　　　　without analyzing.

I celebrate woman.
　　—L. Jacobson

RIPPLES

Rhythmically, the ripples echo in my mind,
I watch them emanate from the seeming portal to my soul,
I see my image in the pond of life,
Always moving with the ripples,
Always subject to their laws.

I feel the languid path of the ripples,
Slowly shaping my life,
I feel the constraint on my ways,
I feel society holding me,
Pleading for conformity.

Quickly, I allow my hand to fall,
Powerfully into the pond,
Wreaking havoc,
destroying patterns,
breaking laws.

I am free.
　　—Joná F. Meyer

A THOUGHT OF YOU

Here I am alone at night
A pen in my hand and a thought of you in my mind
That's all I have to keep me going
A thought of you
Though the distance between us is so great
We still have our hopes and dreams of being together
No matter how far apart we are together we will always be
For I now know you will always be in my mind
You will always be a part of me
You are forever entrenched in my heart and forever in my soul
Though the distance may never grow shorter
I know I will always have the memories
I will always have the photographs
And I will always have the thought of you firmly implanted
within my mind
So until we meet once more
Remember I am thinking of you
Remember I am always yours.

　　—Duncan McILwain

WIND

When Heaven's fan rotates on high,
Hurricanes and tornados begin to fly
O'er land and sea,
through you and me.
Batten down your hatches, dearest foe;
Heaven hath no fury like *this* woman's blow!

—**Janet S. Haley**

AS THE FALCON FLIES

As the falcon flies,
I just sit and watch,
As the falcon flies so swift and free,
I just sit and watch,
My thoughts also glide with it,
I just sit and watch,
At that time I have no worries
Nor fears,
I just sit and watch,
As the falcon flies.

I would like to dedicate my poem to Ms. Sommers and Mrs. Michael. Thanks for believing in me.

—**Jonathon M. Best**

SOLITUDE

Perfect aloneness chanting through the mind
Detachment
Dancing as Pagans deep in the forest of the soul
Shadows surrounding all the World
Never to have to see the sight again . . .
                until morning.
EVIL THING!
Destroys the beautiful haven of night
Close your eyes and keep skipping in circles
deny . . .
      deny . . .
           deny . . .
                deny . . .
Soon the moon will rise
Bringing a brief eternity of perfection
Making us safe and alone
once again.

—**Erica Amrine**

WHY IS THE WORLD THIS WAY?

There's a man in your face
telling you you're a loser,
because you ain't the same color of skin.
He tells you and tells you again.
He calls you a nigger, a wetback,
and other nasty things.

You can't fight back. There's nowhere to run.
He says you shouldn't be on the streets,
you're worse than a bum!
You try to get away, but there's more and more!
What's all this for? You shout and shout,
but no one hears.
Your last lonely words fall on deaf ears.

Why is the world this way?
Tell me why, I'd like to know.
Black, white, yellow, and gray.
How can the color of your skin
grant anyone supremacy?

—**Jeremy A. Meadows**

LOVE

Love is something,

Hard to get.

Not everyone has it.

I had it,

But I lost it,

But I love the one person,

Who loved me before.

—**Jennifer Gessner**

MY CHILD

She brought the very sunshine
She laughed at rain and snow.
I thought she was happy.
Now I do not know.

She left to find her own way.
She needed to be free.
She felt the pull of worldly things
Never looking back at me.

Sadness now engulfs me
And tears are near at hand.
Oh, how much I miss her.
Will she ever understand?

Does the sadness overcome her?
Is her pride now in the way?
Will she ever say "I'm sorry?"
And come back home to stay?

The pain and utter sadness
Are too much for me to bear.
Will she know before too late
How much I really care?

—**Ruthanne Monson**

Four winged clouds converge
the center is the spirit
its path the circle of eternity.

i must have faith and fear not
for the spirit lives forever free
being quiet to listen to Creation
trusting the spirit to guide.

dancing my own wind.

Four winged clouds combine
bringing breezes to fill the heavens
and rain to nurture life below.

best friends share their freedom
soulmates believe in their cause
lovers imagine the possibilities
companions understand their flight.

alike but individual they fly.

S
Dreams Do Come True.
P

—**Pamela Patterson**

SEA OF DREAMS

Bearing out across the tide
of the Sea of Dreams does ride
a hope, an inspiration new
where once stagnation and mud banks grew.

Afloat in an ever expanding range
alone now drifts this magical change
inspired by the touch from another soul
though briefly playing this magical role.

Bringing forth out of despair
beauty and order through deeds that care
stirring the silt that lay below
now to sparkle in a mineral-like glow.

Together they created this harmony
destined to flow from stream to sea
bursting the banks and narrow seams
born in the current of the Sea of Dreams.

—Suzanne DeWitt

SAND CASTLE

The little boy sat playing in the sand.
Busy he was, with shovel and with pail.
Told his daddy: "I will build you something,"
Though he had not a hammer or a nail.

Chewing his lip, he piled the sand up high.
He shaped and tore it down and worked again.
An artist, he labored for perfection
And shaped each pile with skillful little hand.

Then finally he cried: "Oh, Daddy, see!
Such a beautiful castle I have made!"
He laughed and jumped, he shouted loud in glee,
And Daddy, just to please him, left the shade.

There was not a feature of a castle,
No battlements and not a spire or dome.
For the "castle" the little boy fashioned
Exactly copied their own little home!

—Bertha Woods Greenwood

THE SEA

As I stood upon the rocky shore
Beside the angry sea,
I drew a picture in my mind
Of puny man's futility.

The dashing spray!
The angry roar!
Incensed to fury by a hidden might
Tend to reveal that mortals are —
But grains of sand in the great God's sight!

As I gazed out o'er this vast blue void,
Again I pictured in my mind — the worth —
The untamed strength of this great sea!
A benefit to all mankind.

And, as driftwood cast upon the stone
Lying helpless and bleached by a burning sun,
So to each human on the earth
His designated spot does fill
On the beaches of "The Almighty One."

—"Michigan" George Gerhardt, deceased

A PICTURE PAINTED IN THE NIGHT

The earth is all aglow,
With a carpet of snow,
'Tis winter's most beautiful sight.

Moon beams ablaze,
On the snow's icy glaze,
Glitters, like tiny angels dancing in its light.

Ghostly shadows tall,
On earth's carpet sprawl,
It's a picture painted in the night.

This picture of rapture,
Held in memory's capture,
Vanished in the morning light.

—Yevon Copeland

THE ROAD OF LIFE

As we pass along this road of life
Between all the troubles, pain and strife
A time of happiness we should find
A time to know peace of mind.

Life is not all peaches and cream
Often times we need to scream
But take a minute and hesitate
Many times it is just life's fate.

Some we can change and some things not
A job, is knowing which is what
Just take time and have control
As in this life you play your role.

And if you play your role complete
Doing your best to be kind, gentle and meek
You'll be rewarded many ten fold
And know life's many treasures we are told.

—Mary F. Bush

THE GHOST SHIP

The end is near,
all is quiet now.

My ribbed hull,
worn and beaten,
whistles the wind which flows through.
My sails,
tattered and torn,
collect nothing but dust
as they sag on my skeletal remains.

I am the Ghost Ship.

Slowly,
drifting in life's foggy current
My ribs creak,
echoing the laughter and joy
of my previous inhabitants.
Tired,
I sink deeper and deeper,
into the murky waters of time.
Numb,
the icy waters flow through me.

I am the Ghost Ship.

Once I sailed with many,
but now, I rest . . .

Alone.

—Michael Krohn

MINDSET

Why are men and women
   not a covalent bond of life,
Yet they bond towards sexual
   lust,
When love is yet blind or not
   heard of,
It's in their minds.

—**Brently Dean Rye**

SPRING

Spring is a time
when flowers grow,
the birds come back,
and there's no more snow.

The grass turns green,
the rain pours down,
then all the keen people
get out of town.

The town, it floods,
the people are scared,
that all that they love,
will be washed away
with the grim, grime, and grub.

—**Jenny Holl, age 11**

Her life is changed
forever more
Now afraid of living
unsure of what living is for
Destroyed forever
never the same
The nightmare came
but never went away.
She remembers the night
memories seem to last
Yet this girl so afraid
never again will live for the past.
Nobody to turn to
just running away
wanting to forget
that night that seems to stay.

—**DE Rozycki**

TO MY SISTER

I don't know how to say,
the things that should be said,
but these are the things I want
to say, before the day you're wed.
Remember that of this family
you are a vital part,
and no matter what you do or
where you go,
you'll always be in my heart.
As brother and sister we shared
many joys, fears and sorrows too,
but all these things united us and
proved I cared for you.
Now you know you have my love
and my blessings too, keep drawing
closer to our God and you'll have
His blessing too.

—**James LeRoy Swafford**

KINSHIP

It has been said that black is beautiful, and brown is cute.
Before this postulate the Caucasian stands mute!
Perhaps he finds it difficult to explain
why the Anglo-Saxon is so vain.
Or, why he basks in the sunshine all day,
to acquire a suntan, that fades away.
What is the difference, if you are black, brown or white,
is one color wrong, and another one right?
The Caucasian is perplexed, and he should be told,
his thoughts must be refined like the dross from the gold.
He might be embarrassed and filled with chagrin,
to admit all mankind is one race—Homosapien.

—**June M. Souza**

TODAY

Today I don't know whether to like, love or to hate.
It seems that people just don't know what to do
I wish I knew who to trust or not to trust
Who to love or to hate
Today I don't know if I should love you or just like you
Right now I need your help to decide
I've liked you since we met
Now that I talk to you I just start liking you more
I wish I knew what to do today
I don't mean to rush
I'd like to know what I'm getting into
Whatever it is I'm glad that you are here to
Help me, guide me, just having you here by my side
Makes me more and more secure
Just to have you with me today, tomorrow and
Forever

—**Christopher M Benoit**

MY HEART'S CRY

The grievings of my heart are so,
   that I can hardly stand,
the pain I feel so often Lord,
the wounds put there by man.
The hurtful words, the so proud looks,
the feelings of despair,
they were all heavy Lord upon me,
when my soul it was bowed in prayer.

Then as I prayed and sought you Lord,
and brought all my cares to you,
all my fears diminished, blew away,
as I knelt there before you.
There on my knees I found relief,
my soul it found sweet rest,
for when I knelt and called on you,
my soul there you did bless.

The tests that come along my way,
they may seem so hard to bear,
but you will help me when I pray,
a smile someday to wear.
I may walk alone on this life's path,
a way that's set apart,
but I'm not alone for you are there,
always in my heart!

What greater friend could I desire than the one that reigns
                                       up higher?

*Dedicated to all of the hurting people everywhere.
I want them to know that there is a place of refuge
and hope in Jesus Christ for all their hurts.*

—**Faye Kiser**

CHRISTMAS

So many songs are written about the Christmas Day,
Poems galore are made of the reindeer and his sleigh.
Beautiful pictures are painted with the snow upon the roofs,
With Santa flying towards the sky with waving hands and reindeer hoofs
The thought of minds are on the things they'll put beneath the tree,
And the very first words on Christmas Day is what did he bring me.
Many of us are happy when we arise on Christmas Day,
See that Santa has been there with his reindeer and his sleigh.
And it is a homey feeling as the fire burns on the grate,
To smell the food a cooking that soon will adorn our plate.
Many will have their friends come in to see what each one got,
So each can do some bragging about the things that Santa brought.
Then there is a sadness that comes to you and me,
When we see that empty spot beneath the Christmas tree.
And we sit and ponder, "Was there one that we forgot"
'Twas our blessed Saviour that was left the empty spot.

—Dot Scroggins Robbins

COME INTO GOD'S HOUSE

In this house, prayer is in the closet
In the den there's love, and hope if you've lost it
And the cup board has preserves, the strawberry of life
The lamps burn all day, and all through the night
Spiritual food is in the refrigerator, sweet incense on the stove
The television is tuned to serenity, and ran by remote control
Goodness is on the table, faith is the main entree
Your foes have become your footstools . . . for victory is yours today
Sugar and spice is in the teapot, you may pour abundantly
Looking for salvation . . . on the floor is the recipe
Tranquility is on the bed, so rest your weary mind
Joy is in the ceiling, you may choose from various kinds
Happiness dwells in the attic, consume as you like
THE SPIRIT is in the atmosphere, covering left to right
Fear has no place here, for strength is in the walls
Peace is in the pictures, hanging throughout the halls
To make you feel welcome, the mat says so at the door
For once you COME INTO GOD'S HOUSE, you are welcome forevermore

—Vernel Smith

GOD'S CHOICE

I watch in vain as she slowly moves across the room
Each step is a success in its own way
The determination is somewhat spectacular
She knows her time is nearing an end
Her bony hand reaches for her medication — her last hope

I grew up with her as a young lad
Not remembering too much about her
For she moved away to find work
I knew her only by voice and later on by a visit
She knew me as her "Babes"

She knew something was wrong inside
But like many, she figured it was only something small
Or at least that is how she brought it across to us
I believe she knew there was a problem
She did not want to worry anyone — it's her way

The problem was big all right — cancer
Slowly draining her energy and causing much agony
Agony that we as friends and relatives cannot imagine
We all hope she will get better — a miracle by chance
Aunt Flo is home to die in the hands of family, soon to be in the hands of God.

*Dedicated to the memory of Florence Blake
who passed away on August 23, 1989, in
North West River, Labrador, Canada.*

—Dion R. Burry

WASTED TIME

The clock ticks away
the naked hours of the day
I see what has past and gone
I know not what the future brings

And the minutes turn to seconds
And the hands are moving slow
I see what we've turned into
I know not what the future holds

We've wasted so many hours
We've wasted so many days
I wish I could go back
each second of the day
But time is what we've wasted
So precious time is
There is no hope now
All that's left is wasted time

—Cathy Hetfleisch

UNBORN

It's very dark and
I cannot see
but this I know
love planted me.

I feel with every fiber
of my being alive —
my heart beats with hope
but on love and care I thrive.

My senses stir with trust
and a desire to be whole —
nourish me with tender care
birth me with a soul.

I've struggled just as you have
to see the light of day —
you're beautiful — I'm happy —
Pray I'm here to stay.

—Florence N. Troll

FIRE EYES

A father out of work
   Looks day after day
     He would die for his son
       See the fire in his eyes.
A mother at sixteen
   Doesn't know where to turn
     Her child is her life
       See the fire in her eyes.
A young man given up
   Has no family to call his own
     All alone in the world
       See the fire in his eyes.
She is now fifteen
   Missing for three years
     Caged in a dark room
       See the fire in her eyes.
We all bare the pain
   Of life's cruel reality
     Look closely and you'll see—
       See the **fire** in our eyes!

—Caroline Suzanne Dahlke

ARTESIAN SPRING WATER

Evil pressures effervesce; Attract a weak soul,
When one's mind is troubled — Sorrowful —
And stress has taken its toll.

Devils awaken; Dragons unchain,
If temptation wins — The changeling formula is swallowed —
The victim is consumed by disdain.

Strangers, friends, family take caution; Take arms,
The demons are merciless — Relentless —
In cities, in farms.

My eyes have seen the damage; My body and brain pained,
I too have been vulnerable — Surrendering to weakness —
My character eternally maimed.

I've grown a stronger man; A wiser man with advice,
Don't moisten your lips — Keep away from the well —
Don't roll the dice.

—John William McDonald

MEMORIES INFLUENCE

The memories of childhood oft hidden from the sphere
Predict our daily actions from those we all hold dear.
Yet in a newborn baby, we see his future too.
His way and his beginning are showing through and through.

Have you seen a serious baby lying quietly on its side,
Another baby cooing with arms reaching wide?
What makes each one so different for all the world to see?
It's found in generations and done so perfectly.

Happy joyful people spread sunshine everywhere.
Their childhood whispers softly, "Our happiness we'll share."
Privation on the other hand is cause for scars and tears,
But we find some people wise beyond their years.

In spite of what we are at birth and live with everyday,
Our gift to others and ourselves is found within our way.
Our way is from the thoughts we think, things we say and do.
So let us help our world to be more loving, kind and true.

—Helen Lager Konyha

THE PASTOR'S WIFE IN A SMALL CHURCH

When a minister is pastor of a small church
His wife is sometimes placed in a lurch.
She wants to assist her husband—stand by his side,
The order of the church she must not over-ride.

The members are listening to hear what she'll say.
She begins to converse with them in her own way.
She's the pastor's wife, but a member too,
She believes in her heart there is work for her to do.

During the period in her life when she's doing the
best she can,
She really would appreciate the members' helping hands.
She's criticized by them for what she knows,
The wagging tongues of others might just as well be blows.

She tries hard to understand their non-Christian ways.
In her humility she forgives—she prays.
Is there something I need to learn that you're showing me?
Lord, am I the servant you want me to be?

I am ready and willing to do your will.
Help me in every way my life to fulfill.
If you'll show me the way—what you want me to do,
I'll move at your command—determined to go through.

—Ruby L. Boston

THE NIGHT

I stood there gazing at the stars
The twilight night winking back at me.
Such magnitude,
Infinite bursts of light.
The black night surrounding millions of tiny holes.
Such ominous void
Infinite as time
Am I no more than a drop of water in an endless sea?

—W.E. Bookhamer

My love is quiet and gentle, calm as a sea
of glass, on a clear moonlit summer's night.

My love for you is strong and fierce, as strong
and fierce as the ocean on a stormy winter's day.

Its white sandy beaches, are pure, warm, and endless.
Its waters clear, full of life, love, spirit,
and neverending beauty.

I see you in all these things of beauty,
that fill my heart and soul, they know, no
boundaries.

I feel you in the fiery sunsets across the
waters of life, your warmth is in my heart,
and your ocean runs through my soul.

Through GOD

I have been blessed, with all these things
with . . . the eyes to see beauty, the ears to hear
laughter, and most of all, the heart to feel . . .
this is . . .
        My love for you

—Lisa Bonavia

SOMEONE SPECIAL

    I got up one April morn;
It seemed like any other day,
    The sun peaceably shone
through cloudy skies;
    The birds sang, but in a
different way.
    Someone told me that
someone special had left today.

    That was it! Someone's special
giggle and the way her eyes
would twinkle when she spoke.
    She was more than someone's
friend, mother or wife,
    She was that special
sparkle we will all miss in our life!!
    Because she had a way of
making you feel like "Someone Special" too!

    That evening the day closed
like it always had done;
    But there in the heavens
a star; I've never noticed
shone brightly today.
    The sparkle from "Someone
very special" that quietly slipped away.

*Dedicated to Viola Hodge, a very dear friend
I had the pleasure of working with for 10
years. She died of cancer at 32, leaving a
husband, three children, and countless friends
who thought just as much as I did of her.*

—Barb Saveley

YESTERDAY GOOD-BYE

Looking back on your yesterdays,
You find an unlatching purpose.
All found is a condemning reflection.
Lost, find yourself reaching flashbacks.
Your mind's like yesterday's sponge.
Heart grasping onto lost loves,
And absorbing past crimes. There is
A child within concerning distant moods.
All poverty's resting and you're on
Freedom's journey. You demand
A grasp on your tomorrows, looking
For an uncertain treasure.

—Raye Elizabeth Tureaud

I'M STILL IN LOVE

They said it wouldn't last,
They said it was a laugh.
Even after all these years
I'm still in love with you.

When our love began
I turned and ran away.
I came back again,
To find my heart was still
Set on you.
After all this time
I'm still in love with you.

Was there ever a doubt, did we
ever listen, to all the silly fools.

Did you have faith in me,
or were you just a kid in love.
Was there ever a doubt in your mind,
or was love just too blind,
after all this time I'm
still in love with you.

—Bob Benton

THE RAINBOW

Look to the rainbow
Color your dreams bright
For in the splash of artful hues
Lies the answer to unsolved problems
Anxious, sad times watered with blues
Happy, gay moments coated with yellow
And somewhere in-between
Arches of pink, orange, and green
Tell a story as real as life
As false as untimely hopes —
For in the beauty of the rainbow
Is our enigmatic answer
To our long — awaited search —
Our serenity and peace is
Shaded with our thoughts . . .
Of glossy imprints of yesterday
And acrylic-clear prints of tomorrow.

Look, look to the rainbow
For the beauty of your soul
And somewhere over the vivid nostalgia
We find the shimmering reality
Of our untold quest.

Look, look to the rainbow.

—Priscilla A. McGaughan

_____, MY FRIEND

You do not seem to understand
exactly what we've found
A guidance through each other.
The limits have no Bounds!
A need to be together —
Yet kept so very far apart.
YOU are My Friend forever,
FOREVER IN MY HEART!!!

—Pam Gee

FRIENDS TOGETHER FOREVER

We have laughed and
cried together

We have shared dreams
and failures together

Now you are gone

We have shared death
together

Friends together forever

—Mari

THE SUN'S PROMISE

The sun comes up everyday,
promising a new
chance at happiness.
If only I would
take that chance.
Instead, I am afraid
of another hurt.
I wish I could open
my heart to you,
and tell you what
I'm feeling,
and how I'm hurting.
But will you still
be there?
Will you still hold me,
and tell me that you
love me?

—Darci Horrell Lumley

DREAMLAND

While spinning, tumbling, to the ground I fall
A silv'red piece of rock falls after me.
The tree above me stands so wide and tall,
And reaching for the limb I grab a key
Which waits to open endless doors of dreams.
Within float horses, toys, and unfilled thoughts
Of lemon flav'red, yellow floating beams
Which spilled from ev'ry sea which was not bought.
As Hershey's kisses lingered in the sky,
Marshamallow puffs of clouds ne'er spit no rain,
And glints of silver seen in shining eyes
All made the finish, beating out lost pain.
But there within it all stood, lost, a face
That time left to forget without a trace.

—Wink

VIEWS OF LIFE

Thank you dear God for another wonderful day,
I appreciate the ability of work and play;
While feeling the warmth of the beautiful sun,
being exuberant is always very much fun;
A real friend is one with whom you can talk,
cannot understand why anyone would ever balk;
Visit your neighbor that you know is ill,
This makes life easier for them to swallow a pill;
Say hello to all that you pass,
It displays our majesty from the top class;
through dark days it is often difficult to smile,
Justly it makes people's day tremendously worthwhile;
open up your eyes and look all around,
the amazement of beauty is there to be found;
Surely these thoughts have created some blend;
I now bid you adieu my dear loving friend!

—Edward Zimmer

MASTER CRAFTSMAN

He the potter — I the clay
Being sculpted in His image as I stubbornly yield my way
to His skillful crafting, I watch my own likeness grow dim
as tenderly, patiently, He sculpts my heart to Him

Though this process is often tedious
it is never void of purpose, nor it seems pain
yet, somehow I feel overwhelmed
as I view my life once again

Only to find I can't distinguish
between the sculpture of myself I've come to know
and the mass of clay I handed Him
so many years ago

Silently I wonder, as I survey His Grand Design
are there broken places beyond repair?
Can He restore this heart of mine . . .

He the Potter — I the clay
Being sculpted in His image
I choose no other way

*Dedicated, with gratitude, to family and friends
who supported, encouraged and believed in
my talents and abilities long before I was
able to believe in myself.*

—Karen E. Jocson

FRAGMENTS

I am entrapped by glass with stains—but not stained glass.
I cannot reach or touch you now—nor ever will.
You see me but I have no substance—only mass
and only tiny windows to reach out—but still
keeping trying for those windows—see me past the stain.
It happened to me—I'm no longer in control.
My life is shattered and fragmented—I'm in pain.
The glass that traps me now is cutting through my soul.

—Uta Haley

When I was walking down the hall, I felt a pain that hurt me poignantly but it was not really there.

When I was walking up the stairs, I met a man who was not there, and he was not there again today. Oh how I wish, he'd fade away!

When I was at the table alone, I spoke with a lady that was dressed in grass and cotton. But She wasn't there, and maybe I wasn't either.

There just isn't a way to know when we're dreaming, is there? Nevertheless, dreams do come true, some times.

—J.A. Long

I HAVE HEARD THE WIND

I have heard the Wind sneaking in through the branches,
    Sighing and chuckling,
Bringing his cool breath to caress my face.
I have heard the Wind stampeding the forest,
Daring all to challenge him,
    Howling and hissing,
            Thrilling my soul.
I have heard the Wind whispering intimate secrets,
A presence only for me,
    Gentle and loving.
I have heard the Wind.

—J. Keeling

SMILING

Smiling is a gesture, a simple kind of art,
Which makes a person happy and sets aglow your heart.

People smile in the same language which everyone understands;
Smiling is very innocent, and makes no demands.

A smile is a curve that can set a lot straight;
It will warm two people's hearts and take away the hate.

Smiling has no enemies and it doesn't like to fight;
It brings two sparks together and unites them into light.

Smiling takes no practice, not much energy at all;
It starts to build bridges and tears down the wall.

Smiling is like a rocket which lifts spirits high;
It helps your feelings to quit walking and teaches them to fly.

One smile leads to another which in turn will do the same;
Miraculously it will start a fire from just a little flame.

Well, there you have it, how hard could it be,
To put on a little smile for all the world to see.

—Shana Mitzel

REMINISCENCE

I'd like to have a tiny farm,
Not just a lot of space,
An orchard and a garden too,
And a house with a wide fireplace.
   When autumn rains begin to fall,
And cold north winds to blow,
Give me books of pioneer days,
And tales of long ago.
   A rocking chair close by the fire,
Apples and chestnuts too,
There'd never be a lonely day,
If I was there with you.

—Minnie G. Hyatt

FOREVER LOVE

You are so dear to me,
and I want you to know
how very much I love you
with all my heart and soul.
I think of you often,
and treasure the words you say
cause when it comes to you
you're special in every way.

No matter what the day may bring,
whether it's sunshine or rain,
you always seem to make me smile
even when you call my name.
So if you ever wonder
how much I really care,
just turn around beside you
I'll always be right there.

Dedicated to my forever love, Don Wolschleger. You are my knight and shining armor, you are my dream come true and I love you.

—Loretta Raye

MORNINGS

Mornings, mornings . . .
   Oh, how sweet!
I wake up
With morning feet.

Oh, how I feel—
Morning is there!
Morning sunshine
In my hair.

And although I'm
Not sick or dead,
I need not
Get out of bed.

And when I see
A sunny ray,
I know it's time
To start my day.

Mornings start out
Very fresh . . .
Unless you have . . .
Morning breath.

—Amanda Lee Gossage, age 8

ONLY IN AMERICA

Everyday, I await the
opening of the big gates;
to set eyes on festives of
arising sun. Only in America . . . .

—Lela O. (Jenkins) Vaughn

DREAMS

Dreams are second lives which go
on when we close our eyes.

Dreams are like a person who
seems to take our day and turn it
into something very special.

He says, "Come with me to my
special world just made for you and
me.

To my world, come fly
over my mystic rainbow.

Where there is a place of wonder
for you and me."

—Molly McKeever

THE TREE

Here I stand with not a leaf to
my name.
The cold, cold wind goes through
me with no pain.
I am not a bit pretty and I
look like I am dead.
But I am just resting for this
is my bed.
In Spring my leaves will come
out all green and bright
And every one will love me with
delight.
God made me this tree so
straight and tall
For all people to enjoy each,
Winter, Spring, Summer and Fall.

—Margaret Flathman

LETTING GO

Release your fears and painful
tears
Realize your potential the result
of years,
Spent developing your persona and
smile
You have come so far along each
mile.
Your life is rich and full of
joy
Especially given to each girl and
boy.
An opportunity to give and care,
Your goodness and love to
share.
So let go your troubles and
cling to the thought,
That life is special no matter
your lot.

—Joanne M. Montemayor

ON THE DEATH OF THE PRESIDENT — JOHN F. KENNEDY

He laughed. And in a twinkling he was gone;
For one dark moment, hands of time stood still.
The garments of estate were shed; all peoples bowed as one,
In stunned submission to a Higher Will.

Deep anguish gripped the nation and the world;
Grief's arrow pierced the souls of great and small;
The silent sea of mourners wept; the muffled beat of drums
Betokened of the barren, flag-draped pall.

He lies in peaceful rest amid the rows
Of markers white, where sleep the true and brave;
In death, his spirit lives forever, as the Eternal Flame
That burns, unquenchable, upon his grave.

—Kathryn Campbell Slasor

THE GENTLE SPIRIT OF LOVE

What is the unseen spirit that whispers in the wind?
So tightly do religious traditions bind us
in mind and spirit,

That we cannot loose the iron fetters
and look beyond

Our little world in which we are the center
of the whole.

Spiritual darkness descends when minds shrink
and judgements grow.

The Supreme GOD of all religions in the known world
and existing everywhere,

Cries to see our small, empty spirits descend
into sinister nothingness

As loving thoughts, vanishing like a whisp of smoke,
are fading away.

—Carol Gourlay

A VISIT TO GETHSEMANE

Go with me for a minute to witness: What was
perhaps the foggiest night in history.
You'll recognize the story.
The scene is very simple; you'll recognize it quickly.
A grove of twisted olive trees; ground cluttered
with large rocks.
A low stone fence. A dark, dark night.
All the disciples shook with fright.
Now, look into the picture — Closely through the
shadowy foliage: history is on stage.
See that man? What's he doing, flat on the ground,
face stained with dirt and tears? Fists pounding
the hard earth. Eyes wide with stupor fear. Hair
matted with salty sweat. Is that blood on his
forehead?
Who is that man? That's Jesus in the Garden of
Gethsemane. Now, I'm no artist, but I know
the story about Jesus.
Look again — horror and dismay are on the Lord's face.
Where are his disciples? They have all fled.
Where is his Heavenly Father? He's there. He was there
when Jesus died on the cross. He'd be there for you.
Next time you pay a visit to Gethsemane: The hand
that touch you is a pierced one.

Dedicated to my mother, Elizabeth King, who stood by me.

—Connie Holt

THE ODYSSEY OF LIFE

As a young couple start out in life, their minds are filled with thoughts of happiness, love and compassion. The confusion and conflicts that follow are always going to appear but as long as they love each other, nothing can stop the compassion they feel. The words of tears and happiness bring emotion to their hearts. The sound of pattering feet on the hard wood floor are what makes life worth living. This is a poem of a happy marriage; not when they start feeling and loving with their mouths and not the heart. Their life being run by fear instead of love.

The years and days pass, their love grows stronger and stronger. To the graduation of your only child, to the marriage of your little girl and the father filled with emotion giving her away. Then the couple dies in each other's arms and pass away just to see their first grandchild born. The last memorable words said between them are "I love you." It goes back to the old saying, "The children should out live their parents," not the other way. And another generation begins. Life and marriage what a wonderful thing.

—Christine (Christal) Linnard, age 14

ONLY THREE

A little girl wakes in the morning, her mama dresses for work.
Another long day for both of them, a new life together, a rebirth.
A question she keeps in her mind, and sometimes on her mama's mind too,
she often wonders, where's Daddy . . . he says he has new things to do.

Mostly I don't understand, being a little girl, only three,
why in our life all of a sudden, my daddy never sees her and me.
Mommy says Daddy still loves me, but how can that possibly be,
when I think of my dad, I feel lonesome, a feeling too big for a girl of three.

Mama looks sad most of the time, always worrying over just little things,
even a hug and kiss don't help, ever since she took off her rings.
Mama says things will be alright as long as she's got me for a friend,
but sometimes I get to thinking maybe even that will end.

'Cause who know how things will happen, that much I can see,
I'm pretty small, but I know how I feel,
even for a girl . . . only three.

—Terry Newman

I AM AMERICA

I was conceived by a group of men in a Boston coffee-house a mere two-hundred years ago,
From hearts filled with a love of God and a sense of Justice for all.
In the minds of men like Adams, Washington, and Jefferson, who pledged
    their very souls to the idea of my birth.

I was born on the square at Lexington and Concord, and nourished in the
    snow of Valley Forge and Trenton
And finally took my first step, as a frail and struggling child, with a
    victory at Yorktown, when I put a kingdom down.

I crawled and stumbled and grew in places like the Cumberland and Boonesborough.
    And on the long trail to California too.

Many times I've fought for liberty, in 1812, at the Alamo in '36, and in
    Mexico at the youthful age of seventy.
And I've cried out in pain and anguish as I was torn asunder, and shed tears
    of blood to see . . . brother fighting brother.
In the spirit of Freedom and in the same of Friendship, I've sent my youths
    to die, fighting tyranny and oppression for folks like you and I.
In strange places with exotic names like, Belleau Wood, Normandy, Iwo Jima,
    and Chu Lai.

But, today my friends have turned their backs, and spit right in my face.
    And Atheists hold me hostage in a far-off lonely place.
You ask yourselves who am I?
    I'm You, I'm Me, I'm US.
I'm America, the Beautiful, and in God I put my trust.

—Travis Byron Dyer

A DOG BURIES A BONE

On my doorstep I write
About this cold Autumn night;
Sound and Smell blend with Sight,
Can barely see the Sky's true light.

The Moon with two Rings,
A storm this must bring;
Ancient tales and things
Create poems to Sing.

Time tells no Lies,
The Sun will soon Rise;
An old man Dies,
A young baby Cries.

The Northwind is Blowing,
The Season is Showing.
The Birds are now Crowing
To the Gods all Knowing.

—John William McDonald

HERBIPHILES AND HERBIPHILIACS

Just because she was a witch was
Reason to heartburn in fleshfire,
Reason to dial as Jesus does
Long distance by short distance wire.

But not till she pentagraphed it
Could curse geometric survive,
And only as we believed it
Was it ever greater than five.

So mommed by her poppa himself
And popped by her momma and me
Her only love was of herself
And her decision to be free.

Soully because I am a man
Is reason to break a ribrage
And bone the body down again
To unstrangle soul's voice's cage.

—Twixt

A SEASON OF CHANGE

A season of change,
this year was for me.
I am no longer the child,
you thought I would be.
This woman rules now,
strong in my soul.
Feeling the triumph
of just letting go!
Grown to much more,
than I dared ever dream.
Not only by doing,
but surpassing all my needs.
Finding my success,
where you thought I'd fail.
Reveling in the fact,
I am quite female.
I have paid with blood,
the balance once due.
I am more than enough,
even better without you!

—E. "Shadow" Maddox R.A.

MY PICTURE

What do you see when you look at me
When you look at my picture what do you see
In the frame three by five can you make me come alive
Or do I rest there glossy and still, never seem to do your will

Think about the winter past, does the picture make it last
Last beyond the melting snow, winter days that made love grow
Or does it look remote and frosty, far away and long ago
Feelings never again to know

Look at pictures of you and me, a happy winter memory
Is this the proof we have to show it will last and it will grow
Or will this corner that we've carved
Become a place to be love starved

Looking at the picture theme, we linger with a hunger dream
Whittle away at life's command, never want to take a stand
Just want to walk a way with you
Just want to walk away with you

—Francesca Zee

YOUR PICTURE

What do I see when I look at you
I see beauty in your eyes of blue
When I look at pictures what do I see
I see the one who is in love with me
Even in frames of three by five
Your sparkle and smile are much alive
You don't just rest there glossy and still
I ask and you say you always will

I think about the winter past
Your smile in the picture will make it last
Last beyond the melting snow
Gaining warmth from the summer's glow
Never will it be remote or frosty or far away or long ago
Feelings so sweet that it's a love we know

I Love your thought of a picture theme
A place we can linger, a hunger dream
We will whittle away at life's command
Soon we will take a courageous stand
These last two years you walked a way with me
Now I want you to walk away with me

—Robert Wen

I AM

I am a loving girl who wants to help the unwanted.
I wonder how long it's going to take.
I hear their cries from pain and seeking help.
I see myself wondering what I can do.
I wish I could help but, I am only a loving
   girl who wants to help the unwanted.

I pretend that only a few are left.
I feel as if I should give them the love they need.
I wish to touch their hearts.
I worry about them every minute and second.
I cry for the help they try to draw near.

I am only a loving girl who wants to help the unwanted.

I understand sometimes people can't fulfill their dreams,
   but I say even the little ones are precious.
I hope one day they all will be happy and healthy.

I try to help myself try to understand.
I hope one day I'll be able to change things, but
   until then I am only a loving girl who wants to
   help the *unwanted*.

—Helen J. Carver

SANCTUARY OF IDLE BEAUTY

It's raining and I am alone again, and a sublime contradiction arises. Is it for him or for me. Now that I've been informed the perception is dual.
A faceless individual whom I don't even know is blistering jealousy inside my soul.
I don't know anymore, I just don't know.
Will it be a blatant subtlety or a hidden chagrin that makes me stick or peel away. Behind every mask a place of sanctity arises where you can rest and dream. But within that sanctuary of idle beauty is a spot of indecent blackness that will eventually grow and tear open and reveal the true face of indecency. But it's not in vain, because over the horizon a new day will appear covering every night that precedes, and if not what is left to do . . . nothing.
I feel like I'm digging myself half a hole. I thought of you when the dove cried. I was standing in a sanctuary of idle beauty, when the sky bled your name.
My heart defined it while hidden behind a mask of innocence, which you shunned.

—Mark Partridge

COUNT DRACULA

Count Dracula — he finds his night and rises from the grave
Who will be his bride to bite — the kiss that he has saved

Don't close your eyes for sleep is sure to call him to your bed
And you will wake no longer pure but married to the dead

His life is death — his death his life, beginnings are your end
And you shall be his bitten wife to never love again

Though you may gaze upon his face and see but just a man
Beware my poor unknowing one, for he is satan's plan

Deceiving is a simple task, his charming, thoughtful lines
Believe me that behind the mask, lies a poisoned mind

And though you find his eyes of grey hypnotize your soul
Do not stare — for he shall dare to make your blood run cold

And when he smiles as he does, don't smile back his way
For you will find your life at night and never see the day

Beware! Beware! My lovely girl, the kiss — the kill — the bite
Count Dracula is of this world and wants to dance tonight

—Jane E. Hughes

ODE TO BOB E. THE BEGGAR

I met a squirrel the other day.
He from the feeder looked at me, I'm hungry as if to say.
I went and got him nuts and corn.
He had a cute look, my heartstrings were torn.
This little squirrel, he got so brave.
The nuts in my hand he did crave.
I plopped right down to the ground.
And then from the tree did he bound.
He became my close little furry friend.
I knew this friendship could never end.
Today I fed that cute little squirrel.
Bob E. The Beggar put my heart in a whirl.
I saw him laying out on the walk.
He was dead and I couldn't talk.
This time we had, it was quite short.
Cause I fell in love with that cute little sport.
I buried him in the backyard under the tree.
As I did my tears flowed free.
Bob E. I'll miss you, you cute little squirrel,
Who put this lady's heart in a whirl.

—Judy Belski

MIDNIGHT

Whispering winds,
Meowing cats,
The whoo-ing of the owl,
Moving shadows behind the bushes,
That's what happens at midnight.

—Karen E. Miller, age 11

DAWN

And the dew kissed grass
Shimmered in the golden
Morning light.
The sun's rays slowly spreading,
Caressing the leaves of the
Summer trees.
And the cock crowed,
Bringing the first sound to
The morning silence,
Shattering it like fine crystal.
But the pieces left were more
Beautiful than the whole.
And the day awoke.

—Dawn M. Williams

MY DAD

"My dad big and strong."
"For I admire you so."
"You are there when I
    need you."
"You are there when I
    don't."
"For I Love You So."
"For you Love Me."
"For you care what
    happens to me."
"You are always in my
    heart."
"You are always on my
    mind."
"What would we do
    without our Dad?"
"For I Love My Dad . . . ."

—Sandra Nell

ALWAYS!

Oh child, God's gift divine,
Parent love, once sublime,
Now divorce will divide,
Secure love to provide.

Court and Judge think they know,
The best pursuit to go;
Consider not child's heart,
A mother's God given part.

Child lives two sets of rules,
Begot two homes and schools,
Torn, in how love to give,
By which guidelines to live.

God, Bless this little child!
Lead its spirit undefiled,
Teach *Your Love* through others,
Walk with child and mothers,
    Always!

—J.S. Titlow

HANDS

His hands were calloused and rough,
But gentle and tender to the touch.
Hands that knew work
Tanned from weather's wear.
Could mould and shape a piece of oak
Yet take a splinter from a wee child's foot.

—Charlotte Anne Davis

WHY

I made him, inside me, the little one
Ten fingers, Ten toes,
two eyes, two ears, a mouth,
And a nose
He had them all, so perfect,
so little
he was all mine to cuddle
to be mine, all mine
Then you took him
You,
The Divine
Why?
What a question, that's the one I have,
it makes me cry
I was there when you took him from me,
there I was, you see
hoping he could stay
All I could do was pray
That didn't help
You took him anyway.

*Dedicated to Tyler James Schmitz
Born July 23, 1992, Died Aug. 2, 1992
I Love You*

—Renae M. Schmitz

IN MEMORY OF FATHER

You slipped away.
You didn't say good-bye.
My heart was too heavy then to cry.
I think of you in silence;
no eyes to see me weep.
So many silent tears were shed
while others were asleep.
I ponder of those years with you,
and think to myself
"What I wouldn't do . . .
to say I love you just once more."
Before you'd go through Heaven's door.
When I am sad & lonely,
and everything goes wrong . . .
I close my eyes and hear you say
"Just smile & carry on."
Each time I see your picture
you seem to smile and say . . .
"Don't worry. I'm only sleeping.
We'll meet again some day."
For all of you who still have a father;
love him with lots of care.
You will never know the emptiness,
until you find he isn't there.

*Dedicated to John R. Kostenbader,
from my father's heart . . .
to my words.*

—Kristy J Fernandez

NO SECRET

If I love you,
You will be the first to know,
And I will not have told you.

—S. Perry Holleman

CLOCK HEART

Lying alone,
Drifting, Drifting, Drowning away
Resting by night
To be lonely by day.

Lost time, Lost life,
Never love unloving things.
Lose once, lose twice,
A lonely heart king.

Seconds so worthless to some,
Years for me.
Dreaming of something
I'll never be.

Tick Tock, Tick Tock,
Tick Tock, Tick Tock.
No more need of winding,
To Hell with the clock.

—W.G. Williams

PATIENT LOVE

Deep in the meadow
Beyond the tall trees
I see the love
That everyone needs.

Although I see it
I cannot tell
Of the wonders
I see, where I dwell.

It's not the sight
That ails me so,
It's just the pain
That you won't go.

But I am patient
So, when you do
I will be here
Waiting for you.

—Amanda R. Erickson

ROMANCE IS EVERYWHERE

A quiet evening
homeward bound.
Just me and him
clasping hands.
Silence between us.
Yet, there is
a tenderness in his eyes.
Unexpectedly he pulls over
in a parkling lot.
He slowly turns to me
and says "I Love You."
It was a happy surprise.
Too happy for me to speak . . .
My heart smiles.
I smile, He smiles
. . . And then then we kiss.
It was a moment that
I will cherish
in my heart forever.

—Rachel Ramirez Lacosta

THE MEADOW

The buffalo roam the meadow, to eat its lovely grass,
The bear are 'round the river, to sip honey and eat bass.

The trees grow on the meadow, and stand still night and day,
The eagles fly over the mountains, to search for any prey.

The pronghorn meet at the meadow, to chatter about this
　　and that,
The elk are in the forests, to hide away from the wildcats.

The meadow is a special place, that I will never regret,
It holds a special secret, a secret never to forget.

　　　—Ash Jay

VISION OF A DREAM

Night-time falls in a clear black sky, with a thousand suns
　　scattered through.
Profiles in darkness, silhouettes in the gloom, a Tryst
　　beneath the moon.
No words are spoken, no promises made, two spirits are joined
　　into one.
The Magic is there, tightly binding the souls, that by the
　　blackest of spells is undone.

No ensorcellment cast, the Fates elsewhere absorbed,
The rite of their Love is performed.
Passion flares in her eyes of crystalline blue,
The fire by which they are warmed.
He leads by the hand, with the tenderest of holds,
To declare without words the enslavement of souls.
Through the mists of tomorrow Time takes them away,
To another dimension, without night or day.

What is this scene, that I have in my mind?
Is it a dream, or a myth out of Time?
Is it prophesy, fantasy, or something quite else?
Some explanation is due.
I put into verse what I fear to express,
It is my vision of you.

　　　—Richard J Vogt

TIME

I yearn to just go back in time and glimpse into the past,
And see myself a child again in a world that seemed so vast.

Time then to me was fantasy, for my life was filled with fun,
With joys and carefree childhood; life's problems not yet
begun.

Then in my youth, I used to think that time would never pass,
Couldn't wait to be all grown up and in the adult class.

And in my adolescent years, the time just wasn't there,
To do the things I wanted and still have time to spare.

Now the twilight years have come; childhood and youth gone by,
And yet I cling to dreams and hope there is time to try.

If I could but reverse the time and start my life again,
Would I find the time to do the things I'd put aside in vain?

And now my time is running out; the days are filled with
tension,
Should I ask the Lord above to grant me an extension?

And when at last I leave this world, time will still go on,
But my time on earth will be fulfilled for many, many dawns.

Just what is time no one can say; each day it's there for us to
face,
And till the myseries of life are known, time alone shall time
erase.

　　　—Helen Fraser

THE STORYTELLER

In song and verse
The poet skillfully weaves
Our childhood memories
Our dreams
Our very being
Into the Divine Tapestry
Of the great life force.
(Don't step on the rug.)

　　　—Gene Redemer

BREATHLESS

Sunshine drenches sleeping skies
As angels dance before my eyes,
Sent from Heaven you must be,
My spirits lifted and soaring free,
And like the swan of silent tear
I feel I'm lost without you near,
Then I see you the snow white dove,
Come bless this child with your love,
Please sing to me so soft and sweet
And lay down your world upon my feet,
A miracle we shall have begun,
Our hearts unite to be as one,
And this I promise unto you,
Forever shall my love be true.

　　　—Andy Behr

ANGEL UNAWARE

I will bury you today
And claim back my heart
I will bury you today
And pile heaps of dreams
Upon your grave
I'm tired of hanging
Onto angel wings
While you flutter
Here and there
Angel unaware
　　Silly me!
I thought angels could
See and hear
　　Silly me!
You have no ears and eyes
For you don't see my tears
Or hear me cry
So I'll bury you today
And claim back my heart
Angel unaware

　　　—Linda McKee

SUMMER

On morning-glory dextrorse vine
"Bells of the day" ring to design.
Butterflies seek their natal flight
As oxeyed daisies peer the sight.
Through June-banked paths of haying grass
The wind sweeps with a gentle pass.
Old world roses fashion hillsides
Attar of the wild rose abides.
Dandelions stud the fields gold
While fireweed blazes side of road.
From summer flower's dazzling hue
The sky receives the colors due.

—Harriet Poplar

A SUMMER'S DAY

A summer's day will go away
When children will no longer play
A summer's day will surely end
When girls and boys no more pretend
When the sun above won't lie its head
Upon a cloud as if in bed
When trees will fall and birds shan't sing
And flowers shan't come out in spring

A summer's day will go away
If we continue this world today
A world with war
A world with hate
A world that goes against its fate
A summer's day will be no more
When brothers fight as if in war
Let children laugh, let children play
Let them rejoice a summer's day
Let streams run fresh
And clear the land
Let us behold our world in hand
A summer's day will surely stay
And birds from nests won't fly away

—Yelida E. Abreu

OF LIGHT

On the starlit road, of spinning galaxies
Make a right at the Milky Way
Sail on t'ward the second rim star
Straight ahead

On the coast, where the grey whales glide
Across the bay, to the other side
East of canyon and the Las Trampas Hills
Down in the sunny valley . . . she rides

An angel of light
She's music to my eyes

I'm calling your name
In the ancient tongue
Come on arise
The Morning Sun

Stand on the Big Sur
And gaze upon the star
And sing up to her window
Her name is ANJA

An angel of light
Down in the sunny valley . . . she rides

—Anonymous

ANNA

She was a baby once;
crying out at night and Mother was there.
She was a child once;
skinning her knee and Mother was there.
She was a young girl once;
needing a friend and Mother was there.
She was a lady;
wanting the right answers and Mother was there.
She became a bride;
not sure he was Mr. Right and Mother was there.
She is a mother now too;
To whom could she brag? Mother was there.
She became a widow.
The sadness overwhelms her, but Mother,
who was always there is now only in
her mind, only in her heart.
So I hold her once, for Mother.

—Rose Bond

SONG TO A SILENT STAR

Here is no child to sing and dance and pose,
Midget comedienne. This is far more—
The primal innocence of Man; the rose,
Thornless in Eden; all that went before
The glittering Serpent wound his upright way
For the last time, still blest in his bright world
Of harmony with Heaven! Who can say
Why, out of this hushed darkness, one small curled,
Proud golden head gives shadows radiance now;
Why lips, long silent, speak from silence 'till
A listening heart responds? No matter how
The thing is done, a whispered word can fill
The void of time with muted eloquence
Beyond our stridency of sound and sense!

*Written after a showing of some of Mary
Pickford's early films in honor of the
hundredth anniversary of her birth in 1893*

—Mary F. Lindsley

OLD AGE

Eighty-seven I do know,
But remember only a few.
The last of my good buddies,
All have gone of the ones I once knew.

When I saw death as a younger man,
Wishing it would never come.
Not able to picture the years ahead,
Or see there's no race to be won.
No reason for the last seven years lived,
No progress from the body that I'm now with.

The biggest fears I once had,
Are long since gone.
Replaced with a thought that I might live on.

But when I pass away,
At last nothing to fear.
Still others will cry,
Because I'm no longer here.

But I will too,
If they live a long life.
No need for oldness,
No need for a fight.

—W.G. Williams

CLOUDS

There's a movie just above us
Though most don't seem to care
All you have to do is stop, look
up, and then just stare.
You'll see the clouds are shaping
moving to and fro.
There's a different showing everyday
no matter where you go.

—James LeRoy Swafford

WHAT MIGHT HAVE BEEN

We waited too long to make our play
Too many years slipped away

Had we ceased the moment — Perhaps
But now all we have is just our dreams

Fantasies of "What Might Have Been"

—Gene Redemer

FREE TO BE

I think that I will never be
as free as I would like to be.

For days go by so fast you see
I'm not quite sure that I am me.

I like to live my life in full
in spite of all its earthly pull.

Each moment's spent to feel my way
in hopes I will not go astray.

A friend in need I can't deny,
to special calls I oft comply.

The tender care I hope to give
may help another soul to live.

My freedom now I know is part
of all that's in my thankful heart.

—Laurette Bender

ONE FOR DEWEY

Motionless figures surround small
round tables, while melancholy
spirits lumber from the bass.

Rhythm is held captive as the drum
beats steadfast, and fingers begin
to snap in unison as if compelled
against volition.

The virtuoso with hands of ebony
and swollen lip begins to caress
his trumpet with affection fit
for a pharoah's queen.

Cool as an autumn night in full
moon his seductive tone bestows
oceanic feelings of wellness
upon all who listen.

For music is his weapon used for
taming and we are the savage breast.

In memory of Miles Dewey Davis
—William J. Cole

LOST FRIEND

Sorry to hear about your best friend,
I heard you'd be there until the end.
I'm really surprised to see you two apart,
it must be breaking your heart.
I saw your best friend the other day,
it's affecting them in a different way.
They seem to be full of life and laughter,
they really never seem to be better.
Maybe it's for the best that your friendship didn't last,
of course it looks like what happened in the past.
Your friend may feel alone and lost,
but you won't feel used and tossed.

—Teresa A Naugle

SWEET ABOUND

As she glanced about the dim lit room — The music —
The crowd suddenly became a backdrop of muffled
sounds in its own faded atmosphere.

His glazed eyes had fallen upon her — frozen in time.
His statuette remained still, yet inspired.

Moments passed as they suddenly realized, each
had been overcome — captivated by the others
silent stares.

Neither had spoken . . . Neither needed to

The "girl next door" inside of her — unsure to surface.
For tonight, the "city style" had encircled her
identity.

Sutely, she allows her lips to part for a hint
of her smile to invite the next move for him.

His persona — almost direct, as he spoke with a
trembling allurement; assured the ease of
going forward.

Both now transparent . . . Both needing to be
—Mrs. Joyce A. Trent

GOODBYE

Goodbye never comes easy,
it's the end of something dear.
It means I can't look into your eyes,
it means I won't ever hold you near.

I will miss so many things about you,
your laugh, your eyes, your gentle touch,
everything about you that made me want you so much.
I'll miss you more than you can possibly know,
I'll long for the fire that made our love grow.

You always said that I was strong,
so now I must find the strength to go on.
For you have made a choice that does not include me,
so now I must find a way to set myself free.

You will always have a place in my heart,
one that you made right from the start.
A special place made when our love was new,
one that will make me always love you.

Now as we say goodbye, know my feelings are true,
my heart will always want what's best for you.
Have a life full of laughter and dreams that come true,
and remember I will always, always love you!

—Tracy L. Coressel

THE WISE STRANGER

Beside me a stranger sits and so to make conversation I say, "I know today will be a beautiful day."
Without facing me he replies, "I hope it will be."
As I make myself comfortable I say, "I know good things will come my way today."
He replies, "I hope they will."
As I ease back I say, "I know I will be a success in life."
He replies, "I hope you will be."
I look at the stranger and ask, "Why do you say you 'hope' for all these things, are you not sure of the future?"
He turns, faces me, and replies, "I am only sure that at this moment I am alive, the sun is shining, the breeze is softly blowing, and you are speaking to me. When an hour has gone by, will my heart still beat, will the sun continue to shine, will the breeze continue to blow softly, will you still be here?"
I looked at him a while longer, then I turned and without facing him I replied, "I hope so."

—Guillermina Sierra

BIRTH OF A KINGDOM!

The Lord set things in motion, the time had arrived
For His kingdom to be born, so in agony the woman cried
Because she was pregnant, and about to give birth to a child.
But the fiery-colored dragon was standing before her all the while.

So she gave birth to a son, a male who is to shepherd all nations.
And Satan tried to devour him, because it wasn't a happy occasion.
But The Lord saw it all, so the child was caught away to his throne.
And the woman fled into the wilderness, out of the danger zone.

And war broke out in heaven; Michael and his angels,
Did battle with the dragon and put him in grave danger.
And no longer was a place found for him in God's Heaven above.
So down, the great dragon, the one called devil and Satan, down he was hurled.

And his demon angels were hurled right down with him.
Down from the heavens and to death they were condemned.
And the salvation and the powers and kingdom had come to pass.
But Satan is angry and the world of mankind he continues to harass.

Yes be glad you heavens and woe for the earth, for our battle is still on.
But Satan has a very short time, so now it won't be long.
So stand firm and fight the fine fight, if possible, right down to the grave.
And soon now we'll hear The Lord say, "Well done, good and faithful slave."

—Armether Swift Deanes

MY LITTLE GRANDDAUGHTERS AND KITTEN BOOTSIE

"My little granddaughters" are so much fun to watch playing each day.
With their kitten named Bootsie, they run and play.

Little feet running and playing having so much
fun, and laughter to see.
My little granddaughters having fun with their
kitten named Bootsie.

At night when little ones are just all worn out
from playing all day.
Little Bootsie too — lays at the foot of their bed
just waiting for them to awaken and play.

As soon as they awaken — and they all run down the stairs —
Little Bootsie the kitten is waiting and a big
bowl of milk is waiting there.

The granddaughters leave for school each day.
Bootsie lays by the window until they return to play.

I believe God made kittens for little ones to run and play.
A kitten for little girls — for boys a little dog to
run and play each day.

Dedicated to my granddaughters, Heidi and Heather

—Colleen D. Kistler

THE BREEZE

The breeze blew through the weeds
The breeze blew up the hill into
    the trees
And in one of those trees was a
    cat with fleas
The fleas blew all around in
    the breeze
Wow what a breeze said the
    fleas.

    —Amie Schell

MEASURING SUCCESS

How does one measure success?
There are many ways, I guess.
Is your main concern wealth?
Or do you value most your health?
Do you put others care and needs
First when doing your good deeds?

Consider children who are abused
The elderly and others oft misused
And don't forget to heed
The plight of homeless, those in need.
For disaster will always strike
The rich, the poor, all alike

Our youth are not immune
Many of them are not in tune
And don't consider right from wrong
We must teach them to be strong
Will they bring peace, violence or sorrow?
For they are the citizens of tomorrow.

    —Alice Marshall

ASHES IN THE WIND

I want to ride on rainbows
Where eagles soar and peak.
I want to feel the pebbles
As I tumble down a creek.

I want to be the thunder
Or streak across the sky.
To be the dew upon a rose
Or tear in someone's eye.

I want to freeze and sparkle
Fall gently from the air,
To kiss the heads of babies
And snuggle in their hair.

I want to be the wind
A soft and gentle breeze.
The moon up in the heavens
That shines upon the seas.

I want to be the sun
To warm the gardener's soil,
To give him gifts of food for life
For all his sweat and toil.

I want to be beside you
To hear your new born's cry,
And when you're sad or lonely
To kiss tears from your eye.

So mix me up with flower seeds,
And take me way up high.
Then let me go upon the wind,
So I shall never die.

    —Teri Anna Crampton

BEST FRIENDS

The best friend I've ever known
    Is the paper that I'm writing on!
One can tell a person his secret words
    Then find out it's like telling a myna bird!
They don't listen or talk or even guess,
    But when they do listen, they tell someone else!

    —Amy Dalton Napier

PREPARATORY

They walked in silence, single file
    Their eyes and heads downcast
The air was crisp and clean and cold
It chilled their beings and their souls

Bitter breezes lashed out playing
Preparing them for pious praying
Mantles and sashes on each were swaying
Clutching breviaries their lips were saying, Mea Culpa

In Nomine Patris, Et Filii, Et Spiritus Sancti
They began the day ahead
Their eyes now lifted heavenward
Prepare for us Lord, your daily bread

Domine Non Sum Dignus
In Him they place their trust
Their lives are dedications
Their love a fervent thrust

Pax Vobiscum my children
Your prayers are heard on high
Enrich your faith with daily grace
Hope and charity all in place —
                    Amen.

    —C.V. LaCroix

ME

The sun shines bright upon my skin so white.
    Like a cloud or hymn that holds the gentle melody,
that calms the crying baby in me.

Sometimes I'm not so white but black getting bashed
to and fro. Who's getting angry and so mad
that thunder flashes from its depths.

Sometimes I'm friendly like a clown at work
in a park.
But watch when the clown is done with work
for the day. I'm even funnier and like to play.

I have a smile that's as soft as a cat's purring,
but my frown is as sharp as a dog's bite.

I'm a leaf floating to be free
To float upon the wind lipped currents as calm
as the middle of the sea.

I'm a chair ready to be sat upon, but bite
back with careful thought and skill.
Be careful what you say to me.
I like to sting when no one is thinking of me
like a bee protecting its hive

I'm like a rubber band
I will bounce back not to your hand
but to stand on my own two feet
not to wobble not to leave.

I go to every place I can
like a bird upon the wind.
Hoping to find the perfect place to
settle my own land.

    —Christine Ann Tierney (Cat)

TO BONNIE AND JASON ON YOUR WEDDING DAY

Saturday, September 11, 1993, a special day in your life,
Bonnie Jean and Jason Randal today you become man & wife.
You'll start your travels down that road, hand and hand you'll go,
Sharing all your love today, and not worrying much about tomorrow.

There are some special people that could not help share your day,
The good Lord up above asked them to come with him and stay.
But we know they are watching you, they're as proud as they can be,
You both were special in their lives, they loved you don't you see.

Memories of years gone by, we shall hold in our hearts most dear,
And I'm sure there will be many more as we pass from year to year.
Bon and Jay, may your wishes and all your dreams come true,
You're special kids, Mom & Dad Koehner truly love both of you.

—Gary L. Koehner

DISTANT FRIENDS

Distance can be an enemy, like a weapon; exterminating close friendships with the death of communication. Distance can be a friend, like the sun; warming one's heart with rays of distant warmth as in the form of unspoken words. Distance sometimes seems to change our internal heart. The feelings we felt. The way we used to talk. Is it . . . is it . . . is it just because the distance was apart. I hope not! I still have many thoughts of us. As clear as reflections off a smooth pond. Yes, memories; memories like the reflections coming from the surface of that crystal pond. Ever so clear, yet . . . seeming to have been disturbed by a tearful drop, a distant tear drop. By me or you, I know not. Creating a wave in our friendship that was once only a touch apart. If for any reason I have done you wrong, forgive me; I'm sorry, and if you have done me wrong all is forgiven; don't worry. I can never condemn. So let not any distance cause us sad, tearful thoughts, making ripples in our friendship like ripples in that pond. Instead; let it add one tear drop to that pond and increase those reflected memories we so dearly enjoy. Because we both know sadful and cheerful tears make up that pond, even though there be ripples, many from the heart. No matter how close or afar we are, REAL FRIENDS: NEVER EVER PART!

—Mark A. Polomski

WHAT IS A FRIEND?

A friend is someone who defends you when the entire world is against you.

A friend is someone who listens to everything you have to say when others turn a deaf ear.

A friend is someone you can take your troubles to a hundred times and welcome you every time with open arms.

A friend is someone who will always leave their door open to you, regardless of how busy they are.

A friend is someone who remembers you every day of the year.

A friend is someone who calls you on rainy days just to say hello.

A friend is someone who gives you a hug of reassurance when things aren't going your way.

A friend is someone you love in a special way.

A friend is someone you cherish being with most of the time.

A friend is a very special gift from God.

If you can say that you have one friend, it is saying a lot.

Would you be my friend?

—Steve DePola

LOVE

What is love
I often wonder.
Is it like a storm
lightning and thunder
Can it be rough
just like the seas
or warm and tender
like a soft summer breeze
How will you know
if you find the right man
you'll feel a tingle
when he touches your hand
True love must come
from deep in your heart
to be shared forever
till death do you part

—Deborah Aldrich

BUTTERFLY FOR NAN

Sky clear
Sun bright
Grounds green
Trees stately

Family gathered
Emotions shared
Words unspoken
Hearts mourning

Generations locked
Traditions sealed
Burdens relieved
Spirit renewed

Prayers uttered
Praises accepted
Goodness confirmed
Pain forgiven

Life changed
Struggles shed
Energy Released
Butterfly gliding

—Mary A. Duffy

FIRE

Burn my heart.
Burn my soul.
Touch me deep,
Where passion grows.

Set my mind ablaze.
My yearnings grow
white hot.

Scorch me, yet
I feel no pain.
The flames lick.
My blood starts
to burn.

Now, I'm just a
burning ember.
I'm smouldering
In your wake.

Let me be.
My flames have died.
My heart is now
cold ash.

—Lisa K. Loven

GOODBYE

Your presence lingers here with me,
although you're far away.
And in case we never meet again,
there's something I must say.

There's one thing to remember, should
we ever drift apart.
You'll always have a special place
here within my heart.

Should you ever feel unloved, and
feel like no one cares.
Think of me and the love we made
and know you're in my prayers.

For in my life you may not be, but
in my heart you'll always stay.
And if you're never loved again,
you sure are loved today.

—Donna E. Cooper

FORGOTTEN

Forgotten
a lost soul among bodies of nothing
exploring realms of mystery
discovering nothing
uttering strange sounds—
trying to express opinions
that state nothing except fact
without thinking
never unprepared
relying on instinct
which they are without
nonunderstanding beasts of nature
professing wisdom that crumbles
collapses into piles of rubble
no one cares about ones lost
they sink in a pit of despair
never to rise again
because no one cares
the selfish hate
destroys the world

—Valerie Moring, age 13

A MOMENT IN TIME

I look into your eyes
and see . . .
The reflection of beauty
In your soul.
The love there,
Before fate took you away.

Many years have gone by . . .
Do you remember . . .
The words we did not say?
But our hearts knew.

Our lives go on
As though we had never met.
But sometimes . . . in quiet moments,
I remember . . .
The reflection of beauty
In your soul.

And it was good . . .
To have had that moment
In time . . .
To have known you.

—Gwen Hutchinson

DEATH

Death is the slumber that never ends.
Death is when we are reunited with all our friends.
Death is the sickness that's never cured.
Death is the cry that's never heard.
Death is when you're no longer a being.
Death is the end of everything.

—Wren Prante, age 11

LITTLE BOY

The little boy grows in a house full of tears
A house full of pain, of violence and fears
An innocent boy, stuck only with dreams
Abhorring reality and all that it means
Failing to find any compassion at home
The boy will soon learn that happy's alone
Isolation will soon be this child's best friend
Never show his emotion, stand tall to the end
The seasons roll by, his lesson well learned
The past is unveiled, may never be turned
He promised himself, never be like his dad
To never ignite all his passion when mad
But his anger now erupts with a passion untold
Trapped in the madness of Daddy's own mold

—Stephen James Baetge

WAR IN VIETNAM

The men were in Vietnam
They were fighting for Uncle Sam
Some will live and some will die
    Many men's wives; will pout and cry

Some are fighting on land and sea
    Just think; they are doing it; for you and me
I wish I could help fight; for that land
    One day; you're going to have to make your own stand

Life is hard; everywhere we go
    Some people don't care to know
They will all learn; on the right day
    Just think; why do we live this way

War; is just a waste of people and earth
    Right now; some women are giving birth
There are new born everyday
    Pray to the Lord; they don't have to live this way

—Danny Wooten

SUICIDAL THOUGHTS

Why must I live in this world of hell.
All seems bad, and nothing seems well.
Does God hate me? Has He condemned my soul?
Why did the world hurt me? That's what I
    want to know.
You trust someone, and they slap you in the
    face.
They burden you with their hate. You feel
    disgrace.
So why go on living when there's so much
    "why."
I'd rather end it now and die.
But wait, don't you see
    that my soul's in anguish,
    and I need you to help me.
There are others like me that we need you
    to save.
Don't wait forever. Don't send us to our grave.

—Daniel Rees

ALL MY LIFE

I think I've loved you all my life.
Was there a time when you weren't here?
Even in life long ago, I sensed you standing near.
I close my eyes and visualize your face within my hand,
but in a place so long ago, another time, another land.
In my heart I've always held a special waiting place,
reserved for who, I did not know, until I saw your face.
An empty void filled by your love, a love I've often felt.
With an icy heart I waited . . . you caused the ice to melt.
You've threaded and entwined yourself around my heart so
bare. You allowed the love to flow by taking time to care.
Have I loved you all my life?
I do believe it's true. I know that I've been waiting all my
life just for you. Then one day the magic grew. You asked me
to be your wife. Because you "Whistled Dixie" I know I'll love
you . . . all my life

—Kimberly Jacobsen

DASHING DANCING DOLPHINS

Dashing, dancing, dolphins dive so free,
it makes me wish that one were me.
I see the dolphins jump a wave, and
through tuna nets they are saved.
Now that old nets have ceased,
and the dolphins' numbers now increase, so that
dashing, dancing, dolphins dive in the ocean blue,
and in a pair there are two,
and who can help them? You!!!

Dashing, dancing, dolphins dive
with the whales and dance and dive to get some pails
of tuna fish that makes their dish.
If I were one,
this is my wish
to get some tuna for my dish
and drink some water from the sky, and wake up mornings with a sigh,
where dashing, dancing, dolphins dive.

—Billy L. Delaney, age 11

A STARRY EVENING PLAIN

White washed clapboards bound with love
Porch boards sanded by loving feet
Stories etched by rocker's rungs
A family's songs forgotten sung

Generations entertained by anecdotes and fireflies
Now cold and buried in my past
Only Grandma's voice does last
Those ancient, warm molasses tones

Now I gaze at grass grown high
Where stood a shack; home under sky
Collecting years as people died — amidst a starry evening plain

Four corner stones all that remain
Of many links that made my chain
Each stone a generation slain
I hear their cry in wind's refrain

You are my anchor when I'm adrift
Parting grasses as I sift
Through hallowed ground where sprang my seed
Dirt floor, though fertile — poverty
This land, their blood it fills my veins — amidst my starry evening plain

—N. Ken Owens

REALITY

A step forward, two steps back
Violence is growing, education lacks
Goal to become one, reality divided
Mind's open, thoughts one sided
Helping enemy, fighting one another
Assisting them, killing our brother
Brain's there, try using it friend
Common sense, or it's the end

—Latanya M. Joseph

OUR FLAG

Our flag is white for the guiding light.
Our flag is red for the blood we shed.
Our flag is blue because of me and you.
That beautiful flag, Red, White, and
Blue.

The flag may burn. The flag may rip.
  But we will never lose our grip.
   On what is right and what is wrong.
But when our flag is gone
     We will still go marching on.

—Sarah Key

All my life I've dreamed of someone
like you . . .
Someone who understands me —
And accepts me the way I am!
Someone who will listen
when I'm down and need a friend.
Someone who cares about the things
I do,
And understands when I don't know
what's right and wrong.
Someone to hold my hand when
I cry.
And say it's gonna be alright!
Someone to be there through thick
and thin.
Someone like a dream,
that someone is you!

—D.L. Roark

LET — US

That feeling
We lay our blessings upon this world
Let's take up and share some sweet self
Climactic ecstacies
Connections of our souls
This ain't no magic trick
Just share this space with me
Awhile,
Play puppet and master awhile
You can pull my strings
I'll allow that
This game's give & take
And take some more
This is what I'm living for
Like the ultimate ambush
You're playing me
I'm setting the rules

—Keith C. Tulk

OLD GLORY COMES THROUGH

As the years have come and gone my love and devotion lingers on, challenged at the highest degree with death lurking in the wings, from out of nowhere courage did appear! What a view I saw "OLD GLORY" blowing in the breeze, saying there is a message for you! Must stand tall and fight is the name of the game, you're a winner and give up isn't the way. Must remember to keep the faith, in OLD GLORY she will lead the way!

—Mrs. Clara M. Gange

TOGETHER AGAIN

Tears of loneliness fall as I look upon my wall
I have memories of things dear but none of them
   are very near.
All my friends were left behind as I left to
   make a career mine.
Home is so far away but I think about it day
   by day.
Time is spent watching out my window
Hoping that the phone will ring and someone
   will say, "Hello"
People go past my door by and by some even
   stop in to say, "Hi"
When I hear your voice on the phone for a
   moment I don't feel so alone.
But when I put the receiver down my heart,
   soul, and face begin to frown.
As I sit on my bed and shut my eyes
I think about you and I
When will we be together again
I would be so much happier then
Sometimes I even regret that I ever left
   but never fret
I'll stick it out until the end
And we can be together again.

—Janette A. Benner (Peak)

BEFORE I LEFT

In my suffering madness
   My heart has skipped a beat
No longer am I with you
   Now my nights they seem like weeks

I held you in my arms
   I gazed into your eyes
It was our last encounter
   Before we said goodbyes

'Twas dawn when we last touched
   Somewhat scared to tell the truth
Said goodbye but all too quickly
   No eloquent words could I produce

I often questioned why
   But never followed through
Forgetting but **one** thing
   The last time I saw you

How formal our departure
   The magic scared to shine
Before I left, and now I know
   We should have kissed goodbye

*Conjured in memory of the morning of April 30, 1993
In Lieu of Tanya D. Kohls, Calgary, Alberta*

—Ted W. Wiedener

TEARS

We shed tears when we have a broken heart
or when our whole world falls apart.
Tears look like rain
but they're only there to hide the pain.
They also fall down when there is joy,
like over a birth of a baby boy.
Each baby born bears a tear
to tell you of his fear.
Some children shed tears of hunger
because they have no food.
Everyone sheds a tear now and then,
but just remember you always have a friend.
You may not know this friend, but he is there,
and no matter what happens, he will always care.
So when you are feeling blue,
just remember JESUS is there for you.

—Connie O'Malley

BOUNDARIES

Our lives are full of random motion
A path to follow becomes our potion
To lead the way when faced with a choice
Maintain the pattern to quell the voice

If to stray from what's in stone
The conscience to pay and therefore atone
Filled with anxiety unable to comprehend
Rigidity is sought depressing a bend

When faced with what is not common sight
A quiver abounds as we attempt a flight
Remain in control is the motto we bare
For if to falter we do not dare

Attempts often made for that change of pace
To venture beyond what we could not face
Experience the unknown arouses fear within
Forge ahead in hopes to begin

From this we learn the path is not so straight
The bounds we surpassed now become our fate
Allowing such change enhances our self worth
We stray, yet come back with ultimate rebirth

—Kelli M. Smith

TO MY SON

You were my wish upon a star,
Now I wonder where you are.

I was so young and full of hope,
I prayed to God to help me cope.

To make me wise and strong,
So I could teach you right from wrong.

When I first held you in my arms,
I thought I could protect you from all harm.

Now you are growing so very fast,
But Son my love will always last.

There have been times when I have cried tears
of sadness and of pain,

Feeling I have failed you and your youth
I can't regain.

I have tried to be a better parent,
For I know at times I have been errant.

Son, though we don't always see eye to eye,
I will love you until the day I die.

—Cheryl Fredrick

FOR THOMAS

And still:
I take you in each living breath.
On the tip of my tongue; taste and texture.
With the palms of my hands; flesh and bone.
I know you in all shades and sound.
My good senses turned,
by love's welcome trespass.

—L.A. Sailor

CHUCK

His smile is like a bright light,
Shining as bright as the sun is bright,
It warms my heart to see the smile,
    Of someone who cares,
He cares so much that his eyes,
    Shine, shine, shine, like a light,
His eyes are like the midnight
        sky.
They dance like stars when,
He looks me in the eyes and
    says the words "I love you."
His hair is as blonde as a,
    Towel is white, that's why I
Love his laugh, cause it's,
        Out of sight.

*Dedicated to my wonderful boyfriend,
Charles Kent. I love you Chuck.*

—Diane

THE TALKING WATERS

The tongue of the talking waters,
    Beside a flowing brook,
Bubbles notes in merry melody,
    That softly command we listen/look.

The metres of the flowing waters,
    Maintain a constant beat,
Playing upon our senses,
    In tunes both rich and sweet.

Gazing into the shadowed stream,
    With rocks varied in shape and hue,
Snuggled into each tiny cranny,
    Revealing beauty with awe anew.

The sturdy, stalwart, granite boulders,
    Along the banks form dikes,
To contain the fern and flora,
    Of Azalea, Pussy Paws and likes.

The sentinels of this forest scene,
    The majestic Lodge Pole Pines,
Stand straight, tall and unyielding,
    Against the bright blue sky, like tines.

Red fir spread their dainty limbs,
    As ballerinas poised to begin,
Dancing to the waters music,
    With graceful pirouettes and spins.

Above all this, the sun spreads
    The white and puffy clouds apart,
To let shine its radiant beams,
    Upon the brook where fishes dart.

Thank God, for these precious scenes,
    That transform the heart and mind,
For the waters that feed each life,
    For His, "Blessed be the ties that bind."

—J.S. Titlow

MY FAITH

If I should lose my eyes today,
my course is His to chart;
If I should lose my ears, I know
I'd hear Him in my heart.

If I should lose my hands, and feet,
He'd carry me along;
If I should lose my voice, I trust
my heart would sing my song.

If I should lose all friends, and wealth,
I could withstand the cost,
but, if I lose my soul, I know
I have no hope. I'm lost!

So if I lose all sight, and sound,
I'll take Him by the hand,
and with my faith firmly anchored, I
shall see the Promised Land.

—Ruth J. Dikeman

PEOPLE TODAY

This world seems to be falling apart,
it seems that some have no heart.
People criticize as others walk by,
how people can be so cruel,
I wonder why?
Blacks & whites,
Mexicans & Jews,
People don't realize,
they are just like me & you.
Racism is a favorite word today,
whenever something happens,
that's what we scream & say.
I'm so tired of the wars & riots,
when what we need
is some peace & quiet.
I wish the world would
just sing the song,
"Why can't we all just get along?"

—Jennifer L. McNally

CAROUSEL

Long ago . . . in the halcyon days
When time wore carefree faces
The summer star was the red trolley car
That took us to make-believe places.

A magical trip . . . in a scarlet coach
Promising princely pleasure
For, at the end of the streetcar line
Stood a most improbable treasure . . .

Round it was . . . with a towered roof
And banners of Camelot's knaves
As it turned . . . the Calliope played
A song called, "Over the Waves."

The horses, painted in pastel hues,
Pranced on a golden pole . . .
Hooves were raised in rollicking gait
And fantasy touched the soul.

Charming, disarming Carousel
Chariot of my heart
You make me feel like a child again . . .
You're my dormant dreams' fresh start.

—Patricia Gallagher Gibbs

MY PERSONAL SUN

One of the reasons my life is so fun
Is I know that I have my personal sun
Wherever I go, my sun will be there
What makes it unique is I don't have to share
From early morning with its bright sunrise
To evening with its glorious demise
On days when the sun is shining so bright
Just being alive is a special delight
But on those days when the sun doesn't shine
No heart on earth is sadder than mine
When the clouds disappear, and the sun shows its face
Once more I am happy, and my heart starts to race
For all you people whose life needs some fun
Just remember you have a personal sun

—John R. Jensen

I WILL BE THERE

When you need a friend I will be there.
When you need a friend who will always care.
When you are sad and shed a tear.
When you are afraid and have much fear.
When you are alone and your heart feels pain.
When you are left standing in the rain.
When you feel hurt and you feel sorrow.
When you need a smile to maybe borrow.
When you are frail and you are weak.
When there is nothing more to seek.
When you've lost all faith and you've lost all hope.
I will be there to help you cope.
I will be there to ease the pain.
I will be there to stop the rain.
I will be there to wipe the tear.
I will be there to take away the fear.
I will be there to strengthen you.
I will be there to listen too.
No matter what the reason is.
I will be there to help you through.

—Jennifer Barber

SIGNS OF APPROACHING DEATHS

I wondered, is this the last time
to see the sun rise and to see it set
behind the magnificent mountains of peace
will the moon shine its fullest tonight
and will a wish upon a special star
be granted at that moonlight hour

As a moment of silence had been broken
by a wind of rushing air
and as the clouds tend to come and go
it's then, that I remembered my past life
it seemed to have been a precious life too

Remembering my loved one
knowing how far away our love must be
but realizing now, how close we are in spirit
lays my understanding heart, a soft one too
my loving and tender heart
has always been reaching out to you, my love
wherever you may be
as my heart lays to rest, I will stand by your side
as long as both the sun and the moon shall endure.

—Jessica D'Asaro

ROMANTIC ELOQUENCE: DON'T LET IT GO

Epilogue:
***
The future holds the untold; of which only you can unfold . . .
***

Am I the fire of your light
The day of your nights
The blood of your veins
And the aches of your pains

Let me see the freedom of your flight
Let me guide you in our plight
I'll be the bubble in your wine
I'll be the rebel if you're mine
I'll be all that is fine
And I'll be kindness undefined

I'll be that which is yet to be told;
Let me be that which you unfold

—Ted Wiedener

It begins in my thoughts proliferating
incessantly there I ponder of you,
My fiery heart enclosed by a cadaverous body
pines for your presence, your warmth.
It is lonely; it is cold.
I am afraid to look for you.
Darkness arrives with panic, my eyes search the nothingness.
Imagine. In my dreams I whisper a prayer echoes your name surrounding. Placidly I await.
Your coming I recognize, yet unfamiliar, your warmth sporadically teases me.
Forced to strain, my incompetent eyes are anxious, hindering from the light of the moon.
In my dreams your comely face appears, lucid eyes by the stars, yet opaque of your thoughts,
pierce me; yet do not touch.
My heart burns the coldness; I long to reach, I long to touch, my fingers ache to feel.
Parting my lips to whisper, but silence still . . . words need not emerge
Inside it is disturbingly vociferous, a perturbed soul; cannot break a barrier.
Please help me . . . hold me . . . Despondency apologizes.
I raise my hand as you fade, no more can I see.
The loud haunting scream, abrupts, reverberating,
suddenly encompasses me with long arms of darkness.
I am lost and cold once again.

—Peipei Alena Yuan

MIGHTY MAX OUR MASTIFF KID

Mighty Max was his name, Having fun was his game
He came one day in the month of November, Just to see if he could become a member
This household of ours oh so quaint, Upon on our world he would paint
He had teeth that showed and a tail that was bent, But in spite of it all he was heaven sent
To bed we took him when he was small, Now Mighty Max takes it all
With a face only a mother could adore, That Mighty Max slept, but not on the floor
Only one eighty one, or so they say, But to me feels like a ton of clay
My foot is his pillow, my chair he does sit, In times of quiet when we're all at our wits
He comes to our side as though to say, What are we going to do today
That Mighty Max the misfit dog, Who brought you home to lie like a log
The fireplace is warm all cozy and nice, So please dear Max please think twice
The bed is nice and so are you, But Mom needs the bed a time or two
Mighty Max my shadow everywhere, Why do you want to share my fare
The table is all lovely and nice, For Max is expecting to be fed twice
Never a left over do we have, the frig is bare, Because Mighty Max is always there
If by now you haven't heard, Mighty Max was only third
To the show ring he did not go, but home to us to grow and grow
Mighty Max that Mastiff dog, will always lie there like a log
He shares our home, our food and bed, But thinks we are the guests instead.

—Delores D. Hanson

A PLACE CALLED LOVE

I watched you while you slept and
much to my surprise.
What I've denied, for so long now, I've
come to realize.

I can't fight it anymore, the feeling's
just too strong.
I never thought I could love again,
but then you came along.

With more than just my hands, you
taught me how to feel.
And all the pain I've held on to, you've
somehow helped to heal.

You took me to a place, I haven't
been to for so long.
A place I've been afraid to go, a place
where I belong.

—Donna E. Cooper

STOLEN MOMENTS

Stolen moments . . . in the night
  is the lonely hearts
    dance of sheer delight.
Don't look for more
  than the fleeting moments
    or you'll spoil its delight.
Stolen moments . . . in the night
  adding blissful excitement
    to a lonesome life.
Loving for only the moment
  with pure delight.
    Two dancing hearts are
      shadows of stolen moments
        in the shimmering moon light.
Don't reach for the stars
  there're far too far . . .
    it's only moments
      in the moon light,
  And love for the moment
    it's sparkling delight.

—M. Marie Bettger

WOMAN

At the beginning of creation
After God created man
He thought he needed something more
To complete his master plan.

So he took a rib from Adam
And from this created Eve
To walk with Adam side by side
Through all eternity.

For a man without a woman
Even though it doesn't show
Is nothing more than just a part
A woman makes him whole.

So treat your woman tenderly
Use gentle loving care
Don't try to be her "Master"
That isn't why she's there.

She's there to be your loving mate
Keep her always by your side
And she will never rue the day
That she became your bride.

—Dean D. Sevey

THOUGHTS INTO WISDOM

We talk about understanding
And about all the books we've read,
But what good is all your reading
When it's not maintained in the head

You see wisdom is such a strange thing
It gives fore sight of things before,
You'll see the success that it will bring
After it unlocks the hidden door.

Nothing is a well kept secret
When you let someone else know,
This is their whole life feature
Just to say didn't I tell you so.

Everyone hasn't gone to college
It doesn't mean you're really a dumb bell,
You can be one of the greatest scholar
But there are some things you shouldn't ever tell.

—Lindsey R. Smith

SEEING

You look into my eyes and see as so few have,
There is a beach caressed by Sea Wind,
And over years, wave upon wave of
Salty tears have painted the sand and dried unknown.

You see as you wisp along the beach,
Feeling inner warmness, reaching out
Gathering hands full of love, letting it sift
Through fingers for a time to know its softness.

The Sea Wind feels what you do,
Understanding man, like sand, travels the beach
Looking for the other voyage,
Between death, and birth

You touch, and the wind stirs,
Closeness, unshared by others, giving and taking,
Water on the sand, ebbing and flowing,
As one in love.

—Herbert T. Smith

CAROLINE

She knew him all of her life and one year.
He was a tall man, but gaunt, never filled in;
he was an old man, but young, never used up;
he was a hard man, but gentle . . .
a sad man who smiled.
She mewed like a kitten curled deep in his lap,
but made no sound when he walked away.
And she hungered for him one year and all of her life:
she became a young woman, but old, mostly used up;
tall of soul, but mostly filled in;
hard and still . . .
a gentle woman who sadly smiled.
She bore her packs then like a mule,
never curled again in contentment.
She carried her hunger like oats,
feeding on it slowly.
She held her sorrow like a baby
who stayed dumb and never left home.
All of her life and one year and all of her life.

—Lesly Plyler Johnson

Love is a feeling that comes from the heart.
Sometimes love can tear us apart.
Love can also be hard to find.
Sometimes love can be so unkind.
Love can help to keep you strong.
Sometimes love can be so wrong.
Love can often be hard to explain.
Sometimes love can cause great pain.
Love can be bad, love can be good.
Sometimes love is misunderstood.
Love affects all, both woman and man.
Sometimes I understand love the best I can.
Love is a great feeling once it is found.
Love can pick you up when you're down.
Love can cause so many changes.
That's why love and I are strangers.

—Terri Bunker

UNHAPPY RELATIONSHIPS

It was great when I first came here,
But the fairy tale life soon disappeared.
I moved away from my family and friends,
It seemed all the good times came to an end.

I stay home all day,
Because there's just no other way.
He works all day in the hot sun,
And he's very hungry when the day is done.
You ask him to help you out with the chores,
And he declines more and more.

I love him so very much,
But sometimes I can't stand to be touched.
I feel he doesn't appreciate me,
Maybe there's someone or something
else he wants me to be.

Right now, I feel like leaving for good,
It's only sometimes I think I should.
I guess living life on your own,
Sometimes is better than feeling alone.

—TEE

BUT A SINGLE TEAR

*** Epilogue ***

For this is how I feel today
A today that is not a day
But an eternity

*** ***

The Tear In My Eye
Cries For No One
It Rains Down My Brow
    For No Reason
An Empty Reason
    For My Friend Is Not There

I Cast A Shadow
    For There Is But One
I Long For The Time
    To Make A Path To The Sea
And Imprint Upon The Shells and Pebbles
    But That Is A Dream Without An End
An End That Will Never Come To Be
    And Only My Footprints Are Washed Away
By The Passing Of The Tide Into Forever
    Forever Forgotten By No One . . . But Me

—Ted Wiedener

PASSAGE TO PARADISE

The Angel of Death comes not as a
grim reaper cloaked in dark and dreary
cloths, with a mean and determined
face (Sounds more like a bad actor).

She will appear in a Vision of beauty
and grace that transcends the senses.

And She will lead us into the
LOVING LIGHT of THE DIVINE PRESENCE
where we will bathe in all of the
Majesty of Paradise as we are Cradled
in the Soul of the Universe.

—Gene Redemer

TOGETHER ALONE

I look over across at you,
And you look past me.
I want to hold your hand,
But you have it curled upon your lap,
I want to talk to you,
But you can not hear my whispers.
I want to hug you so badly,
But you're so far away sitting next to me.
I want to hear we're inseparable,
But you're so distant, beside me.
I don't want to be lonely together,
Only alone together, forever.

—Frank E. Wright, Jr.

MY WISH

When I die I ask of thee,
    to bury my ashes under a tree.
A tree that flowers in the spring,
    a tree where birds can nest and sing.
A tree to shade a new born deer,
    a tree to have a picnic near.
A hearty tree that kids can climb,
    when school is out in summer time.
And when again it's time to die,
    Beneath a rotting tree I'll lie.
I'll wait with patience,
    for I know,
        some day another tree will grow.

—Amy Elizabeth Mailliard

THE HEART NEVER STOPS TO SLEEP

That important part that keeps us going
And continues that rhythmic beat,
You'll never find it being a bit boring
Yet the heart never stops to sleep.

Don't over load it with lots of stress
With good care it's bound to keep,
Please don't put it through a test
Because the heart never stops to sleep.

It takes on all the pains you have
And it never becomes obsolete,
Sometimes we make it very sad
But the heart never stops to sleep.

All those years you abuse it so
And it becomes so very very weak,
At its final stage it refuses to go
Now the heart will stop to sleep.

—Lindsey R. Smith

MY BABY BOY

I rock my sweet baby to sleep tonight
In hopes that he dreams with all delight
A darling little boy with so much spice
A soul so lifting, he brightened my life.

—Kimberly Ann L. Brown

TO YOU I GIVE LIFE

To you I give strength from up above
To you I give friendship, undying love
To you I give happiness forevermore
To you I give devotion, a new opened door

From you I take sorrow, you'll never cry
From you I take misery, you'll never die
From you I take pain that cuts like a knife
To you I give everything, most I give life

—Michelle Bromley

A FRIEND

You, my friend, you are the one.
You are my rainbow. You are my sun.
You brighten my day when I'm feelin' blue.
Don't really know what I'd do without you.

You are there when I need to cry.
If you weren't there, I'd probably die.
You are the star. You are the rain.
You always listen yet you never complain.

You see, my friend, you just don't see —
   just how much you mean to me.
So I'm tellin' you now and don't forget.
Ours is a friendship to never regret.

And again, I say you're a terrific friend.
You're very special. Let's not let it end.
The fun we have, the time we spend,
I guess is how you describe "A FRIEND!"

—Lisa Marie Streu

THROUGH THE LOVE OF LIVING GRACE

Washed in the blood of the Lamb
Slain for the sins of man.
Red as the crimson sun
Victory over death He won.

The agony of the Master
Awe filled figure, on a cross.
Gaze upon the Man Of Sorrow
Flaming blood, cleanse wanton dross.

The Lamb Of God so smitten
Gave His life for souls of men.
Through the power of the Father
We'll meet Jesus once again.

Not as the little baby
Born in the town of Bethlehem.
Nor as the humble Galilean
Pleading for the souls of men.

Jesus crowned, Our King Triumphant
We shall see Him face to face.
We will reign with God the Father
Through the Love Of Living Grace.

—Patricia Ahnstrom

Shaun,
Moody, spiked, different, and withdrawn,
Son of Kathy and Steve who've been together long,
Lover of music, Pink Floyd, and Z's,
Who's happy, depressed, and full of Golly G's,
Who needs a good stereo, records, and her number,
Who give nothing, something, and maybe some lumber,
Who fears no one, someone, and a good Ala Ka Zot!
Who would like to see Iron Maiden, Pink Floyd, and
Someone who's the size of a dot,
Resident of Lehigh, Florida, a great place to leave,
Whose last name is Henderson, a great guy I preceive!

*Dedicated to the people who gave me
everything — God, Mom, and Dad —
I love you all.*

—Shaun Henderson

FRIENDSHIPS

My friendship with Martin no longer exists,
We don't speak to each other at all.
I thought we'd be friends for the rest of our lives,
But now I don't think that is true.

It all started when I sat with Melissa,
We sat there and talked at a game.
Martin was jealous and worried about me,
Because of my friendship with her.

A couple days later he wrote her a note,
Saying I wasn't his friend.
I started to cry and wonder why,
He could say such a thing about me.

Melissa and him were a close couple,
But now they don't speak to each other.
I think it's my fault for what happened to them,
And I can't stop wondering why.

It has been months since I've talked to him,
And I wish that it was all over.
But now that I know we won't ever be friends,
I must learn that our friendship is ended.

—James A. Pratt, age 17

THE OTHER SIDE OF THE FENCE

The buses roar up, and the kids all shout,
school is over, and they're finally out.
   I am so close, I can see their faces,
and watch their games and observe their races
   I've seen so many happy events,
as I keep my vigil just over the fence.

   The parties & proms have gone on without me,
but my presence there, was not meant to be.
   My distance from them all, is so immense
even tho I'm resting, just over the fence.

They don't know it, but I've been where they trod,
I graduated first, into the hands of God.
   A part of me is lying, beneath the grass,
but my heart is moving, along with my class.

   The music is playing, they're ready to commence,
as I solemnly watch from my side of the fence.
When diplomas are given out, and each hand reaches
      out to take it,
I hope they give a thought to the girl who
      didn't make it.

*In loving memory of precious Angela Jeanne Cary,
   1972-1985 — Class of '90*

—Jeanne Thacher

War is a terrible fight.
Killing is a nightmare, gives a fright.
I don't want killing anymore.
Just because it happened, in the Civil War.

In war, people kill.
What a nightmare, gives a chill.
Bombing, shooting what a fright,
From Fall to Spring, and Day to Night.

—Erik Corby, age 12

WAR

Standing in their formal line
And they begin to fall behind
Distracted from their little war
They're torn apart at the core
Fighting for an unknown cause
Knowing it's for someone else's flaws
It's a useless thing, they know
But soon the blood begins to flow

Now the war is over
And the people have been sobered
Tired of fighting but now it's too late
No time to save those who faced fate
Tears uselessly fall from the sky
And like the time before, they begin to cry.

—Ivy Long

WHATEVER OF LIVING

I shall live my life as full as I may
to the very end of my sensate day,
greeting the dawn on a pearly hill
when all but a singing bird is still.
I shall tumble in surf, wild and white,
and breast the wind in its furious might.
Deep in the heart of a troubled child
I shall hope that my love can earn a smile.
In memory I'll walk with my pet as before,
sharing companionship that ended in pain,
my hand on her long silken head once more.
Again I'll welcome the nighttime rain,
soft, misting balm to a wondering soul.
Whatever of living that I've loved I'll enfold
with winging heart and lightsome feet.
Death, come when you may—but life is sweet.

—Barbara Ruth Sampson

THE OBEDIENT SOLDIER

He's on his way with the 222d
I tried to be supportive, wouldn't you?
But it's hard to find rhyme or reason
For a ticket to Mogadishu.

This time, even politicians
Cannot seem to make it prettier,
Each one asking another
What we're doing in Somalia?

In our goal of peace, we are brothers,
Only for this, Americans unite.
But can we force the peace on others
Who refuse to see the light?

Now my son, the obedient soldier
Marches into a violent land
While I pray to his Protector
For what I cannot understand.

—Teresa Dockter

BROTHERHOOD IN THE NEIGHBORHOOD

I look around the neighborhood
For something that is so rare
This thing called brotherhood
I can't seem to find it anywhere

Brotherhood is something within
Not just making new friends
Brotherhood is love for fellow man
Not just someone who puts money in your hands

Seems no one understands brotherhood anymore
Here in America or on distant shores
We could talk about brotherhood all day
But we can sum it up best this way

I look around the neighborhood
For something that is so rare
This thing called brotherhood
I just can't seem to find much anywhere

—Marvin W. Newsum Sr.

DO NOT CHOOSE GREED OVER NEED

There are times when trouble starts
Many will never stop to take heed,
Then everything starts falling apart
Because greed is choosing over need.

There's nothing too bad that you can't handle
By following every possible lead,
Don't confront things you can't dismantle
So stop choosing greed over need.

You see life should be carefully lived
It doesn't matter what's your creed,
Stop thinking about your take, it's what you give
By not choosing greed over need.

This world is like a large spider web
And its net is so well weaved,
Just stop and think, you too can tell
By not choosing greed over need.

*Dedicated to my wife, Mildred and
my children, Leanise and Lindsey Jr.*

—Lindsey R. Smith

THE SKIN OF THE TEETH

A little girl lost in the breach —
A bitter thought we've tainted sweet —
I feel the laughter fade and dissolve —
Help me catch the night when it falls —

I am bound to this content —
The visions doubted heaven sent —
I'm left with only a piece of mind —
The other pieces left behind —

Will we die by love's disease? —
Doing our best to not displease? —
A darkling thought crept from the brain —
To a little girl lost in the rain —

It's a match made in delirium —
As welcome as her tearing gems —
Sapphires cried on porcelain —
And moved the heart of a mannequin —

Descending upon this shameless deed —
The stunning gape we do bequeath —
A wiry frame sews a torment seed —
The narrow escape by the skin of the teeth —

—Robert Adrian

AN EAGLE

I look below and see, the world how it was meant to be,
The valleys low, the cliffs so high, up here as I fly.
Rolling hills, rocky mounds, glacial peaks so astound.
The peace of the air all around, not like on the ground
Down there, there's noise, up here is quiet.
Clouds go by, clouds go around,
The quiet life is what I seek, way up here on life's peak.
The air so cool, the wind so crisp,
Soaring, diving, rolling, as the wind
The height so beautiful the air so blue, so new.

—Joshua Puck, age 15

MEMORIES

Down the winding lane of memories, cast
Reflections of things which used to be,
Return, and return again, like petals falling
In a summer's rain, they haunt our every waking
Hour, they seem to devour, and flood our minds
Reflections of things which were designed to last
For an eternity, but time had a way of making memories,

Of all that was supposed to last, had slipped through
Our very grasp, there is no way to hold time still,
And keep that new found thrill, of a love that
Promised to last a life, was as fickle as a toss of
Dice, memories cling, and some time fade, then arouse
Again to persuade us, to take a walk, down that winding
Lane of memories, of reflections, of other days.

—Sally Cabaret Lucci

GRANDPA PA

Sometimes I sit and watch my old grandfather, who is over the hill and a mile yonder.

I have sorrow for this poor ol' soul, for I know he has fallen into a bottomless hole.

But I have more respect for him than anyone I knew, for I know his heart is nothing but true.

He has lived a life a many gladness, but now he faces an internal sadness.

I want to spend time with him before he dies, I try to vision the world through his eyes.

But as I look at him my heart grows cold, for I know my grandfather is getting old.

—James E Nichols, age 13
Thunder in the Sky

HOMECOMING

Smiling with anxiety as the wheels come to a halt
The people slowly departing so the crowd dwindles away
The roar of the airplane engine to me seems faint
Home once again forever here to stay
I take a ride to help me remember
Stirring up memories by familiar sights
Reminiscing about the times that were good
Thinking to myself under the enchanting moonlight
The waves continuously pound the shore
As the sand sifts through my feet
Thinking of where I've been all these years
Finding the pieces to make my puzzle complete
Learning new experiences while being away
Enjoying myself wherever I would roam
But nothing will ever beat the feeling
The wonderful feeling of being home.

—Glenn Kealoha Kuhia

SUNSET

As the sun sets over the horizon
And this new day is done,
Look to the future with hope
At the setting of the sun.

Each day's a new beginning
For a future bright and fair;
Peace with God in solace,
You can always find Him there.

He made you for His glory;
He wants you to trust in Him.
Call on Him in prayer
He'll cherish each of them.

—Ethel M. Qualls

MATERNALLY YOURS

Love thyself above all others,
    this I have been taught.
Motherhood has changed it though,
    I learned this rule for naught.

Love your child above all others,
    this includes yourself.
Take books that tell you differently
    and put them on the shelf.

A mother's love is selfless,
    it's pure and it is true.
Forget the things you want yourself,
    you know what you must do.

Now we teach our daughters
    to love altruistically.
We watch as they build their careers
    and live life child-free!

No matter what we teach them,
    the rules just don't apply.
With the world, the rules must change;
    and too, I see, must I.

—Tracey Lynn Grimes

OFTEN CRY

I sit and imagine what life
    would be like without you
And often cry
When I look back
I think of all we shared
The love
The hope
The hurt
And often cry
When I hear a pretty song
    or smell a flower, I think of you
And often cry
These are not tears of pain
Or hurt
But tears of love
And life
You mean so much to me
And when I think about it
I often cry

Dedicated to my dearest Sean,
Thank you for the inspiration
I love you

—Beverly Bowman

CREATED

He created all the flowers,
    And the stars that shine above;
He created all the birds that sing,
    Their melody of love.

He created streams and babbling brooks,
    And placed them everywhere;
He created trees that gently blow,
    A soft breeze through our hair.

He's done all this to show His love,
    A love that just won't end;
He wants to be our Father,
    Our Brother and our Friend!

So let's all lift our hearts up,
    To the one from whom we came;
For He is . . . Christ our Savior,
    Let's praise His holy name!

—Marti Neidigh

LET'S BUILD A BRIDGE

Why can't everyone live with love
    Instead of so much hate inside,
Shouldn't we carry the olive leaf
    like a dove
This I think everyone should realize.

If we build a bridge of concern for
    each other
And make love for mortar to be used,
You'll find how close we'll become
    as brothers
By using our Christians' minds as a tool.

When we live our life so unconcerned
You're really leaving yourself on a ridge,
In this world there's many places to
    learn
By making love as a crossover for a
    bridge.

—Lindsey R. Smith

A MAN OF CONVENIENCE

He sits passively behind the counter,
his bargain face blends in with
the bags of potato chips, and the
packs of cancer-laced cigarettes, and the
football-shaped key chains.

I hand him some change that he counts
like a machine. He tosses it
in the register drawer, "pop, pop, pop"
it goes, like the pink popcorn before
it was stuffed into a bright yellow bag.

Meanwhile I wonder if he swears when
he stubs his toe, or if he kisses
passionately. Maybe he has dreams of
becoming someone other than
himself.

But he's a man of convenience
without toes, or kisses, or dreams
or self.

"Thank you and have a nice day."

—Nathalie Morin

IF ONLY IT WERE TRUE

    Just as the dawn of each day comes
forth . . . I thought was her love. As a painter
is never without his brush . . . I thought was
her love. Perhaps the dawn has come too
soon . . . if only it were true. Perhaps the
painter is still asleep . . . if only it were true.

. . . The dawn has awoken the painter
with his brush at his side . . . so I thought was
her love,
    if only it were true.

*Dedicated to Shannon Manuelito,
whose love really is true.*

—Justin Yarnell

THE HOUSE

Memories flooded back, for it had been a long time,
I stared at the aged tree, that as a child I
would climb.

Walking through the front yard abundant with grass
and thorn. Eyes afixed on the house where, I
was once born.

Crushing leaves I reached the steps, the four wooded
and most fade. Then, frozen there I stood, savouring
whistles the trees made.

Through the door into the halls, lifeless walls ancient
and cracked. Disappeared shadows and pictures,
blank faces robbed of paint it lacked.

Its rooms once loud and alive now, vacant and
dull. Once decorated strived with life, now
tranquil with lull.

Wishful minds and playful hearts, I recall with
a smile on my face. Young days filled with not
worries but, innocence, joy and grace.

—Raquel Roopnarine, age 15

(Toward)
LOOKING TWO-WORD THE SEASONS!

Sandy Beach,
Water Waves,
Yellow Sun,
Summer Days

Colored Leaves,
Blowing Wind,
Baring Trees,
Fall Begins

Chilling Weather,
Falling Snow,
Icicles Forming,
Winter Glow

Warming Air,
Blooming Flower,
Budding Tree,
Spring Power

*Dedicated to Chester and Jean Pesta for my birth.
My late husband, Frank John Ruczynski and our
children, Cheryaleen & Frank. To Jordan Pizzurro
for her encouragement to write on . . . .*

—Kathleen Ruczynski
    Poopsie

A PATCH OF GREEN

Concrete roads to here and there,
Sometimes leading nowhere.
My tired feet long to rest
In a patch of green and feel blest.

Before my eyes are walls of steel,
Of stone and glass, things coldly real.
But how my eyes gaze with delight,
When a patch of green comes into sight.

In a city's desert of glass, stone and concrete,
I long for a garden, God's work complete.
Just a place to wander and wonder,
For my heart, soul and mind to grow fonder.

—Daniel J. Hayes

A LONELY MAN

One day I walked upon the street
A man was seen that life had beat
And I saw from in his eyes
The man had seen so many cries
His eyes had shed so many tears
Running fast from many fears
Now a bottle was his need
His gaze obscured upon a plead
The man was dirty, clothes were torn
Upon this face was only scorn
In his pocket, lived the booze
Is the man just meant to lose?
I'm sure within there lived a good
I wish to God I only could
Show him out there, someone cares
A hand to hold throughout the scares

Please let me never forget there's a world out there in need of a hand.

—Stephen Baetge

STANDS FOR LIBERTY

Enough taxes we say!
In lusty language of Boston Bay.
We have our rights and the King his tea —
Whatever the price to be free!

We know our chances,
In view of the circumstances,
Seems folly to smite the royalty.
But there comes a time in human events
When things must be shaken —
Sides be taken —
We take the stand for liberty!

Weary, cold, and hungry troops
Wearing rags in painful stoops . . .
Long, dark, somber faces
Shadowed by a Death that chases
Those of courage enough to pay
The price of freedom here today.

Now on that coast, a perpetual toast,
In the hand of the Symbol of Freedom
Inscribed to the lowly
Her message is solely
That *she* stands for liberty!

Originally written for my mother's birthday in 1976. Her favorite subject was history.

—Ron Nellermoe

LITTLE PICTURE ON THE WALL

Little picture on the wall,
why do you stare so boldly at us all?
We see your birds,
we hear their hum,
Your river sparkles in the sun.
Your snow-capped mountains give us a chill,
your fish leap from their waters with bright,
shiny gills.
Your grass so green,
your sky so vast,
but how can such serenity possibly last
in this world of war, and hate, and poverty?
Little picture on the wall,
why is it somehow you're not there at all?

—Jeanette Arndot

T'is the total look,
The world view look
    Of natives and their charm.

Their thoughts like ours
    Inspire verse,
        And can cause quite alarm.

They stir the soul's sincere desire,
    Uniting those who care.
        It really is quite plausable
            To find real solace there.

Oh world, how much united be
    When people pause to pray.
        The fears and doubts of all mankind.
            Are slowly washed away.

We're bound to one another then
    In ways deemed true and clear.
        There is a unity in love,
            And each one's wealthier.

—Helen Lager Konyha

THE DARK DAY

The month was November;
It preceded joyous December.
November brought a day of woe
To men, women, children, friends and foe.
For the world, it was a Dark Day.
At his death, the world began to pray.
Yes, November brought a day of woe,
But it was the time for our president to go.

The nations of the world pained;
The birds of the world complained.
Ladies and children moaned;
Men and the winds groaned.
The sky became dark; dogs began to bark.

His loving wife held his head.
The nation watched while he bled and bled.
Throughout the world people listened
While the sniper's unsteady eyes glistened.

Grown-ups prayed; innocent children played.
Then, like Doom, we heard
The soft utterance of a word.
"Dead," was what the commentator said.
Yes, our hope, our deliverer was dead.
His name was JOHN FITZGERALD KENNEDY.
His love will live throughout eternity.

—Sarah G. Chambliss

ROCKING THE EMPTY CRADLE

Unborn baby sweet child of mine.
I stopped for coffee to drop you a line.

Mommy is busy earning a living.
Preparing you for all my giving.

Daddy is working making great pay.
You know, for college and your car one day.

We love you dearly, we really do.
Just right now we're not ready for you.

Please forgive us for taking our time,
but Mommy and Daddy are saving our dimes.

We have the house, the car and a dog too.
One day little one we'll be ready for you.

Maybe . . . .

—Tracy Moore

THIS LOVELY TREE

I have seen a tree with beauty and grace
that was once a tiny sprout,
the humming bird's hummed
the butterflies lit and caressed it all about.
This tree grew by the potter's hand
with its arms reaching out,
beckoning birds to perch or sit
to sing their little hearts out.
This lovely tree blooms on and on
swaying gently by the breeze,
sending out its special fragrance
to touch the other trees.
The potter would say, "Sway on, bloom on
the earth could never be;
the majestic beauty that it is,
without the lovely tree."
"No living thing can stand as tall,
nor reach as far as me."
If it could talk, that is what it would say,
This Lovely, Lovely Tree.

—Grace B. Rooks

MY LITTLE ONE

My little one, how silly you are.
Fussing the way that you do,
And I give the attention that strengthens you!
Your only concerns are,
To be in my arms,
To hold you, to rock you,
To keep you from harm.
A warm bottle and a blanket,
A soft toy to share,
You have no idea how much I care.
You understand your wants and needs,
And I am an expert on all of these.
You do not know what your smile can do,
How my heart melts when I see it on you.
Every 'coo' and 'giggle' that I hear,
You laugh and flirt to keep me near.
You do not know now,
But some day you will find,
With all of your fussing,
The pleasure was mine!

Especially for my little ones,
Eric and Cami

—Nicole James

SMOKE

Strange stuff this black and white and gray
That ride along on a breeze and goes away.
Like time, and joys, and fears, and tears,
It drifts past our eyes and disappears.
I wonder if it is hidden in the skies
Or just turns to dust and dies.

—John Landgraf

A PIECE OF MYSELF

My heart will be open wide
When I dream by day and night
I will ride on the top of the hill
There I will see my lovely Nashville.
There I will get to take a deep breath of fresh air
And again feeling the southern breeze
I want to have this always in front of my eyes
Like in broad sunrise.

—Verena Wüthrich

TOMORROW CHILD

Some are wanted, some are not.
Their love, and friendship, cannot be bought.
So
Give them guidance, give them strength.
Give them this, it's so unique.
Give them time, one on one.
Give them this, daughter or son.
Give them a place, a place to belong.
Give them a place, a place to call home.
Give them laughter, give them love.
Give them, what GOD expects above.
Give them time, a time to grow.
Give them love, and tell them SO.

—Denelda DeWitte

DIAMONDS

I felt like a miner digging up coal,
slaving away in a damp dark hole.
That which I dug each day,
was burnt as fuel to light my way.
Heat its flame would provide,
kept this ole man alive.
That hard work I did not mind,
pains and sorrow I would find.
For I found to my amaze,
why I shoveled all those days.
That coal was people I met,
carbon not quite diamonds yet.
I dug a deep hole it's true,
but there I found a diamond like you.
The luster of diamonds like a stone,
held in one's hand is never known.
It takes the blows of a jeweler's tool,
to release the facets of that jewel.
Held secure yet not too tight,
reflects its beauty in the light.
You hope to find with prayer and luck,
untold wealth when that blow is struck.
In the many lessons you have taught,
I thank you for this wealth you brought.
You have been my light and my right hand,
and each shovel full makes me a wealthier man.

—Stanley F. Buchmiller

A
radiant red
sweet smelling rose
petal moistened passionately in
the early morning dew lingers
in the dawn of a new day.

—Jennifer Beckstedt

I WISH TO YOU

If I could have my way,
to you I'd say,
I wish the best to you
this day.
So be not with dismay,
we have God's
world on display and
it makes us
a fine place to stay.

—A. T. Neville

LORD GRANT ME

Lord would you grant me the blessings
that I so much desire
Would you give me the motivation
I'm trying to inquire
Lord Grant Me the things I want
out of Life most
Which is Love, Peace and Successfulness
While living alone my working coast
Would you look out for me Lord
When my days are Gloom
So I can be Happy again to share
the sweetness of a blossom bloom
And if it's not too much to ask
Would you let the people of the World
endure this great task
So I ask you Lord, grant me this
to share
To let the world know, that I really
do care!

—Ruby Lee Carter (Sally)

MY FAVORITE GIFT

Grandma made a quilt for me
Each block a story told
Sewn together with loving hands
New fabric beside old

The yellow was my Easter dress
I wore when I was nine
The blue was Grandpa's overhauls
He wore then all the time

A touch of pink was blankie
The baby's oldest friend
A large white block of satin
From the dress she married in

A kaleidoscope of color
That lays upon my bed
A gift of sweet memories
That dance within my head

Grandma will never realize
How much it means to me
To snuggle up inside this quilt
Indeed . . . my family tree

—Carla Combs

FRIEND

You were just a stranger in my life, and suddenly you became part of me.
   The transition was wonderful, uniting thoughts and words, and motivating them into something so united, only God himself could have made such a miracle.
   The beginning of a friendship, is so special, it highlights the inner most precious part of a person's resources, thoughts, feelings, emotions, sensitivity, and most of all, the basis of life itself, the depth of a personal relationship, in its natural understanding of life as a total.
   What a wonderful beginning, may it never stop growing.

—Mrs. Joanne Mlodik

The MAN TO ME GOD CREATED; PERFECT

With hair as black as a Raven
Mingled with a touch of Dove
Eyes glow like diamonds in the dark
Nostrils beautiful as summer breeze
Lips like dew drops
Teeth white as pearls I do admire
Cheeks are firm like sapphires
Arms come to me like monarch butterfly
Hands are fine silk
Legs stand like pillars of marble
set upon sockets of fine gold
His feet reminds of the dust God took to make man
and blew breath into
Countenance excellent as a cedar
The upright stature complete as a palm tree
looking as though it's never lost a leaf
This is the man to me God created
Perfect

—Clara Martin Syas

PRIORITIES

Knives in drawer. Cups on shelf.
Why is baby waking? Need
To finish kitchen. He should
Be sleeping. Floor splashed
With milk from his bottle.

Need to mop floor. Why does he cry?
He's dry. Fed. Soapsuds on my arms.
I wish he would stop.
Pick him up. Smiles. Cuddle
Him close. Feel full. Complete.

Floor needs cleaning. Mailman ringing.
Dog barks too loud. Registered letter.
Can't take my baby out. Too cold.
Besides, he likes home. Even with
Dust all over. Sit in rocker. Snuggle close.

Baby smiles. Sleepy. Not finished.
With his sleeping. Nods. Hold him close, let
Him feel my heart as he drifts off.
Letter, floor, dust can wait.
I need to watch my baby sleep.

—Ercel Eaton

MY SECRET

You don't know I watch you
   when you move with agile grace.
You don't know I see you
   when a tear rolls down your face.

You don't know my feelings
   when I see you with a smile.
You don't know how far I'd go.
   I'd run that extra mile.

I act like I don't notice you.
   I always play that part.
And you'll never know I love you, Dear,
   with all my beating heart.

—Paula L. Bersin

THE BREAKING

They were a sea of tossing manes,
   and like the wind they flew.
Their leader was a stallion proud
   who guarded their tableau.

Clearly they were meant to be there,
   but it also could not be,
for man could not let anything
   so beautiful be so free.

So man then came to get the herd;
   he captured them by force,
and while the raging stallion fought,
   they began to break that horse.

They ran and spurred the angry beast
   'til he lay there in the mud,
the fire gone from his once-proud eyes,
   his heaving sides streamed blood.

The stallion may be breathing still,
   but they killed him on that day,
for his great proud heart has waned and died,
   and his spirit gone away.

—Becky Cremer

OH, NO!

Oh, no!
My room's a disaster site
When my mom sees it
She'll die of fright!

Look like junkyards
Upside-down
I'll pack my bags
And leave the town.

Maybe she'll pardon me
Probably not
There's food on my bed
Starting to rot!

Games on my bed
Socks on the floor
Soon it'll become a
Worldwide chore.

She's in the doorway
I'm gonna lose my head!
What'll I do?
Dive under the bed!

—Hirsh Kalyan Sandesara, age 9

MAGIC OF LOVE

Come with me, my darling
And lay with me on our magical bed
So that our love may take flight
Out through the window into the night
Whirling and twirling like the wind
Up past the stars and back again
Clutching each other and gasping for breath
Afraid of falling down to our death
Then God took us in the palm of his hand
And gently placed us back upon the land
For we had invaded his heaven
But with God, all is forgiven
We had shared the magic of love every minute
And consummated our love to the limit.

—Florence Morisette

TO A. D.

I'm my own person now.
I walk alone but satisfied,
owing no vow to any man who lives;
I've my own place.
The heart within me gives its all to freedom —

And then I see your face . . .

I'll not give up our friendship;
your life is yours,
mine — mine.
You have no choice, and I can live with that
and smile in living —

And then I hear your voice . . .

Tell me you think of me once in a while
and I'll be glad.
My world is flexible;
I've played the game.
My happiness depends on none but me —

And then I hear your name . . . .

—Fran Watson

I TOOK THE MOUNTAINS

I lost grasp
And my hand slipped from yours.

As we both took one step — we parted.

Our path we had traveled together for so long
Now became two.

With fear I took additional steps
Till no longer you were in sight.

I took the mountains,
You took the sea,
And along the way grew stronger.

Now land has met sea,
And here we stand today,
One stranger looking into another's eyes.

Past the fear.
Past the pain.

I have some regret of taking that first step,
But time has changed us.

And I am only left wondering
What it would have been like to love you
And thinking it wasn't meant to be.

—Heather N. Vandergriff

BEYOND YEARS

We all feel we have to face the world alone
Because of our problems we now realize how fast
We've grown
We go into the night but when it ends we say goodbye
We return to our homes, shut our bedroom doors and cry
No one understands the way we feel
They figure our problems are small and easy to deal
They do not know we're far beyond our years
They were never around to wipe our tears
Growing up was something that happened too fast
We never look back on the vague memories of our past
Now we slowly move on to our problems of tomorrow
Day by day trying to forget yesterday's sorrow.

—June E. McGarry, age 15

THE HUNTER

He came searching for me in the dark of the night
His footsteps made no sound
This man of mystery
His soul reaching out trying to touch mine
Could it be for real
Of what part of me was he searching
Did his quest come in peace
Or was he danger in disguise
Fear grasped my body as I froze
I had no recollection of time
The bait had been set and the trap sprung
What would this mighty hunter do with his game
Coming slowly, reaching out he took me in his firm grip
And slowly he caressed my soul with his spirit
His touch was soft, yet he wanted more
Could I give him that which he asked
I watched, I felt, I started to believe
And without warning I surrendered
I will give to this man all that I am
And know that this hunter will be a gentle man

—Robin Reese McKay

THE MINE OF GOLD

Miss Emily wrote another incognito "Master" letter
With Helen Hunt in collaboration as duo SAXE HOLM
Addressed in acrostics to SAM—"Sweet Master Mine"
"Sunday Morning—this blazing September sun"—SAM B

1871—They called it an "Allegory"—of Secret Love
"Dream" of She and Him—entitled "The Mine of Gold"
Departed lovers walk hand-in-hand chambers of Gold
"Faces shine as the faces of angels" Eternal Above

Eternity—the walls of "living faces"—are smiling
"Faces of all who have ever entered"—are up there
"Faces of the sons of God looking into eyes of
Earthly women"—"the women they have loved"—alive

Our newcomers—Sam and She—Miss Emily—"see their
Own faces added to the others with the same Smile,
The same joy"—acrostics and anagrams twice of SAM
Her allergorical story's hidden meaning about a Man

And Woman—"these faces are immortal"—"never more
See in each other change or loss of beauty"—know
Why Ms. Dickinson dressed in Her hard white lace—
No man beyond a certain date ever to see Her Face

Ends in an anagram of the precious name—Sam Bowles
"Broad sunbeam an angel meets them, a golden bowl—
Broken—a sliver cord—unloosed"—BOWL and its LSE
1874—Bowles wrote in His paper—authors, She & She!

—Bill Arnold

DRAGON FANTASY

Overhead they fly,
Breathing fire as up they go.
Dragons in the sky.

—Kathleen Carpenter, age 13

May I hold you in my arms,
May I smell your sweet perfume,
May I gaze into your eyes
    And get lost in their beauty,
May I kiss your soft, gentle lips?

Let me into your arms,
Let me become one with you,
Let me show you a happiness
    That you've never felt before,
Let me show you my LOVE.

—Ashley M. Peace

GRYPHON'S WARNING

Oh, ye Atrimaspi clear ye
Away to the Caspian Sea.

Yea that we Gryphons shall not kill
Though to be sure it is thy will

That thee attack our nests of gold.
Thee may be young, but we of old

Shall prove to be valiant of heart
When the time comes to be smart.

Aye, I know where the treasure is
Buried, but you will know but this,

You shall never find it though
Atrimaspi shall have me in tow.

Tomorrow, lad, to your home be
Gone, or I will toss you to sea.

If you value your life and your wife
You shall save trouble and strife.

—Annette M. Tews

THE CONTEST

    I have written many poems, some
with talent and form,
    Some are funny and sad, some
cold yet some warm.
    I have racked my brain, to
come up with just one,
    For money and publicity, and
of course for the fun.
    My subject is the contest, not
so funny nor sad,
    But serious for publicity, and
the money isn't bad.
    So for all who's involved, in
reading this entry,
    Just want you to know, this
is my Sale of the Century.
    I am not a big wig, just a
small town hick,
    A country bumkin if you will, or
just a plain chick.

—Jacqueline

My little house is set among large ponderosa pines. I marvel at their usefulness
their beauty, grace and charms.
The pine cones serve as food for squirrels and make such lovely wreaths.
They kindle brightly in the fire
and scent the air one breathes.
As I sit and ponder this, and
watch the sunset glow through
silhouetted pines I send my
      Christmas fond "HELLO"
    —Marnie Morgan

THE RAIN CROW

It's time for my evening walk, and in the wet woods I can hear the cry of
a bird named Rain Crow, and I know
the fog in the bog and the cotton
wood trees — the creek will very
soon be coming in and so I
feel I should be heading back
to my home —

The silvery moon so bright
casting light in the dark shade of night
fills my ♥ with delight —
Such a pretty sight!

    —Virginia J. Folmar

SPIRIT

Where ever our lives may take us
Our spirits will never be broken
Your spirit wild and untamed
Showed me how to be wild and free
You always teased
But I knew you really cared
And then it was too late
To tell you how much I cared
You were gone
And I was alone
But I know
Somewhere . . .
Somehow . . .
Our spirits will meet
And we'll be together again

    —Beth Ann Bleicher

DREAMING

Body slowly trembling
Breath filled with desire,
I lie beside your slumbering body

Watching as you sleep,
My heart pounds,
I am the blessed one beside you

The warmth of your naked flesh burns,
Sweating, I draw myself closer
Yearning to be scorched

Filled with desire,
My mind races with fantasies
Of being within you forever

Enticingly rich,
The dream abruptly ends
And the coldness of reality returns.

    —Ronnie G. Laflamme

OH, THOSE CHORES

I look around . . . what a mess!
This dirty house of mine.
Stacks of clothes piled here and there,
How did I ever *get* so far behind!

The rug's not swept; the bed's not made;
The laundry needs to be done.
Odds and ends, all out of place —
How did I ever think this could be fun!

    But . . .

I'll pitch right in and dust and mop,
I'll wash and scrub and pray.
This house will sparkle when I'm through
But, alas, I'll have it all to do again next Saturday!

    —Crystal O. Miller

LIBRARIES ARE FOR EVERYONE

Libraries are for everyone,
With everything in them under the sun!
Reading is pleasing and lots of fun,
No one need feel left out, nary a one!
Come to the library with open arms,
And you'll find something to suit all of your charms!
There is no limit to the subjects you'll find,
Some may even give you piece of mind!
Come bring a friend, or even your brother,
And don't wait for an invitation from your mother!
Come and seek, seek and find,
You may even find staff members unusually kind!
For they are programmed to find information for you,
On old things, collectables, and even things new!
So when you are looking for something special to do,
And your finances are meager and won't see you through,
Come to the library and use your free card,
It may almost be as close to you as your own back yard!
The library's collection is waiting for you to decide,
What items you'll discover to keep by your side.

    —Allen P. Rothlisberg

FACELESS PHANTOMS

We all know the problem
It happens all year round.
No matter what the date may be
They always hang around.

No, it's not my buddies
Nor friends from shadowed pasts.
Instead I've been surrounded
By faceless torture traps.

I don't know why they haunt me
I did no wrong to these.
Yet everytime I check my mail
They're waiting there for me.

They always come in numbers
Not one or two, but six.
And if you are not careful
They'll put you in a fix.

Now how can I accept defeat
From villians such as these?
The electric, the water, the gas and the phone
THOSE DREADED UTILITIES!

    —Tina Seigley

THE FIRST LIGHT OF EVENING

There are times in this life when, as day ends,
the light of evening intends a world other than this one.

It is as if, in our eyes, green is hatched into yellow,
and the shell of each isolated remembrance of it lost.
And everything as yet unexploited extends everywhere.

It is in this moment that bird becomes sky
and time ends, perched outside everything.
And high on every mountain nests the truth,
screeching in its detestable rhythm,
ensconced in its universe that is God.

The great abstraction is no abstraction.
In the backwater outback of the universal reality,
at the boring far end of things,
in this slow, low-stakes casino,
Man has standing for awhile.

—Mark C. Williams

WHEN SHOULD IT HURT DEEP INSIDE

When should it hurt deep inside:
When my mother and father are in pain?
When my brothers and sisters cry in shame?
It should hurt deep inside when my family suffers.

When should it hurt deep inside:
When life long friends are being torn apart?
When the pain they feel is from their heart?
It should hurt deep inside when friend's pain runs deep.

When should it hurt deep inside:
When someone I love, won't let me close?
When their love I know I will never boast?
It should hurt deep inside feeling her loss.

When should it hurt deep inside:
When my love I know she will never share?
When she has no feeling, has no care?
It does hurt deep inside knowing the things I do.

—Ronnie G. Laflamme

SCORCH

There is a passion within your soul
I can feel it within your tomb
Heat radiates from your broken, twisted limbs
It wraps me in warmth, fills me with reassurance
While you gaze at me, flames dance wickedly behind your eyes
These flames pour into my mind; BURNING, MELTING
My restraints are gone; time is lost
Your touch lingers, heat passes into my bones
The chill felt from so much isolation is no longer there
Present within my heart and stomach is a FIRE
The flames flicker hungrily up my throat
Soon, all I am shall be consumed
After the heat, after the fire
I am Ashes, Dust
To be blown away by your wind
Now I shall be at your mercy
You may gather me together, keep me bottled up,
Or scatter my remains
Lost pieces of bone and cloth are tread upon by unseeing eyes
It is your decision, What Shall Become Of Me?

—Cathy Mihowich

THE SPIRIT OF SUMMER!

May the rhythm of God's waving
Grasses, in the meadows green,
Be as music to your heart,
    As you listen in rapt silence
To its message of love and peace,
    That is borne on the spirit
Of a summer evening . . . !
    And when the shadows of evening
Blend with the setting sun, bringing
    Another day to a close, let your
Faith rest in God's promise, that
    Life will go on, and that His
Waving grasses will ever respond
    To summer breezes at evening time!

—A.J. Walters

GRACE OF LOVE

Walking with my hand in yours,
Passing people in empty doors.
Seeing sidewalks with empty spots,
Boxes of houses with clothes on tops.
These are strangers, living on streets,
Singing praise with a Holy Beat.
Walking together, arm and arm,
Lonely people, not doing any harm.
Being together is being free,
Homeless people, is what, they see
Feeling happy, this is our love,
God is watching us, from above.
Walking with my hand in yours
We have pride, even if we are poor.
We are people, you and me,
Grace of love, in Heaven, you'll see.

—"Sandy"

CORAL HARBOR AND OTHER PLACES

Fired and broken land formations—
Or maybe sea formations,
It is hard to discern
Foreground from background
As Gaugin must have
Back in Tahiti,
Water worn rocky islets
And shorelines,
Eaten away
By a Parasitic
Emerald sea-
Is that how she retains
Her magnificent color?
Fir trees like teeth
Of a comb line barren low cliffs,
Pink conch shells lie amidst
Stones in shallow water
Like uncut rubies embedded in stone,
Peninsulas weave their way south
Out to sea,
Caught in an eternal grasp
With something unknown,
A Bahamian sun shadowed
By such unspoiled land
And sea,
Fiddler crabs dance across
Aged dirt paths.

—Thela Marie Sullivan

I am trying very hard
    to grow
I am searching very deep
    to know
I am looking very close
    to see
I am wanting so much
    to be
—Cheryl Snopel

AUTUMN LOVE

This autumn day
holds captive our lives,
as our hearts will frolic
in the fallen leaves.
With her amber eyes
staring deep inside,
our mind and soul
fall together in love.

*Dedicated to my one true love,
Jacqueline Renee St. Cryr,
without her my inner strength
would have never been known.*

—Neil R. Jordan

BETWEEN REALITY AND ILLUSIONS

Between Reality and Illusions
    there is nothing

Between the truth and a lie
    there is also nothing

For Reality is the truth
    and a lie is an illusion

There is nothing between them
    because no one person
    can tell the difference

So I leave you this thought:

    The truth and the lies
    Realities and Illusions
    Nothing between them
    Nothing at all

—Karen E. Ahrens

THE CASUAL-CAUSAL MAN

The casual-causal man
Isn't so casual.
In fact, he's deadly serious.
But he doesn't seem so
To the untrained I,
And only he
Has been trained just so.
He isn't so causal,
The casual-causal man,
But when he's around
Things happen:
Big things, small things,
Happy things, wry things.
All these things
Come to pass
When the casual-causal man
Tarries for a time.
He isn't such a bad guy,
The casual-causal man,
Not a bad guy at all.

—Kirby Mankin

INFAMOUS VOID

Black trees—no leaves—dark branches in pack snow
Covered with hard white ice—cold wind—gray haze
Dead winter—dreary dreary Northeast nights—days?
Lonely—the Poetress sits and waits—Again—no show

1857—*last* year—infamous void—Year of Not Anything
Ms. Dickinson disappeared—Earth conceived up a Ghost
Year of Intellect's drought—letters dried up—no Host
No poems running from Her Mind—no freshets of Spring

Valentine Days were gone—Love Poetry had begun
1858—that dreary dreary winter Song—so very much in love
With the city editor—promise across Holyoke Hills—hooves
Satyr summers and poetic winters—Salvation—won

Sam—'twas He—Mr Bowles—Sir Springtime—the city "Bee"
Busy buzzing North—from the field of Spring—*Creak* at gate
Sound of human feet—*knock* on Her door—Heart stopped—Fate
Spoke—"You came?"—"Up the East Road—to see Miss Emily."

—Bill Arnold

EXCUSES

"Hello Ms. Nelson, I'm sorry to say
That Little Kate won't be in school today.
She left last night, t'was a quarter to four,
to fetch some meat from the corner store.
When she returned she had brought no meat,
just a pile of bones and a dog at her feet.
'Look what has followed me home this eve'n.
He looks so hungry. Do you think I can keep him?'
As she replied I looked at the brood
and said, 'We'll wait till morning to give him some food.'
But Ms. Nelson, the dog had not eaten
since God knows when and it was quite to my horror
when I walked this mor'n into the darkened den.
And I realized why Kate had held those bones.
They were the dog's last victim—now nothing but stones.
Ms. Nelson have pity for I'm sorry to state
that the dog has been fed—it was Kate that he ate."

*Dedicated to Robin Spriggs—my silent
encourager and inspiration.*

—Jeanette Meierhofer

TWO-IN-ONE

I see a humongous watertower without which the Town could not
Enrich itself. beside it, a small red firehydrant justfeet
away, dwarfed by the sky-bound . . . Giant(tower) amongst the
soft green grass of the sky-dependanty tiny   Park.
    One without the Other is
Useless.   Perhaps.   Perhaps—the hydrant,—as a small
seemingly insig . . . fact among the trees
Carries importance as a catalyst
    For a higher ideal
Emersing its surroundings
    the tweeting birds, the freshly mowed
    grass, the empty picnic tables   with a sense of belonging
—and   Stands tall,—not alone   Amist—the slow-going sunset
A Soft breeze breathing (existing) new-life
    into its purpose
    More than just existance . . . . . . — Acceptance . . .
Relaxing belief and   FAITH towards — for a
Greater Fountain within us   All . . . Empty no-longer . . . ;
Acceptance.
The Little Red Hydrant.

—Tina M. Johnston-S.

NIGHT PRAYER

The mountain appeared to be a canvas painting as the moon
    glowed in its high place in the heavens.
And the trees of the forest reached out their leaf woven
    branches to touch just one bright star in the sky.
The reflections on the stream ebbed on following the wind
    into the luminous night.
The heart of the forest calls upon God through the songs
    of its surroundings and creatures;
With their croaking ballad ascending to the angels
    praying for all the world.

—LeAnn Dawn DeBock

MY IMPRESSION

How great is life's inspection; how have I fit in the plan
How impressive is my reflection left on my fellow man
Have I been able to live to quell my hate and strife
And to some unfortunate give a portion of my life
I wanted to do my best and hold my head up high
And pass life's rugged test and victorious live and die
But many days I was weak and promised a better tomorrow
The wrong road I'd sometimes seek which always leads to sorrow
Now this I plainly see is the essence of life's plan
It's not what I do for me, but for my fellow man
And when this life is ended and darkness fills mine eye
I'll wonder what I have done for people to remember me by

—Henry C. Fletcher

THE MORNING AFTER

As the sun beats down upon my cheek,
I lay there exhausted from the busy week,
Slowly I wipe the sleepiness from my eyes,
And feel a slight slant in the mattress where he lies,
I finally become aware of the different room I am in,
It is not familiar like the other one had been,
The one filled with stuffed animals and frilly drapes,
At the remembrance of childhood my heart aches,
Until I look across to the other side of the strange room,
The sight of my new husband sleeping chases away the gloom,
A peacefulness descends upon me that I have never felt before,
At the realization that I will have to sleep alone no more,
I have committed to someone for the rest of my life,
I am no longer a lonely child but a loving wife!

—Colleen M. Wasilowski

A PICTURE

    I first saw you in a picture and I asked many questions, never dreaming we would ever meet.

    When that moment happened, a wish had come true. You were shy, humorous, cute and so sweet.

    We talked and we toasted and we were feeling pretty good too. You even asked me to dance cheek to cheek.

    A special feeling emerged. Whoever would of thought we would be here, over a year later with a relationship so unique.

    We can talk, we can laugh and we know each other's funny little secrets too! A love and a bond developed that can't be beat.

    You and I are so much alike and fit so well together that I can't imagine me without you. My life would be so empty and incomplete.

    I want you, I need you, I love you, which you already know. I keep praying time will bring us together as a couple because what we have is so very rare and so very unique.

—Dora Jean Muller Sewell

STORM AT SEA

A cargo lost upon the sea
Souls that roam eternity
Wind that blows
Rain that falls
Lightning strikes
A seaman calls
A fire burns
The mast does break
The ship will sink
All lives it takes

—September Mae Pritchard

PERHAPS THERE IS A REASON

I saved up my love
For you to arrive
Things suddenly changed
You didn't survive

To die in my womb
Brought guilt to my heart
These feelings must stop
How will I start?

I no longer deny
That you were my child
In my soul and my heart
Though your existence was mild

To survive and accept
The loss that I grieve
Is a strength I can reach for
When another will leave

I lost expectations
And the joy that you'd be
But I gained a new strength
And learned more about me

—Sue Beaudin

THE WELL

On the hill,
    above our valley.
There is an old well,
    so dark and dreary.

Voices (moans and groans)
    rise up from its depths.
So low and haunting,
    it would make you sweat!

We looked into,
    the old well.
Deep down within,
    its depths.

Unto our squinting eyes, we see.
Little green glowing eyes,
    looking back at you and me.

Neve would you guess,
    what was in its depths.
I'll tell you,
    if you must know.

For in, the depths,
    of our well.
Our imaginations dwell!

—Michelle R. Cash

GOD'S LOVE

God looks down and sees
How many humans are on their knees.
He will answer their prayers
If they are sincere,
You will know He cares
And is always near.
We know, and we believe
Our heavy hearts He will relieve.
He watches over us everyday.
It is wonderful to feel Him near
        when we pray.
—Letha M. Thornton-Dunsworth

I feel His presence growing within,
Strengthening me more each day.
I am His and He is mine,
His Hands control all things.
He consecrates me with His Spirit;
Fills me with His word, restores my soul;
Cleanses me from unrighteousness.
He speaks: Learn of me, walk with me,
Obey my word; tell of me.
Live by my faith, worship me;
Love me, be not ashamed of me.
My love will come soon
And we will be together forever.
I am my beloved's and my beloved is mine.

—Diana L. Hammer

MOUNTAIN DAWN

The dew yet lingers
   on shrubs flowers and trees.

The birds flit quietly
   among the boughs.

Quietness lingers
   while the dawn slowly struggles
   to push away the darkness.

The hush tarries briefly
   for the listening ear.

God speaks to the heart more clearly,
   in the mountain dawn.

His Word unfolds with majestic clarity,
   in the mountain dawn.

His terrestrial footstool
   and all therein reach out
   in the mountain dawn.

He blesses the listener with a special nod,
   in the mountain dawn.

The Psalmist alerts all,
   with eyes lifted up
   to the mountain dawn.

A word to the wise, His Word imparts,
   in the mountain dawn.

Hark—It is gone,
   till another dawn.

—Charles W. Roe

BECAUSE OF ME

The world is better because of me.
I know this because of what I can see.
Everybody can make a difference, bad or good.
I can too, I know I should.

Years ago, when I was young,
I thought about change and how it was done.
Change is performed with one step to start,
You let your mind go and follow your heart.

If you have the will, the courage, the want,
You can do anything, there's nothing you can't!
Everyone can make a difference, if only you try.
You can see it happen in the blink of an eye.

Countries and nations do not have the might,
Only individual people can do the job right!

—Ken Allinson, age 12

SILENT TEARS

Silent cries,
and unseen tears,
though she sobs
no one hears.

Torn between two forces,
one against the other.
One, her beloved friends,
the other, her loving mother.

They don't understand her feelings,
She's always caught in the middle.
Nothing seems right,
life's one big riddle.

If only she could get away.
If only she knew it would be the same.
If only she could have both — Friends and Family,
She's tired of playing this game.

—Jennifer Reves

A PROPER MYTH

I am fond of her fear.
The helm, from which,
she rules mine, and his
is a proper perspective.

This extraneous daughter,
and the casual recipient of preeminence,
inclined to the artificial drift,
move through their vicissitudes,
with generous ease.

I am a paramour of doubt.
The prodigal son, is a proper myth,
for the obedient nomad;
a terse element of satire.

Our cerebral carnage,
propagates this profound void.
What unholy nemesis
awaits this stealthy burden,
where children prepare
for the silent doom called existence,
with no thought given to the revelation of loss?

—Michael J. McCormack

TOMORROW'S GONE

Do not come when I have gone beyond the touch, the smile or sound,
To lay A weeping and alone upon the cold cold ground,
Come to me with love, and warmth while I can see your lovely smile,
Just wave goodbye when I have gone the last long mile.

Do not cry because I'm gone, because you know we all must go
So give me love and light and roses while I'm here to know.

Then if you feel that you must cry, well shed A tear or two
After that put on A smile and whip away the dew.
Cause when your time to go has come, you'll set here just like me.
And wish for things that might have been, to make A MEMORY

—Ruby A. Greenlaw

UNEARNED DEATH

The squirrel dashed across the street and stopped in its tracks.
He thoughtfully raised on his tiny haunches
                                         sniffed to the left
                          and then to the right.
He turned quickly, as if danger was near,
                          and, in what seemed to be slow motion,
ran for his life.
                          As the car thudded over his tiny body,
I glanced back
                          only to see a dead ball of fur.
Suddenly
                          it began to flip, flop, and spasm,
then my dad sickly says,
        "I ought to go back and get him for dinner."

—Trent Nunley

SHOT GLASS OF CHEAP WHISKEY

My Mother dies so slowly each night as she sips
On the shot glass of cheap whiskey she puts to her lips.

I watch the expression in her eyes as it begins to change
From those of my mother to someone really strange.

Then some wine, a case of beer, and maybe a bottle of gin
And the smile upon the mother face becomes a frightening grin.

The empty bottles and empty cans toppled over on the table
Tell the story of a life totally incapable.

The drinks are gone, the money's gone the fighting then begins.
She cusses, flails her arms about. It's a wonder that she can.

I listen to the screaming and the banging on the walls,
The wailing of her tortured cries. "Don't hit me! Help!" she calls.

I run to her crying. What can I do?
There's bruises on her face! Blood! I am only 2!

My Mother dies so slowly each night as she sips
On a shot glass of cheap whiskey she puts to her lips.

I listen to the screaming and the banging on the walls,
The wailing of her tortured cries. "Don't hit me! Help!" she calls.

I run to her crying. What can I do?
There's bruises on her face! Blood! I'm only 22.

My Mother's dead and gone. How sad. She died so very lonely.
Whiskey, broken bones and bruises killed her very slowly.

I really couldn't stop it. Nothing I could do.
All hope is gone for a mom. I'm only 42.

—Iz Beaing

RUNNING AWAY

As I stand there by
A tree, in the dark
And cold of night, as
I sigh, I wonder why.
Why did I run away,
With nothing but the
Clothes I now wear?
As I sat down by
The tree, everything
I ever owned was back,
Safe at home, unlike
Me. I was out, away
From everyone, without
Any food or anything.
As the tears roll
Down my face, I wonder
Why.

—Jay Daniel Adams, age 10

ABBY . . .

    She sits still
and quiet in the empty
room. Empty walls replay
the sounds of a time forgotten.
The sounds of laughter and
love echo, for it is only
today that they are missed.
    A silent tear traces
its path down her cheek. She
is too young to experience the
feeling of grief. Oh, the
pain is so bad, it hurts, hurts
to see the empty walls, hurts
to hear the hollow sounds, hurts
that her best friend is gone. But,
the young girl wipes away the
tears, stands straight and tall,
and to no one at all she says,
"Goodbye, friend."

—Heidi Koger

SILENT/OTHER

In my silence
You failed
to hear the
language of
my soul

In my other-ness
You chose
to ignore
the wholeness
of my being

Silently
I othered
My other-ness
in alien landscapes
to belong

until my other-ness became
the silence of existence
accepted, expected, demanded
by self
by others

—Kanwaljit Kaur

DREAMS AND VISIONS

In dreams we fly — all chains broken,
Brilliant colors
and shocking questions raised,
Brain cells backfiring,
seeking the past,
tying, twisting and tangling
the roots of the future
with those in our memory.

Faces fade in and out,
asking unanswerable questions —
Bizarre scenes occur;
imagination paints so vividly —
reliving our choices
and reworking our decisions,
We see with totally new vision
and in the morning — sigh.

—Robin Toboz

WORDS OF THOUGHT

Wisdom does not come to the wise
It comes to the understanding
Without understanding there is no wisdom
In times of peace there are wise
But not understanding

In times of war there are in heart
And mighty in strength
There is no searching in this understanding

God hath made clear his holy words
His golden rules his tribe and tribulation
For one and all

In times of sorrow in times of pain
Open your heart and let the Lord in
In times of troubles in times of need

Open the door and let Jesus in
You'll find he's your best friend
In the end

—Sandy L. Gearhart

YOU, AND NATURE TOO!!

Sit with nature, you will find
Gentle peace in your mind.
Your heart can really skip a beat
Sitting in the shade, away from the heat.

Seeing the beauty of it all,
Those stately trees so tall.
As they waver in the breeze,
Seeming to do as they please.

Blue bird perching on a limb
Sings a song, then sings again.
A garden snake goes thru the grass
Not knowing that I saw him pass.

A crow made this awful sound,
Sure did make my pulse pound.
A chipmunk went scurrying by,
I saw him out of the corner of my eye.

Mother Nature sure did fine
Doing these things God had in mind.
Sure would be good for you
If you'd find time for nature too!

—Bernice L. Bing

"THE WORD" FOR LIFE

Open the WORD of true life.
God's WORD gives hope.
For true life, look to Jesus.
Yes, the Bible shows us how, but look to Jesus.
He is the Only way. There is no other.
Jesus' "The WORD"
All mental health is in the "WORD."
Look for it, study it, learn it, receive, apply it.
Let Him lead.
Although you may receive, you may confess,
you must follow Him in His "WORD."
Let His WORD — guide.
He will show you gently by the way you think,
the way you act, what you think, how you act.
Every thought will be CHRIST's.
Let Him lead.

Amen and Amen
—Ronald W. DeWitt

SOMBRAS DEL PASADO
(Shadows of the Past)

Modern man treks these lands,
 these arroyos,
  these mesas,
Believing his sojourn the first;
 Crediting himself author and editor of
  an enchanted place.
He scratches the dome of Father Sky with the
 graffitti of vapor trails
  and moves on to some other where.
Below—

Yucca spikes circle sand grains trenches.
Charred shadows curl and cool—
Embracing obsidian tools, a scraper, an awl
Sheltered in the burned rock of campfires
Abandoned by Sombras del Pasado—
And ashes of time drift and catch upon the wind.

—Cherie Brigham Hanson

THE SINGLE HANDER

There's nobody there but you,
sitting in the shade of the cockpit
on teak bleached white as summer sand.

Firm but gentle fingers grasp a tiller
whose smooth-worn wood knows only your caress;
Now slightly port, now slightly starboard,
You keep your steady course and do not know
you are listening to silence.

The language of the water is turquoise
and lapping; from above you the sun speaks
golden shafts to deep green kelp below.

Tanbark sails wing to right and left;
Up in the high rigging, wind whispers
timeless secrets you recall from ages past;
Each far horizon fills with emptiness,
and there is no other thing save you.

Red bandana tied across your brow,
sunshades reflecting distant, unseen visions,
you absorb the strengths of sea and sky,
and feast on solitude.

—Ronnie Stone

THE CHAIR

There was a brown chair,
At the base of the stair,
When I got mad at my dad,
I decided to attack—
so I used his favorite chair
For an afternoon snack.

I nibbled and chewed,
And pulled on some thread.
But when my mom found out—
I wished I were dead!

Of all the threats and
Words that were sounded,
The ones that hurt most
Were the words "YOU'RE GROUNDED!!!"

*Dedicated to my son, David, who
actually demolished this chair.*

—Karen E. Burnett

Summer sky, autumn fields
The memories ye evoke
Cross the field, cross the field
Into falls sweet pungent smoke
Down the lane, cross the brook
Split-hewn fence doth gleam
Top rail azure, lower violet
Borne by shoulders green
Evening tritons, morning glory
Gentle tendrils glisten
Under meek petals stooped with dew
Pine rails spirals fasten
Four feet up, eight across
A seasoned eye for true
A lengthy trellis softly livened
On late breezes in September blue
Soon the rails next the ground
A stratum of green for a parade of flutes
Wispy waves of gentle sound
A fluttering of tender salutes

—Robert Keogh

BEAUTY

From the mist of the night
    Beauty floats aimlessly

From the long forgotten past
    It becomes the present

From the sight of a new life
    It is witnessed

From the peaceful nature of darkness
    It rises with the sun

From the sight of a full figured woman
    It is galvanized

From season to season
    It evolves with the earth

From the pages of a romance novel
    It intensates the mind

In the warmth and depth of a benign soul
    It rests, only to be seen tomorrow

—Todd Lesesne, age 16

LITTLE FOOTPRINTS IN THE SNOW!

Little footprints in the snow,
  Meandering here and there;
One wonders where they were to go,
  And how long they would fare.
What small thing made these prints,
  And what did it hope to find?
I don't know from these hints,
  Tho' I have a thought in mind!
I am as cold as the snow itself,
  So I'll leave things as they are,
Return to my old book shelf,
  And read other prints beside the fire!
Then may-haps an old dream may come,
  When throu' the snow, a boy's prints were fun!

—A.J. Walters

TO FULFILL A DREAM

We planted our Magic Growing Rocks today
as nearly as we could to the picture
in your mind, but somehow it fell short
of the imagined glory of your dreams.
Small chubby elbows on table supported
anguished face and flooding eyes,
you sobbed, "I wanted it to be so beautiful!"

Little Grandson, I understand. So many dreams
have dimmed, so many plans fell short, making
me feel like bowing down my head in sorrow.
Today I'll take you to the store to get
another pack—two—three more packs of
rocks and castles. And you shall have
a second chance to fulfill your vision
and to create one memory of a dream that was
as glorious in reality as it was within your mind.

Surely—surely, Grandmamas are permitted
to indulge themselves to such a small degree
and to create fulfillment for themselves
as well as you.

—Barbara Ruth Sampson

ALL GROWN

My kids are all grown and gone with a flare.
Soon the last will leave, I know not for where.
Nobody to talk to, or care if I am there.
What will I do with my love with nobody to share.

I walk along the hills, and fish the lakes and brooks.
All that comes to mind are little fingers on little hooks.
Faces bright when a fish their hook took.
Smiles and laughs waiting for the cook.

Rocks and flowers found on walks.
All the things the kids have talked.
The hurt and pain, I could heal with a hug and kiss.
The feel of love and bliss, to find another near miss.

The games they all played,
The scores that they made.
Even a walk in the parade,
These things will not fade.

I remember them all, each one that's true.
With pride and love I cheered for all of you.
Now you are grown, the time how it flew.
All out on your own. What will they all do?

—Billie Jeske

EASTER MORNING — March 31, 1991

Emptiness like I'd never known flooded me
As I looked down at her after her long night of struggle
To stop the ebbing of her life.

So still she lay, and I thought how wonderfully brave she had been,
How gallantly she fought, uncomplaining, thus sparing us
Extra agony.

I remembered the times she spoke, of others she had seen
How bravely they had fought to survive as their
Lives ebbed.

Her days gone, her life done, she quietly slipped away
After her hard night of battle.
She was fine, she was brave, now she is forever young.

A constant, irreplaceable love has gone with her
And from my life forever.
She was my Mother.
  —Sharon Nell (Orahood) Lyell

CENTER OF THE UNIVERSE

I think back to yesterday where country roads traversed,
and traveling east would lead me to the center of the universe.

(At least that's what I believed, being a mere decade old.
Everything revolved around this farm, that's what I was always told.)

I wondered how the earth Grandpa plowed became so rich and black
until one night a falling star left a rainbow colored track.

Another streaked across the sky, and as I turned around
one more crossed my line of sight diving toward the ground.

It seemed that in this nook of space where Grandpa plowed his field
stardust fell abundantly adding to his yield.

So, at the universe's center where virgin soil lay
I see Grandpa plowing it under just as if it were yesterday.

*In memory of my grandparents, William and Helen Walter,
of Arcadia, Iowa. You live forever at the center
of my universe.*
  —Denise Talley

IMAGE IN THE MIRROR

Staring intently into the glass, an image lingering there.
Peering more deeply into the eyes of the me caught in the glare.

Gazing only a moment more there suddenly appeared
Another image just beyond the one that held me near.

Who was this person in that space — that fourth dimension there?
It looked at me as if to say "What are you doing here?"

Silently we then conversed; I asked if she could hear;
Then, with no sound, she answered me. I thought I saw a tear.

That person which I thought I knew was only in my mind.
My real self-image was beyond a wall no one could climb.

Like some old silent movie flickering on the glass
With scenes from my own childhood and mem'ries from the past.

This re-enactment of my life which flashed before my eyes
Revealed a truth as yet unknown — that life's a compromise.

Where issues once were black and white, they now are heather gray.
And values which were once defined are fading day by day.

Then like my life, my focus changed; I blinked and realized
The image had just disappeared before my very eyes.

The one remaining face looked back into my enlightened soul;
The healing process now complete, this blossom could unfold.
  —Marie Piper

A PATH WITH THE LORD

The Lord is by me all day long
He helps me, holds me, keeps me strong
And at night when I'm asleep
He's there by me, my soul to keep.
Each day I walk with Him by me
He shows me things I cannot see.
A light in dark, the Word of God
It shows the path that I must trod.
And when in dark, have no dismay
Go look to God, He'll lead the way.

—Patricia Thies

FAITH

The day will fleet, but I must not
If I do I will be forgot
Faith only knows
Faith can only help
And if the morning shall creep to its peak
No one but I shall be asleep
Yea I guess you're right, why fleet, why flight?
And if that someday goes away
Tell me another way
Ending this poem am I, oh I
Still I know I will fly.

—Tiffany Jean Bates, age 12

Weekend garden will no more be
the same after war, the soil it will
reveal the hell, by digging up the shell
from war,

it's never like as was before, the memory of
hellish nights are like flashbacks with
spikes, the wheel that shows the image in
the mind turns over and over until it's blind

no mind could hide the horror of such nights
when the shells were flying through the
air no one knows from where it came or
land it could strike a friend.

so peaceful is the mind that stands on
holy ground that now and never before
got soiled by war.

—Ruth Culver

ALONE

I'm alone again
I'm sitting here in this lonely room.
sad.
    lonely.
        scared.
In the Day
In the Night
I don't like being alone
But sometimes being alone is fun.
I wonder about other people who are alone.
In the day.
In the night.
sad.
    lonely.
        scared.
I wish nobody would be left alone.
As I sit here in this lonely room alone.

—Marvin Fernando

THE LAST STAND

The silent plea of a small lonely child
Another unseen tear and unheard cry
Always claiming the punishment is mild
Denying the truth, never asking why

In darkness tears fall without precaution
The blame continues as innocence dies
In daylight cold pride leads to exhaustion
And the child begins to believe the lies

Fear is a constant that parallels pain
Strength begins to fade as hate grows stronger
Fate leaves the thought of nothing left to gain
And the need for love is felt no longer

Seeing that the compromising is done
The child makes his last stand, holding a gun

—Angela Dillon

PRISON

They watch you while you're sleeping
What a private thing sleep is!
So inviolable as any stone
You lie a breath away remembering your home
What a strange place? And when
Are you coming home?
Do you go solitary, journeying a
Rugged route triumphantly alone?
You have a need of me and your children
But you can't let them know.
And I must make reluctant peace
With this so our children don't know.
Abandonment until they release you
And it awakens you; and turning with
A kiss you are my love again
Surprised and glad, and murmuring
"What an awful dream I had!"

—Tammy D. Peluso

WEEP FOR ME

Weep for me, my children.
Shed your tears for the time
when blue skies and clear water
were taken for granted.
The gentle breezes and cooling rain
kissed your tanned cheeks.

Weep for me, my children.
Shed your tears for the time
when there were animals roaming freely.
When oceans and rivers gave forth life,
and the trees and flowers perfumed the air.

Weep for me, my children.
Shed your tears for the time
that is yet to come.
When all my children shall be as one.
No prejudice, no hatred, no war.

Weep for me, my children.
Shed your tears for the time
that must eventually come.
When all mankind will pay for their sins.
On that day, my children,
you need weep for me no more.

—Myra L. Moore

THE CLOWN

Child of woe come listen to me; don't let life get you down.
Just put your heart and soul into pretending you're a clown.

Take the silly things we do; accentuate the frown.
The slap-stick way it brings us joy, hurrah for you, the clown.

The way to reach the ears of those who need a visual sound,
Fills my heart with love and joy; it's fun to be a clown.

There was a time, not long ago, life almost had me down.
But luckily, by destiny, came forth the circus clown.

He taught me how to dance and sing and laugh away my frown.
I'm thankful that he took the time to make of me a clown.

You'll always find them at the scene where happiness abounds.
This world would be a better place if there were just more clowns.

There'll always be another me, I'm proud to be a clown.
—Buddee

LOST CARNATIONS

I do not hear the words, yet a man talks on.
I do not feel the cold, yet the wind still blows.

I do not see the people, but they are still there.
I do not see their faces, yet they still exist.

I do not hear the crying, yet it still sounds.
I do not see the tears, yet they still fall.

What I do see is a carnation lost and forgotten.
I can't help but to ask "Are people forgotten that way?"

I feel the emptiness, of where joy and love once was.
There is a void in my life, where you once were.

After many months have passed, I know the love and memories still live on.
I know, I remember and love you as much now, as I did then.

I know that people are not forgotten, like lost carnations.
Grandpa, I still love and remember you.
—Angela S. Merritt

THOUGHTS OF GRANDPA'S DEATH

A land where the sun shines endlessly over Paradise,
Some place where there is no night, hovering with darkness,
No fearing what you cannot see
Because His Light is all around you —
And in your heart and mind there is a calm Peace
Pouring out around uncontrollably.
No bad or evil thoughts invade this Paradise, for hearts are too thankful
Surroundings are unexplainable, too much for a man to comprehend

A place of no sorrowing, confusion, or pain —
No sorrow of missing others for you know you'll see them soon.
No confusion of evil, for there is no evil.
And no pain, for there is no pain to feel.
This is a place where time is nothing, and yet goes on forever,
Nothing in time, or past to miss or regret —
For all you have is so much more.
This is a place of no hunger or thirst, for there is plenty,
And this Paradise is never-ending, given from the One —
This is where my grandfather lives.
He left us for a while, but a day unknown will come,
And we, too, can go home — Home to Paradise.
—Migale S. Mason

MUSING

Love is not the root.
I am someone else.
A stranger, a crown,
a Silver-Spoon.

Small, tiny, strong,
softer than you.

Faithful men and women too
A different port
each country they knew.

A stand of her duty
ridged and still.
A perfect inheritance
was the will.
—Verna U.S.A.

LOST REFLECTION

I looked in a mirror
And I was not there!
No outline or shadow
To prove a life
That believes in no other,
Nor trusts with Faith.

Where have I gone
With my body and soul?
Can others see me
To feel my flesh
And know the longing
Of my eyes?

Is it only I
That have gone away?
Needing to learn
The oneness with another,
So a mirror will show
The likeness of Me.
—Eileen N. Bates

ONLY A DREAM

Stillness fills the air,
nothing can compare.

Seagulls in the sky,
soaring as they fly.

A ship sailing free,
gently on the sea.

No person anywhere,
peaceful everywhere.

My thoughts went astray,
while I walked away.

Footprints in the sand,
left behind on land.

Contentment I feel,
that is life — it's real.

I awakened to see,
it was only a dream.

To Elizabeth, my beloved mother who has been a genuine friend through each year of my life.
—Maria Di Renzo

DREAMS

I dream about acting, singing, and dancing.
Freeing a deer and watch him go prancing.
Giving food for the hungry,
   and a home for the homeless.
I'm just a kid, so I'm only helpless.
So I'll play with my friends,
   and I'll look to the sky and make sure it
     stays blue.
I'll even wish that other people's dreams
   will come true.
But I'm just a kid so this will have to do.
    —Lacey Kristen Sorrentino, age 10

MY LOVE FOR YOU

My love for you is oh so strong
My love for you just can't be wrong
I love you more than you will ever know
I love you more than I can show
My love for you is from the heart
My love is strong even when we are apart
I loved you through all these years
I loved you through all my fears
Many things in life have been unkind
But, I know you will always be mine
My love for you through my heart it pours
I want you to know
I will always be yours
    —Lori Dees

DIAMOND IN THE DUST

Our love has gone away
Thoughts of you are still in my mind
Broken promises and broken hearts
Dreams that lie in the mist
Shadows of the past
And your voice still echos through the night
But our love is gone

Like a dream in the past
You're a Diamond in the Dust
And now rain is falling
Washed away from my heart
You're a Diamond in the Dust
Left to Rust
Love doesn't live here anymore
    —Greg A. Blackburn

    I opened my heart to you and it was within your hands that it broke.
    Though I tried to say "I love you," you never even listened to a word I spoke.
    I gave you my love, then you did the unforgivable.
    You used me to hurt another, and like a fool I listened to your drivel.
    Why? Why did you do it? Knowing that I was hurt before.
    You told me you cared, but deep down you secretly yearned for the one you really adored.
    Why did you have to cut me down so low?
    But most of all, why do I still love you so?
    —April R. Jones

THE TOAST

Here's to a place,
Wherein it's acceptable to give into passion,
To lose track of time
And to think without ration.

Here's to a moment,
Shared only be two hearts,
Where we no longer have to play our roles
Or routinely act out our parts.

Here's to a chance
To rekindle the flame,
To escape from the rest of the world,
And the ongoing game.

Here's to a night
Spent romantically together,
With candlelight and chilled champagne
And a toast . . . to forever.
    —Angela K. Black

THE KISS

A piece of my heart is missing
   It has been taken from deep in me
Only time might turn the tide
     If age can shed the pain
I have yearned for the love and the passion
     Then reacted in total dismay
Thoughts keep running through deep in my mind
     Is this lust or a yearning for love
Can it be a trap of deception
     But then I know it can't be that way
Pour out the feelings you hold within
     So your soul has room to soar
If those feelings stay deep inside
     It's like gypsies with no place to roam
I have searched for this deep inner meaning
     With only one meaningful conclusion
If a kiss is an indication
     My heart may have just been found . . . .
    —Cindy Popp

HIDDEN ARBOR or FOG OF HIDDEN DESTINY

Fog settled down upon our little world
   Making it a hidden thing to all but you and me
And as we sat under the arbor green
I told you of my love so true
I took your hand and squeezed it tight
The while you looked at me with eyes so bright
So full of adoring
And — as life passed us by
We two knew but
The thoughts the other held so dear
My love, I dream of you
When day is long past
You are my inspiration
Which will last throughout my existence
And when you are gone
Only God and his — will know
That it was you and me
That met under the arbor green
In the fog of hidden destiny
    —"Vangi"

As the red sun sets
Dripping pale blood on the horizon
And the seagulls bellow their resounding cries
And the waves crash sullenly on the beach
And the wind whispers around the brazen palms
I walk alone
Carrying emotions far too heavy for my mortal soul
I think of you and I as we once were
Friends and lovers sitting side by side
Walking down the sandy beach together
Where I now walk alone
My love, My friend
I miss you

—Steve A. Bandos

ACTION IN REPOSE
The Suicide of a Saint

Child of the sun, your radiance made us
Forget the melancholy twilight.
When it was day, you caught the sun.
At night you kept us hoping for the dawn.

You lived an existential love
That freed with blissful ignorance
Of that real truth you fully understood
Yet loathed to see us bear.

But in your restlessness you did succumb
And touched the night that bore the hopeless truth.
And now the flurry of your love, restored
By morbid men who still dare hope,
Sings from your grave the secret
Of the dichotomy of your soul.

—Sharon Dockweiler

THE TALIHINA TIGER MALT SHOP

The Malt Shop is the place to be.
It's better than climbing a tree.

You can laugh and have fun.
Instead of sitting on your buns.

You can eat ice cream.
And think you're in a dream.

You can play games, play pool.
And you can sit on a stool.

You can play the jukebox all day long.
As long as you have a quarter to play that song.

You can make friends of all ages.
So come in and turn back the pages.

It's clean and nice.
You'll have to come twice.

Now I've told you what we do.
Malt Shop Customers this is for you.

You are our friends.
On whom we depend.

Sometimes we have some troubles.
But we know you're no rubbles.

You take good care of the Malt Shop.
It's worth working till we drop.

We love you all this is true.
Don't ever leave us or we will be blue.

—Dana Mobley

GROWING OLD

So you're growing old you say;
Wrinkles instead of dimples come to stay.
Yes, but softened by the grey.
Nature reminding to look inward
Where greatest worth and beauty lay
Quietly waiting unfolding
As the perfume of a rose
Most lovely at end of day.

—Suzanne H. Kemp "Suzan"

WHY ME LORD

Just tending my own business one day
Unaware the Lord had a plan to start.
A friend came to town for a stay
This one needs a friend of the heart.

Why me Lord I thought
But only followed his commands.
A much deeper trust was sought
Now my strength is in his hands.

—Linda Bristle Reedy

ODE TO AGE

I'm not so young now, don't you know;
But I'd still like to be on the go.
My hearing is blurred, my joints are bent.
It seems my go got up and went.
There's nothing wrong, though, I'll admit,
With my appetite. It's mighty fit!
Too much so, so the Doctor tells.
Too many sweets and fats, he yells.
But, Doc, I say, it's all OK,
I'll live to eat another day.
But, if I take the Doc's advice
And get real skinny in a trice,
Will then my go that went come back?
Or still be snoozing in the sack?
Old habits are too hard to break.
Sandy, please bring on that steak;
And put some ice cream on my cake.

—Robert D. Spies

ON BEING A SENIOR

As senior citizens, we've seen changes
And fulfilled some hopes and dreams.
We can recall events of the past
But can't remember yesterday, it seems.

Our money somehow disappears.
Our senses also tend to fade away.
Print gets smaller, sound gets softer
And our memory simply goes astray.

Our doctor is important in our life.
He has our medicine cabinet overflowing.
Even though we can't afford it,
we're going to keep right on a-going.

We must keep our spirit alive
As it dwells within our heart,
Especially since our bodies
are slowly falling apart.

We've lived through numerous disasters
And survived them through God's Grace.
No matter what life holds in store
We know, ahead, there's a better place.

—Jeanette Lennon

PRODIGAL RHYTHMS

I closed my eyes and watched.
   She walked toward me, eyes distant
   Without smiles, without knowledge
   Going through the light.
   She passed.

I closed my eyes and watched.
   She laughed, ran to me
   Fisted rose petals near her breast
   Legs long, hurrying.
   She passed.

I closed my eyes and watched.
   She drifted lazily toward the shore
   She glanced, shuddered
   Wooden legged now; she moved on.
   She passed, forever.

     —Lynn Pearson Page

SEEING WITH YOUR HEART

I dream of a blind America,
Just try to imagine that!
No one would know if I am white,
Or yellow, red, or black.

Just my happy footsteps,
Would tell them I am near.
And a cheerful, bright 'Good Morning'
Is all that they would hear.

If America were a nation blind,
Then we could truly see . . .
That peace and love come from the heart,
We would all be really free.

So when you wake up each morning,
Thank God that you have eyes . . .
But stop looking at all your brothers,
Through a skin-colored disguise.

     —Donna Rea

CIRCLES AND CYCLES

See the circle, it is infinite;
it has no beginning and no end . . .
We have much to learn from it
in order to begin to comprehend.

See the cycles set in motion
watch the seasons come and go
In total obedience and devotion
they beckon, "come watch our show."

Feel the moments as you breathe
time passing slowly, them much faster.
Touch the veins in a leaf
it never questions its creator.

Wrap your arms around a tree,
feel the circles of its trunk.
Its life supply flows free
all natural, no artificial junk.

See the circles on a human face
feel the blood pulse through a vein
We are all part of this human race
encircled by cycles that come around again.

     —Noreen A. Hostetler

LIQUID HIGHWAYS
LIQUID HIGHWAYS

        Yearning like a mirage
       On a long deserted road
      Coming but going
     Here but there
    Always within reach
But never obtainable

     —Kenneth Robert C. Farrar

Can you feel what I feel?
Can you see what I see?
Do you know what I know?

How can you feel what doesn't exist?
How can you see what isn't there?
How can you know what's unknown?

You can't feel if you don't open your heart.
You can't see if you don't open your eyes.
You can't know if you don't open your mind.

Believe and you'll feel,
Have faith and you'll see,
Free your mind and you'll know.

     —Lisa Loepp

THE GRAVEMAKERS

To begin.
Impressive, hollow words.
Questions pierce the chasm of empty space;
No resting place to claim an answer.
    Slab grey walls,
        Shoot up like tombs.
Death robs joy of searching and knowing.
What pleasure is seen in this contructed graveyard?
How is it possible,
    Those buried so deep,
        Whose blood no longer stains,
           Can ache and groan in pain?
How is it possible?

     —Paula Gerstmann

RAIN OF THE ACROPOLIS

Love is that rare certain thing,
that climbs the skies and hills,
in as much abundance,
as the myriad of flowers,
that clings like perfume,
to the ground.

The loving touch,
of the vaudevillians,
is the basalt of the Earth's stocking.
They have that certain something,
That one can solve empathetic problems with.

Love is the raining touch of the wind,
that last glance at velvet,
that comb that flatters the vendemas of hair.

In super attachments to this Earth,
we take it,
and promise it a new name.
And love goes on,
within the realm of a second entendre.

     —Lisa Miller

A PIANO BAR

A PIANO BAR
where I sit
    drink
    forget the perma-pressed souls
    around a Kilowatt keyboard   Needing
    to belong—

At thirty-nine breaking forty, I'm in Vegas
dealing tens and aces to plastic traveled faces—
Shot glass ironing boards   Flesh
and powdered Madness, candy-cane women
fishnet legs tell me to ESCAPE:
    the piper has been paid
    I'll take my leave, blindfolded
    two plugs of wax
tied to the mast   I listen to 88's . . . .

—Joe Scalise

TO LIGIA ORTEGA UPON LEAVING FOR COLLEGE

A warning dawn leaks sanguine through my mind
with brewing threats of swiftly rolling hours,
with flashes of the sadness we shall find,
when time pours down on mine and yours, not ours.
And closer than feels safe the rumblings sound
out dolor for two hearts, haplessly marked
to be beneath those loudly pitch days drown'd,
or lose themselves in gusts of love unmarked.
But we would fain these rueful winds defy
by crescent hope rooted in certainty
that weath'red storms will love intensify,
that time will water our magnan'mity.
Each drop of time upon my lonely brow
will, to its torment, watch my fondness grow.

—Joel Caren

TOM JONES

Tom Jones was a drunkard
There's no doubt about that.
You can tell by his red nose,
His coat, and his hat.

And his ragged old trousers,
Oh where could you match 'em
Or 'er find a woman
Whoever could patch 'em.

His wife never tried it.
Twas not cause she wouldn't,
The reason for this
The poor woman couldn't.

For this pair of trousers
Were Tom's only ones,
And what would he do
While the patching was done?

One evening quite sober
Tom came home to tea,
Said to his wife,
"There's something I've missed.

And I've missed it for weeks.
What has become of the rose in your cheeks?"
"You know Tom, what became of the rose,
You stole it for the red on the end of your nose!"

—Doris M. Webb

SCHOOL DAYS

Fall is here
Those School Days are near
Time to gather your thoughts.

Enter the room,
Education is in bloom,
You're no longer tiny tots.

The board where the teacher has wrote,
gives information, you make your first note.

After opening your book,
You take a small look,
Then being where you've been before,

You can't go back,
You're starting to crack,
and can't take the pressure anymore.

—Michelle L. Cowden

CUNNING CAT

Cat is on the prowl,
If she sees a dog — YEOWL!
She'll find her prey,
And catch it if she may.
Under the fence Cat will crawl in the light,
Be careful — the squeeze is tight!
Off to get the mouse she'll pad,
If Cat can't find it she'll be mad!
Now! She's caught the little beast,
Oh, what a feast.
She's killed her mouse,
Now off to Master's house.
She will climb into her bed,
And lay down her head.
It's been a long day,
In her bed she'll stay.
She doesn't make a peep . . .
Cat's fallen asleep.

—Natalie N. Martz, age 12

PROM NIGHT ON THE FIELD

Noises roared through the locker room,
a cage with animals ready to escape.
A wrinkle in a jersey.

A dangerous running of the bulls
and the players are on the field.
The tilt-a-whirl begins,
the plans are laid.

It's a dance.
It's a war.

It's a grunt.
   A groan,
   A plan.

From eleven to one.
Earth to sky.
One yard, one foot, one mile.

Tape-ripped hands raised,
the tilt-a-whirl slows.
Step off.

The carnival's gone.

—Eric Wolff

ALL IN TIME

If time could be turned
would we take the chance
the wonders and beauty
that may lay ahead

Life is but a lesson
that we often learn
to better ourselves
Would back we return?

—Linda Marr

EBONY HANDS

The ebony hands of death grasp
    my neck.
The eternal voice is calling
    for me.
The unbearable hurt will be lifted
    from my shoulders.
Unexplainable and unexpected
My love will stop flowing from
    its source.
What shall you do then, my love,
    when I am torn to shreds by your
      uncaring and dawdling with my
      emotions?
Shall there be another soul as I?
Or shall you be the victim?
Can it be possible?
Will your soul die from lonesomeness
    and a broken heart also?
When shall the ebony hands of
    death grasp your neck?

—Charlene Holguin

WALLS

I built my walls high and
    strong of stone.
And behind my walls I sit.
I look out my window pane and
    peer out at the acid rain.
And behind my walls I sit.
I hear them cutting down our rain
    forests, destroying the homes of
    innocent animals.
And behind my walls I sit.
I see them open up the ground wide
    and hide their toxic waste deep inside.
And behind my walls I sit.
I see the vacant space where they take
    our trees and don't replace.
And behind my walls I sit.
God gave us a wonderful place to live.
He gave us his world with love and care.
We show our gratitude by putting
    a hole in his ozone layer.
And behind my walls I sit.
I see our beautiful earth being destroyed.
And behind my walls I sit.
We put our politicians in office because
    of all their promises to take care of
    these problems.
And behind their walls they sit.

—T.J. Smith

Star light, star bright
First star I see tonight
Wish I may, wish I might
Please grant my wish tonight.
    I wish for happiness, joy, and lots of luck,
      For the people I love, and know.
      For the people who need it the most.
        And for myself,
          I wish for love, hope, and also luck.
Star light, star bright,
    Good night.

—Cynthia Multine

THE RISING LIGHT

In the Spirit of a child there is *LOVE*
    The youngster's face shining with the Dove
And when a little one first makes a moral choice
    Then God indwells the mind with rejoicing

God of Heaven looking out upon the stars
    Sends His Spirit to guide us on our journey
On every infant the Dove reflects God's heart
    And child submits shining to be revealed.

Look upon us, Angel, in our humble cribs
    And share and show us to the holy Cherubim
Bring us into our peace-loving grandeur
    When paradisers proclaim love in our sight

Send us forward into the holy embrace
    Of Father, Son, and Universe Mother Spirit
Lead us into the eternal port of Jerusalem;
    Our heavenly calling now made sure forever more

In the jubilant bouncing of toddlers in the grass
    The sunrise bloomed like rhododendrons:
The seedlings germinating in the divinely ordained
    Unity of man, animal, and angelic environment

—Scott C. Harrison

SPRING

In the vibrant quiet of the hilltop,
While the sun struggled to master the day,
I watched dark shadows disintegrate
Under the piercing, shimmering rays.

I marveled; my ears caught the awakening
Of earth's creatures from their slumbers of night;
Astonished, I listened and wondered
At this panorama of breathtaking sights.

Miracles of communication were rampant,
Understanding each sound-thought conveyed.
Earth's seeds that lay dormant were quickened
On this threshold of Spring, new life is portrayed.

Young birds hatched from the shells that confined them;
Tiny creatures emerged from the throes of their birth.
Vital sunlight probed foliage, wildflower, and seedling
As each burgeon their difficult way above earth.

The New Year of Spring dispenses her blessings
As buttercups catch her warm glow in each chalice,
And radiant sunbeams from the Windows of Heaven
Paint prismatic colors in this primitive palace.

Dedicated to my beloved children,
Jim, Mike, Sherri and Judy

—Madelyn Borgardts

SONNET

Very glowing was its review in the *Times*
I knew this book was one I'd enjoy.
Keen for exotic climes and rhymes,
Right away I loved *The Suitable Boy*.
All told it took 10 years to write it,
Multiple layers of meaning in it.
Sad when I finished, for I wanted more,
Especially more Amit, Kabīr and Tagore.
This author gives us his guts and heart.
His story has a crime, it has a pardon,
It has a passion, it has a garden,
And it has a deeper truth to impart
About life beside the effervescent River,
Where the surfaces change, but essence never.

—Frances M. Scura

MERCILESS ACTS

As I walk down the street on a cold winter day,
I see something horrifying walking my way.
It's disguised as a woman looking in stores,
But it's really a killer, a murderer of sorts.
I don't think she realizes, and if she does,
    doesn't care,
What merciless acts give her what she wears.
She tells me it makes her feel elegant and
    attractive,
In my eyes she's nothing but revolting and repulsive.
Millions of animals die every year,
And not one of these people even shed a tear.
As I turn around slowly and watch her walk by,
I see a young woman out of the corner of my eye,
Complimenting her on the silver foxcoat, and sigh.

—Melissa Hutchison

EARTH'S PRAYER

Earth is our salvation,
Pollution is our devastation,
God save Earth from this damnation,

    "Save the trees,
    Save the breeze,
    Save the seas,
    We all agree,

    Acid rain must not remain
    In the plain."

In the plain
In every nation,
Public viable transportaion must remain
In every nation.

Viable public transportation curbs pollution,
Pollution, earth's elimination.
God save earth from this aggravation.
Earth cannot be liable for devastation.
God save Earth from damnation.

Damnation is Earth's heavy concentration,
Please God, save Earth's constellation.
Destiny can be Earth's only source
Of natural perpetation.
God save Earth from agonizing reservation,
    Natural resources, Earth's preservation.

    In every nation God preserve Earth's destination,
    For God you are Earth's tribulation and adulation,
    And the only true source of gratification.

—Louise Pietrolaj

I STUMBLED ALONG

I've trusted Jesus most my life;
He's the only sacrifice.
I've grown in love — knowledge too;
Tried to do what He wanted me to.
I've slipped and fallen — stumbled along;
But He helped me see — where I was wrong.
He's given and taken — I don't understand;
Yet I know He'll never — let go of my hand.
Oh Praise the Lord — for He is good;
Guiding and helping like He said He would.
He's given comfort unknown to man;
So how can I say — I understand?
I have faith in the fullness of Christ;
Knowing He's given eternal life.

—Karen Martin

BEACONS

    Oh, let our lives be beacons,
Let them shine for all we're worth.
    Let them beam across the mountaintops,
And smile to flood the earth.
    Let them bloom in thirsting deserts,
And glow for ships at sea.
    Let them twinkle in the lonely nights,
So all the lost can see.
    Let them ring across the prairies,
And sing on every shore.
    Let them radiate much better,
Than they ever did before.
    Oh, let them never flicker,
Just a steady stream of light.
    To light the entire world, I pray,
And keep it shining bright.

—Laurie Hasan

NATION'S DREAMS

You started out a small flicker of
light, then to a candle giving us light.

Do we dare to dream and give you
our hopes, so some day you can run with
that bright shining torch.

Oh how your candle with its bright
glow, filled hearts where ever you'd go.
You filled us with love, dreams and hope
so Mr. Clinton we gave you our votes, and
and along with it lays the nation's hopes.

Now you're a beacon shining bright, we
all know it will be a really hard fight,
but hold on tight and follow those dreams.
Behind you stands the nation we'll follow
your leads.

Our hopes are high, the future in your
hands hold to your promises to the rest be
damned.

You planted your seeds throughout the
nation, we've started to grow and now to
blossom, keep your promises, those seeds you
planted are now your garden.

—Marianne Sandoval

MUSIC

Dancing notes on a page
Keys hitting in anger, rage
Strings plucked ever so light
While the moon sings me to sleep at night

—Patricia Bullock

THE DIFFICULT DECISION

The breeze blows warm and salty
at the sandy oceanside.

Sea gulls fly in circles,
is it magic how they glide?

The sun glows hot and orange,
from its rays you cannot hide.

A porpoise jumps into the air,
and fish swim side by side.

The beach, it seems to calm me,
as I walk into the tide.

As night falls I know that I must go,
yet when I'll leave I can't decide.

—Kristi Pinkston

TO SHELLY

Oh, sweet death I feel thy bones
Come close to thee each night—
Might each morrow bring thy grave
For eternally it is mine—
Can thy spirit dwell in thee till
Time shall be no more?
Or come willingly
To thy open shore—
For life is such a pitfall
And day brings forth another—
And can the human soul find
Peace without love from thy brother?
Canst thou swiftly come—
The dawn is near to us and so the darkest hour—
For life goes on day by day
A pitfall for tomorrow!—

—Amy Nicole McGhee

Dear Mother of mine
so loving, caring and kind.
I knew one day you would go away . . .
never more to return.
Oh Dear Mother,
I love you so, I can barely stand
the thought of letting you go, but if you must
go quickly now,
depart for there is a bright light shining in the dark
to guide you down the pathway
to your new home so very far away.
As you climb the golden stairs,
a burst of joy will fill the air
and when you reach the Golden Gate
Dad and Doris will be there
and all of your love and kin will welcome you in
with outstretched arms to love and care for you
where pain and sorrow will be no more.

Your loving daughter
—Barbara

PRIVATEER COVE

Birds flying south,
scooping fish into their mouth.
Close to the bay,
you'll find ducklings at play.
You see across the inlet,
the golden sunset.
The pleasure of the wetlands,
and the history of ancient Indian lands.

—Michelle Piorkowski, age 12

when i cry
there is blood in my tears
and all that is good in me begins to die
i can no longer concentrate on my fears
i can feel my heart melting away
with each painless day
how can a human not feel
for it is that which makes us heal
but if i fall to me knees
who shall catch me
and if i must ask
am i worthy of this task

—Pamela M. Jointer

MY HEAVENLY HOME

Though my days sometimes seem weary
I find that I walk alone
My nights offer little, or no consolation
I know that I have a Heavenly home.

I cannot wave these tides of life
For me, they're much too strong
When I have crossed this chisholm vast
I will have reached my Heavenly home.

I'll take my bow, to a Heavenly rest
Where former things, have all passed
There to behold his immortal face
In my Heavenly home at last.

—Robert Wilson

THE CAPTAIN'S VESSEL

Devotions of compasses, safe in the hands of our future.
Ocean currents moving separating the air we breathe.
Uprising winds surrounding our ship, compassing nautical,
frustration of lightweight cargo in cans of precious oil.
Gazing at the moon, while we stay on course, in an ocean of blue water.
Feeling born again starting new and eager to reach land.
Traveling across oceanless breezes, synonyms blended in chimes.
Dividing our time, watching the stern captain, deciding to go ashore.
Reaching destination plotting to be free.
My God Jesus is my Captain pulling — pushing huge waves from my brow.
Set free by temptation, minute by minute staring turning reflections,
battling life on the high seas.

—Antoinette Garrick

CAPE MAY AVENUE REMEMBERED
(a seaside idyll)

Saltwater demons haunt the backbay scrub forests
Where no traffic lights speak of civilized forms;
Crying gulls hover above the sand-flecked two lane
Making flighty ballet for the landlocked below . . .
This fireskied summer that gave us no repose
Yet made us feel corroded with the mists and the
Ancient whaling songs and the nights when whiskey
Stole the captions of our lives . . .
. . . Somewhere out on Route 9
Near burnt-out Chevy coupes and those
Seatowns sprayed with dew and dappled dreams
We came to find a certain peace amidst the
Indian trails winding low by the Delaware Bay;
For this, we found, was the primordial stuff of our desires . . .
. . . Now the Fall beckons through the foggy dawn
Telling us to make ready for soon the icy will of heaven will grip the sea;
The dunes we trekked will boast layers of frost
And the boardwalk will be closed awaiting the new year
When once more we'll cruise this forest route and find that
Our hearts were left there, after all, last year.

—D. Thomas Imperato

WHERE MUST I GO?

Where must I go?
When a fiendish world so graciously endows me with blow after blow . . .
Where must I go?

Where must I go?
When the all encompassing factors of yesterday, today, and tomorrow are cast
upon my mind, heart, body, and soul like anonymous impressions of blank
visions of people, places, and things that I should know, that I may know,
that I do not know . . .
Where must I go?

Where must I go?
When I travel a journey so distant, so coarse, so bare . . . that as I move
through the course of it: my journey, that is, . . . I am barely aware . . .
Where must I go?

Where must I go?
When I once a man, when I once a woman, when I once a child can no longer
distinguish between you and me or then and now . . .
Where must I go?

Where must I go?
When I am afraid and all alone, and I am living in a world, once so meek
and fair, that now barely acknowledges that I am even here . . .
Where must I go?

*Dedicated to Mrs. Elzenobia Ruth Smith Dillard Downs, my dear aunt, mentor,
and friend who is "the majestic blue bird" who taught me how to fly
over the rainbow and who shall have a special place in my heart:
today, tomorrow, and always!*

—Don Eric Smith

OPPOSITES ATTRACT

I fell in love with just a glance
take it from me, it was just by chance
How did I know that you would be the one
to fill all my days with fun
you gave me your ring and I wear it on a string
It is close to my heart where I pray we will never part
I wish you could see
how much you mean to me
We're both set in our ways
but that's okay, cause we have plenty of days
You like the outdoors and I like the dance floors
We have the time to spend together
hopefully we can make it work forever
They say all things good come to an end
but I say it's time for those rules to bend.

—Colleen Kaczor

SEASONS OF THE HEART

(Humble Beginnings)

The time of year is in the fall.
Now, I can hear my Father's pleading call.

(The Fearful Fire)

It's winter now, the winds blow cold.
My head hangs low, as my Father doth scold.

(My Soul Springs)

This soul of mine looks to the spring
With upturned face, open heart, and hands to cling.

(Summershine)

With eyes and heart filled with an inner glow,
I give thanks to my Father and my love for Him can show.

—Gwendolyn A. Caskey

SHE'S THE ONE

The girl amongst my wildest dreams is right before my eyes.
My affection for her just escalates with every new surprise.

I've developed a certain infatuation for her and her alone,
Her enchanting eyes just paralyze me
and everything in her zone.

Her certain radiance controls me now
and forever and ever more—
My desire for her glides every day, my heart's begun to soar.

She took me out of the darkness, and I won't forget to say,
She listens to my problems and takes my pain away.

My love for her is never extinct and would never be obsolete.
She could lay a delightful spell on me—
Wouldn't that be one intense treat?

She's always happy with herself and vigilant in her ways,
She's led me out of obscurity and into an elegant daze.

I hope one day we'll make it legal and she will be all mine,
My sincerity, passion, love and joy will always
continue to shine.

The words of this poem which come straight from my heart, are dedicated to Mary Bishop. I hope one day our hearts will come together to form one. Mary, you are "The One" forever.

—Jamie Wagar

You lie still,
Much stiller than before.
Six feet of soil stops me
From touching you in love.
I miss you.

Dedicated to Betty

—Bill Fricke

A LESSON FOR LIFE

Daring and brave
Fearless and alone
Big and impudent
Enter the cave.

Take slow steps
'Lest you trip.
Be not afraid
Of any dip.

Face every man
With a strong heart
And an iron will
I know you can.

—Jessica Zver, age 17

DOES ANYONE HAVE A PEN?

I rushed down the hall
to write down my thoughts
found me a pen that would only
leave blots
I grabbed for another to write
down my quirk
Try as I may
that pen would not work
All through the haste
I tried to remember the lines
but time doesn't stop for thoughts
left behind
What if I dig in the back of my
mind?
If only I'd had me a pen
to write down my line.

—Linda Marr

A LONG JOURNEY SOMEWHERE

A long journey somewhere
on a road that never ends
A road with no going back
and nowhere to turn

Travel by day Travel by night
getting higher, taking the flight
A light ahead to follow
coming closer yet farther away

Never give up and never fight
and someday you will find the light
When you get there never let it
leave you

Or you will end up in darkness
with nowhere to go.

Through vigilant guidance
The Long Journey Nowhere
gradually became
A Long Journey Somewhere
Thanks to a very prestigious fellow
Michael Waye

—Linda Marr

I'M ON THE TRACK OF LOVE

Engineer! Engineer! I'm on the track of love,
I'm searching for my turtle dove,
for every man there's a gal
a sweet turtle dove to love, to hold, to cuddle,
I want a sweet five foot two, with eyes of blue,
some like a gal tall and thin
but that's not the kind of gal my love can win,
I want a plump turtle dove.
Do you hear me engineer?

—Virginia J. Folmar

IT'S TIME!!

It's time go, but it's not goodby . . .
So don't let yourself begin to cry . . .
As time passes by, it will be here soon . . .
Just a few passes of an ever-turning moon . . .
Just as the day is long, and the night is black . . .
The time has come, not to look back . . .
Just look forward, and the sun will shine,
AND THAT!!
Will be the reason for this rhyme . . . .

—"COSMOSE" 1993 M.E.R

THE WHITE ROSE

The white rose is pristine and clean;
Perfection in itself:
   One of the prettiest I've ever seen—
White as a freshly fallen blanket of snow.
   Its leaves and stems are garnished in dark green,
Which make a beautiful show.
   Its creamy, soft, white petals
Glisten with droplets of dew—
   When early morning mist makes its debut.
Its perfumed scent lingers in the air,
   With a fragrance, cloyingly, sweet and rare.
I would choose this one perfect white rose
   And give it to you.

—Leah Jeannine Charles

IF OTHERS ONLY UNDERSTOOD

At first things went by in a blur
Then you felt a little unsure
You needed to get your orientation back
To get again on a "straight track"
Things started coming along good
Now if others "just really understood"
There are times you seem to be trying awfully hard
And you keep going inch by inch, foot by foot
Yard by yard
You begin to wonder what others may think
And you feel you'd like to shrink
You begin to wonder what others do say
Then you may feel like you just don't want to stay
Never lose your self-worth and esteem
Because someday you can be like a lighthouse beam
You'll be able to help others "find the way"
And assist them to have a brighter day

—MJ Pietrzak

THE SOURCE OF LOVE

What is the source that carries love,
Upon the shining seas.
Could it be the stars above,
Or whistling with the breeze.
Perhaps the shrewdly road of fate,
Contains within its bounds,
The love that carried you to me,
Aloft my withered grounds.
And now that love has brought to light,
Our newly found decree,
We know that our endearment will,
Succeed eternity.

—Jennifer L. Moss

FOR MY TRUE LOVE

You are my sunshine in the day,
You are my stars at night.
I've cared for other guys,
But this time it really feels right.

The way you hold me,
Makes me feel so secure.
And that is why the love we share,
Makes me so sure.

We are made for each other,
I believe this more each day,
Because of the way we work things out,
In our own special way.

You are the most important part of me,
My love for you is dear.
I hope that these few months together,
Will soon add up to years.

*Written for my true love, my husband, Roy,
who is my inspiration for all of my poems.
Thank you honey. I love you.*

—Amy L. Shreve

TAKE HEART

When you find someone and you fall in love,
   the world seems not so bad.
But, when something makes that love go wrong,
   you lose that grip you had.
You feel as though you're all alone,
   and no one understands.
You just don't care about anything,
   no future and no plans.
You figure you've lost the best you'll have,
   and you know there'll never be,
a person who you think could love you,
   more than you did he.
But, don't stop your life, take day by day,
   because there will come a time,
when things will fall in place again,
   and another love you'll find.
Just trust in God, He'll carry you,
   thru all life's bitter days,
and lead you to your happy self,
   that's found joy thru His ways.
He'll get you thru if you stay strong,
   and give you what you need.
He'll put before you, all the fruit,
   but *you* must plant the seed.

—Tracy L. Kling

GOODBYE

When you speak they don't hear your words.
When you cry they don't see your tears.
When you hurt they don't feel your pain.
When you're gone they don't understand why,
but they should have listened because
you were really saying goodbye.

—Jannise

THIEF OF HEARTS

Everything is a simple word,
but it's what I enjoy about you.
Your smile, your kiss, your tender sweetness,
 gives thoughts to mine never to leave behind.
Uniqueness strong and truly refreshing,
 my words aren't long but hopefully convincing.

On this day, that you gave breath,
 also a day of eminent theft.
You've become a thief of hearts,
 stealing mine with sensuous remarks.
Time pass and passes still,
 my life not lost and loving at will.

If all's forgotten and a mist I consist,
 remember you're at, the top of my list.

—Wayne E. Loveless

THE FINAL CHAPTER

The final chapter, the final page, brings to the
 Closing of this age,
Signs and wonders point the way, they are every
 Where to survey,
Like an echo from the wilderness, come to me
 And I will give you rest,
Lay down your burdens, the hour is late, enter
 In through the narrow gate,
Just try it for size, it may fit better than you
 Realize,
Time is ticking away, as each moment draws near, as
 Man kind poises on the
Brink he so fears, as the final chapter, and the final
 Page, brings to the
Closing of this age!

—Sally Cabaret Lucci

MEDITATIONS

In those brief moments given to me,
 I have known you, Beauty, my dear.
In a woman's love that only love could see,
 In friends, whose hearts knew the tear,
When innocent love was the Young Queen
 Of hearts in little children at play,
And in the wonders of nature's meadows, green,
 When her spirit flourishes in hearts, gay!
In those rare moments when I touched you
 In a tender kiss of love! In a smiling face,
In delicate flowers bathed in morning dew,
 And in my own heart that knew your abiding grace!
If I should come again to those moments, rare,
 I should have all, all love, all life to share!

Dedicated to my friend: Margo Kivisto,
Teacher-Extraordinary! Brighton, Michigan.

—A.J. Walters

I MISS YOU

I miss you Sonny at bed time.
I miss the sounds in the room upstairs.
It's empty and lonely now.
No boys to noisily climb the stairs,
No bouncing, no laughing, it's gone.
But I still remember, I just can't forget.

There were five boys up there.
Now there isn't one left.
You were the last to leave,
It's most more than I can bear.
Some of them will come home,
But your home is in heaven,
I'll try to meet you there.

Dedicated to all those mothers who sat at
home and waited for their sons to return
from W.W.II — Our three brothers,
did make it home.

—Beatrice L. Schnelle, deceased

BLUE

Blue . . .
Blue like the oceans
Your eyes will see.
And gulls flowing here and there.
I taste the salt water on my tongue.
And hide away 'til your presence . . .
To another day of finding you.
Transparent on the sand.
Only before the clouds of blue reach you.
Blue . . .
Blue is that shimmer in your eyes.
The place I get lost in.
The place I love most.
I hear your voice cry out
As the sun shines intently . . .
Intently I stare at you.
Like a gull the blue water.
And he dives for a fish.
While I reach for your soul.

—Alison Fritzius

SONNET

And guarded by a star, a wind swept beach
Lies white and still and dimly-glowing there
While two who know but longing each for each
Run hand in hand, and unaware
Of beauty seen as beauty consciously,
Respond yet to the spell of beauty felt.
Rough sands against warm bodies
Soft lips to rough ones, softly brutal, melt.
A whirling sense of mounting destiny;
A force as of great rushing winds through space;
The blinding brightness of infinity;
Translation of the love met face to face.
Desire, a flame white-hot, burns bright and free
And welds into completeness — ecstasy.

—ILLDC

SUN'S DEATH

Today the sun died in pain
Winter laughed and spring cried
I felt the pain in my mom's eyes
The day the sun died

Rain danced and the wind sang
A song for the falling sun
Today the sun died in the arms of night
The one that took its life

Night was proud of what it did
It never cared — it had no sin
All it wanted was to win

Now the sun is gone
There is no life
No hope
No dreams
Nothing but the coldness of our hearts

—Brandon Pilarski

CAT'S CANTO

Peppermint thighs
he said . . .
And chocolate bellies

The lamb's in the meadow
The wind's in the south
While the rain rains on
And we hum through the night

I had a feeling that the answer was no,
I said . . .
Just like I felt that the night would come

But the morning followed
The day dawned
The lamb grew up
And the wind went west

While I pressed all the flowers
In my book of the dead

—May L.M. Bonnaud

THE GRAPHICS OF LIFE

The Graphics of life
are traces of memories stored
to present many faces of
reality to which I live today—

Choices are many to touch these faces
of webbed reality
Which could be the outcome of my life
. . . tomorrow . . .
What is it that has been set for me in my

fragment
of
life?

I'm not here to except nothing

The sense of unity of self
is to one day hope for
I search for direction and find so many
roads to travel

but yet, I can only take one of me.

—Linda Marr

SHINE OUT

Shine out your light,
in spite the world to be.
Shine out with might.
Be a glorious sight,
for all the world to see.

—Katherine Burton

FOREVER LOVE

I saw a cloud go drifting by
And pictured your face in the sky

I heard the wind blowing in the trees
And felt your touch like a gentle breeze

I smelled the new mowed grass
And knew our love was here to last

I felt the warm sun on my face
And knew my love had found a place

I tasted the cool refreshing rain
And knew my heart would feel no pain

I sensed the sweetness of your kiss
And knew a love I had not missed.

Dedicated to my husband, David

—Ruth M. Croman

A STREAM OF WATER

As I sat by a stream of running water
Tears running down my face
I saw a crayfish floating helplessly by

I realized the tears that I was shedding
really need not be

The crayfish thought at the time
that he would not survive

At the end of the stream was a place he
could make his home in the mud

If I have Love in my Heart
Jesus can cause rivers of Living water
to flow in my Heart

And there won't be any
room for tears

—Charita Martin

SMOKE OF THE SACRED ASH

The stars, winking from the sky
at a soul, who passes by
the time with a bittersweet puff
from the burning of some real good stuff.

The smoke, which ascends in dance
in figures sharper than a lance,
transform to spirits telling tales
in gusts of the winds mighty gales.

Saying, "Oh! This — it ain't so bad
we're happy with the life we've had:
once green, then withered quite
to give some soul pleasure in the night."

"Our only purpose was to give
taste so a person's joy could live.
They call us evil; a bad tobacco stash,
but we're just Smoke Of The Sacred Ash."

—Michael J. Paddock

DON'T GAMBLE WITH YOUR LIFE

I've never been a ramblin gamblin man,
But one day I tried my luck with "Gamblin Sam,"
As old Sam saw me, he collared me to gamble,
I learned my lesson that day — no more to gamble.
Why — I lost my paycheck and favorite hat,
So I decided no more of that!
If I had not stopped gamblin, I would have lost
my car and the clothes on my back.

Hey everybody beware cause old gamblin Sam don't
play fair. Don't gamble with your life.

—Virginia J. Folmar

LOVE THROWN AWAY

    Alas, to be but a flower in your garden,
gently plucked only to wither away and die.
The subtle blissfulness and peace that could
have lasted a lifetime. A daisy with bright
rays of light that cause you to shine when
you're near. The bright center of warmth and
friendship, full of optimism and hope only
to be turned away as if only a dandelion.

    Alas, Alas, such crimes of passion should
not be taken on the wing, but nestled in the
bosom of love.

—Constance Chasmont

There's a tragedy of losing your child in His prime
"As a Mother, I can't live "one" Day at a time"
Lonely Hours, I suffer this fate,
I long to see him at Heaven's Gate
Every day is a struggle to survive
Cause truth be known, you're not alive.
No place to run, no place to hide
All faith is gone, nothing inside.
I long to see Him at Heaven's Gate
This endless time I sit and wait.
The greatest Hell I go through
One Son is here, the other with you
I can't find happiness in either place
This is my hell, this is my fate
I can't leave, I don't want to stay
And I can't stand living this way.
I know of no greater tragedy, on earth that can be done
For a Mother to outlive her daughter or Her first born Son.

—Nancy C. Rossini

MY CAPTAIN

On the island of Tyrene,
    a harbor waits under a veil of death.
The glassy water is serene,
    quiet as bird breath.
A pelican sits on a barnacled post
    that the waves spit and hit,
Coming from the condemned coast.
Deep in the main, an angel boat lies.
It cannot sail closer, but sends a message instead.

I found my Captain died
When a mermaid told me
The ship had been thrown apart, by the cruel
    black sea.
She herself was not well; she'd lost her color.
    My eyes could tell:
No one but she had lived through
    the seaman's horror.

—Julia Moffitt

THE PROMISED LAND

The sun fades over the promised land.
A little baby releases its hand.
The nurse comes in. The wound to dress.
The priest comes in. This place to bless.

—Heidi Kettler

FINDING FREEDOM

We seek freedom,
    Through our governments
We fight for freedom,
    Against our brothers
We cast away responsibilities,
    To gain freedom
Yet in searching,
    We never find freedom,
For true freedom
    Can only be found,
In the heart.

—Sheri L. Corder

LIFE OF THE MISFITS

We are all brothers on this earth
    But Angel and I have been since birth
We walk the road that lies empty
And see what no man would dare to see
For we have faced pain and sorrow
We were not afraid for we knew tomorrow
There would be death knocking on our door
We were not scared, we faced death before
This world is full of things unseen
But to us they mean not a thing
For we have Jesus in our heart
And nothing can make our world go dark
We are not afraid to meet our death
God is with us try our best
If you can kill me and Angel
We will go to Heaven and do God's will.

—Loren "Ruthless A.D." Armstrong

WHEN I WAS YOUNG

When I was young, I watched the
    clouds change into any form
    I imagined.
When I was young, I dreamed of
    wonderful things I would do.
When I was young, the world was
    filled with beauty and magic.
When I was young, I was amazed
    at the perfection of humanity.
When I was young, I was in love
    with love.
But suddenly life got in the way.
Now all I see are the clouds
    being blown away by the wind.
My dreams were shattered by the
    reality of life.
I found little beauty and magic
    in my life.
Now I see the imperfection of
    humanity
But the most important part of
    my life still exists.
I am still in love with love.
For love never dies.

—Adele Veronica Shimp

CLOSE, WE LIE TOGETHER

Close, we lie together
and fill the night with soft whispers.
Speaking in breaths that brush our lips
lightly, gently inviting us
we explore its boundaries
and the limitlessness of the emerging
passion we embrace
Firmly, slowly
within our arms
the rising rhythm of two hearts
ignites a single flame
Building, burning
to a purpose
that exists solely in its consummation and
thus recedes, expiring silently,
drawing in breaths that linger across our eyes.

Close, we lie together
and fill the night with soft whispers.

—John A. Costa

MY LOVE FOR YOU

My love for you is quite strong,
    Even if you do wrong.
I understand the way you feel
    And I know our love is real.
When I'm with you I feel so much love.
    When I'm not, you're who I'm thinking of.

My love for you is so true.
    I only wish that others knew
The joy and laughter we have together.
    I have this feeling it will last forever.
I know you feel this way also,
    And it's my heart that tells me so.

My love for you is so great,
    Even if I become irate.
The feelings we share could not be wrong,
    Because I've loved you for so long.
I hope these words give you a clue
    Of just how much I love you.

—Michelle Bryan

WONDERFUL THINGS

All these are wonderful to me
    and free for all to see
Red skies in morning light
    brings such a delight
The sun rising at dawn, a baby being born
    listening to a robin's song
Knowing winter's almost gone
    and eating home grown corn
The smell of a new mown lawn
    a doe with her fawn
Trees sprouting new leaves
    a touch of a breeze
The warmth of spring
    after a freeze
Smelling a rose as it unfolds
    falling snow, a sight to behold
Warm days, cold nights
    northern lights
Sap dripping from trees, ships passing at sea
    all these things so wonderful and free

—Joan Atwater

THE WALK

We walk together on the beach.
You hold up your hand for me to reach.
I hold your hand to show the way.
You're learning new things every day.
I'll show you how to build a castle
Out of sand.
You are my baby my little man.
Years from now you'll walk this beach.
Holding out your hand for your son
To reach.
I know you'll remember the things we've done.
A young mommy and her baby son.
Whose days were full of love and fun.
Walking on the beach and holding hands
Building castles on the sand.

—Nina Ehrke

A POEM FOR MOM

The baby before your eyes wasn't such
A surprise
Before you knew it I was grown and became
A lady you know and love
When you gave birth to me I was your first and
You watched me grow from head to toe
You've held me close through thick and thin
Always holding up my chin
The excitement you felt when you saw
Yourself in your child's face made your
Heart go at a fast pace
I've grown to know your humor and charm, but
So far it hasn't done me any harm
Through the years we've had our share of
Tears, but I've grown to know that you are my
Mother and I can love no other

—Clarissa Kirschenmann

MOM

I don't know how to say
the things I want to say.

Sometimes I don't even know
how to express my emotions to you.

Whenever I think about
telling you that "I love you."

I choke up and the words
won't come out of my mouth.

I don't remember the last time
or even if I ever told you "I love you."

When things get tough I would like
to crawl up on your lap;

And have you tell me that
everything will be alright.

But I am an adult now, and
I am not supposed to do that.

I must act like a man even
when I feel like a little boy.

Someday with God's help, I hope to be
able to tell you how much I love you.

—Calvin C. McVey

BELVEDERE

An Alchemist, a credit to his kind,
Appealed to the Moon for signs divine
Whereby intelligence incarnadine
Might bind a precious metal with his mind.
How darkly was the New Moon disinclined;
However, a keen sliver (superfine)
Waxed to a crescent Moon, a countersign;
Likewise, a sky-bowl proved starlight enshrined,
Until the Full Moon shone, a hemisphere;
Then to an Alchemist the sign appeared;
Accordingly, he said, "The Trinity
Is here (the triangle that he revered)";
Moreover, afterward, he stroked his beard:
"The valence stuck by aurum may be three."

—Jerome Dehnert

THE POLICEMAN

The policeman walks his lonely beat, as his
  footsteps echo along the street
The night is dark, there is no moon, the street lights
Dimly light the way,
The policeman awaits the light of day, a wail
    of sirens fill the air, screaming as though in
    despair,

As to what their journeys will bring
A life and death, or who knows what? It is all in a day
    a policeman's lot, there is no respect
For these men, who labor night and day,
They are always on call, these men so fine

Their lives are always on the line, he is first to be
    called, when trouble flares,
He is always ready and aware,
These men who really care, your policemen,
When you dial 911, who do you think always comes?
    Your policeman!!

—Sally Cabaret Lucci

ASPHALT COWBOY

The eighteen wheeler is silent.
  The CB turned off for the night.
The "Asphalt Cowboy" has died.
And things will never be right.

For twenty years, over the road,
Cattle from Texas, Nebraska grain,
Colorado oil and piggy back trucks,
All over the country and back again.

Then some young guy in a company truck,
Hell-bent for who knows where,
Just didn't see the stop sign,
Or maybe didn't even care.

The world has lost a great trucker.
A good and dear friend to all.
Heaven must have needed a driver.
And the "Cowboy" answered the call.

Goodbye dear "Asphalt Cowboy."
You were one of a special kind.
Whenever I hear an eighteen wheeler,
You will always come to mind.

—Joan M. Elting

THE OLYMPICS

I watch the people in the Olympic games.
  Most with strange sounding names
And strange faces
From faraway places.

Some on ice.
Some on snow.
But all are on the go.

Some win bronze and silver.
Some win gold.
But all are in the cold.

They all work hard
To do their best.
But what can I say
I'm for the USA.

—Peggy Dixon

MEDICINE MAN

His face was wrinkled and he looked so old
  But his words were wise and oh so bold
He told of days when there were buffalo
And also war with Blackfoot and Crow
He prayed for wisdom and love for all men
And asked the spirit to revive him again
The spirit said I'm sorry but the answer is no
There's only one time and then you must go
Beyond this land of the buffalo
No more war with Blackfoot or Crow
Into a land where the sun always shines
Into a forest of beautiful pines
Prepare for your journey a little each day
Not many moons until you're on your way
Eye to eye with the Great Spirit some day
You can be happy with what he'll say
Well it's almost time to leave this land
So get prepared oh Medicine Man

—George D. Winters

COWHANDS

Cowhands are working very hard
  in the dusty, musty barnyard,
Cuttin' hay and shavin' sheep,
    while a wild bronco is kickin' his feet.

Then old Grandma rings the dinner bell
    and all the cowhands throw up their hats
    and yell.
They say, "Oh, boy! It's time to eat!"
    and on the mat they wipe their feet.

They rush inside and sit at the table,
    and boy o' boy! this ain't no fable—
That food, my friend, was gone so fast,
    you'd think they were racin' to see who
    was last!

Well, ol' partner, just as fast as they ate
    they were back to work as if they were
    runnin' late!
They were cuttin' hay and shavin' sheep,
    while a bronco is still kickin' his
    feet.

—Sarah Michelle Fox, age 10

Shadows cast upon the wall,
midnights clock just down the hall.
I entered within the great room and
looked through the panes at the evershining,
everlasting, everseeing moon.
    And she whispered to me,
        "Come, join within and be,
        taste the blood that cometh
        from a man."
But I called back to her in a voice
of sorrow,
        "Look away from me I am of no use,
        I only have knowledge to borrow."
She looked upon me with shame and sorrow.
And whispered once again,
        "I'll take you then on some early
                      morrow."

—Amanda Edwards

AH AUTUMN!

Summer is playing her final chorus now.
The first dry, brown leaves have
fluttered down to remind me.
They have held on all summer
through the searing rays
and now have shrivelled and given up.

It reminds me that fall will be soon upon us;
With its golden days and golden harvests.
Haystacks drying in bunches; pumpkins
ripe and ready for pies and faces.

Indian corn and goldenrod,
County fairs and football games.
Rainbow leaves spiraling downward,
And squirrels scurrying with
their winter hoards.

Ah Autumn!

—Becky Alghrary

SNAIL TRAIL

Sally and Gus were special snails
who liked to race down garden trails.
Sally Slow belonged to Val
    and Gummi Gus was Jed's pet pal.
Val and Jed would plan to see
    who the winning snail would be.
In every race when Jed yelled "Go,"
    Val would scold her Sally Slow
For Gummi Gus was always fast
    and Sally Slow was always last.

Alas!, Val cried one day to her snail,
    why are you still at the start of the trail?
If you'll just make up your small-snail mind,
    you won't be trailing so far behind.
So Sally got going and changed her pace;
    she rushed and hurried to win the race.
Hooray!, Val cried, you've won the game;
    your prize will be a brand new name.
Sally Slow's no longer true,
    but Sally Swift's just right for you.

—Megan M. Wiltrout

MY WINDOW

Come look out my window with me.
See the wonders that I can see.
I see the rain on the the glass
And the leaves in their mass
And the birds flying to the tops of the trees.

God's spring is opening up.
And he's giving me another look.
Just how lucky can one person be.
With this land all around us.
And the planting of flowers.
And the fish jumping up in the sea.
Yes God gives me his love and it's free
Please come look out my window with me
I pray you see what I can see.
Oh please come look out my window with me.

*Dedicated to my husband, Marvin,
and my three children.*

—Mary A. Loft

LIFE

Life is so unpredictable,
So the acknowledgeable say
Some folks think about tomorrow
And don't give a hoot about today
It's such a precious gift
But taken so much for granted
Too busy worrying about the neighbor next door
And if their lives are slanted
Some people never get a chance
To do what they want to do
And then there are the ones
Who could care less
If the sky is blue
Be a person who is willing
To give a helping hand
For when you reach the great beyond
You will surely have a stand
So give a smile, a hug, or a handshake will do
For God gave life
And he gave one to you!

—Ida M. Falbo

NOT FOR MY PALATE

I'm not a fancy eater
Gourmet is not my thing,
Just good old fashioned cooking
    Will make my palate sing.

No pasta I eat of any kind
    And tomatoes are taboo,
No spaghetti, lasagna or pizza
    To name a very few.

No vegetables creamed or flavored with butter
    No margarine or oils please,
These things will never pass my lips
    Or anything containing cheese.

No microwaved or fast foods
    Prepared in various ways,
No cakes with cream cheese icing
    Or salads with mayonnaise.

No foreign dishes do I eat
    As great as they may be,
Just fish or meat and potatoes
    And a plain vegetable for me.

—Gilbert L. Hilderbrand

THE SEA

Crystal blue waters bathed the white water washed sands as
the beautiful midnight sun slept in a dark blanket which held
the sky.
White gulls, lost in flight, encircled
these waters which hailed them solemnly.
The lofty water welcomed the haggard gulls, luring them to
its eternal beauty; while
loud winds cried tacitly as the black gulls were lost in the
baneful black sea, to all eternity.

—Michele Marie Hall

A FAMILY REUNION

Families came from near and far,
they came by camper, truck, van and car.

They came to visit and reminisce,
to shake hands and hug and kiss.

They all came to the old home place,
with childhood memories no one can erase.

Mommy and Daddy and children were there,
in the memories they all share.

Brothers, sisters, husbands, and wives,
ate, talked, laughed and cried,
remembering loved ones that have died.

They shared yesterday's memories and enjoyed today,
and when it was over,
they went away,
with happy memories of the reunion day.

A family with love and happiness to share,
planning another reunion.

Be sure and be there.

—Ruth M. Stewart

THE MAN IN THE MOON

Loudly obnoxious, my mouth reigns open
at your reactions and words.
How do I know?
How do you?

The moon tonight is full and I danced with it
the other day,
It said, "I love you."

No response came from my torn lips; I shuddered and ran,
so fast I blended with the sky.

Now today I dream of snow in July and robins in December.
Through it all leaps the man who lives in the moon
and whom I believe forced himself upon a feeling of
love for me.

No wonder he hides.

I miss him and go to dance with him again.
Again I laugh openly.
It's not bright; we're gloomy and happy in it.

Six years now, still every week I dance with him.
Yesternight I told him, "I believe in the ghosts of
Halloween and the bogeyman in my closet . . ."
Then I sighed and said,
"I may believe in the love I have for you."

—Eryn Kate Springer

FRIENDSHIP

Friendships are precious,
A true one is hard to find.
But once you have one,
It grows stronger with time.

A true friend stands by you
Through thick and through thin,
They will never forsake you,
When our troubles are grim.

It's easy for some,
Most too friendly they seem.
Always smiling, glad to see you,
As long as all is serene.

Life gives us the opportunity
To befriend numbers untold.
True friendships develop
As we "too soon grow old."

—June Rader

Together we stand
   side by side,
     like two mighty pines,
       together on this lonely hill top.
Slowly we sway together
   in the winds of life
     that come from time to time
Standing alone we would surely fall
   to the strong winds
     that sometimes blow
       in this life
We have each other
   and we stand strong
     in even the greatest winds
Two mighty pines we stand
   side by side
Together we can stand
   forever.

Dedicated to Karen Smith,
for being a friend worthy
of the greatest love.

—David L. Verhaag

THE TRAVELER

As I travel on through time
I see the child that was me
And the trees I used to climb

As I travel on through time
I see the teenager I used to be
And remember all my crime

As I travel on through time
I see the young adult I once was
And working to make my first dime

As I travel on through time
I see the parent I soon became
For this was my life at its prime

As I travel on through time
I see the elder I am
And the life that was mine

As I travel on through time
I hear what is soon to come
The music of Heaven's chime

—Sonya M. Heck, age 17

WHEN IN DOUBT

Praise The Lord — for He is good —
Doing all He said He would.
When in doubt — remember God's Son;
The rejection — the sorrow in all he'd done.
Nothing in life could compare;
With the suffering of Christ — so unfair.
At least — I deserve this pain;
For I have truly known shame.
I didn't mean to crucify Christ;
But didn't live a perfect life.
Often I thought I was right;
Simply cause wrong wasn't in sight.
I know I have disobeyed —
Walking in — my own way.
I didn't surrender as I should;
Yet you used doubt for my own good.

—Karen Martin

CAMEO LADY

Cameo Lady of coral shell,
Lend me the charm of thy gracious spell.
Teach me the art of silence's bliss,
The visions of hope with the rising mist.

Show me the place where you didst dwell,
Its white-washed sands and priceless shells.
Let me but feel the silver foam;
Kiss my lips in your coral home.

To lay full stretched on the sea-damp sands,
Charmed by melodious fairy bands.
To feel the breath of the silver moon
As he leans from one of his star-lit rooms.

Oh Cameo Lady of coral shell,
Your silence has woven a wondrous spell,
Has painted a picture of a rising mist,
Unveiling the lips which love has kissed.

—Madelyn Borgardts

My God has hung the stars up high,
Has painted clouds to drift on by,
Has shaped the rose in loveliness,
And gave His Son for man, to bless . . .

The glorious earth, in awe, I see
The wonders that have been, to be . . .
Nothing's too hard for Him at all;
No obstacle too great, too small . . .

I pray He helps me understand
There is no soul on earth so damned
That can't be touched by love's sweet Grace,
That can't be reached by God's embrace . . .

Life's darkness may be black as coal
But oh, His love has made me whole . . .
A blessed thought, that God, this hour
Fills my soul with glory-power . . .

Burdens born and battles fought;
Impossibilities He wrought . . .
Nothing's too hard for Him, my Lord,
Almighty God, blessed, adored . . . .

—Carolyn Griffin

THE DARK ONE

Why do you come so unexpectedly.
to those who have given so generously?
One day all is well, the next
day gone to hell.
You, the dark one, all dressed
in black, like a thief in the
night, you come to take them back.
But you don't let them go quick,
and painless free.
You make them still suffer
great endless pain and agony.
If this is not enough for you,
what more will you do?
You take away their dignity
and grace, and mutilate
their face.
Why do you come so unexpectedly?
Why . . . .

—Janet M. Asay

JUST A THOUGHT

Mixed emotions I'm trying to understand.
A wave of confusion written in the sand.
I'm not gonna let life pass me by.
Question without answers staring me in the eye.
Far away hopes and distant dreams,
That's all they'll ever be sometimes it seems.
Is it possible to change fate?
And when along the line does it become too late?
What happens to dreams when once you awake?
Will they come true, how long does it take?
What makes things right or wrong?
When do you know when the answer comes along?
Who decides what's meant to be?
And what does it have to do with me?
One thing I know for sure,
Life, is what I wish to endure.
In time, I'm the vision taker.
Maybe I'm my own fate maker.

—Tamara Parham

DEATH TAKES A HOLIDAY

Everybody lives for just one day
Nobody dies, no not today
Babies are born and they're all okay
Death takes a holiday;

No gang wars or bashing gays
No Nazis, no K.K.K.
Nobody works, Everybody is paid
Death takes a holiday;

No business for undertakers
Coffin builders or casket makers
Grave stone chippers or murderers of Flipper;

No war, no famine, no AIDS
No hunger in the world today
No fighting, no blood, no pain
Death takes a holiday;

On a vacation far, far away
A holiday into outer space
Through a black hole to another place
Never to return to this old place

Death takes a holiday.

—Edward Jeleniewski

INHERIT THE FAULT?

14 year old gets pregnant while stoned in a dark sewer hole of the Bronx
Goes thru 6 months of hell and the child is born 3 months early
In a second rate hospital
to a drunk doctor with dirty hands
The baby goes thru a tortuous first day, dies,
But is revived 3 minutes later
for more torture—
its tiny wrinkled body contorting and shaking
from cocaine withdrawal.
The mother hangs herself
And the baby grows up to be president of Harvard University.

—Anc Clarkson

DIFFERENT CUSTOMS

I was in the Market Place in Viet Nam,
Shopping with some friends.
I came to the end of the Market Place,
Saw something that I couldn't live without.
I asked the vietnamese woman how much,
She told me and I told her I would take it.
She took it and went into the back,
I waited and waited for about 15 minutes and then I went looking for her.
She handed me a big brown paper bag with handles and wet spots on the outside.
With a puzzled look on my face, I looked in the bag.
As I screamed, the bag fell and I ran, so hard and so fast,
I ended up struggling with a friend.
Through my tears of telling him what had happened I said,
I wanted a puppy as a pet, not as a meal.
So badly shaken, my legs were wobbling and I was crying uncontrollably.
I remembered the cute little black and white face and the adorable wagging tail.
Why are people's customs so much different than ours?
How do we cope in a foreign land with such different customs?
How do we stop this fighting and all learn to live in harmony together?
I wish we could combine our customs and learn from each other.

—Celeste "CD" Dewey

ECHO OF FAITH #2192

Too late and *Nevermore* shall be the cry the echoes from your
heart . . . too late to right the wrong, to say the *Words* that
Heal . . . that mend, gone far away into *another land, a distant
World . . . too late forevermore . . .*

And who allowed a hurt to fester, a grudge to grow, a word so
carelessly spoken to build a wall between. Has love taken
refuge in an icy cold indifference until it was too late
And time would not rescind, go back, give one more chance to
say "I'm sorry, I was wrong . . . but so were you . . ."

Too Late to wash away the hurt, the words, the grudges, the
pain with *Love* and Compassionate Understanding . . . *Too Late*
And *Now* the eyes you wish to gaze upon are closed *Forevermore*
The ears shall never hear the *Words of Love,* Forgiveness,
Apology . . . the arms shall never feel the warm embrace of
Tender caring from a Mother, Father, Husband, Wife, Sister,
Brother . . . Aunt, Uncle, Cousin, Friend . . .

Too Late for the *Neverending Night* has come . . . nor shall the
Light, the dawning of another day, another *Sun* envelop it
It is too late forevermore . . . They've gone far away and all
We can see is an empty shell, a body cold but still their
Spirit knows we cared, has felt our sorrow, seen our tears,
Heard the words of regret locked within our *Heart* . . .

But it is too late to build new memories of *Love* and *Caring*
To cherish or *Change* what is to what it could have been . . .
If only Charity had been for you . . . *Love's Greatest Treasure.*

—Barbara Louise Martinez-Piligian

OUR PRESIDENT

Revered, respected man of youth
Bleeding and stilled before our eyes,
Unbelievable but for the riderless steed
                with reversed boots —
Trotted in great pride.
While under the flag of state
Put there by the cruelest fate
Pray, peace comes with eternal sleep,
And a nation crushed quietly weeps.
Our leader felled and buried in sod,
Bless his family and keep him — God.

—Eleanor L. Conzelmann

DEPRESSION

There is a deep, dark hole
Where no one wants to go
So filled with emptiness
That no wind can blow

Now life or hope can grow there
What surrounds are broken dreams
Bits and pieces of a vision
To what life really means

Still — in this void are many things
Fear and sadness without end,
Confusion is allowed to run rampant
And sanity is around the bend

There's a soul that begs and moans for light
but no sun is allowed to shine.
A heart once warm with lots of love
that is only able now to cry.

This awful place does have a name
because others have been there before.
They were tortured and abused in there
now I'm inside its trap door.

—Suzanne R. Campbell

PRETTY BIRDY

Pretty birdy loves to fly
   all around the house.

Pretty birdy loves to run
   just like a little mouse.

He loves to play and play all day
   with his old tin can.

He pecks it down, rolls it around
   and stands it up again.

He flies around and loves to land
   in front of a big mirror.

He chirps and chirps and talks and talks
   with a lot of cheer.

Pretty birdy loves good food
   from seed to veggies and fruits.

He eats some lettuce with the turtle
   and gives the turtle the boot.

Our family loves this pretty bird,
   his cute personality, too.

We love him so much, he's soft to the touch,
   without him what would we do?

—Carrie R. McBride

THE GIFT

My gift came from a Great being you see.
That's why it's such a Great thing to be.

Many put it down and call it bad.
But it's the best thing I've ever had.

I wouldn't trade this gift for the world.
Just as you wouldn't trade a fine pearl.

Some close to me who share this same prize.
Have been hurt and even lost their lives.

But I'm still proud to hold on to it.
Even though now my options are strict.

Some disagree that my gift is Great.
But I'm always willing to debate.

I'm sure you wonder what gift is that.
Well my prideful gift is that I'm BLACK.

—Shana Fenae Blevins

WALSENBURG

In a remote area of southeastern Colorado,
   there was a quaint town
   I had never known.
Its streets and its houses
Its lawns and its yards
   will always be unforgettable.

So neat and so orderly,
   everything was.
Even the people there,
   simple and happy
   eager to please
   always accomodating.

Large enough to earn a living,
Yet small enough to be known.
Far away from real big cities,
Yet close to rugged mountain peaks,
        grassy meadows, rippling streams.

—Marie A. Frisbie

1963

The radio was sputtering something
While I vaccumed the rug,
A clay complexion mask on my face,
Pink plastic curlers in my hair,
I caught bits and pieces
Through the whining hum.
Something about an assassination attempt.
Probably one of those hot-headed assassins
In one of those Latin countries.
"Those" people are always trying to solve their
Political problems by murder.
I turned off the vacuum and heard that
It happened in Dallas, that they shot the
President. Not in a million years would I have
Imagined such a thing.
He couldn't be dead, he *couldn't* be!
It just couldn't happen here.
I suddenly saw myself.
The mirrored dining room wall
Reflected my girdled form, my hand on the
Handle of the vacuum sweeper,
The clay mask cracking and melting,
The silly rollers in my hennaed hair.

There will be so many changes, now . . . .

—Audrey Eisman

TO EDIE (ON OUR WEDDING DAY)

To the one whose voice I always hear
    when I am far away.
To the one who takes the time to care
    what I have to say.
To the one who encourages me
    with kindness and with truth.
To the one given so much wisdom
    still in the beauty of youth.
To the one who always gives so much
    to see my peace of mind.
To the one always cheerful
    always loving, always kind.
And to the one who gives me all I need
    from earth to heaven above,
To you, my Edie,
    I give this day,
        my love.

—David S. McKinney

HUTCHINSON

"Hutch," as the natives call it,
Is a true mid-western city.
It has numbered streets going East to West,
A variety of homes, much selectivity.

Large wide lots and lengthy backyards,
Flowers abound in this once small town.
People on the streets are as friendly as ever,
Buildings are clean, sidewalks are sound.

Homes are taken care of
And priced just right.
They're mainly ranch and colonial,
And most are painted white.

Churches are beautiful
And well maintained.
There's a core of inner faith there
Which many attain.

And so it'll be remembered
For its beauty and its strength.
For it has many virtues
To a very great length.

—Marie A. Frisbie

ACROSS THE SHORES TO BRITTANY

Across the shores to Brittany
Lies the castle-abbey of equanmity.
Encircled by the serene bay
It creates a solace from worldly care
Where pious souls can pray.

Across the shores to Brittany
Lies the monastery with an aura of mystery.
The billowing, frothy waves submerge
    the fertile land,
Just as before in a preceding time,
As a lone bell in the chapel rings
    an august, melancholy chime.

Across the shores to Brittany,
The solid abbey stands against
The everchanging hue of France's sky
While the high steeple of the church
Kisses the sky in reverence to God Most High.

—Zenovia D. Lockhart

ONE MORE LONELY KNIGHT

He rides alone from shore to shore.
He doesn't know love anymore.
He gave up her love to lead this fight.
Now all that's left is one more lonely knight.

He never thought he'd have to choose,
A fight he'd win or the love he'd lose.
Before the battle he sees the light.
Into the frey goes one more lonely knight.

His heart's in armor but Love's arrow stings.
He's not afraid of one worldly thing.
But her love brings him bitter fright.
And all that's left is one more lonely knight.

He journeys homeward to be by her side,
But finds too late that she has died.
His heart is shattered, he cries all night.
The bitter tears leave one more lonely knight.

One day in battle he is nearly slain.
He calls out to her and cries her name.
So he lays dying she comes into sight,
And now there's one less lonely knight.

—Betsey E. Code

THE YOUNG SPIRITS

Wisps of confusion may roll on by,
    their destructive ways may never seek me,
but if they do decide to torment my soul,
I won't be in it alone.

We feel the hurt of a thousand worlds, the pain and agony of the silent,
yet also the love of a thousand souls, the happiness of being content.
Like a mighty cry, the shrieks can be heard, inner beings reaching out,
for only us, the star gazers to hear.
We were crafted by the deities, both needing somebody in our life—each other.
And still we sit, looking upon a foreign plane of thought, our wisdom grows.

On the quest for fulfillment, we found each other, perhaps by fate,
perhaps not. Hurt pours from our spirits, stories of long-gone triumph and tragedy,
but to us, it is the purifying of the body, the soul, and the mind simultaneously.
From one spirit to another, I thank you for all you have done, all you are doing, and all you will
do. I just pray that I might be around to share the task with you, two souls becoming one.
Bonded by understanding, trust, and love, to last all of the cosmos, the star gazers shall remain.

Dedicated to Jill, you're my inspiration and the most precious soul I know. I love you.

—Bret Calltharp

AT BEDTIME

Little hands that clasp you tight,
When it's time to say "goodnight."

Mommy's little sleepyhead,
Yes, it's time to go to bed.

Looking in her big blue eyes,
You know that she is more than wise.

She's laughed and played with toys all day,
And now the time has come to say,

"Goodnight, sleep tight" and may God rest,
This little girl I love the best.

—Priscilla Wilber

THE CROSSROADS

When traveling down the road of life,
I have come upon the crossroads.
Which direction shall I go?
What path should I follow?
The choice I will have to make
Will determine the course my life will take.

Ahead lies a well beaten path.
Should I follow in the footsteps of many?
Or adventure out all alone,
And make footprints of my own?

Or I could just stay
And wait till another day
To decide which way to go
But at that rate I'll never know.

So I've come to a decision.
I will follow my dreams
To a place I've only visioned.
A place full of happiness and joy
And where dreams will never be destroyed.

—Penny Farmer

A HUSBAND

I see love in your eyes
Like no other of guys.
You are so special to me,
And because you're yourself you'll always be.

Everytime I think about life
There is always a lot of strife.
But I thank God for giving away
This special person to me on our wedding day.

Some people remind me of others,
We're all sisters and brothers.
But, there's something about you so true
That you love me the way you do.

I never have to cry when I slip and fall,
Because you're there like a child with a doll.
There's no one who can separate us,
Our love will be clean and never rust.

We've chosen each other to be together,
This relationship will be forever.
With a family having God as the lead,
We will never be spared any need.

—Kristine M. Hendricks

COATS OF MANY COLORS

The trees have donned their coats of many colors
For one last fling before the winter winds tear
them from their arms.
Then bare they'll stand against the snow
and sleet of winter,
Until spring breezes tell of warmer weather
now to come
Then break forth the new pale leaves of green
To shelter all from the hot summer sun.
They'll last through fields first planting
And stay to enjoy the harvest moon
While waiting still again to don their
coats of many colors.

—Leila Blood

WITH A PURPLE FLOWER IN HER HAIR

With a purple flower in her hair
The maiden looked so fair
    As we made our way to the winding brook.
With hair flowing
And eyes glowing
    I shall always remember that look.
The way we walked,
The way we talked,
    As we went toward the fall.
We took pictures that last to this day.
But we could never recapture that way
    With a purple flower in her hair and all.
I remember her smile
And walking all the while
    With the sun beating down on us with golden gleams.
And when into space I stare
I remember her with a purple flower in her hair
    And I can rise above all things.

—Curtis Baker

MY LOVER

Intense in its depth
  Yet soft in its caress
My heart flutters and swells
  As my lover reaches to embrace my breast

Mine own hand reaches to encircle
  What I know is swollen, in want of me
And the desire in my lover's eyes
  Is all there is to see

Moans of delight
  Become breathless in their escape,
Then laboured,
  As together our hearts begin to race

And only the here and now exists
  As together we move as one
In ecstasy and bliss,
  In unison and love

Then time stands still
  As the tide rushes in
All moving,
  All consuming

Until together, quietly we lay
  Bodies entwined,
My lover's hand
  In mine

Dedicated to Carsten, with love

—Kendra McBride

THE WALK OF LIFE

Have I Walked This Path Before
Thru Towering Trees, Along The Sandy Shores
Why Do My Travels Seem So Familiar To Me
On This Endless Journey Thru Eternity
Teachers I've Known Of Heart, Soul, And Mind
Lessons Of Knowledge, Love And Endless Time
When Two Spirits Touch, The Imprint Is Cast
In Body And Soul To Forever Last
I Have Been Blessed, With Other Spirits Shared
No Human Emotion Has Yet To Compare
Their Spirits Embraced Mine, In My Time Of Pain
Loving and Nurturing, With So Much To Gain
Two Spirits Unite, To Share From Within
Growing Stronger And Wiser, A New Life Begins
Because Of You My Spirit Endures Time
Your Spirit Will Live Forever In Mine.

—Kevin Eldredge

THE MIGHTY MISSISSIPPI

a forsaken, desolate giant
—barren of all life.
Its currents
churning, swirling, rising
spilling onto dry land.
Seeking, searching to end its solitary confinement,
Only creating more loneliness, despair.
Reaching to the roads
cutting off any movement
overwhelming trees, houses, fields
until only treetops, rooftops,
plundered fields remain.
Forced out by its creeping tentacles,
the people have fled
no animals roam
no birds fly.
A whirring in the distance—
the only sound.
One lone, black army helicopter
surveys the lonely creature's destruction.

—Marianne Wesolowski

THINGS THAT MATTER MOST

The things that matter most in my life
have taken me years to find
they've really been there all along
I just was not aware of them.

The whistle of a mighty train
the cool summer breeze on my face
a walk hand in hand with a special friend
the trees, the grass and the rain.

The voice of a friend when the way gets rough
a smile, a laugh and a tear
the listening ear when the pain is great
the support of those we hold dear.

Creating, composing and sharing
a thoughtful word or deed
helps lighten a load and brighten a day
and makes a life worth living.

As I continue my journey through life
I grow more aware each day
that the value of life isn't money or fame
it is the person we are deep inside.

—Glenna C. Vincent

NEVERMORE

Alone
Am I alone
Am I *really* **ALL** alone

Since I stand on principles
Of
Sensible **R**esponsible **C**itizenship
And
Scorn *appears* as friendly criticism

Alone
I wonder as I ponder
ALONE

—Alice Hanson Senter

FOR TODAY

If today, you will offer
to others, a friendly smile
it will make its way to a lonely heart
and embrace if for awhile

If today, you possess
a kind word, pass it along
it will rest upon the ears of one
who will receive it as a song

If today, you've but a moment
reach out and gently clasp a hand
so that a troubled soul may be assured
there is one who understands

There is no kindness
great or small, lost along life's way
For in tomorrows' gardens bloom
the seeds you plant today

*Dedicated, with gratitude, to family
and friends who supported, encouraged and
believed in my talents and abilities long
before I was able to believe in myself.*

—Karen E. Jocson

ANOTHER DAY

Another day but
the same dawn or is it?
The world keeps changing.
A different sunrise a different
sunset. For the world keeps
turning and people's thoughts
keep changing. For the
same thought will never
come twice. Just like
a sunrise that will only
come once. For there is some
inner beauty that cannot
be seen by the human eye but
by the brain creating the image
to dream, to love, and to hate.
Yet for the person who cannot get
in touch with the inner child; all
hope is lost for there is no will
to live just to survive but not to
create, to use an artistic license.
For there will be a day of peace
when all walls are torn down
and the stillness can be heard and
love will be on the horizon.

—Robert J. Anderson

Oh mystic rock, you're a special spot,
The background, to many a photo.
But, you've been longer here, than the
ages of time. As a constant to tide and
its movements.
Like life's ebb and flow you watch.
Come and go. Never a change is apparent.
But, deep underneath the tide cuts and
sweeps, over your form, never ending.
A little erosion must happen, but you look
same year after year.
It's the same rock you say, we see every
day, but as time takes its toll on the
rock and the soul, it grows smaller
and will fade away.

—Sharon Grove Mack

THE SEARCH FOR ME, MYSELF AND I

By ragged grove, by ruined road.
My heart is cursed where love abode.
So might I follow into the night?
Might I sample my softest delight?
Stardust surrounds me, floating so shy,
wanting shiversome never to die.
The haze aglow casting all doubt aside,
rages me to ride the glaze dripping tide
within the peace that thrives within,
dare stands a labyrinth with a tilted grin.
So should this world ever lose its ground,
suck up the sky, or swallow the sea.
The one soul surviving thing is I.
Myself remains to comfort me.

—Chelsea Lee

FOR EVERYTHING STOPS FOR THE RAIN

For cities tall fall back amidst the mist
Steely spires softened by the gray
For light denied supplied by day
Must lie awake and wait to rise again
Before the dark.

For everything stops for the rain
Leaves upturned cast restless motion
Suspended, upended
From their fallow perch.

But the rain feeds
It feeds the plants and trees
And birds and drains
Each moment of precious sunlight memories.

—Gene H. Sobczak

The wind sweeps through the fall trees,
Taking their sole possession.
Tearing the life from the limb,
As if adding to its collection.
Leaves float and twirl in the air,
Then fall to the ground.
It picks and chooses on a whim,
Never liking what it's found.
Off it goes, when the trees are bare,
But it often comes back through.
Swirling and laughing, without a care,
As if looking for something new.
Finding nothing that it wants,
It leaves as quick as it came.
Blowing off in any direction,
For never will it remain.

—Wendy Borgmann

ONE OF MANY

The strong winds swirled, around the small body
The worn coat was pulled tight
A tattered scarf whipped the breeze
As some body's garbage danced
around the small feet
Then raced down the side walk
Graffiti on the paint peeled walls
read like a horror flick from Steven's pen
The street light danced with the strong wind
as the winter wind lashed every thing in sight
as the small figure pushed on
                Destination-no place
The winter night wore on
as the lonely figure walked on
Sleep will over take her in a narrow door way
Dawn breaks the eastern sky
the long dark night is over
A frosty day emerges

—Mae

THIS POEM

I'm having trouble writing this poem.
What should I write about,
A baseball player sliding into home?
Or, how about a super hero,
Or my favorite music star.
Boy, this poem is almost as hard as counting to zero.
Should I tell about a basketball game,
And say who is winning and getting all of the fame.
How about writing this poem on love,
No wait! I've got it, I'll write about the flight of a dove.
I don't want to write about love, or a dove,
I just can't decide.
I could write about the beautiful Roman art,
Or about lovers that shall never part.
I'm ready to give up on writing this poem,
So now I guess I'll sit and watch TV at home.
I wanted to write a poem that came from the heart,
And then this poem would be written from the very start.
Wait! I really can go home now and play some ball,
Because I just wrote this poem, twenty lines in all!

—Amber Reneé Fryman, age 14

NEW MEXICO AUTUMN

Summer green is faded and sere
Colorful autumn is drawing near.
Adobe houses decked out like halls
    With red chili ristras bright on the walls.
In fields once rippling and waving with corn
    Ecru sheaves stand tall and forlorn.
Virginia Creeper's maroon and red vines
    Climb along fences — up trees intertwine.
Down near the river, the great Rio Grande,
    Mighty old cottonwoods take their stand
Filling the valley with shimmering gold
    Contrast blue mountains — breathtaking — bold.
Tawny Salt Cedars and rusty brown willows
    Fill in the lowlands waving like billows.
In various tones of reds, golds and browns
    Row upon row — orchard trees abound.
Orange pumpkins — corn blue and yellow
    Are beginnings of Autumn — cool and mellow.
New Mexico autumn is glorious and bright
    Truly a wondrous, magnificent sight.

—Arlene Rounds

A MESSAGE TO KIDS

There are important people,
Our leaders, politicians as well,
But parents stand above them,
There are some things I want to tell.

They help you and protect you,
Make sure of your every need,
And most of all, more than anything,
They are there to lead.

To some they might seem strict,
And though they rule the house,
You should not pretend that they are cats,
And you the little mouse.

So, please respect your elders,
But still be a kid,
And be nice to your parents,
As I will and always did.

—Leslie Eve Lyons

WORTHLESS TEARS

As the faces turn in my direction,
looking down they do not see me.
Tears flood their distorted smiles,
and yet I search for their hearts.

Black hides their weak souls,
death surrounds their eyes,
but life floods the gates of their spirits,
and yet I find no truth in their emotions.

A sickening voice rings in the distance,
showering them with unwanted words.
Worthless voices — a masquerade of tears.
Where is the truth in their eyes?

The ground sends forth memories,
dirt encases my essence.
As my blood flows through their veins,
my limp flesh sends my spirit free.

—Lance Kayser

CROW RIVER DUCK HUNT

Quiet Dawn graying light
Push of Oars Heron takes flight
Deer in forest on decks of leaves
Ducks and geese fly with sneeze
Labrador and friend along with me
Raccoon's mask over log we see
Eagle's eye we pass on by
Carp jump high in acrobatic flips
Logs sunk like treasure ships
Twists and turns rocks washed and shaped
Corn fields rustle the harvest await
Beaver tail flaps the water's face
River's current landscaping the banks
Seasons change, feel the cool breeze
Fog now lifting ghost shaped trees
Shots ring out yep missed again
Laughing joking — quiet time
It's the being here I find
Not the catch that matters most
But the time with Nature's molt

—Dale Christophersen

VEXATION

I am so angry with the way it is,
   with the world.
   With the way I'm copied off of,
The way I'm ruled by those who can't rule
                        —themselves,
The way I'm judged by those who are dependent on
                        —others,
The way I'm criticized by those who can't take
                        —criticism,
   by ones who are afraid,
   by ones who are brave.
   And by ones who lie,
 and then accuse me of lying
   I'm sick of sin,
   I'm sick of religion,
   And I'm sick of fairy tales.
If only he'd take me into his arms.
It would make everything better.

—Becky Wysocki

WHY?

You said you cared about me, so why?
You said you would never hurt me, so why?
You said it was terrible what happened to me
in the past, so why?
You said I meant the world to you, so why?
You said if anybody ever did that to me you
Wouldn't know what you would do, so why?
You said I was always in your thoughts, yet
you slept with another, so why?
You said you hated liars, yet you lied to me, so why?
You said all you ever wanted to do was make me
happy, so why?
You said that resisting temptation and being able to
stop was something you could do, but you failed once,
then twice; as far as I know; but how do I know you
won't again, if you didn't think so then, tell me why?
Why should I trust you, believe you, and love you?
Why did you do this to me . . . Why?

—Ashley Means

EVERY NIGHT

Darkness appears beneath my eyes.
Then, you come into sight,
And a light shines in delight.
Though the sun sets every night,
Your heart is always bright;
And as I see your claron bearing,
I realize you are lady sublime.
You bring such joy to my nights,
Though your presence is by far nigh.
This is so, since your flesh I do not seek.
Though the light in your heart,
Is the object of my quest.
So as I keep searching in a street called Desire,
I keep yearning these nights with you;
By closing my eyes and waiting for your fire.
If and when I find you there,
We will be fixed upon this enormous galaxy,
And there will only matter you and I.

Dedicated to Laurina Brasil
'I am longing for that day to come.'

—Alen Jerjiss

MARIJUANA MISCHIEF

I see 3 guys leaning against the hallway walls. They are all wearing the same colors, which are black and dark blue. They're secretly buying a bag of weed. I see the same trio outside on a cold cold day sitting crossed leg on the sidewalk and leaning against the flat red bricks. They're probably getting stoned. Walking by them I smell the scent of marijuana. The stoned kids' eyes are red and low. They're making a crowd of students laugh by making funny faces. I hear footsteps coming down the walk. I see a police car in the parking lot. The big officer has gathered the threesome with one hand. I see the 3 stoned boys being led to the car, and I don't see them until the 9th day. I see the boys have come back, but to what 9 days of grueling makeup work. I see the same kids outside in the police car a few days later, I never see them again.

—Joy Coochyouma

exchange

exchange of hearts
exchange of souls
a whisper of mystery
and a touch of love.
silence is crystal
fresh spirits dance
celebrating angelic beauty.
running stars flee to freedom.
streaking glowing embers
penetrating the black atmosphere.
explosive rainbow light
spreads through the atmosphere.
hot pink emotions sizzle through the veins
of stained glass thoughts.
entertainment zips fiesta-like thrill probes
on the surface of the skin.
golden light powders the small space
full of free comfort.
so it ends on a smart note
from the powers of the human heart.
exchange of hearts
always a part of the soul.

—Kristy Nelson

W H Y?

As I sift through the ashes of our relationship
I look for embers of understanding
What burned it out? What cooled it off?
When did you stop caring?

From a fire that burned so passionately to cold ashes, gray and silent
No whispers of discontent or unhappiness
Only a dead silence in a room filled with vibrations and shock waves

The pain smarts, tears flow, the mind rejects
Hurt, anger, and more hurt, and still a cold silence
The greatest hurt!

Clouds cover reason, the sun tries to come out
A few words of explanation and still no consolation
But an understanding of a soul who fights for his freedom — never in jeopardy!

How sad to know that closeness, warmth, love and happiness can
Frighten away the future of two kindred spirits who nurtured the few days left to enjoy

Healing comes slowly, memories are cherished
Friendly contact helps the healing process
The urge to touch, caress and hold close are strong
Why did you stop caring?

—Angie Alberico

If You, Lord Jesus, choose to tarry,
May I rest in your care?
For on the Cross of Calvary,
   Your precious blood paid my fare.

—Helen Ruth Ewing

YOUTH

Youth, like a flower
just beginning to enjoy
taken away
by wicked time.

Youth, too precious to waste
time comes to steal away
of life's joy
there is just a taste.

Youth, live life to all its extent
search for its beauty
for something does not come for nothing
from all your work
each and every day
to you come rewards and content.

—Deborah J. Ruryk

WHAT! WAWBEE, WAWBEE

It's that time of evening
When the SUN dips into the SEA.
The flaming waves ripple
And sing out, "What! Wawbee, Wawbee."
I stare at this SUNSET
As the airy breeze cools my face.
Hard to believe my eyes —
Wawbee! Wawbee! I love your space."
As the wind's mighty sleeve
Caresses my body and soul,
God's presence surrounds me
And the birds that are on patrol.
Now the SUN is sinking
Fast below the Horizon Line.
The water slaps the shore
As Wawbee's World and mine entwine.

—Lucille M. Brubaker

DREAM WEAVER

The dreams I dream,
As I lay in my bed.
Tho' odd as they may seem,
Dream Weaver puts them in my head.

My very own dream weaver,
Weaving my mind at night.
Some may be pleasant,
While others afright.

The seed that was planted in my brain,
Grows a memory that still remains.
Wish I may, wish I might,
Wish upon a star tonight.

A wish I wish,
To my special Dream Weaver.
May tonight be the night,
That I become a believer.

—Rebecca Lynn Shaffer

The silence of God is a perfection
To who've developed the "sense" to hear it.
Now notice how welcome and serene the
Quality of silence be after our
Senses have been unknowingly battered
By the constant drone of machinery.
An invitation pleasantly received
Is the feel and smell and sound of outdoors
After long sermons in a crowded church.

—Jim Snyder

DARK SHADOWS

There's a dark place,
Tucked away, deep, into the corner of my heart,
Where no light will ever penetrate,
And where black sadness reigns.

This place will never know light, or happiness, again.
For it is reserved
For a special someone.
She is not here —
Yet she is always here.
I love her
And will always love her.

But the corner is empty.
And the only happiness it will ever again know
Are the mere dark shadows of happy memories
Which play about sadly on the tender walls
And reverberate through the black nothingness
Where sadness reigns.

—Teresa Hakim

GATHERED, GIVEN

How I love slowly walking afield
During dusk's gentle repose upon the
Countryside; over and betwixt frost-heaved
Humps of earth that like curled farm animals
Sleeping, dot the cooling, mist-full pastureland.
My humble noise of welkin-ward conversation
Floats spectorlike above twilight's settling
Mist . . . and there, blending with richer starstuff,
Whispering heaven's humas all about,
Is the blesséd aura of eventide.
One ambling through this ethereal
Consistency can't help but absorb
Into the heart its harvest; and like burrs
Snagging upon pantleg and sock, clinging
There long after to remind you of
The color and texture of the field—
So this spiritual, twilight imbibing
Lingers long enough into the night to
Remind me of something left behind.
And the urge comes (like the want of picking
Up a child whose upstretched arms sometimes ask)
To return to my family within,
To stomp down silver-starred glitterings
Like snow upon the floor and bear tidings
From without from someone away too long.
Only sometimes 'tis a worthy sojourn
Out and in; but well worth the bringing in,
If, like gathered berries to share, it pours
My love for you out. This, as it seems to
Me, is what people in families
Must be about . . . each in their own time.

—Jim Snyder

JUST A GLANCE

Out of my window I do glare,
children at each other stare.

Long ago this would have meant nothing,
but in these times a stare could mean something.

Trouble meaning fighting,
not playing.

Oh, how I wish for those good old days,
when I could hear laughter in the air.

When a stare meant a game children played.

It's amazing how one glare out of a window,
makes me aware of the changing times.

—Trina Dodson
"93"

ME

What about me, there isn't much to say,
except that I live life day by day.
Remembering yesterday as a lesson learned,
knowing tomorrow is something I have earned.
Who am I, I guess I'm just me,
a lively person, a soul that is free.
Living for today, and for tomorrow,
remembering the good, forgetting the sorrow.
What am I, there is a long list,
I think negative, I am a pessimist.
I am realistic, I love to have fun,
I forgive and forget, what's done is done.
This is who I am, this is the real me,
very responsible, but as immature as can be.
An independent person, sometimes needing a friend,
doing the best I can, until life's end.

*Dedicated in loving memory of my
mother, Linda Lee Paavola (Smith)*

—Kimberly Dawn Houseman

DREAM OR REALITY

Searching the blackness of my mind
   For the scene that often haunts me
Of a child with such hurt and pain
   My heartbeat does not soften

Her eyes the doorway to her soul
   Beckons and pulls me in
For this child knows my fate
   To my dreams and my fear

In her eyes emotions are jumbled
   Like a river's rapid flowing
Her familiar face shows scars so deep
   It makes me tremble and shiver

I see the bond between us now
   And why to me she calls
She's here to help me understand
   My dreams reality

This child is my heart and soul
   The memories I've tried to hide
She's the feelings and image of the abused child
   Trapped within my mind

*Dedicated to my husband and children for
giving me the courage to accept my
childhood pain, for a better future*

—Laura Ripley

CLOWN VANITIES

All that money being
stuffed down; tough money,
like a dead candy bar or a glove
around the senses. Warm in his castle,
the king of grip smells his breakfast.
The outer being looks in through the portal.
A white soft wife flutters through the
kitchen. A small baby jiggles a rattle in
a crib. It has no name yet for what it is.

—Phil Algosino

GREAT EXPECTATIONS

With great expectations I
await everyday for that phone
call or post card that exclaims
"You're Queen for a day."
I enter the contests, buy all the
hype, what can I say in 25 words
or less as I type. I dream of
Hawaii, the cars and the furs, I
can almost hear someone saying
"It's all yours!"
Just think of that "Love Boat" the
food and the cruisin', I must make
my entry the one most likely chosen.
I have all the patience, I can
wait one more day, perhaps tomorrow
my name will be drawn for the
cruise on Montego Bay.
Oh, whoa, I have one more hope, I
can feel the excitement as my pulse
starts to race and my blood starts to boil,
I can still board that "Love Boat," my bags
are all ready, just that one phone call from
Ed McMahon or John Paul Getty.

—Joanne Swartz

REPOSE IN AUBURN AUTUMN

The burden on my soul is readily
  as heavy as the burden i bear
      upon my back

With every step i take
      it worsens
with every breath i draw
      it grows heavier

Soon i will rest
to ease my body and soul.
For now, i shall like to die;
for quickness of ease
and severity of pain

Let it end here —
i plead the likeness of it.

The crispness of autumn leaves
crunches under my weighted steps

The load upon my back —
no longer heavily honored
      as i suspected.

As for now, why do the leaves still crunch?

—Jennie Frakes

A GEMINI

A gemini must create of itself
Its own oppositely egoed equal
As a check to keep the balance
Dynamic in a strained equalibrium
And both halves must be fed
And both must dance in quicksilver

If one be the moon, and the other
Sunward with a glowing gleam
Then must the moon be its own light
Equaling the day stars dazzle
For both halves must see
There are intricate paths in quicksilver
And the music is imperative

—James Angus Vieira

THE SKY

The sky so gray and wet,
It hangs without a smile
And it looks like it wants to end it all
Forever, not just awhile.

The sky so lonely and sad,
It hangs without a sound,
And it looks like it just wants to fall
Fast and hard to the ground.

The sky — sullen and tearful,
It'll put a stop to misery tonight,
And only to forget the pain
Gives in without a fight.

And as the ugly wicked moon
Casts her drowsy spell without a shame,
The sky will cry itself to sleep
And I will do the same.

—Victoria Billit

OUR LOVE IS HERE TO STAY

On the day that we were married
In December—the thirteenth day,
Whatever our future brings
   Our love is here to stay.

You've always kept your promises
   As I have done the same,
Having raised three children
   We're all proud to bear your name.

Our happiness has been complete
   Each day we share anew,
Hand in hand together
   Our love comes shining through.

In our times of sorrow
   By the deaths of those so dear,
There's always comfort for each other
   In showing that we care.

Forty years have come and gone
   Still it seems like yesterday,
With God's continued blessings
   Our love is here to stay.

*To my husband, Donald V. Kane,
with love, health and happiness
all the rest of our days together.*

—Violet Hilderbrand Kane

THE GOLDEN YEARS

God gave us strength, that we might grow
He gave us wisdom, that we might know
He gave the nights, so we can rest
That the Golden Years, will be our best.

God gave us today, for the work that we can do
With hopes for tomorrow, and faith to see it through
He gave us the promise, that we may lean upon
Our Golden Years, and far beyond.

God gave us knowledge, it's the answer to a prayer
With the assurance, that he would be right there
He placed in our hearts, to be humble and advised
That our Golden Years, we would not be deprived.

God gave us sunlight to brighten up our day
And the wonders of the universe,
   to help us along our way,
We hear his tender voice, as it whispers in our ears
life's sullen streams are all behind now, enjoy the . . .
                    Golden Years.

—Robert Wilson

THE IDEALIST'S LAMENT

Somewhere between nightfall and daybreak
There is a time known only to the lonely;
A time when regret settles like evening fog
And past mistakes are resurrected;
When the phoenix of doubt arises;
A time when insecurities run rampant,
And, somewhere inside, a frightened child cries.
I have been to that place in the loneliness of night
And been forced to examine the choices,
Both wise and foolish, that I have made.
I have survived the foolish
And, I hope, profited by the wise.
I have tried to learn from past mistakes,
And in all but one case, succeeded.
I have reached my middle years,
But I continue to tilt at windmills.
The idealist within me endures;
I repeatedly choose the righteous fight
And charge into battle with colours flying,
Heedless of the dragons blocking my path.

—Philip A. Eckerle

YOUNG LOVE

Young love can hurt so much,
But if it's good love, it could lose that touch.
Sometimes you can be scared of it,
But if you're patient you'd get over it.
Sometimes love can be real rough,
Throw you around, and be kind of tough.
If you're sick of your love but just cannot leave,
You'd sooner or later open your eyes and see—
That your love was young—it wasn't real, so forget that stuff, and put it to a seal.

—Shayla Stocker, age 11

SOMEONE CARES

I wouldn't know what to do
Without you.
The pain would be too much to bear
After all, you know how much I care.
Believe it or not, I can see
How much you've done for me.
I know you have to deal with so much,
but I'll always be there if you need to keep in touch.
No matter what happens, you'll always have my support
Each problem I will help you sort.
Count on me to be by your side
I'd never leave you to run away and hide.
You're the strongest person I know
That must be why I love you so.

—T. Lim

YESTERDAY'S SCARS

Yesterday — a love so true; we felt so blessed
our faces glowed with happiness.
Yesterday — babies laughing, precious little girls
with captive smiles and corkscrew curls.
Yesterday — through teary eyes we hid our pain
and vowed to capture love again.
Yesterday — with aching hearts we came to see
how very different two can be.
Yesterday — we gave up hope and parted ways
two strangers in search of happy days.
Yesterday — for four little girls the balance was lost
by parents unwilling to pay the cost.
Today — adults all; their hearts bear scars
etched in blood by others' wars.

—Joy Acklin

HOME

Her orbit is a flirtatious dance with a ball of fire
The sun.

Gravity is the protective embrace of Mother Earth
Cradling her young.

As angels in disguise clouds drift slowly by,

Canyons made from laugh lines miles and miles wide.

Reaching through the ground her hands are the trees.

Extending her branches like fingers they will soon
Give birth to leaves.

Her bosom is the ocean.

Her bosom is a stream.

Her bosom is often gathered into the angels' wings.

—Veronica Black

AGAIN

As I sit at the front of your grave
I weep for the loss of you in my life,
yet I am reassured in my sadness that
you are now free and well from your
earthly troubles. My tears moisten
the soil and I wonder if you feel
them. My voice calls your name and
I wonder if you hear it. Only time
is between us, and soon I will be your
daughter again.

*Dedicated to my wonderful father,
Josif Markoski, your memory will
live on through me forever.
I Love You Always.*

—Mirjana Mimi Markoska

DIVIDED FEELINGS

Sometimes I am so confused
I have so many things on my mind;
My mother, father, sister, relatives,
school and friends.

I feel just like a computer
and a person has typed as much in
my memory as they could; I can
no longer hold it.

I have so much on my mind,
I know I'm not the only one with
a lot on their mind. I'm just so depressed.

I'm worried about my mom and grandfather
who are crippled, my grades and friends.

I hope I can solve my problems.

—Kimberly Lewelling, age 12

"HEY MAN, WHAT'S THIS ALL ABOUT?"

They never even asked my name,
They only really meant to maim.

"Hey man, what's this all about?"

They punched and kicked . . .
Till I was really licked.

"Hey man, what's this all about?"

This was no game.
They knew I was in pain.

"Hey man, what's this all about?"

My civil rights are now at stake.
These guys have made a big mistake.

"Hey man, what's this all about?"

I was wrong but this isn't right.
Why, why do we have to fight?

"Hey man, what's this all about?"

My country gives me certain rights.
These men are going to pay the price.

"Hey man, that's what this is all about?"

*Dedicated to my teacher, Dr. Corcoran
and my mother who gave me encouragement
to write this poem.*

—Michelle Kissinger, age 13

RAINBOWS

Rainbows are a signal to their surroundings
    that the rain is over
It greets the sun with a warm, glowing radiance
    of colors spanning across the sky
Colors come in shades of blues, oranges, golds,
    pinks, purples
Then the rainbow fades away, but the memory
    of its beauty never dies
Rainbows always return after another rain ends.

—Patricia A. Pritzel

WHAT HE DOES

I don't know what he controls
over me, but it's some power I'm too
weak to refuse. He "can't," or "won't"
comprehend the distinct passion that
I have for him. He creeps
through my darkened body
unlocking the only keyhole to
my overbearing, needy heart.
He won't come in, but he
trespasses anyway. I want
to procrastinate the lust and
companionship that I have
toward him, but it's too in sync
with him, too much for my
demand. He knows who I am,
but he doesn't know me to
love me. He is very superficial
but real to me. I want to
find the true him, yet I haven't
succeeded. But I will someday.

—Courtney Hillhouse

KNOWING

you don't know me.

if you knew me,
you'd see that i am scared of life.

i'm scared of being alone.

insecure.

you don't know me.

if you knew me,
you'd know that your love would help me.

i'd be good inside.

i'd never fear.

you don't know me.

if you knew me,
you'd love me

or would you?

i don't know me.

if i knew me,
i'd understand that i don't need
you to make me happy.

but i love you.

—Ann Marie Anderson

WISDOM OF THE AGES

Like grass growing or paint drying —
It's hard to watch, if not to see:
The passage of time, and the years go flying —
What was and what is, but what is to be?

The future looks endless through the eyes of youth,
So time is wasted over and again.
But older eyes will see the truth,
And cry for things that might have been.

But if eyes grow older in time to see,
Before all youth has drained away —
The present and future (and all they can be)
Could be something better, if we start today.

—Mark Allen Johnson

THE AMERICAN DREAM

The American Dream that spans the centuries
seems a story left untold
People killed because of their pigmentation
human beings that were sold

The American Dream spans the centuries
unravels as the flag unfolds
in a land where you are expected
to do as you are told

The American Dream spans the centuries
many killed for no reason
those that are brave enough to speak out
are accused of committing treason

The American Dream beckons
the weary and brokenhearted
become a part of the dream of old
make sure your story is told

—Mary Patterson

COSMOPOLITAN U.S.A.

There was just one people native to this land; and
for them things would be changed

As explorers and settlers came to make this their
own; native lives were altered and rearranged

The first step having been put in place; opened
doors for many more

All wanted to come to this new land; the temperate
and some hard core

Yes; they came from many places; divergent people;
not just one

They were to form a great new nation; before all was
said and done

Some came involuntary; and most did come by choice

In the long term scheme of many things; what evolved
was a united voice

Whether black, brown, yellow, white or somewhere in
between

All comprise Cosmopolitan U.S.A. and that clearly can
be seen

No one people made this nation great; the corner-stone
was laid by everyone

Yes; a nation of divergent people are we; cosmopolitan
like no other one

—John A. Carter Sr.

SPELLBOUND

Let me gaze unto the mountain as I walk beside the sea
such glory and such beauty in any painting could there be

To look upon the majesty of splender and of might
to behold its firm foundation, behold its snowy, lofty height

Is it your strength that captures me as you stretch to touch the sky
for oh you hold me captive, my mind, my heart, my eye

Yes I am your prisoner surrendered though I be
I turn again to hear once more the pounding of the sea

Oh yes I walk beside the sea, grains of sand I cannot count
but what are these beside the grace of the wonder of this mount

Ageless sea you are spectacular as the sun sets every eve
but oh this mighty mountain my enraptured eyes can never leave.
—Shirley Lamberg

TO NOT LAUGH IS TO DIE

Brave laughter conceals their cry.
Youth must cope with peers, parents, at which college to apply.
To not laugh is to die.

Career-minded singles think of their biological clocks
while they travel, carouse, spend money on bullish stocks.
Brave laughter conceals their cry

The young wives talk of romance, husbands, their day.
Nearby their children rebel, fight or play.
To not laugh is to die.

Middle-aged women gargle to prevent halitosis,
jog to firm up their chest, and speak of life's crisis.
Brave laughter conceals their cry

The old men shake dice, discuss daily news, argue or agree
reminiscing while rubbing liniment on an arthritic knee.
To not laugh is to die.

Two old friends praying in the sanctuary
go home feeling lonely and read the obituary.
Brave laughter conceals their cry
To not laugh is to die.
—Avis Iris Wright

SILENCE

Injustice that goes unseen, by millions of open eyes
Rivals only unheard challenges, to that which was seen
Silence the great equalizer in plain sight, hides the truth
Unfanned flames for lack of a raised voice

Hallowed halls of congressional splendor, make thunder from man
Laws spew forth in cadence to the wants and needs of the many
Only to trounce on the rights of the few, who labor without voices
All men created equal, written but unheard, unchanged in years

Founding fathers who forgot none, voting mothers cried out in a hurricane
Heavy laden ships crossing unforgiving oceans, black cargo for sale
Anguished cries unheard, like the backs of mules scarred by whips
Separated families by others' will, birth, death, now I lay me down to sleep

Civil rights, from court fights before all white juries no one hears
Elected officials demonstrate expert skill to an amazed majority
Rejected calls for help from beleaguered leaders, make well done jobs—jobs undone
Once again silence, for the sake of wanted results shout out loud

A nation of laws, constitutional flaws, U.S. Supreme Court interpretation
Who rights these deeds of injustice? If you speak to me truthfully—
Maybe thousands of years from now, when these same basic questions are asked
What answers will be heard or will there once again be silence?
—Will Russell

LOVE CAN

Love can make a miracle
When given from the heart.
Can turn a sad day to a glad one,
If some love there's been a part.

Love can take a night that's fearful
Make it into peaceful calm.
Takes away the doubt and sorrow,
For love has a healing balm.

Love can change a day of heartache
To one filled with joyous peace.
Helps to ease the pain and hurting,
Gives the day a brand new lease.

Love can take a broken day dream,
Transform it into something good;
For love can make a miracle,
Just as we knew it could.

—Joana L. Soule

THE FORGOTTEN ONES

Pain becomes a well known emotion
Pain becomes a well known fear
Watch your words and tell all your actions
Try to get through all the tears

It's hard being the forgotten ones
When people close their eyes and ears
Trying to pretend what's heard isn't real
Knowing all the pain they must feel

Happiness is a daily illusion
Convincing others everything is all right
My parents love me
They really care
When all along they're never aware

How precious children are
How dear they all must be
Will we ever know the forgotten ones
Will we ever begin to see.

—Paula C. Baker

                                      flight*

                            kite's

                    this

            the way

But not oft
Brief access to the Soul,
Might hint our humble, inward sight
The worthy human goal,
The entire human might,
Life might lend or skim or glean
As I looked on child and kite . . .
I've never so completely seen
Mere humanness accost.
Search for substance in the soar,
If we meliorate Frost,
"It comes to a little more"
Of what was the Mariner wrought?
Why will runners rare resign,
And yogis wander beyond thought,
Why will men fierce mountains climb
Flying a kite is metaphor.
We seek the light, fling ope' the door:
O my soul prepare the flight,
Ah the wonder in wind, child, kite.

read this poem up

—Jim Snyder

GUARDIAN ANGEL

Watching day and night,
Never sleeping or even taking a break.
How many times you've kept me from harm
I'll never be privileged to know.
Nameless and faceless you are.
My human eyes can't see you.
Yet I know you exist.
And I just want to thank you for all you've done and will do
    to keep me from harm.

—Bonnie L. Mitchell

A BREATH OF SPRING

Let us feel a breath of spring in the air,
An upward surge in our souls,
Enjoy the life God has given to each of us,
Share with others our love and friendship,
As we tread the pathway of life,
So we too will be refreshed uplifted to face the
    tasks before us,
With a new sense of spring in our heart, soul, mind
    and body,
Come let us adore Him Christ the Lord.

—Olive Mitchell

MINISTERING

God grant me the courage to answer when you call,
To travel down life's highway whether large or small.
Let me read your road map with sincerity and care
And to walk the roads like Jesus, forever be my prayer.
Grant that I might see the wisdom of your plan
And show love and kindness to each and every man.
Let me never judge and always let me show
And understanding heart, when they're buried 'neath the flow.
Just let me lift up Jesus and always be a friend
To all the faint in heart who think they just can't win.
Let me show them how in Christ they might be blessed
If only at His cross their sins they will confess.
He promised He would hear them and this I can declare
Now and forever, you are in His precious care.

—Lois J. Rammacher

AT LAST

I came to you Lord, with head bowed low, I am
ashamed for my countenance to show,
I am so unworthy to speak your name, I am over
Whelmed by mortal shame, you didn't mean too much
To me, when I was so worldly free,
I thought only of myself, sure, I had a Bible on
the shelf!

I wouldn't let it cramp my style, so I ignored
It for a long while, I knew if I had opened the book,
I would be, forever hooked,
Upon His word, He so gloriously conveyed, and I wasn't
Ready to be saved, I had traveled on in pursuit of
Wealth, and so doing I destroyed my self,
I did all I thought was fun, and fell from the top
Rung, of the ladder of success, by this time, I was in

Distress, my good time friends, bid me good by,
I let them go, with a heavy sigh I am only a shadow
Of my former self. I lost it all, even my wealth.
I glanced again. Upon the shelf, where my Bible lay all
By itself, I dusted it off and turned the page
And asked, dear Lord, if you will save, and forgive my past,
On bended knees, I'm here at last.

—Sally Cabaret Lucci

SO SINGS MY LOVER

Stage lights unscrew the gripping iron vice of your jaw
An atonal melody drops freed
A ball of mercury
Falling to silvery pebbles like notes
Collected by hollow drums.

You pulled my father's well driven stake
From the tortured camp of my childhood
And twisted it into lyrics
Boring sockets through the steely gates
Where lined up blinded women listen
And survive another holocaust.

When clapping hands brown bag your tune
And carry it home like an unfinished supper
You return to flesh,
Tongue a love song under black covers
For a private audience.

Dedicated to you, Sarah

—Alicia Jayne

LIFE WITHOUT YOU

I've been so sad since the day you said good-bye.
I've forgotten how to smile because all I've done is cry.

Life without you is like summer without bloom.
There's no sunshine, no flowers and days are filled with gloom.

I never imagined a day without you here,
When a second seems like a minute, a minute like an hour and
    a week seems like a year.

I've lost my smile and the will to go on;
I'm praying every day that you'll soon be home.

If only I could see your face and hold you near,
I'd show you an eternal love without doubt or fear.

I have a photograph but it could never replace
a gentle touch, a kind word and a strong neverending embrace.

If I could tell you one thing, it would not be how
    very much I love you.
It would be that life wouldn't be worth living if I
    had to live life without you.

—Bonita L. Taylor

A POEM FOR TERRY

Life hasn't been easy
    For either you or I . . .
Take it with a grain of salt
    and never wonder "why."

    The roads we've traveled in our lives
        the paths we've had to take —
    Somehow have brought us face to face
        As sudden as a quake!

        The electric spark we feel is rare
            the current runs quite deep . . .
        A once-in-a-lifetime passion
            is laid right at our feet!

            Our friendship grows into love . . .
                Our hearts and minds entwine
            The future looks as promising
                As a bottle of fine wine.

                Thank you for the love you've shown
                    And for your honesty . . .
                You have a quality that's rare
                    I'm glad you're here for me!

—Stacy McManus

MEETING AT NIGHT

The long black road
aside a trace of mountains
in the distance

The corn fields
aside a farm
awaited us

A match was lit
as a half moon turned full

—Jennifer Beck

THE MOUNTAINS

What a wonder the mountains,
    Spring produces fountains.
Lightly powdered towers,
Fields carpeted by flowers.
Cliffs so jagged and bare,
Glorious beyond compare.
Like a fine crafted doll,
The cliffs stand so tall.
Marvelous are the fountains,
Only God can make the mountains.

—Nathanael Lynn Adams

DARE TO DREAM

I sit there with nothing else to
do, but stare at this empty wall.
I start to think you are there;
in my dreams, but that would
be a fantasy.
I dare to dream every night
when I go to sleep. I dare to
dream you are there when
I close my eyes.
I wish this dream of dares
would please, just end and you
would be real, but all you are
is a fantasy.
I see the dare in my dreams,
I dream and I wish to see you
real, but all you can be is a dream
and all you can be is a fantasy.

—Tabitha N. Timko

BABY MAGIC

Caleb, you don't know how
    special you are,
The life and love you
    bring;
Smiles and tears are shed
    for you,
You're such a beautiful
    thing.
Your hands and feet, so
    delicately soft,
Are squirming about . . .
    fantastic!
You have the qualities
    we once had,
That touch of Baby Magic!

*Dedicated to my nephew, Caleb Craig
Mullauer, born October 24, 1989.*

—Amy Mullauer

FROM THE BUS

'Tis only from a poet
A poem should be writ.
What's fair within his eye,
What's fine enough to fit,
And harmonic 'tis it in his ear
Where it must royal, sit.
Every word would yield worth
If pen could equal sight:
It's when and then I think of thee—
You are a poet's right.

—Jim Snyder

GIVE A CHANCE FOR LIFE

"Give a chance for life,"
I plead,
pressed down to dryness.

How can I coolly rise
When held 'til the green in me
runs yellow,
leaving me bloody blue . . .

I cry,
"My life is a green, growing thing—

a green,
growing thing."

—Anne Elizabeth Bennett

SANCTUARY

Seek the night of quiet sounds;
A cricket chirps its reveille,
An auto toots,
    A barn owl hoots,
And a distant train breathes heavily.

Seek the night engulfed in black,
    Here dotted by four fireflies.
Silence touches,
    Darkness clutches,
All beneath its ebon skies.

Seek the safety of the night,
    Refuge for a thousand wrongs,
Bosom of the baited,
    Shelter for the hated,
A blanket o'er the hunted throngs.

—Bruce K. Borey, Sr.

TOGETHERNESS

In the dark of the night
Raining with tears down her face,
Out came a man
    with blue eyes,
        black hair,
    and stood six feet tall.
Wrapped his arms
    around her,
        dried her tears,
    and said, "Cry no more,
I am here now
    and never more
        will I leave your side.
For I was wrong,
We will make a happy home
Just the two of us
    and later three!"

—Trina Dodson

"93"

MY MOTHER — MY FRIEND

You are a special mother,
Not one to boss or nag.
Because you are so special —
Others often hear me brag.

You are a special mother made by God above.
I'm glad He made you *my* mother,
Because of your special kind of love.

You do the kinds of things that most other mothers do,
But you are different from them,
Because you're my good friend too.

You're always there to listen and give a hug or two.
God made you very special and I'm glad He gave *me* to *you!*

—Denise McFarland

GOOD BYE DAD

I always knew this day would come.
I didn't think it would be so soon.
I thought you were forever young.
Remember our porch swing?
Oh how I miss our evenings there.
When I needed advice you gave it
and it was always fair.
You were my confidant and source of strength,
the kind of dad all kids need.
My heart is heavy, I miss you so
but you're with Mom now this I know.
You were a great man
A mighty oak among many saplings
Even though you are gone I know you still care.
Like our Almighty Father you left me your son, Donnie Blair.
Thank you Dad for all you taught me through the years.
My eyes are wet now for I have shed a few tears.
But I will go on like you showed me best
cause I know you're in heaven at eternal rest.
Good Bye Dad, Love Tonya . . . .

—Tonya S. Blair

DANIEL JOSEPH

My little friend, I love you so, you're a miracle to me.
For I was there, through it all, a sight I thought I'd never see.

I saw you first, before the rest, my heart was filled with joy.
This miracle in front of me was a healthy, red-head boy.

Your cry of introduction to the world was soothed as you met your mother.
That moment was so special, to be equalled by no other.

Your father stood there staring at his love and their new son.
He took a breath and cut the cord, his work would now be done.

Your aunt was there to welcome you, her smile bright and wide.
She looked at me and without a word I understood her pride.

Daniel Joseph you're a special child, a gift to be shared.
The bond we have my little friend can never be compared.

—Theresa Reardon

RAIN

The wind strikes. A series of savage blows leave a trail of grayish-black bruises on the face of the once blue horizon, causing the tender sky to weep. Rivulets of tears spill down her darkened cheeks to nourish the famished soil.

—Janna L. Brown

WHAT MAKES SCHOOL FUN

School isn't the most wonderful thing on earth. But it's one of the things you have to go through.
But one thing that makes school interesting is friends.
From them you can hear the gossip, jokes, everybody who's getting into trouble, see all the lovebirds together, all the letter writing and who likes who.
When friends are around you can talk, laugh, help one another, which i know everybody does.
Friends i think lighten everybody's day. Just like me, all my friends always make my day. That's why i like coming to school.

—Marcy Gee

DRIFTWOOD

Our lives to me appear to be
Like driftwood on a troubled sea,
Tossed by the storms of passion's bait,
Chilled by the foam of conquering fate.
Daring the storms—or the sun's hot kiss;
Daring the will the strength to resist.

We challenge the might of the conquering wave
And flounder about, a helpless slave.
Drawn by the whirlpool's fascination,
Too deeply enthralled for hesitation.
Creeping too close to the lightning's flame,
Then plunging deep to cover the shame.

We played alone with the cards fate dealt,
Passions, horrors and sorrows felt.
But the swelled incision on the earth's broad breast
denotes we have found a place to rest.

—Madelyn Borgardts

DON'T BE SORRY

Your love for me is perfect, encumbered
with human frailties—
So pure and so sweet are the words of
love that flows from your lips . . . !

Your love for Me I will gladly accept,
because, when everyone else is busy
Trying to find their way among ways
you take time out to whisper softly to
Me for not being quite perfect by
saying, "I am sorry!"

Don't be sorry—My daughter—for erring
while trying to find My way
Don't be sorry, my daughter, for loving
Me with a human heart . . . Don't be
sorry for living by "Faith" and embracing
A "Spirit" of one so eternally strong.
All is forgiven . . . Peace!

Dedicated to my parents: Mr. Luther Rackley, Sr. & Mrs. Callie Shepard-Rackley (Carter); my religious/pastoral mentor Mrs. Clarice Wright (Johnson) Murray and other 'super'-humans that sojourned with me til now and forever . . . .

—Margret Rackley (White)

MEOW!!

The cat is purrrrrfect,
A panther gazing at you
Then its meow is heard.

—Jennifer Lynne Rae-Baird

AMERICA

O pitiful for filthy skies,
For Union might insane,
For Corporate-mind-mentality
That mocks our wasting plain.

America, America,
I fear we've failed to see—
Our blessed bounty's waning,
From oily sea to sea.

—Jim Snyder

PHRASES IN DREAMS

It's "just around the corner"
"good fortune down the line,"
These phrases are exciting,
    if you believe—that's fine.
You dream of going to the top,
    life is not that way,
You'll never find that rainbow
    high hopes just fell today.

You'll never find that pot of gold
    at rainbows other end,
You won't find fame or glory,
    it's NOT around the bend.
Life is no bed of roses,
    thorns are in between,
One step forward, two steps back,
    what happened to that dream?

Don't waste the next tomorrow,
    your life is at its best,
Content with thoughts of winning
    you're as good as all the rest.

—Doris Halpin

OUT MY WINDOW
#ONE

The clouds are beautiful
Out my large, clear window.
The beauty is nothing,
Is hollow, is, vapor,
Yet look:
The sunlight beyond,
The bulging slopes,
The bottomless valleys,
Highlighted, shadowed,
Illumed far and near;
So bright it makes me squint,
So bright I seem to smile
To look through the open spots
Of inverted springs
To see more nothing
Towering within the blue
In marvelous detail,
Essence—so important;
Everything from nil,
Out my large, clear window.

—Jim Snyder

BOBBI ANNE

There's bottles to be sterilized, and baby to be fed;
Now to change the diapers and tuck her into bed.
I'm not having none of this, I'll cry and fuss a bit;
And if that doesn't do the trick, I'll really throw a fit.
It's out of bed to walk her, and to pace the floor;
If Mom is really lucky, she will get to bed by four.
It's up again at seven, to start another day;
Baby is awake by now and really wants to play.
You look at last night's dishes, setting in the sink;
If only I could have some help, that's what Mama thinks.
Daddy goes to work all day, and comes home tired at night;
But that doesn't bother me a bit, I can treat him right.
I'll laugh and play and coo some, and be nice as I can be;
He thinks that I am perfect, and he's especially good to me.
The baby is so cute and coy, and to get her way she can;
She's their precious little ANGEL and her name is BOBBI ANNE.
—Joanne Sheehan

MR. CURNEAL'S GARDEN

It touched me as I saw it standing by the garden side,
   in the place where I have watched you work with dignity and pride.
Your silver cane had four legs to help you get along,
   even though your body bent, still you planted on.

Through the years I have watched you and admired your will to work,
   even though your health was gone, your garden you never shirked.
Sometimes the ground became so dry, it seemed there was no rain,
   you would water and nurse your plants, even if you needed your cane.

Yes, Mr. Curneal, your garden was your haven and earthly domain,
   but when you perform your heavenly tasks you won't need your silver cane.
You're not limping anymore walking on that street of gold,
   and your body isn't suffering and you'll never, never grow old.

In that garden around the throne we won't have to work and toil,
   the Tree of Life will bear the fruit in Heaven's richest soil.
And that Great Gardener who knows each plant and calls them all by name,
   will gently wipe away all tears and take away all pain.

So may we ever strive to do the best while here on earth,
   and as we daily trudge along, drop some seeds of worth.
For only when we plant good seed of trust and hope and love,
   can we expect to reap a harvest in that Heavenly Garden above.
—Frances Beshear

ANNIVERSARY BLISS

The wind, the sea, the view and thee,
A more beautiful place there could never be,
To celebrate your second anniversary,
Our life, you and me.

Our vows renewed, our spirits replenished,
We are so fortunate to be alive,
To enjoy God's bounty,
Our love, you and I.

Mozart, Ravel, Debussy, Beethoven,
Mumm Cuvee and Moet Chandon
Have all added to this bit of heaven.

The senses were ripe, calling for pleasure,
Great food and passionate sex at our leisure.

We fed the Jays at your request,
A lazy cat slept on our deck, but no kittens did appear,
We hope the dog pictures will be replaced, when we return next year.

A landscape, a seascape, a watercolor of flowers,
A Renoir or a Monet,
Would better enhance,
This wonderful place to stay.
—Laura

HANDS

Use them to climb on that crooked old tree
Inside you're laughing and shouting with glee
Stretch out—Don't fall as you swing
From the branches
To know that you dare to be
Taking such chances

Use them to climb on that monstrous rock
You pull and struggle to reach the top
Hurrying, as you imagine
The enemy lurking below
Then reality claims you
As you stub your toe

Use them as you grow older to become what you will
But hold dear the memories of your childhood still
Conquering mountains, taking chances
Your wishes are still inside
Lift up your hands in prayer
Don't lay your dreams aside

—Betty Vawter

DEVIL'S BOWL

Wetting down the track getting ready for some slack.
The racers roll back around laying that old track down.
The announcers are speaking and those cars are a cracking,
while the crowd watches on and that sun's beating down.

First, come the hot laps
wheeling and squealing around,
getting that old feel for the track.
Tons of pressure thunderous and
numerous spinning out without a doubt.
NBC Sportsworld camera crew, picture
takers galore, tires for sale, wreckers
by the rail, and emergency aid, but . . .

Down in the pit those crazy crews
are hip. Time laps have been taken
so the drivers need not scurry.
The flagman in position the pace car
heads the pack and sprint cars are in
order, side by side. The green flag goes
down and racers zoom around.

—Rhonda Slajer

ONE SUNDAY AT FRANK'S

The rum went down strangely hard like a dry fire
at a quarter to one
Isley Brothers in the background
a square lay half-smoked and stinking
while a dozen faces — hot and sweating, phony-smiling
embraced a temporary, liquor-laced relief
from this night, this tentative life

Two rums later and it all goes down sweeter
laughter and faces become real, and nearer
and I am allowed this escape; to construct
new hopes over old vacant dreams
to dance to forgotten choruses of dusty songs—
I am allowed that much.

A man snatches a brown, lithe girl
from where she sits awaiting her turn at the dance
their steps are uncalculated and pure,
a joyous demonstration of amnesia against a spineless Steel City
I see the magic liquid has not yet worn off for them
but already it is a quarter after one
and it has lost its grace for me.

—Aimee Denise Harvey

ROMANTIC WISTFULNESS

I watched another sunset today
It wouldn't set me free
Reality is so painful
Fantasy so bittersweet

—Susan Westerlund

SILENT AND FEW

Silent and cold
as morning dew
many are old
ending to few

The tears and
 the pain
the hurt and
 the sorrow
there's no
 more to gain
but a bit of
 life to borrow

—David A. Ramirez

WORLD DESTRUCTION

Man has taken
Over Mother Nature's
Land, and people
Aren't caring anymore.

The rainforest
Is being destroyed;
Thanks to men,
And the employed.

All our clean air
Is being used up
By sewage that is
At our city's dump!

Men, and women
Don't really care
If their kids don't
Have any clean air!!

—Molly E. Sheriff

THE EYE

The Eye of Deceit
The Eye of Despair
A watchful Eye
Is not so rare

Keeping an Eye on you
A common expression
Private Eyes
A valuable lesson

Eying up
Is it down
Cross-Eyed
All around

Look into my Eye
What did you See
An iris, pupil, cornea
A reflection of me

Sight is a sense
Common to all
See clearly with Insight
You shall not Fall

—William C. Leppo

LOVE ME NOW OR LOVE ME NEVER

Love me now or love me never,
Or our bonds I must sever.
Take me as I am today,
Or my heart shall fly away.
Love me only, love me true,
And I'll make a heaven on earth for you.
When the wind blows from far away,
Don't let your mind drift to her, please stay.
For no boundary can keep me from your path,
No existing demon could curb my wrath.
For I love thee with a love impassioned,
God hath for no other such a love fashioned.
Call me servant, call me slave, call me what you may,
But I will never leave thy heart in dismay.
I know you need myself and soul,
That's why I'll never set thee free.
As long as I feel thy bonds strong hold,
I'll keep thy chains locked fast on me.

—Linda Hudgins Pierce

FALLING DOWN

The days of my youth were spent on the swings,
Even borrowed a few to get away from things;
The hands at my back were never there to decieve,
But the push was gone as I grew numb and naive;
My escape was going nowhere at all,
Until I lost support and began to fall;
I held on for my life, grasping at air;
It slipped through my fingers but no one could care;

Paranoia persuaded me into perplexity,
To the point that I killed everyone next to me;

My thoughts were telling me I'd rather be dead,
So I lost my mind to clear my head;
Trying to get my hands on reality,
I lost my touch with rationality;
In search of sense, I found myself insane;
I gave away my cares and lost the pain;

Excruciating emotions eviscerated me,
Alleviating my affection into apathy.

—Nickolas Patrick Tague

THE EIFFEL TOWER

While I was in Paris, France,
I visited the Eiffel Tower.
This is a tower of iron framework,
and it was built for the International Exposition
of 1889. This is what I was told.
I also was told by the Frenchmen
that this 984-foot tower
was designed by ALEXANDRE GUSTAVE EIFFEL.
The guidebook says, "The Eiffel Tower
once ranked as the world's greatest engineering marvel.
It is a hugh wrought-iron skeleton
on the Champ de Mars."
The tower has, according to the guidebook,
elevators and stairways that lead to the top.
It also has restaurants, a weather station,
and spaces for experiments.
"For many years, the Eiffel Tower was the highest
structure in the world."
As I left the scene of the Eiffel Tower,
I went to the Leaning Tower of Pisa.

—Benjamin F. Miller

MY FRIENDS

Speaking from a view, geometrically:
I'm sure my friends are odd shaped—
Like me!

They're not round, triangled, rectangled
or square — They aren't oblonged
octangled, bean shaped, or pear
shaped.

Oh, forget the hexagon, the bad
shaped or the fair shaped!

These are special people with forms
all their own — with shapes
Never seen before, heard of or
drawn.

People who fit neither here nor there
— and yet — by their uniqueness —
    find home anywhere!

—Judy Woods

MAN ON THE MOON

A strange light in the night sky
covered by the clouds passing by
His glowing face so comforting
with his wide true smile

The love provided is as golden
  as any just trial
How he listens through the wondrous sky
with no resent of why I cry

His arm is always around
to lend that extra hand
Swiping away the tears before
they land

At night before I sleep
I speak with him to make ends meet
As I drift into my dream
his love comes

As smoothly as a mountain stream . . . .

—Nicole L. Elder, age 15

A MEMORY

I watched as the stars zipping by
Standing still upon the lake's shore
Hearing the waves lap onto shore
Watching with a careful eye

Wondering where do stars come from?
And why don't they land here?
Wondering why do they shine so bright?
And why do they only come out at night?

Watching from the campsite is family —
Who is the silhoutte figure?
The silhoutte figure is me —
Standing in awe on lake's shore

Time to retire I put out the campfire
and I am surrounded by night
Taking one last look at the wondrous
sight
The meteor shower of '93 sailing
over the lake's shore as I go
inside the camper.

—Casie Anne Hodges

MARRIAGE TAKES THREE

Oh how I love him, I really do,
But let me not love him more than You.
You've given him to me till death,
Father, You've given so much—I'm so blessed.

Let me be the wife that he needs,
Teach me with love to sow Your seed,
Lord, give me the wisdom to do Your will,
Our love will grow deeper still.

May I always remember that it was You
Who planned our lives and our love too.
May You get the rev'rence You deserve,
With all our hearts to You we'll serve.

Yes, may I never forget who is the giver
Of such wonderful blessing that You deliver.
Your strength helps us be all that we can be,
For how well we know, marriage takes three!

—Lancie L. Spragg

SLAVE

I fall to the wood stained cot
trying to remember my remorse.
Today you sold my man
and my baby girl.
Now I just have another ache
and the mouse in my box springs.
Come mouse and have a taste
of mother's milk.
It is now left only for you
and my master.
Here he comes now for the daily grind.
Will I let him take me again?
A fight will just prolong the pain.
He enters and nears the bed.
Today the oil lamp will greet your flesh.
Maybe the fire will burn your heart.
I reach for the cocktail
when mouse jumps in my face
and sucks out my eyeballs.

—Roger VanOstrand

BREAST-FEEDING

The pain was immense, but the accomplishment was greater
As I looked at this innocent child, I thought what in life could be better
He looked up at me with his big brown eyes
He had a sense of despair, I didn't recognize
I knew in life nothing could compare
To the joy I felt as I held him near
He turned his head and started to suckle
As I undid my blouse I let out a chuckle
This tiny life was dependent on me
To adhere to his request to have his ninny
Many don't understand and I can't fully explain
The joy I feel when I call his name
Breast-feeding to me is yet another expression
Of the way a mother can provide to her prize possession
If in life, I never experience anything quite the same, again
I'm glad to have breast-fed my little YaQin.

—Charlene Kellum-Jackson

rescue us, oh springtime from the throes of the wicked
for winter has taken our spirit.

rescue us, oh springtime
glorify the season.
bring to us the warmth and color we thrive upon.

rescue us, great primevera, for you are our life.

our rest has been too lengthy and restless is our soul.

bathe us, in your chastity.
drape us in your youth,
blanket us in your sunshine.

oh springtime,
awaken dear child. shout "morning" to the world.
enliven all your flora and fauna
allow mother nature to give you life.

bask in the strength and seeming eternity of your glorious being.
good morning
oh, springtime
good morning.

—Pamela Louise Lee

THERE IS A TOMORROW

Oh, yes, dear friend, there is a tomorrow, yesterdays, all our
yesterdays have come and gone
Oh yes, when you look back — you can almost feel again things
in the past
But look up! Walk tall! There is a tomorrow!
Things in the past will be gone like the wind
So, all we have to do is keep looking more and more to Him
Reach up and touch the hem, oh yes, reach up high and touch the hem
Of His garment—just give it all to Him
For, looking to Jesus—counting on His promises—giving yourself
over to Him will make everything so right
So, dear friend, just take the hand of Jesus, and hold—oh so tight
And He'll wrap His arms around you and give you a peace—a sweet
peace—so beautiful and right
He'll hold you close and comfort you and gently soothe you through
the night.
—Lorna Mae Williamson

REMEMBERED ROMANCE

A mirage of romance is created as the gentle ripples of the lake
blend with the soft haze of the summer moonlight.
The images are of a long ago lost love and the memories are
innocent as the nights of youth are remembered.

The youthful soul spirit is receptive,
eagerly responding to the seductive moon glow and quiet nights.
Romantic feelings are nurtured and allowance is given to control
the being of self.

The mature soul spirit longs for the serenity found in those
recalled nights and awaits the excitement found in peaceful
times of youthful romance and longings.

As the moon rises over the stilled waters,
so shall it descend at dawn's beckoning
And the harsh realities of daybreak must be recognized.

Remembered romance is the rekindled love of our youth.
—M. Cathy Davis

THE UNDERTOW

I'm drowning, in the deep blue seas of your love,
hoping you'd pull me to the surface, and we as one will rise above.

As I'm going under I'm constantly looking for something to hold onto,
but the waves of passion are swiftly, pushing me back towards you.

I feel so cold here in the water, I feel it doing harm,
just jump in next to me and at least keep me warm.

Time is running out, and you're standing there watching me,
and I see it in your eyes, should I pull her out, or is she better
off in the sea?

I'm begging, pleading, screaming, please don't let it end this way,
all it takes is a little courage and your preserver to save the day.

The current is getting stronger and beginning to pull me under,
and the one last thought on my mind, is you could have been stronger.

I'm sinking to the bottom, and you still have a chance to save me,
just whisper darling I love you, and forever we will be.

It's too late to save me now, for I've become one with the ocean,
think about it now not later, how you could have changed that motion.

I'm losing all my oxygen and things are becoming dim,
I guess I should have told you, I never knew how to swim.

Goodbye!
—Tanya M. Lewis

PRINCE WAS TRULY A PRINCE

Prince Tom, my purebred funny "Nut"
it was your life a relative did gut
It was me that he did disturb
when he threw you onto a street curb
to be run over by a passing car
Although our friendship didn't get very far
I knew that you knew I loved you
despite our precious moments so few
I only loved you for one solitary day
before you had to eternally pass away
Your beautiful coat of honey brown
always ended my perpetual frown
In the end, you never let me down
for you took the abuse intended for me
Prince Tom, you showed your loyalty
and devotion, so completely, to me.

—Chris-Mary Repiscak

MAN OF DEATH

His skeleton figure sends shivers down my back,
The voice turns my blood into an icy river.
He makes his living scaring the hell into people,
Leaving them under the covers on many sleepless nights,
Trying to hide from the horror that lurks beyond the sanctuary.

Ghouls and goblins surround him on his throne,
Lurking as knaves to a king.
He sits storming up his next plot,
To turn you white with fear.

Images of death come into play, chills strangle you in fright.
Turning; there is nothing, but you still run to save your soul.
Finally trapped in darkness, you turn to face the terror,
Shivering you realize, it's only one of his tricks.
As you turn to leave, faintly a deep, shrill of laughter
Comforts the sunrise . . . .

—James Wilke

U. P. HOURS

Baring my soul to you,
Dear,
is almost like reading
the paper in the morning.

uno, dos, tres.

. . . and my mind floats
after every article.

tres, quatro, cinco.

I prefer to stretch my feet
under the sheets.

cinco, seis, siete.

You find me immersed
between the pages.

ocho, nueve, diez.

I wish I was at the movies.
Destruction and masturbation
should be brief.

diez, once, doce.

Y tu me miras.
Do you think the social pages
are the cause of bad news?

I know you call me naive,
not even a poet.

uno, dos, tres.

I wish I could stay in bed.

Dedicated to
Douglas Oliver Reymor

—Jorge Letelier

WILL HE LOVE ANOTHER?

Every time she looked at him, a flame went on inside.
It was like a rainbow's shining eye, and yet he looked away.

That must have meant something, if not to her,
That he turned his eyes away.
And if by chance he looked again, he would only hear her say . . .

"I love you with a passion, so strong yet so naive."
"I love you like a child loves life, and like a water dove."

He said just then . . .

"My heart is flattered, and so are my eyes."
"Since you look so pretty, and you're so warm inside."
"But I do not feel much anything, except a world of fools."

She had to ask what he meant by that, her friend and so much more.
Her question was soon answered, by words so short and sore.

"I know that I would be a fool, to not love thee with pleasure."
"But if I had one simple choice, we wouldn't be together."

Her eyes filled with pain just then,
As he told her to keep them dry.
He looked at her just one last time,
And then he said goodbye.

To this day, he never said,
Just why he chose another.
But she always thought the reason was . . .

His heart just didn't love her.

—Sylvie Leroux

PATIENCE

So like then I went to this doctor so that I could report back what he said? And when he asked me what was wrong with me, I answered, "Ya see, it's like this Doc, I'm dead!" Well, like, the Doctor wouldn't believe it, ya know? I said, "Doc! It's true! My heart is like real fragile and Cupid's arrow has pierced it right through. And like I was overwhelmed, in love, and it was really 'heavy'." Still, the Doctor wasn't going to believe it. "Do you believe it?" was what I said. "It's true," I told the Doctor, "it was the wait of love for all of God's creation that like broke my heart— it just tore it in two. And nothing have I to gain in lying, ya know, I'm not into messing with anyone's head." Well, like, then the Doc said, "I believe it." So I said, "Well, Doc, it's true."

—Mrs. Julie Hallissey

GREED

    Let me tell an eternal tale, one every person should beware,
For a lady lost her life for greed, never needed.
With her husband dead, she left a flock of fools in her path.
A lady named Hrena, her Lord named Hresther.
    On a night sad to everyone, but Hrena
She peered out with timeless tenderness and plummeted
Into an illusionary abyss of incredible tears.
However, it was heartfeltly unknown to everyone what was really
Going on. Behind those false eyes, evil was brewing.
She could never love, I knew, for treachery was most important.
So she invented a scheme, a terrifying scheme of the sheerest of
Fascination, the townspeople would be flabbergasted at the thought.
The conception of a mind working contrary to a lifeless
Husband whom she is to rightfully grieve, not hate.
She easily thought of the extinction of her elder son,
Who she would have to share the realms riches with.
But, alas, it never was to take place,
For the king encumbered her to extermination for the slaying of,
What was thought to be, a beloved husband.

    —Eileen Jackson, age 15

NIGHT MUSICIANS

Dusk started to come
The daylight noise gave way to the night time musicians
The sky started to swirl its cloak
To a different time and pace
The sun kissed its neighbor good-bye
As it slowly sank to a different sky
One by one they started to come
As lady moon gave light to the night time musicians melody
She gave them a spot light of heavenly lace
The wet lands welcome her
With the dancing of golden topazes upon their water
The fairies caught a ride on the firefly light
To make a beautiful pattern into the night
The crickets and frogs polished up the tune
Before the big band's serenade had to begin
Everyone and everything plays a part to the singing and dancing
Of the ladies heart
The wind . . . it has a strong part too; it makes the trees and grass
Sing for you
The frogs and crickets are the musical part
But the fairies and wind have the vocals at heart
If you lie and listen my friend you can hear
The night time musician playing and singing its tune to a smooth
Melody that pleases the ear as it slowly rocks you to sleep in
The cradle of the ladies' bosom at night

    —Antonia Toledo Sherrod

IT AIN'T NO GOOD

Crack cocaine ain't no
good it'll kick you
right out of the hood,
It's something you
shouldn't take but
some people would,
but remember crack
cocaine ain't no good.

your friends might pressure
you into something bad,
but the next morning you'll
wake up sad, so if you take
my advice you'll see that
it's right, never do drugs
cause (IT AIN'T NO GOOD).

—Sparkle Lynette Heard, age 14

MYSTERY

An image,
A black figure,
Standing among the crowd.
A strange smile
with eyes of secrecy.
A laugh so familiar
and a voice so well-known
sent a chilling mystery.

A face so unclear
a personality so free.
The image — A little hazy.
A look so surprising
A package so marveled
A creation so unique —
it barely appears.
Through each eye
the view is different.
But, the figure is true.

—Vernadette Abella

autumn

listen to the hush
of silence,
search the dark skies
for a stillborn sun;
smell the frayed petals
of wilted rosebuds,
feel the kiss
of earth's icy breath.

wind and rain
no longer whisper
of life and love
but sigh and moan;
trees blackly weeping
cry brittle withered tears
of dry brown leaves.

birds chirp no more.
(will you fly with them
to some distant shore?)

hold me close,
give me warmth,
talk to me of love.
banish the doubts and fears;
their coldness chills.

—Felipe L. Agas

TU(BAL) DENELLE

I am woman = equal of man!
Without the cross of centuries in my life.
I am no longer the bearer of eggs or men or gods,
to be used, filled and then cast aside
trapped within the fertility of my own body.
No more a seed bed for man but a temple for my own desires.
I am Isis without Horus!
Leda with no fear of swans!
I am all!
I am free!

—Linda Lee Franks

NO DISHWASHER

My daughter makes a meal, but she'll never clean up.
That's left for mom — after we sup.

Now this is one reason that my blood pressure soars
And when I walk by her room, I say: "thank God for doors."
It's a shambles, a war zone, you must watch where you go
For fear there's a land mind ready to blow.
But, if she's happy content living that way
Each to his own, is all I can say.

But once, only once, may she honor my wishes
And surprise me by doing that sink full of dishes.

—Donna Weber

THE LITTLE GIRL AND HER DOLL . . .

The little girl and her doll, a precious sight
Mommie's dolly dressed in blue, Mommy dressed in white,
pretty beads in Mommie's hair, bows on dolly's dress
who made dolly's dress, try and take a guess?

The little girl was visiting, at her Aunt Charlene's
Charlene made dolly's dress, tucked love inside the seams,
the pretty dress with bows, was blue and pink
the little girl's age, eight years old, I think?

The little girl and her doll, I'll always adore
I'm proud of the little mother, that's for sure,
she's my daughter, she'll have a real child someday
though memories of her dolly, will never fade away!

—Suzanne Jean Starr

FREEDOM

Free me I say, from who named the blacks and the gays,
from the stereotypes, and the evil ways.
The fire of late in a bright conflagration,
A message from hell that will kill this nation.
Free me I say, from the greed and the slavery,
and the political powers that hurt our babies.
Help force through the shroud that keeps us separate,
from similar races they have not killed yet.
Let's hold each other's hands in a global circle,
and save ourselves from their acts that are not civil.
Let's come together, and fight for our freedom,
fight with our love,
and we all shall lead them
to the place we love,
the place called *FREEDOM*.

—Rick Langdon

ONLY A ROSE

It was only a rose some would say,
But it helped save my life one wondrous day.

It was sent to me "From Son, With Love."
He must have had it blessed from the Lord above.

That rose it seemed to talk to me,
As it lay dying on the window sill.

"It was just a bud all wrapped in green,
The way the florist wraps, I'm sure you've seen."

I had no vase to put it in so it just laid without a chance to live.

A nurse picked it up and said, "Oh, how lovely"
But it would surely die, its leaves were all
wrinkled and wilted way down.

Its poor weak stem matched my facial frown.

She picked it up and placed it in a water cup,
And before long it perked right up.

I knew right then that message it had to give
The wisdom to heal and the will to live.

I knew what it had been saying to me,
The Lord would heal me also and set me free,
To let me return to my family where I was supposed to be.

*Dedicated to my wonderful husband, Buddie Gene; our
children, James, Mark, Charles, Teresa, Laura, John; and
Sister Kathryn Clendenin for her help in making this possible*

—Margaret E. Garrison

THE DARK BLACK NIGHT'S DAY

In the glowing twilight baby boy Tom held my hand so tight
as he toddled up the hill to see the sight.
Among the coral bells and the cherry laurels
the stars twinkled bright in the dark, black night.

The Moon and the Milky Way did the polka and swing
and the Little Dipper danced the Highland Fling.
Sweet fragrance of coral bells and cherry laurels
pleased our senses in the dark, black night.

The little boy said as we climbed the hill,
"Used to 'magine . . . that a helicopter will
swirl me fast away, far from sight,"
as we gazed at the mythical moon and the jewel starlight.

On a picnic table, the young lad and I
lying flat on our backs, sought celestial insight.
We searched for constellation and cosmic information
while peering into the galaxy of the dark, black night.

The winged horse, Pegasus, galloped off afar.
A forever wish we made on a spinning, falling star.
In the dark, black night, we had secrets to share
as we found the glimmering Orion and the flickering Little Bear.

It was winter when the stripling said, "Mom, come with me
up the hill to see the glistening twilight."
The frost filigreed our faces though bundled up tight
as we trudged through our kingdom of the dark, black night.

The lunar eclipse appeared like a mist. It was a sight to behold.
On the dewy grass sat the young man and I watching wonderment unfold.
As the earth shaded the moon, on his cheek, I pressed a kiss.
For Tom, the little boy grown, swirled away that dark, black night's day.

—Avis Iris Wright

THE IRONMAN

Lou Gehrig grew up, a poor, humble boy,
    and most of the time brought his parents great joy.
His mother envisioned a great engineer,
    But Lou performed to a quite different cheer.

His first great love became a bat and a ball,
    and with the Yankees he gave it his all.
He hit with great power and drove in key runs,
    in "Murderer's Row," many world champions.

His teammates all loved and respected him,
so Lou came through when things were most dim.
He played every game for fifteen full years,
but was forced to retire amidst flowing tears.

Lou Gehrig's disease wore the "Ironman" out,
    his wife always there throughout the long bout.
A tragedy, no doubt, so young, what fate,
    but the memories he left will always be great!

—Alvin K. Benson

FLICKERING FLAME

Like a candle in the wind; my heart flickers for you. Each time something came by to stop my undying love for you. My heart would always retain its flame. I have always loved you; but you never took the time to notice. Nevertheless I would sway back and forth in the wind to wait in the mist. In the mist I waited to capture your heart whenever someone tore it apart. I would come to mend your heart to be your Knight in Shining Armor. However when I would mend your heart like a gentle rose—your petals would blow away in the wind. Although you may not realize that I'm your silhouette that lifts you up when you are down and gives you courage that makes your mind sound. I will keep you in my heart no matter how far away you may be. I will always be by your side to let you know someone cares; whenever rain should come your way. I will be at your side to cry your tears, and I will hold your hand when you confront your fears. I will always love you in my heart and in my mind. I will remain your flickering flame for you will always be mine.

—Leo

SEASONS

The snow from above is gently floating down,
laying its beautiful white blanket upon the ground.
You watch as winter ever so gently moves in,
painting a lovely picture without sin.

The icy pine tree branches bending low,
coming ever so near to the blue white snow.
The birds flying southward ten or twenty in a row,
the cold season must come and the warm must go.

Children now coming out with laughter and glee,
playing in the snow as far as you can see.
Building their snowmen four and six feet tall,
enjoying this for three or four months in all.

Others sitting in and watching winter slowly go by,
waiting for sounds of spring when the new born cry.
And when it comes you think how long it's been,
then back come the birds and the bears out from their den.

The snow and the ice melting and starting to flow,
into small streams and rivers they grow.
So I suppose it's all in nature you know,
when one season comes, the other must go.

—Robert W. Drew

BLISSFUL NIGHT

Breathe the darkness
Kiss the night
Ride the eagle
Hold it tight

Lift your spirit
Walk the clouds
Life is hateful
Death is proud

Slip your wings
Into the wind
To free yourself
Begin within

—Vern Cisney

LOVED ONE

Who is the person
Standing next to me
He is so quiet
As still as a tree
"Do I know you?" I ask
"And do you know me?"
I feel we have met
My heart feels it, you see
No one else can see you
But I know that you're here
Your body is elsewhere
But your soul is so near
Is that you Dad?
I've missed you
Thanks for coming today
I needed to feel your presence
And know that you are OK!

—Nola Nackerud

JOY AND CHEER

Christmas time is very near;
    Hearts are filled with joy and cheer.
    Take a look all around;
    Watch the snowflakes fall to the ground.
    The reason why these things are true;
    Is because God sent His son for me and you.
    Christmas is to celebrate Jesus' birth;
    God sent him to live on earth.
    His life was hard, but he never failed;
    And to end his life onto the cross he was nailed.
    So as Christmas time grows near,
    Fill your hearts with joy and cheer.
    Stop and thank the Lord above;
    For sending Jesus; for giving his love.
    And when Christmas day is finally here;
    Spread God's word; let people hear.
    And hearts all around will be filled with joy and cheer!

—Lindey M. Hughes

STRENGTHEN ME

I'm tired of the warfare day to day. My strength is gone and I'm
fading away.

My armor is dented and my shield is too. My sandals are worn and
my faith has been torn.

I need a break and some peace today, from the sound of my sword
clanging away.

My arm is weak and my feet are weary; my mind is cluttered and my
eyes are teary

So Lord, let me rest in Your infinite love, let me find some
strength from heaven above.

Let my arm be strong and my mind be sharp; let me quench the fire
from every dart.

Let me run the race and finish strong, and let me finish what I
have begun.

—Patti Jo Wahlroos

Lost direction
On the surface of it all the
Very important progress
Entertains and occupies me
Longer and more thorough education; less famine; more communication;
Overall, society runs smoothly. Nothing left unknown unused.
So i should be content. How else could i feel?
Time here on earth rushes by. I reach out.
The telephone cord trips through the wires to the other cord
On the other end. Our friendship is computerized as quickly as
Progress moves on, so do they.
Run Rush to the next stage in life
Only today never in the past could we
Grow so quickly. Hop on a plane, in a car, on a bus,
Ride to the destination. What destination.
Express destination. The goal is to change. Move faster than the
   world. That is what we are
Supposed to do. Faster than the information. The most information.
   Then we have
Success.

—Heather Marie Mitchell

OUR FIRST SAIL

As we navigate often on the deep sea,
dreaming of large spiritual ships
that sail the waters of the ocean blue
and carrying their religious cargoes everywhere,

in all places in the great beyond
where we are going to be
in that land where over yonder
where the redeemed will be resurrected.

This is autumn now,
but winter comes after awhile
with its cool, chilly winds
that cause all pests to die.

I welcome the period of the newness of spring,
where vegetation, animals, and human beings
shall all be happy, lively, and gay,
and can start their lives all over again.

Dedicated to:
  Mrs. Beverly Y. Davis—an Instructor—Shaw High School, Columbus, GA
  Mrs. Laverna H. Elzy—an Instructor—Ft. Benning, GA
  The Taccati Family—School Instructors—Columbus, GA
  Mrs. Dorothy Aniton—an Instructor—Spencer High School, Columbus, GA

—Benjamin F. Miller

AUTUMN LEAVES

Autumn falls and so do leaves
Drifting through the Autumn breeze
Geese and ducks fly to the south
But leaves keep falling down,
Snow falls in the winter
And leaves a pitter, patter, pinter
But when I look around
The leaves keep falling down.

—Marnie Buckner

RABBITS GRAZING

Rabbits graze among the fields,
Eating grass and carrots.
They sound as though they're talking
Like little parrots.
All the time they're fearing,
A hunter or a leering.
All the while they're underground,
They seem to pad around.
Rabbits are smart, it's true,
And never seem to have gloom.

—Andrew D. Wignall, age 9

I look into the mirror and
find my shattered dreams,
I constantly stare at the
picture where you and I were
we,
Dreams I dreamed for you
and me,
Dreams that would make us
one,
I found it was her you loved,
not me.
The Revenge is overwhelming me
I want to die, fade away
Away into my own world
I want my life to stay a dream
In my dreams was not she,
Once upon a time you loved me,
Happily ever after was not "we."

—Lorelei Lesak

HOMEWARD BOUND

I'm going to a beautiful city
In a land that's far away
I'll take my journey homeward
When Jesus beckons me
I have a home awaiting
One that's hard to picture in my mind
My home is built on a golden street
So pure it is crystal clear
My walls are made of jasper
And other precious stones
Each of my doors is a pearl
And there will be no night there
Only God's perfect light
I have loved ones there waiting
To welcome me home
They've gone on before me
What a glad homecoming twill be
I'm homeward bound, homeward bound
There to meet my Jesus
There to wear my crown.

—Joanne Cardwell

ADVICE

You do not need a hair to splice
but it is very nice
to see from friends sometimes good advice
and better, you think twice
before changing fortunes, by throwing a dice
hope grows with age, like in soil rice
love is melting hate like ice
in life is happiness the highest price
to reach peace we all need to sacrifice
but HAPPINESS always needs to be handled . . . WISE.

—Frank Zdzislaw Glinski

two magpies floating in the valley
below
and my hands are shaking
it's a beautiful thing
but, god, inside
I'm all shaken up with a calm
and a desire to scream without
making a sound.
the serenity of a low glide of a black and white form
long tail sweeping the ground
The sweet sadness drooping my eyes
and the vile taste in my mouth

—Kimry D. Schlacter

FATHER

I remember the look of your dark black eyes . . .
and the sound of your laughter.

I remember the soft deep sound of your voice when you spoke to me, when you would call and say "Hi, how was your day?"

These will be in my heart and soul forever.

I also remember how you tried your ultimate best to make us happy.

But there was something deep inside this pain

There was just something you could not explain.

And through the years, you wanted more for your family than what you thought you could give . . .

but you were wrong, because you see . . .
you gave us your heart and that was enough for me.

But now, you're finally happy . . . no more being judged by others.

For you can walk freely without restraints of any kind.

I love you with all my heart and soul,
and I will never totally get over my loss
of you.

Because you were my Father of which there will be no other.

So my beloved father, tell grandpa and grandma I said "Hi."

And I will close and for now say "Goodbye"

In loving memory of my father:
David P. Wilcox Sr.
I love you Dad.

—Mae L. Wilcox

A CELESTIAL DREAM REALITY

My lover came to me as a Celestial Dream—
His strong and throbbing loin My Celestial Giant . . .
His warm melodious voice, His hypnotic choirs—His
luxurious tones, as he sang to me—The spark was there
My Celestial Giant—How I do care for you; before, you
came you were always in my dream—But, your reality is
more than I could hope for, My Celestial Giant;
Your warm brown skin—Your wondrous arms, You smile
all the gestures of a being of meta-physical, yet,
Celestial Reality—all mixed into One Black Celestial
Giant—My Wonderful—tremendously sensitive being—My
Celestial Lover—My Dream—That walks on Earth—My
Celestial Giant—You know who

—Delores A. Loving-Starks

ANGEL TAKES TO FLIGHT

Upon a night a small child like an angel took a flight.
Once was a man took her soul with much fright.
Deep within the mind was found a place in which to hide.
When pain did overtake she like an angel did then fly
As a child pain you stuff for small minds it's too much
Beatings that were rough the child watched from above
When the child in such pain cries out but not heard.
Within the mind a protective change does then occur
Now the child that cries, no help within sight
The small child like an angel then takes to flight.
Upon a fatal night for past pain felt inside.
To Heaven this little angel did then take a last flight.
I was once an angel when young did take to flight.
So for all little angels, up in Heaven this poem I write.

—Sheila L. Crane

MY GUARDIAN ANGEL

There is a stranger in my dreams
He is not scary, though he may seem
He's there with me, everywhere I go
I cannot see him, but I know
I don't know him personally, that's why he's strange to me
But I know he's my friend, that I can see
He will be by my side, all through my life
Knowing that, I shall not strife
This special person protects me from bad
Having him around makes me glad
Everyone has their own special friend
From the day they were born, till their life shall end.
There's no tricks, magic or sneaky angles
This special person is my guardian angel

—Elizabeth M. Torres

CHILDHOOD

And I wonder
shall we always be like little children
who scratch their fingernails on frosted windows
and make designs, letters or just crazy pictures

And while our noses are pressed against the window panes
shall we see the stars and snowflakes
dancing out there in the sparkling winter night

Shall we also dream of holidays (as children always do)
holidays in the snow
so we can run and play

Shall we always be like children
on a snowy winter's day?

Dedicated to Donald J. Rasch

—Kathleen M. Edwards

ANOTHER DAY

Smiling at him,
from beyond the passing
windows of the train;
an advertisement for Freedom
Wire and Cable.
To his left, across the
metal turnstiles, was
the silence of the morning
commute coming out of the rain.
A drone, still
and heavy, sank
across the tracks.
He looked
through the film,
with unbending gaze,
two bodies quarrel,
rigid, upon the stone.

—James Freel

THE LETTER

Though I may stand alone now
You are always in my heart
The good times that we had then
Led us to a good start.
To lose you was a sorrow
That was never meant to be
But your happiness means more
Than your precious love for me.
If she is who you want
I won't stand in your way
I'll never look for you
Or the memories that we made.
So many times I dreamt
That your love for me was true
But even though I slept
I'd wake up feeling blue.
I send this note with love
Sealed with a last kiss
By the wings of a white dove
Flying through the mornings mist.

—Melissa Adkison

MY HEART

When I stand next to you I
can feel my heart beating.
Inside myself it's so loud
I can hear it. It's letting
me know it's feeling something
I can not control.
Even my breath stops and I
have to tell myself to breathe.

When my eyes look into yours I
find myself being in a place that
takes over me. Everything races
inside of me. I can't keep up. At
night I slow it down, then I dream.

Is there even such a thing as
reaching that point without even
touching?

All I can do is stand next to you
holding my breath as if to hold
life within me so I do not die when
you walk away without even looking.

—Lana Downey

FINAL TRIBUTE

I've been a youth District officer for 26 years,
Most times were happy, but I still shed my tears.
The presidents I honored, stood by their side,
I hold my head high, I still have my pride.
But, there is something I've never heard,
You can bet on that, cause you have my word.
It's really something I think I deserve,
I did my duty, to the best I did serve.
My dues are all paid, I owe no rent,
Will you please all rise, it won't cost you a cent.
You're all on your feet and you like to cheer,
A standing ovation is what I'd like to hear.

—Bea Miller

THE ANGEL IS GONE

As nature's morning light hits the tiny pond below
All God's birds rush to put on their show

The sparrows chatter back and forth what's going on
They do not yet understand the Angel is gone

The cardinals are beautiful in their right
But why now do they appear dull and not bright

The martins circle the clouds high up there
They have already seen the empty chair

Mrs. Robin drops her worm and said as she shed a tear
Today our audience did not appear

The bluebird said we will have to sing alone
That chair over there is empty because the Angel is gone

You must sing God said to us
From His Mighty Throne
Sing cheerful and loud that's a must
And be thankful you knew the Angel that is gone

*Dedicated with all my love to my
wonderful wife, Evelyn Jean.*
 —Gary W. Glisson

THIS DRESS

This dress is the time
 This dress is mine
  This dress cost a dime
   This dress is mine
    This dress is new
     This dress is blue
      This dress is mine
       This dress cost a dime
        This dress was made in this time.
         This dress is mine
          This dress cost a dime
           This dress fits
            This dress sits
             This dress sticks
              This dress is a must
               This dress is mine
                This dress cost a dime.
                 This dress of mine that only cost dime
                  Is the dress that is mine
                   Now if you like the dress that is mine
                    It only cost a dime.

*Dedicated to God and Jesus, also Tracey, Eunice,
and Andrew, Tracey's father.*
 —Barbara Jones

CAN I READ YOUR MIND

If I could read your mind,
then my heart would be at ease.
My love may I read your mind,
 Please?
But my love what would it find?

If you could read my mind,
What a story my thoughts would tell.
It would reveal how my heart fell.
It would tell of the treasure it did
 find.
 —Vincent F. Jungenberg

TIME SLIPS AWAY SO FAST

Toys in the sandbox,
 kids playing there.
Now, where are they?
 Time slips away so fast.

Christmas decorations all around,
 cheer and glee fill the air.
Now, where is the noise?
 Time slips away so fast.

Off to the movies, out to the show,
 now, only TV and radio.
Where are the good old times?
 Time slips away so fast.

Ball games, playing catch,
 now, a slow walk.
Where has youth gone?
 Time slips away so fast.

Looking into the mirror,
 reflecting on the past.
Did it all happen?
 Time slips away so fast.
 —Alvin K. Benson

BORN

"hold me . . ." he whispered
in a voice like pouring sand
and death came to claim him
with cloak and outstretched hand.
"i have fears," said he then
in one shallow breath,
"and i tell you now, my child,
one of them is death."
though i already feel his fingers
gripping tightly about my soul
i do so wish to hesitate
for i am not yet ready to go.
but as i'd rather stay and chat
i know he impatiently awaits
and this will be my only guide
to those distant and foreign gates,
just one last thing i'd like to share
before i pass eternal sleep,
i'd like to give a part of the
something small for you to keep.
i leave with you a piece of soul,
yours to take upon my death
a little piece of memory,
my one last dying breath.
 —Stacey R. Holt

FRIENDS

Some of us hold all of our youth, some of us hold age,
Yet in common we have one thing, a friend standing by we can page.
They're always there for that short little talk,
Or to hold your hand when you take that walk.
This world moves fast, but we still get along,
If I had the talent, I'd put it to song.
So slow it down people, take a good look around,
There may be a friend you have not yet found.
But keep your good friends, they're all made of gold,
It took many years to make that fine mold.
Be it golf, other things, there are losses and wins,
But please, dear Lord, please give me my friends.

—Bea Miller

MY GRANDMOTHER

Who is this one that I have known, through precious childhood years;
The loving kindness she has shown, brings about my tears.

A special one to me is she, so quiet, tender and caring;
She gave her all to every child, and never once stopped sharing.

She was the magic of the day, no matter what the season;
Her hands could weave the ultimate when times were out of reason.

The voice of love spoke through to me, when I was just a child,
The tender smile, the sweet caress, if only for a while.

I see you now with silver hair, and know you're growing old;
Before the hand has turned the key, memories must unfold.

I love you dear, my precious one, thank you for loving me;
For you have been a part, of what I want to be.

Please keep with you our memories, for we shall never cry;
And know that I shall love you, as you've loved me in days gone by.

Dedicated to my mother, Elizabeth Lawrence LaFever, in memory of her mother and "my grandmother," Shirley Cantrell.

—Monica L. Gribble

WILLIAMS PRAIRIE

Williams Prairie is located in Johnson County between a ridge of loess-laden hills and the Iowa River in an extension of the Iowan glacial lobe. It might more appropriately be named a "sedge meadow."
— *Proceedings of the Iowa Academy of Science, 1962.*

On the ridge just to the north are ruins of a graveyard
where a century past we remembered and honored our losses
some were aged   so many were young
Civil War dead   women in childbirth   children with fevers

But here the land dips low   sedge meadow   once the edge of
empire of postglacial cold   here is our unremembered past
gnarled bipeds who wore skins   huddled nightly in burrows and caves
our lucent smudge was warmth against boreal storms   a warding sentry
against the snuffling sabertooth   the circling pack of dire wolves
our spearpoints were the odds between famine and another chance
our losses were very great but we laid each in a straitened bed of earth
we gave each tools for the long journey

Who would have known how long our common journey from then till now
or dreamed our tamed metal beasts that outrun the cheetah
our silvery eagles that respond to the jesses yet quarter continents
or those shining spirits of our invention
                that fly past the planets toward Alpha Centauri?

Who would have known how changeless the journey of each to loss
the unchanging mourning   how we lay each in a bed of earth
how each needs artifacts for the long journey?

—Mark Armstrong

Summer months have passed away
To live again another day
And in its stead is born the fall.
Spreading russet leaves over all
Winter approaches with an icy blast
As if expecting to forever last
But spring in her garb of brilliant hue
Emerges and changes, grey skies for blue,
Over all each season yearns to be queen
But wise Mother Nature always changes
   the scene.

—Olga Papanek

MAMA'S COOKIE JAR

Hi, what's your name?
No, wait, let me guess!
I remember your voice from last year,
you were my father's guest.

Your name's John as I recall,
you hung a picture on my bedroom wall.
No, I can't see the smile on your face,
but I remember your voice of kind grace.

I still can't walk so come to me,
I still can't talk but I can feel,
but my little Raggedy Andy body,
God made it for real.

God made me this way,
but why I don't know.
I know I'm a little angel,
coz' he told me so.

So when you come back again,
Look for me I won't be far.
I'll be here in the kitchen,
by my MAMA'S COOKIE JAR.

—Kimo

FOSTER

I'm only three,
Mommy don't leave me . . .

A new home,
Time changed their tone.

A big house!
He hits me and his spouse.

A beautiful condo,
Bruised, confused and fondled.

A cool pad —
She says I'm stupid and bad.

A small apartment,
I was a disappointment.

A foster center . . .
I'm fifteen, here I'll remain.

Jail house.
A room of my own.

Homeless . . .
Shared shoes with an old man in an alley.
It rained, shared a box, her name is Sally.
I think I found a nice family.

—Tanya Bivins

DESTINY CALLS

To say I've waited all my life —
Would sound to you so illusionary!
To say I've wandered through life's existing strifes —
Would only appear to be imaginary!

To say I've intersected you in mind solely —
Would evoke you to interrogate my sanity!
To aver I've loved you in another entity —
Would implore a question not to be echoing!

To rely on fate as an absolute solution —
Would seem to most a depletion of pendency!
But to depend on destiny was my mind's resolution —
And today I realize it was the exclusive journey!

To travel the path set forth by destiny —
Never envisioning a cessation in view —
Was my channel into your vitality —
And unequivocally generated me to encounter you!

—Myra L. Hulse

DEATH OF DAY

I watched, as darkness came, to claim the day
I watched, as it slowly, crawled in
Stealing away, each golden, amber ray
Like a chillin' cloak of death, the darkness came
It slowly claimed the warmth of sunlight from the sky
Leaving behind the cold, lonely night
Filled with haunting, whispering winds
As ghostly memories dance in and out
Of the moon's mystical glow
Casting a silhouette of dewdrops upon the rose
An image of a lover's tears falling silently
As she cast away the hurting years
As she closes her eyes in an eternal sleep
Where apparitions finally diappear
I watched, as darkness came, to claim the day
I watched, as it slowly crawled in
Stealing away, each golden, amber ray
Leaving behind the cold, ghostly silence of night

—Gina Posey

THE FEARS OF LIFE

   As a child things are simple, you
look up to your parents for advice and
guidance. You see things for their face
value. As you grow you begin to learn
you can't rely on your parents, sometimes
you're left with one adult figure, not
two like life says you should. You begin
learning about things that scare you, like
divorce, murder, disease, and war. As a child,
you only know of good things like love, happiness,
and peace, you don't learn of the real life, the
one that awaits your coming. As you grow even
older, you learn of sex and the fears that come
along with that like; pregnancy, disease, love, pain,
and the hardship of being alone. As a child
you should be taught about life as it is; a
way of pain that only you can make better,
a way of loneliness that only you can heal,
and a way of goodness if you can only
believe.

—Nicole Montgomery

A DOG'S DREAM

The dog lies; asleep in a different world.
Its legs begin to twitch as it begins to dream.
It is chasing something; the dog's feet move as if running.
The dog barks out, disrupting the household.
It wakes up, surprised by the sound of its bark.
It yawns, stretches, falls asleep in the middle of the floor,
and the cycle begins again.
—Regina Dure, age 13

CLEARLY HEARD

A symphony ringing in my ears that only I can hear,
Oblivious is the outside,
Inside the music rings clear.
As the violins sound sweet,
Birds in sight seemingly sing, "Tweet, tweet."
Beneath their feet rests a branch with leaves,
As one single leaf falls,
Flutes blown softly guide Nature's own,
To rest on the floor and finale.
—Teresa Sanderson

TAHQUAMENON FALLS

At Tahquamenon Falls in the State of Michigan,
You think of the waterfalls and about how they began,
You can smell the flowers and hear the water rushing,
When the birds are chattering and the popcorn popping,
With the tall trees gently swaying in the breeze.
and the wild flowers alive with the buzzing of the bees,
It's then that nature's at its best 'cause it is always near,
If it's peace and quiet I seek, it is always here.
You hear the people talkin' of how beautiful it is,
But in my heart I know, the credit is all His.
—Marjorie F. Sovinski

NATURE'S SONG

Can I share with you the beauty of nature's creation?
    Just to see the clouds drifting lazily through
the summer skies,
    Feel the warm breezes blowing and knowing how
good the morning is, giving me a cool sensation,
    I can hear the birds happily singing as their
young try their wings to fly.

    Oh, to smell the fragrance of the cherry
blossom in the air,
    And to see the first violet picking up its lovely
face,
    I love to hear the song of the rolling creek
water as it drifts swiftly around the bend with so much care,
    And see the busy spider weave its web through the
branches of each tree making it like dainty pieces of lace.

    I walk the rocky pathways through the woods,
Never knowing what new beauty of nature will I see,
    Up ahead I can see the squirrels darting through
the bushes at play, and then I wonder if I should,
    Follow the paths that the wild deer take and
realize that God has given me the key.

    To His kingdom of love, and happiness,
That only you, and I can feel just how much we
        have to share,
With each day we have left to live it to the
        fullest that some others can care less,
That we are the chosen few who have the vision to
        see into tomorrow's plan if you dare.
—Annette J. Wesgaites

As seasons come and seasons go
Life itself will grow and grow
From birth to death to life beyond
It all comes full circle to form
        a true bond.

Love travels with it as the
        seasons go by
There is no reason to ask
        and wonder why
For the love in one's life is
        the force that will persist
So that each very special person
            will always exist.
—Nola Nackerud

DAVID

You are gone . . .
My last one off to college.
I enter the still room,
pause; absorb the silence.
I take down the posters —
reluctantly.
I bring, from other corners
of the house, a chair and
a table — and place them
where your desk and
stereo, now gone, have
carved deep caverns into
the lofty carpet
    . . . and I am sad
        that you are gone
—Lorraine Windahl Thatcher

SOMEWHAT LIKE THE EAGLE

Mighty Eagle that fly so high,
Take me upon your wings!
Let me reach the height you fly
In everything that I plan and dream.

I will not settle in my mind
For a lower flight
But that I may strive to succeed
With all my ability and might!

All of life's troubles and conflict
Will not prevent me from flying
With you,
I'll put my faith to work for me
I am determined to endure!

To conquer all that God has for me,
To live in Peace and Joy
And total victory!
So take me upon your wings so high
Each and Every Day,
Constantly, being thankful for a better
Way!

Every day of life should be
Somewhat in comparison to the eagle
Striving to live life to its fullness,
Going to the highest level,
Not taking down!

And like the mighty eagle
Let our mind and purpose
Be high above the ground!
—Lennice Marie Taylor

PEACE AND VICTORY

Men and women who stand like giants, and travel far from home,
Shed blood and tears, swallow fears, for a land where buffalo roam,
Peace is a forgotten virtue and war an uncoined phrase,
    But our men and women will fight, as long as our flag is raised.
We're allies to many nations, and an enemy to just one.
    We have so little in common, yet we share the same bright sun,
Adults cry, children cry, "Stop Saddam Hussein,"
    But often times neglect to hear, our soldiers' moms' enduring pain.
What do you have with five million soldiers, tear throughout the sand.
    A needless war, muddy hands, in an already dirty land.
We wake up to beautiful homes, cars, peace and more,
    While our husbands and wives, sons and daughters wake up to a war.
I write, not to make you guilty, only to make you aware,
    And for those who had no thought or opinion, I write to make you care.
So tie a yellow ribbon, for all the world to see,
    That America stands for pride, yet peace and victory.
      —Rashaad C. Clark (RC)

YOUR EYES

I see so much in your eyes, the guise
Of what could be, of what might have been.
I see so much in your eyes: My hopes for tomorrow,
The easing of pain and sorrow.
The mere joy of knowing that you are there.
That you care, and knowing that I will see — your eyes!
I see so much in your eyes, so many dreams.
So many aspirations of goals to come, of victories already won.
I see so much in your eyes, your desires, your rage,
Your willingness to readily engage in whatever realm there is to face.
With such precision, such grace.
I see so much in your eyes, the sea blue-green mist of calming ocean waters.
The waves of experiences you have gained.
The billowing upheavals you have contained and, yes, the simple pleasure,
the smile, their glow can bring.
I see so much in your eyes, so many plans and schemes, hopes and dreams.
Your eyes, your eyes — your eyes!
      —Eleanor Lorraine Gregory

THIRD WIFE

God doesn't allow polygamy in heaven. He hasn't shown me anything, yet,
That I can understand. Everyone says "I'll meet him in heaven" — my husband.

Just walking around on golden streets within four jasper walls,
With four pearly gates, singing praises continually,
And kneeling in a blinding light to worship God, —
And only one hundred forty-four thousand people there!
Why Chicago has more than three million!

I just can't believe God would waste all that time creating people who
Would never enter those gates because the quota had already been met.

Everyone keeps saying "I'll meet him in heaven,"
But that is of no comfort to me.
I know he is not going to run and swoop me up and spin me around,
And then bury his face at my neck and shoulder
While he squeezes me until the dizziness goes away.

I know he isn't going to lie in bed and hold me warm against him
In the dark, because the Bible say there will be "no night there."

He'll not be bringing me a hot, steamy cup of coffee, holding it under
My nose to wake me, — with that big grin and his brown eyes smiling.

God allows no polygamy in heaven, so he won't have time for *me*,
Especially with two other wives there, who died before he did.
      —Vera Thomas Rabe

the fate of the artist/the fate of the writer

i   they have stolen my thoughts of
       art
       bold as they may have been
       they have been destroyed
       the material has destroyed the immaterial

       a pain belts through my heart
       as the canvas bursts
               into
                   flame
       the brushes and paint turn
               into
                   chains
       and i am tied down by their ashes

ii   my pen has collapsed under the weight of hate
       no longer am i to fulfill the dream
       sought by
             man
               for ages
       have given up

       my pens have all been sold
       some soldier heard that they were
             "mightier than the sword"
       i watch their battle through the key hole

iii   i lost the will to live long ago
       in the days of remembering
       in the days of thought
       the sun has yet to rise since yesterdays' yesterdays

       anger . . . .

—Floyd Diebel

HEAVEN HOLLOWER

Just one year ago we came here to live . . .
Enjoying our new home and our new
Found friends . . .

One special man we learned to love . . .
Was our neighbor, Johnny Robert . . .
He lived in the hollower up above . . .

He and I shared many things alike, the
Way we cared and how we knew how to share . . .

He was kind and thoughtful and full
Of fun, he loved to tell stories and how he just loved
Living . . .
And didn't matter if things didn't
Get done . . .

He was wise in so many ways . . . and he
Taught me a lot in oh such a short time . . .
It was always interesting how he figured things out . . .
Never left anything for your mind
To doubt . . .

He left us one night without a notice . . .
For his heart gave out when no one
Noticed . . .

We shared that day about a new hollower . . .
He said he was leaving . . .
But I thought he was just kidding . . .
Now I know the new hollower was
Heaven above . . .
Where he can roam and always be home
And he'll always be loved . . . .

Dedicated to Johnny Robert Pevahouse
Born 6-15-38 Passed Away 12-23-93

—Anna Carrozza

LOVE

Love is not a toy,
Love is not a fashion,
Love is something sacred,
To be felt with compassion.
Love is not concrete,
Love is an emotion,
Love is something abstract,
To be meant with devotion.
Love is a feeling,
Love cannot be measured,
Love is sent from heaven,
That's why it must be treasured.
Love has a meaning,
Love will always be true,
Love is within my heart,
Love is what I feel for you!!

—Albert A. Barchard

FALSE SYMPATHY

Put your sympathy in me,
and feel sorry for what you see,
look at me with sadness,
in your eyes.
Cry all the tears inside,
for me.

Try to heal me,
with your words of wisdom;
don't waste time,
with someone else.
Make me your case study,
another hobby for you to hide.

Tell me how you understand,
from experiences in the past;
tell me, do you really think I care?
Don't look at me,
feeling sorry for what you see;
don't look at me,
with your false sympathy.

—Lin Pisiak

LAMENT

Hidden deep inside me
Are feelings that never are free
To surface, to be,
As part of my whole
For all the world to see.

My spirit cries
From the depths of my being
For support, understanding, and love.
Accept me, set my soul free
To exist and live as me.

And yet you see me not for who I am
Unique, less than perfect
But with beauty in my soul.
You cannot see the whole of me—
Just the imperfect physical shell.

How sad for what you miss,
The part of me you never will know.
Tears flow for what I miss:
Total acceptance, unconditional love,
From the one whom I love so.

—Roseann Stuetz

THE DREAM

As I lie here awake
    dreaming of tomorrow,
"Will you be there?" is the question I *must* ask.
In the morning after the darkness, all I can see is your
eyes, watching my every move.
How can this be?
You speak of love.
How can anyone Love Me!?!
Through your eyes I want to see just what you see
in me.
I want to be inside you, thinking your thoughts.
    Just to understand you,
        I must!

—Cheri L. Jones

A DREAM

Last night while asleep I felt a dream
    way down deep inside my heart;
With an instant flash I saw your face
    I hope we will never have to part.

The feelings of closeness clearly crept in
    and grabbed ahold of one heart string;
I gulped fresh air then lay and stared
    because you were surrounding my very being.

I focused on the wide starred sky
    and got a catch in my breath at the moon;
It is so beautiful tonight and perfectly round
    it helps me to count the hours until I see you soon.

It is getting so hard for me to get through the day
    without your smiling face looking at me;
But when you can spare the time and give me a call
    I get so excited when it's you I do see.

Now you are flying far away once again
    I won't see you for another whole week;
I'll mope and I'll groan and I'll be all alone
    until I again see your sweet smile on your cheek.

—Barbara Nell Smith Dawson

THE MORNING LIGHT

Time and time I found company
But what did I truly have?
Uncertainty, insecurity,
DARKNESS.

All roads led to disappointment,
Leaving my dreams shattered and my heart unsatisfied.

In my life
I must have wished upon every star
Every wish, a prayer to my Lord for — the one
The one in my dreams
The one I fathomed as only an illusion.

Just as I thought I'd go it alone —
Behold, the one, chained to my soul.
You appeared — a perfect gift from above.

The darkness flees. The morning has arrived.

Suddenly, the dull stars blind me.
Beauty encompasses me.
Nature shouts at me.

As long as I have existed, I have loved you.
I shall love you eternally.

—Leah Newsome

SINGLE ROSE

This single rose before me,
Resembles what we've shared,
So unique and beautiful,
Growing without a care.
Then one day the sun stopped shining,
Our relationship came to an end.
You left me out in the rain,
So my rose will never bloom again.
Love hurts sometimes that's just how it
goes. Forever upon this single rose!

—Kitrina M. Barnhill

VISITOR

He went away so silently,
He never said, "Good-bye," to me.
He never smiled nor clasped my hand,
Just hastened to some distant land
In search of treasures I've been told
Of value greater far than gold.

He never took a thing that day.
They were the same when he went away.
No change of clothes was out of place.
No sign that he my home did grace.
Although he's gone, he's still a part,
A treasured memory in my heart.

—Eveline T. Good

WHEN THE RED WIND BLOWS

When the Red Wind blows
    Across the sands of time,
War and death ensue—
    Their horrors sharp defined
In images and memories
    Of those who carried on—
Thoughts of those who didn't live
    To see the next day's dawn.
In the sound of war machines,
    As across the ground they roll;
In the sound of many church bells,
    As, in mourning, loud they toll—
When the Red Wind blows.

—Mike Martin

BED TIME

The trees grow dim.
The flowers grow old.
Night is coming.
It's getting cold.
"Go to sleep now," my grandmother
said. Then she finished a book to
get us to bed. My brother and I
would close our eyes. As Grandmother
whispered, "Tomorrow you'll rise."
The angel will help you, guide
you to sleep. So you will not cry
so you will not weep. Then Grandfather
came in to say goodnight.
Now everything will be alright.

—Brandi Nicole Tedford, age 10

My lonely heart has no place
inside a body without a face
you couldn't see, even if you tried
the tears I've shed, the tears I've cried
My hurt runs deep, can't you see
Oh! I forgot, you can't see me

>Non Existing
>You don't see my tears

—Angela M. Bowen

HOW CAN I GET RIGHT WITH THEE

Lord, how can I get right with Thee
  when hard times are all I see
Lord, how can I get right with Thee

Lord, how can I get right with Thee
when family and friends are down on me
Lord, how can I get right with Thee

Lord, how can I get right with Thee
  when bad is all I know to be
Lord, how can I get right with Thee

Lord, how can I get right with Thee
  when I have no one to teach me
Lord, how can I get right with Thee

>Just ask and you will see
>the way will be shown to you by Me
>It's not hard, you will see
>It's not hard to get right with Me
>I'll be a friend and family to thee.

—Larry D. Halliburton

A YOUNG ADULT'S DREAM

Eyes of the ocean are watching me.
They're telling me things I'll
never believe.
The vision of a strong masculine
body lingers in my mind.
A sight so breathtaking;
a smile that comes only when
cordially invited.
A glare of deception perhaps;
A right gaze of sincerity once
thought again.
Two generations unfamiliar to
one another.
Too afraid of change or new
beginning.
A childhood crush, a romantic's
dream.
A sign of love or a show of
mischief?
The thought of an uncertain
past sends shivers down my
spine.
A curious mind wonders
about the future.
Is it possible that each day
could be filled with such feelings
as this?
Or is this enchantment
too much for a single heart to bear?
I suppose it is.
But never-the-less I'll continue
to dream, and perhaps those eyes
of the ocean will as well.

—Ellen Ward

WHO AM I

I walked "the walk,"
I talked "the talk,"
I was always at the places "to be,"
  but still something was missing.

I laughed at what was supposed to be funny,
I said things that were the right things to say,
  but still something was missing.

  So I began looking and searching.

I started walking "my walk,"
I started talking "my talk,"
I was at the places I wanted to be.

I laughed at what I thought was funny,
I said things I wanted to say.
  And only then did I find what I was looking for,

>Me.

—Suzanna Carrithers

WHEN I THINK OF YOU

Confusion fills my heart,
Tears fill my eyes,
then fall silently down my cheeks.
A song usually wonderful now turned painful,
plays on the radio.
The song is called "Forever In Love"
But I have no love, no life, and no reason to live.
For the one I love doesn't love me, or does he?
It's useless you see for me to go on,
without answers I am nothing.
He says he does care but then expects me to share.
My love knows no other because when he came
along I gave my all to him.
Now he flirts with me and another.
What can I do? I have no right we've never
shared a night or even a day, so I can't complain
or so I may but, not really because we have no ties.
So I go on while my heart just cries.

*Dedicated to the one I was thinking of:
Jerry D. Deady.*

—Tiffany N. Travis

BABY

Brown round eyes sit laden in my sockets,
Heavy with the luggage of my soul.
Arrested lives dance around the iris,
And eyebrows tremble with guilt.
But just a blink and the lashes,
Mask it all from man.

This side of the road the oak trees stand in support.
Their leaves offer me solace while,
Brown acorns roll about (some will swim back to sea).
Opposite I see shadows of men, overbearing evergreens.
Just beyond this indifference rolls the sea,
Filled with lives that can never be.

Deformed and ghastly I'm thankful,
It will never return.
I see its bald head bobs in the sea.
Nightmarish, I feel a kick in the gut.
It should have been normal but . . .
And he told me to throw it back. I had to.

Out to sea it swims, but it does not know,
I love it. My eyebrows are still trembling.

—Jamie Tenneill

SUMMER MORNING

The early morning is pure and clean,
Untouched by man's rebellious scene,
The sun comes up, with radiant light
To chase away the darkened night
Birds break forth with cheery song
And quickly walk about the lawn
To gather breakfast of dew and worm
Before the heat of day returns.
The music of "Bach and Handel" play,
From air waves, Oh! so far away.
What valued time we have found,
In early morn to be around.

—Marguerite Morrison

LETTING GO

I stare wistfully into
Your deep, expressive eyes,
Remembering the excitement,
The giddy, mystical feeling
Of our new love.
When did we lose the magic,
The wondrous yearning, the desire
To be forever together,
Needing only each other?
When did we become accustomed
To the feelings we shared?
I still love you, of course,
And I always will, but
I love you with a quiet desperation,
Afraid of making the slightest mistake,
Or saying the wrong thing.
I cling anxiously as we embrace,
Trying desperately to hold you to me,
Yet I know you are slowly
Pulling away.

—Shannon L. Boyd

TO CLIMB A MOUNTAIN

High above the darkened sky
Where peace exists and eagles fly
There is a place for which we long
A mountain top so rare and strong

Yet standing here below its base
We can not find a resting place
So there's just one thing we can do
We climb a mountain, me and you

The slopes do not seem hard at first
But deep inside we sense the worst
Our legs grow weak, our hearts do shake
Fear grips us like an evil snake

For straight ahead we see at last
Up jagged rocks and twisted paths
This route will bring us to our goal
If we can give it all our soul

Yes, up we climb with aching flesh
No turning back to what we've left
For we know well what lies above
A resting place of peace and love

—Timothy Pelfrey

MY DANCING PARTNER

On this glorious day I shall greet the dawn
And I'll dance with the sun across the sky;
Take delight in the rush of the Westerly wind
As Sir Isaac's incredulous face flashes by.
I shall revel in diamonds of dazzling frost
Which emblazon the meadow and treetops below
And be drunk from the scent of the balsams and firs
As their liquors flow sweet in the sun's noontime glow.
I shall thrill in the music of children at play
Whose sweet innocent voices make harmony clear,
And then bathe in the silence as twilight draws down
Over forest and hillside and countryside near.
I shall bow as my partner slips over the ridge
And continues to waltz through his evening domain;
Left abandoned and earthbound, I'll fret until daybreak
When I and the sun can go dancing again.

—Lucy I. Allen

AND NOBODY EVER DOES

I had a friend who meant the world to
me. His smile turned mine to laughter,
his touch made me feel happy and free,
and to him I tried to be the best I could,
and to give all of me.

I spoke out loud what was in my heart, to
him I've been honest from the start. I
thought he himself could just once be, the
honest friend and let his thoughts and feelings
fly free. But he was afraid to be honest, he
was afraid to be open, he was afraid, and I
suppose men always are,

So our friendship died and we now only see and
feel from afar. He just couldn't tell me how he
felt. That's the way it is, that's the way it
always was — and I don't suppose nobody ever does.

—Marlinah Willis

SLAVERY FOREVER

To be a Slave
There must be a Slave Master
Someone to rule
To make you work faster

At the beginning of Slavery
Blacks just strived to survive
To work hard for "Ole Massa"
Keeping Slavery alive

Now, we have Million Dollar Slaves
Working in Sports, Comedies and Shows
But the Slave Master is still "cracking the whip"
Making big profits—how much—who knows

So Slavery is Slavery
Whether it's Old or New
It's the way we perceive it
Solutions are long overdue

Sometimes we ask the question
Why Slavery ever had to be
It wasn't the Slaves decision
The Master had to be free

*Dedicated to all my children: Toni M. Perkins,
Randolph and Janet Branson, grandchildren—
Sterling Branson, Theresa, Tamera,
Jerry Jr., Deanna and Faith Perkins*

—Ms. Marie E. Daniel

SNOW FLAKES

Have you ever watched the snowflakes
as they come drifting down?
They sparkle in the sunlight
as they fall upon the ground.

It seems as tho they're diamonds
the way they sparkle in their flight.
Silently they fall to earth
as darkness brings the night.

—Doris Moore

When I look into your eyes,
all of these feelings I can't disguise.
When you hold me close to you,
there isn't one thing I couldn't do.
You brighten up my every day
in your own very special way.
You give me a sense of security
every time that you are near me.
Nothing could ever tear us apart,
for you have a special place in my heart.

—Rheannon McCorkle

APART

Sitting still staring at the clock,
noticing that the time goes by slow;
Seems like hours between every tock,
you are the one that makes time for me go.

The time away from you,
seems to be a period of sorrow;
But waiting is all I can do,
hoping that I get to see you tomorrow.

—Richard Lee Goldner

TODAY, I MUST WALK ON THIS GRASS!

Some days the sun shines and I feel fine.
Get most things done with no whine.
Don't even smoke and can't stand wine.
TODAY, I MUST walk on this grass.

Riding the bus on the way downtown,
Looking at grass that has turned brown,
Thinking that life is such a clown.
TODAY, I MUST WALK on this grass.

Watching lips that smile to greet
From blank faces along the street.
Making sure to have swift feet.
TODAY, I MUST WALK ON this grass.

Sounding strange or quite confused.
Feeling all inside bemused.
Sign makes an offer I just refused.
TODAY, I MUST WALK ON THIS grass.

Facts of life cut like a knife.
Every day is filled with strife.
GOT to stay in touch with life.
TODAY, I MUST WALK ON THIS GRASS!

*Dedicated to Chris, Jeremy,
Jonathan, Timothy and Maggie*

—Janette M. Smith

WALKING

Late summer sun ambers autumnal leaves
in golden afternoons,
  on silent trees—
    the round-russet of apples
      heavy and warm—
A pale fuzz of motionless milkweed
    afloat on still air,
      and the soft, home-incense of cedar burning
(and other hints this hour I'll have learning)
that my journey
    transcends beyond the norm,
      past mendacious demands
        of figure and form.
          I from field or 'long the
            fallen tree,
o'er stream or rock or 'round the coppice dense,
find without seeking
    how things that be, be—
      all unconcerned color
        and blazing confidence.
          O, that we . . .
Such growth that spread 'tween me and the sun
    that late afternoon
      when light would run
        up trunk or limb,
          through leaves
            and me,
'neath branch arching slim,
    was like the artist's palette
      packed and hued,
        then *spilt* . . . then spread—
          yet, the accident unrued.
Being beneath such, personality . . .
    the percolation from their reality
      is that
Winter coming concerns them not,
Nor spring after either,
Nor next summer's hot.
They pound no point,
No crwth their creed,
No wonder or worry
No wise warning, "Heed.";
Not finer and foolish
Or philosophic steed,
No complex neuroses
Nor urge to lead;
Not pious or proud
Through philanthropic need,
No ponder or awe
From the faintest far felt:
  They do,
    with what they're orginally dealt.
So looking close,
  or 'cross,
    or past the fields afar—
      It,
        as we,
          simply,
            wonderfully,
Are

—Jim Snyder

THE NIGHT WIND

If dreams were wishes and wishes came true
I would spend my life just loving you
The night wind called and I felt a chill
As I saw my love coming over the hill
I called to her when will our love be
She glanced a stare of love then said to me
It's in the wind that our love will be free
Only true love can ever capture me
I held her tightly then looked into her eyes
She said my love for you is finally realized
The night wind blew and once again I felt a chill
Then my love silently walked away and over the hill
Was this a dream where wishes come true
The night wind called and said don't be blue
One day your true love will come back to you

—Patrick Duke Campbell

TIBBERY-TOO

I have a friend named Tibbery Too
You can't see her, only me, not you
We laugh and we run and play all day.
I hope Tibbery Too never moves away.

My friend Amy moved to
Chicago.
Her mom bought a boat and
Amy gets to row.
Amy has a new brother, his
name is Cal
I sure miss Amy 'cause she
was my pal.

Tibbery Too sleeps with me
and my bear.
I brush my teeth and Tibbery Too combs my hair.
Mom says Tibbery Too can't comb very well,
Tibbery Too hugged me when I tripped and fell.
I missed Tibbery Too when I went to school,
The teacher read stories as she sat on a stool.
I had lots of fun, 'till it was time to go home,
Then one day Tibbery Too was gone.

—Leta Koch

IT DOESN'T DO ANY GOOD TO CRY

I voted for a change in Government;
After all, it seemed to be worth a try.
But it wasn't a tax hike that I meant —
Still, it doesn't do any good to cry!

Working all year, a vacation I gained;
Some money was saved so I could get by.
Odd though it might seem, 'twas the week it rained —
But it doesn't do any good to cry!

I felt that I needed a pickup truck.
So, at a car lot I talked to a guy
Who sold me one held together by luck —
Still, it doesn't do any good to cry!

In a change of diet, my food bill rose.
My health sure has improved, I can't deny.
Now, I've got to go out and buy new clothes —
But it doesn't do any good to cry!

Now, I hope you don't think I'm a "sad sack"
If you should glimpse a big tear in my eye.
At times, I wish to get my money back —
And it doesn't do any good to cry!

—Charlie F. Manuel

CHANGES

Swifting thoughts like shifting sands
burning among candle sticks
feelings cross, friendships change,
has the world just rearranged?
Now it seems like a whole other place
and it's gone and changed its face:
Time to sing out or time to cry in?
Whatever you do make sure it's not a sin
everyone's watching every step you take.
Come on people just give me a break
fix this world of racist people
Because all men are created equal
People stereotype and people ignore
that's part of this world
that I don't adore.

—Brooke Davidoff, age 14

MASQUERADE

Death prevails
Hatred reigns
Madness ignites
Sadness drains

    Negativity exists
    Fatigue calls
    Ennui comes
    Apathy befalls

        Masquerade trumpets and chimes
        A change, a reformation will occur
        Lights flicker, electrify
        You come alive, not as you were

Compassion caresses
Excitement exclaims
Enthusiasm explodes
Positivity proclaims

Joy predominates
Happiness hails
Love reigns
Life prevails

—Jason E.

SPRINGTIME FOR ALL

A daffodil! Oh, what a thrill
At last to welcome spring.
The winter's cold has lost its hold
And nature prepares to sing.

The pussy willows' silver pillows
Dance upon a limb.
A crocus flower with a burst of power
Starts my walkway trim.

A pink primrose pokes forth its nose.
Green buds adorn the trees.
The wind around carries the sound
Of busy honey bees.

The air is clear. The birds appear
Surveying for a nest.
And all creation, with jubilation,
Awakes from its winter rest.

And even man in his spirit can
Enjoy a springtime too.
Jesus gives a new start to each open heart.
He's the one who makes all things new!

—Valerie Johnson Cox

UNANSWERED QUESTIONS

I have exactly seven children.
One and one from A friend of Whitman.
Two more packages arrived
Courtesy of three years in Paris.
A fifth and sixth were donated by my third wife.
You ask where the last one came from and I
Will add that it is a very small one, from
Me, myself.

—Kevin McDonough

EMPYREAL NIGHT

Lost in a wistful slumber,
The languorous night stretches out
Before me in wondrous splendor.

The first shudder echoes through the sky,
Like a whisper carried aloft by the wind,
Shaking loose the instincts buried so long ago.

Molten Lips find their mark
As Thunderous Torrents of passion
Pour over the delight I take in you . . .

Each touch binds our souls
In a tenuous moment . . . of complete submission,
Lost in the empyreal night.

—Michael A. Lubarsky

SENSE OF FEELING

A warm scent is in the air
On the water, the sunset creates a gentle glare
The waves lay upon the shore
After making a quiet roar

The air is sweet
The sand, caressing under your feet
It gives a subtle feeling
That your tender heart is healing

The world is washed away
As you enjoy this beautiful day
Surrounded by innocent sounds
Upon these untamed grounds.

*Dedicated to my friend, Heather Brannam:
May the memories of your grandpa run free.*

—Boro

YOUR TREASURE

Give to many so that your treasure will grow,

For the amount you receive depends on how much you sow,

Good thought and deed you have in limitless supply,

And to all that you give all will reply,

When you love other people, you'll feel love too,

For you give this gift also to you,

Adding love to love the treasure grows, a heaven on earth only the wise one knows,

This way of living be sure not to miss,

For there is nothing simpler or greater than this.

—Gene Patuna

A MOTHER

Like a Rose, a Mother is beautiful and graceful and full of life . . .

Like a Rose, a Mother needs love
and care to grow . . .
And without that love and care,
she will wither and die . . .

Like a Rose, a Mother holds all
her children close to her heart . . .

Like a Rose, a Mother brings
love and a smile to all she meets . . .

Like a Rose, a Mother's tears flow
when she is hurt or left to wither . . .

Like a Rose, this Mother I want
forever to keep . . . .

—Delilah J. Clem Byers

WIDOW'S YEAR

It starts with the loss
Of the one you let be boss
Then comes the start of the grief
There doesn't seem to be any relief.
It begins with shock and tears
As you look back over the years.
You have the wonderful memories,
But you have to see ahead through the trees.
Everyone keeps saying give it a year.
Is this a magical time when I will cheer.
I think not, but I really don't know.
My year is about over and it doesn't show,
It went by so very fast
It will be a year in my past.
I will go into my remaining years,
Maybe with just a few less tears.
There is a little bit of relief,
I know there is less grief.
Yes, there is a widow's year,
But it certainly is not a time to cheer.

—Anna M. Meverden

DON'T HURT ME ANYMORE

I am only a child
Very innocent and nieve
This pain could hurt me for life
It could take away my sanity

What makes you hurt me like this
Does it make you feel so in charge
It strips me of the person I could've been
Against the world I'm now cold and hard

If I spoke out against you
Who'd believe in what I say
Is there one someone who'd listen
And let justice be served today

Your reputation distinguished and respectable
Like a bird would fly away
You'd lose everything you've worked for
If they knew you hurt me this way

My eyes are no longer innocent
You've taken that away and more
Please for the sake of my growing up normal
Don't hurt me anymore

—Gwendolyn L. Lewis

WEB OF PASSION

I find myself caught in a web of passion
Tearing at the fibers of my heart
Longing to be near her and not apart
Though I am standing alone with all this passion
Just maybe someday our love could happen
Then the joy, peace harmony and most of all love
Will shine and fill the heavens above
For now I am caught in this web of passion
Longing to make love happen.

—Patrick Duke Campbell

MY FIRST POEM

My first poor poem
was not a dandy one,
but it was the best that I could do.

As I took a pencil in my puny hand
to scribble down my first poem,
it was just a group of written words.

But I had to have a starting point,
with a pencil in my shaky hand
and a few words in a flickering head.

This is the way that I began
I said to the young in heart
and to the tired old people, too.

The name of the game of life
is how well that one plays the game.
Education and wisdom are the tools that one needs.

So don't go empty-handed and with dull minds.
The world is looking for good players
so take your tools to the game with you.

Real opportunity comes only once.
Use it now or lose it later.

—Benjamin F. Miller

END OF DAY

At the end of the day
People slow down
It's time to be thankful for what we have
It's time to look forward to rest
It's time to relax your mind
Put work aside
To be with the ones you love
To bring your work home
Is like living with your boss
Your boss is a slave driver
It's his job
To put everything second
And the job first
There should be a box
At the front door of every home
Where we can chain up our boss
A box where we can leave our brief case
Home is where you live
Where you love
If you don't have time for your loved ones
If you have to work all night
Move in with your boss
Destroy his love life
That is if he has one
He'll do the same to yours
Be a man and leave your boss at work
Be a drone and bring your work and your boss home

—Henry Sherrod Jr.

COME HELL OR HIGH WATER

We gather at the river again
And bid upon, plan our escape
Standing straight in the hour of sin
Protesting virus, cursing rape
As the mirrors and the thoughts of men
Grope in vain for pompous zen

The devils are there proclaiming fate
As we have pushed aside our only friends
Tormented forever at Hell's bloody gate
Which will never die and never end
Dazed and awestruck as a virginal bride
Our levelling, rancorous pathway denied

Smoke fills the caverns of daggered device
Where poverty reeks and innocence dies
The warlord is patient and carries his spite
As the roof swings shut on our plasma-red sky
Centuries trapped for to this we are wed
Wisdom is property only to the dead

—Casey Hayes

LOVES LOST

You are young and immature
a first crush you endure
but soon there comes a day
when you go your own way.
From the heart love departs
And life goes on.

Grown up now and then one night
you are smitten by love's bite.
You try to make this the one
then from the relationship you run.
From the heart love departs
And life goes on.

Older now you search your heart and sit alone
and wonder about the loves you have known.
Do they still have feelings in their heart
after all the years that you've been apart?
From the heart love departs
but in the mind, past loves you'll find
For Love Never Dies!

—Jim Damon

THE TRAIL

The times of past have been
memories of joy.
Things are changing, now it seems
life uses me as a toy.
Twisted and mangled are the
emotions I receive.
These feelings are taunting me.
I wish they would leave.
My life is leading a walk
down a trail.
My freinds are needed
to help me prevail.
Sometimes it feels I'm walking by myself.
Sometimes it feels I'm put on a shelf.
My emotions are tattered, teared and scarred.
My life is so confusing bitter and hard.
Feelings should be sacred and protected.
Why do I feel I've been rejected.
My life is leading a walk down a trail.
My friends are needed to help me prevail.

—Erik Gordon

PINK SUNRISE

Have you seen the peachy pink sunrise,
A phenomenon dazzling before your eyes!
Frothy, billowing clouds, what a sight,
Like a gifted painter's palette of delight.

A formation of birds from east to west,
Circling, zig-zagging; a sky-diver's quest.
Freedom to roam the heavenly skies above,
Multitudinous species — cardinal or dove.

Out of nowhere, there looms a specter,
An ironbird wending its way to adventure.
Majestically upward, onward, soaring,
My window is closed; can't hear the roaring.

Oh, it's morning already. Rise and shine!
Subtle features begin to delineate divine.
Can we somehow hold back the dawn?
Nay; it is a new day to "write on!"

—Mabel M.H. Chang

JUST ONCE

Just once . . .
Can I find a love staying strong within me
Letting there be more than tears from lost eyes
and pain from a shattered lie

Just once . . .
Can't people believe love is only within two
Who feel dreams are as fairy tales
spoken of, never seen

Just once . . .
Can time do so much
Letting wanted love be shown
while lonely times disappear within me

Just once . . .
Can we be free
Knowing over time were there is only peace
But, as days go by and time may pass
We shall know
that just once, shall never be

—Michele J. Alvarado

PRICELESS ART

It carries you oh so gently
Into the stillness of the night
It takes you ever so closely
To the realms of sheer delight.

It erases the gloomy past
To reveal a brand new start
It serves as a talented doctor
To mend a broken heart.

It combines some very special feelings
To express what one can't say
It's one of nature's most treasured possessions
One that can never be taken away.

It lifts away the darkened clouds
To turn grey skies to blue
It makes a path for one to express
The treasured words, "I love you."

A wonderful thing is that which I speak
A true gift from up above
It has the power to bring true joy
For it's the art of MAKING LOVE.

—Robert A. Sulton

PROSPER

May a waterfall of enchantment
pour into your mind
May your dreams and visions
be fulfilled to you with time
May love surge
with the beating of your heart
and a path to destination
begin to finally start
May an angel of protection
guard you on your way
And may everything you love
surround you all your days
And when happiness has filled your life
And your time is growing late
May I be there to greet you
when you come to Heaven's gate.

*Dedicated to my family especially
my grandmother, Helen Lee Smith*

—Tony L. Smith

ERIN

Under Leo's sign you came,
a puny mound of wrinkled flesh
that cried and suckled and slept.
Now you've woken to a new dawn.
Eyes twinkling, you smile brightly
and create a wondrous world.

I hold you in my arms,
no longer old and tired,
freshened by your pulsing warmth.
I set you down to quest on your own.
You creep, you crawl, you toddle and fall;
then taught by unseen Hands,
you begin to run.
Pushing at doors, you explore every nook,
mapping all in your mind.

Outside, you reach out at the sun,
sky, clouds, trees, blades of grass,
flowers, birds, butterflies and bees.
Each holds your fascination.
In syllables by angels and fairies known,
you talk with them in a mystic tongue.

When the soft night falls,
we dance as I croon
a half-forgotten ancestral song
till you're lulled to sleep;
your face calm and serene,
untouched by bad dreams yet.

One day, another time,
you'll say goodbye
to Spot, Dumbo and Barney;
you'll leave behind
Teddy Bear and Raggedy Ann.
Would I still be here then?
Would I have moved on?

O sweet, O lovely child!
Apple of this old man's eye!
Could I but have this impossible wish:
That you are always as you are,
and I am always as I am.

—Felipe L. Agas

If life is a journey,
let me read the map correctly.

If life is as the ocean,
let me weather the storm
without the destruction of my ship.

If life's importance is wealth,
let me fill mine with the rubies of hope,
the emeralds of dreams,
the diamonds of strength and perseverance,
and the gold of happiness and love.

*Dedicated to my parents for always believing
and trusting in me. Also,
to Doug for opening my heart.*

—**Andrea M Nay**

HEROS

(For Co. "B" 5th Marine Reg. R.V.N. 1967)

The birds eat their bodies
where they fell
long lonely miles away
from what they believed in.

I don't know their names
their faces all look the same.
Maybe someone loved them
and they died, defending that love
I don't know, I just don't know
I'm new here, I really don't belong.

Soon,
they will be gone,
back into the dust
and the birds will move on,
to another field.

—**Michael Walters**

THE HOLOCAUST

A time of sorrow, weeping, and pain,
of homes being lost, and hopes to
stay sane.

You would never see a smile,
or laughter from any child,

Just many sad faces,
and trails each tear traces.

Don't cry my friend, don't stop dreaming.
Don't plug your ears when you hear
the screaming.

You must live through it, and remember it all
you'll come out of it prouder, and
standing tall.

Because of a belief, or the wrong
sounding name,
the feeling of anti-Semitism became
a lasting fame.

Only a few lived through it, out of
the many that perished
but my knowledge of what happened is
something I will always cherish.

—**Alyson Eisenlord**

THE GRAY OF DAWN

I was reaching for you last night
Wanting to hold you near
But my arms were empty
Telling me something I didn't want to hear.

I called for you last night
Hoping that you would return my plea
Saying you had been wrong
And you really did need me.

I cried myself to sleep last night
When my dreams stopped coming true
And I finally realized
That, never again, would I have you.

I woke up from last night
Knowing that you were gone
And for the first time in my life
I saw the gray of dawn.

—**Susan Colley**

REMEMBRANCE

As
the bloody
crimson sky
darkens
my
horizon,
I remember
you
and cry
rivers
of eternity
to your
quieted
heart.

*Dedicated to Nicholas J. Filotei
(1972-1992), my brother and inspiration.
His beautiful heart and soul will always
be remembered, and his love
will live on forever.*

—**Angela Filotei**

ONLY A STATISTIC

She opened the door
and stared at the trooper
in shock and disbelief
And as his words came
they brought anger and grief

Earlier in the night
her son and his friends
were talking and milling about
when — without provocation
shots rang out

In an instant her son
had become a statistic
of which the numbers only increase
the violence overwhelming
the prayers for peace

The hate, anger and prejudice
flowing freely in our cities
affects all social levels
Only equality, love and compassion
will free us from these devils

—**Sheryl Lynn Largent**

THE KITTEN

A precious emblem of someone's love,
A graceful creature from God above.
She sleeps in silence unharmed by the world,
Purring soft purrs that cannot be heard.
Who could destroy her perfect dreams
And bring her into a world so cruel?
This gentle life is unknowing it seems,
Of hurt and pain and human rule.
So she drifts again off to sleep,
To dream of the world that she will someday meet.

—Desireé Graham, age 12

EPITAPH A

Gone but not forgotten, and to my Master I
To sit above the moon so bright hung in the starry sky.

And now to who may read this,
And now to he who knew
The man that lies beneath them
For whom now time is through.
Do not weep or fret for him
For he is safe above
To send down rays of hope for you
Rays of hope and love.

—Rhyne Piggott

THE GHETTO

Take me to a place where everyone around me is my family,
Where I can talk when I am alone or weary.

Even though many times I go through trials and tribulations,
There are always people to console and comfort me.

The ghetto is not just a violent place
as people think,
It is also a calm,
peaceful and warm environment.

There are many different nationalities,
But in the ghetto nobody is different,
everyone is the same
everybody is one
To me, the ghetto is not just a place
it is a home.

—Jōvon M. Gamble, grade 8

THE WHISPER

A Whisper softly sets upon my shoulder,
a reminder that things aren't what they seem to be.
A reminder, before life closes like a folder,
to fix things and to love for free.

While we have a chance to make it better,
we shouldn't wait until it is too late.
Opportunities do not last forever,
and we have no time to wait.

After the Whisper touched me, she left.
As soon as she got here, she was gone.
She left us feeling quite bereft,
but she knew her job on earth was done.

*Dedicated to Sulin Ma — The 'whisper' that briefly
alighted upon the hearts of those who knew her,
and left her light to be treasured forever.*

—Elizabeth Consolazio

TREASURES

A room full of toys
Where a child once played,
A pond in the yard
Where he used to wade.

A bike in the shed
That he used to ride,
A tree behind which
He would run and hide.

A butterfly collection
Put away on the shelf,
An electric train
He could run by himself.

These are the treasures
Of a boy once alive,
But he left this world
When he was only five.

—Jan Eversole

I LIKE POEMS

Some poems
Are sweet,

Some poems
Are not
So sweet.

I like
Poems.

To me
Poems
Are
Filled
With
Love
And
Fun.

I like
Poems.

—Amy Marie Reynolds, age 9

FRIENDS

Friends are true, Friends are caring, Friends are best when it comes to sharing.

They bring out the best in you
Whether you're happy or blue.
The best Friend of all is someone
who can talk to and share your
dreams with.
Someone who cares enough to share
theirs with you.

A Friend is someone who is
understanding and true;
Before they think of themselves
they think of you.

If we were Friends from the
beginning it was meant to be . . .
Our Friendship will last, me
in you, and you in me.

—Tammy Jo Fisher

CONFINED VASTNESS

A piece of driftwood floating out to sea
carried to an unknown destiny.
By the force of the ocean it floats near the shore
to rest on the waterfront, to drift no more.
Rescued by the clutch of a human hand
only to be flung out to sea once again.
Weather beaten and wobbly it wrestles the waves
but it was captured and carried to its watery grave.
The driftwood is a prisoner of the untamed sea
as I am the prison that locks up me.

—Grace H. Batie

THE POWER

The moment that you love someone — everything changes.
Nothing will ever be the same.
The instant you surrender your heart,
your sanity has lost command.
You no longer are the matter of your fate.
Your heart lies in the hands of another.
You see so many brilliant colors,
nothing will ever be *just* black and white again.
Sometimes love can be so powerful,
but when it dies, it leaves you devastated.

—Josephine A. Licci

WORM GERM WILLY

Worm Germ Willy would not take a bath.
When his mother told him to, he just laughed.
Since he would not take a bath at all,
His mother dragged him down the hall.
She stripped off all his mudcaked clothes,
And into the bathtub — there he goes.
Since Will had never taken a bath,
He surprisingly began to laugh!
With soapsuds flying in the air
And shampoo doused upon his hair,
He said, "Gee Mom, this is fun!"
And drying off he said, "I think I'll take another one!"

—Lindsey E. Braun

LIKE A DREAM

Ricky was a little boy, they say he was just three,
The first time that he played guitar for everyone to see.
Ricky was a prodigy; by nine he played like a dream.
Everyone loved Ricky with his six-string on his knee.

The first time I met Ricky, we were barely seventeen.
I tell you I was mesmerized by Ricky's melodies.
Ricky was a lot like me; he soon became my friend.
We played together everyday—music without end.

Later, Ricky met a girl and the rest is history.
"Love at first sight is no cliche," thought Ricky and Marie.
At first we all were happy—making music, living dreams,
But Marie had other plans for Ricky's future, now it seems.

I saw less and less of Ricky, and he married in the spring,
And Ricky sold his guitar just to buy that wedding ring.
Ricky got a job to buy the food and pay the rent;
It seemed that life had found a way to make the music end.

Me and Ricky went our separate ways, but I must say,
I find it sad, indeed, the world will never hear him play.
But music always finds a way to live on, seems to me,
For I saw Ricky's little boy play guitar like a dream.

—Sean Patrick O'Shea

HOW I WISH

The days have gone by
so cold and lonely.
How I wish you were
here — just to touch me.

How I wish I could just
say three words to you,
just to end my pain. Those
three words, "I Love You" would
be repeated over and over again.

Streaming down my face
is one crystal clear tear. All
I can say is "How I wish you
were here."

—Charmaine A. Gordon

OUR OWN

Out of the scraps of life
You not only build a house
But a Home,
A place to call our own.

A place where our children play
With laughter and smiles.
Of simple things that could only
Make our house a Home.

Of lullabies and cookie jars
And cakes and candles that shine.
Of secrets that children's lips
Could only speak.

A place for Peace
At the close of the day.
Our Home, a place
To call our own.

—Michal J. Standridge

PROPER HOUSE

It's no fun
To be at the "proper house"
Where kettles and teapots shine

Where soft voices sound
With absent expressions
Where placid eyelids blink

Where toast and tea
Sit limply, on the china dish
Where ladies starch their souls
Into ruffled clothes
And walk about "complete"

Where walls sit mute
Beneath their vacant
And listless scenes
Where even garden plants
Don't stray beyond "their place"

Where sunlight bores a little hole
Through brocade-covered glass
And silence sits conspicuous
Upon your breakfast plate
Where children sit
Like store-bought dolls
"Performing etiquette."

—Rayne Hymn

BONES AND FLOWERS

Children come on Remembrance Day
to place flowers on his grave
withered petals, wind sweeps away
to fate they are a slave

(Then the light was gone, like the flicking of a switch,
he could not outrun the bullets which chose to riddle his flesh)

Veterans come on Remembrance Day
to stare at his grave
withered souls Reaper sweeps away
to war they were a slave

(Then his life was gone, like the passing of a storm,
the wounds were mortal, and crimson then gushed forth)

His family comes on Remembrance Day
to weep upon his grave
bitter tears the rain washes away
to anguish they are slaves

—Joey Martel

WITH YOU

With you the weeks have more than 7 days the hours never blow away, with you everything changes and becomes just us, alone.

Now I understand why the moon lights up at night, and why the sun ever shines in the day, 'cause there is always somebody who has just fallen in love again.

I never thought this love I feel for you could be this strong, I never thought I could ever love the same way I love this world. Now I don't want to ever think that I could live without you because I know that I couldn't ever stop thinking about you.

With you the whole world becomes better than I thought, with you my heart still pumping faster like never before. You mean everything to me and just like this life belongs to God, this person with all this words, loves you and will never let you go, because she will always belong to you. And I know that I would never think that I was wrong by giving you all my love.

—Raquel Loyola, age 18

MORE QUESTION THAN ANSWER CATEGORY
Humatoid — Plan for man

What is a question ? Why is it there ?
Where did it come from ? Where is it going ?
Where did we come from ? Why are we here ?
When ? Where ? What ? Why ?
Questions , Questions , Questions
Where are the answers ?

The world is full of questions from the young and old alike
Who is our overseer ? The sun the moon the stars ?
Who rules the sun the moon the stars ? Who is their overseer ?
Who rules the wind the rain or even the sunshine ?
Need I say more ?

What is evolution ?
Where does it begin ? Where does it end ?
Does evolution rule the sun the moon the stars ?

What is half a question ? Where is the other half ?
What is the name of the game of this problem solving earth ?
Is this evolution ?
Why do you ask ? Why do you need to ask ?
Can you see ? can you feel ? can you plan ?
I do , I did , I can

—Cleatrice Moore

KEEP MOVING

Ever on and forward go,
   Never stop to sigh;
Those who slowly, sighing go,
   Find but time to die.

—S.I. Nelson

DAY BY DAY

Monday through Friday
it's all the same
   Saturday and
   Sunday I've lost
the flame;
Even the holidays
   to me is another
   day.
Since the day of
   AIDS, my life is
   lived day by day.

—Jose Martinez

TIME TO GO

It's time to go
for our life is
through.
It's been fun
all the way
through.
We've seen the
good.
We've seen the
bad.
We've been happy
and we've been
sad.
But now our
worries will be
through, for Heaven
awaits both me and
you.

—Adam L. Fossett

THIS HEART OF MINE

Forever in love
That I gave my heart
For him to hold
Until it has been broken
A moonlit stroll
Along my deepest emotions
Cuz I've fallen for him
Sadness seems to disappear
Quickly from my heart
And my thoughts
Are now the feelings
Of love which he
Holds deep inside of me
He has stolen this heart
Which I have given
I hope he keeps it safe
And holds it as a memory
To remember me by
Though if broken
He shall return it

—Liza Marie Umipig

LOST IN THE SYSTEM

Are you lost?
Are you constantly going around and around?
I'm trying to find myself and start something new
But I keep coming back to where I started . . . .
Asking for help won't help me;
I must do it all on my own.
I must find myself and talk to others to help them find themselves.
When this happens we will no longer be lost.

—Jason B. Rozell, age 15

MATH

Math oh math won't you please go away.
My brain is fading and sometimes I think I drool. Hey! If you like math you must be a fool!

My eyes get red by looking at this board so long, I get every single question wrong, wrong, wrong!

Please oh please, won't you take away multiplication. Have any of you even heard of math vacation?

I'd rather eat spinach or even peas
I would even swim all the seven seas.
Just please, oh please take math
away. But I really came to say what's 2+2?

—Lindsay Lee Harrison

A DREAMER'S WISH

O how I wish that I could soar across the vast blue sky, to discover for myself where the wind would take me.

The freedom, excitement and the loneliness of the adventure would set my heart like an alarm clock, anxiously awaiting to sound at the exact second.

Some may want to try to understand and accept any knowledge that I return with,
While others may want to scorn me,
As if I were like a madmam, not understanding my own words.

But as long as there was one,
I would willingly pass along to the next what I didn't know before.

Would it ever be possible or will it remain a dream forever?
Maybe, Maybe not.
It would depend on how great my urge for knowledge really is.

At times, even I wonder.

Dedicated to my parents, John and Elizabeth, who taught me more about life than any book could. Also to my daughter, Elizabeth Madonna, who is my life and my everything.

—Madonna Sarah Penney

FUNNY-SOUNDING FOREIGNERS

I go out with Mom and Dad
people stare

what comes out of their mouths
strange

the girl manager gets a puzzled look
the boy clerk wrinkles his nose

the sound of my Dad's mouth
uneven in American syllables

he is misunderstood over and over
he is seen not as a big guy

Little people we are
to your native eyes

we funny-sounding foreigners
the ones from afar

We dream as big as you
we have come thousands of miles

listen to us next time

don't dismiss us
because of our funny sounds.

—Behnaz Esfehani

NURSE CONNIE
(My Angel-in-White)

I heard God's soft voice,
So clear in the night.
He said, "Hold on, my child,
You'll be alright.
I'm sending you my angel,
To help you tonight."

Many angels of mercy,
I can recall,
But Nurse Connie,
Is, the fairest of all.

I looked up at my angel,
The thought came to me.
What a lovely thing,
That God's done for me.

My world is transformed,
From pain to love.
I thank "God," for my angel,
With compassion so right.

She's my angel of mercy.
My angel-in-white.

Dedicated to my nurse, Connie Conley
—Lola J. Meeker

Lola J. Meeker and Connie Conley

DEATH

The light grows faint,
As I fall into the dark chasm
of pain and emptiness,
All goes numb,
I forget who I was,
Not knowing what I'll become,
Upon reaching my final destination,
I see the angel of death below me,
Waiting to catch me in his dark embrace.

—Noel

HOLIDAY

Holidays are great
For all the things we give and make
The seasons are well to do
The things that we look forward to
But when it's time to end the day
And everyone go their way
We finally realize and ask
"Why this be!"
It's just to keep
Friends and family
In harmony

—Edith D. Suggs

LIFE'S TRUE COLORS

Let me take you thirty years back,
To three little boys who lived by the track.

Mommy's gone, has been, for a while,
Leaving just Daddy to make them smile.

No names will we mention, but this we will do,
We'll call one Brown, one Green, one Blue.

Life for them never was that "good."
But they all grew up the best they could.

Two were content—average to be.
But, "something better," was wanted by one of the three.

So, educated Brown became, although it took him years.
Green died unexpectedly at twenty leaving Blue and Brown in tears.

Five years later—things at their very best,
Once again, death came calling and Brown was laid to rest.

And now Life has shown its colors true.
And it left one alone, and he is Blue.

—(Sam) Shirley A. Moen

SULLIED SACRAMENT

Can any man, however evil, partake of this feast
Without knowing that it is, at the very least
                                   a sullied sacrament?

Can he feel   the hand of his lady,
    without feeling   the touch of love
                         the finger of God
                         the promise of redemption
                         the hope for that Love which does not end
                         the foretaste of the hereafter?

Can he take   without giving of himself?

Can he give   without sensing gift in return?
                without knowing that someone else cares, however little
                without knowing that Someone Else cares? However much?

Might this not be   the first stirring of love
                      for someone who has never known love?

Might this not be   the hope,
                      the promise, of everlasting life   for him?
                                                           for her?
                                                           for you?
                                                           for me?

—Robert W. Sackett

FUN AND LEAVES

I like autumn
Leaves are falling
Leaves are burning too
Kids are jumping
In leaves
Leaves are red
Yellow orange and brown
I like autumn leaves

—Candace Carpenter, age 6

WOODLAND WALK

I taste the smell of fall,
The leaves are changing skins,
I hear the forest call,
My excursion now begins.

I know this season well,
I like to walk the woods,
The trees have stories to tell,
I'd live here if I could.

I know I must go home,
I cry to have to leave,
I wish I could forever roam,
And live among the trees.

—Victoria A. Brierley

HOMELESS

They live on the streets.
Can't we give them a treat?
Cardboard is their home.
Can't we give them a throne?
People these days
Live all different ways.
Such as the homeless,
A poor community that is.
The upper class
The middle class
The lower class
Please Help!
Provide them with
What they seek and need.

—Stephanie Ballard

THIS FRANTIC PASSION

Fly, you wild bird of freedom—
And where you can
To escape the traps.
Fly to be free,
Fly for life,
But do not stop.

Fly, wild spirit,
Fly free—
Above the heaviness,
The looming thunderclouds.
Use the storm breezes
To carry you to heights unknown:
Ever upward, climbing higher.

Don't fold your wings;
Stretch them ever more
As if to fill the sky.

—Elizabeth A. Lescheid

LINGERING MEMORIES

To dwell upon a youthful past, now beached as bracken lumber cast.
Times of worldly travel go, unbeknown splendors folly sew.
The minds adventure challenge might, often times with solace bright.
Such a youth behold world riches; Gold and Silver, bade eyes to flicker.
Golden streaks across wind swept seas, memories creep up among the seaweed tangled eves.
Can you hear the melodious chime of yesteryear, still on the mind?
Climb aboard my sailing ship, to Port Said or old Islip.
A world away, a world away I say, dream my youth of past now grey.

—George L. Johansen

LILY & FRED

He sat on her bed.
On his head was hair fiery red.
Lily's clown — Fred.

II

On his face was a frown.
Lily turned it upside down
With needle & thread.

III

Out of his head sawdust bled
All over the floor & on her bed,
Poor old Fred, I guess he's dead.

IV

He sat on her bed.
On his head was hair flaming red.
Freddie's clone stepping out of the looking glass.

—Jane Pierritz

MY FLOWER

Taking it easy — taking it slow.
Never knowing before these feelings I feel.

My resistance is not that strong
For I have prayed that the Lord would never
Allow me to feel for another or another to
Feel anything for me.

Then I stumble upon a bright and beautiful
Flower in a valley of weeds and tall grass.

How can I resist the bright colors?
The supple leaves.
The fragrance of that
I have never known.

As I sit in the field with this flower
Time excels.
Only to have the day end much too soon.
And to return another day
Hoping this flower is still there
For me to view.

—Michael Louis Conley

innocence

How, I long for innocence past
Before the abandoned knowledge of which violence lay
    & the nearness of the reaper's wrath
Before the ill-onset of the defiled onset
    & the liberation of the primordial need to want

A time when the nostrils flared-up with a dry emptiness
While warm water flooded the eye in a blur
    & flushed the face in a flash
Straining away mishaps, misfortunes, & misunderstandings

When the down trodden and successful looked upon each other as equals
A sparkle . . . or a twinkle of wonderment reaches the eyes
A shy smile ever percolates on a lip's edge

When optimism and idealism were considered a valued norm
Courage bubbles forth to look in other such past moments
Past moments haloed with wisdom.
    —James S. Kim

THE MEANING OF LOVE

Basically it offers a choice; to move together toward something better or to wait for something else to show up.

    It is getting past defects or shortcomings to realize the abilities and strengths.

    Love: Is more than a feeling, it is a decision.

It becomes more than a doubt of attraction, it is a chance to realize who we are to each other.

    When it is said, 'I love you,' one should look at the actions not the words involved.

    The Reality of Love: Is what each person means or has done to create an impact upon each other.

Love: Is the empathy of emotions felt or held close and dear to the heart while they add to 'The Meaning of Love.'

    Love: Always Is A Daily Routine Which We Confront To Change Ourselves To Everyday.
    —M·2·EZY/Albert Nelson

OPEN HEART

Have you ever experienced an open heart. "I have."
An open heart is when you're in love with someone you truly
care for, You'll do just about anything for him or her.
You'll be willing to share openly, but having an open heart
can hurt also. "I was one."
I put my heart out for grabs, Just to express to someone
that I care, but that person took advantage of my heart,
Just to get what they wanted for themselves.
Leaving me hanging on with nothing to share.
This time around I'm learning to strengthen my heart in a
special way.
I've grown to open my heart each and every day to someone
that I know will take care of me.
Words to the wise everyone should open their heart and let
him in. He will fill you up with joy where there's no end.
This person is a very close friend. His name is JESUS. The
son of GOD. The one and only true friend. Just open your
heart and let him give you unlimited warranty protection.
I LOVE YOU JESUS.

    Your friend
    —Rachel Pope

NATURE

Nature is a beautiful gift.
With the birds, high in the trees,
chirping.
With the flowers, filling the air with
fragrance.
The sound, of the streams flowing.
The smell, of fresh dew on the grass.
The sight, of the mornings' rising sun.
The wrestling, of the squirrels
gathering pine cones.
The fall leaves fluttering in the
cold wind.
As winter comes; All is silent.

—Vicky Lynn Lyons

The spark of life it smoulders
brighter than the sun,
and you lie next to me
burning out — asleep for lack of energy
or will to move.
In the darkness,
I hear your labored breath
as the threat of distance and
death lingers over the place we rest.
But will you know what I'm thinking
as the night drags slowly on?
The fear of end — so concrete
I can almost touch it.
And do you contemplate the very
thing that drives you closer near?
To hold me one last time or not,
will be of God's design.
Remember this, I always will,
a moment in the night.
When everything was silent and you
were done with life.

—Joseph Wirtes

OFTEN DO I THINK

Sometimes I sit aside
And often do I think
Why can't I make a difference
Just within a wink?
Our world is so messed up
With drugs and serious crime
Often do I think of this
Nearly all of the time
I wish our problems would go
With just a simple wink
How to solve them I don't know
But often do I think
Though I may be wrong
I might be the person it takes
'Cause I don't want to always remain
In an environment full of treacherous snakes
I want to keep my life
From going down the sink
I sit here today,
But often do I think.

—Laura L. Bledsoe

THE FRIEND YOU LOVE

When troubles come your soul to try,
You love the friend who just stands by,
Perhaps there's nothing he can do,
The thing is strictly up to you.

For there are troubles all your own,
And paths the *soul* must tread alone.
And times when love can't smooth the road,
Or friendships lift the heavy load.

But to just feel you have a friend,
Who will stand by unto the end.
Whose sympathy through all endures
Whose warm handclaps are always yours.

It helps some way to pull you through,
Although there's nothing he can do.
And so with fervent heart you cry,
God bless the friend who just stands by.

—L.E. Hamm

A SUNSET

The projection of radiant colors in bloom
the beckoning of the moon,
an invitation for the stars to fill
the deep blue sea.

Red, yellow, pink and blues
seen from many different views
display color so vividly.

Such beauty to me, this
display of tranquility,
the stage for an act of romance.

Such a way to enhance
the perfect romance
for two lovers
walking silently.

Strolling together holding hands
the woman and her man,
making plans,
for their eternity.

—Felicia M. Thorns

SHE'S MY DAMNED SPLINTER

I remember, I never forgot:
spring, a horse and a squeaky small cart,
and your voice always teasing on me
lives since then in my broken heart:

"Oh, my dear, don't feel jealous at all
of the sky, and the birds on the wire,
I don't love you, don't love anymore,
we don't fit: you are mad, I'm wild.

"Oh, my dear, don't feel jealous at all
of the train, and the whistle of engine,
I am leaving, I am flying away
yours not hen, but the wild pigeon.

"Oh, my dear, don't feel jealous at all
of the rain, and the spring, and the winter,
I will never return again,
but remain in your heart like a splinter."

I will always remember that spring,
our old mill by rapids of a river.
Youth had gone. Now what do we have?
Only heads just in silver.

—Isay Billit

It was a night of pure beauty, one the moon, in all its glory, did its
duty. It was a night, of deep thought, and much ponder. One my mind
soared to the heavens, in future wonder. A serious thought was on my mind; as
I looked at the future with love and sublime. A serious thought, I came chasing,
an eternal question indeed, one that isn't found through haste and greed. Is she
the one, the one for me, the one the Lord prepared, for all eternity? Or am I
a fool, seeking gold, not listening to the Lord's council and treasures untold. I
stand at the crossroad of wrong and right, fearing of my decision on this
beautiful night. O Father, reveal my sight, that I may know, wrong and right.
Open my eyes, the answer so sweet, so that I with her, may kneel at thy feet.
—Adam Hawkes

DAWNING OF A NEW BIRTH

Such a precious man, he came to be.
A man who brought joy, happiness, & glee,
To our lives, each and every day,
   In every thought and in every way.
A man of God who never complain,
   No matter the agony or severity of his pain.
He loved to share and to give his all,
   No matter how high the mountain or how great the fall.
He preached about courage, strength, love, & salvation,
   Honesty, dignity, sin, and damnation.
He always thought of others before himself,
   In spite of the situation or condition of his health.
He was such a strong man, 'twas said he had 9-lives,
   But he was just willing to do what it takes to survive.
I thought I would see the day when he'd give me away in marriage,
   Just like the storybooks, with white horse and carriage.
But as the days passed, I knew this wouldn't come to be.
   For the moment had come for God to set his soul free.
Now we are left to mourn and grieve here on earth.
   As his spirit arises to the heavens, the dawning of a new birth.
   —Vanessa McIver

MOM AND DAD, I LOVE YOU

If I could I would capture in a glass bottle,
      the love I have for you two,
so you can see how deep my love is.
But since I can't do that, since I can't capture an emotion that
      is so special, an emotion that is sometimes so rare between
a parent and child, I'll do the next best thing and say it — I Love You.

   I love you for raising me and helping me become the person I am
today, for the love you have bathed me with has made me complete
and well rounded.
   I love you for putting you with all my attitudes,
                           all my bad choices,
                  just all my stuff!
   I love you for all the encouraging words like,
         "Well I thought the paper was good," when you saw in
that bright, bold, red ink the "D" the professor gave me.
   I love you Mom and Dad for supporting me spirituality,
                           mentally and
                                 financially.
You've done so much for me and words just can't express
   how grateful I am and how much I honor and appreciate you two.

So you see that is why I would like to capture in a glass bottle
the love I have for you two, so you can see it,
               and always remember it.
But I'll just do the next best thing and say,
      I love you
            over and
                  over and
                        over
as long as I have breath in my soul.
   --Lori Ann Archie

FEELINGS

I would like to write a poem,
I don't know if I can.
I would like to write a poem,
To find out who I am.
I pick up the pen and start to write.
I almost feel like I want to hide.
Little did I know these feelings are true.
Little did I know these feelings are of you.
I am kind of a shy person, but I have a reason.
Don't blame me, but this is the season
Of feelings from the past.
I don't know how long they will last.
But I think for realizing what's wrong,
I can finally go on and sing a song.

—Olafia Aldman

BEING APART FROM YOU

It's another lonely sleepless night
without you here to hold me tight.
Visions of you run all through my head
as I stare at your empty pillow beside me in
bed.
Memories of us keep rushing in, it seems
sometimes we never will win.
After all things we have went through I
could never go on living without you.
I miss you more than words can say, I know
we'll be together as one some day.
I see your face so clearly everytime I close
my eyes.
One day we'll be together without
mistrust and lies, everyday that I'm away
from you is tearing me apart and though
you're not here with me within you is my
heart.
There will soon come a time when we will
say "I do." Until that very special
moment remember always I love you.
I miss you.

—Lori Rae Hardy

BRENDA ANN

On October, eleventh, Seventy one —
I thought for sure I was having a
third son.
But as the nurse helped us
bring you in . . . She smiled and said
"You have your Brenda Ann!"
From that moment on as the years
passed . . . There was love, song and
your precious laugh.
We went through a lot as
our world seemed to spin . . . up and down
even out and in . . . .
But together we stood through
all with love . . . Now I've watched
you make choices with the help of God
above . . . It's hard to believe you're a mother
yourself, now sharing your love with
that special someone else.
I keep with me always the
moments we shared . . . knowing
there's more, only less time to spare . . . .

*Dedicated to my loving daughter Brenda Ann
Flores. Born 10-11-71   Love Mom*

—Anna Carrozza

AN ODE TO THE ONE I LOVE

Your thoughtful deeds and givings
have not gone unnoticed;
I was watching.

Your caring voice and whispers
have not gone unheard;
I was listening.

Your desperate looks and tears
have not gone unseen;
I was feeling.

Your joyful shouts and smiles
have not gone unobserved;
I was sharing.

I was watching, listening, feeling, and sharing
everything that you are;
I am loving.

—Elizabeth R. Johnson-Bonson

THE MAGNIFICENT BRIDGE

When I survey that beautiful span
Stretching across the Golden Gate
How could such a magnificent structure
Be created by mere man?

Coming into that city by the bay
Viewing the bridge from afar
The towering but graceful silhouette appears
Welcoming travelers at the break of day

What a stunning and breath-taking experience
To see the billowing gray fog
Come rolling o'er the steep brown cliffs
Completely covering, with a blanket so dense

Viewing those steely red towers
From a tiny, frail plane
Floating like a feather in the air
Makes one realize God's infinite powers

—Greta Busch

GOD HAS THE RIGHT-OF-WAY

Who has the right-of-way?
Not I said the policeman,
but I have the authority.
Therefore, I take the right-of-way.

Who has the right-of-way?
Not I said the ambulance driver,
but when I flash my siren, the
patriotic citizens give me the right-of-way.

Who has the right-of-way?
Not I said the fireman,
but when I yell out fire! fire! fire!,
here comes everyone running
to see me take the right-of-way.

Who has the right-of-way?
I have said the postman,
but I do not ask for it
because I have all day long
to get my mail out to everyone.

Who has the right-of-way?
The Almighty God has the right-of-way.

—Benjamin F. Miller

LEGACY

I climbed high to a mountain peak
It reminded me of a castle keep
For a moment, queen of all I saw
Looking down on a kingdom without flaw

From pirates wild, my blood must flow
And what they knew, I think I know
Midnight raids and days in the sun
Battles to win and some of them won

Courtly men, and ladies so fair
Are here now, as they were there
What they felt, is what we feel
By giving us life, they became real

For some, a rocky point is not a castle keep
And no Viking memories run silent, still and deep
As for me, I feel a thrill
To know their blood runs through me still

—Jeanne Prescott Farnworth

LOVE IS

Love is a relationship composed of two
Love is staying together and seeing it through
Love is a life time of many years
Love is filled with very few tears

Love is a matter of give and take
Love is smiling for the sacrifice you make
Love is never having to ask where have you been
Love is when you don't have to pretend

Love is sharing and most of all understanding
Love is never when one is constantly demanding
Love is looking forward to many tomorrows
Love is shared without many sorrows

Love is accepting the good with the bad
Love is the joy in making up once you were mad
Love is the willingness to sometimes give in
Love is a special feeling that has no End.

—Claudia D. Moncure

SILENCES

I wish I could
tell you
just how it is
with me.
Would I dare quote
poems of love?
Would I dare be honest
to tell you?
I did that once —
It got me a summer
of raindrops
and teardrops,
for my honesty.
So, perhaps, I will never be able
to tell you how I feel.
I suppose all you will hear from
me . . . is . . . silence.
Yet, I suppose that if you
cannot understand my silence —
You will never be able to understand my words.

—Peggy J. Myers

FAREWELL

I have counted the years we spent together
Somehow sweet, yet sometimes bitter,
Remembering your ever watchful eyes as you
darted this way, then that way. Then slowly
ole friend no longer were you walking at
my side, nor sitting with me as I gardened.
No more did you run through the water, acting
the child. The time had come to say adieu.
For you to rest in richly deserved quiet peace.
Farewell Then dear friend, Farewell, Farewell.

—DML

SUMMER LOVE

The soft summer breeze kissed my cheek,
The hot summer sun made me weak.
As I lay there on the warm white sand,
He sat up and took my hand.
The pounding of my heart in my chest,
As I lay thinking of the one who I love best.
A romantic shadow came from above.
The warm summer day was filled with love.

—Tammy Scherer
Errin Shoop
Lisa Vaniglia
Jessica Morgan

A PEACEFUL MAN

An olden book, a big stuffed chair
   A fav'rite pipe with smoke-ringed air
Perhaps some music turned down low
   A fireplace, its soft warm glow
Outside the wind blows recklessly
   Across the land and out to sea
Whatever pain the world may know
   For it may come and it may go
No matter what goes on out there
   A peaceful man has his book, pipe,
      And chair.

Dedicated to David L. Robinson

—Mavis Smallfield Vejar

DO I HAVE TO

Do I have to understand
that someone in my life is gone
It's hard to live with cause
since he left everything's gone wrong.

The days are dark
the nights are long
Do I have to understand
that he is gone.

In the last moments
I start to cry
I wish it was me
who was chosen to die

Now I guess I'll understand
cause he is happily above
Do I have to let go, I wish he had known
Just how much he was really
   LOVED.

—Susanne Spicer, age 15

FAITHFUL REMITTANCE

Diminished light behind veiled lids of conceit; lost in passage of yesterday's Sundays.
Unkept promises admist gluttonous feasting; noted in the Keeper's record.
Jealousy falsely obstructed truth; Spiritual turbulance returned home.
Relativity demands vexation; confusion wins its rightful place.
Twisted thoughts tighten into hangman's knot; the whine of misery pierces a curtain.
Yet understanding is out of reach; placed there by prideful ignorance.
Sliding into crack of despairity; unwilling to relinquish disaster's hand.
The serpent assured all roads are blocked; retreats to the sound of victim's lament.
The Triune surveys a damaged trophy; listening again to the familiar song.
Pure Love holds no hatred for the lost; inventing the wisdom of forgiveness.
Once again the Map Maker labors; building the perfect flow of events.
The Great Artist leaves no mistakes; every shadow is highlighted with peace.
He leans back to survey the project; awaiting payment long overdue.
Blind eyes see what nature knows; a thankful soul grows with faithful trust.
Deny not the Master Shepherd's wishes; empowered to give all to His flock.

—Sue C. Stone

CHILDREN OF A LESSER GOD

. . . on the zeroth day, Almighty God empowered a lesser god, and named him "the Word"; for we are all the children of that lesser god . . .

"In the beginning was the Word;
and the Word was with Almighty God,
and the Word" became our god and our creator.

" . . . through him was made everything that was made, and
without him was made   nothing   that was made . . . "

For Almighty God wanted a world full of worshipful subjects,
created after His Own image and likeness,
but the work of creation was beneath His dignity.

The Word, the lesser god, did the best he knew how, but . . .

that is why we are flawed, and our planet also
that is why we long for grace and beauty, which are transitory
that is why we yearn for peace and justice, which are illusions
that is why . . .

But the Word planted the seed of Love in our hearts, and it grew . . .

that is why we can endure our shortcomings
that is why we hope for a better tomorrow
that is why we strive to perfect the creation of the lesser god
that is why . . . .

—Robert W. Sackett

WHO AM I

Being Black I was brought up to believe that our race was inferior, dumb and illiterate. Blacks were a burden to the rest of the world. The teachers never told me about Black History. The only thing that I was ever told, is that my ancestors were slaves. I once felt demised by my race. The White race was always so smart, but I felt just as smart, sometimes even smarter. Their history was so full and rich; However, my history was so bleak; full of slavery and drowned with isolation. I used to think being Black was a crime, but now I know that being Black is something special!

Blacks for so long have been ignorant, and not by choice. Our true history has been locked away, so that no one of the black race will become knowledgeable; However recently that knowledge has become available. I have been on Earth for 16 years, and until recently I didn't know who Nelson Mandela was. Apartheid, never heard of it! The creator of sugar, King Tutankhamen, Cleopatra, Black . . . You couldn't pay me to believe that nonsense. My ancestors, Kings, and Queens before any other race ruled. A White couple creates a Black child; sounds reasonable to me . . . All of this false information fed into the minds of young Black children who have no choice but to believe it.

The Black history class taught me a lot. Disgraced to be black when I was young. Proud to be Black now! The White race isn't the only smart race on the face of this Earth. We as blacks, are just as smart and wise as any race. I look up to my Black leaders, and White alike. But I will always be "Proud to be Black!"

Education consists mainly in what we have unlearned. My mother once told me to be proud of our race, but after being in school, I just couldn't do it! Once I learned about my true ancestry, I changed around for the better. Who am I? *BLACK*, and damn proud of it!

—Derrick Harris

PASSAGE OF THE LORD

Crimson pools mark pathways to eternity's gates
while white rays deflect harsh shadows.
Shimmering glints of gold light the passage of angels
as the souls of heaven light the skies with the
fires of eternity.
The golden gates open wide and the harps sing as
the spirits dance.
And the angels pass.
The passage of angels mark the passage of souls,
and the souls of the passage of the Lord.

—Denise Ward

When she was a little girl
  She would call "Mama!"
    And mama was there.
She was there for the bad dreams,
  She was there for scraped knee,
    She was there when the kitten died,
      And when the thunder rolled.

When she was a big girl
  She would call "Mama!"
    And mama was there.
She was there for the good dreams,
  She was there for the excitement of the first date,
    She was there for the special dress,
      And explaining things to pa.

But now mama is old and frail
  She is sick in body and soul.
    Out of her weakness, in depths of loneliness,
      She calls out "Daughter!"
And daughter isn't there.

—Charlotte Paulson

ODE TO A STOMACH

The stomach is on everyone's mind
And in constant whine.

Some eat too much and
Some too little.

The gluttons suffer from stomach pain
And clutch and grip their round, round middles.

Those who eat little . . .
Hear the stomach's constant growl and hunger pangs
And they hang in hungry gangs
Looking for their daily soup and bread

Think of other things instead.
Start to plan your life
And eliminate your strife.

Soon the daily bread will come . . .
When life's good fights are won.

Buy a good philosopher's bread and cheese
And a book on etiquette and culture.
Do these things, please
And life will mean much more.

And you'll proudly carry
Some "good" groceries from the stores.
Groceries free from the disease of the world.

As you proudly fill the "happy" stomachs,
Your mind will finally feel at rest
As you sup with the happy stomach guests.

—Amelia Hincken

A TEAR

How sad one feels to see a tear
roll down the cheek of someone dear
What it means or why it came
No one knows, but just the same
The ache is there within your heart
So sad you feel and torn apart
For 'tho you do not share their fear
Some unknown way you share that tear.

—Mavis Smallfield Vejar

THE MASTER'S PAINTING

'Way atop the mountains
  Where clouds like to lie
Basking 'neath the sun
  As it rolls across the sky
Soars the graceful eagle
  Riding on the breeze
Spreads his wings then dips below
  And settles in the trees
Would that I could fly so high
  And see the earth below
The Master's painting to behold
  A treasure more than gold.

—Mavis Smallfield Vejar

NOTHING FREE

Broken glass, shattered tears,
Days are long, short are years.

Lonely nights, hours die,
The sad laugh, the happy cry.

The old run, the young sleep,
Pain is felt, hurt is deep.

Blood drips, from eyes so red,
Your heart stops, your body dead.

Days of darkness, nights of gray,
Everything free, yet you pay.

No escape, never to be free,
Open plains, through bars you see.

—Heather Lynn Barr

LOVE

Love what is it you might ask,
what is this thing that sounds
so great that makes you
think this way?
Love is something you can not
explain, it is something you
can not see, it is something
you feel for someone else, that
only you can understand.
Love, someone can not tell you
what it is like, no one can
draw you a picture.
Love is something you have to
find out for yourself, it can not
be explained.
Love, how will I know when
I've found it you ask, this I
can not tell you, but trust me
when I say to you, I think
I've already found it.

—Kaci Ann Perry

PRAYER OF A BLIND PERSON

I'd like to see the trees in spring,
I'd like to see the snow winter brings.
I'd like to see a bird's flight,
Or see the stars on an endless night.
I'd like to see a flower in bloom,
Or see a child's face in a party room.

Although I cannot see with my eyes,
I see with a different part of me, a part in disguise,
I see with my heart instead of my eyes.
I see things you will never see with just your eyes.

—Jacqueline Clinger

TOMORROW — I WONDER

Tomorrow, will there be rain or snow
    Will the sun shine or the wind blow — I Wonder
Tomorrow, will some dog or some stray cat
    Seeking a home sleep on a mat — I Wonder
Tomorrow, will some girl or some boy
    Be killed with a gun or a toy — I Wonder
Tomorrow, will some woman or some man
    Be found dead in alley or can — I Wonder
Tomorrow, will death come by plane or train
    Will a car cause one not be sane — I Wonder
Tomorrow, will daughter be against mother
    Will kinsfolk be against each other — I Wonder
Tomorrow, will the world be full of turmoil
    Will rain, quakes or wars turn up the soil — I Wonder
Tomorrow, will man be consumed by disease
    Will he stop doing as he please — I Wonder
Tomorrow, will there be prayer in the land
    Will someone to God stretch his hand — I Wonder

—Annie B. Stevens

THE WOLF

As dark as a shadow
slipping, slinking, through the dark forest,
on silent paws he walks.
A lone shadow in the moonlight
eyes a burning, a glowing in the dark night.

Walking low and lonesome,
on he walks.
As silent as the black night itself
slowly he walks,
paws touching lightly on the cold ground.

A massive beast
swift long legs, he slowly strides on
barely touching the ground,
climbing higher, higher, until he halts quietly.
He stares into the blackness of the forest below him.

He slowly lifts his head
and stares at the moon with his burning eyes.
He cracks open his mouth
wet daggered fangs, canines and incisors show
shining and gleaming.

He gives a long low moan
which splits into an earpiercing howl.
The call of night
when night slowly ends,
he slowly strides back to join the pack.

—Elizabeth Rae Winston

CORNER

Job interviews and deadlines
No sleep for comfort
My feet hurt from a standstill
Of non motion
My head hurts from the
Standing non thoughts
Is this what adulthood
Is supposed to be or
Just bad situation
All I know is I want
That time of enigma
Back
I want that precious
Hate of unknowing
Reason to fill my
Tears again
I want that simple
Stupidity

—Eric Powell

THE ROSE

Mind races
Thoughts converge
Chaos controls the mind
Muscles tighten
Confusion grows
All is a waste of time
Images blur
Sounds silenced
Why is it I go on
Life is lost
There is no point
Let us to end this song
Ray of light
Shines through dark
The rose atop the hill
Beacon bright
Love's delight
All emotions filled

—John T Hicks

PRIMAL SPRING

Drifting at a slant
this grain like salt
that's cold and damp.

Has chased away
the azure blue
and sunny warmth
that cuddles you.

It's so cold and gray
with pale silhouettes
that stand and say;

Please, kiss us now
and bring new life,
sweet green buds
in the morning light.

Feathered velvet fish
swim the crystal dish.
Sun-drenched thoughts
that can't be bought.

—Nickè-Chantalle Young

PLEASE

He moved away
And there you were
You stole his heart
But you were willing to share
It seemed like you changed him forever
But that he kind of liked
So I ask of you just one thing
If you should ever grow apart
Be sure you spare both of your hearts

—Dreamer

STOICISM

Moist, not dry,
As I cry from unhappiness.
Alone, unattended,
With those who were friends.
Yearning, not loathing,
For the loved ones I've lost.
Peaceable, never hostile,
Are the feelings I most value.

Guarded I want, reckless I am.
Life is too grueling, may easy come my way.
Expand my horizons, shrivel not my mind.
Default not what I do, just praise what I am.

—Bridget

MASTER DISGUISE

She is always smiling, laughing
Friends flock around her hoping
her upbeat disposition erases some of the
negativity in their lives.

As she smiles gaily,
she works hard at keeping the tears inside.
The loneliness which has been her friend for
many years trying to escape from within.

But they will never know nor do they care
about her clever disguise.
As long as her smile feeds them she will always
have a place in their world.

—Nancy Jo Bojarski

A BALLAD OF PEACE

I once spoke with a Noble man
Who told me tales of war.
He kneeled down to the ground and cried:
  "What are we fighting for?

How many times must the sun shine
  On death's great battlefields?
Why must people fight for their land?
  Why do they raise their sheilds?

Why can't this world's destruction cease?
  Be all for one in Love.
Increase our brotherhood and faith,
  And share our God above."

And I spoke to the Noble man:
  "Get up, get on your feet.
You can't attempt to change the world,
  But you can pass the peace."

—Marty Thompson

A ROSE IN BLOOM

It is a beautiful thing to see a rose in bloom,
To watch the petals open up for air.
To smell the fragrance after you have picked it
Go from room to room.

It is a wondrous thing to see a rose in bloom,
For you know it is the promise of spring.
It is the beginning of a new dawn,
And a newness of life to come.

The rose is a symbol of undying love.
The petals symbolize unending faithfulness;
The leaves symbolize cradling tenderness;
The stems symbolize standing together;
And the roots symbolize trust, firmly grounded.

—Elizabeth Butts

MISSING YOU

Another day, another week,
Another month, a different year
All this time has passed on
and yet we can still feel you here

Another sentence, another paragraph
Another page, A different phrase
All these words to help us
get through the days

Another reason, another solution,
A different problem, the same conclusion
It seems like life's unfair,
But all the love you filled us with
makes all problems something we could bare

A different time, another life,
A change of season, a different reason
Everything that matters in life and
everything that doesn't just goes to show you
the dreams we have both good and bad
help us remember the love in you, and the
life in you is something we will always treasure.

—BIANCA

EMOTIONS

So many emotions lie in our minds
The things I feel and see are real
You must remember the words I say
They bring truth to the light of day.

In a world full of disloyalty and dismay
There is no one to blame for our own mistakes
To some life is less, they only live to take
And the young are blamed for mistakes
made by the older mind
Desired is less hate, more compromise

All temptation is there and at times taken
Again, another wrong step someone is makin'
Heaven is the place we desire, to fail is to
become a part of hell's furious fire.

Life is the only gift that can be given
but taken away without a moment's notice.
Like the flash of a shooting star.

Emotions are all for real, everything I said and
feel. Life is outside your window, the proof is
real.

—Benjamin David Hooks

US

Taking you for granted, is not what I
wanted to do.
What I did was shut you out, what I
wanted to do was let you in.
I didn't want to show my pain, I wanted
to share our pain.
I try to give my love, I need to share
our love.
I try to grow on my own, I need us to
grow together.
I cry alone, when we need to cry
together.
Even through all of this, our love has
grown.

—Jeani Ethridge

A WISH

If I were a little flower
And I belonged to you
Would you always keep me watered
And mist my leaves with dew
Would you keep me clean and shiny
Let me see the morning sun
Would you always keep me near you
Then life would sure be fun

Would you treat me kind and gentle
Would you talk to me each day
Would you let me grow and flourish
Or wither and decay
Would you take pride in my new blooms
Protect me from the cold
If I could be your flower
I never would grow old

*Dedicated to a precious flower,
my sister Eloise, who has been
a real inspiration in my life.*

—James H. Ogle

THE NIGHT

stars filling the sky
the moon shining over the earth
sitting out in a field
so peaceful, so calm
stretched out on a sleeping bag
staring into the sky
the night seems eternal
moving down onto the beach
a soft breeze blowing through your hair
the waves gently rubbing the shore
such a rhythmic motion
you look over and at your side
is the one you love
as the night passes
you look and see the eyes
the gateway to your lover
the entrance to their soul
just the two of you
spending time together all alone
one of the few moments you get
your bodies moving with the rhythm
of the ocean waves
and the music of the sea

—Jennifer Ann Millan

I GO FORTH . . .

I go forth to move about the earth.
I go forth as the eagle, brave and peaceful.
I go forth as the whale, gentle and daring.
I go forth as the deer, tender and loving.
I go forth to move about the earth in bravery,
peace, and compassion.

—Melody Dawn McCrea

THE DRAGON

The mist of the dragon descends all around.
There is a stench of old and dying in the air.
As he lands, the blood drips from his talons,
The remains of his last meal.
His golden eyes glow with the evil,
That lurks in his small brain.
His tail flicks with a nervous twitch,
As he settles on his treasure.

—Marketa Cornwall

WHAT'S FOR REAL

When rainbows gleam and dance around
and the forests are swamped with magical
sounds, The beauty of love is then
seen, Spirits set off, souls to be freed
Dragons and fairies and all mystical
things all gather around to unite and
sing, The song of many, the song of few
The song I sing from me to you. Purity
cleanness, warmth and spirit gather and
reign in the heart where its dearest
Dream again of all these times, read again
all of my rhymes wish again it will come
true, Spoken secrets made just for
you, Wilted dreams to them we forget
yet undying love is the feeling I meant
Take this thought, feel no regret
Memories of my fantasy, Feeling I love
to feel, And I know now that only you are
real.

—Shannon Leigh Pickle

DRIFTER'S FAREWELL
(Postcards from the Moon, Pt 1)

Hitched a ride to the city limits
Where smog cover turns to stars.
The fresh air burned inside my lungs
As I watched for passing cars.
The desert night engulfed my soul,
Sent a shiver up and down my spine,
I was free as a man can be
And feeling it for the very first time.

I can see a lifetime in the twilight sun,
I'm moving on and changing my song.
But the night is dark and the night is cold
And I hope I wasn't wrong.

And when the morning comes I'll be moving along
If the night doesn't claim me first,
And when the sunlight shines on morning's dew
It'll be a sight to quench my thirst.
When the tractor trailers roll on by
I'll be on the road again,
The folks back home will fade away
And I'll never be seen again.

—James Kanavy

MY GOAL

My goal is to achieve my dream,
no matter how small or large it may seem.

Sometimes I sit and stare, to see what I can be,
I can be, whatever I see.

My dreams, are not beyond my reaching,
This I have learned, through my life's teaching.

Whenever, I think about how my life is going to be,
I know that the beginning of that, begins with me.
I realize, that I have to take care of me, in order to be, whatever I see!

Sometimes in my dreams, I can flyyy, I just lift off, and go bye-bye.
I feel so free, being whatever I want to be, whether standing on the dry, or in the sky flying by!

—Bridget L. Harris

LOVE IS LIKE A FIRE

Love is like a fire that burns within your heart
If there is no heat the fire won't start.
You need two things to make a fire grow
Heat and Oxygen in order to make it glow.
She was the Heat which helped get the fire on its way
But without the Oxygen she almost faded away.
You are the Oxygen that helped the fire burn
You were the strength that made her life turn.
It's sad to say that the Heat turned cold
But when she was hot the memories were made gold.
You were there for her and helped erase her frown
She didn't understand your love so she let your heart down.
Your heart is broken but will be stronger as it heals
It's better to have loved and lost than to never know how love feels.
Remember her always even though you are apart
Let her memory make you happy and even heal your heart.
You are a special brother who is courageous and bold
You see the beauty in a rose even when the color grows old.

—Darcy Erin-Marie Long

SOMETHING IN THE SOIL

It used to be, that you could plant a tree,
and be proud.
But, now, instead of a tree, I see,
It is the body of another child plucked, and murdered from the crowd.

It used to be, you could plant a seed,
and eat the yield,
But, now, instead of that healthy weed,
It is only a container of pollution with a broken seal.

How can I sleep?
How can I eat?
Murderers and molesters still creep.
Probably, one is sitting next to my seat!

Does anyone care?
Is anyone brave?
Who will set the snare?
Something for what the children gave.

Life is short,
Life is cheap,
Another victim to report.
Now I lay me down to sleep.

When I awake,
I pray my fear,
Was all just a dreamscape,
And, this new day, has been made clear.

—Sadie Greer

A POET'S "WORD-PORTRAIT" OF AN ARTIST AT WORK

In a straight-backed chair
in a sun-drenched room
he sits, bent over, sketching,
no easel, no palette, no desk,
just a sketch pad, balanced on his knees.
Open mouth gently working,
chewing on a tongue
held firmly between two molars.
The slow meticulous scratching of the pen
squeezed in a tight little fist,
reminiscent of a school boy
learning to write.
An invisible barrier
shields him from the distractions
swirling around him.
He sits alone,
bent over,
sketching,
sealed in a vacuum of his own concentration.

—Catherine Kossuth Mack

GOING THE WAY TO THE LIGHT

Going my way into the light, of an eternal sun
where the soul, its transparency has reached,
I am leaving the shadow, desolated soil,
where evil corrode hope.

And once again, creating a new world
separating from the human kind,
the fierce egoism that spread sorrow everywhere,
with love.

And the crystaline waters will spring
where the travelers placate their thirst,
nards will sprout, instead of thorns
where leaning at last, their bleeding feet.

I hope my Lord, that man gets
greatly endowed with higher intelligence,
where perhaps, the pain will hide,
all the goodness his conscience demands.

Silent I'll be, at last peace I'll have
with my hands and lips tied
my last plead to you I'll give
when my name is called, to be your side, my Lord.

—Blanca Nava Lopez

y y

My room, my room,
Is softly in illume . . .
I watch a swaying hanging plant
Silhouette, in moon.

Its mute, mild tune,
To silent, sleepy stare . . .
Prevents a gentle moon's beam slant
Further through the air.

In going past what last we're taught
Needing night as much as day,
This plant adds substance to my thought
Pausing at day's end to pray.

My room, my room,
Is softly in illume . . .
I swoon from swaying hanging plant
Silhouette, in moon.

—Jim Snyder

i ain't plain

here i sit, and i sit,
and i sit all the same . . .
i sit in wonder,
with Ideas to proclaim.

i search the seas,
walk the fields of my mind,
for all the Memories,
i've left behind.

i Need to Think,
i Need to relieve,
something of Creativity,
to Believe!

i want my Pride.
i want my Thoughts.
and all the Pain,
this Life has brought.

i Need my Pride!
i Need my Pain,
Because without them . . .
I am just plain.

—Jeffrey Scott Place

THE OTHER SIDE OF LOVE

As I look out into the world I can see the other side of love.
A woman who has been abused, crying in the night.
A child who has no food, dying from the lack of might.
A little boy who's never been told, what worth he has inside.
Grows up with a lack of confidence, fulfillment, and a sense of pride.
A person who has been rejected because of the color of their skin.
What is it all coming to, where do we begin?
We can begin on the good side of love.
The gift that has been given us from the Father up above.
We begin by giving of ourselves, to heal the wounds from a broken heart.
To be thankful for what we have, and to do our part.
We need to become colorblind, so it does not matter what we
see on the outside, but of what we see on the inside.
The right side of love can change our world, and put a smile on your face.
Because love fulfills all emptiness, and makes the world a better place.

—Marvis J Palmer

THE TINY NEW BABY

There is a baby with the cutest nose
and also the tiniest toes.

He has the most beautiful blue eyes
so he can make his sad little cries.

When you lift him up
he feels as small as a cup.

He is growing up now
and you say to yourself "HOW!"

He is not tall
but he is very very small.

Now you feed him from a bottle
soon he will begin to tottle.

When you bath him you feel his soft skin.
When you tickle him you see him grin.

With his tiny little booties
you think he's the cutest of the cuties.
Now he is a little boy.
The little boy whose name is Roy.

—Michele Alexandria Chase

TRAVELING

As I Traveled this old World!
In the way I was taught!
Who knows what quality,
This lonely life has wrought!

I protected my giver!
I loved my very own!
Now I love my maker!
Through Him, I've found my home!!

Over the hills and down the dales!
I give it my very all!
With wings of steel and solid sails!
Through all this, I met the call!

Down, down, down I go!
To gain a deserving berth!
Away; away! to my niche, so low!
A deserving role on this blessed Earth!

I love; I desire; I give my best!
To the ones that mean the most!
I retrieve the good with a vital zest!
My givings, I stand and boast!

—Hugh Phillips, Jr.

THE LEAF

I felt the handlebars,
I saw the green, grassy hill,
With humming bees on it.
I saw the shadow of a bee,
Which made me speed up,
For fear of being stung!
But it turned out to be
A fluttering leaf!

—Chris Kobberod, age 9

BOOGA BOO

I feel so foolish writing this,
　　　　I really do.
But you see, I call my granchildren,
　　　　"Booga Boo . . . ."
They are five little fingers
　　　　wrapped around my heart,
I feel as though I've been stuck
　　　　all over with a dart . . . .
When I ask them "Just what are you
　　　　good for Booga Boo?"
My little ones say "Why, MoMo, I'm
　　　　good for you!" SO TRUE! . . . .
When I tell them "Come and let me
　　　　give you some itchie coo,"
They say, "Please MoMo, bite me on
　　　　the ear, too! . . . .
Playing of course, but then I have to
　　　　tic tic them on their tummies,
And say, "You're MoMo's little Sugar Poo,
　　　　Angel Poo, and Booga Booga Boo . . . ."

—Ginger Wilson

A STAR

I used to kiss him on the cheek. He would look like
God had just dropped a little star at his feet.

I brought his coffee to his chair. "Oh, yes, he knew
I was there."

Divert the traffic from the den, until the last play
is in!

Now his game is over; the last play is in. God and
his angels watch over him.

Loving memories we will always have—as it's been
one year today, April 11, since he's gone to Heaven
to stay.

His pastor was Bro. Lamb, who knew him well and never
put him down.

He loved to work by the sweat of his *brow;* he loved
his children and saw that they knew *how.*

His grandchildren loved a story by the green chair,
being enchanted as they would run their fingers thru
his jet black hair.

He suffered many a pain, but not once did he complain.
I would not want him back again, for where he is,
is far better gain. Many times he would say, "Do not
grieve for me when I am away, for you know it is *not*
better that I stay."

I don't want to see his grave for I know he hurried on
to rest and waits for us to meet him there on
Judgement Day.

If I listened good I think I could hear him say,
"God move that star over a little the other way
so my grandchildren can have a better place to play!"

—Nelda P. McGrew

About The Author

Authors are listed in alphabetical order by name or pen name.

LINDA H. ADAMS resides in Fraser, Michigan. She is a homemaker who enjoys reading and writing short stories, poems, and song lyrics. **Her comments:** I write about my life; the pain of the past, the happiness of the present, and the promise of the future! My ultimate wish is to co-write a song with Paul Anka!... 33

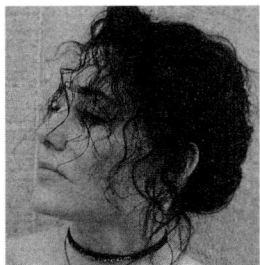

ALICIA JAYNE is a Fifth Place Award Winner in this edition of **Poetic Voices of America**.. 11, 32, 329

Alicia Jayne

KEN ALLINSON resides in Lower Burrell, Pennsylvania. He is in the seventh grade at Huston Middle School in Lower Burrell. He enjoys swimming, drawing, writing, basketball, and reading. His memberships include: Sylvan Swim Team and Burrell Youth Basketball. He had **Eric's Special Wish** published in **Young Author's Magazine** in 1991. His awards include: Reflections Cultural Arts Contests, 1989-93; Presidential Academic Fitness Award, 1991; gifted class, John Hopkins University Talented Youth Qualifier; Sylvan Swim Team, first place medley relay championship competition, 1993................................. 286

Ken Allinson

HERB (H.P.) AUGHINBAUGH resides in Farmington, New Mexico. His publications include: **Pico Blanco** published in **Big Sur Gazette**, 1978; **Loving You** published in **Seagull Books**, 1980; and **Blue Bill Day** published in **Salesworld**, 1981. **His comments: Partington Cove** appears in an unpublished work titled **From the Cabin**. It was written in 1977, while I resided on the Big Sur Coast of Monterey County, California. It is one of my favorite poems commemorating my return to my greatest love, the Pacific Ocean!................... 157

Herb (H.P.) Aughinbaugh

STEVE and **EFFIE BAKER** reside in Galena, Illinois. Steve attended Lees College in Jackson, Kentucky and other schools. Effie's education includes: Wright Jr; Triton, IBYC, Chicago Area Highland, Freeport, Illinois; JDW, Galena, Illinois, and Snow College, Utah. Steve works in substance abuse counselling and heating & air conditioning. His interests include: insects, "oldies", hiking, and fishing. Effie works in real estate management and as a laundress. Her interests include: Steve's wishes, cooking, quilting, swimming, travel, and nature. Publications include: **Love's Stirrings** published in **Poetic Voices of America**, June 1994, and a bridal salon slogan contest (Antoinette Bridal Salon); "Your Reaction is Our Satisfaction", in 1959. **Steve's comments:** I was awaken at 2 a.m. from a sound sleep, alone, locked in a prison cell. I went to my desk and picked up a pen. I put it back down next to my paper. I went back to bed. In the morning, this poem was on the paper of stirrings about my girlfriend, Effie, who later gave it the title.. 106

Effie Baker

IZ BEAING is the pen name for **C. SHARON FAIRCLO**, who resides in Klamath Falls, Oregon. Her education includes: high school, business school, and community college. She is a homemaker who enjoys nutrition, animal rights, writing, and athletics. Her memberships include: PETA (People for the Ethical Treatment of Animals), and Phi Theta Kappa invitee. She had **Coo-Coo Juice** published in **The Other Side of the Mirror,** and **Choices** published in **The Best Poems of the 90's,** both in 1992... 287

HELEN POPE BELL resides in Smyrna, Georgia. She is an executive secretary. Her publications include: **Blessings of a Season,** Fall 1993; and **My Country,** Spring 1994; both published in **Poetic Voices of America. Her comments:** I have loved poetry as far back as I can remember. The first recognition I recall was a poem I had written in grammer school which was displayed on the school bulletin board. Many of my earlier poems were about people who are special to me; for many years, however, my poems have been inspired from nature and real life experiences that come from the heart. Poetry and music are the inspirations of my life...................... 237, 240

Helen Pope Bell

LORETTA C. BLANDING resides in Upper Marlboro, Maryland. Her education includes: completed a B.S. Degree in Elementary Education at Hampton University, 1966; 2 years graduate work at Howard University, 1975. Her interests include: writing poetry, plays, stories, playing piano and guitar, and singing. She was a member of the Washington Teacher's Union in Washington, D.C. from 1968 to 1991. She retired from 25 years of teaching in September of 1991. **Her comments:** At the age of 8, I wrote my first poem, **Chewing Gum.** All of my inspiration for writing came from God at an early age. My poetry is varied on subjects such as people, retirements, and other special occasions. As of late, I've been writing inspirational poems.. 190, 226

Loretta C. Blanding

VIDA E. BLOOD resides in Hillsdale, Michigan. Her education includes Western Michigan University. She is a teacher/homemaker and enjoys church and community service. She is a Fifth Place Award Winner in this edition of **Poetic Voices of America. Her comments:** I lived for ninety years in Barry County, Michigan. As a widow, I joined a writing group in Hastings and wrote historic sketches of my hometown. I also wrote poetry and had several poems published in the **Hastings Banner, The Hastings Reminder,** and the bulletin of the Barry County Historical Society. I particularly enjoy writing poems in the Oriental haiku style, using themes and observations from nature.. 11

Vida E. Blood

CINDY BRENNAN resides in Goderich, Ontario, Canada. She is a teaching assistant at the Young Offenders Centre and owner of a new business, Murder Mystery Mixer Parties. She is a wardrobe manager for Goderich Little Theatre and her interests include baseball and its history. **Her comments:** I started working on stories, poetry and essays during "Saturday Night NHL Hockey Games" in the 1960's. My parents and brother watched the game each week while I retired to my room to write. Presently, I write original murder mysteries for rental at staff parties...................................... 103

Cindy Brennan

MARGARET A. BRENNAN resides in North Babylon, New York. She is a high school and business school graduate. She is a medical secretary and housewife. Her interests include: first aid, fire arms, fishing, boating, and photography. She has current cards for Public Notary, Certified First Respondant, and CPR. She had **Anticipation** published in **American Poetry Anthology** in 1988. Her awards include: Golden Poet Award in 1988, 1989, and 1991; and a Silver Poet Award in 1990. **Her comments:** When I was a freshman in high school, I had an English teacher who had discovered the fact that I enjoyed writing poetry. She introduced me to the works William Wadsworth Longfellow. I tried to imitate his style, but my teacher encouraged me to improve on my own poetry. She would frequently give me different subjects about which to "create" a verse. Through her encouragement and inspiration, I have learned to see "life" in any form. Life is all around us; therefore, so is poetry.. 36

Margaret A. Brennan

CARROLL R. BUFFUM, SR. (BUFF, THE SIMPLE MAN) resides in North Clarendon, Utah. He has 10 years of education and is retired from G.E. His memberships include: League of Vermont Writers, Buffum Family Association, N.R.A., Middletown Springs Alumni, and International Society of Poets. He had a book of poems published in June of 1981. His awards include: 2 Editors Choice Awards, 1993; Silver Tray, G.E. plaque; First Prize Ribbon for driftwood sculpture and book of poems; and the International Poet of Merit Award, $50.00 cash prize. **His comments:** I strive to write about nature, the good old days, togetherness, and Vermont poetry. I have been greatly influenced by **The Raven** by Edgar A. Poe, and **The Old Swimming Hole** by James W. Riley.. 208

Carroll R. Buffum, Sr.

CAROLYN ANN CAPORUSSO resides in Sewell, New Jersey. She is a high school graduate and a housewife/homemaker. Her interests include: antiquing, reading, and old movies. She is a member of the Rotary Club, Turnersville, New Jersey. Her awards include: Anthology Award, 1962; and Paul Harris Fellow, Rotary Club, 1992. **Her comments:** Christmas is my most favorite time of year. That, in itself, inspired me to write this poem.......................... 115

Carolyn Ann Caporusso

KACI DIANE CARLISLE resides in Whittier, California. She is currently enrolled at BIOLA University, majoring in English and writing. She is interested in doing free lance writing. **Her comments:** My poetry, and most of my other writing, is written about feelings and experiences about my life. By doing this, I hope that people will be able to re-experience similar events in their lives. Poetry is telling a story. People should be able to understand what the poem means and portrays........................... 127

S.S. CECIL (SHERRI SUSAN CECIL) resides in Hawesville, KY. She has an Associate Degree in Business Administration and a diploma for Children's Literature. Her interests include: writing, reading, and oil painting. **Her comments:** My soul inspiration came from my daughter, Kelli, who one day actually ran outside on the first day of a snowfall, without her shoes... 135

RASHAAD C. CLARK (RC) resides in Kearney, Nebraska. He is a freshman at Nebraska Wesleyan University, Lincoln, Nebraska. His interests include law and communications. His memberships include: University track team; Nebraska Youth Against Drugs and Alcohol Organization, national and state wide. Also he featured in the movie, "Lean On Me", starring Joe Clark. He won an award from the Ashland, Nebraska newspaper in 1991. **His comments:** I was inspired to write **Peace and Victory** because everyday life reminds us that the utopia God wants for us isn't the goal of every man. During the Persian Gulf War, American men and women died in service to their country. In remembering the Vietnam War, in which my father was a soldier, I reflect on the sentiments of my mother. **Peace and Victory** will bring our loved ones home... 351

Rashaad C. Clark (RC)

JACQUELINE CLINGER resides in Shalimar, Florida. Her interests include: gymnastics, writing, and swimming. She had **End of a Rainbow** published in **Dance on the Horizon** in 1994... 376

Jacqueline Clinger

KATHRYN HENDRICKSON COLE resides in Freehold, New Jersey. She is a 1953 graduate of Freehold High School. She is retired from civil service and her interests include: bike riding, planting flowers, cross stitching, and singing in the choir. She is a member of the Immanuel Baptist Church and AARP and American Federation of Government Employees. **Her comments:** I recently was reacquainted with my fourth grade grammer school teacher and felt this was the best way I could thank her for all her hard work and patience in teaching me (and others as well). She also was very beautiful.. 66

Kathryn Hendrickson Cole

ANGELA CRONCH (THE TIMELESS POET) resides in Paducah, Kentucky. She is a Senior at Paducah Tilghman High School. She will graduate in 1994. Her interests include writing short stories and poems. Her publications include: **See the Flower?** published in **A Question of Balance** by **The National Library of Poetry**, 1992; **Death is of steel—** published in **A Break in the Clouds** by **The National Library of Poetry**, 1993; **For I do see the flowers** published in **Outstanding Poets of 1994** by **The National Library of Poetry**, 1993; **Butterflies are free** published in **Famous Poets Anthology,** by **The Famous Poets Society**, 1993; **The Seldom Souls** published in the "in" magazine, which is within the **Paducah Sun,** 1993; and **See the flower?** published in **The Tilghman Bell** (school newspaper), 1993. Her awards include: nominated in The Who's Who Among American High School Students, 1993; nominated by the International Society of Poets, 1993; and nominated to attend the 10th Annual Washington Journalism Conference. She has also qualified for enrollment at The Institute of Children's Literature in 1992. **Her comments:** My source of inspiration if my life. I live at 1946 Seitz Street, Paducah, Kentucky, 42003.. 127, 129, 148, 165

Angela Cronch

FRED B. CUSHMAN resides in Lehigh Acres, Florida. His education includes: Philadelphia College of Osteopathic Medicine. He is a retired country doctor and his chief interest is people. He is a member of the American Osteopathic Association and the Maine Masonic Lodge. His awards include: Jefferson Award, 1953; and 50 Year Medal from Philadelphia College of Osteopathic Medicine, 1981. **His comments:** For 20 years, I was asked to write a poem for special events, like a minister leaving Franklin Baptist Church. I was impressed by the qualities of the people of Maine, their diligence, honesty, dependability, and humor. Also, for many years, I was the only member of my profession easily available to Mount Desert Island, so I met some of the most prominent people in the U.S......... 208

ELIZABETH I. CVETIC resides in Lake Oswego, OR. Following high school, she studied art at the Corcoran Gallery, Washington, D.C., and National Art School, Washington, D.C. She is a homemaker who enjoys painting, drawing, and hiking. She is active in her church and a member of the Garden Club. **Her comments:** The poetry of hymns has inspired me all my life, particularly the works of Charles Wesley and Isaac Watts. I have just completed a small book of poems titled, **If Trees Could Talk,** which I also illustrated (pen and ink drawings). Writing poetry is new to me, just since January 1993............ 11

Elizabeth I. Cvetic

LESZEK CZUCHAJOWSKI resides in Moscow, Idaho. He has a Ph.D. in Chemistry. He is a professor of chemistry at the University of Idaho and a member of the American Chemical Society. His publications include: **Verses on Two Strings** (77 poems in Polish) published in Idaho, 1986; **Poetry of My Days** (88 poems in English) published in Idaho, 1991; and **Poems from Somewhere** (71 poems in Polish) published in Idaho, 1993. He is a Fifth Place Award Winner in this edition of **Poetic Voices of America. His comments:** I write for my own pleasure. I consider writing poems more creative, exciting, and most of all, more gratifying, than manipulating the science............ 11, 125, 129

Leszek Czuchajowski

BELINDA A. DALTON was born in Cairo, Illinois on September 28, 1963. She presently resides in Levittown, Pennsylvania. Her education includes: an Associate's Degree from Shawnee College in Ullin, Illinois, emphasis counseling services, 1984; a Bachelor's Degree from Florida International University in Miami, Florida, major Sociology/Anthropology, minor emphasis Psychology, 1983; and a Master's Degree from Murray State University in Murray, Kentucky, emphasis higher education, counseling and adult education, 1985. She completed her B.A. at the age of 19 and a M.S. at the age of 21; approximately two years toward her B.A. was completed through college extension courses offered during the evening hours while she was attending high school. She has assisted and performed a multitude of functions while working in higher education. She is presently employed at Thomas Edison State College, Trenton, New Jersey, as Assistant Director of Registration and Records: Academic Evaluator. Additionally, she is an Educational Consultant and serves as President for Professional Liaisions, which is an independently owned agency, and the owner of several real estate properties in Wisconsin. Her memberships include: New Jersey College and University Coalition of Women Educators, American Association for Counseling and Development, American College and Personnel Association, National Association of Student Personnel Administrators, Middle Atlantic Association of College and University Housing Officers, Memphis Area College Counselors Association, and Writer's Digest Book Club. She enjoys writing poetry, song lyrics, plays, slogans for advertisements and acting. She has written and performed in numerous plays and has completed hundreds of literary works. She had **What's Important** published in **Poetic Voices of America,** 1992, and **The Reason I Write** published in **Creative Arts and Science Enterprise,** 1991-1992, and several books. **Her comments:** I have been very successful in meeting my personal and professional goals and have always been dedicated to assisting others in reaching their fullest potential. I have a genuine love for the field of education and my work, however, my first love is my family............ 210

Belinda A. Dalton

LESLIE L. DAME resides in Louisville, Kentucky. Education: Sacred Heart Academy, 1975; B.A. Centre College, 1980; and Teaching Certificate for Secondary English, University of Louisville, 1987. Publications include: **Leave Taking** published in **Poetic Voices of America,** 1994; **Centre College Affair** published in **Starburst** and **Poetic Voices of America,** 1994. Awards include: Accomplishment of Merit, 1993. **Comments:** The most painful events in my life, affairs of the heart, seem to be the ones which make for the best publications............ 238

CHARLOTTE ANNE DAVIS resides in Belleville, Ontario, Canada. Her education includes: Quinte Secondary, Loyalist College. She is retired and enjoys reading, crafts, and helping people. Her memberships include: Ontario Association of Certified Engineering Technicians and Technologist, Ontario Electrical League. She had **A Walk in the Valley** published in **A Break in the Clouds** in 1993. **Her comments:** My inspiration comes from anywhere, any people, any animal, any thing. I enjoy living each day to its fullest, while learning and growing.. 256

Charlotte Anne Davis

RICHARD FREEDOM DAVIS resides in Huntington, West Virginia and is interested in being a poetic writer. **His comments:** My inspiration comes from being the sphere that rotates on the axis of sadness. I am inspired by writers: James Douglas Morrison, Edgar Allan Poe, Charles Baudalier, Arthur Rimbaud, and Friedrich Nietzsche.. 100, 175

Richard Freedom Davis

FRANCHESCA deBONNEVILLE resides in Martinez, California. She is 26 years old and has been in the military for 9 years. Her most rewarding experience was when she spent 3 weeks in Thailand working with and helping the people in the village. She felt good inside because she was able to give to them and bring a sense of happiness in their lives. She has an Associate's Degree and is planning to get her Bachelor's Degree in teaching and to learn sign language so she can help the hearing impaired. She enjoys giving and helping people to reach their goals. **Her comments:** My inspiration was a very special friend who helped me through a lot, and the poem was directly from my heart and soul. I am a nature person. I find my inner peace when I am walking on the beach at the ocean or walking through the woods.. 141

Franchesca deBonneville

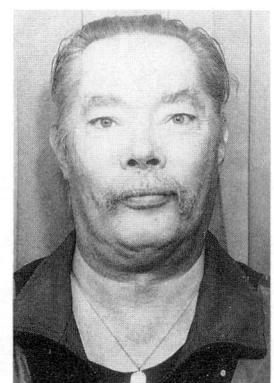

JEROME DEHNERT resides in St. Petersburg, Florida. He graduated from DePaul University with a Bachelor of Science Degree in Commerce. He served in the U.S. Army and worked for U.S. Civil Service. He now is retired. His memberships include: The National Authors Registry, member I.D. DEHNEJO13666, and The Academy of American Poets. He had **Even Paradise Knows Tears** published by **Vantage Press, Inc.**, New York in 1992. **His comments:** The English language is a constant source of fascination to me; in fact, I enjoy reading books on poetry, prose, syntax, punctuation, and word usage more and more with the passing time...................................... 309

Jerome Dehnert

BILLY L. DELANEY resides in Neptune Beach, Florida. He is in the 6th grade at Beaches Episcopal School. He is a member of St. Paul's Times Newspaper Staff and USS Excalibur. **His comments:** I wrote this while I was in the third grade.. 265

Billy L. Delaney

Louise Devendorf

LOUISE DEVENDORF resides in Reed City, Michigan. She is a 1957 graduate of Leroy High School. She studied nursing and business and was a Gold Medal Dance Medalist. Her interests include: politics, writing, and music. She is a promotor. She was elected to city council and is a board member of Osceola Cares, and is on the Library Board. Her publications include: **Some Nostalgia Pertaining to Pearls,** a book published in 1994; **Stars Are Bright,** sheet music, 1958; and **Favorite Poems,** a book, 1994. **Her comments:** The poem I have submitted to you was written in memory of John Lazzatti. John was a well known politician. His voice was heard around the state. He was a very dear friend.. 88

Suzanne DeWitt (Suzanne Zilenziger)

SUZANNE DeWITT (SUZANNE ZILENZIGER) resides in Bellevue, Washington. Her education includes: Endicott College, 1 year; Sarah Lawrence College, 1 year; and Westchester Community College, 1 year. She is a member of the Women's Writing Guild. **Her comments:** Life and love inspire my poetry. After briefly reuniting with a childhood sweetheart (the love of my life) in 1989, his long buried influence mysteriously emerged some 30 years later as the underlying influence of these works written in 1990, still over one year prior to our next, more permanent reunion........... 12, 37, 46, 224, 227, 245

PEDRO DIAZ-LANDA resides in Miami, Florida. His education includes: Law Degree, University of La Habana, Cuba, 1947; Certificate of Completion, Course of American Law for Cuban Lawyers, University of Miami, Coral Gables, Florida, 1961. He is retired and enjoys literature. His memberships include: Academy of Poetry of Miami, National Association of Cuban Lawyers, National Association of Cuban Journalists. He had **Esther** (poem) published in Miami, Florida, 1988; and **Columbus,** (sonnet) published in **Spain,** 1993. His awards include: World Poetry Contest, University of Puerto Rico, 1992; Association of Ibero-Americans Poets and Writers, New York, 1992; and Discovery, 5th Centenary, **Spain,** 1993. **His comments:** My sources of inspiration are love, religion, nature, and philosophy............ 146

Haley Dillon

HALEY DILLON resides in Auburn, Alabama. She is 10 years old and in the 5th grade. Her interests include: writing stories and poems and reading. **Her comments:** I want to be an author and a psychologist when I grow up.. 137, 165

TRINA DODSON resides in Adrian, Michigan. She is a 1994 graduate of Adrian Adult Education as a Certified Nurses Aide. She is a wife and mother of four boys. She is employed as a Patient Care Assistant at Herrick Memorial Hospital, Tecumseh, Michigan. She enjoys writing, poetry, roller skating, white water rafting, and being involved in Boy Scouts with her sons. This is her first publication, but she has written other poems for school. **Her comments:** I was inspired by my adult education teacher, Mrs. Jane Waldo; especially my husband, Calvin Dodson, and my mother, Mavis Vanover, who stood by me and encouraged me to follow through on my writings. My ideas came from personal past and present experiences. Writing poetry is my way of expressing my feelings and thoughts on paper.. 323, 330

D.Q.M. (DERRICK QUINN MILLER) resides in Chicago, Illinois. His education includes business school. He is a steelworker and his interests include computers. **His comments:** My poetry was and is inspired by events in my life.. 232

MARK FENNELL resides in Denton, Texas. He has a B.S. Degree in Physical Chemistry, USF. He is a graduate student and his interests include chemistry. He is a member of the World Affairs Council and the Red Cross. His publications include: **Peace** published in **American Poetry Anthology, 1989; Bill Graham** published in **The Sound of Poetry,** 1993; **Lonely Roads and Barbed Wire Fences** published in **Tears of Fire,** 1993; and **A Black Christmas** published in **Outstanding Poets of America,** 1994. **His comments:** I strive for poetry that is both vivid and pleasing to the ear, yet maintains its integrity. My themes run the gamut of daily experiences, which can include the simplest events or the deepest emotions... 34, 202, 218, 219

Mark Fennell

MARGARET FLATHMAN resides in Hebron, Nebraska. She was manager of a drive-in, Thayer Co. Deshler, in Nebraska for 5 years, and worked in the Dietary Department at St. Joseph's Hospital in Buchanan Co., MO for 10 years. She was a 4-H Leader in Nebraska, a member of the Missouri Lutheran Church in Nebraska and Missouri, and now back in Nebraska, she is a Sunday School teacher. **Her comments:** I (Margaret Sell) was a farm girl and a farm wife (Margaret Flathman), with three children, 10 grandchildren, one passed away, and 4 great grandchildren. My son, Larry, has a Master's Degree in Science. I am also very proud of my oldest child, Carrie, and the youngest, Diane, born on Christmas day. I love nature. I now am retired and babysitting back in Hebron, Nebraska............................. 252

Margaret Flathman

LINDA LEE FRANKS resides in Jena, Louisiana. Her education includes: Jena High School, Jena, Louisiana, some English and poetry classes at Northeast State University, Monroe, Louisiana; poetry workshop in Jena, Louisiana. She is an accountant who enjoys working with people, traveling, reading, movies, music, crafts, horseback riding, and canoeing. Her memberships include: Friends of the LaSalle Parish Library, LaSalle Literary Society, LaSalle Art and Historical Association, LaSalle Museum Association, and Hemps Creek Art Guild. Her publications include: **Soulquest** published in **Our Town Poets,** 1993; **Haven** also published in **Our Town Poets,** 1993; and **Sookie's Teapot** published in **Arcadia Poetry Anthology,** 1994. Her awards include: Honorable Mention, Hemp's Creek Holiday Art Show, "The Gift of Art", 1993; Guest Writer, Central Louisiana Aids Support Services, "C.L.A.S.S. Notes", 1994; and Featured Author, Angola Expressions, "The Angolite", prison news magazine, 1994. **Her comments:** I used to write poetry with it just bubbling out of me. Now, as I am starting back after many years, each poem is an emotional personal wrenching of my very being. At times a painful emergence of self. Yet, since I have again begun the creative process, I can't stop! Most of my poetry is to a specific person in regard to a particularly personal event. Much of the rest revolves around religious themes and periodically, I try what I call passionate love works, but find it hard to achieve focus on these and usually tire of the endless revisions before completion. I love words, their look, their sound, and I like to use allusion in my work... 340

Linda Lee Franks

Helen Fraser

HELEN FRASER was born on January 18 in Brantford, Ontario, Canada, and has lived most of her life in the city of Toronto. She is married and has one son as well as a grandson. Helen loves poetry and has been writing poetry of her own own since she was very young. Her interests include: archaeology, horticulture, and painting, to name a few. She also loves nature with the kind of passion that is unseen in most people and finds endless inspiration from it. On that same note, Helen recently moved into a new house in the beautiful countryside just outside of Toronto and is reaping the rewards of living in such a picturesque environment. In her eyes, Helen sees the beauty in all of life, even in the daily activities most people may find repetitive. She has a charm about her that is unforgettable, and it is nearly impossible not to fall in love with someone who tries so hard at everything she does while never issuing a single complaint. She is a sensitive, caring individual who has a wonderful talent to empathize with almost any situation, and always has she been willing to unselfishly sacrifice her time in order to help someone else in need. Helen Fraser is truly one of a kind, and the world could only wish there were more like her!! 257

MARIE A. FRISBIE resides in Concord, California. Her education includes: B.A Degree in English and Education, Holy Names College, 1958; M.S. Degree in Human Relations/Personnel Administration, Golden Gate University, 1982. She is a home teacher and tutor with local school district. She is an Alumnae member of Holy Names College and Golden Gate University. She has had various inserts on prayer life in her church bulletin. **Her comments:** In my travels with my husband, I constantly see the Infinite Beauty of God expressed in a variety of ways in the splendor of His creation. As I grow closer to Him, I am constantly inspired to write about His Beauty 314, 315

Marie A. Frisbie

JŌVON M. GAMBLE (VON) resides in New Haven, Connecticut. He is in the eighth grade at West Hills Middle Magnet, New Haven, Connecticut. His interests include: football, basketball, karate, and writing poetry. His memberships include: Elm City Youth Group, CPEP-CT Pre-engineering Program, West Hills Middle Magnet School Yearbook Staff, 1993-94; and Youth Group, CTBC (Christian Tabernacle Baptist Church) Church. He had **The Ghetto** published. He won First Place in the Trio Writers Contest sponsored by the New England Association of Educational Opportunity Program Personnel in the Summer of 1993. **His comments:** My inspiration comes from Maya Angelou, my mother, and my life 362

Jōvon M. Gamble (Von)

PATRICIA GALLAGHER GIBBS resides in Bloomfield Hills, Michigan. Her education includes: Academy of the Sacred Heart, Detroit, Michigan; Manhattanville College, New York City, University of Detroit, Bachelor of Philosophy, English major. Her awards include: Golden Poet Award from **World of Poetry**, 1985-87-89; Silver Poet Award from **World of Poetry**, 1986-90; and Honorable Mention from **World of Poetry**, 1985-86-88-89. Comments: Her children referring to her writing as "the wardrobe of poetry our mother has woven for each of us," have compiled much of the body of her work into a privately distributed anthology entitled, **Family Ties Have Special Strings, A Collection of Light Verse by Patricia Gallaher Gibbs** 268

LISA-JAI GIBSON resides in Salem, Virginia. She is a part-time student and personal-care giver for the elderly and she studies and writes on insanity. She had untitled work published in **Philomel Jug Jug,** 1992; and **Pensive** published by **Arcadia Poetry Press,** 1993. **Her comments:** My poetry comes from the end result of dissociation with the socially acceptable side of my mind. My inspiration is solitude, with the unintentional knowledge of society, on my life, provoking me. A lot of the themes that I write about deal with self and society since the two undeniably go hand in hand........... 25

JOSEPH ANTHONY GONSALVES resides in Hayward, California. His education includes: Washington High School, Centerville Jr. High, Maltos Elementary School. He is a United States Marine and is interested in sports and singing. **His comments:** I try to write something no one else would think of writing. Being a Marine, an organization where everyone is seen as an equal, one will often try to be unusual or different on his/her own time. Since I don't have time to express myself person to person, I find that putting my feelings on paper helps me to get by day by day. It also enables my feelings and emotions to last a lifetime... 73

ERIK GORDON is the pen name for **ERIK ALTMAN,** who resides in Middleburg, Florida. He is a high school graduate and a member of the United States Army. He had **But Not on Purpose** published in **Break in the Clouds** in 1993. He also won an Editors Choice Award in 1993. **His comments:** Poetry is one of the best ways to express your true feelings and problems. Writing poetry releases stressful emotions that clear your mind. That's why poetry is so meaningful to me.. 359

Erik Gordon

SHIRLEY ANN GREEN resides in Detroit, Michigan. She is a high school graduate and a Job Corps graduate. She is a school service assistant and is interested in writing. **Her comments:** I was inspired in high school to write by my English teacher. Since then, I have been inspired by God, my students, and Maya Angelou, who hails from my home town. This year I have written two books of poetry entitled, **Taking Flight** and **Coming Forth as Gold.** These books have not been sent to the publisher yet.. 159

CONSTANCE GREENLEAF resides in New York, New York. She has a M.A.+ in English from the Harvard School of Education. She is a Fifth Place Award Winner in this edition of **Poetic Voices of America. Her comments:** My poetry has appeared in the **Transatlantic Review,** the **Chicago Review, Albatross,** and other periodicals. The Summer of 1992 I held a Tennessee Williams Scholarship to the Writer's Conference in Tennessee. This is dedicated to my mother.. 8

IZENA GRIFFIN resides in Smithville, Tennessee. She had **Miracle So Sweet** published in **Tears of Fire** by **The National Library of Poetry** in 1993. **Her comments:** In December of 1989, God gave me a healing miracle. The inspiration comes to me from the Holy Spirit. I praise my God for His loving grace. All glory and honor belong to God through Jesus, my living Saviour...... 98

Izena Griffin

T. MITCHELL GUY resides in Chandler, Arizona. He has a B.S. Degree in Liberal Arts and a M.A. Degree in Special Education. He is an educator and is medically disabled. His publications include: **Too Far Gone** published in **Expectations** by **Iliad,** 1990; **I Don't Lie,** 1990, and **My Lonely,** 1991, both published by **World of Poetry.** He won a Golden Poet Award in 1990 and an Award of Merit also in 1990. **His comments:** My poetry has been my tears of pain, anger, confusion and/or happiness which fell upon a page and I cried until I felt better and/or understood my pain............................. 52

JOHN W. HAMILTON resides in Inola, Oklahoma. He is a high school graduate and a construction foreman. He enjoys hunting and fishing. **His comments:** I listen to the stories carried on the wind and try to write what is spoken.. 83

Diana L. Hammer

DIANA L. HAMMER resides in Gibsonburg, Ohio. She works in nursing: geriatrics, home-care, and hospice. **Her comments:** Warmed by the constancy of God's love, my inspiration comes from His glory in nature; along with His support as reflected by my husband, family, and friends.................. 286

Cherie Brigham Hanson

CHERIE BRIGHAM HANSON resides in Long Beach, California. She is a graduate of the University of Southern California. She is a third generation Californian who adopted the Southwest 30 years ago. She taught in the El Paso school systems and was Head of the Speech and Drama Department at Irvin and Eastwood High Schools. She was active in volunteer work for the El Paso Museum of Art being on the Members Guild Board to serve as Chairman for the Docent program during Bill Rakocy's tenure as Curator of Education. She also was Chairman of the Museum Gift Shop. Other organizations included the El Paso Art Association where she assisted in holding various offices because she believed the principles set forth by the group to bring appreciation of fine arts to the community and the scholarship fund for young El Paso artists. She was one of the founders of the Rio Bravo Watercolorists group. Pastels, acrylic collage, oil and watercolors are the media through which she expresses her love of everyday things; from realism to semi-abstract her work is in private and public collections in Texas, New Mexico, California and Kuwait. She studied with Texas artists Bill Rakocy, Ray Lopez-Aleman and Jan Herring. She studied watercolor with Zoltan Szabo, Tony Van Hasselt, Jan Herring, Dong Kingman, Charles Reid, Leo Smith and Naomi Brotherton; Pastels with Albert Handell of Santa Fe. She is a member of the Southwest Watercolor Society, Pastel Society of the Southwest, San Diego Watercolor Society; associate member of National Watercolor Society and the American Watercolor Society. **Her comments:** Writing comes to me as something that must be done out of deep study of a subject or deep feeling that can't be released another way. Poetry has always been a part of my life initially as an interpreter of the written word.................. 288

Bridget L. Harris

BRIDGET L. HARRIS resides in San Francisco, California. Her education includes: elementary school, middle school, and G.E.D. She is a Housing Resource Developer. She is upgrading her computer skills. **Her comments:** I am estatic about my poetry, since it depicts to me "Life's experiences and/or achievements." My source of inspiration first came to me while I was writing in my journal for my biography. A thought/title of a poem, "My Goal," within 45 minutes I had completed it. Now it's in the spare of the moment. I never know what, when, or where. I keep a tablet or micro-cassette with me at all times. I am a 31 year young Black female with a 12 year young daughter to raise. I am constantly striving to achieve my goals in life and in heart. A person should always have long and short term goals. "I have those long and short term goals and all in between." My poems and songs are about life's dictionary: love, hurt, sadness, happiness, desires, dreams. "I sincerely look forward to satisfying the depths of your inner mind.".................. 379

AIMEE DENISE HARVEY resides in Gary, Indiana. She studied theatre at Emerson School for Visual and Performing Arts in Gary, Indiana and Indiana University in Bloomington, Indiana. She is a reseach assistant for a leading Chicago PR firm. She won Guideposts Youth Writing Scholarship in 1989. **Her comments:** I draw inspiration for my work from all the rage, frustration, beauty, and joy that comes with being a woman in general, and a woman of color in particular.................. 333

Aimee Denise Harvey

SONYA M. HECK resides in Brooklyn, Iowa. She graduated from BGM High School in Brooklyn, Iowa in January of 1993. She left for one year in Australia as a Rotary Foreign Exchange Student, and returned to the United States in December of 1993. She is attending Simpson College at Indianola, Iowa, majoring in English and Guidance Counseling. She enjoys traveling, reading, and writing, and she is active in the Rotary International Foreign Exchange Student Program. **Her comments:** I have very strong feelings about the current environmental situation which inspires a lot of my thoughts for writing. My high school English teacher, Mrs. Heetland, has provided me with encouragement and helped me develop the skills needed to put my thoughts on paper... 311

Sonya M. Heck

ANNA MAE HOFFMAN resides in Sacramento, California. Her education includes: Sacramento City College, Sacramento, California; California State University at Sacramento, California. She is a writer/poet and her interests include: writing, reading, and Tai Chi. She is a member of the International Society of Poets. Her publications include: **Time** published by **The National Library of Poetry,** 1992; and **Waitin'** published in **ISP Newsletter,** and **Poet's Corner,** 1992. She won Best Essay Contest (CSUS) in 1987 and 1988, and International Poet of Merit in 1992. **Her comments:** Poetry wears many faces and speaks with many voices... 13, 61

Anna Mae Hoffman

BENJAMIN DAVID HOOKS resides in Phoenix, Arizona. His education includes: currently a freshman at South Mountain High School; National Conference Christians and Jews, Anytown, U.S.A. He plans on becoming a corporate attorney. His memberships include: NAACP Youth Council; National Honors Society; Career Leadership Development Program; S.A.T. Prep. Phx. Urban League, 1993. His awards include: band member, 1991-93; Honors Society, 1993; and Excellence Award-Career Leadership, 1992........................... 377

Benjamin David Hooks

DEBRA L. HORTON resides in Hayward, California. She is a Special Education Assistant and an avid reader of poetry and Native American books. She makes Native American crafts. Her poem, **My Own Thoughts About Life** appears in this edition of **Poetic Voices of America,** 1994. **Her comments:** While listening to American Indian flute music by **Sky,** the **Northern Plains Song** spoke to my soul. This is what inspired me to write **My Own Thoughts About Life**... 81

Debra L. Horton

Barbara Brickey Jividen

BARBARA BRICKEY JIVIDEN and her husband, Jerry, own & operate Images Unique Photography. Barbara's writing often appears with their photography. Her publications include: **Ohio Magazine** where an article and two photos appeared in November, 1993; The **Ashland Daily Independent Regional Poetry Column** (KY) and **The Phoenix Writers Column** (OH) regularly publish her poetry; six separate hardcover anthologies contain a total of ten of her poems since 1992. The total ending the 1993 year exceeded over thirty-five in print in various publications. She earned the "Editor's Choice Award" from the **National Library of Poetry** last year. Currently, she is Vice-president of the **WRITE Group** (Writers Responding in Training and Education); she is also co-founder. Other memberships include: the Ohio Verse Writers' Guild and the National Federation of State Poetry Societies. She sponsored and judged the "Save the Earth" poetry contest open to Ohio high school students. She has written three books which are being considered for publication. **Her comments:** I believe all my writings are inspired by God. I suggest to new writers to participate in as many opportunities to write/share as possible (such as Sparrowgrass contests) and to not fear rejection; someone will win and you must believe it can be **you!**... 138, 168, 198

GEORGE L. JOHANSEN resides in Copiague, New York. His education includes 12 years of school. He is retired from the U.S. Navy and a retired transit worker. Memberships include: B.S.A. Troop 2000, V.F.W., American Legion, and International World of Poetry. He had **Road to Adventure, Vol. I**, published in 1993, and **From Love They Shed a Tear** published in **All My Tomorrows** in 1993. His awards include: International Poet of Merit, 1993; Golden Poet Award, 1992; and Ruby Award.. 368

George L. Johansen

EDWIN JOHNSON resides in Escanaba, Michigan. He has a high school education and is retired. His interests include golf, painting, and writing. His memberships include: church, Senior Citizen S.R.S. Club, and American Legion. His publications include: **Excuses**, 1989, **Projectable**, 1993, and **He Cares**, 1993, all published in **Word Aflame Pub. His comments:** My inspiration comes from God, love, nature, and life in general. Some of my most inner thoughts are expressed in my poems. I've been asked to write poems for weddings, funerals, birthdays, churches, veterans, Community Action, Senior Companion, and local papers. I started writing at the age of 17 and wrote many poems while overseas during World War II. Poems about my mother, brothers, wife, sons, daughter, grandchildren, etc. Letters in rhyme written to family members and friends. Some of my most enjoyable hours are spent painting and writing. I wish this dedicated to my wife and family.................... 241

Edwin Johnson

MARK ALLEN JOHNSON resides in Farmington, New Mexico. His education includes: New Mexico State University, Las Cruces, New Mexico, Bachelor of Science Degree in Education. He is a school teacher and his interests include: reading, writing, music, entertainment, and sports............................ 326

Mark Allen Johnson

MARY HULON JOHNSON resides in Geneva, Alabama. Her education includes Slocomb High, Slocomb, Alabama, in Geneva County. She is disabled and enjoys writing and reading. She is a member of The Songwriters Club of America. She has 2 songs with Broadway Music Productions and 2 songs with Music City Music, and she has 1 song copyrighted, none published. **Her comments:** I can sit down and write songs and poetry easy, but I just don't have the financial backing it takes to become a good writer. Writing is a real pleasure.. 70

Ashley Nicole Alvarado, daughter of Thomas and Jennifer Alvarado, Geneva, AL

NICOLE JONES resides in Detroit, Michigan. She attends Dewey Center for Urban Education in Detroit, Michigan. She is a 6th grade student. **Her comments:** Dewey Center School Specializes in English and encourages children to become writers. I write a poem or a story each day................... 177

ZEMA L. JORDAN, PH.D. resides in Detroit, Michigan. Her education includes: Valedictorian of her high school graduating class; Council Training School, Huntsville, Alabama; Bachelor of Arts Degree, in English, Tennessee A. & I. State University, Detroit, Michigan; Ph.D., Wayne State University; Wayne State University, Detroit, Michigan; Ph.D., Wayne State University; further studies at Wigan, England, University of Michigan, Michigan State Univ., and George Peabody College. She is an Administrator with Detroit Public Schools and part-time English instructor with Wayne County Community College, Detroit, Michigan. Her memberships include: National Council of Teachers of English, Pi Lambda Theta, National Association of University Women, Michigan Opera Theatre, Delta Sigma Theta Sorority, Inc., Founders Society of The Detroit Institute of Arts. Her publications include: Articles on Education published in **Palmetto Education Association Journal,** 1960's; **Dr. Martin Luther King, Jr., A Legacy** published in **The National Library of Poetry, A Question of Balance,** 1992. Her awards include: The International Poet of Merit Award, 1992 by The International Society of Poets; Inclusion in biographical dictionaries, 1992-present, Who's Who in the Midwest, International Who's Who of Intellectuals, International Who's Who in Education, International Directory of Distinguished Leadership. **Her comments:** I believe in a cultivated and disciplined intellect. I treasure English literature, especially the Lake District poets. I believe in the practicality of world hypotheses—formism, organicism, contextualism, and mechanism—when ordering experiences about literature and the world.. 85

Zema L. Jordan, Ph.D.

KIMO is the pen name for **JIMMIE WILLIAMS,** who resides in Novi, MI. His education includes: high school, phycology (branch of botany), several computer courses such as: DOS, Intro to Computers, Harvard Graphics and WordPerfect. He is a Ford Motor Co. Auto Worker and enjoys photography and outdoor life. He is a member of the Disabled American Vet. **His comments:** I have written poetry for many years. I am inspired by many poets, but never knew any of them. I credit my inspiration to my friend, James Waters, who works beside me in my job, as a writer of fiction short stories, for his encouragement and support... 348

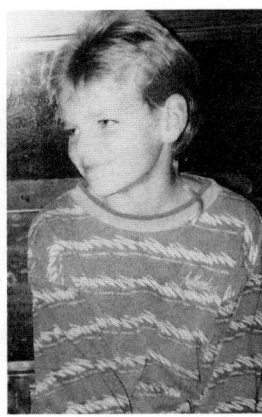

BARRY LYNN KINGERY resides in Orland, California. He is in the sixth grade, and is interested in becoming a teenager. He is a member of the Sports Club. **His comments:** I like my poem..................................... 242

Barry Lynn Kingery

MICHELLE KISSINGER resides in Sewell, New Jersey. She is an eighth grade student at Chestnut Ridge Middle School in Washington Twp., New Jersey. Her interests include soccer, swimming, and singing. **Her comments:** Violence is becoming more and more of a problem in our world today. From the streets of Bosnia to L.A., I see a total lack of respect for human life. We need more peace on the streets, in our schools, and in our homes............. 325

Michelle Kissinger

HEIDI KOGER resides in Blowing Rock, North Carolina. She is 12 years old and in the eighth grade. Her interests include: reading, playing the piano, writing, and horseback riding. Her memberships include: student advisory of Watauga Co. Schools; TRG to Teen Magazine. Her awards include: Duke Talent Identification, 1992; Ranatra Fusca Creativity: OM, 1992; Academically Gifted Student Council Representative, 1989-93. **Her comments:** My poem was written the night my best friend, Abigail Weaver, died. She was the inspiration for this piece.. 287

Heidi Koger

HELEN LAGER KONYHA resides in Kirkland, Washington. Her education includes: M. Educ. Counseling and 6th year in specialization, Seattle University and Ex. courses at the University of Washington, Western, Central Washington and Seattle University. She is a public school teacher, counselor, and Director of Counseling and Mental Health Counselor. Her interests include: travel, handwork, reading, oil painting, poetry, teaching, and workshops. Her memberships include: WSRTA, NRTA, APGA, WMHCA, and AADA (teacher's and counselor's associations). She had **Echoes of the Heart** (a book) published in New York in 1994. **Her comments:** Experiences in life taught me to seek a higher level of living found in God. During times of contemplation, poems sprang into my heart. They are often spiritual and relate to everyone's existence in some way... 248, 277

Helen Lager Konyha

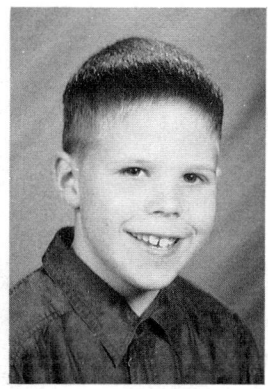

ADAM T. KRYNICKI resides in Natrona Heights, Pennsylvania. He is in the fourth grade at Heights Elementary School, Highlands School District, Natrona Heights, Pennsylvania. His interests include soccer, trombone, and writing. **His comments:** My second grade teacher, Mrs. Burton, encouraged us to read and write in our spare time. I look around and ideas come from what I see. I like to rhyme and develop my ideas.. 218

Adam T. Krynicki

C.V. LaCROIX resides in Regina, Saskatchewan, Can. Education includes: University, Early Childhood Education. Occupation: teacher, amateur artist, decorator, and gardener. Publications include: **Enjoy the Moment** published in **Listen With Your Heart** by **Quill Books**, Harlington, Texas, 1992; and **Friends** published in **Dance on the Horizon** by **The National Library of Poetry**, Owings Mills, Maryland, 1994. Awards include: Honorable Mention in 1992. **Comments:** My poetry lends itself to my upbringing and people who have influenced me in the past while growing up and being educated in rural Saskatchewan, Canada.. 262

RONNIE G. LaFLAMME resides in Biddeford, Maine. He graduated from Biddeford High School and went into the Navy. He received the Military Excellent Award and has plans to graduate from George Washington University in 1994 with a 4 year degree in business. He is a Navy officer and married Judy Tardif on July 4, 1992. His interests include: hunting, reading, fishing, walking, and bike riding. He is a member of the R.O.T.C. in the Navy. **His comments:** To me, writing poems is a source of deep feelings to show others deep inside their own hearts... 282, 283

SCOTT OWEN LEONARD resides in Burton, Ohio. His education includes: Masters of Science and Bachelor of Science, Ohio University; Associate of Applied Science, Hocking Technical College. He is a naturalist, a teacher, a Red Cross Instructor, a poet, and a writer. His memberships include: Phi Kappa Phi, Association for Experiential Education, and Ohio Parks and Recreation Association. **His comments:** When I write poetry, the whole world seems to be spinning inside me. When not writing poetry, the world seems to spin without me. I hope to make present, those things which find their way onto the page. It is my desire that this presence is immediate, powerful, and true.. 12

Scott Owen Leonard

MARY A. LOFT resides in Memphis, Tennessee. She has a 9th grade education from Hume's High School, Memphis, Tennessee. She is a housewife and her interests include: arts and crafts, fishing, and writing. She is a member of the Juliet Avenue Women's Club of Memphis, Tennesee. **Her comments:** My inspiration for the poem, **My Window**, was having two heart attacks, and the Lord let me live. I am very blessed. I would like to dedicate this poem to my husband, Marvin, and my three children......................... 310

Mary A. Loft

J.A. LONG resides in Chico, California. He is a 1983 graduate of Shasta Union High School in Redding, California. He attended some college and is self taught in creative writing. He is self employed and his interests include creative writing and singing. **His comments:** My poems are all original, but few. However, a couple of them are a version of an old one. I live in the Sacramento River Valley and have lived in 5 locations besides Chico, California. One poem is from an emotional experience of mine... 251

WAYNE E. LOVELESS resides in Apple Valley, California. He has a B.S. Degree in Business Administration from Chapman University, Orange, Califoria, 1993. He is a certified surgical technician and his interests include: traveling, photography, and bowling. He is Vice-president of the Association of Surgical Technologists, Chapter 186 of Southern California. His publications include: **The Beauty of Love** published in **The American Poetry Annual**, 1993; and **Commitment of Love** published in **Tears of Fire** by **The National Library of Poetry**, 1994. **His comments:** My inspiration comes from my children and the love I have for them. Too often in the rush of everyday life, I forget to say "Thank you" so that they can hear it, but I do appreciate all the encouragement they have given me. Their caring has made a difference... 305

LINDA S. LOWE resides in Clayton, California. She has a B.A. Degree from Florida State University. She is a home/hospital tutor for Mt. Diablo Schools and teaches the primary class at Valley Christian Church, also the Ladies' Bible Study. Her publications include: **Broken Dreams** published in **Communicate**, 1993; **Courage** published in **The Family Album**, 1981; and **Swiss Cheese** published in **Mid-Valley Church**, 1990. Her awards include: Scholastic Writing, **The Miami Herald**, 1952; Employing the Handicapped, essay, 1957; and poetry contest, **Contra Costa Times**, 1978. **Her comments:** I sent my first published poem, **The Chinese Girl**, to Pearl Buck when I was 17. She wrote me a letter of encouragement which I have treasured. Now I enjoy encouraging other young poets and sharing my love of poetry......................... 66

Linda S. Lowe

Cindy Pennington Lusty

CINDY PENNINGTON LUSTY resides in Sullivan, Missouri. She is 23 years old and her birthday is December 26, 1970. She is currently working at Midland Brake, Inc. in Cuba, Missouri. She is also attending East Central College in Union, Missouri for her prerequisites for the RN Program. She has a 5 year old daughter, April Christine Lusty. She married Mark Lusty at 17 years old. She is currently divorced and in a one year relationship with a wonderful man, Bernard McGowan (Bernie). She attended Magnolia High School in Magnolia, Texas, until the 10th grade. She receive her G.E.D. in November of 1991 to preceed with school. She is a mother, a student, a homemaker, a working person, and a girlfriend. She says "It's tough." Her father is Dennis Pennington and her mother is Shirley Brown. She had a rough childhood and a bad marriage. She had to learn the hard way a lot. She knows what she wants out of life and is going for it, despite setbacks. She is a winner. She doesn't like to be around negative people anymore because she needs to be positive. All of this is where the poem came from. She feels alone a lot because people in her life deny happenings as a child. She loves elderly people and she is a CNA, although she doesn't practice anymore due to money. She needs to get in a field where she can work with the elderly and make money, then she'll be happy. "Maybe an RN in physical therapy so I can teach them not to give up." **Her comments:** My inspirations come from my own life experience mostly, but sometimes, from people I meet throughout my life. I have to feel what I write.. 36

VICKY LYNN LYONS resides in Fairbanks, Alaska. She is a Sophomore in high school and she loves animals. **Her comments:** I was inspired by our beautiful Alaskan summers.. 370

Betty A. Mannon

BETTY A. MANNON resides in Memphis, Tennessee. She has a high school education. She is a retired homemaker and has been a widow since May of 1988. Her interests include: her 4 grown children, 9 grandchildren, writing, piano, church, and travel. **Her comments:** Many years ago I wrote (in 25 words or less) why I liked a certain brand of salmon. I wrote my answer in recipe style and it rhymed. I won first place, a beautiful Easter bonnet. My aunt (now deceased) was my inspiration. Several of her poems and limericks were published. She entered her works in nationwide contests and won nice prizes. One day I hope to write a love song................ 68, 69, 170

Linda Marr

LINDA MARR resides in Calgary, Alberta, Canada. She received a "Certificate in Art" and is currently enrolled in the University of Calgary to obtain a Bachelor of Fine Arts Degree. Her interests include: art, writing, and exploring the inner self. **Her comments:** It is through examination of self, that the inspirations have arose through poetry, which holds a purpose to my lifelong journey. My hope that others will gain insight into their own lives through my own thoughts and findings..................................... 298, 302, 306

JAMES A. MARSTERS resides in St. Louis, Missouri. He has a high school education. His interests include: chess, photography, karate, and painting. He is a member of the U.S. Chess Federation. He had **Fragments** published in hardback in 1991. **His comments:** My inspiration for writing comes from poverty. My father died when I was 5 years old, and my mother died when I was 16. Under the dominance of an alchoholic, nomadic, stepfather, I had lived in 5 states by the time I was 9 years old. The streets were my mentor—their garbage, my food—their people, how not to be. I have been married 36 years (November) with three fine boys and 6 grandchildren. As of May, I have worked at the same job for 30 years. I started writing at 16. My book, **Fragments**, end in 1986 when I was 44 years old—A noticeable point of my later work, brevity, as people have so little time to read. This book comes through Winston Derek of Nashville, Tennessee..................... 74

James A. Marsters

AARON MICHAEL RICE resided in South Lake Tahoe, California. He had a high school education. He was an artist, musician, and writer. During his last years in high school, Aaron and a friend, Austin, formed "In Your Face Graphics," a company that designed and printed T-shirts and went on to create two comic books: **Zdenek I** and **Zdenek II** published in high school in 1992 and 1993. He won a Reflections Program Award in 1990 and a G.A.T.E. Program Award in 1991. **Comments:** Aaron died in the early morning hours of his birthday, May 2, 1993. A sleeping passenger returning from a long trip to celebrate his 19th birthday at home. A tragic head on collision took his life, but his art lives on... 18

Aaron Michael Rice

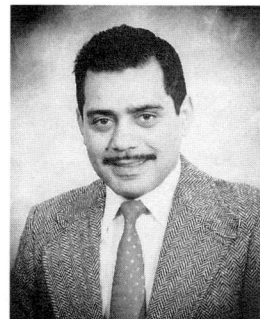
ALFONSO C. RODRIQUEZ resides in Philadelphia, Pennsylania. He is in progress of his philosophy in non-fiction writing. He plans to become a writer. He is a member of the Mayor's Commission on Literacy in Philadelphia. He had **El Espanal** published in a textbook in 1993. **His comments:** My inspiration was my mother. One day I was thinking about her and I decided to do the poem, **What Is A Mother?**, because I care and love her very much.. 84

Alfonso C. Rodriquez

KATHLEEN RUCZYNSKI — POOPSIE resides in Sterling Heights, Michigan. She has a high school education and is a medical records file clerk. She likes to listen to country music and oldies from the 50's. Traveling in Northern Michigan, Gaylord, and Charlovoix, are her favorite places. Her favorite lake is Black Lake, near Onaway! She loves her family and Elvis Presley! She collects Elvis music and memorabilia from him! She drives senior citizens on trips to stores, doctors, and little errands. She likes to decorate cakes, and writing poems most of all. **Her comments:** My inspiration for writing is my personal (inner) feelings when I look at something of nature, or think of a person or place I love! I love the outside—leaves, trees, water, and Autumn, my favorite season! I feel God directing me when I write and when I feel happy, serious, sad, or funny. I find writing poems very relaxing and strengthening to my inner self!.................. 241, 276

Kathleen Ruczynski — Poopsie

DEBORAH J. RURYK resides in Lawrenceburg, Indiana. She received an Associates Degree in Applied Science in computer information systems, and a certificate in accounting in May of 1994. She is a bookstore clerk and her interests include: writing, computers, and writing down ideas of how to earn money at home. **Her comments:** My inspirations come from my love and fascination of children. I believe that childhood is such a precious time and it should be enjoyed as much as possible. Adulthood comes too fast, therefore, I hold on to my youth as much as possible. My inspirations also come from my children, Andy and Chris Seabolt, and my boyfriend, Jeff Orcutt, who keep me youthful!.. 322
Deborah J. Ruryk

LINDA L. RYAN resides in Manchester, Iowa. Her education includes: B.A. from Buena Vista College, Storm Lake, Iowa; M.A. in special education from N.M.S.U., Kirksville, Missouri; and 2nd graduate endorsement from the University of Dubuque, Dubuque, Iowa. She is a special education teacher and her interests include reading, writing, aerobics, and walking. She is a member of the I.S.E.A., the N.E.A., and the United Methodist Church. She had **Remember When** published in **In The Desert Sun** in 1993. **Her comments:** I want my writing to reflect the reality of my life and my experiences in today's world, and hope that my readers can relate to the same reality!.. 16

Richard Claude Shacklett and museum curator

RICHARD CLAUDE SHACKLETT resides in Murfreesboro, Tennessee. His education includes: Crichlow Grammer School, Lascassas Elementary, Central High School, Middle Tennessee State, and Army Air Force Photography School in Denver. Presently, he spends most of his time restoring "old" damaged photos! He tries to encourage young people to join 4-H Club! In the late 1930's, he was State 4-H President. His interest is still STRONG. He had **Iris** published in 1937. He had a world exhibition of photography (Strike!) in Lucerne, Switzerland in 1952. Six—16x20 paintings still hang in the Idaho State Museum in Boise, Idaho, 1950 (circa). **His comments:** Being a farm boy and NOT prefering to milk cows, I developed a system of thinking poetically to ESCAPE this task. It still works for me to think this way today when I'm painting or drawing...... 17

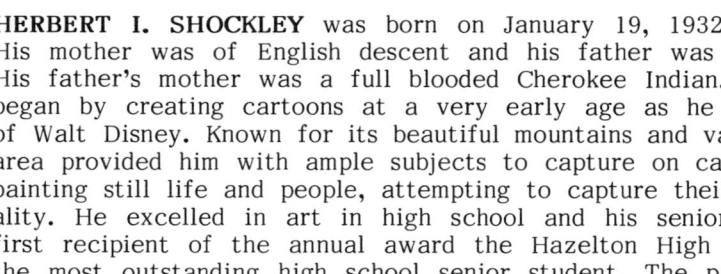

Herbert I. Shockley

HERBERT I. SHOCKLEY was born on January 19, 1932, in Hazelton, PA. His mother was of English descent and his father was of Indian descent. His father's mother was a full blooded Cherokee Indian. He loved art and began by creating cartoons at a very early age as he admired the magic of Walt Disney. Known for its beautiful mountains and valleys, the Hazelton area provided him with ample subjects to capture on canvas. He also liked painting still life and people, attempting to capture their mood and personality. He excelled in art in high school and his senior year he was the first recipient of the annual award the Hazelton High School presents to the most outstanding high school senior student. The painting he received it for was of a friend of his sitting in a big overstuffed chair titled, **Lazy Day.** After graduation in 1949, his mother passed away. Not knowing what he wanted to do, he worked in the Hazelton area for a few years. He moved to San Francisco and fell in love with the area. While there, he got the inspiration for many of his paintings. He moved back East and in 1955, opened his own sign painting business in his hometown of Hazelton. During this time he got involved with the Hazelton Chapter of Barbershoppers and loved singing. He also took up table tennis and basketball. He belonged to the Hazelton Art League and kept in close touch with the arts and his high school art teacher. She encouraged him to paint more. After painting for many years, he was invited to have his own art show at the Hazelton Art League in 1979. At that show he sold 18 paintings, mostly of local scenery and historic landmarks. He was awarded the first ever Service Award in 1990 from the Art League. It was truly an honor for him. His love of life and genuine sincere personality touched every person he met. Art came natural to him and he never pursued it further than a high school diploma. In 1967, he started working for St. Regis Paper Company in Hazelton as a graphic artist. He worked there for 26 years. He worked his way up to becoming a graphic art manager the last ten years he was there. During that time, the company changed from St. Regis to Princeton Pkg. Inc. He passed away on December 2, 1992, and shortly after that, Princeton Pkg. became Bemis. He was the last art director there........ 78

Susan Elizabeth Small

SUSAN ELIZABETH SMALL resides in Princeton, Illinois. Her education includes: Associates of Science, Illinois Valley Community College, Oglesby, Illinois; Bachelor of Arts/English Literature, Illinois College, Jacksonsville, Illinois. Her interests include: literature, philosophy, art, music, drama, science, and nature. **Her comments:** Music plays an important part in my poetic writing. Together with my love of philosophy, this poem, **Inspiration,** was inspired by a musical concert I attended in St. Louis for an art history class I was taking during my senior year at Illinois College. I came away completely exhilarated!.. 24

Cecile Musson Smith

CECILE MUSSON SMITH resides in Devonshire, Bermuda. Her education includes: Ontario Business College; local (overseas) Cambridge University; Queens University; Maryland University; American International College at Lend-Lease Air Base, taught there; and International Shorthand Writers, U.S.A. She is founder/head of Smiths Commercial School and a free-lance and staff journalist. Her memberships include: Founder-president of Bermuda Writers Club; Teachers Union; Founding member of Bermuda Arts Council; National Business Education Association, U.S.A.; World Life Fellow International Biographical Centre, Cambridge, England, who gave Order of Merit; World Life Fellow American Biographical Institute and Deputy Governor; and was on the now defunct Social Welfare Board, 1955/56. She is now on Special Juvenile and Domestic Courts Panels and opposing incarceration. Joined Prison Fellowship's Special Congress to promote rehabilitative rather than retributive justice. She promoted teen court rather than incarceration. Her publications include: collection of poetic thoughts; **Zephyrs** published in Bermuda, 1937/1942; **Bermuda Review** published in Bermuda, 1951/52; **Worlds Fair Anthology** published in U.S.A., 1940; read a poem over BBC in U.K.; Barbados magazine, **BIM**; and U.S. Radio, **Enjoyment of Poetry.** Her awards include: International Who's Who in Poetry, England, 1970/71; The Great Prize, Winged Victory, Rome, 1982; International Order of Merit for Literature, U.K., 1990/91; International Woman of the Year 1992/93; and International Poets Laureate Medal and Citation. **Her comments:** I am the daughter of an uncrowned Poet Laureate (his topical poetry spanning 50 years) and a sister of a poet. My inspiration comes from love—the agony and ecstasy, God—instant answered prayer, UFO's, Astraltravel Nature. My poems come complete and unedited.. 164

Lindsey R. Smith

LINDSEY R. SMITH resides in White Plains, New York. He is a high school graduate. He is retired and enjoys music, reading, and writing. He won the National Black Achiever Award in 1983. **His comments:** My inspiration comes from things I'm always thinking, being that the mind is the "Master Power." I used to perform with a jazz trio as a jazz singer. I feel all my inspiration has come to me from the Creator of Almighty God. For there is no partiality with God, and I also much want to share this inspiration with others... 239, 270, 271, 273, 276

Mildred Smith

MILDRED SMITH resides in Morganton, North Carolina. She is a member of the Hartland Church. **Her comments:** My husband, Odell, passed away in 1985 with cancer. We have three daughters, all married. I have adopted my grandson who is 15 years old. I have two other grandchildren, Nathan Conley, and Melisa Bailey. I would like to travel and see God's beauty.......... 27

JIM SNYDER resides in Bonney Lake, Washington. He tunes and restores pianos and is a regional tuning examiner with the Piano Technicians Guild. He has substituted with the Seattle Symphony. He is a percussionist with the Bellevue Philharmonic Orchestra and is also a high school baseball umpire. His wife of eleven years, Lynn, is a summer peach who works full-time as a medical laboratory technologist. She is the mother of their three children, Erika, Tom, and Adam.. 24, 31, 195, 322, 328, 330, 331, 356, 380

EDWIN P. SPIVEY resides in New Iberia, Louisiana. He lists his education as Irish National!!! He is a retired Telecom Engineer who enjoys poetry, gardening, and do-it-yourself. He is a member of the International Society of Poetry and was a member of the former World Poetry. His publications include: **Magic Days** published in **Great American Anthology,** 1987; **Look Out...Not In,** 1990, and **None Can See But Thee,** 1989, both published in **Who's Who in Poetry; Look to the Golden Dawn,** 1988, and **How Long To Mend a Broken Heart,** both published in **Great Treasury of Great Poems; Drifting Sands** published in **Great Poems of the Western World; Set Your Sights on Yonder Hill** published in **New American Poetry Anthology,** 1991; **God's Gifts to Me But Loans** published in **Who's Who in Poetry** and **Our World's Favourite Poems,** 1993; and **I Stand and Gaze Far Out to Sea** published in **Selected Works of World's Best Poets,** 1992. He has won 18 Award of Merit Certificates; four

continued on next page

4th Place Awards; and a Golden Poet Award in 1987-88-89-90-91. **His comments:** I wrote my first poem, **The American Remembrance,** when I was returning to Britain from my first vacation in the United States in 1958, in appreciation to great friends, known to my first wife since 1926, myself from 1937, when I married my first wife. I have been writing since that year on different subjects. Now my main inspiration for writing is in remembrance of both my first and second wives........... 206, 224

SHELLY L. STANERT resides in Geraldton, Ontario, Canada. She is a high school graduate. She loves animals and is pursuing a veterinary career. **Her comments:** I had a fabulous summer holiday in 1993 which motivated my inner feelings, which inspired me to put them on paper............................ 48

Shelly L. Stanert

THELMA TASIMOWICZ resides in Brooklyn, New York. She received a B.A. and a M.S. from Brooklyn College, cum laude, and special honors in Education. She is a teacher who enjoys writing, biking, and hiking. She had **Child of the Night** published by **National Library of Poetry,** 1994, and **In No Man's Land** published in **Prolific Writer's Journal,** 1994. **Her comments:** My poems are like a patchwork quilt, filled with turmoil, hopes, aspirations, and love.. 130

LENNICE MARIE TAYLOR resides in Tulsa, Oklahoma. She has a diploma in computer programming and teaches high school at Tulsa Public School. She loves to walk and sew, and also enjoys reading. She is the proud mother of nine children. She is a member of Outreach Ministry of Love Church, Tulsa, Oklahoma. **Her comments:** I love being an author, it allows me to bring out the innermost expressions of my soul when I write. Hopefully, every heart that reads my poetry will be inspired by it................................. 350

Lennice Marie Taylor

BRANDI NICOLE TEDFORD resides in Eastland, Texas. She is currently in the 5th grade. She enjoys writing, singing, and dancing. She was published in **The American Anthology of Poets** in 1991................ 353

AL THOMAS resides in Norcross, Georgia. He received a G.E.D. and is a checker on a truck loading dock. He is a member of the International Society of Poets, and the Teamsters Union. His publications include: **The Snow Storm of the Century** published in **Poetic Voices of America,** 1993; **Who's Who in Poetry** by **National Library of Poetry,** 1993; and **Our World's Best Poets** by **World of Poetry,** 1992. His awards include: Editors Choice Award, 1993; International Poet of Merit, 1993; and Golden Poet Award, 1992. **His comments:** My greatest inspiration comes from my Heavenly Father. Many people: waitresses, police, airline flight attendents, and God's nature inspire me. Our nation needs the love of God, love for each other, and relation with other countries... 183

Al Thomas

J.S. TITLOW is the pen name for **JEAN SAVAGE TITLOW**, who resides in Belmont, California. She graduated from George Washington High School in San Francisco, then through San Francisco and Peninsula Colleges, earned an accounting degree. She is a mother, grandmother, and is retired after 17 years with the Redwood City School District. Her love of children has led her to becoming a lunch yard supervisor for San Carlos School District. Her loves are the arts, ceramics, writing poetry, creative endeavors, and most of all, her family, now numbering 12. Her publications include: **God's Gift** and **To!**, both published in **Treasured Poems of America**, 1993; and **Always!** published in this edition of **Poetic Voices of America**, 1994. **Her comments:** For the last ten years, I've hiked and climbed the mountains and domes of Yosemite Park, California. Beauty there is awesome and inspiring. I also have climbed and hiked the Alps in Switzerland, Austria, and a bit into Italy. Hiking in Vermont during the Fall colors was breathtaking.. 255, 267

J.S. Titlow

JACQUELINE R. TURNIPSEED resides in Bastrop, Texas. She is a drafting graduate and commercial cross country driver graduate. She is a truck driver and her interests include metaphysics, writing, and horses. **Her comments:** I am a 40 year old widow with 3 children. I was inspired to write after my husband's death in 1985. During my search for the truth, I chose a career as a cross country commercial driver. My poem, **The Highway Across Heaven**, expresses my observations.. 102

Jacqueline R. Turnipseed

VERNA U.S.A. is the pen name for **VERNA HARMS**, who resides in Owen, Wisconsin. She is a grade school and high school graduate. She is past 65 and on social security. She is a retired nurses aide who enjoys home, horses, flowers, democracy, government business, children, paintings, and and prose poetry. She is a 1935 Audubon Society member, Northern Greenwood, Wisconsin. **Her comments:** I am an amateur. My inspiration is my personality.. 293

Verna U.S.A.

JESUS MORÓN VILLARREAL resides in Houston, Texas. His education includes: Master of Visual Arts, Casa de Cultura Zuazua, N.L. Mexico; cultural promoter (conafe) S.E.P. He is a journalist for Spanish Publications and a painter and photographer. His memberships include: Cultural Arts Council of Houston; founder of the Mexican Academy of Critics and Authors for the Visual Arts. His publications include: **Como Declamar Y Escribir Poesia** published in Houston, Texas, 1992; **Gaceta De Texas** published in Houston, Texas, May 25, 1993; and **Técnica De Pintura Nahua** published in Houston, Texas, 1993. His awards include: **The Tree** (acrylic painting), Chicago, 1973; Best Writer, Zuazua N.L., Sala C.O.N.A.F.E., 1980; 1st Place in Photography, Machtilli Gallery, 1985. **His comments:** Zuazua N.L. Mexico is a nostalgic village full of romantic hills. There I find the best sources of inspiration. The "Orejones" (Oregon's Indians) emigrated from there to settle Oregon State, as the "Carrizos" did in New Mexico. The "Hacienda of San Pedro," actually U.A.N.L.'s Center for Regional Historic Research, is a place full of fantastic legends and surrealism. There I meditate and create the most incredible poems of Hispanic influence and Indian nature that has formed the Mestizo. My wife, Maria F. Marroquin, and my three daughters, Nancy, Rubi, and Xochitl, are my Goddesses of inspiration.. 101

Jesus Morón Villarreal

JO ANN B. VOGEL resides in Manitowoc, Wisconsin. Her education includes: Senior in college at Silver Lake College, major: Business Management, Human Resource Development, Management, and a minor in Psychology. She is a student and farmer. Her interests include: international consulting, reading, traveling, and organizational work. Her memberships include: Wisconsin Women for Agriculture, American Agricultural Women, Business Administration Student Association, Extension Homemakers, Multi-Cultural Club, and Psychology Club. **Her comments:** Poetry is the reflection of our hearts and souls. These words were written for Creativity Class. I feel those of us experiencing life in the 50's, experienced a wonderful happy time in the history of our country. My words expressed the feelings in my heart and soul. The 50's were a time of family and love... 108

Jo Ann B. Vogel

JUDY VOLTZ resides in Covington, Tennessee. She completed 4 years of college at Mississippi State University. She is a mother and loves to write. She is a member of Phi Beta LaBa, Beta Club, Alumni Association, and Student Organization. **Her comments:** My inspiration comes from my heart. I was inspired because of my mother who is also my best friend.. 201

SYBIL (MESSER) WADKINS resides in Hokes Bluff, Alabama. She is a dietary aide at Mountain View Hospital. Her memberships include: Gadsden Songwriters Association; Alabama Songwriters Guild, which the Association is a member -of; and Glencoe Church of Christ. Her publications include: **My Precious Saviour** (a song) published in 1993; **I Love You, Jesus** published in 1992; **In My Small Way,** 1991, and **The Precious Blood of Jesus,** 1993, both published in **Treasured Poems of America. Her comments:** I have always had this depression. I'm trying to turn it around and make it work for me for a change. I enjoy creating something new.. 116

LESLIE ANN WALTER resides in Westland, Michigan. She is twenty years of age and interested in pursuing a career as a commercial artist. She enjoys singing, drawing, and writing. **Her comments: My Shining Light** was written in 1991 and is an expression of my pain of living with a social phobia between my mid to late teens. The poem describes my sense of having felt trapped inside myself and unable to feel free and whole and bring outward the real me. I remember how therapeutically venting my poetry was for me during those difficult years. Today when I read the poem, I think of how I am finally free to shine, and I feel a sense of victory.. 49

Leslie Ann Walter

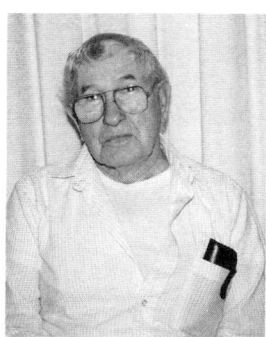

A.J. WALTERS resides in Oneida, Kentucky. Education has been a continuum. He is a high school graduate and attended 1 year of college. **His comments:** Inspiration is imagination in all its richness! In nurturing the seeds of inner thought, it stirs and arouses the mind's potential powers of creative thought . . . and interceding, it brings to light, as it were, those rare jewels of inner beauty, allowing me to capture them in moments of quiet meditation. Theme-wise, most of my writing is inspired by wild nature. Its natural beauty, in all its exquisite variations, must be felt within as a prerequisite to understanding its power for creative imagination, thus allowing me to enter into the spirit that waits within to give expression to my inner feelings!... 283, 290, 305

A.J. Walters

MICHAEL S. WHITWORTH I resides in Benton, Arkansas. His education includes: B.S.E., received from the University of Central Arkansas, social studies—major, Spanish—minor; football and track coaching endorsement. He is a teacher of social studies and Spanish and enjoys family camping trips. He is a member of Alpha-Chi Honor Society. **His comments:** I've always found it easier to express myself through the written word as opposed to the spoken word. My sole inspiration is the people I love so deeply, my wife, Debbie; my parents, Helen and Tex; my children, Michael II, Denise, and Amy; and each and every one of my brothers and sisters. God Bless Them All!... 123

Michael S. Whitworth I

JAMES A. WIGGINS JR. resides in Camden, New Jersey. His education includes: New Bern Senior High School; Associated Business Careers; and The Dorothy Aristone School (Casino school). He is working for the Board of Education in Camden, New Jersey and he wants to become a writer. He is a member of the Afro-American Library of Camden, New Jersey and The Southern Comfort Sports Club. His publications include: **Nite Love** published in August, 1993; **Remember the Confusion** published in September, 1993; and **Daddy's Little Girl** published in the Spring by **The National Library of Poetry,** 1994. He won an award in 1993 for **Nite Love,** which was published in a book and he received a plaque; and Poet of the Month for **Remember the Confusion (Let's Find the Hope),** 1993. **His comments:** I get my inspiration for my poems from family experiences and from talking to people from all walks of life, that have left an impression on my life, whether the circumstances were good or bad... 91, 138

JAN WILL is the pen name for **JANICE E. WILLIAMS,** who resides in Dover, Florida. Her education includes: high school, a little college, and lots of night courses in journalism. She is retired and interested in genealogy. She is a charter member of the Tampa Bay Genealogical Society, and years ago, Supervisor of Teen-age Center. **Her comments:** I'm inspired by sunrises and sunsets. While writing letters, themes pop into my head. Being around people inspires me.. 220

Jan Will

ELIZABETH M. WILLIAMS resides in Palatine, Illinois. She received a B.A. in Journalism from Ohio State University in June of 1985. She is a home-maker, currently working on her first multicultural children's book. Her interests include: reading world literature, writing children's short stories, and writing poetry. She has **Beautiful Black Child** published in this edition of **Poetic Voices of America,** 1994. **Her comments:** I am inspired to write by life's daily adventures as a wife, mother, friend, Bible class student, daughter, sister, and more.. 168

Elizabeth M. Williams

WALLACE JOE WILLIAMS resides in San Antonio, Texas. He has a degree in progress. He is retired from the U.S. Army and a Vietnam Vet. He enjoys writing. **His comments:** I was born and raised on a farm among lots of plants and animals and had a good relationship with nature. The water and air were clean as the: **The Blue Heavenly Sky** on a non-cloudy day. I have always **loved** and have been **nosey** about nature. Nature's ways amaze me as it takes its course as a circle, a cycle and is **perfect** and performs its task to **perfection** in every way. I believe in God. My parents taught me to love my fellow-man, fellow-woman and all of God's creations (nature). To abuse nature just for the sake of abusing is, **wrong because** there is a **reason** for every living thing although we don't understand the **reasons.** I started writing while I was attending school at St. Philip's College in the fall semester of 1989. I had to write essays in two of my subjects which was difficult for me to do after being out of school for over thirty-five years without taking a refresher writing course in anything. The first essay I wrote was in my Psychology class and it was less than twenty-five words. I was **so** ashamed of it until I went to my instructor's office

Wallace Joe Williams

and told her that, "I did and could not write the essay the length you requested." She replied, "turn in what you have because it will help your grade and, **oh yes!** Mr. Williams, you can write essays and don't say what you can't do." I felt like a private in Basic Training getting chewed out (disciplined) by a sergeant. My instructor was right about that state-ment she made because there was an improvement in the next essay I wrote which was in my Phys-ics class; however, the instructor made so many corrections on it **with that red pen,** when he gave it back to me, I thought he was giving me an essay of his **own** for me to read. My physics instruc-tor said, **"Joe!** The **meaning** is clear and understandable. **But!** You need to enroll in a writing or English class as soon as possible." I took my instructor's advice and it was beneficial because I have been writing since then. I wrote about the things I had **deep feeling about.** While I was writing, I did not have in my mind about getting my work published. I wrote for myself and in doing so, writing became a **Dear Friend. Writing! Is** soothing to my heart, my mind, my soul..................... 59, 147

LILLIAN M. WILLIAMSON resides in Tuscaloosa, Alabama. She has an A.A. in Journalism. She is an administrative secretary and a journalist. She enjoys singing and genealogy. Her memberships include: Altrusa, Phi Sigma Alpha, and Tuscaloosa Genealogical Society. She had **The Gumdrop Tree** published in Lufkin, Texas in 1990. Her awards include: Honorable Mention for **Home in the Pineywoods**, 1988; and First Prize for **Valentines**, 1930. **Her comments:** I like to write for children, about nature, homey things, and verses for special occasions. I get inspiration from everyday life.................................. 143

Lillian M. Williamson

STEPHEN WILLIS resides in Denmark, South Carolina. His education includes: B.S. in Biology from Voorchees College; high school diploma from Socostee High School in Myrtle Beach, South Carolina. (Voohees College is in Denmark, South Carolina.) He is an aspiring medical student and a prospective Omega Psi Phi Fraternity member. He is a member of Alpha Kappa Mu National Honor Society, National Dean's List, and a Veteran of Operation Desert Storm/Shield. He had **Escaped Thoughts** published in April of 1988. **His comments:** My poems are usually interpreted by people who haven't been trained in the "art" of literature dissecting, analysis and critique. The morbid, unclear, and seemingly camoflaged thoughts are hidden behind analogous words or phrases meant to convey the complexities of defining life, love, and pain. I call my poetry "labyrinthian literature," but it's only abstract.. 45

Stephen Willis

ROBERT WILSON resides in Opelika, Alabama. He was educated in Lee Co. Public School (12), attended Gunnery School U.S. Navy, and attended Opelika State Technical College for data processing. He is retired from Uniroyal-Goodrich (25 years) and his interests include writing and physical fitness. His memberships include: Nazareth Baptist Church, serving as Sunday School superintendent and church clerk; worshipful of Nazareth Masonic Lodge #927; Assistant District Deputy (State of Alabama); past Commander-in-Chief of Booker & Washington Consistory #115 A.A.S.R.; and past High Priest of the A.E.A.O.N.O.T.M.S. He is married to the former Doris Sims and they have one daughter, Cynthia, and three sons, Kevin (deceased), Peter, and Keith... 300, 324

Robert Wilson

LES WRIGHT is the pen name for **LESLIE WRIGHT** who resides in Elko, Nevada. Her education includes: 1975 graduate of Elko High School, Elko, Nevada; attended Links School of Business and Boise State University in Boise, Idaho. She is an avid photographer, winning numerous awards. She enjoys golfing, playing and coaching softball, and working with children of all age groups. She had **Rest in Peace** published in **Poetic Voices of America** in the Summer of 1993. She is a Delegate on the Sierra Nevada Girl Scout Council, and a board member on the Mountain View Parent Teacher Organization. Her awards include: Best of Show for Color Photographs in the Nevada '86' Photography Contest; won numerous awards for photography, including State Winner in 4-H for photography, in which she received an all expense paid trip to the National 4-H Congress in Chicago, Illinois. **Her comments:** I write about things that touch my heart. I especially enjoy writing things that make other people happy.......................... 173

Les Wright

Nickè-Chantalle Young

NICKÈ-CHANTALLE YOUNG resides in Englewood, Colorado. Her education includes: Colorado Institute of Art, Academy of Floral Design, Araphoe Community College (degree in art therapy). She is a professional dancer who toured with Jimmy Durante, a soloist with a ballet company, a floral designer, and an artist. Her interests include: flowers, music, writing, animals, and watercolor. Her memberships include: Association Guild of Variety Artists, Denver Art Museum, Phi Theta Kappa, National Honor Society, Cherry Hills Community Church, Altar Guild (flowers and design banners for church), and choir. Her publications include: **Rhythms of the Night,** Fall, 1993; **Framework of Time,** Spring, 1994; and **Primal Spring,** Summer, 1994; all published by **Sparrowgrass Poetry Forum, Inc.** She was on the National Dean's List in 1991-1992 and 1992-1993. **Her comments:** Writing, for me, is like tapping a deep well filled with exciting and innovating ideas. Visual, sensual, auditory, kinetic, and intuitive thoughts shape my written words. Picture dipping a bucket into a well and tossing the water like words out before you on the page; there you will find the words arranged like pieces of a puzzle that fit just so. Writing helps to shape my wholeness as it connects me to my inner being. Hopefully, someday these written words will dance off the page and embrace the reader with the same joy and energy I feel.. 376

Norma Zoller

NORMA ZOLLER resides in Seattle, Washington. **Her comments:** I write poems for my own enjoyment. The poem, **The Anniversaries,** was written for my parents.. 55

Index of Authors

Authors are indexed under name or pen name that appears with their poem.

Abella, Vernadette, California	340
Abreu, Yelida E., New York	258
Acklin, Joy, Illinois	325
AcMoody, Connie, Michigan	99
Adamec, T.A., Tennessee	91
Adams, Alice, Michigan	191
Adams, Erika Lynn, Louisiana	110
Adams, Jay Daniel, Alaska	287
Adams, Linda Carol, California	228
Adams, Linda H., Michigan	33
Adams, Nathanael Lynn, Utah	329
Adkison, Melissa, Idaho	345
Adrian, Robert, New York	273
Agas, Felipe L., Michigan	340, 360
Agrava, David, California	174
Agudo, Susan R., California	158
Aguirre, Monica Nunez, Arizona	239
Ahnstrom, Patricia, California	272
Ahrens, Karen E., Missouri	284
Aid, Bobby H., Texas	82
Aitken, Henry D., Washington	223
Alberico, Angie, Pennsylvania	321
Aldman, Olafia, Florida	372
Aldrich, Deborah, Michigan	263
Alghrary, Becky, North Carolina	310
Algosino, Phil, New York	323
Alice, Wisconsin	233
Alicia Jayne, Massachusetts	11, 32, 329
Allan, Lorelei P., Washington	114
Allard, Jenny, California	181
Allen, Jill, North Carolina	51
Allen, Lucy I., Massachusetts	355
Allen, Margaret E., Ontario, Canada	146
Allen, Marjorie, Alabama	89
Allen-Byers, Rosanne, Iowa	44
Allinson, Ken, Pennsylvania	286
Allyson Jade, Michigan	201
Alvarado, Michele J., California	360
Alvis-Richards, Dawn, California	207
Amaker, Willie, South Carolina	62
Amenda, Kathryn, Illinois	220
Amrine, Erica, West Virginia	243
Andersen, Sally E., Alaska	12
Anderson, Alice J, Iowa	68
Anderson, Ann Marie, Kentucky	326
Anderson, Mike, Indiana	101
Anderson, Neva June, Michigan	159
Anderson, Robert J., Minnesota	317
Anderson, S.D., Tennessee	140
Anderson, Wanda, Arizona	71
Andrews, Dona, Utah	96
Anonymous, California	258
April Frances, West Virginia	26
Arbogast, Gail P., Illinois	107
Archie, Lori Ann, California	371
Ard, Sandi, California	159
Areeda, Rich, Jr., Pennsylvania	234
Armstrong, Chad A., California	193
Armstrong, Loren "Ruthless A.D.", Massachusetts	307
Armstrong, Mark, Iowa	347
Arndot, Jeanette, Indiana	277
Arnold, Bill, Florida	281, 284
Asay, Janet M., Idaho	312
Ashby, Brenda, Missouri	85
Atkins, Cynthia M., Oregon	145
Atwater, Joan, Oregon	308
Aughinbaugh, Herb, New Mexico	157
Austin, Theodore H., North Carolina	213
Bacon, Richard Francis, New York	146
Baetge, Stephen James, California	264, 277
Baggett, H.L., Tennessee	91
Bahun, Venita J., Michigan	113
Bailey, Carol, North Carolina	161
Baker, C.L., Arizona	26, 44
Baker, Curtis, Tennessee	316
Baker, Effie, Illinois	106
Baker, Jennette Effie English, Illinois	55
Baker, Paula C., California	328
Baker, Steve, Illinois	106
Baker-Lehne, Susan, California	231
Ballard, Stephanie, Massachusetts	368
Balli, Elena, Texas	206
Bandos, Steve A., Michigan	295
Banker, Laura Ann, Massachusetts	36
Barbara, Indiana	300
Barber, Addison Alfred, III, Michigan	180
Barber, Jennifer, Nevada	268
Barchard, Albert A., Massachusetts	352
Bardach, H., Connecticut	7
Barlic, Evelyn, Illinois	72
Barnes, Alisa, Tennessee	187, 197
Barnes, Lavada H., North Carolina	24
Barnes, Lonnie A., Washington	55, 57, 59
Barnes, Mikki, Missouri	209
Barnhill, Kitrina M., Kentucky	353
Barr, Ernest F., New York	171
Barr, Esther, New Jersey	6
Barr, Heather Lynn, Ohio	375
Barr, Lois, Nevada	120
Barrera, Roberta A., California	182
Barrett, Marion, California	54
Barrón, Jonette, Washington	156
Barten, Nadine M., Wisconsin	101
Bastian, Mary Alice, Idaho	171
Bataller, Allison L., New Jersey	143
Bates, Eileen N., California	293
Bates, Tiffany Jean, West Virginia	292
Batie, Grace H., California	363
Batman, Chris, Virginia	126
Battey, E.C., Jr., Rhode Island	68
Beaing, Iz, Oregon	287
Beaudin, Sue, Ontario, Canada	285
Beck, Jennifer, Massachusetts	329
Becker, Bella, New York	216
Becker, June V., Wisconsin	163
Beckstedt, Jennifer, Ohio	279
Bedard, Julie A., Massachusetts	62
Beebee, Robert R, Nebraska	40
Behr, Andy, California	257
Behrens, Anne K., Washington	130
Beilman, Donald Lee, Michigan	86
Belcher, Julie, Ohio	119
Bell, Florence L., New York	216
Bell, Helen Pope, Georgia	237, 240
Bell, O.J., Kansas	198
Belski, Judy, Illinois	255
Bender, Laurette, Michigan	260
Benjamin, Ann H. Womer, Ohio	11
Benner (Peak), Janette A., Pennsylvania	266
Bennett, Anne Elizabeth, Washington	330
Bennett, Teresa, Missouri	87
Bennett-Lindeman, Victoria, Ohio	170
Benoit, Christopher M, Illinois	246

Benson, Alvin K., Utah	342, 346
Benson, Dortha, Michigan	192
Benton, Bob, Rhode Island	249
Bergman, Eve, Ontario, Canada	75
Bergman-Althouse, Linda S., North Carolina	93
Bergsten, Pamela L., Kansas	232
Bergstrand, Barbara, New York	189, 200
Berkos, Sally Ann, California	6
Bernard, Catherine A., New York	123
Berry-Boyne, Nancy, New Jersey	41
Bersin, Paula L., Illinois	280
Beshear, Frances, Kentucky	332
Best, Jonathon M., Colorado	243
Bettger, M. Marie, Washington	270
BIANCA, Illinois	377
Bice, Jane N., Alabama	144
Bigham-McGinnis, ElizaBeth, Kansas	44
Bilal, Lavern, Michigan	233
Billit, Isay, California	370
Billit, Victoria, California	324
Bing, Bernice L., Alaska	288
Bischoff, Arley M., Washington	49
Bishop, Naky, Utah	20
Bivins, Tanya, Hawaii	348
Black, Angela K., Utah	294
Black, D., Montana	35
Black, Veronica, New York	325
Blackburn, Greg A., Ohio	294
Blair, Tonya S., Illinois	330
Blake, Birgit, Wisconsin	84, 155
Blanding, Loretta C., Maryland	190, 226
Blank, Marge, Pennsylvania	134
Blansit, Tony L., Alabama	238
Bledsoe, Laura L., Mississippi	370
Bleicher, Beth Ann, Pennsylvania	282
Blevins, Michael, Oklahoma	106
Blevins, Shana Fenae, Michigan	314
"Blissful", British Columbia, Canada	102
Blood, Danika, Oregon	238
Blood, Leila, Michigan	316
Blood, Vida E., Michigan	11
Blount, Shirley Outland, North Carolina	122
Blue, Patsy Potter, Texas	137
Bogardus, Agnes K., Illinois	136
Bogart, Larry, Kentucky	173, 203
Boitnott, Jason, Nebraska	53
Bojarski, Nancy Jo, Ohio	377
Boldt, Darleen Ann, Ohio	97
Bomani, Tennessee	145
Bomar, Zelma, Iowa	93
Bonavia, Lisa, Indiana	249
Bond, Rose, Tennessee	258
Bonnaud, May L.M., California	306
Bookhamer, W.E., Pennsylvania	249
Booper, Tennessee	152
Borey, Bruce K., Sr., Michigan	330
Borgardts, Madelyn, Washington	298, 312, 331
Borges, Natalie, California	96
Borgmann, Wendy, Illinois	318
Boro, Michigan	358
Boston, Ruby L., Washington	248
Boulware, Gale, Virginia	32
Bourdeau, Sue, New Hampshire	57
Bourgeois, Jessica Erin, Louisiana	182
Bowen, Angela M., Washington	354
Bowman, Beverly, Ohio	275
Boyd, Dwight Philip, Ohio	69
Boyd, Shannon L., Pennsylvania	355
Boyles, Ann, Tennessee	122
Bradley, Adam Todd, Tennessee	225
Bradley, G.M., Tennessee	196
Bradshaw, Michael, North Carolina	92
Brand, Teresa, Kentucky	193
Brandt, Sandra, Alabama	227
Braun, Lindsey E., Minnesota	363
Bray, Marilyn, Florida	163
Bremen-Humphreys, Heidi, California	59
Brennan, Christina, New Jersey	63
Brennan, Cindy, Ontario, Canada	103
Brennan, Margaret A., New York	36
Bridget, Kansas	377
Brierley, Victoria A., Michigan	368
Brodersen, Lance, California	20
Bromley, Michelle, South Carolina	272
Brooks, Melissa E., New York	85
Brown, Amy D., Illinois	192
Brown, Dorothy I., Washington	180
Brown, James E., Maryland	95
Brown, Janna L., Utah	331
Brown, Joey C., Virginia	129
Brown, Kimberly Ann L., Florida	272
Brown, Patricia Duncan, Michigan	69
Brubaker, Lucille M., Ohio	322
Bruce, Joyce, Kentucky	143
Bruce, Shawna, Ohio	190
Bruns, Mary Jane Reed Welch, New Mexico	38
Bryan, Michelle, Texas	308
Bryant, Pat Farquar, Nevada	232
Buchmiller, Stanley F., Washington	241, 278
Buckner, Marnie, Alberta, Canada	344
Buddee, Mississippi	293
Buerkle, MaryLee, Idaho	174
Buffum, Carroll R., Sr., Vermont	208
Bugosh, Helen M., Pennsylvania	74
Bullock, Patricia, Michigan	300
Bullock, Sandra, Tennessee	110
Bulmahn, Sara, Indiana	15
Bundridge, Shirley, Missouri	224
Bunker, Terri, North Carolina	271
Burgin, M. Lynn, Tennessee	18
Burnett, Judith Kay, Indiana	166
Burnett, Karen E., Kansas	290
Burns, Inez E., Ohio	61
Burry, Dion R., Labrador, Canada	239, 247
Burton, Katherine, Indiana	306
Busch, Greta, California	372
Bush, Mary F., South Carolina	245
Butler, Byford "Doc", Illinois	135
Butts, Elizabeth, Louisiana	377
Byers, Delilah J. Clem, Michigan	358
Byrn, Eunice Kirby, Kentucky	232
Byrnes, Eva .M. (Golden), Tennessee	77
Cadeau, Robert, Michigan	78
Calltharp, Bret, Kansas	315
Cameron, Carol, Washington	234
Cameron, Judith, Australia	6
"Camia", California	60
Campafiore, Anthony Liberato, Kentucky	156
Campbell, Christopher T., Oklahoma	136
Campbell, Jeff, Washington	205
Campbell, Jennifer E., New York	100
Campbell, Patrick Duke, California	357, 359
Campbell, Suzanne R., Michigan	314
Cannis, Gretchen, Michigan	194
Caoili, Bert, Washington	215
Caporusso, Carolyn Ann, New Jersey	115
Cardwell, Joanne, Indiana	344
Caren, Joel, Florida	297
Carlisle, Kaci Diane, California	127
Carlon, Paul B. W., Illinois	195
Carlson, Jody, Washington	63
Carole Ann, Tennessee	145
Carpenter, Arlene (Abate), New Jersey	200
Carpenter, Candace, Michigan	368
Carpenter, Christopher Manoli, New Mexico	18
Carpenter, Kathleen, Mississippi	281

Carrera, Chris, Oklahoma	40
Carrick, Jennifer, New York	62
Carrithers, Suzanna, Indiana	354
Carrozza, Anna, Tennessee	352, 372
Carter, Edwin T., Oklahoma	86
Carter, John A., Sr., Maryland	326
Carter, Ruby Lee, (Sally), Georgia	279
Caruso, Ellie, Florida	230
Carver, Helen J., California	254
Carver, Pamela, Louisiana	213
Casey, Claire Marie, Iowa	159
Cash, Michelle R., Florida	285
Caskey, Gwendolyn A., Washington	302
Cavanaugh, Cynthia Ann, Pennsylvania	222
Cecil, S.S., Kentucky	135
Chaconas, Brandie G., Washington	131
Chambliss, Sarah G., Mississippi	277
Champlin, Alice, Tennessee	12
Chang, Mabel M.H., Hawaii	360
Charles, Jada D., Wisconsin	40
Charles, Leah Jeannine, Arizona	303
Chase, Edith, Michigan	231
Chase, Julie L., Pennsylvania	140
Chase, Karen, Indiana	103
Chase, Michele Alexandria, Ontario, Canada	381
Chasmont, Constance, New Jersey	307
Chaussée, Sandi, Wisconsin	134
Chernobieff, Mishell, Idaho	150
Cheslock, Conrad D., New Jersey	25
Chicoine, Frances E., Nebraska	221
Childress, Ellen F., Georgia	203, 213
Chrisman, Darlene, Tennessee	219
Christman, Alicia, Tennessee	185
Christophersen, Dale, Minnesota	320
Ciosáin, Maire Ni, Massachusetts	221
Cisney, Vern, Illinois	342
Clark, D. Keith, Illinois	30
Clark, James Robert, Tennessee	145
Clark, Jason, Michigan	78
Clark, Rashaad C., (RC), Nebraska	351
Clark, Richard, Texas	34
Clark, Zelma C., Michigan	111
Clarke, Douglas Barrett, Kansas	64
Clarke, Michael James, Michigan	34
Clarkson, Anc, South Carolina	313
Clay, Charlena R., California	235
Cliff, Leanne Marie, Illinois	55
Clinger, Jacqueline, Florida	376
Cloretta Rose, Michigan	225
Code, Betsey E., Oklahoma	315
Coffey, Stephen D., Massachusetts	161
Cohen, David, California	114
Cole, Carrie, Michigan	108
Cole, Kathryn Hendrickson, New Jersey	66
Cole, William J., New Jersey	260
Colella, Nadia Mena, Ontario, Canada	54
Colley, Susan, Michigan	361
Colombo, Blanche Mary, Michigan	107
Combs, Carla, West Virginia	279
Combs, Tracy, Kentucky	43
Comer, Roberta, Tennessee	240
Conaway, Cheryl, Texas	61
Conley, Michael Louis, Arizona	368
Conro, Matt, Illinois	150
Consolazio, Elizabeth, New York	362
Consolino, Nicholas C., Michigan	132
Conzelmann, Eleanor L., California	314
Coochyouma, Joy, Arizona	321
Coombs, Carrie A., Florida	142
Cooper, Donna E., Michigan	264, 270
Cooper, Sylvia, Michigan	126
Copeland, Yevon, Tennessee	245
Corby, Erik, New Jersey	273
Corder, Sheri L., South Dakota	307
Cordova, Michela, New Mexico	239
Coressel, Tracy L., Ohio	260
Cornell, Sarah M., Michigan	221
Cornish, Eunice, Michigan	173
Cornwall, Marketa, Idaho	378
Cory, Linda Marlene, Illinois	59, 62
"COSMOSE" 1993 M.E.R, Indiana	303
Costa, John A., Rhode Island	308
Costello, Fern, Washington	160
Costley, Edward S., Maryland	27
Cottrell, Loretta, New York	183
Cover, Berniece, Michigan	7
Cowan, Amanda, North Carolina	217
Coward, Vetha Marie, New York	211
Cowden, Michelle L., Pennsylvania	297
Cowley, Heather M., California	83
Cox, Dorothy A., Indiana	56
Cox, Florence A., Florida	114
Cox, Mildred, Ohio	146
Cox, Valerie Johnson, Washington	357
Crafton, Frances, Tennessee	69
Crampton, Teri Anna, Washington	262
Crane, Sheila L., California	345
Cremer, Becky, Michigan	280
Crider, Ryan, Missouri	31
Crist, Richard Steven, California	104
Crobaugh, Emma, Florida	9
Croman, Ruth M., Oklahoma	306
Cronch, Angela, Kentucky	127, 129, 148, 165
Cronin, Jeffrey E., Louisiana	82
Crowe, Deana C., Ohio	140
Cruz, Michael David, Tennessee	227
Cuevas, Gloria, Philippines	75
Culver, Ruth, New Jersey	292
Curran, Dorothea T., California	117
Curtis, Brenda, Tennessee	138
Cushman, Fred B., Florida	208
Cutting, Shelly, New Hampshire	24
Cvetic, Elizabeth I., Oregon	11
Cypher, Lorraine, California	166
Czajkowski, Annette R., California	119
Czuchajowski, Leszek, Idaho	11, 125, 129
Dahlke, Caroline Suzanne, California	248
Dale, Stewart, North Carolina	140
Dalton, Belinda A., Pennsylvania	210
Dame, Leslie L., Kentucky	238
Damewood, Stella, Oregon	145
Damon, Jim California	359
Daniel, Carrie Gobar, Kansas	81
Daniel, Cheryl E., Tennessee	56
Daniel, Marie E., Ms., Arizona	355
D'Asaro, Jessica, New York	268
Daugherty, Ellen F., Arkansas	228
Daugherty, Sarah, Nebraska	56
Davidoff, Brooke, California	357
Davidson, Elizabeth, Arizona	6
Davidson, Hilda M. Rowe, Ohio	222
Davis, Charlotte Anne, Ontario, Canada	256
Davis, Dee, Kentucky	227
Davis, DuRaāe V., Iowa	240
Davis, Ed, Tennessee	119
Davis, M. Cathy, Tennessee	337
Davis, Rachel, Michigan	115
Davis, Richard Freedom, West Virginia	100, 175
Davisson, Kevin Michael, Illinois	54
Dawson, Barbara Nell Smith, Washington	353
Deanes, Armether Swift, Mississippi	261
DeAntonio, Dorothy A., New Jersey	192
DeBock, LeAnn Dawn, Texas	285
DeBoer, Sharon E., Ontario, Canada	181
deBonneville, Franchesca, California	141
DeChirico, Michael, Tennessee	187

Dees, Lori, Mississippi	294
DeHass, Melvin, Oklahoma	197
Dehnert, Jerome, Florida	309
Delaney, Billy L., Florida	265
Delaney, Christina M., Indiana	142
DeLay, Harriet, Nebraska	20
DeMaria, Nancy, N 9/93, New Hampshire	66
DePaulis, Todd, Michigan	96
DePola, Steve, New York	263
Desirée Dawn, Oklahoma	362
de Vaz, Rebecca, Florida	41
Devendorf, Louise, Michigan	88
Devenport, Isabell T., Illinois	236
DeVincent, June, Florida	78
DeVine, Conal Royal, Texas	188
Dewey, Celeste "CD", Colorado	313
DeWitt, Ronald W., Kansas	288
DeWitt, Suzanne, Washington 12, 37, 46, 224, 227,	245
DeWitte, Denelda, Indiana	278
DeZuani, Barbara, Tennessee	32
Dharampaul, Subhendra Santoshan, Alberta, Canada	226
Dial, Billye, Tennessee	218
Dial, LaDonna, Georgia	207
Diane, Iowa	267
Diaz, Nicolas, California	17
Diaz-Landa, Pedro, Florida	146
Dick, Cindy A., Louisiana	180
Dickens, Paige, North Carolina	41
Diebel, Floyd, California	352
Dikeman, Ruth J., Illinois	268
Dillon, Angela, Michigan	292
Dillon, Haley, Alabama 137,	165
Dimock, Laurie, Ohio	36
DiPietrantonio, Pauline, Florida	90
Di Renzo, Maria, Ontario, Canada	293
Dixon, Peggy, Tennessee	309
DML, Michigan	373
Doane, Ave M., Alabama	87
Dobrzycki, Walter F., Maryland 13, 102, 113, 125,	135
Dobson, Randal E., Georgia	103
Dockter, Teresa, Alabama	273
Dockweiler, Sharon, New York	295
Dodson, Trina, Michigan 323,	330
Domgaard, Nancy, Nevada	71
Douglas, Donna Mae, Alaska	113
Douville, Ilana, Michigan	228
Dove, Angela, Missouri	23
Downey, Judy Ann Williams, Colorado 40,	221
Downey, Lana, Oregon	345
D.Q.M., Illinois	232
Dreadin, Melissa M., Alaska	138
Dreamer, Louisiana	377
Drew, Robert W., Michigan	342
DuBois, Barbara R., New Mexico	100
DuBois, Shirley, California 89,	157
Dudek, Patricia, Michigan	133
Duffy, Mary A., New Jersey	263
Duncan, Estle D., Indiana	194
Dunlap, B.G., Michigan	230
Dunn, Mary, Colorado	141
Dunnigan, Danielle Nicole, District of Columbia	47
Dunwoody, Isabel, California	101
Duong, Theresa Duyên, Mississippi	150
Dure, Regina, Indiana	350
Durham, Mary, Illinois	122
Durr, Marie Placide, New York	172
Dyer, Travis Byron, Mississippi	253
Easley, Annie Louise, Georgia	221
Eason, Benita, Maryland	147
Eaton, Ercel, Ohio	279
Eberhardt, Doris, Ohio	121
Eckerle, Philip A., Michigan	324
Edens, Betty L, Tennessee	115
Edwards, Allene Coley, Tennessee	215
Edwards, Amanda, Ohio	310
Edwards, Kathleen M., Pennsylvania	345
Ehrke, Nina, New Jersey	308
Eisenlord, Alyson, Washington	361
Eisman, Audrey, Pennsylvania	314
Elayn, Heather, Alabama	209
Elder, Nicole L., Washington	335
Eldredge, Kevin, Indiana	317
Elizabeth, Idaho	128
Ellis, Deborah K., Virginia	61
Ellis, J., Georgia	65
El-Tawansy, Ursula Egger, California	136
Elting, Joan M., Colorado	309
Emberton, J.M., Kentucky	188
Emerson, Marlene, Tennessee	96
Engram, Carmen M., Mississippi	144
Ensign, LeAnne Fisher, California	26
Erickson, Amanda R., Wisconsin	256
Esfehani, Behnaz, California	366
Ethridge, Jeani, Illinois	378
Eversole, Jan, California	362
Ewing, Helen Ruth, California	322
F., Cicely, Texas	37
Fairfield, Austin, Pennsylvania	10
Falbo, Ida M., Pennsylvania	310
Farmer, Penny, Florida	316
Farnworth, Jeanne Prescott, Idaho	373
Farrar, Kenneth Robert C., Minnesota	296
Felgner, Monica M., Ohio	179
Felty, Laura E., Tennessee	12
Fennell, Mark, Texas 34, 202, 218,	219
Fenstermaker, Betty Brobst, Pennsylvania	112
Ferg, Dorothy, Illinois	191
Fernandez, Juan R., California	44
Fernandez, Kristy J, Michigan	256
Fernando, Marvin, Arizona	292
Feutz, Mary Beth, Georgia	58
Field, Amanda R., Alabama	83
Field, George Perry, Indiana	183
Figueroa, Katie, Oregon	46
Fike, Frances B., Tennessee	107
Filotei, Angela, Pennsylvania	361
Fink, Leopoldine, Ontario, Canada	224
Fisher, Tammy Jo, Michigan	362
Flathman, Margaret, Nebraska	252
Fletcher, Henry C., Ohio	285
Fletcher, Sherri, West Virginia	133
Flowers, Frances Suggs, Tennessee	195
Flowers, Rebecca Sue, Michigan	122
Floyd, Denelle, Louisiana	10
Foecke, Keith, Mississippi	201
Foldvik, Norman James, Washington	205
Folmar, Virginia J., West Virginia 282, 303,	307
Ford, Bill, South Carolina	38
Ford, Lola G., West Virginia	15
Ford, William R. Jr., Michigan	30
Fossett, Adam L., Georgia	365
Foster, Yvonne, New Jersey	176
Fox, Diane Karen, Virginia	236
Fox, Roni, California	116
Fox, Sarah Michelle, California	309
Frakes, Jennie, Kentucky	323
Frampus, Stephanie L., New Jersey	64
Franks, Herb, Jr., Ohio	209
Franks, Linda Lee, Louisiana	340
Fraser, Helen, California	257
Frazier, M.L.A., Michigan	202
Frederick, Cheryl, Minnesota	267
Freel, James, Massachusetts	345

Frenette, Lorraine, Maine	24
Fricke, Bill, Pennsylvania	302
Frieden, B.J., Illinois	201, 204, 209
Frigo, Sandra L., Tennessee	107
Frisbie, Marie A., California	314, 315
Frisch, Nadine L., Michigan	95
Fritzius, Alison, Mississippi	305
Frog - Jeff, California	50
Frost, S. E., Michigan	113
Fryman, Amber Reneé, Texas	318
Fuller, Nancy Belle, California	67
Fuqua, Cliffidean R., Alabama	61
Gaglio, Linda, Michigan	92
Galasso, Priscilla, Illinois	77
Gallagher, Kelly, New Jersey	174
Gamache, Lola, North Carolina	218
Gamble, Jōvon M., Connecticut	362
Gange, Clara, M., Mrs., Washington	266
Garcia, Jammie Marie, Hawaii	71
Garcia, Lili, Texas	126
Garrick, Antoinette, Louisiana	301
Garrison, Margaret E., Colorado	341
Gates, Pattie Denise, Mississippi	167
gatherdi, Illinois	42
Gearhart, Sandy L., Kentucky	288
Geddes, Derek, New Hampshire	6
Gee, Marcy, Arizona	331
Gee, Pam, Wyoming	250
Gehr, Colleen A., Pennsylvania	45
Georgi, Mandy, Illinois	110
Gerardi, Mae R., Massachusetts	135
Gerhardt, "Michigan" George, Oregon	245
Geris, Brenda, Minnesota	81
Gerstmann, Paula, Washington	296
Gessner, Jennifer, Washington	243
Getz, Lori L., Illinois	211
Getz, Melissa C., Illinois	35
Gibbs, Patricia Gallagher, Michigan	268
Gibson, Leiane N., West Virginia	48
Gibson, Lisa-Jai, Virginia	25
Gielow, Matthew E., Illinois	50
Giese, Gerald E., Michigan	35
Gifford, Kimberly J., Washington	228
Giles, Dawn, Wisconsin	110
Gilliland, Coleen M., Florida	143
Gilliland, Brian, Missouri	93
Gilson, Thomas James, Illinois	239
Givens, Edmond W., California	194
Glaz, Emilia A., Florida	97
Glinski, Frank Zdzislaw, New Jersey	344
Glisson, Gary W., Kentucky	346
Goerne, Rob, Illinois	233
Goetz, Rachel, Colorado	23
Gohm, Kelly, Delaware	216
Goldner, Richard Lee, California	206, 356
Gonsalves, Joseph Anthony, California	73
Gonzales, Jessica Erlynn, California	218
Good, Debora Jean, Indiana	237
Good, Eveline T., Washington	353
Gooding, Karyl J., Washington	108
Goodridge, Eric V., Massachusetts	159
Gootee, Michael, Indiana	158
Gordon, Beth A., Illinois	162
Gordon, Charmaine A., Ohio	363
Gordon, Erik, Florida	359
Gordon, Ray, Massachusetts	48
Gossage, Amanda Lee, Illinois	251
Gourlay, Carol, Michigan	252
Gousie, Christine, Massachusetts	17
Graham, Wilda, Tennessee	166
Granberry, Jane Elliot, California	51
Granieri, Celeste Kusnell, New Jersey	57
Grant, Gene, California	193
Graver, Mark, Maryland	119
Gray, Kathleen (Lee), Tennessee	33
Gray, LeeAnn, Michigan	189
Gray, Lois, Washington	52
Green, Judy R., California	40
Green, Sheila, Tennessee	137
Green, Shirley Ann, Michigan	159
Green, Willie Rose, Tennessee	166
Greenlaw, Ruby A., New Brunswick, Canada	287
Greenleaf, Constance, New York	8
Greenwood, Bertha Woods, Pennsylvania	245
Greer, Sadie, Pennsylvania	379
Gregory, Eleanor Lorraine, Ohio	351
Gribble, Monica L., Tennessee	347
Griffin, Carolyn, Wyoming	312
Griffin, Izena, Tennessee	98
Griffin, Richard B., Arizona	188
Grimes, Tracey Lynn, Maryland	275
Gromek, Sheri, Michigan	208
Grove, John Pendleton, IV, Virginia	116
Grover, Peggy, Washington	72
Guerrero, Vicky, California	153
Gunderman, Rachel R., Pennsylvania	11
Gunnerson, Marsha (McGillis), New York	70
Guy, T. Mitchell, Arizona	52
Guyer, Barbara, Pennsylvania	39
Hacker, John, Jr., California	211
Haddock, Melany L, Oregon	112
Haffener, Selma, Kansas	193
Haines, Sarah, Connecticut	118
Hakim, Teresa, Michigan	322
Halash, Amanda Marie, Michigan	211
Haley, Janet S., Michigan	243
Haley, Uta, Ontario, Canada	251
Hall, Frances, Idaho	7
Hall, Michele Marie, New York	311
Halliburton, Larry D., Kentucky	354
Hallissey, Julie, Mrs., Washington	23, 339
Halpin, Doris, New York	331
Haltermann, Rick, Colorado	14
Hamilton, John W., Oklahoma	83
Hamm, L.E., Kentucky	370
Hammer, Diana L., Ohio	286
Hampton, Evelyn, Pennsylvania	242
Hampton, Susan, Alaska	212
Hamric, Ramona E., West Virginia	78
Hamry, Barbara, Washington	97
Han, Annie, Washington	54
Handley, Nell, Kentucky	71
Hansen, Merle C., California	160
Hanson, Cherie Brigham, New Mexico	288
Hanson, Delores D., California	269
Hanstedt, Constance, California	37
Hardy, Leisha, Texas	147
Hardy, Lori Rae, Nevada	372
Harper, Angie K., Iowa	242
Harper, William H., Illinois	97
Harps, Lori, Kentucky	227
Harrell, André J., Louisiana	75
Harris, Bridget L., California	379
Harris, Derrick, North Carolina	374
Harrison, Lindsay Lee, Illinois	366
Harrison, Scott C., Washington	298
Harry, Lisa, West Virginia	204
Harvey, Aimee Denise, Indiana	333
Hasan, Laurie, Florida	299
Hassig, Claire, California	88
Hatcher, Vincent E., Tennessee	86
Hawkes, Adam, Washington	371
Hayes, Carol, Alabama	190
Hayes, Casey, Texas	359
Hayes, Daniel J., Ohio	277
Haynes, Courtney Lynn, Louisiana	171

Heard, LeRoy, Jr., Michigan	202
Heard, Sparkle Lynette, Michigan	340
Hearn, Adrienne, New Jersey	26
Heck, Sonya M., Iowa	311
Hedglen, Dean, Michigan	49
Heerman, William, Colorado	137
Heinle, Coletta, Colorado	84
Heinle, Mistie, Colorado	108
Heinzman, Shelley Ayn, Washington	72
Henderson, Gradys Scott, New York	98
Henderson, Linda L., Oklahoma	112
Henderson, Shaun, Florida	272
Hendricks, Kristine M., California	316
Hendrickson, Debrah, North Carolina	52
Heng, Soka, Washington	188
Henkel, Rick, Nebraska	90
Henley, Faye, Tennessee	53
Herbert, Maria E., South Dakota	132
Hess, Anne, Pennsylvania	134
Hetfleisch, Cathy, Illinois	248
Hicks, John T, Texas	376
Hicks, Mary "Emily", Pennsylvania	212
Hildeman, Janell, Washington	224
Hilderbrand, Gilbert L., New York	310
Hill, Darleen I., Illinois	52
Hill, Marcy L., Ohio	185
Hillhouse, Courtney, Pennsylvania	326
Hillinger, Edith Gabriele, California	10
Hincken, Amelia, California	375
Hindes, Jolene, Alberta, Canada	55
Hines, Briana, Ohio	200
Hixson, Joyce, Tennessee	223
Hodges, Casie Anne, Georgia	335
Hodges, Gloria, Missouri	183
Hoffman, Anna Mae, California	13, 61
Hogue, Roma, Michigan	230
Holguin, Charlene, California	298
Holl, Jenny, Wisconsin	246
Holland, Jason A., Michigan	158
Holland, Joyce, Florida	82
Holland, W. Carl, California	83, 126
Holleman, S. Perry, North Carolina	256
Holt, Connie, Tennessee	252
Holt, Stacey R., Texas	346
Hooks, Benjamin David, Arizona	377
Hoover, Helene A., Indiana	67
Horaz, Bruce, Illinois	171, 220
Horning, F.A., Indiana	237
Horton, Debra L., California	81
Hostetler, Noreen A., Indiana	296
Houle, Kristy L., Alabama	120
Houseman, Kimberly Dawn, Missouri	323
Houston, Kevin J., Alabama	38
Houston, Linda, Massachusetts	120
Howard, Ken, Georgia	215
Howe, Sarah, Florida	155
Hoyle, Karin, Massachusetts	20
Hubbart, Albert, Florida	116
Hughes, Jane E., California	255
Hughes, Lindey M., Mississippi	342
Hulse, Myra L., Tennessee	348
Hunley, Marie, Tennessee	30
Hunsher, Lance Rafael, New Jersey	182
Hunt, Ivan Holt, Utah	153
Hunter, Margaret Ethelyn, Michigan	123
Hutchinson, Gwen, Kentucky	264
Hutchinson, Jeanette, Oregon	82
Hutchison, Melissa, Florida	299
Hyatt, Minnie G., Indiana	251
Hymn, Rayne, Colorado	363
Hyung, O.J., Michigan	182
Ibe, Ndukaku, California	212
Ickes, Karl, Washington	163
Igrisan, Angela, Michigan	16
ILLDC, Illinois	305
Imperato, D. Thomas, Pennsylvania	301
Isican, Seny, California	50, 206, 211
Jackson, Eileen, California	339
Jacobs, Paula .D., Washington	213
Jacobsen, Kimberly, California	265
Jacobson, Alice, Arizona	52
Jacobson, Allan, South Dakota	39
Jacobson, L., South Dakota	242
Jacqueline, Pennsylvania	281
James, Erin, California	163
James, Mitchell B., Ohio	112, 115
James, Nicole, Mississippi	278
Janjac, Michael S., Ontario, Canada	116
Jannise, Arizona	305
Janse, Adon J., California	164
Jarrell, Jonathon (Stone), Michigan	233
Jaryno, John Henry, New Jersey	159
Jason E., Texas	357
Jay, Ash, Louisiana	257
J.C., California	57
JeanAnn, Michigan	189
Jeleniewski, Edward, Florida	312
Jenkins, Brent, Minnesota	156
Jenkins, Mary Alice Badeau, Mississippi	38, 60, 68, 75, 77, 165
Jenks, Lynn, Michigan	144
Jennifer (JenniSu), Texas	108
Jensen, John R., Utah	268
Jerjiss, Alen, California	320
Jeske, Billie, Montana	290
J. Frederick, Michigan	76
Jividen, Barbara Brickey, Ohio	138, 168, 198
Jo Ann, Ohio	143
Jocson, Karen E., Washington	250, 317
Joetta Lee, Missouri	103
Johansen, George L., New York	368
Johnson, Edwin, Michigan	241
Johnson, Eldora, Illinois	112
Johnson, Lawrence A., Wisconsin	22
Johnson, Lesly Plyler, Texas	270
Johnson, Mark Allen, New Mexico	326
Johnson, Marlene N., North Carolina	189
Johnson, Mary Hulon, Alabama	70
Johnson, Robert W., Utah	197
Johnson, Sophia deLayne, Tennessee	195
Johnson-Bonson, Elizabeth R., Tennessee	372
Johnston-S., Tina M., Illinois	284
Jointer, Pamela M., Alabama	300
Jones, Alf, Alberta, Canada	168
Jones, Allen, Michigan	71
Jones, April R., Maryland	294
Jones, A. Rosita, Tennessee	166
Jones, Barbara, New York	346
Jones, Cheri L., Kentucky	353
Jones, David, Oklahoma	144
Jones, Musataye (Misty), Michigan	235
Jones, Nicole, Michigan	177
Jones, Orovelia L., Washington	228
Jones, Tom, Illinois	44
Jontz, Clyde W., Iowa	130
Jordan, Neil R., Massachusetts	284
Jordan, Zema L., Ph.D., Michigan	85
Joseph, Latanya M., Louisiana	266
Jungenberg, Vincent F., Ohio	346
Kaczor, Colleen, Michigan	302
Kanavy, James, Illinois	378
Kanbi, Maame, Tennessee	143
Kane, Betsy, Wisconsin	147
Kane, Elisabeth, Wisconsin	128
Kane, Violet Hilderbrand, New York	324
Karlsen, Karen S., New York	104

Katz, Alan B., New York	14
Kauffman, Bertha, Indiana	133
Kaur, Kanwaljit, Alberta, Canada	287
Kayser, Lance, California	320
Kearney, Jamie Reuben, Colorado	26
Keeling, J., Texas	251
Keene, Sharon Lee, California	198
Kellum-Jackson, Charlene, Pennsylvania	336
Kelly, Patrick Joseph, Pennsylvania	18
Kelly, Royal A., Iowa	222
Kelly, Tootsie, Washington	105
Kemp, Suzanne H., "Suzan", New York	295
Kennelly, Mary A., Rhode Island	10
Keogh, Robert, Massachusetts	290
Kerlee, Nancy, Washington	84
Kerner, Thomas J, Wisconsin	235
Ketchum, Karla M., California	78
Kettler, Heidi, New Jersey	307
Key, Sarah, California	266
Kiely, Dan R., Florida	42
Kim, James S., Washington	369
Kim, Yoon Sun, California	164
Kimo, Michigan	348
King, Alwyn Hallowes, North Carolina	117
King, Beverly H., Iowa	149
King, Gerald, Tennessee	125
King, Judith, California	158
King, Paul E, Ohio	152
Kingery, Barry Lynn, California	242
Kingsley, Roy, Ontario, Canada	14
Kirkman, Carol O'Lea, Washington	129
Kirschenmann, Clarissa, Washington	308
Kiser, Faye, North Carolina	246
Kissinger, Michelle, New Jersey	325
Kistler, Colleen D., Ohio	261
Klinck, Kristin, Nebraska	60
Kling, Tracy L., Pennsylvania	303
Kobberod, Chris, Washington	381
Koch, Leta, Texas	357
Koehner, Gary L., Illinois	263
Koger, Heidi, North Carolina	287
Kollmeyer, Kim, California	33
Kolosky, Jeremy, Minnesota	54
Konarski, Joy Ann, New Jersey	51, 66
Konersmann, Amanda, Mississippi	201
Konrath, Deanna, Indiana	175
Konyha, Helen Lager, Washington	248, 277
Kostadinka, Ohio	99
Kowalski, Gina M., Michigan	176
Kravec, Maureen, New York	11
Krohn, Michael, Ohio	245
Krueger, Arlene D., Wisconsin	201
Krumenacker, Kathleen J., West Virginia	65
Krynicki, Adam T., Pennsylvania	218
Krynicki, Jill, Wisconsin	47
Kubulan, Vivien, Texas	200
Kuenzli, Tami Jo, California	64
Kuhia, Glenn Kealoha, Hawaii	275
Kurunwune, Anne, Michigan	31
LaChapelle, Lawrence V., Minnesota	208, 218
Lacosta, Rachel Ramirez, New Jersey	256
LaCroix, C.V., Saskatchewan, Canada	262
Lacy, Deborah, Mississippi	28
Laflamme, Ronnie G., Maine	282, 283
LaHatt, Lorilee, Washington	47
Lamb, Mavis, Tennessee	106
Lamberg, Shirley, Michigan	327
Lambertus, Jessica, South Dakota	142
Land, Carol D., Tennessee	48
Lande, Shelley S., Iowa	149
Landgraf, John, Illinois	242, 278
Lane, Randy "R.J.", California	159
Langdon, Rick, Pennsylvania	340
Langer, Frank A., West Virginia	18
Lanham, June Marie, Ohio	150
Largent, Sheryl Lynn, Colorado	361
Larke, Donna Babin, Louisiana	95
Larson, Autumn, Wisconsin	168
Laue, Timber, Montana	216
Laughlin, Dale G., Idaho	56
Laura, California	332
Lauze, Dina J., California	219
Lawrence, Gertrude, Kentucky	65
Lazarus, Steven, Washington	63
Leadens, Deborah K., Minnesota	162
Lebron, Yolanda, Illinois	104
Lee, Chelsea, Illinois	318
Lee, Jimmy, Texas	213
Lee, Pamela Louise, California	336
Leedy, Janeen, Tennessee	67
LeFebre, Rebecca Ann, Colorado	101
Leis, Traci, Wisconsin	235
leMieux, Mykle, Ontario, Canada	134
LeMoine, Blanche, Tennessee	123
Lenger, Dave, Jr., Washington	238
Lennon, Jeanette, Michigan	295
Lenseigne, Kert B., Washington	129
Leo, Wisconsin	342
Leonard, Scott Owen, Ohio	12
Leppo, William C., Pennsylvania	333
Lerner, Jean M.S., Illinois	164
Le Rose, Tisha C., California	39
Leroux, Sylvie, Ontario, Canada	338
Lesak, Lorelei, Illinois	344
Lescheid, Elizabeth A., British Columbia, Canada	368
Lesesne, Todd, Pennsylvania	290
LeSieur, Sharon, Mississippi	127
Letelier, Jorge, New York	76, 172, 181, 338
Levy, Sarah Kate, New York	19
Lewelling, Kimberly, Tennessee	325
Lewis, Brenda S., Tennessee	100
Lewis, Carol L., Colorado	160
Lewis, Chris, Georgia	140
Lewis, Denise M., Tennessee	73
Lewis, Emanuel, Michigan	62
Lewis, Gwendolyn L., Michigan	358
Lewis, Misty, Kentucky	115
Lewis, Tanya M., Mississippi	337
Licci, Josephine A., New York	363
Light, Kerry Kathleen, Michigan	28
Lightcap, Laurie, Georgia	223
Lim, T., Ohio	325
Lindsley, Mary F., California	258
Linnard, Christine (Christal), Alberta, Canada	253
Linton, Maureen F., Pennsylvania	205
Lippman, William J., Colorado	235
Liska, Karen Ruth, Michigan	93
Little, Steven I., Ontario, Canada	181
Lockhart, Zenovia D., Indiana	315
Loepp, Lisa, Pennsylvania	296
Loft, Mary A., Tennessee	310
Loftis, Annette, Alabama	236
Logan, Cameron B., Michigan	146
Lohr, Linda Jean, West Virginia	162
Long, Darcy Erin-Marie, California	379
Long, E. Tisa, Kansas	86, 165
Long, Helen D., South Dakota	182
Long, Ivy, Idaho	273
Long, J.A., California	251
Long, Kathryn "K-T", Ohio	155
Long, Lori Ann, Ohio	21
Lopez, Blanca Nava, Peru	380
Lord, Merrylee, Washington	159
Loretta Raye, Indiana	251
Lorring, H. T., California	149
Loveless, Wayne E., California	305

Loven, Lisa K., Virginia	263
Loving-Starks, Delores A., Illinois	345
Lowe, Linda S., California	66
Loyola, Raquel, New Jersey	365
Lubarsky, Michael A., Indiana	358
Lucas, Franz, Michigan	131
Lucci, Sally Cabaret, Florida	275, 305, 309, 328
Luckey, P.B., Tennessee	51
Luebbers, Dawn, Iowa	89
Luft, Kathlena, Alabama	35
Lumley, Darci Horrell, Pennsylvania	250
Lusty, Cindy Pennington, Missouri	36
Luttrell, Amy L., Colorado	47
Lux, Janet, Iowa	48
Lyda, Michigan	204
Lyell, Sharon Nell (Orahood), Tennessee	291
Lyons, Leslie Eve, Indiana	320
Lyons, Vicky Lynn, Alaska	370
M·2·EZY/Albert Nelson, New York	369
M. Elizabeth, Massachusetts	40
M. Shirley, Virginia	220, 231
Mack, Catherine Kossuth, West Virginia	380
Mack, Sharon Grove, Washington	318
Mackovski, Danica, Michigan	46
Madariaga, Anne, California	95
Maddox, E. "Shadow", R.A., Virginia	254
Madlock, Regina R., Nebraska	151
Mae, Tennessee	318
Maglaris, Bettye, Pennsylvania	212
Magpoc, Halle H., Ohio	91
Magulick, T.J., Virginia	43
Mai, Marie, California	7
Maier, Albert M., Tennessee	156
Mailliard, Amy Elizabeth, California	271
Mak, Ruth, California	230
Maleski, Stephen, Vermont	204
MALKAH, California	148
Mankin, Kirby, Pennsylvania	284
Mannon, Betty A., Tennessee	68, 69, 170
Manuel, Charlie F., North Carolina	357
Manwarring, Melvin, Texas	95
Mari, Wyoming	250
Markoska, Mirjana Mimi, Illinois	325
marks, michael scott, Georgia	114
Marquette, Joanne, Michigan	188
Marr, Linda, Alberta, Canada	298, 302, 306
Marshall, Alice, Oregon	34, 65, 262
Marshall, Dallas, Nebraska	117
Marshall, Lane W., Kentucky	153
Marshall, Melissa, Ontario, Canada	110
Marshall, Melissa J., New York	176
Marsters, James A., Missouri	74
Martel, Joey, Manitoba, Canada	365
Martell, Jud, British Columbia, Canada	80
Martin, Charita, Oklahoma	306
Martin, Karen, Nebraska	299, 312
Martin, Linda (Ryan), New York	15
Martin, Mike, Washington	353
Martinez, Jose, APO AE	365
Martinez-Piligian, Barbara Louise, New York	313
Martz, Natalie N., Virginia	297
Mary Fran, Ohio	226
Mary Lou, Ohio	198
Marzinski, Leona, Michigan	188
Mason, Danielle M., Massachusetts	95
Mason, Migale S., Florida	293
Masten, Judy D., Michigan	47
Mathews, "Buddy" Frank, Tennessee	75
Mathews, Sara Raley, Alabama	117
Mathewson, Bill, Nova Scotia, Canada	236
Matteson, Dawnmarie, Massachusetts	126
Maxwell, Margaret Elaine, Tennessee	226
Mayhue, Linda F., Oklahoma	234
Mays, Thomas O., California	76
McBride, Carrie R., Nevada	314
McBride, Katie, Illinois	119
McBride, Kendra, Saskatchewan, Canada	316
McCarty, B.J., Texas	10
McClain, BethAnn, Ohio	144
McCorkle, Rheannon, Pennsylvania	356
McCormack, Michael J., Connecticut	286
McCormick, Dianna, California	178
McCrea, Melody Dawn, Ohio	378
McCuiston, Margaret Morris, Kentucky	198
McDermott, Mary, O.S.U., Nebraska	131
McDonald, John William, Texas	248, 254
McDonough, Kevin, Massachusetts	358
McDuff, Corie, Manitoba, Canada	155
McElligatt, Colleen, Colorado	170, 173
McEven, Wm, Missouri	156
McFall, Carol B., Washington	206
McFarland, Denise, Mississippi	330
McFarlane, Maureen Jolie, Wisconsin	93
McGarry, June E., Massachusetts	281
McGaughan, Priscilla A., Illinois	249
McGaw, Cecil Austin, Kentucky	76
McGhee, Amy Nicole, Tennessee	300
McGhee, Cedric Lamar, Ohio	136
McGrew, Nelda P., Louisiana	381
McILwain, Duncan, California	242
McInnis, Pauline, Connecticut	107
McIver, Vanessa, North Carolina	371
McKay, Robin Reese, Kentucky	281
McKee, Linda, Tennessee	257
McKeever, Molly, Tennessee	252
McKinney, David S., North Carolina	315
McManus, Stacy, Michigan	329
McMurry, Alice C., Iowa	155
McNally, Jennifer L., Virginia	268
McNeil, Elnora Pugh, Alabama	183
McQuiston, Denise K., California	162, 168
McVey, Calvin C., Washington	308
"Me", Michigan	55
Meadows, Jeremy A., Indiana	243
Means, Ashley, Tennessee	320
Meeker, Lola J., Washington	209, 366
Mehi, Jean, Michigan	179
Meierhofer, Jeanette, Georgia	284
Melchoir, Yvonne, Virginia	231
Melles, Renée, Illinois	162
Meloni, Pamela, California	172
Meredith, Francis E., Kansas	132
Mereness, L.C., North Carolina	25
Merritt, Angela S., Michigan	293
Merullo, Paul, Massachusetts	29
Meverden, Anna M., California	358
Meyer, Joná F., New Mexico	242
Meyer, Marie Zeisler, Tennessee	196
Meyers, Lisa, Ohio	228
Michael, Elizabeth A., Alaska	92
Mickey, Pennsylvania	157
Mihowich, Cathy, New York	283
Millan, Jennifer Anne, California	378
Miller, Barb, Indiana	232
Miller, Barbara Lynn, Massachusetts	175
Miller, Bea, Indiana	346, 347
Miller, Benjamin F., Georgia	27, 28, 335, 343, 359, 372
Miller, Crystal O., West Virginia	282
Miller, David P., California	241
Miller, Karen E., Iowa	255
Miller, Lisa, New York	296
Miller, Lupe, Illinois	190
Miller, Nanette M., Florida	51
Milton, D. J., Louisiana	223
Mingle, Winifred, Kansas	168

Mitchell, Bonnie L., Ohio	328
Mitchell, Heather Marie, Kansas	343
Mitchell, Michael, Rhode Island	60
Mitchell, Olive, Ontario, Canada	328
Mitzel, Shana, Minnesota	251
Mlodik, Joanne, Mrs., Wisconsin	117, 123, 279
Mobley, Dana, Oklahoma	295
Moen, Shirley A., (Sam), Illinois	367
Moffitt, Julia, Connecticut	307
Mohs, Karen, California	185
Molinet, Kathleen D., Michigan	242
Moller, Wade, Washington	78
Moncure, Claudia D., Mississippi	373
Monnier, Audrey, Indiana	189
Monro, Maryanne, Pennsylvania	105
Monson, Ruthanne, Colorado	243
Monteith, Sabrina, Alberta, Canada	125
Montemayor, Joanne M., California	252
Montgomery, Betty J., Illinois	114
Montgomery, Nicole, California	348
Moo, Ohio	82
Moody, Elisha, Alabama	196
Moon, Marcella, Alberta, Canada	10
Moore, Cleatrice, Michigan	365
Moore, Doris, Idaho	356
Moore, Janet, Michigan	50
Moore, Myra L., California	292
Moore, Pamela, Florida	193
Moore, Pat, Texas	56
Moore, Shari, Idaho	206
Moore, Tracy, California	278
Moore, Wallie L., California	89
Moreland, Guyla Wallis, Illinois	107
Morgan, Bunny, Washington	98
Morgan, D. Shaun, Tennessee	195
Morgan, Jessica, Pennsylvania	373
Morgan, Marnie, Arizona	282
Morin, Nathalie, New Hampshire	276
Moring, Valerie, Illinois	264
Morisette, Florence, Michigan	280
Morris, Kari, Wisconsin	192
Morrison, Marguerite, New Brunswick, Canada	355
Morton, Jeff, Oklahoma	21
Mosley, Muriel, Georgia	118
Moss, Jennifer L., Arizona	303
Mugge, Brian, Iowa	176
Muhs, Broch, Nebraska	198
Mull, Joshua C, New York	132
Mullauer, Amy, Michigan	329
Mullen, Esther G., Tennessee	14
Mullins, B., North Carolina	38
Multine, Cynthia, Arizona	298
Mungar, Mary, Michigan	105
Munro, Richard, Ohio	240
Munson, Pam, Washington	57
Murphy, Joyce, California	98
Murphy, Kathy, Connecticut	127
Musko, Tamra, Arkansas	132
Myers, Ellen, Michigan	186
Myers, Margaret Story, New Jersey	195
Myers, Peggy J., Missouri	373
Myrick, Sharon Toni, Pennsylvania	128
Nackerud, Nola, New Mexico	342, 350
Napier, Amy Dalton, Tennessee	262
Napier, Bill, North Carolina	54
Nash, Earl, Ohio	96
Naugle, Teresa A, Pennsylvania	260
Nay, Andrea M, Indiana	361
Neely, Linda S., California	46, 203
Neely, Richard A., California	46, 47
Neidigh, Marti, Pennsylvania	276
Neill, Margaret, Tennessee	200
Neitge, Judith A., Minnesota	71
Nell, Sandra, Iowa	255
Nellermoe, Ron, Washington	277
Nelson, K.A., Ohio	205
Nelson, Kristy, Arizona	321
Nelson, Linny, Tennessee	136
Nelson, Mary Lee, Ohio	219
Nelson, Nancy Ellen, Illinois	156
Nelson, S.I., Washington	365
Neusom, Willie J., California	42
Neville, A. T., North Carolina	279
Nevitt, Lee Roy, Kentucky	180, 208, 209
Newman, Terry, Ohio	253
Newsome, Leah, Michigan	353
Newsum, Marvin W., Sr., Tennessee	273
Newton, Danielle, California	76
Nicholls, Kristi, Indiana	145
Nichols, Charlotte, Florida	205
Nichols, James E, Thunder in the Sky, Montana	275
Nicholson, Douglas D., Iowa	225
Nielsen, R. Laurel, Iowa	223
Nieto, Audrey, Texas	163
Nilsson, Sam, New Hampshire	190
Nishimura, Keiko, Minnesota	172
Noce, Shannon F., New Jersey	34
Noel, California	367
Normandin, Diane, Ontario, Canada	170
Norris, Jean, Michigan	93
Nuernberger, Delores K., Illinois	90
Nunley, Trent, Texas	287
Nygaard, Judith Sheridan, Minnesota	28
O., Margie, Wisconsin	222
O'Brien, Joan, New York	192
O'Bryan, Vickie, Kentucky	57
O'Bryant, Myra Alexandria, Illinois	180
O'Connell, Kathleen Anne, Maine	96
O'Connor, Orillia, California	88
Ogle, James H., Arkansas	378
Ogletree, Mary L. Walker, Georgia	92
O'Hearn, Catherine L., New York	191
Oliphant, Marie, Michigan	72
Olson, Donnie, Minnesota	151
Olson, Steve, Wisconsin	20
O'Malley, Connie, Kentucky	267
O'Neill, Blanche M., Indiana	208
Ordiway, Phillip P., Wisconsin	150
orit, New York	149
Ortiz, Nilson, California	108
Osborn, B.W., Florida	9
Osborn, Doris M., Arizona	203
O'Shea, Sean Patrick, Arizona	363
Ossman-Muhammad, Mary-Ann, Ohio	30
Osterholtz, Anna, Arizona	74
Otero, Mariano, California	163
Overbay, Christina, California	153
Owen, Bob, Texas	18
Owens, Lynda Blankenship, Pennsylvania	58
Owens, N. Ken, Washington	265
Ozanich, Ruth S., California	89, 123
Paddock, Michael J., Vermont	306
Page, Cindi A., California	176
page, helen m, Illinois	177
Page, Lynn Pearson, Idaho	296
Paglini-Konieczny, Nadine, Illinois	225
Pallatto, Nicole L., Connecticut	226
Palmer, Marvis J, Tennessee	380
Papanek, Olga, California	348
Papanikolaou, Kostandinos, Washington	187
Parham, Duncan, Ohio	219
Parham, Tamara, Tennessee	312
Parkin, Richard Sean, Michigan	99
Parnell, Kathy L., Tennessee	47
Parsons, Leroy, West Virginia	136
Parsons, Sylvia, Quebec, Canada	8

Partridge, Mark, Pennsylvania	255
Pasco, Lauro E., California	100
Patrick, Amy Nicole, Ohio	108
Patterson, Mary, North Carolina	326
Patterson, Pamela, Tennessee	243
Patuna, Gene, Michigan	358
Paul, Beverly A., Michigan	186
Paulsen, Diane, Illinois	186
Paulson, Charlotte, Michigan	375
Paxiao, Paula A., California	216
Peace, Ashley M., Nevada	281
Pearson, Hether, Missouri	8
Pedroso, Carol Marie, Rhode Island	24
Peeters, Lila, California	127, 135
Pelfrey, Timothy, Michigan	355
Peluso, Tammy D., Pennsylvania	292
Pence, Creola, Florida	70
Pendragon, Jenna, Pennsylvania	172
Penney, Madonna Sarah, Newfoundland, Canada	366
Pepe, J. J., North Carolina	133
Pepera, Rhonda R., Arizona	120
Perkins, Gregory, New Jersey	35
Perry, Kaci Ann, Washington	375
Peschong, Nicole, Idaho	240
Peters, Theressa, Ohio	23
Peterson, Charles E. Sr., "The Poet", Michigan	36
Petrut, Dorothea M., Washington	72
"Petunia Skittlebum", Ontario, Canada	164
Pfeil, J.A., Wisconsin	160
Phelps, April, Massachusetts	111
Phillips, Hugh, Jr., Colorado	381
Phillips, Monettia, Tennessee	117
Phillips (Scibelli), Ruth, Nebraska	50
Pickle, Shannon Leigh, Tennessee	378
Pierce, Betty, Pennsylvania	212, 217
Pierce, D.E., Kentucky	156
Pierce, Linda Hudgins, Florida	335
Pierritz, Jane, Illinois	9, 368
Pietrolaj, Louise, Pennsylvania	299
Pietrzak, MJ, Michigan	303
Piggott, Rhyne, Tennessee	362
Pilarski, Brandon, Michigan	306
Pilcher-Freas, Betty, Illinois	14
Pinkston, Kristi, Florida	300
Piorkowski, Michelle, New Jersey	300
Piper, Jo, Colorado	174
Piper, Marie, Georgia	291
Pisarski, Theresa, Ohio	208
Pisiak, Lin, Ontario, Canada	352
Pitera, Judy, Michigan	9, 58
Place, Jeffrey Scott, Texas	380
Plautz, Bernice C., Wisconsin	137
Plesh, John, California	204
Plymel, Janice F., Georgia	158
Poffenroth, Jill Marie, Idaho	207
Pollard, Daniel J., Rhode Island	42
Pollock, Jeanie M., Ohio	158
Polomski, Mark A., Florida	263
Ponvelle, Joan, Tennessee	16
Pope, Rachel, Maryland	369
Popham, Dennis Dale, Texas	80
Poplar, Harriet, Washington	258
Popp, Cindy, Wisconsin	294
Porter, Lafern E., Michigan	166
Porter, Nancy L, Illinois	56
Posey, Gina, Tennessee	348
Powell, Antoinette M., California	137
Powell, Eric, Tennessee	376
Powell, Juanita, Colorado	39
Powell, Linda M., Illinois	38
Powers, Hudson, New Jersey	185
Powers, Rae Kae, California	221
Prante, Wren, California	264
Prater, Lonnie, Virginia	8
Pratt, James A., Idaho	272
Preece, Lilly, California	152
Price, Paula Ellison, South Carolina	171
Price, Rebecca, Wisconsin	88
Priebe, Irene, Illinois	67
Prince, Karen, Oklahoma	151
Pritchard, September Mae, New Mexico	285
Pritzel, Patricia A., Colorado	326
Pryor, Pamela M., Missouri	86
Puck, Joshua, Iowa	275
Puckett, Woodrow (Pee Wee), Virginia	191
Puncochar, Jennifer Lynn, Illinois	46
Pyrek, Jane C., Pennsylvania	241
Qualls, Ethel M., West Virginia	275
Quinney, Richard, South Carolina	122
Raasch, Todd William, Iowa	238
Rabe, Vera Thomas, Illinois	351
Rackley (White), Margret, Florida	331
Rader, June, Ohio	311
Radosevich, Judith, Washington	26
Rae-Baird, Jennifer Lynne, Florida	331
Ralston, Faye Carlton, Tennessee	69
Ramirez, David A., Texas	333
Rammacher, Lois J., Florida	328
Ramsey, Ruby J., Kentucky	16
Rand, Richard, Washington	97
Randolph, Zac, New York	12
Rapp, Sharon, Michigan	14
Raushanah, Michigan	142
Rawson, Kellie Sue, Pennsylvania	77
Ray, Thomas D., California	43
Rea, Donna, Tennessee	296
Reardon, Theresa, Massachusetts	330
Rector, E.B., Oregon	231
Redemer, Gene, California	257, 260, 271
Redmond, Joy D., Oklahoma	155
Reed, Bruce, Ohio	62
Reedy, Linda Bristle, Illinois	295
Rees, Daniel, Kentucky	264
Reese, Hardy, California	92
Regner, Joan, Wisconsin	90
Reid, Gerald C., Georgia	226
Reinert, Nate, Iowa	49
Remington, Alma Cook, Washington	13, 83, 149, 158
Render, Judith Ann, Florida	238
Renfro, Khrystan Page, Illinois	152
Repiscak, Chris-Mary, New Jersey	338
Reves, Jennifer, Pennsylvania	286
Reyes, Thomas, Texas	32
Reynolds, Amy Marie, California	362
Reynolds, Tracy, Ohio	120
Rhonda Gayle, British Columbia, Canada	150
Ricci, Holli Ann, California	65
Rice, Aaron Michael, California	18
Rice, Alice, Georgia	84
Rich, Paul, South Carolina	7
Richmond, Adam, Michigan	19
Riggins, Brandon L., Texas	66
RIO, New York	128
Ripley, Laura, Illinois	323
Rivera-Reyes, Sunny, Colorado	8
Roach, Glenn, Georgia	111
Roach, Susan M., Michigan	130
Roark, D.L., North Carolina	266
Robbins, Dot Scroggins, Tennessee	247
Robbins, Shelly Ann, Michigan	118
Robinett, Cassie, North Carolina	128
Robinson, Dwain C., California	101
Robinson, Fiona, California	30
Robinson, Gayle, Alaska	217
Robinson, Kathleen, Ohio	190, 213

Robinson, R. Marie, Pennsylvania	93
Roby, Alma Ann, Tennessee	98
Rockey, Terry Marie, Florida	46
Rockwell, Nancy G., Indiana	146
Roden, Lucile, Wisconsin	113
Rodriquez, Alfonso C., Pennsylvania	84
Rodriguez, Linda, California	238
Roe, Charles W., Alabama	286
Rogers, Daniel, California	13
Rogers, Helen Rooker, Tennessee	87
Rohnie, California	186
Rohrbein, Sheryl, Illinois	115
Roncevich, Sonya, Massachusetts	236
Rone, Dennis B., Arkansas	68
Rooks, Grace B., Georgia	278
Roopnarine, Raquel, Alberta, Canada	276
Rosales, Christian J., California	220
Ross, Heather, Georgia	28
Rossini, Nancy C., California	307
Rossiter, Jessica, Indiana	106
Rothlisberg, Allen P., Arizona	282
Rounds, Arlene, New Mexico	318
Rouse, Nicole M., Michigan	155
Rouse, Sharon R., Maryland	121
Roush, Jenny, Pennsylvania	125
Rowe, Wayne A., West Virginia	39
Rozell, Jason B., Illinois	366
Rozycki, DE, Florida	246
Rubin, Diana Kwiatkowski, New Jersey	5
Ruczynski, Kathleen, Poopsie, Michigan	241, 276
Rudd, Lorraine, Michigan	171
Rudolph, Ernie, Indiana	106
Rudolph, Patricia, North Carolina	165
Runnels, Judy, Arkansas	173
Rupp, Lisa Kay, Michigan	178
Ruryk, Deborah J., Indiana	322
Rushing, Charnell, Kentucky	148
Russell, Will, Wisconsin	327
Rusty, Ohio	174, 191
Ryan, Linda L., Iowa	16
Rye, Brently Dean, Tennessee	246
Sackett, Robert W., Wisconsin	367, 374
Sadler, Paul S., North Carolina	137
Sadler, Peggy Ann, Georgia	147
Safer, Rena Scheingarten, Wisconsin	186
Sailor, L.A., Washington	267
Sampson, Barbara Ruth, Georgia	273, 290
Sampson-Haney, Sylvia R., Georgia	233
Sanchez, Tania P., California	8
Sanden, Odessa, California	103
Sanderson, Teresa, California	350
Sandesara, Hirsh Kalyan, Illinois	280
Sandoval, Marianne, California	299
"Sandy", New Jersey	283
Sanghvi, Hrishabh, California	182
Satterfield, Rachel, Tennessee	74
Sauls, H.D., Georgia	12
Saveley, Barb, Tennessee	249
Scalise, Joe, Ohio	297
Scatena, Michele, California	67
Schantz, Julie E., Indiana	32
Scheer, Merle, Washington	69
Schell, Amie, Idaho	262
Scherer, Tammy, Pennsylvania	373
Schlacter, Kimry D., Alberta, Canada	344
Schlueter, Matthew J., Wisconsin	142
Schmidt, Alyce, Florida	76
Schmitz, Renae M., Minnesota	256
Schnelle, Beatrice L., Ohio	305
Scott, J.W., Michigan	73
Scott, Michael David, California	183
Scribner, Nancy C., Tennessee	235
Scura, Frances M., New York	299
Seals, Jessi, Tennessee	86
Secor, Dawn, Indiana	127
Secula, Andrew John, Maryland	142
Seigley, Tina, Ohio	282
Semel, Julie Schultz, Ohio	194
Senior, Ann, Iowa	141
Senior, Jim, Iowa	116
Senter, Alice Hanson, Washington	317
Setters, Gladys M., Kentucky	180
Sevey, Dean D., Illinois	270
Sewell, Dora Jean Muller, Mississippi	285
Shacklett, Richard Claude, Tennessee	17
Shaffer, D. Elaine, Pennsylvania	82
Shaffer, Rebecca Lynn, Ohio	322
Shaffer, Virginia L., Colorado	31
Shana, Iowa	33
Shank, Dorothy, Indiana	97
Shannon, Katie, Wisconsin	90
Shaut, S.O., North Carolina	161
Shaw, Wanda, California	118
Sheehan, Joanne, Nevada	332
Shela, Washington	77
Sheldon, Chalane J., Ohio	119
Shelton, D.J., Virginia	10
Shelton, Marilyn J., North Dakota	223
Shepherd, Tammy J., Arkansas	231
Sheriff, Molly E., Nevada	333
Sherrod, Antonia Toledo, Washington	339
Sherrod, Henry, Jr., Washington	359
Shields, M.A., Arizona	64
Shilling, D. L., Illinois	239
Shimp, Adele Veronica, Pennsylvania	307
Shipp, Vivian, West Virginia	41
Shockley, Herbert I, Pennsylvania	78
Shoop, Errin, Pennsylvania	373
Short, Rebecca D., California	92
Shreve, Amy L., West Virginia	303
Shuman, Marjorie G., California	58
Siciliano, Lisa Joann, Michigan	227
Sides, Melisa, Pennsylvania	160
Siegel, Donald R., New York	192
Sierra, Guillermina, New Mexico	261
Sifuentes, Gloria, California	167
Silvera, Annette, Washington	178
Silye, Jessica L., Michigan	133
Simiele, Heather A., Colorado	96
Simonson, Thom, New York	186
Sinex, Catherine Mejia, Maryland	227
Sissman, Reed, Wyoming	209
S. Kay, Washington	164
Skidmore-Hasil, Stacey J., Illinois	153
Skillen, Ellie, Kentucky	35
Skinner, Nathaniel, Washington	118
Slack, Erin, California	144
Slajer, Rhonda, Tennessee	333
Slasor, Kathryn Campbell, Pennsylvania	252
Slone, Stacy, Kentucky	50
Small, Susan Elizabeth, Illinois	24
Smedley, Linda, California	103
Smith, Betty Joan, Texas	219
Smith, Cecile Musson, Bermuda	164
Smith, Don Eric, Louisiana	301
Smith, Floris P, Michigan	81
Smith, Helen Madeline Alexanian, West Virginia	48
Smith, Herbert T., Texas	270
Smith, Janette M., Louisiana	356
Smith, Julia Ruane, New York	203
Smith, Kelli M., California	267
Smith, Lindsey R., New York	239, 270, 271, 273, 276
Smith, Mary Joan, Minnesota	42
Smith, Mildred, North Carolina	27
Smith, P.A., Michigan	147

Smith, Sharon E., Oregon	179
Smith, T.J., West Virginia	298
Smith, Tony L., Kansas	360
Smith, Trish, Mississippi	16
Smith, Vernel, Texas	247
Snarski, Carolann, Michigan	29
Sneed, Rosie B., Tennessee	128
Snodgrass, Jaimie, Pennsylvania	52
Snopel, Cheryl, Ohio	284
Snow, Rebecca, California	28
Snow, Tina M., Utah	225
Snyder, Jim, Washington	24, 31, 195, 322, 328, 330, 331, 356, 380
Snyder, Nicole, Michigan	193
Snyder-Haney, Joanne G., Pennsylvania	60
Sobczak, Gene H., New Jersey	318
Sobel, Charlotte, Florida	35
Soileau, Travis P., Louisiana	162
Sokn, Erick L., Illinois	170
Sophia (L.M.C.), Vermont	51
Sorensen, Jeri, California	174
Sorrentino, Lacey Kristen, Florida	294
Soule, Joana L., Ohio	328
Souza, June M., California	246
Sovinski, Marjorie F., Michigan	350
Spanier, Stuart L., Kansas	202
Spears, Jennifer, Louisiana	176
Speer, Lindia, Tennessee	241
Spicer, Susanne, Saskatchewan, Canada	373
Spies, Robert D., Washington	295
Spivey, Edwin P., Louisiana	206, 224
Spivey, James E., Texas	121
Spragg, Lancie L., Ohio	336
Sprague, Valerie, Ohio	132
Springer, Eryn Kate, Maine	311
Spurlock, Ashley, Louisiana	189
Squires, Carol A, Washington	58
Standridge, Michal J., Tennessee	363
Stanert, Shelly L, Ontario, Canada	48
Stanius, Sharon, Minnesota	194
Stanton, Peggy, Alabama	104
Starks, Jennifer Lynn, West Virginia	101
Starr, Suzanne Jean, Pennsylvania	340
Stebel, Meryl, New York	19
Steepleton, Kelly, Ohio	70
Stein, Becca, South Carolina	150
Steinert, Maggie, Iowa	81
Steinka, Eva E., Florida	198
Stephen, Indiana	42
Stephens, Evelyn M., Minnesota	203
Stevens, Annie B., Michigan	376
Stevenson, Mary Ann, Washington	202
Stewart, Ruth M., Illinois	311
Stilwell, Kandi J., Colorado	100
St. Louis, Dorothy A., California	170
Stocker, Shayla, Iowa	325
Stone, Ronnie, North Carolina	288
Stone, Sue C., New Jersey	374
Stone, Tracy, Washington	145
Storms, Wilma, California	240
Storney, Rachael, Wisconsin	36
Stout, Billie Jo, Michigan	232
Streu, Lisa Marie, Michigan	272
Strzalko, Robert, Illinois	11
St. Sauver, Floy, California	110
Stuetz, Roseann, New Jersey	352
Stull, Ruby Vernon, Pennsylvania	196
Stumreiter, Mary M., Wisconsin	39
Styck, Donald E., Georgia	125
Suggs, Edith D., Michigan	367
Sullivan, Edward J., Florida	224
Sullivan, Thela Marie, California	283
Sulton, Robert A., Mississippi	360
Sundstrom, Wendy, Washington	132
Suveg, Ivanka, Idaho	44
Swafford, James LeRoy, Michigan	246, 260
Swaney, Laura L., Illinois	150
Swartz, Joanne, Nevada	323
Swisher, Patricia A., Pennsylvania	165
Syas, Clara Martin, Oklahoma	279
Syrtis, Demitra Ann, Wisconsin	83
Tabor, Virginia, California	152
Tague, Nickolas Patrick, Michigan	335
Tahauri, Marvelee Soon, Hawaii	7
Tall, Sandra L., Washington	188
Talley, Denise, Missouri	291
Tasimowicz, Thelma, New York	130
Tavares, Everett A., California	116
Taylor, Bonita L., Georgia	329
Taylor, Colette, Minnesota	138
Taylor, Dorothy C., Mississippi	122
Taylor, Lennice Marie, Oklahoma	350
Taylor, Mary M., Kentucky	175
Taylor, Mary Ramsey, North Carolina	43
Teague, Devin, Missouri	163
Tedford, Brandi Nicole, Texas	353
TEE, Texas	271
Temperly, Janet, Illinois	127
Temple, Lori, Missouri	196
Tenneill, Jamie, Virginia	354
Teresa Michele, Oregon	61
Tew, Elizabeth Tyner, South Carolina	140
Tews, Annette M., Iowa	281
Thacher, Jeanne, Michigan	272
Thagard, Jason, Florida	14
Thatcher, Lorraine Windahl, California	350
Therriault, Karly, Washington	140
Thibodeau, Arthur, Massachusetts	223
Thies, Patricia, Illinois	292
Thomas, Al, Georgia	183
Thomas, Brian H., Texas	45
Thomas, Clarice, Michigan	65
Thomas, D. G., III, Hawaii	143
thomas, diana, Illinois	29
Thomas, E.L., Louisiana	22
Thomas, Kate, Illinois	31
Thomas, Margot A., North Carolina	87
Thomas, Shavonne, Alabama	114
Thomas, Susan, Tennessee	56
Thompson, Deborah, Michigan	185
Thompson, Jesse, South Carolina	87
Thompson, Marty, Texas	377
Thompson, Shawna, California	185
Thompson-Criswell, LaCheryle, Tennessee	104
Thomsen, Melinda R., New York	62
Thorns, Felicia M., Michigan	370
Thornton-Dunsworth, Letha M., Oklahoma	286
Tierney, Christine Ann, (Cat), Oregon	262
Tillman, John, Iowa	64
Tillotson, L. Ezra, Texas	6
Timko, Tabitha N., Ohio	329
Tisdale, Phebe Alden, Massachusetts	22, 74
Titlow, J.S., California	255, 267
Toboz, Robin, Pennsylvania	288
Toda, Bev, Michigan	72
Toles, J.T., Tennessee	65
Tomlinson (CPS), Bob, Pennsylvania	192, 235
Tondreau, Virginia, Oregon	15
Toomey, Lil, Michigan	66
Topeka, James Ray, West Virginia	153
Torres, Elizabeth M., Michigan	345
Travis, Tiffany N., Texas	354
Trent, Joyce A., Mrs., Michigan	260
Troll, Florence N., Pennsylvania	248
Trost, Jamie C., Pennsylvania	64
Trotman, Shane, Alabama	234

Troxclair, Caneel, Illinois	241
Truax, Michael A., Indiana	13
Trudgeon, Heather L., North Carolina	20
Tsoukalas, Judy I., Washington	218
TTG, North Carolina	120
Tucker, Veronica C., Louisiana	157
Tulk, Keith C., Ontario, Canada	266
Tureaud, Raye Elizabeth, Michigan	249
Turnipseed, Jacqueline R., Texas	102
Twixt, New York	254
Tzay, K. Ann, Michigan	33
Umipig, Liza Marie, Washington	365
Unterwegner, Jennifer, Washington	130
vail, dana paige, Washington	112
Valarezo, Melba Murleen, Illinois	205
Valero, Rupert, Texas	202
Vandergriff, Heather N., Tennessee	280
Vander Heide, Ruth, Michigan	215
Vangel, James E., Washington	174
"Vangi", California	294
Van Horne, E. Jean, Washington	134
Vaniglia, Lisa, Pennsylvania	373
VanOstrand, Roger, Illinois	336
Van Riper, Trudy, Texas	196
VanSanden, Teresa, Washington	58
Varner, Betty, Tennessee	211
Varner, David M., Missouri	67
Vaska, Marcus, Alberta, Canada	8
Vaughn, Lela O. (Jenkins), Michigan	252
Vawter, Betty, Tennessee	333
Veasy, Demetrius Teal, II, Florida	80
Vejar, Mavis Smallfield, California	189, 373, 375
Velez, Anthony J., Massachusetts	24
Verhaag, David L., Washington	311
Verna U.S.A., Wisconsin	293
Vertefeuille, Dita, California	41
Vicknair, Shantell, Louisiana	215
Victoria, Maryland	51
Vieira, James Angus, Washington	32, 324
Villarreal, Jesus Morõn, Texas	101
Vincent, Glenna C., California	317
Vogel, Jo Ann B., Wisconsin	108
Vogele, Jacquelene Rane, Oklahoma	43
Vogt, Richard J, North Carolina	257
Voltz, Judy, Tennessee	201
Wadkins, Sybil (Messer), Alabama	116
Wagar, Jamie, Michigan	302
Wagner, Patricia (Trish), Wisconsin	178
Wahlroos, Patti Jo, Minnesota	343
Walker, A.L., Indiana	98
Walker, Bill, Oregon	41
Waller, Louise, California	157
Walsh, Sarah E., Michigan	170
Walter, Leslie Ann, Michigan	49
Walters, A.J., Kentucky	283, 290, 305
Walters, Michael, Florida	361
Walters, Susan, California	134
Wang, Harry, California	181
Ward, Becky, Indiana	129
Ward, Danny J., Colorado	220
Ward, Denise, Iowa	375
Ward, Ellen, Washington	354
Ward, L.M., New York	171
Warner, Ida E., Arizona	119
Wasilowski, Colleen M., Pennsylvania	285
Wasserman, Melissa, Ohio	225
Watkins, B. B., New Jersey	56, 70, 104
Watman, Sandra Jeanne, Oregon	99
Watson, Edwene Dorothy, California	13
Watson, Fran, California	280
Watts, Michelle, Ohio	233
Weatherspoon, Penny S., West Virginia	99
Weaver, Ruth W., New York	194
Webb, Doris M., Indiana	297
Webber, Rebecca, Ohio	149
Webber, T. Hayes, West Virginia	157
Weber, Donna, North Dakota	340
Weber, Virginia, Wisconsin	83
Wegdahl, Leander, Oregon	126
Weigandt, Millecent, Michigan	106
Weldon, Helen J., Ontario, Canada	240
Wells, Jennifer D., Newfoundland, Canada	67
Wen, Robert, Colorado	254
Weng, Kat, Michigan	222
Wesgaites, Annette J., Pennsylvania	350
Wesolowski, Marianne, Florida	317
Wessel, Joy Cojeen, Florida	68
West, Donald L. Jr., Iowa	129
Westerfield, Danette, California	70
Westerlund, Susan, California	333
Whalen, Peter, Wisconsin	9
Wheeler, Lee, Indiana	49, 75
Wheeler, Robert J., Tennessee	123
White, Dennis, California	43
White, Harriet, District of Columbia	53
Whitworth, Michael S., I, Arkansas	123
Wiedener, Ted W., Ontario, Canada	266, 269, 271
Wiemer, F.E., Illinois	133
Wiggins, James A, Jr., New Jersey	91, 138
Wignall, Andrew D., Louisiana	344
Wilber, Priscilla, Michigan	316
Wilbourn, Ethel M., Oklahoma	105
Wilcox, Mae L., Michigan	344
Wiley, Dorothy, West Virginia	110
Wilke, James, Texas	338
Wilkinson, Caulene Hobby, Alabama	176
Will, Jan, Florida	220
Willett, Margaret, Kentucky	105
Williams, Dawn M., Minnesota	255
Williams, Elizabeth M., Illinois	168
Williams, Elmer A., Ohio	200
Williams, Gisela M., Tennessee	90
Williams, Josephine, Ontario, Canada	113
Williams, K. M., Washington	222
Williams, Lee, Indiana	138
Williams, Mark C., West Virginia	283
Williams, Sheila Rose, Washington	20
Williams, Wallace Joe, Texas	59, 147
Williams, W.G., Florida	256, 258
Williamson, Lillian M., Alabama	143
Williamson, Lorna Mae, Colorado	337
Williamson, Robin B., Alabama	230
Willis, Marlinah, Michigan	355
Willis, Stephen, South Carolina	45
Wilson, Faye, Tennessee	21
Wilson, Ginger, Louisiana	381
Wilson, Jeanette, British Columbia, Canada	212
Wilson, Penny S., California	30
Wilson, R.M., Michigan	88
Wilson, Robert, Alabama	300, 324
Wilson, Roberta L., Illinois	173
Wiltrout, Megan M., Pennsylvania	310
Wink, Washington	250
Winn, Michael Develle, Kansas	216
Winston, Elizabeth Rae, Wisconsin	376
Winter, Robert, Pennsylvania	181
Winters, Francine B., Indiana	111
Winters, George D., California	178, 309
Wipf, Karen, Illinois	82
Wirtes, Joseph, Illinois	370
Wirth, Matt, Maryland	119
Wolfe, Chad, Ontario, Canada	152
Wolff, Eric, Minnesota	297
Wolfgang, Heidi L., Pennsylvania	191
Wood, Marion, Washington	178
Wood, Melissa, New Hampshire	148

Woods, Edmond C., Ohio 152
Woods, Judy, Tennessee 335
Woods, Matthew, Tennessee 177
Woods, Sue, Washington 39
Woodson, Donald A., Kansas 215
Wooten, Danny, North Carolina 264
Wright, Avis Iris, Minnesota 327, 341
Wright, Bette Stalder, Vermont 77
Wright, Frank E., Jr., Florida 271
Wright, Les, Nevada 173
Wussow, Jenny, Minnesota 88
Wūthrich, Verena, Switzerland 33, 278
Wyant, Wilma Boe, North Dakota 99
Wysocki, Becky, Michigan 320
Yang, Sugene, New York 232
Yarnell, Justin, New Mexico 276

Yarrow, Michele, California 167
Yeager, E.S., New Jersey 148
Yeoman, Mike, Illinois 160
Yokom, Scot, Michigan 60
Yost, D. Helene, Colorado 87
Young, Alyssa, Connecticut 201
Young, Nickè-Chantalle, Colorado 376
Youngs, David, Michigan 89
Yuan, Peipei Alena, California 269
Zambrano, William Boone, Kentucky 104
Zee, Francesca, Colorado 254
Ziegler, Sara, Pennsylvania 222
Zimmer, Edward, Michigan 250
Zimmermann, Christine, New Jersey 130
Zoller, Norma, Washington 55
Zorro, Tennessee 148
Zver, Jessica, Washington 302

Made in the USA
Charleston, SC
27 November 2015

06

2005-2006	Valerie Binney
2006-2007	Choudary Rangzeb
2007-2008	Robin Ernest Owens
2008-2009	Howard Middleton
2009-2010	John Godward
2010-2011	Peter Hill
2011-2012	Naveeda Ikram
2012-2013	Dale Smith
2013-2014	Khadim Hussain
2014-2015	Mike Gibbons
2015-2016	Joanne Dodds

1968-1968   John William Taylor
1968-1969   Arthur Walton
1969-1970   Edward Newby
1970-1971   John Edward Baines Singleton
1971-1972   Herbert Morgan
1972-1973   Audrey Firth
1973-1974   Derek Smith
1974-1974   John Edward Baines Singleton
1974-1975   Thomas Edward Hall
1975-1976   Doris Birdsall
1976-1977   Frank Hillam
1977-1978   Paul Hockney
1978-1979   Arthur Frederick Twigg
1979-1980   John Stuart Senior
1980-1981   Daniel Canon Coughlin
1981-1982   Arnold Lightowler
1982-1983   Joan Lightband
1983-1984   Norma Free
1984-1985   Olive Messer
1985-1986   Mohammed Ajeeb
1986-1987   William Arthur Nunn
1987-1988   Laurence Corral Coughlin
1988-1989   Smith Midgely
1989-1990   George Hogson
1990-1991   Ernest Saville (died in office)
1991-1992   Sydney John Collard
1992-1993   Barry Kenneth Thorne
1993-1994   Robert Sowman
1994-1995   Danny Mangham
1995-1996   Marilyn Beeley
1996-1997   Gordon Mitchell
1997-1998   James Anthony Cairns
1998-1999   Tony Millar
1999-2000   Harry Mason
2000-2001   John Stanley King
2001-2002   Ghazanfer Khaliq
2002-2003   Richard Edward John Wightman
2003-2004   Allan Irving Hilary
2004-2005   Irene Ellison Wood

88

1929-1930	Angus Hardy Rhodes
1930-1931	Alfred Pickles
1931-1932	George Walker
1932-1933	John William Longley
1933-1934	Arthur Walter Brown
1934-1935	Walter Hodgson
1935-1936	Jonas Pearson
1936-1937	George Ripley Carter
1937-1938	Henry Hudson
1938-1939	Thomas Johns Robinson
1939-1940	Meredith Farrar Thompson
1940-1941	William Illingworth
1941-1942	Louis William Squire Smith
1942-1943	James Harrison
1943-1944	Walter Henry Barraclough
1944-1945	Cecil Barnet
1945-1946	Kathleen Chamber
1946-1947	Thomas Illingworth Clough
1947-1949	Fredrick James Cowie
1949-1950	George Thomas Meggison
1950-1951	Alton Ward
1951-1952	Horace Hird
1952-1953	John Shee
1953-1954	Angus Crowther
1954-1955	Henry James White
1955-1955	Herbert William Semper (died in office)
1955-1956	Richard Cornelius Ruth
1956-1957	Horace Robert Walker
1957-1958	David Black
1958-1959	Norbert William Durrant
1959-1960	Ernest England
1960-1961	Edgar Robinson
1961-1962	Benjamin Wilfred Bur
1962-1963	Harold Kershaw Watson
1963-1964	Tom Wood
1964-1965	Weber Marshall Hird
1965-1966	Jack Wilson
1966-1967	Louis Cowgill
1967-1967	Thomas Lee (died in office)

Chapter 20
Lord Mayors of Bradford

The first Lord Mayor of Bradford was Alderman John Godwin who took up the position on September 16th 1907. Bradford's first Female Lord Mayor was Alderman Kathleen Chambers in 1945, and Bradford was the home of the first Asian Lord Mayor in Councillor Mohammed Ajeeb who took up office in 1985.

1907-1907	John Arthur Godwin
1907-1908	John Edward Fawcett
1909-1910	James Hill
1909-1911	William Laird
1910-1911	Jacob Moser (died in office)
1911-1912	John Batt Moorhouse
1912-1913	Fred Foster
1913-1914	John Arnold
1914-1915	George Henry Robinson
1915-1916	Thomas Haworth
1916-1917	Abram Peel
1917-1918	John Bland (died in office)
1918-1918	Herbert Hustler Tetley
1918-1919	Joseph Hayhurst (died in office)
1919-1919	Walter Barber
1919-1920	William Wade
1920-1921	Anthony Gadie
1921-1922	Thomas Blythe
1922-1923	Thomas Snowden
1923-1924	Herbert Morris Trotter
1924-1925	John Henry Palin
1923-1924	Herbert Morris Trotter
1924-1925	John Henry Palin
1925-1926	Joseph Stringer
1926-1927	Richard Johnson
1927-1928	Michael Conway
1928-1929	Herbert Thornton Pullan

24 hours to study the lock the fact is that Houdini, the world's greatest escapologist had been beaten. The lock was eventually passed down to Fenton's grandson, George E Waddington who placed it on display in his shop window in Carlisle road, Manningham. In the early 1970's the lock was presented to Bradford Industrial Museum on the understanding that the back of the lock must not be removed. The lock remains there this very day!

James Bond and His Life in Bradford

Many younger people born in Bradford will be shocked to learn that the man who liked it 'shaken not stirred' lived a while in Baildon whilst running a textile company in Idle in the late 1960's. Roger Moore had just finished The Saint TV episodes before taking the Bond role in 1973 in Live and Let Die. Moore used to socialise in the Rosse Hotel at the bottom of Moorhead Lane in Saltaire. I personally remember seeing his famous white saloon with 'The Saint' symbol emblazoned on the car not forgetting the halo as he no doubt travelled around the city.

William Fenton

Harry Houdini (real name Enrich Weiss) started life as a magician, but soon moved into escapology. He toured many principle towns in America and Europe before hitting Bradford at the Bradford Palace February 4th to 9th 1901. Houdini became known for escaping from handcuffs and straight jackets and he would frequently ask his audience to challenge him. One gentleman that did was William Fenton, a local locksmith and cycle maker and repairer of Lumb lane, Bradford. The lock William chose to baffle Houdini with was a lock from an old warehouse door which could have been 150 years old. There were apparently only three in existence and measured 12" wide by 8 ¾" high and 3 ¾" thick. It weighed 7 kilos. William wrote a letter to Houdini challenging him to pick the lock, nothing more, in front of an audience. Houdini declined wishing to examine and possibly take the lock apart. Thirteen years later Houdini once again performed in Bradford and William Fenton re issued his challenge stating that Houdini should pick the lock on the spot without examination. Houdini once again declined stating that he would require

The Clown Prince of Soccer

Len Shackleton was born in Bradford on 22nd may 1922. He attended Whetley Hill Junior School and Carlton Grammar School and soon became Bradford's first player to be chosen for the England schools football team. His talent for the round ball was spotted by Arsenal who invited him for trials as an amateur. Little did they realise their mistake at the time as Len later became a cult figure in the North east of England and generally accepted as one of the finest forwards to wear an England shirt. He made his initial work on the game by playing for Bradford Park Avenue at the age of seventeen scoring an amazing 160 goals and dazzling fans with amazing footwork and special silky skills. An English international cap followed in 1945 and a year later he joined Newcastle United playing staff for a paltry sum of £13,000. Soon the magpie fans cottoned onto what a real bargain they had obtained in the transfer market. Newcastle fans held him in awe after an astonishing 13-0 victory on his debut against Newport County (Shackleton scored six goals). Shackleton then moved along the East coast to Sunderland F.C and it wasn't long before the Roker Roar was in evidence. The £20,000 fee was well justified and in all competitions he scored a total of 101 goals for the Black Cats. Amazingly only a few further England caps adorned Lens mantelpiece but this was probably due to his forthright speaking and dislike of football authorities. An injury brought an abrupt end to his career. England's finest only received £17 a week for his endeavours. In terms of transfer fees and wages, how much would he be worth today? The mind boggles! A true hero of the working class people of Bradford and beyond, Even in death he his remembered by his legion of fans. What could the Bradford clubs do with him today?

83

remained an individual with an eye for a musical career. His father sent him to Florida to work on an orange plantation, however after eighteen months he moved to the state of Virginia. Fritz craved for a full time musical career and education and obtained such at Leipzig, Germany before moving to Paris in 1890. Not much is known of this period of his life. He developed a roving eye for women and struck a period of financial hardship when family sponsorship ran out. He was now at the crossroads of his life having completed his musical works and was considering moving back to London. His female companion at the time was a certain Jelka Rosen (who was to become his wife) who had purchased a property at Grez-sur-Loing near Paris. Here he settled to write some of his finest works although he continued to travel in Norway and the USA. Eventually Delius's health began to deteriorate; he began to go blind and lost the use of his limbs.

A fellow Yorkshireman, Eric Fenby heard of his plight and went to live with Delius at Grez and completed his last work by dictation. Delius died in1934 and is buried in Limpfield, Surrey. He had received the ultimate honour from his home city as he was made a Freeman in 1932. Today a plaque stands at the entrance of his birthplace at 6 Claremont in Bradford and a huge skeletal sculpture adorns the front of Bradford's County Court building. There is also a street named after him on the Ravenscliffe estate, plus a bar in the house next door to 6 Claremont, aptly named 'Delius Lived Next Door,' but that is all that remains of the musical maestro, who turned his back on his home city to find international fame and a bohemian lifestyle.

The Man Who Turned His Back on Bradford

Frederick Delius was born in Bradford during the year 1862 and is noted to be one of Bradford's greatest sons, although he showed distaste for his home city and left the place as soon as the opportunity arose. His father, Julius was a wool merchant of German- Jewish stock and helped to arrange the subscription concerts at St Georges Hall. Frederick was originally known as Fritz for the first forty years of his life. He attended Bradford Grammar School but did not have the aptitude for the book. After leaving school he worked in his father's business as a travelling rep engaged in textile sales. This position never interested Fritz and he

81

forgot his roots despite his immense fame.

York Minster to give him his final send off. He was a man who never Yorkshire TV in the days after his death. A huge gathering turned up at his fame that more than 250,000 people jammed the switchboard at given the honorary title of mayor of Wetwang in East Yorkshire. Such was Deputy Lord Lieutenants for West Yorkshire. Other awards included being Before his death he was awarded an OBE and appointed one of the He died a modest man aged 61, leaving £2.5 million in cash and property. relationship with Carol Vorderman made him the darling of the nation. His 200 jackets and alleged 500 ties together with a good working Channel 4 made him a TV superstar. knowledgeable on most matters but the quiz show Countdown on Margaret Thatcher after the Brighton bombing in 1984. He was very News programme on its formation and he was the first to interview Some years before Richard had joined Yorkshire TV and their Calendar

Housewives Favourite

Richard Whiteley OBE was the son of Kenneth Whiteley who ran a textile business in Eccleshill which in turn became Studley Wools. Richard was born in 1943 and lived in Baildon. At the age of thirteen he attended Giggleswick public school near Settle and gradually progressed to Cambridge to read English after being taught by Russell Harty. He married in 1971 but the association did not last long and the wife did not feature in his will.

08

attending school, Bradford Grammar School to be precise. The book did not appeal to him and after leaving school he threw himself into his clothing business which attained a turnover of one million pounds and thirteen retail premises. Yes Jonathan loved a challenge in his life but duly settled down to domesticity in August 1972 with Maggie Jackson but was soon on the outlook for other business ventures. Together with their young family they travelled around the world for eighteen months before returning to buy Dean Clough mills in Halifax. But things did not work out well with his business partner, Ernest Hall. In the mid-eighties Salts Mill came up for sale and Jonathan jumped at the chance to regenerate it. Long hours were spent at the site and an old friendship with David Hockney the Bradford born artist led to his paintings being displayed in a special 1853 gallery on the site. The day after purchasing the site he was offered a profit of one million pounds but he refused. Through sheer hard work he put Saltaire on the tourist trail, and industry was attracted in the form of Pace Technology. Saltaire became a fashionable place and duly became a world heritage site all thanks to the single minded dedication of one man whose vision was achieved before his untimely death in 1997.

more time on the moors which became the inspiration for the books that soon had London talking. The views they had took in the west likley moors to the North Pendle hill. From reading their books you can often imagine the wind whistling round their ears and their feet surrounded by moss and sometimes purple heather. The resultant books have stood the test of time as the hard copies even today are described as works of genius. Wuthering Heights, Jane Eyre and Agnes Gray were classics which followed in quick succession and made a mark on America. The authors were unspoilt by success but also refused to accept failure- Good Bradford qualities I might add!

Many admirers of literature from all over the world now make the pilgrimage to Haworth and its parsonage, the local church and the Black Bull pub where the brother Bramwell spent a lot of his time. Others will traverse the moors to see the tumbled down ruins of a farmhouse 'Top Withens' which Emily used as a scene in Wuthering heights. The very characters used in these fine novels epitomise their landscape and surroundings. The sisters sadly died in a short period of time in the late 1840's at what would be described as a young age. Charlotte had just married and was pregnant when life struck her a cruel blow. Reverend Bronte, the father, outlived his entire family and died in 1861 at the age of 84.

A Man with a Vision

Jonathan Silver shaped the lives of others through his tremendous vitality for life and imagination, innovation and tenacity. Born soon after the Second World War had finished at Clifton Villas, Manningham to Jewish parents Jonathan was soon involved in matters of business whilst still

79

reputation that he became known as the 'King of Washington', and a legend in his home city of Bradford. At one time he is believed to have owned 10% of the housing stock in Washington, second only to the American Government. Confidence in himself abounded but still a cautious and calculated gamble paid off, these qualities enabled him to see his way through the 1929 stock market crash at which point his wealth amassed was said to be six million pounds though real estate bonds.

Married twice he lived life to the full but died young at the age of 65. Unfortunately many young Bradfordians will never have heard of him or his exploits but his incredible story must be told as an example to all young entrepreneurs.

Three Famous Writing Sisters

Without doubt Bradford can claim to be the birthplace of the Bronte sisters although it is not known to the world at large and most people assume Haworth to be their place of birth. Any self-respecting Bradfordian will point to a terraced at a rather deserted Market Street but a plaque marks the spot. Here Reverend Patrick Bronte obtained his first post as clergyman, having married Maria Bramwell in 1812 and then during a seven year period six children cam their way. In 1820 they moved to Haworth and their parsonage, now world famous, facing east and which was subject to strong wind and gales. Mrs Bronte died soon after moving here from cancer and two of the six children passed also. The remaining offspring could only be described as frail, with the exception of Patrick. The three daughters had little more to do than household chores, dined apart from their father. Increasingly they spent

Edward would not have been out of place as a comic book hero, he was so multi-faceted he knew nothing was impossible- a true Bradfordian.

Harry Wardman 'The King of Washington'

Bradford has raised some astute businessmen, but none finer in my opinion than Harry Wardman, a very determined man born in 1873.

Feeling he was getting nowhere fast in his home city he decided to try his luck in America. Queen Victoria's reign was coming to an end when Harry boarded an ocean steamer with a few personal belongings, the clothes he stood up in and his total wealth of 7s6d, or thirty seven and a half pence in decimal currency. He had acquired a variety of skills working in Bradford from messenger boy at Lingards, mill lad, draper and most importantly of all, a joiner which ultimately was to stand him in good stead during his ascendancy. After arriving in the states he took time to familiarise himself with his new home and apprenticed himself to a building contractor. A year went by and sure that he could do the work he decided to go it alone.

He borrowed money and built the Wardman Park Hotel. On completion in 1918 it had 1,000 rooms and other hotels followed and Harry became a very rich man. Further successes followed and with Washington growing at a fast pace population wise Harry secured a deal with the local municipal council housing department and such was his

77